The Global Seven Years War, 1754–1763

MODERN WARS IN PERSPECTIVE

General Editors: *H.M. Scott and B.W. Collins*

This ambitious series offers wide-ranging studies of specific wars, and distinct phases of warfare, from the close of the Middle Ages to the present day. It aims to advance the current integration of military history into the academic mainstream. To that end, the books are not merely traditional campaign narratives, but examine the causes, course and consequences of major conflicts, in their full international political, social and ideological contexts.

The Global
Seven Years War,
1754–1763

Britain and France in a Great Power Contest

Daniel Baugh

Routledge
Taylor & Francis Group

LONDON AND NEW YORK

First published 2011 by Pearson Education Limited

Published 2014 by Routledge
2 Park Square, Milton Park, Abingdon, Oxon OX14 4RN
711 Third Avenue, New York, NY, 10017, USA

Routledge is an imprint of the Taylor & Francis Group, an informa business

Notices
Knowledge and best practice in this field are constantly changing. As new research and experience broaden our understanding, changes in research methods, professional practices, or medical treatment may become necessary.

Practitioners and researchers must always rely on their own experience and knowledge in evaluating and using any information, methods, compounds, or experiments described herein. In using such information or methods they should be mindful of their own safety and the safety of others, including parties for whom they have a professional responsibility.

British Library Cataloguing in Publication Data
A CIP catalogue record for this book can be obtained from the British Library

Library of Congress Cataloging in Publication Data
Baugh, Daniel A.
  The global Seven Years War, 1754-1763 : Britain and France in a great power contest / Daniel Baugh. -- 1st ed.
     p. cm. -- (Modern wars in perspective)
  Includes bibliographical references and index.
  ISBN 978-0-582-09239-6 (pbk.)
  1. Anglo-French War, 1755-1763. 2. Seven Years' War, 1756-1763. 3. United States--History--French and Indian War, 1755-1763. 4. Great Britain--Foreign relations--France.
5. France--Foreign relations--Great Britain. 6. Great Britain--Foreign relations--1714-1837.
7. France--Foreign relations--1715-1774. 8. Great powers--History--18th century. 9. World politics--18th century. 10. Imperialism--History--18th century. I. Title. II. Series.
  DA500.B38 2011
  940.2′534--dc22

                                                                                    2011006092

ISBN: 978-0-582-09239-6 (pbk)

Set in 10/13.5pt Sabon by 35

To my wife Carol

Contents

List of maps

Preface and acknowledgements

The annihilation of General Braddock's army by Indian warriors accompanying a small body of French soldiers near Fort Duquesne; the French conquest of Minorca after which Admiral John Byng was executed on grounds of negligence; Clive's triumph in Bengal, the first step towards British dominion in India; Wolfe's defeat of Montcalm at Quebec which led to British possession of Canada; the remarkable capture of Havana where yellow fever thereupon took the lives of most of the captors – these are prominent military events of the global Seven Years War. In reality, however, the number of land battles in this war was quite small and the troop numbers involved were usually quite limited. In the naval war there were only six fleet engagements: three in the Atlantic and Mediterranean, three in the Indian Ocean. The battles mattered – some may be called decisive – but this book will also pay close attention to the challenges of mounting expeditions and sustaining lengthy campaigns in difficult circumstances. In the British case there was also the challenge of maintaining supremacy at sea, and in the French case of trying to avoid its consequences. This was a war in which strategic and operational planning, careful logistical preparation, and adaptation to unfamiliar campaigning conditions were absolutely necessary for success.

The war exhibited the attributes of a great-power contest. The statesmen on each side considered it their duty to gain, or avoid losing, advantage in every part of the world where British and French interests lay. If this had not been so, London and Versailles would have managed to settle a dispute over control of the wilderness region called Ohio even though it produced bloody skirmishes between Canadians and Virginians. But the negotiation for devising a settlement failed. (Consequently, 1754 must be considered the year in which the global Seven Years War between Britain and France began.) On the other side of the world in India, although hostilities involving French and English East India company forces which had begun before the war were terminated by a local agreement in 1754, the fighting resumed as soon as the declaration of war arrived from Europe.

The Seven Years War occurred at a time when European monarchs had substantially consolidated their realms and managed to depend chiefly upon their own armies instead of hired mercenaries. These armies of the Crown, when they could not feed off conquered territory, had to be sustained by the royal treasury. Monarchs were expected to defend and possibly extend their realms, but they generally lacked financial means and could not, or dared not, exploit popular national enthusiasm or make the kinds of demands on their subjects that would be made a half-century later. Eighteenth-century warfare was 'limited' somewhat by aristocratic civility and moderation but mainly by the reluctance or inability of governments to make heavier fiscal demands upon privileged political and social classes. Wars tended to be long, and after three or four years most states were scarcely able to sustain campaigning costs. The notable exception was Great Britain, partly because its army was relatively small, but mainly because its financial system was well developed and reliable. This system was significantly nourished by resources generated outside the realm by maritime and colonial commerce. Other powers of Europe had begun to take notice, and were therefore anxious to retain and improve their own overseas assets and opportunities. It is the conjuncture of heavy wartime demands on state treasuries and realization of the importance of transoceanic resources that fundamentally accounts for the special character of the global Seven Years War. At the operational level this special character was most strikingly exhibited by British military successes made possible by unprecedented penetration far up rivers by ships of the line; the famous instance is Quebec; a far less famous instance, though it prepared the way for sweeping change in India, is pictured on this book's cover.

I have chosen to tell the story of the war chronologically while making allowance for the fact that campaigns were going on simultaneously worldwide. My plan from the beginning was to examine both sides. The narrative tries not to presume that what happened had to happen. Instead, it seeks to present the circumstances and mixture of considerations in which decisions were made. Those who were engaged in making the decisions are quoted in their own words where possible. To expose the British cabinet's paths to decision-making (throughout the book the word 'cabinet' is used very loosely, to describe the body of statesmen, small or large, who had to decide) I have relied on the Newcastle and Hardwicke papers deposited in the British Library – the only manuscript collections I have systematically gone through. The task was lightened by P.C. Yorke's invaluable three-volume *Life and Correspondence* of Lord Hardwicke published a century ago. There is unfortunately no equivalent archive on the French side, for reasons that are interesting and will be explained later. My efforts to probe decisions made at Versailles have chiefly made use of the magnificent multi-volume history of the war written over a century ago by Richard Waddington, who addressed the problem with great acumen and immense scholarly labour.

It has often been observed that wars are a testing ground of a nation state's capabilities and efficiency. Here were two great nation states of the eighteenth century, seemingly comparable – their people talented and intellectually advanced (the Seven Years War coincides with the first flowering of the French Enlightenment) and their war capabilities impressive. Yet, as the research and writing of this book unfolded, I became increasingly aware of how differently the two states performed in directing military affairs at the highest level. Management of policy and strategy at Versailles was often ill-advised and fumbling. The government of Louis XV seemed complacent – inclined to act as if France were inherently invincible regardless of what was happening in the wider world. The court could not bring itself to believe, despite one setback after another, that France might not be able to find a way to achieve 'an honourable and reasonable peace'. Although there were numerous Frenchmen who considered their nation to be engaged in a great-power contest, Louis XV and his entourage seemed more focused on other things – such as military reputation, the king of France's standing in Europe, his status as a Bourbon, and the authority of the Church. In Britain, there was certainly concern about military (and naval) reputation, but the attitude towards the war was markedly different. Even before William Pitt took the helm, the British government was very serious about winning it, or at least not losing it; for Britain's statesmen, along with the public, never ceased to consider France the more powerful country, even in the midst of overwhelming victory.

A word about bibliographical references may be of use. All quotations are linked to footnotes. Full citations are usually to be found in the chapter's Notes on Sources or in the list of Abbreviation and Short Titles. The works mentioned are those on which the book's discussion of the topic at hand is based. Primary printed sources have been used as much as possible.

Place names are generally spelled in accordance with present-day maps, but where a French place name is familiar in English the English spelling is employed (hence Quebec, not Québec). I have modernized spelling and punctuation in a few cases for the sake of clarity and comprehension.

I wish to thank the staff of Cornell University's Olin Library, especially the circulation, reference and map departments and interlibrary loan services, for their unwavering helpfulness, and also wish to mention how much I have benefited from the (Ivy League's) Borrow Direct system. Encouragement from my Cornell History Department colleagues during this long project has been much appreciated. In London the staffs of the British Library Manuscripts Room and the British National Archives (formerly Public Record Office) were helpful and efficient. I was fortunate to be able to make use of the Institute of Historical Research as a place to study in London. In Paris, my effort to discover the motives of French policy in 1755–6 by recourse to the Archives du Ministère des Affaires Étrangères was facilitated by Yves-Marie Bercé and expertly assisted by the archival staff. A Cornell University research fund made available to professors emeritus helped to support travel to these overseas archives.

My wife joined me on road trips to survey sites in Canada and New York State. Our visit to the Fortress of Louisbourg National Historical Site was particularly informative thanks to guidance from members of the staff. Nicholas Westbrook, Director at Fort Ticonderoga, generously provided us with a comprehensive tour of key locations relating to the 1758 assault; this included Mt Defiance where he pointed out the likely position of Lieutenant Clerk's proposed battery.

I could not have faced the daunting challenge posed by this book's global reach without hoping to consult the particular expertise of many historians. It is a pleasure to acknowledge at last their generosity. For responding to my queries and offering valuable suggestions I warmly thank Ian K. Steele, James Pritchard, Christian Buchet, Nicholas Rodger, Daniel Usner, David Syrett, Alan Jamieson, Clive Wilkinson, James Vaughn, Karl Schweizer and Matt Schumann. (Schweizer and Schumann's *The Seven Years War: A Transatlantic History* (London and New York, 2008) did not appear in time for me to benefit from it.) Kent Hackmann, Jeremy Michell and Javier Cuenca generously provided me with findings from their unpublished research. To Tim Le Goff, John Bosher and Joël Félix I am particularly grateful both for their responses to queries and for sending me offprints, extracts and copies of their published work. I am also grateful to Carole Séguin of the National Archives of Canada for sending me photocopies of some microfilmed correspondence between Mirepoix and Rouillé in early 1755. Jonathan Dull generously provided me with a typescript copy of his *The French Navy and the Seven Years' War* before it was published; although my interpretations and emphases have sometimes differed, the book has helped me in important ways and its bibliography is the most comprehensive available.

For reading and commenting on sections relating to India I am immensely grateful to Peter Marshall, Gerry Bryant, and my Cornell colleague Robert Travers. My colleague Jon Parmenter did the same for portions involving American Indians, as did Ruddock Mackay for the sections dealing with Hawke's blockade, Lagos Bay and Quiberon Bay. My sons Charles and John each read a chapter and made useful suggestions, and at my request, my daughter Nancy Baugh Fortunel read the first six chapters and gave me much valued advice on matters of readability. In addition she and her husband Christian helped me with a number of French phrases that I could not confidently translate. Also my daughter-in-law Anja translated a German phrase that baffled me. Finally, I wish to record that the book has benefited immensely from the alert and intelligent editorial scrutiny of Barbara Massam.

During research trips to London, Mrs Terry Masterson made my accommodation in Kew Gardens as restful and pleasant as could be wished. Above all, my old friend Roger Knight with his wife Jane repeatedly extended their wonderful hospitality. The work of a historian is essentially solitary, but it was my great good fortune to have frequent breakfast-table conversations with Roger which, among other things, nourished my research and brightened my outlook. Over the many years in which I was engaged on the book Ruddock Mackay remained a steady, supportive, email correspondent and also provided sound advice on naval and navigational matters.

My debt to my academic editor, Hamish Scott, is enormous. It was he who suggested that I write this history (of the only war I truly wished to examine closely). He has read my chapters carefully, and not only saved me from numerous errors concerning continental European matters – those that remain are my fault – but also provided manifold useful suggestions of all kinds. His patience, well-tempered criticism and cordial encouragement were vital. My wife, a careful proofreader, scrutinized every chapter, sometimes twice. On many mornings she allowed time for patient listening as I tried to find my way through a confusion of ideas by saying them out loud while hoping, as often happened, that she would interject an essential question. Her support despite a receding finish line never faltered.

CHAPTER 1

Introduction

The Seven Years War has been called 'the Great War for the Empire'.[1] It certainly was that, but the war for empire was part of a great-power contest between Britain and France. By the middle of the eighteenth century these great rivals, the two most advanced monarchies of Europe, were both inclined to measure power in terms not only of armies and European territory, but also seaborne commerce, naval prowess and financial stamina. This fact made the Seven Years War a maritime and global contest as well as a European one. Sir Winston Churchill's chapter on the war in his *History of the English-Speaking Peoples* bears the title, 'The First World War', which is an accurate name for it.[2] By the end Britain held positions in North America and India that would have an enormous impact on modern world history, so looking back upon it the war is understandably seen as a contest for empire. But the ultimate object of statesmen in London and at Versailles was to maintain or increase security, power and influence in Europe.

Any war's history, but especially that of a great-power confrontation, ought to be viewed from both sides. Although the French side has been well documented regarding campaigns in North America, it is less so for other parts of the world, and when it comes to finding reliable information about how decisions were made at the court of Louis XV the French archives are generally unhelpful. Considering that the king of France ruled over one of the most advanced and sophisticated societies of Europe, the

---

[1] By Prof. Lawrence Henry Gipson; this is the title he gave to vols 6, 7, and 8 of his fifteen-volume history of *The British Empire Before the American Revolution*.

[2] Winston S. Churchill, *A History of the English-Speaking Peoples, Volume 3: The Age of Revolution* (New York and London, 1957).

degree of obscurity that shrouded French high-level decision-making is remarkable – in fact, quite unusual when compared with the practices of most other courts of Europe at the time. Between Britain and France the contrast with respect to surviving evidence is extreme. British archives provide an almost daily record of British high-level decision-making. For the court of Louis XV we have not much more than a few private memoirs plus letters dispatched to French ambassadors abroad. The main cause of this scarcity is deliberate suppression at the time, not accidental archival destruction later.

War was formally declared in spring 1756, but British and French troops clashed in North America during 1755, and the British seized French ships at sea in that year. Indisputably, then, the war encompassed eight full years of organized Anglo-French hostilities. In America the war is known as the French and Indian War, begun in 1754 (though the French began deploying military forces near the British colonial frontier in 1753). This book's initial plan did not allocate much space to the origins of the war. The matter seemed settled; along the contested frontiers of New France and the British colonies hostilities were inevitable. Nevertheless, the questions of why organized violence erupted when it did, and why a full-scale Anglo-French war resulted, ought to be reopened. Since neither London nor Versailles wanted war in 1755 the common assumption has been that the governments of the home countries were simply 'drawn in' by their governors in North America, as if helplessly. Yet this assumption, as will be seen, is falsified by strong evidence. Furthermore, it is puzzling that the principal dispute was focused on a wilderness region of the interior beyond the mountains about which statesmen in London and Paris knew almost nothing and had hitherto cared less. Equally puzzling is the failure of the attempt in early 1755 to negotiate a settlement of this dispute. In view of all this, the book's narrative will commence in the years 1752–3.

North America's emerging importance

Underlying geopolitical considerations had recently raised North America from a lower colonial priority to a continent worth fighting over. After the peace of Aix-la-Chapelle of 1748 which ended the war of the Austrian Succession everyone expected another major war between Britain and France to occur before long, but no one predicted that it would be brought on by disputed claims in a scarcely mapped region west of the Appalachian Mountains of North America.

English settlement of North America, begun a century and a half earlier, was undertaken with government approval but with hardly any financial support, the land grants costing the king nothing. One significant exception was the conquest of New Amsterdam in the 1660s and 1670s, made possible by the Royal Navy. Renamed New York, the acquisition brought the entire seaboard between Nova Scotia and South Carolina under British rule. Otherwise, the Treasury did not spend money on founding new colonies or on promoting settlement in North America until a small government subsidy was provided for the foundation of Georgia in 1733 and parliamentary grants were made, beginning in 1749, for settling Nova Scotia. The population of British North America grew rapidly, both by natural increase and by an immigration policy – or non-policy – that permitted foreigners to pour in.

It was the British government's aim throughout to keep the costs of territorial administration and defence low. During the long period of Anglo-French peace after 1714 colonial governors often asked London to help them develop frontier defences, but very little help was given. It is clear that the British government considered the wilderness frontiers of North America to be a nuisance. The few colonists who ventured to trade with Indians beyond the settled frontier were expected to provide for their own protection. Colonial assemblies seldom spent any money or effort on helping them. For its part, the British government simply wanted to keep the interior frontiers quiescent, hoping to ignore any problems. This attitude summed up Britain's territorial policy in North America down to about 1750.

Britain's concern was not territory but commerce and shipping. By means of the Navigation Acts of 1651, 1660 and 1663 the British Atlantic colonies became linked in a maritime-imperial system. Successive British governments valued this system because it increased seaborne commerce, generated wealth that helped support public finance, and enlarged the British merchant marine, which provided a reserve of trained seamen that was essential to the navy. It was a system of 'traffick': that is, trade *and* shipping. The priority given to the latter is revealed by patterns of enforcement; those aspects of the Navigation Acts which concerned shipping were quite strictly enforced while those concerning commodities were often revised or left unenforced in order to adjust to market demands and maximize traffic. French West Indian molasses, for example, went to New England without a prohibitory duty being enforced, but only British vessels could legitimately ship it. It was carried mainly in New England vessels, which accounted for almost a third of total British merchant tonnage. (American colonial shipping enjoyed the same privileges under the Navigation

Acts as shipping of the home country.) Thus, the maritime-imperial system, though its trade was concentrated within the British colonial orbit, was open enough to stimulate economic growth and prosperity. To provide currency throughout the system, contraband trading with Spanish America to acquire silver coin was permitted, though deemed illicit by the Spanish authorities. Noting how an absence of regulatory rigidity had contributed to commercial success, Edmund Burke, in 1775, warned against unin-formed legislative meddling, and attributed the growth of British Atlantic trade and colonial prosperity to 'salutary neglect'.[3]

In the century preceding 1750 British policymakers accorded far less importance to the American mainland colonies than to the West Indies, where tobacco, sugar, coffee and indigo produced by slave labour, along with contraband trade with the Spanish empire, generated the most wealth. Yet during the first half of the eighteenth century British North America became an important export market for British manufactured goods. In 1700 its population was 234,000; in 1750 the figure was 1,206,000 (964,000 if the black population is not counted). Although, in 1700 the West Indies purchased more of the home country's goods (by value) than the mainland colonies did, in 1750 the mainland colonies con-sumed more than double the West Indian figure. In *The Wealth of Nations* Adam Smith supposed that British goods sold well in America because it was a captive market; but by mid-century British goods would have outsold most European goods in America without one.

At mid-century, when it came to be realized that North American colonists were purchasing vast quantities of British manufactured goods and that the trade fostered a large shipping traffic, influential members of the public began to think that these colonies of settlement ought to be allowed to expand. The French possessions to the north and west of them should not, therefore, be allowed to stand in the way of their growth. When land speculators in Virginia, among whom was George Washington's uncle, put forward a petition for a substantial land grant on the western frontier in the name of the Ohio Company, George Montagu Dunk, Earl of Halifax, who was head of the Board of Trade, recommended royal approval. He noted that the petition spoke of founding new settlements and building a fort within seven years. He commented – this was in 1749 – that it 'would be a proper step towards disappointing the views and checking the incroachments of the French, by interrupting part of the communication from their lodgements upon the great lakes to the river

---

[3] Speech on Conciliation with the Colonies, 22 March 1775.

Mississippi'.[4] Although the frontiers were no longer being ignored at the Board of Trade, most British statesmen at this time did not care in 1749 whether the Ohio Company would actually carry out this scheme.

Canada's utility for France

At about this time the court of Versailles was being advised on the subject of North America by a well-informed expert. His name was Roland-Michel Barrin, comte de la Galissonière, an admiral who had recently served two years at Quebec as acting governor-general. He wrote a long memorandum, a 'Memoir on the French Colonies in Northern America', that was read before the king and council in December 1750. His main point was that the expansion of the British mainland colonies constituted a dire threat to the French West Indies and also that the growth of American trade was augmenting British maritime power to a degree threatening to France's superior standing in Europe.[5]

He began by stating that although Canada was unprofitable, 'motives of honour, glory and religion' did not permit its abandonment, but the argument he made for supporting Canada was geopolitical. La Galissonière set forth some bleak realities. Whereas the tropical colonies (he named Saint-Domingue and Martinique) clearly added to French wealth, improved the trade balance, and furnished revenues to the state, Canada was a drain on the French treasury and would probably continue so for a long time. He quickly passed over the fisheries since everyone recognized their value. The problem was the interior. Geographical disadvantages prevented export commodities from being produced there at competitive prices, so there was nothing except the unevenly profitable fur trade. In sum, Canada was 'a barren frontier'. Yet it possessed one great attribute, he said: it provided 'the strongest barrier that [could] be opposed to the ambition of the English'.

Ultimately and quite self-consciously, La Galissonière's argument pointed towards finding some way to cope with British naval strength. It was the greatest source of danger to French power: 'If anything can, in fact, destroy the superiority of France in Europe, it is the English naval forces; it was these alone . . . which caused France to lose the fruit of the entire conquest of the Austrian Low Countries at the close of the last

[4] Quoted in Jennings, *Empire of Fortune*, pp. 12–13.
[5] Lamontagne, ed. *Aperçu structural du Canada*, pp. 93–112. The quotations are my translations from this French text.

war.'[6] He evidently believed that French leaders had hurried to sign the peace treaty of 1748, in which they gave up the military conquest of the Austrian Netherlands, because two crushing British naval victories in 1747 signalled an end to French trade and colonial communications.

France, however, could not hope to match the British navy: 'We must not flatter ourselves that we can long sustain the expense of a navy equal to theirs; therefore, the only recourse that remains is to attack them in their possessions'. The need for doing so was becoming more urgent; the power of the British colonies in North America was 'daily increasing', and 'if means be not found to prevent it', they would soon swallow all of France's transatlantic colonies. By this he meant that they would take over the whole West Indies, too:

If we do not halt the rapid progress of the English colonies of the Continent or, what comes to almost the same thing, if we do not form a counterweight capable of containing them within their bounds and of forcing them onto the defensive, they will have, in a short time, such great facilities that they can make formidable armements on the Continent of America, and it will take them so little time to carry large forces either to Saint-Domingue or to the island of Cuba, or to our Windward islands, that there will be no hope of keeping them except at enormous expense.

No one questioned the importance of these islands where the production of sugar and coffee generated a vast and profitable commerce. France had depended upon forts and militias rather than naval power to defend them, but La Galissonière realized that such methods were far from invincible; their defence ultimately depended on the difficulties that enemies experienced when carrying 'from Europe troops capable of subjugating them'. Britain's North American colonies, however, as they grew in strength would enable the French islands to be attacked with relative ease.[7]

Already the produce of those colonies enabled British Caribbean peoples, garrisons and warships to be supplied more reliably and at considerably less cost than by sending the same commodities from Britain (and before the Seven Years War ended British North America would in fact play an important role in attacks mounted on French and Spanish West Indian islands). It was necessary, La Galissonière reasoned, to curb the growth of those colonies and harass them. With this in mind France

[6] Ibid. pp. 96–9.
[7] Ibid. pp. 97–9.

should 'augment and fortify Canada and Louisiana', recognizing the two factors that gave French combatants there an advantage. The first was alliances with the Indians, 'who love us until now a little, and fear us much more, than they do the English' but understand that it is in their interest that 'the strength of the English and French remain nearly equal'. The second was 'the number of French Canadians who are accustomed to live in the woods like Indians, and are thereby not only well fitted to lead them to fight against the English, but to wage war even against these same Indians when necessity obliges'. These advantages were somewhat 'accidental', yet no expense should be spared to maintain and improve them.

The unchecked progress of the British in America, La Galissonière concluded, would 'very certainly give them superiority in Europe'. French Canada and Louisiana were a bulwark against that progress, and only by reliance on those colonies could France 'make up for the lack of maritime strength'. New France would be unable, however, to serve this important function in its present condition. It needed investment, population growth (even if it meant sending *'femmes de mauvaise vie'*), and expanded settlements along the Illinois river where an abundance of crops could be grown.[8]

Obviously, La Galissonière's argument for sustaining Canada was broadly geopolitical – to restrain the growth of Britain's economic power and indirectly its sea power, which threatened the supremacy of France in Europe. The memorandum aroused very considerable interest at the court of Versailles, and it clearly looked to the future. But it also spelled out ways in which Canada's resources and defences needed to be immediately strengthened, and in fact the governors-general were already engaged in the work, with ministerial approval as will be seen in Chapter 3. The policy was in operation in Canada before the memorandum was presented to the council of state at Versailles.

This French policy would transform British attitudes towards empire in North America. French activity on the frontiers of the British colonies, together with recognition of their importance as a growing market for British goods, would introduce ideas about imperial territory into popular consciousness. The church-and-state issue, which in former days had profoundly divided Tories and Whigs, became secondary to excitement about trade, empire and maritime supremacy, and now, at mid-century, the trade became entwined with territorial imperialism. The territorial aspect was given political immediacy by the nature of the peace treaty of 1748. Both sides had wanted to end the war in a hurry, so at Aix-la-Chapelle

[8] Ibid. pp. 98–9, 112.

they allowed numerous disputed claims in the wider world to be set aside and referred to a Boundary Commission. Contentions over North American boundaries were thus formally placed on the political agenda, in an atmosphere of intense rivalry with France.

A global contest

Although the Anglo-French Seven Years War erupted in North America, it became global. In due course there would be fighting on four continents including Africa. The Royal Navy played an essential role everywhere. Ships operated in every ocean except the Pacific and even ventured there in the final months of the war when an expedition from India attacked Manila. The Mediterranean, though not as important as in the preceding war, saw moments of significance. The Caribbean was, from the beginning, an arena of contention for ships large and small, and eventually became a scene of important British conquests. Nevertheless, until Canada was surrendered in 1760, North America remained the principal theatre of operations.

While French strategy in North America was basically defensive, in Europe it soon became offensive. After a few months' hesitation, the government of Louis XV decided to make a major military commitment in Germany. Ostensibly the king's motive was to assist his new ally, Austria, which he personally very much wanted to do; but it was clear from the outset that the French plan was mainly focused on occupying Hanover, King George II's beloved fatherland. France's idea was to force Britain to accept a negotiated peace, and it certainly appeared to be the swiftest and most expedient way to bring the war to a satisfactory end. To help Hanover and oppose the French the British eventually sent troops. In 1761 close to 22,000 campaigned on the continent alongside Hanoverians and Hessians under a general borrowed from the Prussian army. Almost the entire cost of this combined army was borne by the British Treasury. For all these reasons a history of the global Seven Years War must include campaigning in Europe to some degree. But it should be understood that when people in London and Paris spoke of the 'war in Germany', it was the war fought in the north-western sector, loosely designated Westphalia, that they meant. It was there that the French hoped to gain victories which would compensate for anticipated losses overseas. Further east in Europe, the Seven Years War consisted of a bitter and exhausting struggle between Prussia and her adversaries, mainly Russia and Austria. This war in central Europe, in which Frederick the Great of Prussia amazingly found means to overcome setbacks and keep on fighting, is not covered by this book, although it cannot be entirely ignored because Britain formed an alliance with Prussia and sent Frederick subsidy money, while France gave direct support to Austria.

In this global contest dominance at sea was essential to British success, not only to protect supply lines but also, and more visibly, to carry out seaborne expeditions. Under conditions of naval superiority the British army and navy, in the Seven Years War, pioneered the development of effective specialized methods and tactics for amphibious landings. In the Hughli River of Bengal as well as the St Lawrence River of Canada the navy was an essential partner in military success, and in the Caribbean, on the French coast and on the coast of southern India the navy's role was critical to the outcome of military operations.

In the last instance, on the Coromandel Coast, three Anglo-French sea battles involving substantial squadrons took place, but otherwise there were very few major naval battles in the Seven Years War, the reason being that the French navy scarcely ever challenged the British to a contest of broadsides. The British were, nevertheless, committed to a perpetual war at sea, which, in the most important theatre, involved tedious, usually uneventful (except for storms) cruising off the French coast. The French navy's strategy was to wait – to remain in port until wind conditions assured escape – and in returning to port to hope that efforts at evasion would succeed. Combat when it occurred mainly featured single-ship actions. In the war's later years, thanks in large part to a decisive naval victory in November 1759 at Quiberon Bay, British cruisers and priva-teers were able to operate inshore. Until then, however, departing French warships and supply transports were not easily intercepted, and it is a mistake to speak of a British 'blockade' until the year 1759. Every history of the Seven Years War has acknowledged in a general way that the Royal Navy seriously hampered French efforts to carry supplies and reinforce-ments to its beleaguered transoceanic colonies, but this book offers details of the failures and successes.

In terms of numbers the British navy did not achieve an extreme preponderance over the French until 1758, for reasons that will be explained in Chapter 9, but it never made sense for the French to engage in avoidable combat even in the years when the naval imbalance remained moderate. One reason was the superiority of British naval gunnery, but the main reason was the French navy's mission-oriented strategies which avoided a contest for sea control.

Sea warfare's greatest challenge concerned health. Given its limited presence at sea it would seem that the French navy should have suffered less from sickness than the British. Its mission-oriented pattern of operations was mainly 'out and back', and French squadrons spent a lot of time in port. Only warships sent to the Indian Ocean were expected to remain overseas for any length of time. Those heading for Canada or the West Indies were generally stocked with a six-month supply of victuals and expected, after two or three months, to return without basic replenishment except for taking on water and acquiring, if possible, fresh provisions to ward off scurvy. There were not many exceptions. One would think, then, that health could not have been a problem for the French navy, but it was indeed a serious problem. On mobilization typhus spread among the crews, and was carried to sea where it continued to exercise its malignancy.

Potentially, health was a greater problem for the Royal Navy because it was a cruising navy and a ship's time at sea could last for months, thus introducing the deficiency disease of scurvy. The strategy of the Western Squadron, which cruised out of sight of land off the French coast for long periods, invited this disease. The strategy was put into practice as soon as hostilities began, and continuous presence whenever a French squadron was known to be mobilized was crucial, because if the French learned that the squadron had returned to port they would sail. At the war's beginning the squadron was usually forced to return prematurely to Portsmouth or Plymouth because too many sailors were sick, dying from typhus as well as scurvy. By the third year of the war the incidence of typhus diminished, but the problem of scurvy remained; the disease, caused by a deficiency of vitamin C, would commonly take hold of a man after about five weeks, and he would become completely disabled and die if not relieved by fresh food. In 1759, however, the Western Squadron under Admiral Sir Edward Hawke stood off Brest for six months and practically no one became sick. Pairs of ships shuttled back to Plymouth or Torbay for refreshment, but this proceeding did not fully account for the almost magical good health of the squadron, which stemmed from a huge effort to provide fresh provisions to the ships on station, arguably the most remarkable victualling achievement in eighteenth-century naval history.[9]

A sailing ship of the line (invincible to any opponent except another ship like it), if loaded with provisions for six months or more, could go anywhere in the world where it was able to replenish drinking water. Continuance in a foreign theatre depended mainly on three things: cleaning the hull to enhance speed and to defeat *teredo navalis* (the wood-boring

---

[9] Described in Chapter 12.

worm), resupplying damaged masts and keeping the crew in health. Regarding the first two, a naval base with storehouses, a mast pond and careening wharves was highly desirable. Sustained health required adequate victuals, fresh provisions to defeat scurvy and potable water. British naval administration had developed by this time the means of supplying what was needed to a degree that the French navy could only envy. Sea power may be measured in numbers of ships and depended ultimately upon the test of battle, but without an enduring presence on station, made possible by adequate shore facilities, it could not be very effective. In this sort of endeavour – patrolling and cruising – the Royal Navy, particularly during the first half of the eighteenth century, had developed a number of advantages. One was that the Admiralty had established permanent bases overseas. The French navy had none. Its warships could use private facilities for repairing ships overseas, but there were no colonial navy yards under royal administration until one was established in 1787 at Martinique.

Shortage of ammunition was not a common problem. Occasionally, when ships were employed to bombard shore targets, or when the navy's guns and ammunition were loaned to an expeditionary army ashore, shortages could develop, but not in sea battles. In the Anglo-Dutch wars a century earlier, shortages had been experienced, but in the Seven Years War, even in hard-fought naval engagements involving frightful bloodshed, this was not the case.

On land, maintaining an army's health was often a serious problem, but the greatest challenge arose from transport requirements. The French found out how hard it was to move a large army deep into Germany. If a force was of moderate size, not burdened with heavy artillery and trained to march expeditiously, it might be able to meet its provisioning needs along the way by requisition, but distance took its toll, especially when numbers were large. Since the French army's chief aim in this war was to conquer and occupy Hanover, an objective much further from a French border than the Austrian Netherlands where French armies had been used to campaigning in the past, depots and magazines were necessary, and long supply lines had to be protected. Carts, wagons, teams, fodder and forage – these words and their French equivalents were repeatedly uttered by frustrated generals on both sides. It was almost impossible to bring sufficient quantities from the rear, so it was rare for an army to advance until 'green forage' emerged, often not until June. Without the vast amounts needed to feed horses, cavalry could not assemble, provisions could not be hauled and artillery would remain immobile. Foraging parties had to fan out for many miles along the line of march, and when they had finished, the resulting terrain was commonly described as a 'desert'. As the French minister of war wrote to his commanding general in Westphalia in 1758, 'You can rest assured that I go to bed thinking about forage and get up again still thinking about it.'[10] The deeper into Germany the French armies advanced, the longer the supply chain became, and the more necessary it was to obtain local supplies.

In terms of cost, campaigning in Germany was cheaper for the French army than for its Hanoverian and British opponents because the French did not pay well for their requisitions, and almost never promptly. Fifty years earlier under Louis XIV, and fifty years later when Napoleon campaigned, forced requisition was seen by the French government as the ideal way to wage war – let conquered people bear a large portion of the cost – but in the Seven Years War this practice was not militarily efficient, the chief difficulty arising from the resistance of local farmers, who sequestered their carts and wagons as well as food. The demands of British and allied German forces also provoked resentment and resistance even among a more sympathetic people – it was inevitable – but the British were generally known to pay for what they took.

In North America the burden of the offensive lay upon the British, or one should say British and Americans because combat forces depended significantly on colonial – commonly called 'provincial' – troops to help bring up provisions and guard supply lines. This was a war, as Professor John Shy has observed, 'in which geography created problems of communications and supply so great that the principal task of generalship was in simply moving a force of moderate size into contact with the enemy'.[11] Except for wood, water and green forage, the wilderness provided for none of an army's needs. Provisions for a campaign had to come from the rear, and there were no roads through the forests.

Therefore, provisions such as guns, mortars and projectiles for a siege had to be transported in almost every case on water. Although short roads could be cut through the forested terrain, it was nearly impossible for an army to reach a distant objective without water transport. The only exception was the campaign across Pennsylvania in 1758 which went over the mountains to Fort Duquesne on a road built by order of General John Forbes. It was an arduous and controversial endeavour, fraught with

---

[10] Marshal Belleisle to Marshal Contades, 6 Nov. 1758, Kennett, *French Armies*, p. 105.

[11] Shy, *Toward Lexington*, p. 87.

delays and disappointments.[12] The assault on Canada proceeded entirely on water: up the St Lawrence River, and also upon the rivers and lakes of northern New York. In the latter arena the essential means of transport was the bateau – a long wooden boat of shallow draft, usually 25 to 40 feet long, which was capable of surviving moderate rapids.

Needless to say, waterways and the portage roads connecting them were vulnerable to enemy attack. Such attacks, usually in the form of an ambush, were almost always guided by Indians, men who could find their way through vast forests where everyone else was blind. Canadian fur traders and French missionaries penetrated the North American interior, so most tribes were either neutral or aligned with the French, especially in the early years of the war. Having difficulty obtaining Indian scouts, the British army formed ranger battalions, recruited mostly among American colonists. It is to the credit of General Jeffrey Amherst, whom military historians have commonly criticized for slowness, that his troops made their way northwards to Canada in 1759–60 without the blood-stained setbacks suffered in earlier campaigns. On the other side, Canada's rivers and lakes provided enviable interior lines of communication for the defenders.

Except for the campaigning in Europe the Anglo-French Seven Years War was a war on water – not always fought on water, but in the sense that offensive operations were made possible by water transport. Water transport's relative efficiency underlines the advantage of amphibious operations. Army officers disliked them – all risk, little glory, it seemed to them – but without them the British could not have won the Seven Years War. The attacks on Louisbourg and Quebec were obvious instances, as were those in the West Indies. Less well known is the importance of water-borne supplies to the success of campaigns in India. The exception proves the rule: a great obstacle to French penetration of north-western Germany was the lack of suitable waterways. The major rivers of Westphalia run north and south. Although the Lippe and Ruhr flowed to the Rhine from the east, they were not navigable far enough eastwards. Near the head-waters an invading force became completely dependent upon teams and wagons. In contrast, when the British and allied German forces controlled the Weser and Ems rivers (which flow south to north) they could use them to bring supplies from North Sea ports.

In both North America and north-western Germany the logistical prob-lems at the extremities shaped the character of the fighting: there were

[12] Because this overland campaign was unique it is given close attention in Chapter 10.

small actions, often brought on by attacks on supply lines, but few major battles. (Prussia's war saw many more battles, partly because the Prussian army was well trained for rapid movement, but also because the geography of the rivers in central Europe enabled the Prussian army to overcome long distances more readily.) Both in Westphalia and in North America battles, skirmishes and sieges could be decisive for a campaign's ultimate success or failure, but generals of the time could never safely ignore transport and logistics.

Geography and policy

Admiral Sir Herbert Richmond, a career naval officer who turned his enquiring mind to the historical study of navies and war, came to the following conclusion:

Powerful, therefore, though the arguments of technique may be, the arguments of policy are more powerful. In the long run errors of policy have far more far-reaching effects than errors of strategy, errors of strategy than errors of tactics, and errors of tactics than errors of technique.[13]

By 'technique' he meant weaponry and skill in its use as well as tactical arrangements. Richmond's most important historical work, *Statesmen and Sea Power* (Oxford, 1946), was inspired by this 1938 pronouncement. The book, originating in the Ford Lectures at Oxford in 1943, explored the interrelationship of British policy and strategy from Elizabeth I to the Second World War. Especially when the French side of the Seven Years War is considered, it is easy to conclude that 'errors of policy' had 'far more far-reaching effects' than errors of strategy and tactics or the effectiveness of available weaponry.

In considering policy one must start with the fact that in the eighteenth century France was the most powerful nation in Europe and perhaps the world. In 1750 her population and useful land area were three times those of Great Britain. France could mobilize an army of more than 300,000 whereas Britain, even as she drew upon Ireland, could scarcely raise 80,000. To be sure, the Royal Navy at its peak in this war mustered close to 80,000 sailors, but France possessed the second most powerful navy to complement her very strong army. Russia was, of course, far

[13] Herbert W. Richmond, 'Some Naval Problems', *Nineteenth Century and After* (Feb. 1938), pp. 202–3.

larger and more populous than France, but Russia's economy was backward whereas that of France in many respects was advanced. The intellectual and cultural life of France was regarded as pre-eminent, and in the 1750s the French Enlightenment began to shine brightest. Practically every educated Englishman could speak and read French – not so, the other way round.

Though the British admired the French (not politically), they were afraid of the power of France, and with reason. A half-century earlier Louis XIV had waged prolonged wars in which one of his principal goals was to overturn England's 'Glorious Revolution' of 1688–9. The form of defence that England evolved and embraced after 1689 was unique in the world. Its main elements were maintenance of a superior navy and formation of coalitions with continental allies. Those allies expected to receive British subsidies, and Britain expected them to be sufficiently concerned about French military power to be willing to confront it. The navy and the subsidies required a great deal of money, so a third principal element of British policy was that it should promote wealth and prosperity. Prosperity helped to keep the House of Commons and the public contented, and wealth facilitated the collection of taxes and enabled support of the national debt. Britain's war-making capacity and endurance depended heavily on her effective system of public borrowing. Seaborne commerce was seen as essential to prosperity, and a powerful navy was understood to be not only crucial for the defence of the realm from invasion, but also for protecting the commerce that provided profits for sustaining the cost of defence, a relationship that La Galissonière fully understood.

France was a maritime as well as a land power, and her western ports enjoyed quick access to the ocean. The principal British port, London, was literally up a sleeve (La Manche), the French word for the English Channel, and numerous small ports for harbouring privateers were sprinkled along its French side. Great Britain's insular situation enabled her to adopt a naval basis for national defence, and although the location of London did not afford easy access to the oceans, it encouraged this choice because the centre of seaborne commerce and finance coincided with the centre of government. Since France's principal oceanic ports were distant from the centre of government at Paris, maritime and colonial concerns were less in view. Nevertheless, in the mid-eighteenth century the educated public in France began to pay attention to the maritime sphere. Growing fascination with voyages of discovery would be a symptom of this trend, but the main concern was the ominously growing power and prosperity of Britain. By 1750 French public opinion judged Britain to be France's principal enemy.[14]

For its part the British nation continually feared a French invasion. If the French had occupied Ireland, they would not only have increased their ability to disrupt British shipping but also possessed a staging area from which an invasion of Great Britain could have been launched. Close as France was to the south coast of England, a direct cross-channel invasion was hazardous. Prevailing winds readily enabled a French battle fleet for escorting an invasion force to sail up the Channel, but the same wind pattern meant that such a fleet, if it encountered a strong opponent, could not count on retreating, and there was no large, protected, deep-water roadstead on the French side to provide safe refuge. If France possessed the southern Netherlands, she could develop the estuary of the Scheldt into such a refuge, and Great Britain's island defence would have been much more difficult and expensive. Defence against invasion was the main reason why British policy always aimed at preventing the French from occupying Ireland and the Netherlands.

No sensible person in England doubted, in principle, the value of allies for the purpose of countering French military power on the European continent, but questions of purpose and degree were fervently contested. Would a prospective ally actually undertake to confront a French army? Would it assist, if necessary, in defending the Netherlands? And there was the question of Hanover. King George II was also Elector of Hanover. He had been born and brought up in the Electorate and his heart remained there. Although the parliamentary statute that had placed the house of Hanover on the throne of England specified that the British government was not obligated to defend the king's German Dominions, as they were called, the reality was that if they came under threat, George II's English ministers were morally bound and subject to predictable royal pressure to look after the safety of those lands. On the eve of the Seven Years War British statesmen could not avoid considering how a war would affect British concerns in Europe, but their attention was focused on the Netherlands and Hanover. Some statesmen might talk about the European balance of power, yet, with the notable exception of the Duke of Newcastle, most agreed with popular opinion that the global war to preserve and amplify shipping, trade and prosperity, not the diplomatic posture of the continent of Europe, was of primary importance.

---

[14] Dziembowski, *Un nouveau patriotisme français* shows that the emerging French patriotism of this era was decidedly Anglophobic.

CHAPTER 2

Statesmen and regimes

Structurally, the English constitution with its permanent tension between Parliament and monarch appeared unsuited for war. The absolute monarchy of France seemed better equipped to achieve unity in matters of policy and strategy, and also to command resources more readily. In this war France did gain certain advantages from her absolutist institutions, but these benefits were more than offset by a lack of public trust in royal finances, and by errors and inconstancy of policy. The system needed a coordinating leader with authority, and Louis XV neither met the need himself nor found someone who did until too late. Except during the final year of this war the quality of British governmental leadership conferred a decisive advantage.

Such quality was not guaranteed by the British constitution. The king had the right to choose his ministers while the House of Commons had the right to deny those ministers the funds necessary to support their administration. In the preceding war George II had stubbornly insisted on retaining ministers whose policies displeased practically everyone in Parliament, and it was only by a unanimous resolution to resign their offices that a body of politicians who had assembled strong parliamentary support managed, in early 1746, to force the king to accept a new ministry. Occurring in the midst of the war of the Austrian Succession when it was going badly for Britain, this singular episode was one of the most important constitutional events of the century. The new administration was able to salvage something close to a draw at the peace of Aix-la-Chapelle in 1748.

Three British statesmen stood above all others in importance during the Seven Years War. United they overcame the complexities of waging war in the constitutional monarchy, and their individual and collective actions exhibited the essential characteristics of the British political system at its best. They deserve detailed introductions. (Generals and admirals will be introduced later, when they come on stage.)

The Duke of Newcastle

Thomas Pelham-Holles, 1st Duke of Newcastle, was the leading minister during almost the entire war. Born in 1693, he attended Westminister School and Clare College, Cambridge, and had fond memories of both. He and his half-brother, Henry Pelham, along with a trusted associate, the Earl of Hardwicke, had led the group that forced the king to yield in 1746. By 1754 George II no longer regarded Newcastle with resentment, mainly because the duke was now inclined to pursue a foreign policy well suited to protecting the king's beloved Hanover. Having gained the king's confidence, Newcastle enjoyed easy 'access to the closet' (that is, a standing invitation to discuss politics and policy privately with the king) as well as permission to supervise the disposal of a large portion of royal patronage. Much of this patronage, directly or indirectly, could be employed to ensure support for the government in Parliament. Yet Newcastle also commanded, thanks to enormous inherited wealth and property, considerable patronage of his own. Of course he sat in the House of Lords; but the key point was that he controlled approximately 17 seats in the House of Commons. This may not sound like a lot in a body with 558 members, but most seats were unlikely to change hands. A man capable of throwing so much weight into the parliamentary balance was bound to be a desirable colleague in any administration, and Newcastle was eager to serve. From his first appointment as a secretary of state (there were two) in 1724 he spent a total of 38 years in high office.

At first glance, the duke's personality seems comprehensively unfitted for a career in politics and government. He was visibly emotional. In conversation he gushed and sometimes grasped men by the hand or cheek. Because he was paranoid about threats to his political position the slightest hint of a challenge threw his thinking into disorder. Along with this went a continual fear of being blamed and a disposition towards self-pity; and he was sadly deficient in political backbone.

Yet Newcastle also possessed qualities and inclinations that were desirable for carrying on the everyday business of a politician. Gregarious, open-hearted, affable, delighting in the obligation to entertain, he loved to greet and be greeted. He knew hundreds of people among the political classes, not only the elite who gathered at Westminster but also lesser men in counties like Sussex and Nottingham where his influence was dominant – men who mobilized the vote for candidates he favoured. Wealth and patronage did not automatically secure allegiance. In electoral matters he was a good judge of situations. It may be disconcerting to see Newcastle, prior to the election of 1761, talking about who – himself or the new king's mentor, John Stuart, 3rd Earl of Bute – would get to 'choose the House of Commons', but that is how he thought about it when he selected nominees for constituencies. Obviously, he worked at politics and enjoyed the work. Conversations were not enough; he had to read and write countless letters, but in this regard, too, Newcastle was indefatigable. Someone remarked that he was 'a jealous lover of paper', and how true that was. His political and governmental correspondence, not counting his other collected papers, runs to over two hundred thick quarto volumes.

People who remarked on the duke's personal foibles – almost everyone did – also acknowledged that he was honest. He did not enrich himself by holding high office; on the contrary, he spent his vast wealth in maintaining his position. The greatest mistakes of his career, however, stemmed from this goal; that is, from his passionate desire to remain at the centre of power. He was jealous of men whose talent might grow into rivalry and was therefore reluctant to allow a strong and influential person to become leader of the House of Commons.

At the beginning of hostilities in 1755 Newcastle was secretary of state for the Southern Department and the leading minister. Though he was well informed about international relations, timidity often undermined his judgement, and his capacity for cunning was meagre. In 1757 he became First Lord of the Treasury in the Pitt–Newcastle administration. Was this a case where birth, wealth, ambition and capacity for managing patronage had the effect of installing incompetence in high office? Newcastle was not incompetent. When his mind was not clouded by political anxiety he could be quite perceptive, and he was hard-working and intelligent. A good listener, he possessed a remarkable ability to recall important conversations and commit them to paper afterwards. These memoranda, usually in the form of letters to colleagues, were generally honest notwithstanding his personal dislikes and prejudices; and besides, if his letters had not been faithful to the truth, colleagues would, he knew, quickly find out. His letters and papers deal with policy and strategy fully as much as patronage and are even useful for discovering what was being thought at Versailles because Newcastle had a well-connected informant there who reported via Cologne throughout the war. At the centre of power and fond of activity, the duke played a vital coordinating role: in effect, he functioned as the cabinet secretariat.

He possessed one other very important attribute, which may be considered a saving grace. He knew his limitations. As First Lord of the Treasury he employed well-informed assistants who were in touch with leading financiers of the City of London. The key point was that the financiers trusted Newcastle. In matters of diplomacy and strategy he learned rather early in his career not to rely solely on his own thinking, but rather upon the wisdom of a highly intelligent and learned personal adviser – someone who liked him, was willing to be patient, and could persuade him by employing a deft mixture of courtesy and firmness that did not offend the duke's sensibilities.

The Earl of Hardwicke

That person was Philip Yorke, 1st Earl of Hardwicke. In 1755 he held the office of Lord Chancellor, the highest judicial post in the kingdom, and had held it for 18 years. His origins were middle class. His father and mother were well placed in the city of Dover and sent him to school in London to study under one of the finest schoolteachers of the time. Instead of going to Cambridge, he studied law. He found the materials to be tedious, but mastered them and was soon recognized as a young man worthy of patronage by senior members of the profession. He rose rapidly and became a distinguished jurist, still renowned today for his establishment of the English law of equity on a consistent foundation which, although conservative, could deal dependably with property disputes in an increasingly commercial society. The work of the Court of Chancery was arduous. After a temporary political necessity caused him to resign the Lord Chancellorship in 1756 he chose, nine months later at the age of 66, not to take it up again.

For many years he had held a second, very time-consuming job as a statesman. In 1740 Sir Robert Walpole had suggested to Hardwicke that he might consider becoming the next prime minister. He certainly possessed some of the requisite qualities and talents. Said by many to be handsome, he had a sonorous voice and combined gravitas with unpretentious good humour. He could speak cogently in the House of Lords where his influence was tremendous. He had a well-trained mind, could write easily in Latin, and his English prose was clear, forceful and economical. Over a period of two decades it was Hardwicke who wrote the King's Speech for the opening of Parliament. He was diligent, patient, courteous and a good judge of people, but he preferred not to be in the forefront of politics, so he turned away Robert Walpole's suggestion. Nevertheless, he played a major role in steering George II's choice of ministers. He helped manage the threatened mass resignation of 1746, and from then until Henry Pelham's death in 1754 he along with Pelham and Newcastle dominated the cabinet. When Pelham died he guided the leadership into Newcastle's hands and continued to serve as the duke's right-hand man. His role in the Seven Years War was that of adviser – a regular participant in the inner cabinet meetings, but also a regular recipient of the contents of what would now be called the dispatch box. 'Your Father, though at Wimpole,' Newcastle wrote to Hardwicke's son at The Hague, 'gives the tone to all we do, and is so good as to let me have freely and most ably his thoughts upon everything; and we generally, sooner or later, follow them.'[1] An opinion has been passed down from the eighteenth century that Hardwicke was not a statesman of the first rank. Neither his cabinet colleagues nor King George II would have agreed.

A word should be said about cabinet efficiency. The great men in high government office all had London residences, but since they were fond of going off to their country estates it might be supposed that they thereby allowed the conduct of affairs, even in wartime, to slow to a casual, aristocratic pace. In reality the three men most concerned with the direction of the Seven Years War made sure this did not happen. Newcastle's country house, Claremont, was south-west of London in Surrey, Hardwicke's Wimpole was north of London, near Royston in Cambridgeshire, and William Pitt's at Hayes was to the south-east in Kent, but communication was prompt, by mounted messenger. The highly trusted messengers were familiar to them, often referred to by name (perhaps not their real name). Letters and papers moved back and forth in a day or two. Newcastle sometimes sent off documents to Wimpole without waiting for his clerks to make copies. If he needed them back quickly together with Hardwicke's advice, two days were required, the messenger having to stay the night.

As Lord Chancellor and member of the court of appeals for adjudicating the legitimacy of prizes captured at sea Hardwicke was directly familiar with matters maritime. More important was the fact that Admiral Lord Anson, First Lord of the Admiralty, was his son-in-law; they often conversed informally. His son Joseph was another important source. Joseph Yorke had made a creditable career in the army (though his very rapid promotion was of course mainly due to his father's political

---

[1] Newcastle to Joseph Yorke, 5 Sept. 1760, Yorke, *Hardwicke*, II, 558.

standing). When he left active duty he served as under-secretary at the British embassy in Paris, and after spending four years there went on to become British minister at The Hague where he became a fixture. The Hague was the information centre of Europe. Joe, as his father called him, corresponded regularly with the whole family – his father, brothers and sisters – and also directly with Newcastle, reporting news that came to The Hague from Paris as well as forwarding and commenting on reports of military and diplomatic developments in Europe. Thus, Lord Hardwicke was someone with personal access to up-to-date information; he was also familiar with modern as well as ancient history. In sum, he was capable of developing well-informed, insightful perceptions of the war on land and sea as well as foreign affairs. It will be evident in the chapters that follow that his advice was usually validated by events. As an astute historian remarked over 70 years ago, Hardwicke was 'the best strategist in the cabinet'.[2]

He was a man who acquired wealth by intelligence, industry and thoughtful preparation; he had been a successful barrister, and as Lord Chancellor he earned his salary by long hours at his desk and on the bench. As some people noted at the time, he was frugal, a trait of which he left evidence by the cheap paper he used (frustrating to a historian because he wrote on both sides and the ink soaked through from the back, rendering some words illegible). If Hardwicke neglected hospitality in the broad social sense, his excuse was that he preferred to spend scarce leisure time with his wife and children. He had five sons and two daughters, and large family gatherings – what Joe from afar called the 'Wimpole Congress' – provided his favourite moments. Contemporaries who considered him avaricious found their best evidence in the public favours he sought and gained for his sons. Eighteenth-century aristocratic standards presumed that sons of high social rank should marry money, but Hardwicke carried it too far. Joe wanted to marry the daughter of a Russian ambassador, with whom he apparently fell in love, and besought his brother Charles and sister Elizabeth (Lady Anson) to plead his case with 'Papa and Mama'. Yet the match was judged unsuitable, not because the lady was Russian, evidently, but because she had no fortune. Joe and his brothers held their father too much in awe as a man to challenge his goals as a patriarch. Though the sons were intelligent and conscientious, their future careers would be somewhat limited by diffidence. Joe and Elizabeth were exceptions; they were less solemn – actually cheerful and optimistic. After his

[2] Pares, 'American versus Continental Warfare, 1739–63', p. 168.

request to marry was refused the heartbroken son forthrightly criticized his family's temperament. He wrote to his brother Charles, 'I have told Papa in a letter, and I insist upon it, that I have a fundamental objection to all the family, myself included, and that is a cursed way we have of overthinking everything, which . . . deprives us of a thousand things which sweeten the lives of our fellow creatures.'[3] Eight years later when his parents offered him an arranged marriage to a lady worth £40,000, he refused.

Hardwicke's role as an adviser on war policy will be evident throughout this book, yet it may be contended that he performed an even more important role: that of brokering and sustaining the government that enabled the British constitutional monarchy to achieve victorious results far beyond initial expectations. It was Hardwicke who manoeuvred George II into accepting a Pitt–Newcastle administration and patiently laboured to hold it together. His role in this has been too little remarked. There were moments when William Pitt did things that the former Lord Chancellor could not bear, such as Pitt's proposal regarding habeas corpus in March 1758, but on the whole it was his intimate friend Newcastle who most frequently tried his patience. Hardwicke warned Newcastle that he did not want to come up to London 'upon every occasion of Mr Pitt's being necessary to be talked to' and thus to be 'perpetually the middle man', 'constantly employed to expostulate'. But he took time to write countless letters to calm the duke down, urging him to put in perspective the trivial slights and imagined insults of which he was continually complaining. On one occasion, however, he did show open anger; it stemmed from Newcastle's failure to defend Joe from a false accusation. The duke, stupefied by fear and weakness, had shied away from telling Pitt the truth about why Joe had written only to him about an inconsequential diplomatic development which, Pitt claimed, should have been communicated to himself as secretary of state. In the end Hardwicke had to ask Anson to convey a stiff message to Newcastle. It was: tell Pitt the truth or 'I will not set my foot within the House of Lords. I will not come near the Court, nor hear one word upon any public business.'[4] The message worked, and the trust and friendship of the two great lords resumed.

[3] Joseph to Charles Yorke, 26 Dec. 1752, in Yorke, *Hardwicke*, II, 185; see also II, 154.
[4] Hardwicke to Newcastle, 29 Oct. 1757, Hardwicke to Anson, 14 Nov. 1759, ibid., III, 39, 88.

William Pitt

William Pitt (the Elder), born in 1708, created Earl of Chatham in 1766, was a great man. George II, however, disliked him intensely. Pitt built a parliamentary reputation in the mid-1740s by condemning the way in which Hanoverian concerns twisted British foreign policy, and the king deeply resented it. The circumstances and political manoeuvring that drove George II to accept Pitt as the leading minister responsible for war policy are highly relevant to the story of British wartime success. As mentioned, Hardwicke played the key role in the manoeuvring, but he did not like Pitt much, and Newcastle was afraid of him. Pitt's speaking style exhibited an attitude of command which, though impressive in a large forum, was discomforting in private conversation. The other ministers when describing their meetings with him often thought it necessary to remark upon whether he had been 'civil' and 'rational'. Often he was both, but his tendency toward vehemence, especially in talking to Newcastle, was not helpful.

The friction between the twin pillars of the Pitt–Newcastle administration was not entirely Pitt's fault, however. Pitt understood what Newcastle had to do to mobilize patronage and keep well with the king, but the duke habitually disregarded the things Pitt had to do to maintain his reputation and influence with the public. Deep down, it seems that Newcastle felt Pitt's role to be unnecessary: having 'chosen' the House of Commons, Newcastle tended to suppose, though he knew better, that its support was secure. Hardwicke had to remind him again and again that in wartime circumstances Pitt's leadership in that house was indispensable. In sum, Pitt understood what Newcastle was inclined to forget – that it was in the national interest for each to remain strong in his own sphere.

Judging by his popularity, one would suppose that Pitt's sphere was Britain 'out of doors', that is, public opinion at large. He had ostentatiously rejected the usual spoils of office while presenting himself to the public as a true patriot. He greatly depended upon a favourable press. London had two or three dozen newspapers. Paris, in contrast, had one official newspaper and one other; the content of both was supervised by the government. Across the Atlantic at this time, eight to a dozen newspapers were published in the British colonies, none in New France. There was virtually no censorship in England; the situation was nothing like that of the first half of the twentieth century when governments controlled war news. Pitt did not write or commission pamphlets; he let others do that for him. The capital was the key to public opinion. In matters of high politics the provincial newspapers freely drew upon the London press. It was necessary for Pitt to reckon with both London and 'independent country' opinion.

The sphere of direct and vital importance to Pitt, however, was the House of Commons. It was there that he made his speeches, and his reputation as a war leader, like Winston Churchill's, has rested heavily on those speeches. Pitt must be placed among the half-dozen best parliamentary orators in all of British history. Tall and thin but not handsome, he had a strong and supple voice, theatrical gifts, and a rather frightening eagle eye. Two developed capabilities made him incomparably effective. One was his capacity to call to mind a large body of prepared material and present it with beautifully adapted rhetoric. The other was his alert sense of the particular audience of that House. Some speeches, disorganized or lacking in brilliant touches, did not go well, but most did, and when a performance by Pitt was expected, members and gallery watchers flocked to attend.

Many of these speeches, or parts of them, were recorded for posterity only because Horace Walpole, the talented letter writer, was fascinated by Pitt's performances and wrote down as much as he could. These speeches were not mere declamations of a demagogue; they were packed with information. In one of them, of which we have an unusually complete record, Pitt undertook a purposeful review of the entire history of the war. Before embarking on tedious details he had the wit and wisdom to warn his audience that he wished to remain cool and calm, adding playfully: 'I will endeavour to be dull if I can.' Long, clear, faithful to the facts, it was a tremendous speech.[5] In his speeches Pitt never willingly misrepresented facts, but he eagerly embellished arguments, and sometimes got carried away, saying things he could not have really meant. He admitted that this occasionally happened. Care must be taken, therefore, to avoid taking any particular phrase in his speeches as representing his considered opinion. Instead, one must view the whole, and this is all the more necessary because the reporting of his speeches was woefully deficient and sometimes fanciful.

Pitt was not just a superb orator, nor was he content simply to serve as the government's leader of the House of Commons; he insisted on taking the lead in directing the war. The greatness of his performance in that role has usually but not always been recognized. When it came to details, he was not a brilliant strategist, but he did catch on quickly (as

[5] See Schweizer, 'An Unpublished Parliamentary Speech' (cited in Chapter 15), p. 98.

some war ministers in those days did not) to the required rhythms when preparing expeditions bound for distant theatres. He depended on the responsible department heads and did his best to instil urgency but could not control war administration. He was rarely in a position to choose the generals and admirals who would command operations, but was determined to defeat complacency and to prevent political or social favouritism from operating to excuse those who failed in their duty. This required political courage and on occasion brought personal pain, but the lesson conveyed to senior officers in both services was important: political and personal connection or claims of seniority would not be allowed to excuse failure. Another point: while his cabinet colleagues tended to overestimate the enemy's capabilities and often thought Pitt's ideas were too daring, he usually proved to be right, and this may have been his most important strategic contribution.

Pitt seldom wrote down his ideas about strategy except in official letters he wrote to generals and governors abroad. His broad war aims may be found in his speeches, though this is not always a reliable source. He sometimes spoke about such matters to Newcastle, who reported what he said to Hardwicke or to William Cavendish, 4th Duke of Devonshire, a trusted and sensible colleague. The remarks that Newcastle recorded must be used with caution since they were made in particular contexts to a man who, more than anyone else in high office, differed with Pitt on fundamental questions of strategy and foreign policy.

Although Newcastle had paid attention to transoceanic concerns earlier in his career, he was, before and during this war, a devoted continentalist, always anxious about the fate of the Electorate of Hanover and looking to reconstruct an alliance system for countering the power of France regardless of the availability of suitable partners. Pitt viewed Hanoverian influence with great suspicion and was sceptical about allies until they proved they would fight. Ambition for high office compelled him to speak out or remain silent on these matters according to political circumstances, but he approached diplomatic and military necessities on the continent with reluctance, and it was this attitude that most consistently directed his choices of policy and strategy. Pitt's strategic choices showed that it was never his wish, except on one occasion of impatience, to try to win the war in Germany. His strategy there was to help Prince Ferdinand fight a defensive war, both to consume French resources and to limit France's conquests, which she would use to recover some of her lost overseas possessions at the peace table. It is this that defined the difference between his conception of grand strategy and Newcastle's; the latter habitually focused on the continent and never stopped wishing that Britain would try to win the war there. While Pitt famously remarked, in November 1761, that 'America has been conquered in Germany', he was, at that time, making a plea to the House of Commons in order to prevent support of Ferdinand's army from being abruptly cut off. He continued to make this plea, but it did not mean that he had ceased to give priority to the navy, overseas trade and colonial possessions.

Pitt's ideas about the interrelation of these three elements in a nexus of power were (like practically everyone else's) somewhat incoherent, but it was a merit that his 'mercantilist' notions were not doctrinaire. His ideas about 'empire' were diffuse. In respect to grand strategy he took his cues from unfolding events and circumstances, but the wish to contain or diminish French power, especially at sea and overseas, always dominated his thinking. It was a striking moment for Pitt and for British strategy when he realized in 1745 that superior sea power could be used not just defensively but offensively to choke off shipping and 'absolutely to ruin' French trade to North America.[6] Thereafter, in Pitt's eyes, whatever else British policy might aim at – for instance, keeping France out of the Netherlands – the navy must be kept strong.

When only a boy at Eton, Pitt had begun to suffer from gout. He impressed his teachers as a good student, went to Oxford for an unhappy year, then to the university at Utrecht where he valued his studies and experience, and on to France. He became fluent in French while residing in Besançon and Strasbourg. Afterwards he became a young army officer, serving only briefly and in peacetime. His immediate family never had much money, but his grandfather, who had made a small fortune in India, saw promise in the young man and nominated him to a parliamentary seat he had bought: the depopulated borough of Old Sarum. Family connections put him in touch with the Grenvilles. Hester Grenville had no sisters and five brothers, all of whom loved her, and Pitt, luckiest of men, was able to marry her in 1754.

It was a late marriage: he was 47 and she was 34. Her dowry was small and the couple was usually hard-pressed for money, but she was a treasure. She understood his quest for greatness and supported it heart and soul. In the family circle Pitt's formal façade was wiped away by a deep affection for her and the infant children. Five lived to adulthood. Of the three boys John would become a well-liked 2nd Earl of Chatham, William

[6] Speech in the House of Commons, 21 Nov. 1745, Marie Peters, 'The Myth of William Pitt' *JICH* 21 (1993), 37.

would eventually be prime minister for a total of nearly 19 years, and James as an ambitious young naval commander would die of fever in the West Indies. The great men responsible for the higher direction of the war on the British side, all three, were fortunate in their wives – loyal companions who were competent to run the households (no small task in those days). Hester combined personal tenderness with an excellent head for business and was in the opinion of Thomas Coutts, the banker, 'the cleverest *man* of her time'.[7] She put up with her husband's absences – some necessary for his duties in London, some odd and unexplainable though he was completely faithful to her – but the greatest burden upon her came during his later years when he was devastated by a mental illness that would almost certainly be diagnosed today as manic-depressive. During the war years he appears to have been manic; it annoyed his colleagues but may have given him extra energy at important moments. From 1766 to 1768 he suffered from long bouts of deep depression during which he was worse than useless, and Hester's care and durable courage were indispensable. Although he was unusually susceptible to gout, only once in a while did it seriously affect his ability to conduct the war.

The duc de Choiseul

The only French statesman who exercised a dominant and durable role during the Seven Years War was Etienne-François de Stainville, duc de Choiseul. A few others possessed great abilities and were dedicated to the nation's service, but they were not given sufficient authority or did not stay in office long. Choiseul was France's leading minister for 12 years, from December 1758 to December 1770. To have remained in the highest ministerial position at the court of Louis XV for such a long time was an achievement in itself. In his case it was accomplished by intelligence, energy, alertness, finesse, personal charm and treachery masked by good humour. The ministries that Choiseul headed at various times – foreign affairs, war, naval – required attention to business, especially foreign affairs, but his survival depended to a large degree on absence from the desk so that he could circulate at court and spread his abundant wit and charm. Speedy decision-making was his habit; he dashed off letters with brilliant ease, though sometimes with too little consideration and attention to detail. A man who could manage the business of state effectively yet spend many hours participating happily in the pleasures of the court

[7] Ayling, *Elder Pitt*, p. 406.

perfectly suited the taste of Louis XV and the woman to whom he handed most of the power of awarding and denying favours, Jeanne-Antoinette Poisson, marquise de Pompadour.

Choiseul came to power after many, perhaps most, of the crucial diplomatic and strategic decisions had been made and at a time when the war was beginning to go badly for the French. The manner in which decisions were made before his time revealed all too abundantly an absence of co-ordination and foresight at the highest level. In 1755 no one seemed to be in charge. In 1756 and 1757 the leading minister was François-Joachim de Pierre de Bernis, but everyone knew how beholden he was to Pompadour and some said that she was 'prime minister'. In 1758 the abbé Bernis argued for a policy that she did not favour. At length it was arranged for him to become cardinal Bernis and he was dismissed. There is no question that in December 1758 Choiseul's leadership was much needed.

Louis XV was a sincere man of good will, but he wished to avoid boredom, and Pompadour, though her physical bond to him as mistress had lapsed, was careful to keep him amused by providing entertainments and concubines. He was willing to work at governing and wrote a great many letters, but he did not wish to bear the burdens of leadership. He received advice from many sources and attended meetings of the council of state. No minutes were kept, and such was the king's desire for secrecy that when ministers were dismissed he asked them to send back the letters he had written to them.[8] Decisions were sometimes made in meetings of the council of state, which was composed of senior, one might say super-annuated, statesmen, but it is clear that many important decisions gained royal approval before the council learned of them. These institutional practices were inherited from the reign of Louis XIV. Unfortunately for the French navy there was no inherited equivalent of the British Board of Admiralty, that highly useful centralized office of naval information and authority. The great point about the council of state is that it was an advisory, not an executive, body, and therefore, unlike the British cabinet, it did not take responsibility for departmental coordination. As 'loyalty of ministers to one another was scarcely prescribed in theory and certainly did not prevail in practice',[9] the king needed a chief minister, but France

---

[8] Antoine, *Louis XV*, pp. 450–1. It seems that he destroyed these letters. As Michel Antoine comments, this may have been more important than revolutionary turmoil as a reason why so little documentary evidence has survived concerning high-level deliberations during Louis XV's reign.

[9] Butler, *Choiseul*, pp. 392–3.

did not have one until the duc de Choiseul managed to acquire the role. Among the great powers of Europe at the time France was unique in this respect except for Prussia, but Frederick II oversaw and coordinated almost everything whereas Louis XV oversaw and coordinated almost nothing.

Before Choiseul, Pompadour was the key personage. Her power was enormous. She could even influence, decisively on some occasions, the choice of generals to command major campaigns. She was intelligent and a lavish patron of literature and the arts, but had no education in matters of state, and she was not a chief minister in the fullest sense because the king did not expect her to secure ministerial cooperation and she did not undertake to do so. Her overpowering concern was to maintain her position. From a selfish viewpoint this was understandable: loss of the king's favour would mean disgrace and banishment, and no one understood this better than she because if a minister acted in a way that she perceived as threatening her position she procured his dismissal. The result was a system of government in which lack of coordination among ministers was joined to fear of precipitate and unwarranted dismissal. Rumour, intrigue and jealous faction could too readily trump merit.

Ministers rarely wrote letters and memoranda on policy issues for each other's eyes or, if they did, they got rid of them. They may have been influenced by the king's desire to keep his own correspondence secret. While in the British case a historian may reliably trace the progress and motives of high-level decisions, often on a daily basis, by reading cabinet members' correspondence, in the French case recourse must often be had to memoirs, which were generally written long afterwards and were commonly filled with self-serving distortions. Although the French government's departmental files of this era are quite extensive, the surviving material above that level is minuscule, except for diplomatic dispatches. In some instances, however, ongoing policy arguments at Versailles were observed and reported by foreign ambassadors.[10]

Born in June 1719, Choiseul was brought up in Lorraine and had family ties to Austria as well as France. One grandfather was a French navy captain who was killed in the West Indies. As comte de Stainville, the boy was educated at the elite Jesuit school in Paris, Louis-le-Grand, where secular culture and light-hearted entertainment were by no means shunned. He acquired intellectual tastes attuned to the Enlightenment and

---

[10] Over a century ago the French historian Richard Waddington found a rich source in the Austrian ambassador's letters, preserved in the state archives at Vienna.

had no qualms when it appeared politically useful for him, later in life, to assist the movement for banning the Jesuits. In 1730, he entered the army as a lieutenant. He was small and baby-faced – attributes not normally associated with impressive military bearing – but on active service, of which he saw a great deal during the wars of the 1740s, he showed himself to be a brave and resourceful officer. By favouritism but also by merit he rose in seven years from subaltern to the equivalent of major-general at the age of 28. After the arrival of peace in 1748 he married the granddaughter of a war contractor. He was fortunate in her character as well as her wealth; everyone liked her and he loved her, though her faithfulness as a wife did not deter him from pursuing other women at court. Evidently he had no children either by her or anyone else.

He soon looked for an ambassadorship and in 1753, thanks to Pompadour's intervention, was given the post at Rome to which others had a better claim. When he managed to mediate a solution to a problem that had vexed relations between the king of France and the papacy for a long time, his reputation for diplomacy was established. He was ambassador at Vienna when recalled to France in late 1758 to serve as foreign minister. It was Pompadour who got him elevated to a dukedom and manoeuvred to place him in this high office. The war had begun to go badly, and she needed someone competent in business who would be congenial and loyal. It helped that Choiseul was adept as a courtier. Deceit and recovery from missteps came easily to him and he met all situations with remarkable aplomb. A viewer of the portrait painted when he was 44 may be struck first by the baby face, but secondly by the eyes and mouth, which suggest a man of amiable temper who simultaneously amuses and deceives.[11]

Choiseul was effusive in conversation and prolific with his pen. In letters to his ambassadors he freely expressed his policy intentions, but his situation as a foreign minister dealing with many allies and potential allies often required that he should tell Vienna one thing while telling Madrid another and Copenhagen a third. The letters to his ambassador at Madrid, the marquis d'Ossun, who was a trusted friend of long standing, are informative, but it is safest to define Choiseul's policy preferences by what he did rather than what he said. That method, however, also entails uncertainties. Until January 1761, he was not sole director: at the war office there was a powerful and much respected war minister, Marshal

[11] The portrait by L.M. Van Loo painted in 1763 is on the cover of Chaussinand-Nogaret's *Choiseul*.

Belleisle. Belleisle's death that month gave Choiseul supremacy, even over Pompadour, people said. (It helped that Choiseul, along with his charming wife and sister, dined regularly with the marquise, who much enjoyed their company.) Yet he still had to be alert to the wishes of the king, and although Louis XV's wishes can sometimes be deduced from evidence, it is very difficult to determine whether he cared strongly enough about something to override Choiseul's recommendation. In contrast, George II's opinions, moderate or vehement, were regularly reported to colleagues, mainly by Newcastle. Did Choiseul at certain crucial junctures bend to the king's wishes? Certainly, and he undoubtedly anticipated those wishes when feasible, but how hard he tried to persuade Louis XV to change his mind is not known, at least for the wartime period.

From the beginning of his time in office he said repeatedly that his goal was to obtain a 'reasonable and honourable peace'. He meant this truthfully no doubt, but the definition of 'reasonable' belonged to him and the king and, as events showed, it allowed for plenty of expensive warmaking in the attempt to make the British government reasonable. It was well known that Pompadour very much wished to please the Austrians, who, until near the war's end, wished to keep the war going, and also that Louis XV was eager to consummate a Bourbon Family Compact with Madrid. Choiseul's conduct in the peace negotiations with Britain in 1760 and 1761 may be interpreted as accommodating their desires. Yet his policy also indicates that he was not a man of peace but a man of war, who believed that a wartime alliance with Spain was a winning formula. It is quite possible that he did not keep the king adequately informed of the risks he was taking in 1761 as he negotiated secretly and separately to form a military alliance with Spain. Two and a half centuries later, these uncertainties regarding his motivation and management remain.

Choiseul was given a weak hand when he entered office, but he acted as if he could win the game. His optimism seemed to please the king and Pompadour, but the reality was that every military initiative he undertook turned out badly, and he chose to keep on playing. It is therefore impossible to consider him a competent war minister. Argument for his greatness must be based, instead, on the diplomatic skill with which he maintained France's alliances with Austria and, despite adversity, with Spain. He also procured, by unflappable skill and patience, far better peace terms than Bourbon military performance deserved.

The latter success was owing to a degree of British war-weariness, but more particularly to the Earl of Bute. A year after George III came to the throne (succeeding his grandfather in late October 1760) Lord Bute began to dismantle the Pitt–Newcastle administration. Newcastle's weakness and Pitt's lapses in political judgement paved the way for this, and the result was the rise to power of Bute, the 'royal favourite', who could expect the young king to grant whatever he asked. Bute's goal in 1762 was to end the war quickly by pursuing a policy of appeasing France. (The characters of Bute and George III will be viewed in the context of their conduct, displayed in the book's closing chapters.) All in all, it may be said that France began the war with a disconnected and incompetent government, and ended it with a unified ministry dominated by Choiseul; in contrast, Britain acquired a successful and popular government led by Pitt in close cooperation with Newcastle and Hardwicke, but under a new monarch this was replaced by an unpopular, though politically invincible, government directed by Lord Bute, the royal favourite.

CHAPTER 3

Origins: the contested regions, 1748–54

Generations of historians have regarded the hostilities that erupted in 1755 as a continuation of the war that ended in 1748. Too many points of contention worldwide had been left unsettled by the treaty of Aix-la-Chapelle, and both sides wanted to end the war quickly, so lingering disputes were assigned to a joint Boundary Commission for resolution. The commission was charged not only with North American issues but also the question of the 'Neutral Islands' in the West Indies, islands of the Lesser Antilles that had been unofficially abandoned by Spain and belonged officially to neither France nor Britain. Madras was restored to the British at Aix-la-Chapelle, but the region of southeastern India in which it was situated called the Carnatic was a scene of continuing hostilities long after news of the peace arrived.

Given the rising intensity of Anglo-French overseas rivalry, it was a safe prediction that the Boundary Commission would achieve practically nothing. In North America the French claimed all territory to the west and north of the established British colonies. Included were the Mississippi valley, the Ohio valley, the area south of Lake Erie, the Lake Champlain corridor and the Atlantic maritime region. In the interior the French had established many settlements, trading posts, forts and garrisons, but most of the vast expanse was wilderness in which the only settlements were scattered Indian villages. Nevertheless, as a matter of principle the French claimed all territory drained by a river and its tributaries if some part of that river had been first explored by a Frenchman, regardless of whether any French explorer had ever gone near the headwaters. (This 'watershed principle' was later allowed to prevail in the distant northern reaches of the Mississippi and Missouri rivers – hence the balloon-like configuration of the Louisiana Purchase of 1803.) The headwaters of the Ohio River and its tributaries lay near Virginia settlements and also in territory claimed by the colony of Pennsylvania. When the French tried to solidify their claim to these regions by military positioning they provoked a dispute that escalated into the Seven Years War. At first, however, in 1749, the focus of contention was the maritime Atlantic region, which the French called Acadie.

Acadia and Nova Scotia

British forces had captured Port Royal on the Nova Scotia peninsula from the French in 1710 (renaming it Annapolis Royal), and the treaty of Utrecht (1714) awarded possession of the peninsula to Britain. The rest of Acadia remained under French rule (approximately the modern province of New Brunswick). By the treaty of Aix-la-Chapelle (1748) the French kept Île St Jean (later Prince Edward Island) and recovered Île Royale (Cape Breton Island), while Britain's formal possession of Nova Scotia was confirmed.

When peace came in 1748 the British government immediately launched a scheme of immigration to Nova Scotia. No time was wasted; the first set of transports sailed from England in May and arrived in late June 1749. Most of the immigrants were demobilized British soldiers and other unemployed persons. Very few were familiar with agriculture, and many soon boarded vessels for New England. The new governor who came out on this first voyage, Edward Cornwallis, urged that in future German and Swiss farmers should be sent. This was done. The voyages of 1750 and 1751 carried Germans, mostly recruited from the Rhineland. An absolute requirement was that all should be Protestants. The project was ambitious and its expense was subsidized by the British Treasury. The principal objective was to settle around a superb harbour called Chebouctou on the south-eastern coast. The settlement was named Halifax, after the Earl of Halifax, who was chairman of the Board of Trade, the department in charge of the project.

All in all, about 4,000 state-sponsored immigrants arrived within three years. More would have been brought across if circumstances had not forced a curtailment. Nova Scotia was thus launched as a British colony peopled largely by German immigrants. As is well known, other colonies of British North America had, over time, received streams of immigrants including many Germans. Nova Scotia was unique in that it was the only one in which the colonizing was directly organized and carried out by the government and paid for by government money.

Why did the British government do it? One reason was to take possession of Chebouctou as a potential naval base. A second reason was political pressure. The giving up of Cape Breton did not please a highly vocal segment of public opinion in London, and this was a way of responding. It was a gesture of substance that betokened official commitment to a British presence in the region and was aimed partly at mollifying New Englanders. Cape Breton with its fortress capital Louisbourg had been captured by New England troops with Royal Navy support in 1745. Although the London government reimbursed the New England colonies for the expenses they had incurred, there was the moral factor that a conquest for which 1,300 colony troops had died was restored to France. (All but 100 of them died while garrisoning Louisbourg through harsh winters after the capture.) Moreover, the French recovery of Louisbourg meant that once again there was a fortified base from which, in time of war, New England's northern fishery, shipping and coasts could be easily attacked. A base at Halifax could help neutralize these threats.

Although Governor William Shirley of Massachusetts had wanted to see Cape Breton Island as well as all of Nova Scotia settled with British or foreign Protestants, the project launched in 1749 was confined to the Atlantic coast of Nova Scotia. The peninsula was an empty wilderness. The Indian population was thin (probably not more than 1,000). Officially the British were merely settling a territory that the French government had ceded; there was no encroachment. The trouble was that British possession was ultimately the result of a conquest made 40 years earlier, and in the western sector of Nova Scotia near the Bay of Fundy dwelt numerous Acadians. These were settlers of French lineage and Roman Catholic faith who had carved out homesteads and chosen to remain when the peninsula was ceded to Great Britain by the treaty of Utrecht in 1714. At that time they had numbered about 1,800; by 1749, through natural increase, the number was close to 11,000. (There were perhaps 4,000 others in French-controlled Acadia.) The population grew at an even faster rate than that of Pennsylvania, yet did so without immigration. The cause was a rapid natural increase under conditions in which epidemic diseases were absent.

In 1714, the treaty stipulated that those who chose to remain under British rule were to be allowed to retain their religion (their priests were appointed by the bishop of Quebec) and title to their lands; this was confirmed to them by a British royal proclamation. They believed that their conditional pledge to His Britannic Majesty allowed them not only to practise their Catholic faith but also to be considered a separate people and permitted to remain neutral. Neutrality was important, and accordingly they refused to agree to bear arms. Over the years British authorities in Nova Scotia, backed by orders from London, tried to make them acknowledge this obligation to bear arms and serve in the militia. Acadian delegates were summoned to Halifax and it was insisted that they must take the full, unconditional oath. If they did not do so, they were told, they must expect to be deprived of their lands and expelled from the province. But when they refused the threatened penalties were never imposed. One reason was British uncertainty as to whether it was legal to deprive people of their property if they failed to agree to bear arms (they did take an oath acknowledging the sovereignty of the king), but, as will be seen, there were other more practical reasons why the Acadians were not compelled to take the unconditional oath.

During 30 years of peace, from 1714 to 1744, the Acadians were not seriously troublesome to British settlers and authorities. In fact, they usefully supplied fresh food to the garrison at Fort Anne and Annapolis Royal. They generally got on well with the local Indians and intermarriage sometimes occurred. Their communities were strongly united by pervasive family ties and cooperative undertakings. Because of their French peasant background and Catholic faith they had a strong sense of proud independence, forged by isolation and frontier hardship. But they accepted the fact of British governance and recognized some of its benefits. It would have been useful to bring them into the management of local government in their communities, but the Board of Trade insisted, in keeping with the Test Acts that prevailed in Great Britain, that no Catholic could hold public office.

When war between Britain and France erupted in 1744 British authorities became worried: Acadians not only continued to refuse to participate in armed defence but were accused of failing to warn British garrisons of imminent attacks. It was known that in some cases they made information and provisions available to the attackers. But military duress accounted for a good deal of this cooperation with the enemy and, to the great annoyance of French and Canadian authorities, the Acadians regularly refused to take up arms against the British. Thus, there were reasons for the British authorities on the spot to consider that even in a dangerous time of war the wisest course was to trust the Acadians to remain neutral. Governor William Shirley of Massachusetts had been devoted to the idea of their being expelled because he was sure that if a French force appeared they would all heartily support it. But there had been no evidence of that, and in 1746 when it appeared that a French force was planning to attack, even he saw the practicality of treating them well and hoping they would remain neutral. As he informed the Duke of Newcastle, 'an attempt to drive all the French inhabitants from their settlements, should it succeed, would in effect be driving 5 or 6,000 men to take up Arms against his Majesty's Government there every Year during the War'.[1]

Cornwallis's instructions of 1749 required him to compel the Acadians to take the full oath. When the three months allowed to them for deliberation elapsed their delegates answered that they wanted to continue under the existing agreement. The governor responded that this course was no longer acceptable, but neither he nor his successor followed up with punitive action. Even in time of peace the measure was impractical, for reasons that will become clear in a moment.

The British objective of developing a naval base at Halifax posed no immediate threat to the Acadians because they were concentrated on the other side of the peninsula. A more intrusive plan was proposed, however, namely to place Protestant German settlements in the midst of the Acadian people, particularly on the Chignecto isthmus. After obtaining convenient legal opinions the British decreed that the Acadians dwelling on the isthmus had no valid title to their lands. If this plan had been carried out, many Acadians would have been dispossessed, some of them dwelling in a disputed borderland. The British would therefore have been guilty of a provocative encroachment.

As it happened, the British government did not send settlers to the isthmus or any other locations near the shores of the Bay of Fundy, and in late 1751 the Board of Trade ordered recruitment of German immigrants to be suspended; there would be no voyage of 1753. These decisions, and also the decision not to penalize the Acadians resident in Nova Scotia for refusing the full oath, stemmed from an awareness of the goals of the French, to which we now turn.

In the seventeenth century French colonial policy had ignored the Acadians – they were viewed as useless subsistence farmers in an out-of-the-way location – but the eighteenth-century decision to develop Louisbourg led to a policy of encouraging them to migrate to Île Royale (Cape Breton) so that they might produce food locally for the fortress city. A delegation of Acadians surveyed the island and concluded that farming there would be far more onerous and less productive than it was near the Bay of Fundy, from whence they were already shipping food to Louisbourg (chiefly by New England vessels). When Louisbourg was returned to the French in 1748 the governors of New France anticipated that the British

---

[1] Shirley to Newcastle, 21 Nov. 1746, Faragher, *Great and Noble Scheme*, p. 233.

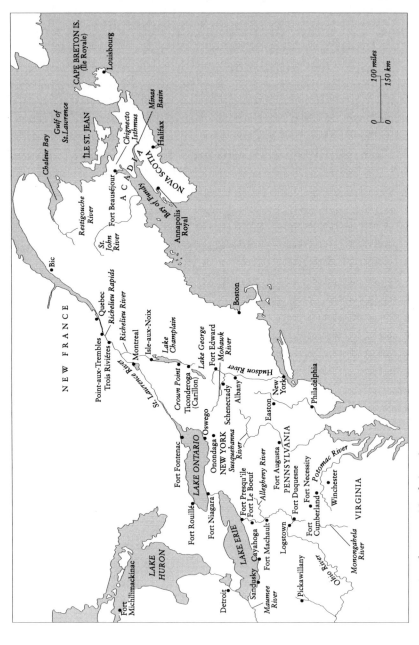

MAP 1 *North-eastern North America*

would prohibit Acadians in Nova Scotia from supplying the city, and in 1749 Governor Cornwallis, carrying out instructions from London, did in fact impose such a prohibition. The governor-general at Quebec sensibly ordered the commander of a small garrison recently placed on Île St Jean (Prince Edward Island) to entice Acadian farmers in Nova Scotia to move there. Yet, even though that island's climate was more suitable for agriculture than Île Royale's (because the cold Labrador current cannot reach its sheltered surrounding waters), very few Acadians were willing to move from their existing farms and communities. A powerful reason why Governor Cornwallis did not punish and expel Nova Scotia Acadians for refusal to take the full oath thus becomes evident. If he had, he would have helped the French to achieve a goal that they had been pursuing for decades with very little progress – removing Acadians from under British rule.

The treaty of Aix-la-Chapelle stipulated that the Acadian population in Nova Scotia should be left undisturbed, so the French effort to entice emigrants violated the treaty. Enticement was a mild infraction, however, when compared with other measures of a wholly different character that were also approved and supported by the governors of New France. These were carried out under the inspired and ruthless direction of the abbé Le Loutre, a man of God and of France.

Jean-Louis Le Loutre came to Acadia as a missionary to the Indians in 1738. From his location in the heart of Nova Scotia, at Shubenacadie, he operated with remarkable success, converting a large following of the local Micmac Indians to the Roman Catholic religion. Until war erupted in 1744 he maintained untroubled relations with the British governor at Annapolis Royal, but thereafter his conduct was strongly partisan, and his zealous Indian converts appear to have been eager to engage in guerrilla war. After the return of peace in 1748 Le Loutre continued to encourage Indian violence against the British regardless. His response to the new British settlement at Halifax was to incite the Indians to attack it: 'I shall do my best', he wrote to the minister of marine and colonies at Versailles in late July 1749, 'to make it look to the English as if this plan comes from the Indians and that I have no part in it.' That was not easy to do, especially as the written declaration of war that the Micmacs sent to Cornwallis in September – their complaint was that British settlements were encroaching on their God-given native lands – was written in flawless French.[2] The resulting Indian raids were sporadic, but sufficiently threatening to have an effect of confining British settlements to small enclaves.

[2] *DCB*, IV, 'Le Loutre', p. 455; Gipson, V, 189.

Le Loutre tried to frighten Acadians into emigrating to Île St Jean. He hinted that Indian savagery might at any moment be turned on them. Though they chose not to leave Nova Scotia, their fears were heightened. 'One thing is sure,' concluded the intendant of New France in a letter to the minister of marine and colonies, 'without this missionary . . . the Acadians . . . would be very tranquil and so would the English be at Chibouctou [Halifax] and on very good terms with the Indians.'[3]

Le Loutre was extraordinarily zealous and enterprising, but his actions accorded with secret directives from French governors. Jacques-Pierre de Taffanel, marquis de la Jonquière, governor-general at Quebec, saw to it, quietly and under a false pretext, that military supplies were sent for the use of the Micmacs. He even suggested that some loyal Acadians 'dressed and painted like Indians' should participate in raiding so that – he assumed they would be found out – Acadians would be suspected of treachery and expelled. All the while he was reassuring the governor of Nova Scotia that 'far from encouraging the Indians against the English', he was doing his 'best to keep them at peace'.[4] How much did Paris know? The minister was certainly kept informed. In fact, as early as August 1749 a memorandum was read before the king which outlined steps for defeating British efforts to improve their hold on Nova Scotia, steps of the sort that Le Loutre was pursuing.

It soon became unsafe for Le Loutre to remain at Shubenacadie. The mission centre was only 40 miles from Halifax, and in January 1750 the British put a price on his head. He moved to the Chignecto isthmus. There he operated quite openly, directing his Acadian and Micmac followers to assist a military force that had come from Canada under the command of Jean-Luc de la Corne.

Although La Corne was ordered to encourage Acadians to emigrate from Nova Scotia, his primary mission was to defend the isthmus. The only feasible line of communication from Quebec to Louisbourg when ice closed the St Lawrence River was via the St John River to the Bay of Fundy, across the isthmus to Baie Verte, and through or alongside the Northumberland Strait to Cape Breton. La Corne wanted to move as many Acadians as he could to the west side of the Missaquash River, which cut across the isthmus. His force was already in place in April 1750 when Major Charles Lawrence arrived by sea at the head of the Bay of Fundy with 400 soldiers. To prevent Lawrence from occupying the village of

---

[3] Quoted by Gipson, V, 192.
[4] Frégault, *Canada: The War of the Conquest*, p. 168. Stanley, *New France*, p. 65. Also Faragher, *Great and Noble Scheme*, pp. 257–8.

Beaubassin (near present-day Amherst) Le Loutre's Indians were ordered to put it to the torch. To induce the Acadians dwelling to the east of the Missaquash to migrate westward Le Loutre ordered houses and barns to be burnt. Homeless refugees poured into French territory. La Corne had an order from Quebec requiring refugees to take an unqualified oath of fidelity to the French king and immediately enrol in the militia. Many did. Others migrated to Île St Jean where actual militia service would be unlikely. As a result, the rate of migration to that island surged: its settler population had been only 650 in 1748; it was 2,200 in 1752.

Major Lawrence protested to the French commandant against these scorched-earth methods, but his force was heavily outnumbered and he withdrew. He returned in September with reinforcements. His landing was opposed by some Indians and Acadians led by two priests, one of whom was Le Loutre, but it was only briefly delayed. In the spring and summer of 1751 both sides were vigorously building forts: Fort Lawrence east of the river, Fort Beauséjour near its west bank. At first, French strength was the greater: the combination of Canadian troops, recruited Acadians and Le Loutre's Indians kept the British garrison on the defensive. There were numerous raids and skirmishes, including a deadly ambush of a British officer by Indians and Acadians while he was proceeding to meet a French officer under a flag of truce; the killing was bitterly remembered by the British. Under these conditions there was no point in trying to settle any German farmers near Chignecto.

During the latter half of 1751 the French at Chignecto found themselves in a weakened condition. Their numbers created a problem; they could not feed all the soldiers and Acadian refugees that were concentrated in the area around Fort Beauséjour and their external food supplies were being intercepted by British armed sloops of war. Still, London would not authorize an attack on Fort Beauséjour, nor Paris on Fort Lawrence. The rival commanders settled down to a long stand-off. A line formed by the Missaquash River and extended to Baie Verte became the provisional divide between British and French territory while the two governments awaited a decision from the Boundary Commission.

Notwithstanding their problems of subsistence the French were firmly established in the isthmus and locations west of it. British attempts to dislodge them from a settlement at the mouth of the St John River were desultory and ineffectual. On the rugged Atlantic coast, however, British settlements were becoming solidly established. These suffered from occasional raids, particularly the settlement at Dartmouth (next to Halifax) which was attacked in May 1751 by a party of Micmacs who arrived by sea and killed men, women and children. Yet, all in all, despite the abandonment of the plan to settle Germans at the Chignecto isthmus and sporadic Indian attacks, the British were winning the contest for supremacy in the peninsula. Le Loutre went to France for a year and Indian violence slackened; Acadians became less frightened and more willing to seek some arrangement with the British governor. For one thing, they had heard reports of the misery of their brethren who had become refugees at the isthmus. Even when sporadic Indian terror recommenced upon Le Loutre's return from France in late 1753, the Nova Scotia residents stayed put, and many Acadians who had fled to the west side of the Missaquash sought to return eastwards to their former homes. In June 1754, a body of the latter approached the commander at Fort Lawrence, asking if they could resume their residence under some arrangement that would not require their taking the full oath. They now dreaded its consequences more than ever: if they took it, they said, they would 'every day run the risque of having their throats cut and their cattle destroyed' by the Indians.[5] The British commander said that it was not in his power to grant a special arrangement regarding the oath, but advised them that they could return and take their chances. They retraced their steps to Fort Beauséjour where they immediately complained to Le Loutre of the great hardship under which they had fallen and spoke to him of their desire to return to their farms. Soon afterwards some Indians informed them that if they went back to British territory they would be regarded as enemies and treated accordingly. So they stayed, envious of their brethren who were able to remain under British rule. As will be seen in Chapter 5, this situation would not last.

The Seven Years War when it came was not triggered by activities in this region. From 1752 to 1755 the garrisons at the head of the Bay of Fundy did little more than eye each other warily. Nevertheless, Nova Scotia was not forgotten in Britain: the French hostile actions had been reported in the London press, and monetary support for the colony was a distinct item in Parliament's annual appropriation. The perception that it was under threat increased London's sensitivity to any instance, valid or supposed, of French aggression in North America.

The New York frontier

The shortest and easiest line of communications between Albany, New York and Montreal, Canada was the water corridor formed by Lake George (Lac Saint Sacrament), Lake Champlain and the Richelieu River. Lake

[5] Gipson, V, 203.

George flows out to the north, so by the watershed principle the French could claim practically the whole corridor. They established Fort St Frédéric at Crown Point on Lake Champlain in the 1730s. Forts that the British had built in the vicinity of Lake George a half-century earlier were in ruins, and Fort Edward on the Hudson River would not be established until autumn 1755. In the period of peace after 1748 some Indians, supported by the French presence at Fort St Frédéric, raided southwards; the Mohawks who were settled near Lake George and in the northern Hudson Valley suffered from these raids, as did a few English colonists, and both were losing confidence in British colonial willingness and capacity to protect them.

At the south-eastern end of Lake Ontario stood the New York trading post of Oswego (then commonly called Choueguen), and directly north from it, near the origin of the St Lawrence River, stood Fort Frontenac (now Kingston). Each place was vulnerable to a well-mounted waterborne assault. Oswego was first established in the early 1720s. It lay at the end of a long passage up the Mohawk River involving Lake Oneida and some troublesome portages. The security of this route from attack depended heavily on the good will of the Iroquois Confederacy. As a means of travelling from Albany to Montreal the route via Oswego was not only circuitous (around the massive Adirondack Mountains) but also more difficult.

The existence of Oswego tormented the French because many of the beaver pelts upon which the economic life of Canada depended were carried by western Indians to Fort Frontenac and Montreal. Oswego offered an alternative market; it allowed pelts to be diverted from Canada to New York, and this was no small matter: by experience the western Indians found 'English' goods – especially woollen cloth, blankets, copper kettles and firearms – to be more plentiful, cheaper and generally of better quality. The competitive British advantage was especially strong in time of war, the root cause being British naval curtailment of French transatlantic shipping. Even French goods that got through were more costly because of high insurance charges, while British transatlantic trade in wartime was relatively secure.

Antoine-Louis Rouillé, the new minister of the marine and colonies in April 1749, was sure that Oswego meant the ruin of Canada. He wanted immediate action taken and went so far as to outline a method to his governor-general, the marquis de la Jonquière. The idea was to persuade the Iroquois leadership that the trade through Oswego was a means used by the British to reduce them to subservience and make them vulnerable to usurpation of their lands. If the Iroquois could be made to realize this, they would wish to wipe out Oswego on their own. Of course, the minister observed, the governor-general would have to proceed with great prudence and circumspection so that French complicity would be masked. La Jonquière knew, however, that the Iroquois would reject this scheme because they were determined to preserve neutrality in peace as in war. Even so, Rouillé remained zealous for it. A year later he again suggested that this 'ruse' (his own word) might be put into practice. Instead, La Jonquière concentrated on improving the portage at Niagara and building up a trading post at Toronto (Fort Rouillé) whereby the Indians could trade their pelts for goods before traversing Lake Ontario. Yet it is interesting to see how far the minister in Paris was prepared to go, notwithstanding the return of peace, to defend the fur trade from English competition.

The French had thought of attacking Oswego during the war of 1744–8, but fear of provoking Indian hostility restrained them. This consideration remained influential in the early 1750s. The Six Nations of the Iroquois, whose pre-eminent 'camp fire' was at Onondaga, not far from Oswego, dominated the region, and neither side dared to disturb their resolute neutrality. As soon as organized hostilities appeared inevitable, however, the New York frontier became the prime focus of military campaigning in North America. Both the British and the French planned attacks in the region in 1755 and 1756. But until then neither side was inclined to press its claims by military positioning.

Ohio: the French predicament

Hardly anyone expected a dispute over the Ohio region to produce a great war. In mid-eighteenth-century usage, the Ohio River, which the French commonly called 'la Belle Rivière' (Ohio being a Seneca word for 'beautiful'), included the Allegheny River of today. Thus, it referred to a river flowing 1,100 miles from modern Pennsylvania's northern border past the Forks (now Pittsburgh) and then south-west to its connection with the Mississippi. The Ohio region, as the phrase is used here, stretches westwards from the Appalachian Mountains to the Wabash River, and northwards from the Ohio River to Lake Erie; it measures nearly 450 miles east to west, and 200 miles north to south. It contained no British or French settlements at this time and its Indian population was thin, having been sharply reduced by the Iroquois wars, but in the 1730s and 1740s fragments of tribes journeyed westwards to the region, especially Senecas of the Six Nations.

The French had no direct interest in the region. Their interior traffic between Canada and Louisiana stayed to the west of it, making use of the

Maumee and Wabash rivers from Lake Erie and the Chicago and Illinois rivers from Lake Michigan to reach the Mississippi. The main commodity was deerskins, for which the British colonies could find markets but not the French. Yet the French had a strong political reason for barring British traders: their presence made it very hard to keep the resident Indians loyal and quiet. Ideally quietude was achieved by alliance arrangements. The tribes recognized the Canadian governor-general (whom the Indians called Onontio) as their 'father' and accepted him as a mediator who could forestall tribal wars. The duties of the 'father' were manifold: attending long ceremonial conferences; providing presents for the chiefs and their people; making European goods available at reasonable prices, measured in beaver pelts; and forgiving a Frenchman's murder by accepting a ritualized formula that involved regret. Clearly, it was necessary to be patient, and some governors-general and commandants thought they could achieve pacification more simply by instilling fear and subordination. Experience taught those who remained in America long enough to recognize that reciprocity and generosity were more suited to the limited measure of French power.

The presence of British traders allowed dissident groups in the region to find an alternative to the French system, and because British goods, especially woollen blankets and shrouds, tended to be of better quality and cost fewer skins and pelts in exchange, French traders were at a competitive disadvantage. This pressure became extreme during the Anglo-French war of 1744-8. In the years preceding that war the minister at Versailles tried to reduce the cost of the Indian alliance network: the periodic presents to the chiefs were reduced in value, and trading posts were leased to contractors, who raised prices. In 1745 Indian trade goods from France began to be affected by British harassment of French Atlantic shipping. On the frontier French excuses were meaningless to the Indians. What they saw was that their 'father' was no longer taking care of them as promised, bringing too little and charging too much. There was anger and frightful violence. George Croghan, the most experienced English trader, reported: 'Another French Trader has since been killed . . . the Frenchman offering but one charge of powder and one bullet for a beaver skin to the Indian; the Indian took up hatchet and knocked him on the head.'[6]

---

[6] Quoted in White, *Middle Ground*, p. 200. The term 'English', for all its faults, will be sometimes used when discussing Anglo-French contentions in the interior; it should be taken as referring to people based in British America whether of Scottish, Irish, English, Dutch or, quite often, German extraction. The French and Indians most commonly called them 'les Anglois'.

The Indians often turned to British supplies. Croghan had trading contacts at Sandusky and Cuyahoga (Cleveland) on Lake Erie. Officials at Quebec wanted these connections eradicated and counted on loyal Indians in the Detroit area to do it; but they reneged. Increasingly the French feared a massive, English-inspired Indian conspiracy, which might unleash violence and slaughter upon all their French frontier posts in the west. But Indians along the Lake Erie shore began to fear the French. In November 1747 they sent a delegation to Philadelphia seeking help; chiefly they asked for powder and lead. It is to be doubted that Croghan and other Pennsylvania traders were promoting a conspiracy since they were prospering by peaceful trade, but they did encourage Indians to align with the English. Some wise precautions were taken by the French commandants at the western posts and general massacres never occurred, but small parties of Frenchmen were slain, and remembrance of the larger threat remained fresh in French minds when peace returned.

The trading posts on the Lake Erie shore felt vulnerable to a surprise attack, so the focus of trading moved south to Pickawillany at the headwaters of the Great Miami River. This town, rather large at 400 families, was politically dominated by a branch of the Miami tribe, the Twightwees, who, under a leader whom the French called 'La Demoiselle' and the English called 'Old Briton', were closely tied to English interests. Not only were deerskins traded here, but also some of the beaver pelts that came down from the upper Great Lakes.

To the French authorities the diversion of beaver pelts to the English through Ohio was ominous. This economic threat was accompanied by a strategic one, for by undermining Indian allegiance it threatened security all the way to the Mississippi River and thus the severance of Canada from Louisiana. Indians were absolutely vital to the furtherance of any and every colonial activity in the interior wilderness, whether commercial, agricultural or military. Their acquiescence was a minimum requirement, and Indian hostility, though it might not be actively continuous, could be devastating. Moreover, near-term relief from the violent effects of Indian hostility was seldom obtainable without help from other Indians.

When news of the peace arrived in North America, La Galissonière, who was interim governor-general, drew up a plan for an expedition to the Ohio River. Receiving authorization from the minister of marine and colonies, he went ahead, and in mid-June Lieutenant Pierre-Joseph de Céloron de Blainville left Montreal with 15 officers and cadets, 20 French regulars and 180 Canadian militia. A month later he began the difficult portage from the shores of Lake Erie to Lake Chatauqua, and from its eastern end he portaged again to the upper 'Ohio River', near what is today Warren, Pennsylvania, the point where La Galissonière had ordered him to begin. Céloron was instructed to proclaim as he journeyed down river 'the renewal' of the king of France's 'possession . . . of the said River Ohio, and of all the lands on both sides'. In furtherance of this mission he carried with him a number of metallic plaques on which these words were inscribed as well as words indicating that the original claim was kept current by the treaties of 'Ryswick, of Utrecht and of Aix-la-Chapelle'. (None of these treaties of 1697, 1714 and 1748 warranted any such inference.) He planted the plaques at prominent locations along the river as far as the junction of the Great Miami River.[7] There he turned northwards to call upon La Demoiselle at Pickawillany on his way back to Lake Erie. Speaking for the governor-general and the king of France, he told all Indians he encountered that the land belonged to France and that the English who came into it would be expelled.[8]

Céloron's instructions required him to chase away any English traders he came across and to urge the local Indians to do the same. By this means, he told the Indians, peace and tranquillity would be restored to the region. On one occasion early in his travels, however, some of them responded that they could not possibly shun English traders; they could not survive the coming winter without access to trade goods and a gun-smith, and the only traders and gunsmiths they ever saw were English. Céloron did not have a good answer and recorded afterwards that he was greatly embarrassed by what they said. He promised, however, that French traders would be coming to them in the spring to supply their needs. It was a promise he felt the need to repeat in many villages as he made his way down river.

Although Céloron was courteous and diplomatic, the mere proximity of over 200 armed Frenchmen terrified the villagers and they commonly took to the woods. His chief interpreter often had to be sent ahead to calm them; otherwise he could not have carried out his orders to assemble them to hear his announcements. The village leaders adhered to the formalities of welcoming and of courtesy, but they could not conceal their fear and mistrust. At Pickawillany they were particularly cool to him, yet practically

---

[7] Text of inscription in *NYCD*, X, 189. Photograph of a surviving plaque in *Collections of the State Historical Society of Wisconsin*, vol. 18, edited by Reuben Gold Thwaites (Madison, 1908), p. 44.

[8] Céloron's Journal, in *Ohio Archaeological and Historical Society Publications*, vol. 29 (1920), pp. 344–5.

everywhere, even there, he had heard expressions of good will towards the French. He knew, nevertheless, that these were not to be relied upon, and when he drew near to Lake Erie a chieftain said to him: 'My bitter sorrow is to be the only one who loves you, and to observe that all the nations to the southward are raging against the French.' Upon his return to Canada in early November Céloron recorded a sombre conclusion:

All I can say is that the Nations of these localities are very badly disposed toward the French and devoted entirely to the English. I do not know by what means we could bring them back. If we employ violence, they will get warning and take flight. . . . If we extend commerce, our traders could never give merchandise at the prices given by the English.

He estimated that any attempt to introduce French traders into the region would probably be counter-productive. The post at Detroit would suffer, and it would be hard to stop French traders from dealing illicitly with the English. In any case, it would be difficult to maintain trading posts in the Ohio region and expensive to keep them viable.[9] On due reflection, then, he did not think it advisable to keep the promises he had made about sending French traders to the region.

Céloron's mission, as conceived by La Galissonière, had three objectives: to establish a French claim to the Ohio Valley, to purge it of English traders, and to gather information about Indian attitudes while impressing them with the king of France's resolve to command their allegiance. Ostensibly he succeeded in accomplishing the first, and it should be noticed that by having him start near the headwaters La Galissonière was affirming the broadest possible territorial claim to the Ohio Valley, a claim that the French rested upon explorations by René Robert de La Salle, who left no evidence of going higher upriver than the mouth of the Wabash.[10] Céloron completely failed to accomplish the second objective (the Indians refused to help send the traders away), and could only bring back gloomy intelligence about Indian allegiance.

Céloron made his report to La Jonquière, who took over from La Galissonière. At first, the new governor-general was inclined towards severity; he planned to punish the dissident Indians and refuse pardon to those who had used violence against Frenchmen. His colleague in Louisiana, Pierre de Rigaud, marquis de Vaudreuil (whose jurisdiction included

---

[9] Ibid. esp. p. 482; also Frégault, *Grand Marquis*, pp. 356, 360.
[10] The evidence of La Salle's exploration of the Ohio is critically examined in Charles A. Hanna, *The Wilderness Trail* 2 vols (New York and London, 1911), II, 87–91.

Illinois), agreed. Therefore Pickawillany must be crushed; otherwise it would become 'un nouveau Chouéguen' (Oswego), fully as dangerous to the fur trade and future of France in America.[11] There was also a renewed fear in the west of a massive conspiracy. The commandant at Vincennes warned the commandant at Detroit that he should 'use all means to protect himself from the storm which is ready to burst on the French; that he is busy securing himself against the fury of our enemies'.[12] La Jonquière ordered detachments of troops to be sent westwards to join with allied Indians in the vicinity of Detroit in order to attack English traders in northern Ohio and their Indian friends at Pickawillany. But food shortages and Indian reluctance caused these plans to be cancelled.

In this situation La Jonquière shifted to a policy of moderation. It was the preferred policy of Charles-Jacques Le Moyne, baron de Longueuil, whose forebears were Canadian; he would become acting governor-general upon La Jonquière's death. Longueuil believed that armed intervention in the Ohio region would only serve to alienate the Indians. The alternative was to revert to the alliance methods of former times – pardons, fair-dealing and friendship – and these methods did prove effective again in the west, but the Ohio region constituted a more difficult challenge. To the Ohio River the governor-general sent a well-qualified emissary to engage in friendly conversations designed to win the Indians over and discourage them from trading with the English. Phillippe de Joncaire had been brought up in an Indian community, his mother being a Seneca, and had been Céloron's mainstay as interpreter in 1749. In autumn 1750 he began to travel the same route. Expecting to devote three years to this mission, he moved very slowly down the upper part of the river, spending many days at a time in villages.

On 20 May 1751 he came to the pro-English Indian village of Logstown, 20 miles downriver from the Forks. The timing of his arrival was particularly unfortunate. Two days before, the leading Pennsylvania trader, George Croghan, and his interpreter, Andrew Montour, had arrived there for a big conference, bringing substantial presents that the Pennsylvania Assembly had voted for the sake of Indian good will and allegiance. Committed to his mission, Joncaire reminded the assembled Indians that Céloron had asked them to have nothing to do with English traders and to banish them from the region. This met with a blunt reply: the English, a chief told him, were invited to come and trade. Later the Indian leaders

---

[11] Frégault, *Grand Marquis*, pp. 360–8.
[12] Longueuil to Rouillé, 21 April 1752, *NYCD*, X, 247.

at Logstown, Iroquois who had migrated, pointed out that although, as they were informed, England and France had made a general peace less than three years before, it was the French who persisted in disturbing the peace in the region by sending soldiers and capturing English traders. Besides, they asked, 'Is it not our Land? What right has Onontio to our Lands?'[13] Joncaire was in no position to remonstrate; he moved on. Notwithstanding their boldness, the Indians at Logstown were afraid of the French and asked that the government of Pennsylvania erect a 'strong trading house' for protection of their families in case of war. Two months later the Onondaga leadership of the Iroquois Confederacy raised the issue of territorial possession at a conference with La Jonquière and told him that they would 'not permit any nation to establish posts' in the Ohio region: 'we alone ought to enjoy it, without anybody having the power to trouble us there'.[14] In his response to the Iroquois representatives the governor-general failed to correct them on this claim, thus leaving the impression that the region did in fact belong to no one but the Indians. For this error La Jonquière would be pointedly rebuked by the minister at Versailles, but the old admiral died in March 1752 before learning of it.

Joncaire's reports about the disposition of Indians on the Ohio River when joined to anxieties about conspiracy and the growing influence of Pickawillany suggested that the methods of peaceful negotiation and generosity were not working. There was agreement that Pickawillany should be eradicated. The problem, as Céloron reported from Detroit, was that the local Indians were reluctant to undertake this task; they told the French that they must gather more troops. Letters from Longueuil, the acting governor-general, to Rouillé emphasized the unreliability of allied Indians for this kind of mission. When he wrote these letters Longueuil did not know that two French subalterns from the region round Michillimackinac in northern Great Lakes were planning an attack.

Of the two the leader was Charles Langlade, an adventurer who had chosen an Indian wife and was influential among the northern tribes. Under his urging and guidance a force of about 240 warriors came down Lake Huron, across Lake Erie and into Ohio. On the morning of 21 June 1752 they fell upon Pickawillany. Surprise was complete. Many inhabitants were off working in the cornfields and most of the warriors were away hunting. Only about twenty men were left to assemble at the

[13] Gipson, IV, 214–15.
[14] Report of a conference held 11 July 1751 between the Onondaga chiefs and La Jonquière, NYCD, X, 233, 235.

stockade, and after some fierce fighting they had to capitulate. Seven English traders were captured; two of them soon managed to escape and five were eventually imprisoned in Canada; another was killed and scalped. Fifteen Miamis died in the fighting, including La Demoiselle, parts of whose body the victors ceremonially boiled and ate. This violent and unforgettable raid threw fear into English traders and seriously under-mined the coherence of anti-French communities in the region, and it was achieved by Indians under only two Frenchmen. How the situation would have evolved cannot be known, however, because at this point Versailles took over the direction of French policy in the Ohio Valley.

Ohio: the French solution

Vaudreuil had told La Jonquière that the task of winning the allegiance of the Ohio Indians by good will would be hopeless as long as the English continued to trade with them. The same point had been made, very force-fully, in a letter written to the governor-general by Captain Charles, comte de Raymond, stationed at Fort Miami on the Maumee River:

While there is a single Englishman in all the rivers mentioned, whatever efforts you may make you will never succeed in driving off the Indians whom the English have drawn there and whom they are daily drawing there however large an army you may be able to march against them. If numbers are overwhelming, the Indians will take to the woods, and as soon as the army has passed, they will return.

He added:

But once the English are driven off . . . the Indians being no longer supported by the English and no longer finding the goods that they need will be obliged to go back to their villages among their tribes, and the French can without any hindrance make settlements in the most proper places to secure this country.[15]

If this were not done, Indians would inevitably be drawn to the more attractive trade goods of the English, among which would undoubtedly be firearms and ammunition. No Frenchman could imagine tranquillity under such circumstances.

Events reported to Versailles before news came of Langlade's success at Pickawillany indicated that for the mission of driving off English traders

---

[15] Raymond to La Jonquière, April 1750, Pease and Jenison, *Illinois on the Eve*, pp. 181–2.

Indians were unreliable, so the task would have to be accomplished by Canadian troops. And as Raymond advised, attacks on dissident Indians were fruitless. Putting it all together at Versailles, Rouillé decided, in early 1752, that the correct method for bringing the Ohio region under firm French control was to expel the traders using Canadian troops. This appeared to be the only viable solution.

There was a legal difficulty, however. Article 15 of the treaty of Utrecht had specified not only that the inhabitants of Canada must not molest the Iroquois, who were under British protection, but also that both sides should be allowed freedom of commerce with the Indians. In order to employ force for banning English traders from the Ohio Valley while avoiding violation of treaty terms, it was necessary for the French to insist on territorial possession. This was why Céloron planted the plaques. Although he did not announce French possession to the Indians, a plaque was found and turned over to English traders who translated its inscription for the Iroquois to hear.

These considerations shaped the instructions given to the new governor-general, Ange Duquesne de Menneville, marquis Duquesne. His first object was

to make all possible efforts to drive the English from our lands in those regions and to prevent them from coming there to trade by seizing their goods and destroying their posts. Secondly . . . to make the Indians understand that we have no designs on them, and they shall have the liberty of going when they wish to trade with the English, but that we will not allow them to receive the English on our lands.

It was added: 'If you attain these two objects you will assure the tranquillity of our possessions' in the Ohio country. There were to be no punitive expeditions or measures against 'rebel' Indians, since such actions might provoke a general Indian war which would be more dangerous to the French than the English. To make sure there was no mistake Duquesne was explicitly informed that this constituted a fundamental change of policy and that in executing it he was to employ *troupes de la marine* and Canadian militia rather than Indians. These instructions were approved at Versailles in April 1752 and issued to him on 15 May 1752; he carried them with him to Canada.[16] A letter from the minister to François Bigot,

---

[16] The quotations are based on the 15 May document, a dual-language version of which is printed in ibid. pp. 631–5. The draft approved in April (printed in *NYCD*, X, 242–5) did not specify use of troops rather than Indians.

the intendant at Quebec, dated 9 July made the position clear: 'the king has judged it proper to prescribe an altogether different policy to M. le Marquis Duquesne . . . [One] must begin by expelling the English traders from the Ohio River.'[17]

Duquesne, 52 years of age, was the son of an admiral and grand-nephew of a very great admiral. He was recommended by La Galissonière, who undoubtedly played a large role in drafting the instructions. His temperament was well suited to a policy of firmness backed by organized force. Canadians found him proud, arrogant and overbearing. Immediately after his arrival in July 1752 he summoned the militia and set about their discipline, for he planned to mount a very large military expedition to the Ohio. All told, he mobilized 2,000 troops and only 200 Laurentian Indians (those dwelling near the St Lawrence River).

In view of Canada's resources it was a huge undertaking. The pre-parations not only involved calling up the men and requisitioning food, but also tasks that were, literally, groundwork. The quantity of necessary supplies meant that the portage road round Niagara Falls had to be upgraded. Numerous large bateaux had to be built above the falls for transit across Lake Erie to Presqu'Ile (Erie, Pennsylvania). From there a 21-mile portage road capable of wagon traffic had to be carved through the wilderness to the headwaters of the Rivière aux Boeufs (French Creek), and at that point smaller bateaux would be needed for transit of supplies to Venango (now Franklin, where French Creek joins the Allegheny River). The expedition was clearly intended to result in permanent occu-pation of the upper Ohio. The plan called for three forts merely to protect this access route: Fort Presqu'Ile, Fort Le Boeuf (Waterford) and Fort Machault at Venango. The prime objective was the Forks, where a fourth fort was to be built. Considering the scale of preparations it is appropri-ate to call this operation 'The French Invasion of Western Pennsylvania'.[18]

Duquesne issued detailed orders in autumn 1752, and the works at the Niagara portage were hurried along during the winter. Construction of the road from Presqu'Ile to Fort Le Boeuf was begun in March 1753. Although a great deal was accomplished during the winter and early spring, much of the work on the long portage road remained to be done by the troops who arrived at Presqu'Ile in June. On 3 August the road was ready for service. Indians with their horses were hired to help move the

---

[17] Rouillé to Duquesne and Bigot, 9 July 1752, Pease and Jenison, *Illinois on the Eve*, pp. 645–6, 651.

[18] The title adopted by Kent, *French Invasion*.

wagons, but the burden of portage labour fell heavily on the soldiers. Duquesne himself paid tribute to the Canadians who carried it out, later remarking to the minister:

The Canadians are the only people in the world who would be capable of sleeping in the open air, and able to endure the immense labor which this detachment performed in transporting baggage on two portages, one of seven leagues and the other of three leagues.[19]

Fort Le Boeuf was built in July. Although in August the campaign was a month or so behind schedule, its further progress still seemed quite promising as construction of the pirogues (a narrow, shallow-draft boat) and the fort at Venango began.

At this point, however, misfortune struck hard. While the absence of summer rains had made construction and ground transport easier, there was insufficient water flowing in the Rivière aux Boeufs for the bateaux, so the bulkier supplies could not be moved forward. The dry weather persisted into the autumn. Worse, the troops were now succumbing to sickness in alarming numbers. Even the commander, Pierre Paul Marin, died. The cause of this dreadful sickness is not clear. Probably 'camp dysentery' from septic water played a role, also influenza and pneumonia. By the beginning of October only 800 of the 2,000 men who had left Canada were fit for service, and except for 300 left behind for garrisons, the surviving troops were ordered back to Montreal. Upon their arrival in November Duquesne himself remarked on their miserable appearance.[20] Still, the foundations had been laid for a formidable advance the next year.

On 31 October 1753 Duquesne reported to Versailles that the mere rumour of the coming of his troops had brought some Indians in the region to submission. The Iroquois leaders at Onondaga were arranging to come to Montreal to ask his forgiveness.[21] The invasion had not met with any organized opposition. Duquesne had not expected any, knowing that if the English were to respond they would be slow to mobilize. He urged his new commander, Captain Claude-Pierre Pécaudy de Contrecoeur, to move down to the Forks as early as possible in the spring.[22]

---

[19] Ibid. p. 27.

[20] Ibid. p. 67. Duquesne mentioned 'fevers and lung diseases'.

[21] Duquesne to Rouillé, 31 Oct. 1753, Pease and Jenison, *Illinois on the Eve*, p. 844.

[22] Duquesne to Contrecoeur, 27 Jan. 1754, *Papiers Contrecoeur*, p. 93.

In sum, the French invaded the upper Ohio River in order to drive out English traders and keep them out. It was a military solution to a problem of Indian relations connected with trading. The invasion was a major undertaking and it provoked, as will be seen in a moment, protests in London as well as authorization of military action by the colony of Virginia. When Virginia's action proved inadequate the British government moved towards war.

The standard interpretation of the war's origins tends to emphasize the pressure of British westward settlement, the implication being that the French moved into the Ohio Valley to halt it. The chartering of the Ohio Company in 1749 is cited as the particular source of alarm. Words like 'expansion' and 'penetration' have been commonly used by historians without making clear that those words could only refer to penetration by traders rather than settlers. English trans-Appalachian settlement was a threat but not yet a fact when the French government made its decision in 1752. Because the English reputation for settlement expansion was well known, the Indians worried about it as much as the French did. The tribesmen regarded compasses as instruments of oppression; explorers and surveyors learned to use them covertly. Céloron, Joncaire and others repeatedly reminded the Ohio Indians of what they well knew – that the English were likely to encroach on their lands. And because both the French and the Indians of the Ohio region realized that there was no credible prospect of French settlement there, French spokesmen found it tempting to allow Indians to think of the region as 'their land'. As we have seen, La Jonquière got carried away when he said to Iroquois representatives that the French would never settle on their lands without first obtaining permission.

It needs to be asked why the French chose to occupy the upper Ohio (or Allegheny) region, an area close to the backs of the colonies of Virginia and Pennsylvania and thus likely to cause provocation. The reasons can only be inferred. One was geographical convenience. It offered the easiest point of access to the whole river from Canada; no Frenchman knew of a better one, and in fact there was none better. A second reason was the utility of placing a barrier across the main avenues of access as the best way of stopping English traders from coming into the territory; most of them came from Pennsylvania. A third was to exercise the French claim that Céloron had staked out.

Another question is why the scale of the expedition was so large and entailed the establishment of forts. Rouillé's letter of 9 July 1752 condemned the failure of Duquesne's predecessors to send 'sufficient forces', so he could hardly be blamed for making the invading force formidable. In fact, it was the establishment of forts and permanent garrisons, not the size of the operation, that upset the French court. When Versailles received Duquesne's outline of his plan, which included forts and garrisons, the official reaction was one of dismay and disappointment. On 30 June 1753 Rouillé informed the governor-general that although His Majesty would not presume to prescribe what should be done about the forts, assuming the plan succeeded, His Majesty would rely on his 'zeal and prudence' regarding their future utility. The king hoped, however, to see the forts destroyed unless circumstances rendered them indispensable to the security of the region. This letter indicates that the French government was mainly concerned about the ongoing expense and the possibility that Indians of the interior would react adversely. No mention was made of a possible British reaction.[23]

The letter could be taken to imply that Duquesne had exceeded his orders, yet one should hesitate to accuse him of this. The instructions issued to him in mid-May 1752 said nothing one way or the other about forts and garrisons; he was required 'to make all possible efforts to drive the English from our lands in those regions and to prevent them from coming there to trade by seizing their goods and destroying their posts'. How was Duquesne to interpret this? He undoubtedly realized that yearly seasonal expeditions, however impressive and frightening, would allow English traders to operate during the winter. Durable prevention required a permanent presence, which was unthinkable without forts. The instructions given to the governor-general did not specify the means; those were left to him, but in view of the objectives which the ministry had stated in its original instructions, his plan represented a logical course of action. It gave greater certainty of establishing a stable and controlling influence over the Indians. Duquesne also knew that he would be blamed if he failed to keep English traders out. He chose not to take that risk, and in any case it is quite possible that La Galissonière had spoken to him about the necessity of forts and garrisons before he left Paris.

It is significant that Duquesne was told to keep 'the affair of the Ohio River . . . confined to the king's troops and the English traders'.[24] Inevitably, the operation would also require a large number of Canadian militiamen, but it was clear that the governor-general was not to rely on Indian warriors. By substantially excluding Indians the instructions

[23] Gipson, IV, 270–1. French National Archives, Paris, AN Col. B97, fo. 265.

[24] Rouillé's letter of 9 July 1752, Pease and Jenison, *Illinois on the Eve*, pp. 649–51.

defined a campaign which pitted French troops against English traders. Duquesne did not make this decision; it was made in Paris, and seems to have been decided without thought of the possible consequences. On the whole, the invasion of the Ohio Valley seems to have been carried forward without much consideration of how the British might react.

Virginia responds

It was not until mid-June 1753 that reports of a French military presence at the Ohio's headwaters reached the governors of New York and Virginia. Governor Robert Dinwiddie of Virginia immediately wrote to the Board of Trade, the administrative centre for colonial affairs. Lord Halifax read it on 11 August 1753 and immediately sent extracts to the Duke of Newcastle together with a long memorandum itemizing instances of peacetime French aggression. He placed special emphasis on Dinwiddie's report that the French were now building forts. The Ohio region, he reminded the duke, belonged to the Iroquois who were under British protection by an agreement which the British had taken care to record in the treaty of Utrecht. The French had no right to claim the territory and place forts in it. Newcastle convened a meeting of the cabinet. It was resolved that the several governors in North America should be alerted about 'the settlement said to be intended to be made by the French on the River Ohio' and told to 'do their utmost to prevent by force these, and any such attempts, that may be made by the French, or by the Indians in the French interest'. A circular letter was accordingly sent to governors by a secretary of state, Robert D'Arcy, Earl of Holdernesse on 28 August. It asked them to find out whether the recent reports were well grounded, to be on guard to defend their colonies where necessary, and to resist any encroachment or building of forts on their territories by 'the subjects of any Foreign Prince or State'. If forts were in fact being built and the French refused to desist, the letter continued, 'you are then to draw forth the armed Force of the Province, and to use your best endeavours, to repel force by force'. Yet at the same time the governors were strictly forbidden to use their armed forces anywhere that was not 'within the undoubted limits of His Majesty's dominions'.[25] Since it was 'His Majesty's determination not to

---

[25] The text of the circular letter is printed in *NYCD*, VI, 794–5. It shows that London initially supposed that the composition of the expedition was 'a considerable number of Indians . . . supported by some regular European Troops'.

be the aggressor' and the western boundaries of those dominions were uncertain, this last injunction effectively imposed restraint.

Governor Dinwiddie, however, received a special letter. It advised him to 'use his utmost endeavour' to erect a fort on the Ohio as soon as possible and to respond to any hindrance of this project by drawing forth the militia. 'Europeans not our subjects' who might be found engaged in erecting 'any fort within the limits of our province of Virginia' were to be peaceably warned that they must depart, and if they did not, he was not merely permitted but enjoined to use force: 'we do strictly charge and command you to drive them out by force of arms'.[26] The cabinet accomplished all this in just three weeks. For a governing aristocracy accustomed to treating August as a month of repose in the country during time of peace it was fast work, indicative of a sense of urgency.

On reading these orders two months later, Dinwiddie realized that he could hardly have wished for stronger or more specific directions to do what he wanted to do anyway. His first task was to learn the full truth about the activities of the French and, if necessary, warn them off. For this mission he needed someone to journey northwards immediately. Major George Washington of the Virginia militia, 21 years old, volunteered. He left Williamsburg on 1 November, acquired a Dutchman as French interpreter, and by arrangement met with Christopher Gist near the Pennsylvania border. Gist was familiar with local Indians and the back country, and proved invaluable as a guide. They went forward on horseback; the baggage went by water where possible. They called at Logstown where they managed, after awaiting resolution of complex protocols of Indian diplomacy, to get four pro-English Indians to accompany them. At Fort Machault, Washington met and dined with Captain Joncaire, who told him that he would find the French commanding officer at Fort Le Boeuf. This meant a further 40-mile journey in cold drenching rain and across swollen streams and half-frozen swamps. The small party reached the fort on 11 December and Washington was courteously received by the interim commander, the elderly Sieur Legardeur de Saint-Pierre, to whom he presented the letter he carried from the governor of Virginia.

The letter began with a blunt but dubious statement that the lands in question were 'notoriously known to be the property of the Crown of Great Britain' and ended by demanding that the French make a peaceful departure. Saint-Pierre replied that he was where he was by orders of the marquis Duquesne to whom the matter must be referred. On the return journey

---

[26] Printed in Freeman, *Geroge Washington*, I, 275.

Washington and Gist, finding their horses exhausted, decided to make haste without them and set out on foot with backpacks. The venture proved to be perilous, arduous and bone-chilling. An Indian 'guide' they happened to meet proved to be treacherous, and it required an all-night hike to escape him. Soon afterwards, Washington had his first experience of white-water navigation, which culminated in an icy bath in the Allegheny River. But they kept moving southwards on foot and reached a friendly trading post at the end of the month. Washington got back to Williamsburg on 16 January 1754 and delivered Saint-Pierre's non-committal letter to the governor.

While returning, Washington had seen caravans moving towards him across the north-western Virginia frontier. He was witnessing the unfolding of Dinwiddie's other urgent mission – to hurry construction of a stockade at the Forks. The Ohio Company's 1749 royal charter had specified that the company would promote settlement on these lands and build a fort, but no plans and contracts were drawn up until the summer of 1753. Because recent directives from London made the job urgent, workers and supplies were on the move in the dead of winter.

Much more important than the delivery of the French commander's reply was Washington's confirmation that forts and a wagon road from Presque'Ile had been constructed, and that 220 canoes and small bateaux were at Fort Le Boeuf ready to come southwards in the spring. Dinwiddie sprang into action. By the end of January he had called for recruitment of 200 provincial soldiers and begun arrangements for provisions. He also dispatched letters to seven fellow governors, each of whom was asked to send military assistance; Dinwiddie promised them a cooperative inter-colonial mode of command. As yet, however, his own assembly had not voted money for an expedition. In November he had asked it to provide for a suitable armed force but, annoyed by a fee he had imposed on certain real-estate transfers without their approval and wary of devoting public money to the defence of a private company's land scheme (in which the governor himself was known to be financially involved), the Virginia House of Burgesses had refused. In mid-February, however, when furnished with Washington's report, they granted £10,000.

Washington, now ranked lieutenant colonel in the Virginia militia, was already recruiting and trying to train men. Dinwiddie was convinced of the need for haste. In early April Washington made his way up the Potomac River toward Winchester where he found to his dismay that nothing had been done to provide wagons. After commandeering wagons he pressed forward to Wills Creek (Cumberland, Maryland) where he found that the contract for pack horses had not been fulfilled.

While waiting for the horses he received a report that 800 French soldiers had come down the river. On 17 April they had found militia Ensign
Edward Ward and 40 workers at the Forks constructing a stockade.
Courteously but firmly the English were required to leave, which they did.
At this point a less determined and energetic man – and a wiser military
man – than the 22-year-old Washington would have paused to reflect
upon the situation. Since the race to the Ohio was now clearly lost,
the original goal of deterrence was unattainable. There was no longer
any point in hurrying forward with a mediocre band of soldiers through
110 miles of mountainous terrain to a place where French forces were
overwhelmingly superior. It is not easy to understand why he continued
on, let alone understand why he anticipated success. It is possible that he
expected more Indian help than he got.

Washington made his rendezvous with some Indian allies under
Tanaghrisson, the 'Half King', the same Mingo (i.e. an Iroquois who had
migrated to Ohio) chieftain who had accompanied him to Fort Le Boeuf.
Washington and his men were 60 miles west of Wills Creek in late May,
in the valley of Great Meadows, where he laid out a rudimentary
fort. Various reports made him intensely aware that he might be attacked,
and when he learned from Tanaghrisson's scouts that a band of French
soldiers were nested not far away in a hidden encampment he marched on
a rainy night to the place, which was a glen about half a mile away from
the travelled road. On the morning of 28 May 1754 Washington, leading
44 soldiers and a small band of Indians under Tanaghrisson, approached
the camp. Shots were exchanged, but Washington had the advantage of
surprise, and the Half King's Indians had gone to the rear of the glen
and blocked escape so that 21 French troops were taken prisoner. One
Virginian was killed and 13 Frenchmen, including Ensign Joseph Coulon
de Jumonville, their commander. The incident, though it marked the first
drawing of blood by French and British colonial troops in what would
become a war, might not have been of much significance if the French had
not claimed afterwards that Jumonville's purpose was innocent: to present
a declaration warning all Englishmen to stay off lands belonging to the
king of France. Written by Contrecoeur, it was addressed to the commander of the English troops, informing him that he must expect to be
compelled to leave by whatever means would be 'most efficacious for the
honour of the king's arms'.[27] According to French accounts Washington,
after a ceasefire, shot Jumonville who was already wounded and was

[27] Printed in *Papiers Contrecoeur*, p. 130.

protesting that his purpose was to present a declaration. By this account Jumonville was simply murdered.

No historian can be sure about what really happened that morning, but it seems fairly clear that the exchange of musket fire killed only a few men and that Jumonville and most of his troops were killed after firing ceased. It also seems likely that they were killed by the hatchets and knives of Tanaghrisson and his Indians, possibly while Washington and his interpreter were trying to translate the declaration. The bloody events that occurred in a space of 20 minutes cannot be confidently narrated, but it is clear that Washington and Tanaghrisson acted offensively. On the other hand, Jumonville's mission was not entirely innocent. The young officer was undoubtedly sent both to gather military intelligence and to deliver the declaration. Such a dual mission was not uncommon, but it was normally carried out as openly as possible and with fewer than a dozen soldiers and scouts, to avoid the appearance of a threat. Hearing reports that the French had come to the Forks with a considerable number of men far better trained than his own, and that detachments were spreading out, Washington (as he mentioned in his report to Governor Dinwiddie) was bent on attacking the enemy force before it attacked him. Nevertheless, at the glen he allowed the Half King and his warriors to be deployed in positions where he could have little chance of restraining them, and for that he may be held responsible.

Despite indications that many formerly friendly Indians were now too afraid of the French to join him, and even though his only reinforcement thus far was a company of regulars from South Carolina, Washington moved forward. On 28 June, however, he knew he must turn back. A strong French detachment from the new French base at the Forks, Fort Duquesne, was reported to be heading towards him. He regained Great Meadows on 1 July but now realized that the location of his unfinished fort and trenches was faulty. His men were exhausted by the hurried retreat under heavy burdens of equipment, so he could neither retreat further nor manage to reposition the fort in time to defend against an enemy onslaught. Fort Necessity, in the Great Meadows, deserved its name for many reasons.

Against the 600 French and 100 Indians who attacked on 3 July Washington commanded only 284 effectives (all told, 400 men were with him). Drenching rain made the defenders' location even worse: the trenches filled; powder could not be kept dry. When the French commander, Captain Louis Coulon de Villiers, offered to discuss the situation Washington had no choice but to accept. Messengers went back and forth in the night.

The paper stating the terms of capitulation that Washington eventually signed was scribbled in French – Washington could not read French – and blotched by rain (it has survived). The paper contained an admission by Washington that he had ordered the killing of Jumonville. He always claimed afterwards that he did not knowingly make any such admission, and it seems unlikely that he would have done so. Evidently, trying to read aloud a scribbled, rain-spotted paper by candlelight, his Dutch interpreter failed to say or make clear that it contained the word *assassin*.[28] The damage was done, however. The French version of 'l'affaire Jumonville' provided a story which French diplomacy would be able to exploit: Washington had not only started a shooting war, but also, it appeared, had committed the brutal atrocity of killing a surrendered and well-intentioned courier.

The articles of capitulation were obviously signed too hurriedly, un-doubtedly because the French terms, given the helplessness of Washington's position, were generous. He was formally forced to admit defeat and withdraw, to agree not to cross the frontier within a year's time, and to agree that the Ohio Valley belonged to the king of France. Coulon de Villiers was Jumonville's older brother and naturally intent on vengeance; however, he knew he must not slaughter surrendered troops and also that it would be difficult to feed and transport them. Two hostages were kept, but the remainder of Washington's little army – 30 had been killed in the battle – were allowed to return to Virginia.

Coulon de Villiers was aware that he should not provoke a war, but otherwise he was under no restraint from Duquesne. Neither the governor-general nor the naval minister had expected an organized British response. The first notice of a British protest was Dinwiddie's letter that Washington carried to Fort Le Boeuf, which Captain Marin forwarded to Montreal in January 1754. Reading it, Duquesne dismissed it as absurd and chose an active man, Contrecoeur, to replace the deceased Marin. Hearing a few weeks later that the English might be building a storehouse near the Forks, he had ordered him to go downriver as soon as weather permitted. If no structure yet existed, he was to 'spread terror' so that subsequent operations would be easier, but Duquesne emphasized that it would be a very bad beginning if some building were suffered to be built 'under our nose'.[29] Contrecoeur had anticipated these orders and managed

---

[28] Freeman, *George Washington*, I, 406–9. Volume II's frontispiece is a photograph of part of the capitulation paper.

[29] Duquesne's instructions of 15 April 1754 to Contrecoeur, *Papiers Contrecoeur*, pp. 114–15.

to interrupt the Virginia Company's worker-soldiers in mid-April, forcing them to leave. Contrecoeur's report of this action delighted Duquesne. He was equally pleased to learn of the victory at Fort Necessity and described it as a 'jolie affaire', saying, 'Everything has happened according to my wishes.' It would, he said, implant a good lesson in the minds of the English and the Indians.[30] He may not have known perhaps that Fort Necessity, marginally situated within the Ohio watershed, was in the foothills of the Allegheny Mountains beyond the first ridge, but it was not a fact that would have troubled him. He urged Contrecoeur to be alert and consolidate his defensive position while chasing out English traders and speaking firmly to the local Indians. Not until October 1754 did the governor-general receive an order from Versailles telling him to avoid any action that might give the English cause for complaint. On the 30th of that month he conveyed this to Contrecoeur, who could not have received it before December. This order was sent from Paris on 19 August, over the signature of a new minister of marine and colonies, Jean-Baptiste de Machault d'Arnouville, who replaced Rouillé in late July. The order came far too late, of course, to calm the British reactions.

Rouillé has been commonly labelled a man of peace, perhaps because the Duke of Newcastle supposed him to be such, but with respect to Ohio his record was far from that of a pacifist. Under his administration both La Jonquière and Longueuil were criticized for failing to stifle English trading. He appointed Duquesne, a man well known to be demanding and aggressive – in modern idiom, a 'hawk', as he proved to be. Duquesne was recommended by La Galissionière, another 'hawk', and Rouillé approved both the appointment and the invasion of the Ohio Valley. Although he subsequently said that he wished that the governor-general had not made the expedition so large and expensive, his ministry did not diminish the appropriations that continued to support it.

The people of Virginia were not disposed to renew the contest. Although Governor Dinwiddie went to work on new plans, people were suspicious of his motives and utterly averse to serving at arms or approving the needed taxes. As hard as Dinwiddie tried he could not move the House of Burgesses to authorize an autumn campaign. Assistance from other colonies proved to be feeble and the Virginia force began to melt away. In mid-September Dinwiddie knew he must give up any thought of an autumn campaign. He looked to London for help. If the issue had been

[30] Duquesne to Contrecoeur, 11 May, 25 July 1754, ibid. pp. 125, 221–2.

left to the colonies, the surrender at Fort Necessity would have postponed Anglo-French conflict over the Ohio question indefinitely.

A contest in India: Dupleix's project

In the eastern Caribbean there were four 'Neutral Islands' – Dominica, St Lucia, St Vincent and Tobago – to which neither the French nor the British had undisputed title. The treaty of Aix-la-Chapelle had called for them to be evacuated and left undisturbed. Although successive governors at Martinique refused to force French settlers to leave St Lucia, and British merchants at Barbados ventured to cut timber on Tobago, there were no overt hostilities, and a definitive settlement respecting the four islands was left to the Boundary Commission.[31] What occurred after the peace of 1748 in India was very different.

Madras (now Chennai) on the Coromandel Coast, which the French had captured in 1746, was returned to the British by the treaty, and both London and Paris expected peace to prevail, but hostilities in India did not really end. Whatever might be settled in Europe, the Indian state system's dynamics generated armed conflicts between rival claimants, and the regional governors of the English and French East India companies were strongly tempted to take sides. With the support of their councils they retained a body of European as well as native troops, and although direct Anglo-French military confrontation was to be avoided in peacetime, the temptation to join in alliance with local princes, who had observed the relative military efficiency of these companies' troops and were willing to pay their cost of campaigning, was irresistible. As part of the arrangement the companies would be given important trading and revenue benefits.

Early in 1749 the exiled raja of Tanjore offered the British company a small trading port in return for military assistance which he would pay for. The governor and council at Fort St David (Madras had not yet been reoccupied) accepted the offer and sent troops to help his cause and take possession of the port. While this was being done, the French governor at Pondicherry, François-Joseph Dupleix, entered into arrangements to assist Chanda Sahib, recently freed from Maratha captivity, in making good his claim to rule the Carnatic (the region between the western mountains and the Coromandel Coast) from Arcot. In mid-July, French company troops (400 Europeans and 2,000 sepoys) marched to join 12,000 Indian soldiers

<hr />

[31] For the contention over the Neutral Islands in this time of peace see Pares, *War and Trade*, pp. 195–215.

under Chanda Sahib. On 1 August the combined force fought the presiding nawab's forces at Ambur (near Vellore), a battle in which the nawab was slain. Chanda Sahib soon occupied Arcot, and Muhammed Ali Khan, young successor to the slain nawab, was forced to withdraw. French troops played a decisive role in the victory at Ambur, and Dupleix gained not only handsome rewards for himself and his officers but also for the French company – a right to revenues drawn from territories close to Pondicherry. To these acquisitions he added others by the end of 1749.

These successes encouraged Dupleix to pursue a plan to use military force to extend the company's influence throughout the Carnatic. Since it was likely that neighbouring princes would form an alliance with Muhammed Ali Khan and seek to restore him, Dupleix resolved to attack him, and by the end of 1750 forced him to take refuge in the walled city of Trichinopoly. Chanda Sahib now ruled the Carnatic under French protection.

At Fort St David the governor and Rear-Admiral Edward Boscawen (who had not yet taken his squadron home) observed these developments, and when Dupleix tried to establish a French foothold in an enclave near Madras they became alarmed. It was obvious that the French governor's next objective would be Trichinopoly, to eliminate Muhammed Ali Khan. Thomas Saunders, governor of the company's trading base at Masulipatam, came south to interfere. Soon, a bold project was suggested to him by Robert Clive, who had come out to India as a commercial 'writer' but found his *métier* in the company's army. Clive proposed a thrust at the ancient capital city of Arcot, the idea being to distract French forces from their siege at Trichinopoly, 150 miles away. Clive's six-day march from Madras to Arcot with only 200 British troops and 300 sepoys, his unopposed entry, and the skill with which his small garrison defended its dilapidated walls in autumn 1751, made his reputation. Of itself a minor operation, the defence of Arcot nevertheless changed the military situation in the Carnatic. Saunders was able to persuade a Maratha mercenary captain to assist Clive in the field and help him win a signal victory in December. From then on, although the contest would go back and forth, with Trichinopoly subject to repeated French threats, Dupleix's chances of success diminished. The greatest blows were struck on 9 and 13 June 1752, when considerable French and native forces became cornered at Volconda and Srirangam and were compelled to submit to a complete surrender. One result was the execution of Chanda Sahib; another was that Pondicherry was destitute of troops for its defence. Its vulnerability did not matter, however, because neither side dared to assault the other's base, which would have been too blatant a violation of the treaty of Aix-la-Chapelle.

Since throughout the campaigning the French company could deploy more troops (Europeans and sepoys), why did Dupleix fail? His sepoys, recruited and also commanded by native chiefs, were less reliable than the better paid sepoys of the English company, who were commanded by British officers. But money was the biggest factor. Chanda Sahib needed it to pay and feed his own army as well as the French forces assisting him, so he habitually paused to collect revenue (or tribute demanded at gunpoint) from local jurisdictions. Dupleix's finances became severely distressed in 1751. As he lamented, the territories from which revenue was to be drawn were devastated by the campaigning and native allies could not fulfil their pledges to cover the costs.[32] Chanda Sahib was not an efficient ally and, in addition, Maratha incursions from the north-western hill country caused serious setbacks.

The English company also experienced difficulties when it sought to convert Muhammed Ali Khan's promises to cover campaigning costs into actual payments, since he also was short of funds, but its European and native troops were better skilled and disciplined. Dupleix's willingness to let Charles Bussy go inland to the Deccan in January 1751 was a serious mistake, not only because he took part of the army with him but also because the remaining French forces in the Carnatic were deprived of their best general. Bussy was an engaging, patient diplomat who took the trouble to study the culture of India. He was also a superb judge of when to strike militarily. Thanks to him French influence in the Deccan flourished, but before long he was much needed in the Carnatic. Dupleix's plan required domination of the Carnatic by his Indian allies, but the region could be too easily penetrated by forces on its perimeter, and the British, fearing that their trade in the region would be stifled if Dupleix succeeded, were prepared to seek their cooperation.

Dupleix was not in a position to ask for financial help from Paris. He had assured the French company's directors that the expenses for his project would not require company money. His plan had been to present them with a fait accompli, and they did in fact congratulate him on his early successes, though always with an expressed wish for resumption of peace. But as the campaigning dragged on and the expenses mounted, what could he say? It is not surprising that he was reluctant to report adverse events. Thus, compared to his British adversaries he was at a

---

[32] Vigié, *Dupleix*, p. 363.

great political disadvantage. Governor Saunders could justify his military expenses to the directors in London as a necessary counter to French aggression that threatened future British trade, but Dupleix could not avoid the appearance of having caused his own troubles.

A resilient optimist and in many ways a brilliant man, Dupleix had helped the company prosper ever since he had disembarked at Pondicherry in 1722 at the age of 25, but he was foolish to withhold disappointing information from the directors. Reports of armed clashes in the Carnatic appeared in British newspapers, and the French company's London agents could easily convey them to their superiors in Paris, who began to believe British and Dutch newspapers rather than Dupleix's letters. Even before they learned of the disaster at Srirangam the directors, joined by leading ministers at Versailles, were warning Dupleix that he must abandon his policy. After they learned about Srirangam in January 1753 they amplified their warnings and pointedly reproached him for failing to keep them informed.

When Dupleix read these letters at Pondicherry he was furious. It was now pointless to disguise his goals, and in a memoir – a treatise really – he explained his policy and its rationale. The document was aimed more at the court of Versailles than the company directors because, he said, the king's honour and the interests of the nation were at stake. His most important argument was not without merit: the French company could not maintain profitability merely by trading; its capital and credit were too limited; the loss of just one vessel and cargo wiped out a year's profits. The only remedy was to give military support to a local prince and gain in return a permanent right to collect a territorial revenue. This money would provide for the company's fixed costs so that trading could be profitable.[33] He might have pointed out the company's inability to carry on seaborne commerce in wartime because of British naval superiority, and hinted that war was to be expected from time to time, but he was writing in peacetime and knew that company officials did not want to think about this. In any case, Dupleix's focus was not on developing trade: he said nothing about promoting textile production in the areas he hoped to control; his concern was land revenues. What he did not see was that his policy was ill-suited to political conditions in the Carnatic where rival claimants frequently disturbed the region and French forces would not be

---

[33] This memoir, dated 16 October 1753, is discussed and critiqued by Marc Vigié (*Dupleix*, pp. 427–8) as well as Manning, *Fortunes à faire* (pp. 214–15). Dupleix hoped that it would be distributed widely in Paris.

large enough both to assist allies and to ensure collection of territorial revenues.

A question being asked in Paris was whether other nations trading in India would permit the French to establish such a system. Since British troops were already opposing it, the answer was clearly negative. The alternatives seemed, however unrealistically, simple and obvious: the French company could either pursue tranquillity and trade within existing internationally acknowledged limits or it could follow a policy of aggrandizement which would entail a prospect of several years of war against Indian princes and the troops of other European companies. To the directors the choice was clear, and their view was conveyed to Machault, the controller-general of finance. Machault was reminded that Dupleix was not the sort of man who would change his ways, and after consultation with Rouillé, Étienne de Silhouette and leading company officials he made the decision (at the very moment when Dupleix was writing his long memoir) to recall the governor and restrict the troops to defensive roles. Charles Godeheu, who had served in India, was appointed to take over from Dupleix (and given secret orders to arrest him if necessary). Embarking on 31 December 1753 he reached Pondicherry on 1 August 1754. At the time French influence in the Carnatic was still significant, but Godeheu ordered a pull-back and the British agreed to a truce, following which a preliminary treaty was drafted. The terms benefited the British in the Carnatic, but Bussy was allowed to keep his influential position in the Deccan.

Clearly, both the ministers at Versailles and the company's directors wanted the hostilities in India to end. When Dupleix's project met with effective armed resistance and became costly he lost credibility. Besides, directors and shareholders knew that he and Bussy were acquiring personal fortunes in return for their military services while the company was approaching bankruptcy. When they learned that money sent out for use as trading capital had all been spent for military operations the directors' patience was at an end.[34] Dupleix's supporters in Paris argued, as he did, that the king's honour and the nation's interest were involved in this contest, but Versailles also had to consider relations in Europe: Denmark and the Dutch Republic, having companies that traded in India, were objecting to the French company's aggression. Their main concern, however, was the future of French East India trade. It was judged that the British did not intend to stifle their trade in time of peace and that trade

---

[34] Haudrère, *Compagnie française*, II, 740.

could not be carried on profitably if Dupleix pursued a policy that kept hostilities alive.

During 1753 the French company responded to an overture from London and sent emissaries to try to negotiate peace terms. The French ambassador, the duc de Mirepoix, assisted the negotiations, receiving his instructions from Machault, by now the foreign minister. Though the French offered to pull back in the Carnatic, they were determined to retain Bussy's influence in the Deccan. The longer the talks continued the more the leadership of the English East India Company believed that the French were not sincere. Letting the talks drag on, the Secret Committee at India House began discussing a plan for forcing a complete French withdrawal.

No firm orders were issued until after it was learned that Godeheu was to be accompanied by a very considerable fleet of French East India Company ships carrying no fewer than 1,600 recruits – more men than had gone forth to Pondicherry in all the preceding years of peace. The British ambassador at Versailles had been forewarned by French officials that a large reinforcement was to go out for purely defensive purposes, but no one in London believed the purpose would be merely defensive and news of it had an explosive effect. English East India stock dropped 7 per cent in one day. Newspapers accused the French of outrageous deceit, and Parliament demanded that the negotiations be halted for three months. The French were taken aback. In their desire to avoid military weakness in the Carnatic they had provoked a strong British reaction. A naval squadron under Rear-Admiral Charles Watson and a regiment of about 700 regular army troops sailed for India on 24 March 1754. Fortunately, by September when the squadron and transports arrived, Godehue was already arranging a truce with the British. As it happened, the presence of this British naval force would have momentous consequences for the Seven Years War and British domination of India.[35]

[35] See Chapter 9.

CHAPTER 4

Risking war, 1754–55

Although the rivalry of the two great powers was intense, each side had good reasons to avoid war at this time. As this chapter will show, the British colonies, except for Massachusetts, were militarily unprepared, and Newcastle's diplomatic efforts to protect the Netherlands and Hanover were failures. On the French side there were many reasons to hesitate, but above all there was the ominous fact of relative naval weakness. Yet when the opportunity arose early in 1755 to negotiate a settlement of the Ohio Valley disputes neither side would yield. It will not be hard to see why Newcastle, though personally anxious for peace, could not afford to accept France's proposals. The puzzle is to explain French firmness. Did the French government truly intend to risk war over the Ohio question? It appears that Versailles was captivated by some potent illusions.

Unreadiness of the British colonies

The British government would have preferred to see its colonies deal with the problem on the upper Ohio, and at first glance one would think that British North America, with a population of 960,000 not counting slaves, could have found a way to force Canada with a population of only 60,000 to withdraw from the forts. Eventually this might have occurred, but in the near term it was impossible. To understand why, we begin by observing that Canada was far better prepared for war-making.

Military service was woven into the fabric of Canadian government and society. Practically every able-bodied man was a member of the militia, which was organized by parishes, and it was not uncommon for *habitants* to be called up. The captain of the militia company was head of civil government in his parish. Among Canadians of higher social rank young men commonly sought commissions in the *troupes de la marine*. All the French officers mentioned in the previous chapter were members of this body of colonial regulars. These officers were accustomed to hardship and familiar with wilderness campaigning. By the mid-eighteenth century they were nearly all Canadian-born, very often sons and nephews of officers. Active service was essential, however, and early promotion could come only by valour in action.

The commander-in-chief of the *troupes de la marine* was the governor-general, who was usually a naval officer. La Galissonière, La Jonquière and Duquesne had all served at sea. (The reason why La Galissonière became acting governor-general was that La Jonquière had been forced to surrender his flagship to Admiral Anson in the battle of 3 May 1747 and was made a British prisoner of war.) As the name implies, the *troupes de la marine* belonged to the minister of the marine and colonies (to whom the governor-general was responsible), not to the French army. Although connections at Versailles were sometimes developed from afar by the families of officers, every commission and promotion had to be recommended by the governor-general.

There was a council of Quebec and an assembly where remonstrances could be voiced, but the governor-general could ignore their advice and complaints, especially on military matters. When the marquis Duquesne arrived in 1752 he quickly made himself unpopular, proving to be arrogant and demanding. He did not like Canadians, and they quickly learned not to like him. Translating his instructions into a plan of action, he pressed his demand for mobilizing the militia. They served without pay, and a visitor to Canada in summer 1753 reported that the populace had taken to the streets against the governor, crying out with 'seditious Libels and satirical Sonnets' against him 'on account of their being arbitrarily bereav'd of their children'. Action was taken to silence them.[1] The fact that the harvest had been bad and food was short did not deter Duquesne, though purchase of supplies resulted in inflation. Thus, despite protests from Canadian officers, adverse conditions and hardships imposed on the people, the governor-general was able to carry out his plan.

The difference between his powers and those of British colonial governors was profound. In January 1754, when Governor Dinwiddie

[1] From a letter of 24 Dec. 1753 by a resident of Massachusetts, who left Canada on 18 Aug., to Governor William Shirley, *NYCD*, VI, 826.

realized the magnitude and character of the French invasion of the upper Ohio, his orders were swift and vigorous. Nevertheless, Virginia's military effort was feeble and inept. This might have been predicted. Notwithstanding their vastly superior basic resources, the British colonies were incapable of mobilizing and deploying military expeditions. Every official of New France understood this, and Duquesne had counted on it; he was sure his troops could consolidate their hold on the Ohio Valley before the British could effectively respond. The astonishing thing is that Governor Dinwiddie did not seem to understand it. He was full of military confidence and so was young Washington. Their hearty spirit was perhaps commendable, but their abundant confidence was inexcusable.

The inability of Britain's North American colonies to mobilize forces against the French incursion is explainable under four categories: money, troops, Iroquois diplomacy and colonial disunity. First, money: colonial legislatures were parsimonious and suspicious. The Virginia assembly's reluctance reflected a lack of concern for the trans-Appalachian frontier; most Virginia colonists lived near tidewater. Moreover, the governor's motives were suspect: he and his friends, it was believed (not without cause), hoped to profit from frontier land speculation. When the House of Burgesses did vote £10,000 for an expedition in February 1754, it was admitting, in effect, that there was an issue of defence involved, but, as we have seen, after the initial expedition failed the assembly declined to authorize a second one. In New York, Pennsylvania, Maryland and other colonies where the governors perceived frontier threats in early 1754 the assemblies refused to support the cost of defence. Quaker pacifism was a factor in Pennsylvania, but assemblies in other colonies commonly refused to vote for military preparedness without reference to religious ideology. The exception was Massachusetts. There the legislature had given Governor William Shirley money for an expedition up the Penobscot River (which turned out to be a wild goose chase prompted by a false rumour). In early 1755, as will be seen, Massachusetts would readily vote to support a force of 2,000 men. It is clear, however, that Massachusetts expected to be compensated by the British government. Shirley told the legislature that this was a near certainty, and his promise seemed credible because Massachusetts had recently received recompense for the costs it had incurred in the capture and occupation of Louisbourg (1745–8), much of it coming in the form of hard cash. But Massachusetts was focused on Cape Breton, not the Ohio Valley. In October 1754 the Virginia House of Burgesses voted £20,000 to match a British grant of funds for taking action on the Ohio, but perhaps they would not have done so if Dinwiddie had told them the full truth – that the £20,000 promised from London was in fact a loan, to be repaid by an excise duty levied in Virginia.[2]

Secondly, there was the problem of troops and trained officers. American colonial lore is filled with frontier images in which practically all farmers and traders possessed firearms. While it is true that western settlers were familiar with muskets and sometimes rifles for hunting, they were at this time ignorant of the most rudimentary aspects of warfare. Three generations earlier, experience of warfare in Virginia had been quite common, and a visitor in 1750 might well be 'astonished at the Number of Colonels, Majors, and Captains that you hear mentioned', but these titles sprang from a militia that had been reduced to a system of political and social formalities.[3] Frontier warfare had become practically extinct; the nearby Indians were now quiet. As George Washington remarked: 'Virginia is a Country young in War. Until the breaking out of these Disturbances has Lived in the most profound, and Tranquil Peace; never studying War or Warfare.'[4] Washington himself had never studied war; before late 1753 his frontier experience was as a land surveyor.

When Governor Dinwiddie called the militia of the north-western counties to arms in early 1754 there was consternation. The men claimed that under existing law they had no obligation to serve outside the borders of the colony. Since Dinwiddie's orders from London implicitly placed the area around the Forks within Virginia's borders he could have legitimately compelled the militia to serve, but it was not feasible politicalically: the recalcitrance of men on the militia rolls, voters all, was amply supported by the gentlemen of the legislature. Washington had a Virginia militia commission, but the troops that went forth under his command were separately recruited volunteers, not militia. There was another problem. Like most British colonies, Virginia lacked administrative means to organize and transport food and ammunition for a substantial expedition. Transport on the western frontier involved long hauls over mountain roads no better than paths and much could be excused; but in learning how to deal with problems on a scale needed for military operations Virginians started from a condition of almost complete ignorance.

Diplomatic relations with the Iroquois Confederacy, a third category, were important not only because good relations with Indians on all

---

[2] Titus, *Old Dominion*, pp. 58–9, 168.

[3] Ibid. pp. 4–5, 32–7.

[4] Colonel Washington to Lord Loudoun, 10 Jan. 1757, W.W. Abbot *et al.*, eds, *The Papers of George Washington: Colonial Series* 4 (Charlottesville, VA, 1984), p. 90.

sectors of the wilderness frontier were vitally necessary, but also because of the nature of Britain's claim to the Ohio region. French authorities acted as if their rights under La Salle's watershed claim were absolute. The British, however, had no independent claim of their own to the region. The Iroquois nations had conquered the territory by about 1700, and in due course the Confederacy acknowledged subservience and dependence upon Great Britain in exchange for protection of this conquest. The British government stretched this into a claim of responsibility for peace-keeping in the region and managed to get it formally recognized by the French in Article 15 of the treaty of Utrecht. At Onondaga, the anchor of the Iroquois 'Covenant Chain', the leaders of the Six Nations, though not admitting subservience, were reluctant to deny the claim openly because they looked to British colonial governors for protection against French incursions. In the Ohio region, however, the Onondaga council's influence was, by 1750, diminished; resident Iroquois chieftains in Ohio were making key decisions. The most numerous inhabitants, commonly called the Mingos, were of the Cayuga and Seneca nations; they had migrated from western New York to the southern shore of Lake Erie and spread southwards. They were loosely aligned with the English not only through trade but also because of the Iroquois Confederacy's claim over the region. The Ohio region had also become home to the western Delawares and to some Shawnees – the latter were uncooperative with everybody – but both groups, like the Mingos, traded with the English.

When commissioners representing Virginia's colonial government and members of the Ohio Company wanted to solidify a trans-Appalachian claim, and gain permission to establish a fort and trading settlement, they went to Logstown, an Indian settlement 15 miles downriver from the Forks. They did address the Iroquois centre in New York (near Syracuse). An Onondaga representative attended the negotiation at Logstown. Tanaghrisson, the Half King, the leading negotiator there, was a Seneca chief whose authority in the upper Ohio region was recognized by the Onondaga council. Although Tanaghrisson accepted treaty terms at Logstown in June 1752, he was far from happy about it – neither he nor the Confederacy's leaders liked the idea of settlements of any kind – but like many Ohio Indians he did not want to yield to French authority, and he knew that his followers would be defenceless without the arms and ammunition which English traders supplied. In early September 1753 Tanaghrisson led a delegation to Presqu'Ile (many weeks before George Washington went) to tell the French commandant of the fort that he was occupying Iroquois lands and had no right to be there. In response the commandant, Marin, had treated him with contempt.

As the French invasion progressed and Virginia responded, Tanaghrisson and his followers took an active part alongside Washington, but most of the Indians in the region asked themselves a fearful and urgent question: Can we count on English protection? When French troops arrived in force the greater part of them abandoned the English, judging that there would be no effective English military presence. They judged correctly. Even Tanaghrisson had his doubts, but he was committed. With his death in October 1754, apparently of natural causes, the English side, having lost heavily at Pickawillany, no longer had active friends among the Ohio Indians. The government of Pennsylvania retained a hope that the leaders of the Iroquois Confederacy would take a stand against the French incursion on the Ohio, but the emergency in the Ohio Valley made it necessary to try to cultivate allies among the Indians who were on the spot, not only Mingos but also Delawares. Nevertheless, a desire to consult the Onondaga council delayed diplomatic action.

British colonial disunity was one reason why the Indians doubted whether the British would act quickly enough. Tribal leaders often complained that different governors were sending different signals. The French invasion did prompt a degree of cooperation between Pennsylvania and Virginia. Before 1753 Pennsylvania traders and their official supporters in Philadelphia had been telling the Indians, just as the French were, that Virginians were intent on settlements that would eventually dispossess them of their hunting grounds. But upon news of the French invasion the governor of Pennsylvania decided to let the Virginians advance (into what is now western Pennsylvania) because Pennsylvania traders were in need of protection and the Quaker-dominated assembly in Philadelphia remained unwilling to pay the cost of a fort and garrison. It had already turned down an Indian request for one in 1751. Virginia was thus given permission to act, but nothing more.

The Earl of Halifax at the Board of Trade had been aware of the general problem. News of the French incursion on the Ohio, coinciding with reports from the governor of New York about Iroquois reluctance to come into an active alliance, enabled him to obtain permission to send a circular letter to all governors 'whose interest and security is connected with & depends upon' the Indians to meet in conference. The governor of New York was to organize the conference and choose its location. Indian grievances were to be addressed, but above all the 'Covenant Chain' with the Six Nations was to be renewed on a broader and firmer basis. The

British government would provide money for amassing presents. In effect, the Board of Trade was pushing for a unified British colonial agreement with the Iroquois: the conference was to fashion 'one general Treaty to be made in his Majesty's name'.

These directions were issued on 18 September 1753. The conference was to convene in June 1754 at Albany, not far from the heart of Iroquois country. Each colonial delegation received from its governor a set of instructions which were distinctly focused on the task of improving Indian relations in this moment of emergency. The result was what has become known as the Albany Congress, which met in June and July. It is remembered in American history because it acquired a second agenda – a rather ambitious 'Plan of Union' for the purpose of ensuring the common defence of British colonial America. Many of the delegates were highly respected men, among them Benjamin Franklin. A proposal for a plan to provide a unified posture of defence was in fact adopted at Albany, but it was rejected in short order by practically every colonial assembly. An essential difficulty was the assignment of the quotas that would apportion the burden; populous and wealthy colonies would be required to raise more troops and funds. Agreement on such a matter by colonies whose characters were diverse and whose apprehensions of a frontier threat were dissimilar was not to be expected.

While this proposal was on its way to London for possible parliamentary approval the Board of Trade was developing a plan of its own, which Lord Halifax submitted to the Duke of Newcastle for consideration. The duke consulted John Carteret, Earl Granville, and Lord Hardwicke, both of whom favoured the plan. It envisioned unified and mandatory colonial cooperation. But Newcastle also consulted others, many of whom feared that such unity, even if minimal and for purposes of defence only, would develop into a structure that would encourage a spirit of independence from parliamentary authority. Newcastle decided not to put the measure before Parliament. Thus, this fourth cause of British colonial unreadiness remained. Virginia was left to act alone.

Britain raises the stakes

Parliament was not due to meet in 1754 until mid-November, and Newcastle, now alone as leading minister after his brother's death, had been thinking about taking action since the end of June when word arrived that the Ohio Company's construction team had been driven from the Forks. 'We must assist the Northern Colonies from Hence – the French must be

Drove Out', he wrote in a July memorandum to the king. Subsequent news of Washington's capitulation at Fort Necessity sent him into a rage:

All North America will be lost if These Practices are tolerated; And no War can be worse to This Country than the Suffering Such Insults as These. The Truth is, the French claim almost all North America, and from whence they may drive us whenever They Please, or as soon as There shall be a Declar'd War. But that is What We must not, We will not suffer.[5]

The idea that British colonists could be driven from North America was absurd, but it seemed clear that Virginia could not cope with the French incursion.

On 11 September 1754 Newcastle and Hardwicke agreed that a high-ranking British officer should go to America along with 'a number of Half-Pay or other officers, with money, arms and ammunition'. This idea, favoured by Hardwicke, was to help the colonists fight better and give them greater resources. Newcastle favoured (though Hardwicke disagreed) sending regiments of regulars to America, but he knew that George II would oppose the idea. His only hope was an approach through William Augustus, Duke of Cumberland, the king's son who was captain-general of the army. Newcastle privately distrusted and disliked him, but consulted him anyway. Cumberland responded by drawing up a plan which he showed to his father. To everyone's astonishment the king was enthusiastic. Although the plan involved sending two regiments to America, George II nevertheless looked upon it as 'the Highest national Service'.

Two regiments of the Irish establishment (part of a Protestant force originally formed for the defence of Ireland) were to be sent to Virginia, about 1,000 men. They were to be recruited up to full strength (1,500) in America. They would be commanded by Major General Edward Braddock – Cumberland's personal choice – who was to be appointed commander-in-chief of all North American forces. To the two regiments would be added the seven Independent companies – units of the British army which were already based in Nova Scotia, New York and South Carolina – plus numerous provincial troops raised in the colonies, such as those recruited in Virginia. The mission to be undertaken first was to expel the French from their forts on the Ohio using the Irish regiments in cooperation with Virginia provincials. After that, the regulars would

---

[5] Newcastle to Lord Albemarle, ambassador at Versailles, 5 Sept. 1754, Clayton, 'Duke of Newcastle . . . and the American Origins', 590.

move to northern New York and dislodge the French from Crown Point on Lake Champlain. The colonial regulars stationed in Nova Scotia, assisted by New England provincials, would then attack Fort Beauséjour and push the French off the isthmus. Newcastle accepted this strategic plan, but insisted on a pause after the French were driven from their forts on the Ohio so that a settlement with Versailles might be then negotiated.

Hardwicke thought the plan too provocative: it might bring on a general war. Newcastle considered it to be sufficiently restrained because it envisioned a pause for negotiations and was limited to areas where (according to British views) French forces had no right to establish themselves. Since the initial thrust would be launched towards the Ohio where French 'encroachment' was deemed outrageous, the British government could justify its action in European diplomatic circles. The preparations would be kept secret for many weeks, the duke presumed, and the whole scheme would be 'as cheap and as inoffensive' as could be pursued 'consistently with doing it effectually'.[6]

A week after this plan was approved by the cabinet (26 September) Cumberland produced a more aggressive one. The assaults on the upper Ohio, Crown Point and the Acadian isthmus were now to be made simultaneously. Since Newcastle saw his limited approach being set aside he now shared Hardwicke's misgivings about the danger of a general war. He tried to persuade the king that this plan was too dangerous. Whether the king might have changed his mind cannot be known because on 8 October the cabinet was ambushed by an official notice published in *The Gazette* by direction of the secretary at war, a notice that summoned officers of the regiments destined for America to report for duty.

The mistake of allowing this advertisement to be published was so egregious that someone at the War Office should have been severely disciplined. Published notices of this sort were routine in time of war, but this was peacetime. Hardwicke was incensed. He remembered that during the earlier discussions 'it was agreed . . . that everything should be done with as much secrecy and as little éclat as possible'.[7] He strongly suspected that the published notice was not a mistake but a ploy by Henry Fox, secretary at war and a close associate of the Duke of Cumberland, to commit the British government to enlarged military activity and thus to ensure himself and Cumberland a position at the centre of affairs. Newcastle and Hardwicke had never trusted Fox and had contrived to make decisions

---

[6] Clayton, 'Duke of Newcastle . . . and the American Origins', 593–4.
[7] Hardwicke to Newcastle, 13 Oct. 1754, Yorke, *Hardwicke*, II, 282.

without him. What had happened was a sufficient ground for censuring his conduct as irresponsible, but that was hardly possible because Fox was the royal duke's political right arm. Newcastle, to his credit, tried once again to persuade the king to reconsider his son's provocative plan for North America, but failed. Though secrecy was gone, the cabinet saw where the power lay and adopted the plan.

Parliament was due to reconvene in five weeks, and the press was filled with expressions of mistrust of France and indignation over her aggressive activities in America. Newcastle, knowing how hard it was to stand up to this, felt cornered. His best hope for moderation had been the king. No one had a stronger motive than George II for insisting on a less provocative approach, since a general war could place Hanover in jeopardy, but the king was allowing his son's scheme to go forward. With the prospect of a belligerent House of Commons on one hand and an inability to contain the aggressive proposals of the Duke of Cumberland on the other, Newcastle was forced into a policy that risked war. We have seen that Governor-General Duquesne was essentially following orders from Paris when he ordered the military occupation of the upper Ohio Valley. It is equally evident that the aggressive British response was organized in London. The idea that governors in America had foisted a war on the home countries is clearly mistaken.

In late November the British plan became even more aggressive. By this revised plan, after conquering the Ohio forts a portion of Braddock's army was to go north, cross Lake Erie, and capture Fort Niagara. From Oswego a New England provincial force was to proceed westwards on Lake Ontario to assist in the Niagara operation. Lord Halifax had recommended its capture, and strategically the idea had merit, for it was certainly a vital point: if the British held Fort Niagara, Canada's fur trade from the west would then have to come by the more difficult overland and river route from Lake Huron.

The simultaneous three-pronged offensive was of itself impracticable, even without an expedition to Niagara. Cumberland and his advisers were ignorant of the strategic difficulties of campaigning in North America, and Newcastle certainly lacked the geographical and military knowledge needed to challenge them. He did understand very clearly, however, that a thrust at Niagara was not a measured response to unjustified 'encroachments', but a blow at the vitals of the French empire in North America. He also knew that long-standing usage had given the French a strong case for claiming the Niagara passage as belonging to them. If this feature of Braddock's secret orders were to become known in Paris, the French could proclaim to the world that Britain was planning an aggressive war to dismantle New France. A general war would thus appear inevitable. Although the preparation of a British force to be sent to America could not be disguised, Braddock's orders were secret, and Newcastle realized how essential it was to keep them secret if any hope of avoiding war was to be preserved. A speedy diplomatic settlement could make those orders irrelevant.

The futile negotiation

Rouillé, minister of foreign affairs since late July 1754, quickly learned about the War Office advertisement. In a meeting in mid-October with the British ambassador, William Anne Keppel, Earl of Albemarle, he asked why troops were being sent to America. Albemarle answered that the British had a right to send troops and arms to America as the French had so often done. When the ambassador described the French actions on the Ohio as 'hostile unjustifiable proceedings', the minister responded that the French 'only retook possession of their own, and endeavoured to confine us to our limits', and that the Ohio river 'could never be looked upon as the boundary of the British possessions'. Albemarle reminded him that the treaty of Aix-la-Chapelle had left the limits to be settled by boundary commissioners: 'Upon my asking him, in virtue of what principle they took upon them to prescribe our limits to us, when I understood that both Crowns had named commissaries to settle those points, and that during their negotiations nothing was to be attempted on either side, I found the reproach stung him, not knowing how to answer or evade the question.' By late November Rouillé was becoming worried. He wondered when the British expedition would sail and asked Albemarle whether there were means 'of accommodating these things in a friendly manner'.[8]

Albemarle died suddenly on 22 December 1754 of what seems to have been a heart attack. Versailles thereupon ordered its ambassador to return to London. This man, Charles Pierre Gaston François de Lévis, duc de Mirepoix, aged 55, had served in London for six years. He was well liked and trusted by British statesmen. It seemed obvious that the French court was genuinely interested in reaching a negotiated settlement.

Mirepoix's instructions, however, were entirely unsuited to the purpose. They were accompanied by a long memoir, and in both his

---

[8] Albemarle to Robinson, 23 Oct., 27 Nov. 1754, Pease, *Boundary Disputes*, pp. 55–8.

instructions and the memoir all blame for aggression was placed on the British. No fewer than seven times the current troubles were attributed to 'the forcible undertakings of the English governors' and words to that effect. The English 'had sought to invade'; the 'French governors . . . have done no more than defend the lands of the king and repel force by force'; the 'rights of the [French] king over the invaded territory are incontestable'. Jumonville's assassination was 'the work not of the Indians, but of the English' and was 'inexcusable'; the ambassador was required to demand satisfaction as well as 'proper reparation'. The British were planning a complete destruction of the French position in North America, aiming 'to break the communication of the colonies of Canada and Louisiana the more easily to wrest them from France'. The current crisis on the Ohio could have been prevented by proper action of the British government: 'England should have ordered . . . [its governors] to leave things as they were before the war and abstain from all forcible undertakings' and wait until the claims could be 'adjudicated in the manner prescribed in the Treaty of Aix-la-Chapelle'. In sum, Mirepoix was furnished with a catalogue of declarations, accusations and demands.[9]

The British were not surprised by the French claim of indisputable possession of the Ohio River, but it was troubling that the instructions offered no path forward except a proposal, reiterated many times, that both sides should now 'abstain . . . from all forcible undertakings' and await the decision of the Boundary Commission. A cessation of arms at some point during the negotiation was to be expected, but the French were asking for it as a first step, and to the British cabinet this seemed outrageous. For the last two years the French had been establishing a durable military position on the upper Ohio, and now they were saying, after blaming the present crisis on Britain's failure to restrain her governors, that everything should be put on hold until the Boundary Commission reached a verdict.

Newcastle was incensed. Four months earlier he had anticipated that the French would take this position. He had given full vent to his suspicions in a heated letter to Albemarle:

Mo[nsieu]r Rouillé presses The Renewal of The Negotiation with The Commissaries: and assures You That The strongest Orders are sent to

[9] Pease prints the instructions and memoir, both dated 30 December 1754 in full (ibid. pp. 60–83, quotations pp. 67, 73, 71, 61). Max Savelle (*Diplomatic History*, p. 58) comments that the instructions were 'scarcely calculated to bring about the desired accommodation'.

Their Governors, and Officers, To give no Cause of Complaint. . . .
[Thus] they get into Possession by Force. And afterwards, or at the
same Time, to shew their pacifik Disposition, they offer to refer the
Discussion of those Rights to Commissaries. I own, I am quite sick
of Commisssaries.[10]

Rouillé had been earlier warned by Albemarle that if there was to be a
negotiation the British would insist that the French relinquish the forts.[11]
Soon after Mirepoix arrived in London he became aware of the main
outlines of the British position and advised Rouillé:

They will demand as a condition of the armistice that the fort we have
established be demolished and that we evacuate all the settlements we
may have lately made on the river Ohio; they will perhaps consent that
the whole [Ohio] territory should remain prohibited to either nation
until [the issue is basically decided. They] will absolutely refuse the third
article . . . [settlement of the dispute by the Boundary Commission].
They will demand that it be treated court to court.[12]

This was an accurate rendering of the British position, but if the
negotiation were to be carried on between the two governments (court to
court), Mirepoix had a problem. He had been given scarcely any guidance
on boundary questions, no briefing about the geography in question, and
supplied with maps of poor quality. Thomas Robinson, the secretary of
state with whom he chiefly dealt, possessed copies of French maps of the
American interior as well as recent British ones based on new information
from colonial experts. Robinson explained to Mirepoix – to the latter's
amazement – that the headwaters of the Wabash River and the upper
Ohio (Allegheny) were separated by 'more than three hundred leagues'
(900 miles), an expanse which encompassed practically the whole of the
region in dispute. Robinson further informed him that the French had
used only 'three routes in communicating between Canada and Louisiana',
two of which, via the Great Lakes, connected with the Illinois River, not
the Ohio; the other, via the Wabash, he was informed, joined the Ohio far
to the west. The outlines were not entirely clear in Mirepoix's mind, but
he grasped the point: 'The English say the French have never seemed to

[10] Newcastle to Albemarle, 5 Sept. 1754, Pease, *Boundary Disputes*, pp. 51–2.
[11] Robinson to Albemarle, 12 Sept. 1754, Gipson, V, 324–5.
[12] Mirepoix, in a memorandum for Rouillé, 16 Jan. 1755, Pease, *Boundary Disputes*,
pp. 97–8. Here and elsewhere I have altered Pease's translation slightly.

lay claim to the lands near the sources of the Ohio River.' Robinson appeared to have mastered the details and was '*fort au fait de la question*', so the French ambassador could only listen and answer that he was not provided with the instructions necessary to enable him to discuss rights and boundaries.[13]

Knowing that political pressures for further naval and military escalation were building in London, Mirepoix urgently asked for powers to carry on court-to-court boundary negotiations, at least on the subject of the Ohio.[14] The French king and council gave him the authorization, but Rouillé's letter (3 February 1755) conveying it dismissed its utility. Mirepoix should not worry about geographical details: '[A]s the essential point to conclude is that which concerns the territory of the Ohio River, all that we can tell you on this subject is that it belongs incontestably to the king.' Rouillé went so far as to add that Louis XV would not flinch at the possibility of war: 'His Majesty eagerly wishes for peace . . . but if he is forced to make war he will fear neither the expense nor the danger.'[15] Mirepoix believed (at this point correctly) that Newcastle and Robinson were in earnest about trying to reach a settlement, and he had therefore gone ahead with a tentative discussion of boundaries. He seemed to sense that Versailles would authorize court-to-court negotiations. Indeed, it is likely that he was also receiving letters via a back-channel directly from the king and madame de Pompadour.[16]

When Mirepoix's authorization arrived on 6 February the British government acted immediately. Three cabinet meetings in four days were devoted to outlining a proposal. The result was speedily conveyed by Robinson to Mirepoix, who wrote the same day (10 February) to Rouillé.[17] The main element of the British proposal was this: before the British government would issue orders for its colonial governors to desist from further military actions, both sides must agree to withdraw from the Ohio region, returning it to the status of 1714 (the treaty of Utrecht). The result would be a neutral zone, in which all English or French settlements

---

[13] Mirepoix to Rouillé, 16 Jan. 1755, Pease, *Boundary Disputes*, pp. 87–97, quotations at pp. 87–8, 91.

[14] Mirepoix to Rouillé, 23 Jan. 1755, Waddington, *Louis XV et le renversement*, p. 75.

[15] Rouillé to Mirepoix, 3 Feb. 1755, Pease, *Boundary Disputes*, pp. 102–8, quotations pp. 107–8.

[16] Waddington (*Louis XV et le renversement*, p. 64) suggests that the private letters from the king reached Mirepoix through his wife, who was a friend of Pompadour's.

[17] Mirepoix to Rouillé, 10 Feb. 1755, ibid. pp. 76–7.

and forts were to be demolished, stretching all the way from the Allegheny Mountains to the Wabash River.[18]

While this proposal was being considered in Paris it was also under-going close scrutiny in London. Lord Halifax, president of the Board of Trade, had a strong personal interest in American affairs and also had access to the latest and best geographical information. Robinson con-sulted him and learned some disturbing things. Apart from the fact that there was no obvious way to determine where a line defined by 'the back of the mountains which enclose the British colonies' might be drawn, Halifax pointed out that the mountains were not configured as the cabi-net evidently thought. At their 'North Eastern Extremity' the 'Apalachean [sic] Mountains' did not approach the Great Lakes but curled eastwards and became ill-defined. The most important concern was that a boundary based on the mountains was likely to cast a third of the 'Province of Pennsylvania' and all of western New York (the latter belonging indis-putably to the Iroquois nations) into the proposed neutral zone.[19] He had other objections, but this one appeared to be very serious (and in fact conformed to geographical reality).

Newcastle and Robinson had made a serious mistake in allowing a boundary proposal to be presented to the French ambassador without having Lord Halifax and the Board of Trade review it first. Undoubtedly, consulting Halifax at this point was diplomatically injurious, but from a political standpoint it was a necessary precaution because French 'encroachments' had become a much-heated public issue. If the negoti-ations were to succeed, the details would quickly become known; mis-takes of ignorance would be lacerated in the public press. Newcastle and Robinson were aware that Halifax was an ardent imperialist. As a check on him they asked Lord Hardwicke – discerning yet desirous of a peaceful accommodation – to evaluate Halifax's information. Hardwicke was certainly no expert on American geography, but he and Robinson, meeting on 16 February, had at hand a recent map created by Dr John Mitchell. Mitchell, a botanist turned cartographer, had been born in Virginia and strongly supported British territorial claims in America, but with respect to geography his map was a remarkable product of research; it set a standard that lasted many years. Hardwicke became convinced that Halifax's concerns could not be ignored: 'if that Map be correct, [it] makes the Apalachian or Alligany Mountains a most uncertain and

[18] The cabinet minute of 10 Feb. is printed in Pease, *Boundary Disputes*, pp. 110–11.
[19] Ibid. pp. 111–14.

dangerous Rule', the Lord Chancellor reported to Newcastle.[20] As a result, the cabinet met again on 20 February, this time with Halifax present, and adopted significant alterations. The proposed eastern boundary of the neutral zone was now to be a meridian extending from Cuyahoga Bay (today, Cleveland) south to the 40th parallel and from thence south-west on a diagonal just south of the approximate course of the Ohio River. The British were thus rejecting not just the 'back of the mountains' as determining the eastern boundary but in effect claiming possession of the upper Ohio Valley.

This was a substantial alteration, and the British leaders did not inform Mirepoix about it straightaway, for if the French had chosen to accept the proposal of 10 February only to learn that the British had withdrawn it, they could advertise the faithlessness of the British government in every capital of Europe. It was wise to wait for the French response to the earlier proposal, which was due to arrive soon.

That response, dated 19 February, was a formal proposal: a 'Draft of a Preliminary Convention' approved by the king and council, which was to provide the basis of a two-year suspension of arms.[21] The French did indeed seize upon the British willingness to 'retire behind the mountains' for the eastern boundary. For the western, since they had long used the Wabash for communication, they required full possession of both banks, a concession the British would have no difficulty in allowing. If the response had been confined to making these points and had left others to further discussion, the British cabinet would have been in a very awkward position, for the ministers would have had to decide whether, for the sake of reaching a settlement, they would be willing to set aside the alterations they had adopted in their meeting of the 20th.

The problem never really came up because the French in their response of the 19th did not accept the terms the British had offered on the 10th. Their 'Preliminary Convention' proposed a neutral zone that was much smaller and situated entirely in the eastern sector: it would consist of a band of territory between the back of the mountains and the Ohio (Allegheny) River. This meant that the French would evacuate the upper Ohio forts but that the expanse of land west of the river to the Wabash would not be neutral; it would be recorded as belonging to France. As a result most of the Ohio territory over which the British had assumed supervisory powers under the treaty of Utrecht would become French.

[20] Ibid. p. 115.
[21] Contained in the 19 Feb. packet from Versailles, ibid. pp. 116–35.

Nevertheless, the British might have accepted this arrangement if the French had allowed a condition specified by the cabinet on the 10th, namely that no 'Corps of Armed Men' would be allowed to enter the Ohio territory, but there would be liberty 'for both the English, and French, to pass and repass, in a peaceable Manner, for the sole Purposes of Travelling and Trading'.[22] The French 'Preliminary Convention' did not allow this: its Article 3 prohibited free passage by soldiers or traders of either side.[23]

Rouillé, in letters accompanying the 19 February response, made much of France's sacrifice in giving up the forts, but the magnanimity was diminished by his pronouncement that 'the rule must be general and recip-rocal; and while we demolish forts built in a country [the Ohio] which patently belongs to us, the English must demolish those they have built' in lands where possession is disputed. He specified Oswego and the estab-lishments at Chignecto, Baubassin and Minas (the last on the Nova Scotia peninsula) as instances, but made no mention of Fort St Frédéric near the south end of Lake Champlain.

Summing up, in its counter-proposal the French government did not accept Britain's offer of 10 February. Rouillé's 'general and reciprocal' rule regarding forts might have been set aside, but the issue of free passage for English traders was something that the British government had never failed to insist upon. To be sure, the French offered to give up their own right to trade in the Ohio region, but, as noted in the preceding chapter, they were at a trading disadvantage there, and many Canadian authorities advised against attempting to do so anyway. How a denial of free passage would have been enforced was certainly a question, but it is clear that the French remained focused on prohibition, and if the British had acquiesced, the French would have gained a long-sought objective while being relieved of the expense of maintaining forts and garrisons. The tendency of historians to focus on proposed boundaries for the neutral zone has obscured the issue of whether English traders would be allowed access to the Ohio territory, which was the original cause of the crisis.

It has been said that 'Rouillé had, in effect decided to accept Robinson's proposals of 10 February as the basis for negotiations'.[24] In the French response of the 19th, which reached London on the 23rd, he accepted only one feature of those proposals; on all other points the two sides

---

[22] British cabinet minutes 9 and 10 Feb. 1755, ibid. pp. 109–11.

[23] From Versailles, 19 Feb., ibid. p. 119; see also pp. 128, 133, 142.

[24] Clayton, 'Duke of Newcastle . . . and the American Origins', 601, n. 129.

remained far apart. Between 23 and 28 February Mirepoix was engaged daily in discussions, and he picked up hints that the British ministers were changing their demands.[25] Finally, on 7 March, Robinson presented to him the British decision made in the cabinet meeting of 20 February. After reading it the ambassador told him that there was now little hope of an accommodation, and warned Rouillé to advise the court to prepare to defend Île Royale and Louisbourg. Evidently, the British leaders understood by 7 March, and perhaps as early as 23 February, that there was practically no hope of an accommodation. Rouillé's reaction to the revised terms was as strong as might have been expected: 'We see with regret, Monsieur,' he remarked to Mirepoix, 'that war alone can end our differences.'[26] He told his ambassador that he could listen to further British proposals but make none of his own. In subsequent weeks Robinson did make concessions, some of which were not trivial and gave Mirepoix hope, but Rouillé would not bend on matters the British considered crucial. Besides, the British were still insisting that a two-year suspension was not admissible: only a permanent settlement of both the Ohio boundaries and the Acadian boundary of Nova Scotia would suffice. In the end the French reverted to their original demands, denying the validity of practically every British claim of rights in the disputed territories.

If Versailles had accepted the British terms that were dispatched on 7 March along with certain minor concessions subsequently provided by Robinson, France, by a resulting treaty that would have replaced the vague provisions of Utrecht, would have been guaranteed the following: Acadia without the Nova Scotia peninsula, full possession of the St Lawrence passage and of the usual lines of communication between Canada, the Great Lakes and the Mississippi Valley, and the right to develop Illinois undisturbed. In view of the relatively small size of the French population in North America, this outcome has the appearance of a favourable arrangement, and France's reiteration of her claim to the entire Ohio watershed – almost as dubious as the British claim to it was – seems in hindsight to have been extremely unwise.[27]

Given the problem of Indian allegiance that the French faced which, as they well understood, stemmed from the competitiveness of British trade goods, there was logic in Rouillé's steadfast refusal to grant English

---

[25] Mirepoix to Rouillé, 28 Feb. 1755, Pease, *Boundary Disputes*, pp. 138–43. Also Waddington, *Louis XV et le renversement*, pp. 78–9.

[26] Rouillé to Mirepoix, 17 March 1755, Pease, *Boundary Disputes*, p. 161.

[27] This opinion was expressed by Prof. L.H. Gipson (Gipson, V, 336–7).

traders the right 'to pass and repass' in the territory. Yet he was well aware that there was a growing uneasiness at Versailles about the expense which had been incurred in trying to keep Ohio Indians under control. On 31 March 1754 Rouillé wrote a letter to Duquesne expressing this anxiety with a strong warning: 'Unless the excessive costs of the upkeep of the colonies are reduced, the French government will abandon them.'[28] But Rouillé did not want to do this; the forts on the upper Ohio had been built under his administration and he believed that France could not afford to evacuate them unless the British were willing to agree to prohibit colonial traders from entering the Ohio territory. When, during the negotiations, he did offer to dismantle them he included, as we have seen, some complications. For the sake of peace he might have been willing to withdraw these contingent demands if the British had agreed to bar their traders from Ohio. The British government never agreed to this. To be sure, it preferred not to deprive colonial Indian traders (chiefly from Pennsylvania) of their profits, but this was not a vital branch of British commerce. Rather, it felt it must not yield to the French on this issue, because by the bold move of establishing forts on the upper Ohio River the French were evidently announcing that British North America was to be confined to the eastern seaboard.

Britain and Europe

Newcastle and Robinson had sincerely hoped for an accommodation, not least because of Britain's diplomatic predicament in Europe. To understand why, one must go back to the previous war and the way it was brought to an end. Although Britain won that contest in the colonial and maritime sphere, France was the clear winner in Europe. Under Marshal de Saxe, a field commander of remarkable ability, French armies overran the southern Netherlands. The Dutch Republic, despite the danger, had stayed neutral, and it was only when the French invaded Dutch territory in April 1747 that neutrality was abandoned. A popular uprising toppled the pacifist regime in Amsterdam and installed William IV of Orange as stadtholder. The British government, which had quietly aided the stadtholder's party during the turmoil, now had hopes of military success. An allied army of 180,000, outnumbering the French, was to be assembled, and the British and Dutch agreed to split the cost of bringing 30,000

[28] Minister of Marine and Colonies to Governor Duquesne, 31 March 1754, quoted by Freeman, *George Washington*, I, 414.

hired Russian soldiers across Europe to take part. These plans were not fulfilled. The new Dutch regime could neither mobilize enough trained soldiers nor raise enough money. It turned to London for a loan, but Henry Pelham considered it hopeless. The inability of the Dutch to organize a meaningful effort even to defend their homeland determined the British government to end the war as quickly as possible.

In London the policymakers realized that Louisbourg would have to be given up. Other sacrifices might be necessary, and therefore when France offered moderate terms as preliminaries for peace in April 1748, it was looked upon as a deliverance. Although Louisbourg was to be returned to France (and Madras to Britain), the great attraction to the British was France's offer to withdraw her army from the Netherlands. Britain's ministers embraced the offer so eagerly that they directed their representative at Aix-la-Chapelle to sign straightaway without hearing from Britain's ally, Austria. They did not wish to wait the month needed for dispatches to be exchanged with Vienna, and they knew that the Austrians would almost certainly raise objections. Naturally, everyone in the cabinet agreed that once the preliminaries were signed, as they were on 30 April, a strong effort should be made to placate the Austrians and bring them into a comprehensive final treaty.

Newcastle, in Hanover with the king at the time, convinced himself that Austria could be persuaded to accede. His optimism was not shared by the statesmen in England, and in fact the Austrians did demand unacceptable conditions. Communications between Hanover and Vienna were slow, and the ministers in London worried that France might become disgusted with the delay and withdraw the terms. In early August they met together and feelings were intense. The consensus was, as Henry Pelham bluntly advised his brother, that nothing would bring the Austrians 'to their senses but a conviction, that we will act without them, if they do not concur'. A week later he wrote: 'I own, Brother, it has given me great concern, to see you run so fast into declaring, that we will do nothing without the court of Vienna, let them be never so obstinate.'[29] A precipitate action by the empress-queen, Maria Theresa, cut short the dispute. Dealing directly with Versailles, she suddenly and without notice arranged to pull her 30,000 troops out of the Netherlands. Their cost had been partly met by a British subsidy, and Newcastle now saw that his patience was to no avail. He informed the Austrians that if necessary Britain was determined

---

[29] Pelham to Newcastle, 4, 11 Aug. 1748, Coxe, *Administration of Henry Pelham*, II, 14, 17.

to sign a definitive treaty without them. Knowing that she could not go on fighting without British subsidy money, the empress-queen signed the treaty. When she acquiesced her anger and resentment were palpable.

British statesmen had known what they had to do. Allied efforts to defeat the French army in the Netherlands had completely failed, and the dreadful weakness of the Dutch Republic was fully exposed. Britain's immediate problem could be solved by taking advantage of France's attractive offer, and the cabinet speedily accepted. But Maria Theresa was abruptly compelled to give up her effort to regain Silesia from Prussia. Perhaps British statesmen should have been more patient and given Vienna time to understand Britain's view of the situation, but they were unwilling to risk delay. The consequence was that two of the three powers which for decades had formed the backbone of the Grand Alliance against Bourbon France were no longer to be relied upon: the Dutch Republic was exhausted, Austria alienated. Thereby, Britain not only lost her long-standing foundation for sustaining a European balance of power, but also lost her principal means of defending the southern Netherlands.

The southern Netherlands (approximately modern Belgium) had always been a matter of serious concern to Great Britain strategically. The provinces had formerly belonged to Spain, but when peace was made in 1713–14 the acknowledged king of Spain was a Bourbon. Britain and the Dutch Republic therefore arranged for the southern Netherlands to be transferred to the Habsburg empire, the purpose being to keep the territory from being dominated by France. The terms of possession were spelled out in Barrier treaties of 1713 and 1715, the purpose being to defend the Netherlands against French invasion. By these treaties the Dutch were responsible for garrisoning the Barrier fortresses and the British for providing some money, but the main burden fell on the Austrians, who were required to provide 25,000 troops plus a monetary subsidy to the Dutch. Vienna also had to accept limitations on the commercial development of these provinces. All this had rankled for a long time, and now, in late 1748, the British and Dutch were setting aside Austria's concerns while focusing on their own. When, full of resentment, Maria Theresa withdrew her troops the Barrier became denuded of defenders, a situation that put the Dutch Republic itself at risk. As Hardwicke remarked to Newcastle a year later, an insecure Barrier 'will be one of the greatest temptations to that Power [France] to begin a new war, when she is ripe for it; for she may immediately, with little trouble or expense, march two armies into Holland'.[30]

[30] Hardwicke to Newcastle, 30 Aug. 1749, Yorke, *Hardwicke*, II, 16–22.

Dire as the post-war outlook was, Newcastle believed he could fashion a diplomatic remedy. In November 1748 he set to work, first conferring with Willem Bentinck, who was the political leader of the Orangist party and chief adviser to the Dutch stadtholder, William IV; the stadtholder's wife, Anna, was George II's daughter. He then journeyed to Hanover where he talked with his friend, Philip von Münchhausen, a leader of the Electorate's governing council. The plan, as it evolved, called for an elaborate scheme of alliances and required Austria's cooperation. Newcastle hoped that the anger at Vienna would cool. The system he devised to win back the favour of Maria Theresa involved engagements with, and subsidies for, some of the lesser states of the German empire.

In a long letter to Hardwicke he laid out his plan and asked for advice. The Lord Chancellor did not like it. The subsidies for German princes, whoever they were, would, he pointed out, probably prove to be valueless if war threatened, for the princes could easily change their minds. He emphasized the two obvious underlying problems: the Dutch Republic was weak and Austria was unlikely to cooperate. Knowing that Henry Pelham was determined to tighten the budget to restore post-war finances, Hardwicke suggested that whatever money the Treasury could spare should go towards helping the Dutch rebuild the Barrier. That, he said, would be 'thought by many to be a much more material object for Great Britain than securing a few of the German Princes'. The other matter to be given priority was to 'keep up our Marine'. He continued:

I think it is the great point of all; for I am persuaded that one principal view of France in making the Peace, when they did it, was to give time to restore and raise theirs. I am therefore clearly of opinion that no expense should be spared upon that head, not only for keeping up and increasing the number of ships, but also for securing and having in readiness a proper number of seamen, for want of which our Fleet has been at some times almost useless. Nothing will tend to keep France so much in awe as steadily and effectively to pursue this measure, especially if there could be any hopes of having a Dutch fleet to join us. France has already felt this, and knows that her trade and colonies must always be in the power of the superior force at sea.[31]

Hardwicke also considered Newcastle's proposed system to be too weak to survive under pressure unless it included Prussia. But getting Prussia and Austria on the same side was impossible, as they both knew.

[31] Hardwicke to Newcastle, 30 Aug. 1749, ibid. II, 21–2.

Therefore, Hardwicke preferred a plan that would be more directly focused on British interests and clearly designed to deter the French: the Barrier should be maintained to the extent possible, naval superiority should be established beyond challenge, and France should be warned that her seaborne trade and colonies would be seized if she invaded the Netherlands.

Newcastle did not follow Hardwicke's advice. A strong navy, he asserted, could have no influence on continental affairs. The opposite, however, could be the case: 'France will outdo us at sea, when they [*sic*] have nothing to fear by land; and they can have nothing to fear there, if we can have nothing to oppose them.'[32] He cited the weakness of 'the Republic of Holland' as a reason why a more broad-scale 'System ought to be formed', and therefore went ahead with his comprehensive plan of 'collecting and connecting . . . our allies upon the Continent'. He spoke of it as a restoration of the 'Old System'.[33] Yet what he was trying to do differed from the 'Old System' in an important respect. That system had been a Grand Alliance aimed at containing French power; Newcastle's system aimed at 'the Preservation of Peace'. This formulation categorized the system as one of generalized war prevention or, in modern terms, 'collective security'. Newcastle considered France and Prussia to be the two powers most likely to disturb the peace of Europe, but in fact he focused on Prussia as the principal source of danger.

This focus suited George II and his Hanoverian ministers. They feared and detested Frederick II of Prussia, looking upon him and his efficient army as the greatest threat to Hanover's safety. Newcastle agreed with George II that Frederick must be controlled by fear. The king wanted to join the Austro-Russian alliance (formed in 1746), which everyone knew to be hostile to Prussia. Hardwicke pointed out to Newcastle that the king's joining it would 'be said to provoke Prussia to no purpose' and thus 'contradict your own Principle' of trying to ensure peace in Europe.[34]

---

[32] Newcastle to Hardwicke, 2, 6 and 10 Sept. 1749, BL Add. 35,410, ff. 140–54, quotation at fo. 153. Yorke, *Hardwicke*, II, 22–3 prints fragments. The sentence has been frequently quoted as the classic expression of the argument that naval superiority required continental intervention.

[33] BL Add, 35,410, ff. 143, 145. The 'collecting and connecting' phrase is from Newcastle's original outline of his ideas in a letter to Hardwicke dated from Hanover 6/17 Nov. 1748 (ibid. ff. 86–7). The summaries of these letters in Yorke, *Hardwicke*, II, 9–10, 22–3 are inadequate.

[34] Hardwicke to Newcastle, 26 Sept. 1749, BL Add. 32,719, ff. 187–8.

Newcastle again rejected Hardwicke's advice; he chose not to dissuade George II, in 1750, from joining the Austro-Russian alliance (after he had made sure that it would include the defence of Hanover). The Electorate's safety and the remote chance of restoring good relations with Austria were driving British foreign policy.

At Vienna, defence of the Netherlands clearly became a secondary concern. A rising star in Maria Theresa's counsels, Wenzel Anton von Kaunitz, insisted that the recovery of Silesia must be the principal object of Austrian policy; therefore Prussia, not France, was the real enemy. This Austrian priority shifted the fulcrum of the balance of power eastwards towards central Europe, but in the near term Vienna would try not to offend the British, and thus Newcastle's hopes were kept alive.

Despite misgivings the duke's cabinet colleagues loyally supported his alliance policy. A subsidy for Bavaria sailed through Parliament without a division, Henry Pelham arguing the case in the Commons and Hardwicke in the Lords. A year later, in February 1752, when it came to the debate on the subsidy for Saxony, Pelham again spoke in support. This time opposition was voiced, but the government won the vote handily, perhaps because Pelham promised that no further requests of this kind would be made. Thus, Newcastle's colleagues closed ranks behind him. He was the vital nexus of their political hold on government, and everyone knew that his policy was congenial to the king. In any case, it was hard to mount an argument against a diplomatic system designed to keep Europe at peace, and the amounts of subsidy were small.

The duke's system involved subsidizing certain German princes who were 'electors of the empire' to gain their votes in favour of naming the empress-queen's young son as eventual inheritor of the imperial throne. This 'imperial election scheme' proved to be a fiasco. Frederick II's strong reaction to it frightened everyone, and France, as might have been expected, also objected. Even Maria Theresa turned away; she was anxious to see affairs in Germany remain calm and also could not help feeling that Newcastle's initiatives were a British and Hanoverian intrusion upon her imperial authority.

She made no offer of any significance to help restore the Barrier. At first, the Dutch were willing to try to refurbish and garrison the fortresses, but they reduced their effort when they realized that the Austrians would contribute nothing. The Austrians, for their part, asked that certain annoying restrictions imposed on their Netherlands commerce should be removed, but, to Newcastle's disappointment, the Dutch government would not grant this request. Since the British government was unwilling to contribute unless the Dutch showed a commitment, and the Dutch would not do so unless the Austrians agreed to contribute, matters were at a standstill. In due course, seeing that the Barrier was likely to remain weak, Dutch leaders became more and more persuaded that neutrality was their best hope: perhaps France would consider a neutral Dutch Republic more useful than a conquered one.

Newcastle increasingly concentrated on holding Prussia in check. His excuse was that Frederick was a known warmonger while Louis XV in 1748 had shown himself to be a man of peace. He became so convinced that the king of Prussia alone was likely to break the peace that he contemplated a policy whereby Britain would offer subsidy money to the Russians to enable them to maintain an army poised on Prussia's borders to keep Frederick fearful. This idea was encouraged by the Hanoverian ministers and also Maria Theresa. The risk of course was that Frederick would feel so seriously threatened that he would take a desperate, preemptive, peace-shattering step. Newcastle's cabinet colleagues could see the danger, as Hardwicke did, and also see that the duke was in thrall to George II's Hanoverian concerns.

Henry Pelham refused to provide money for a Russian subsidy. Newcastle, cautioned by Hardwicke, hesitated. He realized that continental peace was his main goal. Besides, he never forgot domestic political considerations for long, and was aware that the more his policy could be seen as focusing on Prussia and the safety of Hanover, the more vulnerable it was to parliamentary opposition. Defence of Hanover was a German-born monarch's object, while defence of the Low Countries was a 'British object', and in the eyes of the public and Parliament France, not Prussia, was the enemy to fear.

Newcastle seemed to have given up all hope of diminishing the vulnerability of the Netherlands. His diplomatic schemes could be judged as a means of favouring British as well as Hanoverian interests if there had been any real prospect of restoring good relations with Austria, since this might have led the way to Austrian assistance in the Netherlands. But Vienna's price – a strong continental commitment against Prussia – was too high. As a result, practically the entire burden of defending the Barrier would fall on Britain, and the cabinet was unwilling to accept it. Thus, there was not much that Newcastle could do. Obviously, in early 1755, when negotiating over the situation of Ohio, Newcastle had strong reasons to worry about the safety of the Netherlands. It must be observed, however, that his accent on protecting Hanover rendered his administration politically vulnerable, and he knew it. As will be seen shortly, this tended to make the duke and his colleagues think that they must not yield to the French in America.

In one area of Europe, however, the situation was more promising. Newcastle's eyes were chiefly on northern Europe, but he knew that Spain was important. At first glance one might think that good relations with Madrid should have been impossible. Britain and Spain had been at war from 1739 to 1748, and under the Second (Bourbon) Family Compact of 1743 Spain was France's ally. There was, however, a turning point in 1746 when the accession of Ferdinand VI brought a change in Spanish policy. When peace came in 1748 Spain charted a new course. The Family Compact was allowed to decay, yet at the same time British proposals for an alliance were rebuffed. Only the alliance with Portugal was sustained, solidified by Ferdinand's wife, Queen Barbara of Braganza.

Thus, Madrid decided to stand clear of the European power systems in a posture of neutrality and independence while it devoted attention to building up Spain's domestic economy and her navy. The revived navy was not designed to oppose the Royal Navy, but was meant to serve as an instrument of independence by offering a modicum of protection to the empire in America. In effect, the Spanish government chose to trust Britain not to seize Spanish territory and to keep her contraband trading with the Spanish empire within reasonable limits. This policy may seem hazardous and naive, but it was true that the British government was not at this time interested in acquiring Spanish possessions and desired, instead, commercial relations.

In 1748, during the negotiations at Aix-la-Chapelle, Newcastle had not paid adequate attention to forging a settlement with Spain, but some of the damage was soon repaired by Benjamin Keene when he resumed his post as envoy at Madrid. The Anglo-Spanish commercial treaty of December 1750, negotiated by Keene, put Britain's trade through Cadiz on a good footing. Remaining unsettled were the questions of continuing the *asiento* (the South Sea Company still wanted to send its annual trading ship), Spain's 'right of search' in the Caribbean, and recompense to British merchants for their ships unlawfully seized after the war ended. *Guarda costas* (really Spanish privateers) commissioned by officials in Spanish America frequently made unwarranted seizures. Ferdinand was not in good health and placed his trust chiefly in José de Carvajal y Lancaster, the foreign minister, who was a central figure in these negotiations. He understood that the principal methods used in trying to prohibit British trade with the Spanish empire in America, that is, seizing the British vessels, was expensive, invited corruption and did not work.

To meet British objections he agreed to certain remedies, one of them being to provide compensation to British shipowners and merchants out of royal funds. The marquis de la Ensenada, minister of the navy and the Indies, was determined to build up Spanish defences and mistrustful of Britain; he may have influenced the reluctance of authorities in America to carry the remedies into execution. But when General Ricardo Wall, ambassador at London, went home to take over foreign affairs from the deceased Carvajal in mid-1754 visible progress was made. Madrid proceeded slowly but was honestly trying to remove the more serious causes of British discontent.

One issue was impossible to resolve, however: the right of British logwood cutters on the shores of the Gulf of Honduras (now Belize) to possess fortified settlements. The Spanish regarded their presence as an unauthorized encroachment on imperial territory; the British answered that it had gone on for many decades without threatening Spanish sovereignty. The wood was chiefly valued as a source of dye in the English cloth industry, a vital commodity. Madrid did not wish to deny the British access but did wish to control sales. As the regulated Spanish price would be a monopoly price (there was no other source), the British would not accept such an arrangement. Both sides agreed to negotiate a solution, but Spain insisted on prior withdrawal of the settlers. The issue lay dormant during the early years of the Seven Years War, but all Spanish ministers, including Wall, thought that the British were in the wrong, and the dispute arose again in 1760 when it would have serious consequences.

In the early 1750s the issue played a role in the dismissal of Ensenada. Although he cooperated with Carvajal in upholding the policy of neutrality and independence, his inclinations were unmistakably pro-French, and when Carvajal died in March 1754 there was reason to suspect that Ensenada would steer Spanish policy towards affiliation with France. Ensenada had provided grounds for his dismissal, however, when, without informing Carvajal or the king, he ordered officials in America to organize an attack on the logwood cutters' settlements. He later protested his innocence, but it seems certain that he authorized an attack (which was made), and although it is possible that he informed Ferdinand, the king did not recall the fact and Ensenada was banished from the court on 20 July. As a result, Wall, who was a friend and protégé of Carvajal's, became foreign minister and had no significant rival as dominant minister.

These transactions at the Spanish court ensured that by the summer of 1754, when reports of Anglo-French hostilities in North America reached

London, British relations with Spain were in good order. Wall had spent his early private career in London and despite his being Irish happened to be pro-English. Called to high office at the court of Madrid, he was always happy to talk with Keene, who was well liked by everyone except the pro-French faction. Fluent in the Iberian languages, familiar with the ways of Spain and Portugal since the early 1730s, alert and perceptive, Keene was a first-rate diplomat. Moreover, he was not afraid to tell secretaries of state in London, very courteously and clearly, what they should and should not expect from the Spanish government. He played an important behind-the-scenes role in conveying the information about Ensenada's misconduct to the king and queen. His achievements earned him a knight-hood and an ambassadorship.

Keene could not have accomplished so much without some favourable underlying conditions. Most important was the queen's ineradicable mis-trust of the French. Queen Barbara had considerable influence over King Ferdinand, and her dislike of the French was shared by most people at the court of Madrid, who resented the air of superiority the French exhibited and were also wary of their manoeuvring to guide Spanish policy. Besides, France had neglected Spanish interests at Aix-la-Chapelle almost as much as the British had done, yet had taken no material steps to repair the damage. Another underlying change was diplomatic. In June 1752, Spain, Austria and Sardinia signed the treaty of Aranjuez, which effectively ended a long-standing contention over territories in Italy. France was left out of the negotiations. The treaty reflected the changing goals of Austria and Spain, the former now focusing on Prussia, the latter on her domestic economy and navy. As a result of this treaty Britain would no longer be useful to Austria as an ally in the Mediterranean because the Royal Navy would not be needed as in the 1740s to try to prevent Spanish military supplies from reaching Italy. A former source of contention between Britain and Spain in European affairs was thus eliminated.

When the threat of war loomed in 1755 the French began intensive efforts to regain Spanish support. Newcastle and the cabinet understood how important it was to keep Spain neutral, and when the London negotiations over North American disputes reached an impasse in March 1755 Sir Benjamin Keene at Madrid was the first minister abroad to be given a full and detailed account by Robinson, the secretary of state. London was well aware that Versailles would be supplying its Spanish ambassador with a different version, and this was certainly the case: 'I will tell you further', Keene later wrote to his friend, the British consul at Lisbon, 'that, since the negotiations began, the French Ambassador's advices of the state of the negotiation did never once agree with those I received from our Court.'[35]

Britain did not need Spain as an ally but was anxious to prevent Spain from becoming France's ally. The most important reason was naval power. Britain did not need, or particularly want, Spanish naval assistance, but France most definitely did. It was not just a matter of ships. The theatre of war that would be most affected was the Caribbean where the Royal Navy would find it far more difficult to protect British trade and stifle the enemy's if French cruisers and squadrons were to have access to Spanish bases and supplies. If Spain did adhere to neutrality, the French might consider themselves to be at such a great disadvantage in a solely maritime and colonial war that they might choose instead to act against the Netherlands, or perhaps Hanover.

London under pressures, Versailles under illusions

With the Netherlands vulnerable and Hanover's safety in doubt Newcastle was anxious to avoid war, but he could not afford to yield to the French in North America mainly because he feared the pressure of public opinion. A pamphleteer wrote in 1752: '[W]e have almost introduced a new criterion of virtue and vice, regarding not more their moral Differences, than their influence on Trade.'[36] A few decades earlier a rampant enthusiasm for seizing Spanish wealth and possessions had held sway, but it had now given way to an acute sense of trade rivalry with France. Since mercantilist thinking no longer supposed that there was only a fixed amount of trade in the world, attention was focused on the increasing totality of global trade, and it was a fact that the value of France's overseas commerce was increasing faster than Britain's. French plantation production in the West Indies surged after the return of peace in 1748, and the volume of French re-exports to northern Europe became greater than ever. Thanks to the restoration of Cape Breton, the tonnage of French fishing, more profitable than the Canadian fur trade, now exceeded British, and the fisheries had strategic importance because they enhanced the supply of skilled mariners. Thus, the French were catching up and threatening to overtake. The British public viewed commerce and maritime superiority as essential to

---

[35] Keene to Abraham Castres, consul at Lisbon, 12 June 1755, Lodge, ed. *Private Correspondence*, p. 410.
[36] *Reflections on Various Subjects Relating to Arts and Commerce* (1752), quoted in Harris, *Politics and the Nation*, p. 272.

national survival and prosperity, and believed that the French were bent on diminishing that superiority. Everything that France was doing at this time appeared to justify this conclusion.

The British public's conception of 'empire' encompassed all forms of overseas commerce but was now strongly focused on colonies. For reasons mentioned in the introductory chapter, the defence of colonial trade was acquiring a territorial accent, especially in North America where it was realized that the population consuming British goods was growing rapidly. News of French harassment and boundary limitation, whether occurring in Nova Scotia or the Ohio region, fell upon a public mind that was disposed to react strongly, and the British press gave full play to the news of the armed conflicts of 1754. The *Gentleman's Magazine* provided two somewhat different maps of North America within six months, in July 1754 and January 1755, showing the interior rivers and lakes in considerable detail: the first marked the 'Fort taken by the French'; it was labelled 'Fort Duquesne' in the second.[37]

The London press of the eighteenth century was a very large fact of political life. It has been estimated that, in 1750, around a quarter of London residents read newspapers. These newspapers were carried into the country, and provincial newspapers freely copied their contents. In addition, there was an outpouring of pamphlets, on all sorts of subjects. Between 1740 and 1760 'around 160 pamphlets were published on the subject of Hanoverian influence on British foreign policy . . . [and] just over 100 on North America'.[38]

In each case the number must be considered large, but the greater number devoted to Hanoverian influence is interesting, for it reminded Newcastle that the policy of his administration was bound to appear more intent on protecting Hanover from Prussia than the Netherlands from France. To try to defend such a policy in Parliament would be problematic in itself, but to do so while yielding to French pressure in North America would be politically suicidal.

When Newcastle reacted so furiously upon learning that the French had established forts on the Ohio and had overwhelmed Washington's Virginians at Fort Necessity, he may have been genuinely angry at the French, but he undoubtedly feared popular pressure. His administration did not have a firm hold on Parliament. Henry Pelham had been a trusted leader of the House of Commons who could effectively defend ministerial

---

[37] *Gentleman's Magazine*, July 1754, p. 321, July 1755, p. 296.
[38] Harris, *Politics and the Nation*, p. 117, n. 60.

policy in debate, but he died in March 1754 and the administration found no replacement. Sir Thomas Robinson tried, but he was bewildering in debate and the posturing manner of his speaking style was an embarrassment. While the administration had a steady parliamentary majority based on patronage, this was likely to be insufficient when there was popular excitement over an issue.

As will be seen, Lord Hardwicke believed that the best thing to do would be to elevate William Pitt from paymaster of the forces to secretary of state and thereby bring his voice to the government side. Newcastle knew that Pitt was a spellbinding speaker, but also knew that he would insist on a share of power. In any case, George II deeply resented Pitt's anti-Hanoverian rhetoric and was likely to refuse. If Newcastle chose to promote Henry Fox, the other man with the talent needed to deal with the House of Commons, it could possibly make the situation worse, because in that event Pitt, knowing he had been bypassed, would be all too ready to attack. Under Henry Pelham, Pitt had been tamed. In the mid-1740s he had railed against the ways in which British policy was being biased by Hanoverian interests, but he had calmed down. Now, however, given the tilt of Newcastle's diplomacy, Pitt could argue that Hanover was still trumping British interests. The best solution was for the government to act with firmness against French pretensions in America and thus maintain popular and parliamentary support.

France, for her part, was not ready to fight a war with Britain in 1755. Although during the years of peace money had been allocated to rebuilding the navy, no one at Versailles believed it could cope with Britain's, and Spanish assistance was unlikely. Since the French army was by all accounts the strongest in Europe, the best strategy from a power viewpoint would be to offset the near-certain losses in the colonial sphere by invading and occupying the Netherlands or Hanover. French interests did not call for war at this time, however. There was no power or combination of powers which might threaten France in the foreseeable future, and there was no territory worth seizing except the Netherlands. The trouble with launching an attack in the Netherlands was that France would clearly be the aggressor, and Louis XV and Pompadour were personally averse to starting a European war in that way. Because people at Versailles saw no good reason to incur the expense and disturbance of a war in Europe they hoped that Louisbourg and Canada could hold out for a long time.

It is therefore hard to imagine how the arguments presented by La Galissonière could have persuaded the French government that it had no choice but to risk war in 1755. The thinking at Versailles on this question deserves close examination, even though the decision-making process remains opaque. First and probably most important, French ministers believed that Britain would yield. Secondly, there was a substantial body of opinion in France holding that further increase of British power in America had to be prevented, even at the risk of war – opinion that accorded with La Galissonière's. We shall consider these explanations in order.

When Governor-General Duquesne became worried in 1754 about the intensity of the British reaction to the forts and mentioned the possibility of war, Machault, the new naval and colonial minister who was now his chief, advised him in a letter of 6 November that he was wrong to think that there was danger of a rupture: the British government, he averred, was bent on maintaining peace.[39] Machault was probably focusing on Britain's extremely disadvantageous diplomatic situation in Europe. As for Rouillé, from the beginning he had assumed that Britain would not risk war. He had seen no need to defuse the crisis by granting what the British negotiators were most emphatically and repeatedly requesting, namely an immediate withdrawal of the garrisons from the upper Ohio. In fact, Rouillé used the military occupation as a bargaining tool – a proceeding that the British cabinet, fearful of public opinion, considered intolerable.

Mirepoix had informed Rouillé by the end of February if not earlier that Newcastle and Robinson were citing public opinion as a significant problem. The foreign minister considered it a dishonest excuse. All European diplomatic experts knew that the British often introduced the possibility of public and parliamentary objections as a tactical ploy for refusing to yield points at issue. Rouillé understood this; he told the French ambassador at Madrid that it was only a pretext, adding that the ministry needed only to 'cause this fermentation which had no reasonable foundation to cease'. To Mirepoix he suggested: if 'the English nation were exactly informed of the facts . . . it would be less stirred up and would do us more justice'.[40] When he told Mirepoix that for the sake of peace the British ministers must ignore the public's clamour, the ambassador responded that he did not think Newcastle and Robinson could do this.

[39] Machault to Duquesne, 6 Nov. 1754, Waddington, *Louis XV et le renversement*, p. 38.
[40] Rouillé to the duc de Duras at Madrid, 25 Feb. 1755, Black, 'Anglo-French Relations', 75; Rouillé to Mirepoix, 19 Feb. 1755, Pease, *Boundary Disputes*, p. 135.

The British public, he observed, was 'very touchy on the subject of American colonies and commerce' and it was extremely difficult for the cabinet to dismiss their concerns. He then commented that the situation of ministers in England was very different from that in France: whereas French ministers acted in safety under royal authority, 'Newcastle and Robinson would answer with their heads for the consequences of any treaty to be concluded'.[41] Responding on 5 March, Rouillé said he was aware of 'the degree of influence that the clamours of the nation could have' on British conduct, but nevertheless insisted that the British ministers must stand up to it. They must act to lessen '*la fermentation populaire à Londres*'.[42]

Reading this, and aware that the two sides were far apart, the ambassador became alarmed, and on 13 March wrote vehemently in reply. He admitted that ideally France should not have to depend upon the caprices of the English nation and the weakness of its ministers; nevertheless, he added:

[I]t is quite certain that it is not, as one supposes it to be in France, the minister who prescribes the impressions of the public. The king of England and his ministers would like very much to avoid a rupture, but they have not dared or they have not known how to handle it, not at all. That, Monsieur, is exactly the truth. I am on the spot; I ought to know the terrain after more than six years in England, and you can be assured that I am not mistaken in my conjectures.[43]

Rouillé was unmoved. He answered on 17 March in a manner implying that the British ministers were simply trying 'to justify to the eyes of their nation the prodigious cost of the armaments now preparing in England'. If they were 'able to maintain their credit' only by the treaty terms they were proposing, they would, in his opinion, not long remain in charge of the government. 'For . . . of what utility . . . is the sincerity of the pacific intentions of Messieurs de Newcastle and de Robinson, if they . . . have not enough strength to sustain them against the popular clamour?' He seemed to be ignoring the probability that if the Newcastle administration fell from office it would certainly be replaced by a less hesitantly bellicose one.

---

[41] Mirepoix to Rouillé, 28 Feb. 1755, Waddington, *Louis XV et le renversement*, pp. 78–9.

[42] Rouillé to Mirepoix, 5 March 1755, Black, 'Anglo-French Relations', 74–5.

[43] Mirepoix to Rouillé, 13 March 1755, Waddington, *Louis XV et le renversement*, p. 81.

Evidently this did not matter, because it was in this same letter that he concluded that 'war alone' could 'end our differences' and ordered Mirepoix to break off negotiations. If 'they are determined in London to kindle a war', he wrote, nothing France could say would prevent it. Moderation, he added, would be taken as a sign of timidity.[44] It appears that by 17 March the foreign minister considered war inevitable. As insurance the government had ordered troops to be gathered for embarkation, and ships to be made ready. Yet no one seemed to think the danger of an attack was immediate or, perhaps, even probable. Apparently, Machault's remark to Duquesne in November 1754 that Britain was bent on maintaining peace continued to represent the thinking at Versailles.

This complacency may have been sustained by a misleading piece of intelligence. When the French learned that the British planned to send two regiments of regulars to America and that General Braddock was to be the commander-in-chief, they asked what his orders were. No one in the British government would answer that question, or at least not truthfully, but by the beginning of January 1755 Rouillé may have thought he had secured the information needed: the French chargé d'affaires in London had managed to purchase a précis of Braddock's orders from a disgruntled government clerk. The purchased version of the orders was, however, a false document. Its content was organizational and defensive; there was no hint of the multiple assaults that would have exposed the highly aggressive nature of Braddock's orders.[45] If Rouillé had got hold of a true version, his long-standing fear that the British would use the first excuse that came along to reduce New France would have been confirmed. The false document may have misled him into supposing that there was time to wait.

It is impossible to know whether the French foreign minister genuinely believed that the British would back down. In mid-March when Rouillé expressed to Mirepoix his belief that the negotiation had no chance of

---

[44] Rouillé to Mirepoix, 17 March 1755, Pease, *Boundary Disputes*, pp. 160–2.

[45] Many historians have reported that the French secretly learned the nature of Braddock's orders by this purchase. The document, and accompanying letter from the chargé d'affaires saying how he managed to buy it, both sent to Paris in cipher, is in the French Foreign Ministry Archives, Paris (AE, Corresp. politique: Angleterre, 438 ff. 2–8). Hitherto, only Pease has noticed that these were not Braddock's true orders (*Boundary Disputes*, p. lv). It is likely that the allegedly disgruntled clerk reported the fact that he had been approached to his superiors and that Robinson thereupon caused a false version to be drawn up.

success, did he intend it as a negotiating gesture or was it a genuine assessment? It is interesting that the king of Prussia believed that Rouillé and Mirepoix were deluding themselves and was willing to bet ten to one that Britain was ready to go to war.[46] He was probably not alone in this opinion.

If Rouillé had serious doubts about the chances of a successful negotiation, did he share them with Louis XV and Pompadour? It is believed that Mirepoix communicated with Pompadour and the king by a back-channel, but did the ambassador candidly express his growing alarm? Both he and the foreign minister would have been tempted to avoid conveying bad tidings. To push further this question of who at Versailles was kept accurately informed, it seems possible that no one outside the naval and foreign ministries, and perhaps a few people in the war ministry, knew that the outlook for peace was becoming bleak. René-Louis de Voyer de Paulmy, marquis d'Argenson, who had intimate court connections and strained to hear every piece of news, was completely in the dark regarding the negotiation. Throughout the month of March the couriers from London were anxiously awaited, but opinion at Versailles does not appear to have reflected the seriousness of the situation. The mode of governance provided no regular means of altering Rouillé's stance – indicative of a systemic flaw that did not require the foreign minister to keep his ministerial colleagues correctly informed of developments.

Rouillé's removal from the ministry of marine and colonies to the foreign ministry in late July 1754 had been an accident of court politics, but it meant that the man who had presided over French policy in the Ohio region found himself in charge of the negotiation, and also that he remained in close touch with the same advisers. He was 70 years old with no experience in foreign affairs, and d'Argenson was convinced that he would be controlled by the first commissioner of the foreign office, Jean-Ignace, abbé de La Ville, whose attitudes were hawkish. Rouillé would be 'nothing more than de La Ville's echo'. D'Argenson's apprehensions focused on a broad suspicion of the influence of a 'war party' at court; de La Ville was known to be in regular communication with military officials at the war ministry. Yet Rouillé was also in touch with La Galissonnière, who was living in Paris, and no one in France knew more, thought more, or cared more about the future of New France than this admiral. He had played a key role in the decision to send troops to the Ohio Valley.

---

[46] Waddington, *Louis XV et le renversement*, pp. 94–8, 103–4, 111–12.

There was, however, a broader source of influence on the foreign minister. The question of containing the growth of British naval and colonial power was a vibrant topic. It received considerable public exposure, most notably in articles in the *Observateur hollandois* (produced in Paris) which urged the importance of limiting British sway in America. This idea had enough adherents, some of them highly placed, to constitute a second explanation of Rouillé's firmness. The belief was that because Britain was bent on acquiring a monopoly of world trade France could not afford to ignore a chance to limit British colonial expansion. Pompadour, a patron of Machault, may have been a supporter of this point of view. Rouillé undoubtedly held it himself. Public interest in the negotiation is therefore easily explained; it was not a topic about which no one at court knew or cared. But it is to be wondered whether the king and other ministers knew the full truth about what was passing between Rouillé and Mirepoix.

On 30 March d'Argenson, hearing rumours of French troop movements near the Netherlands border, wrote in his journal that 'all this has the smell of the counsels of favourites [*mignons*] who wish to make their fortunes by war'. He then sadly reflected on the way arguments which seemed correct, but were actually invalid, appeared to be directing the policy of France. In this instance:

It is eight years since the King was dying with desire to promote peace, and today he courts a universal war. It is believed beyond doubt [at court] that our enemies are frightened by this perspective of a prompt and general war, if we let the English attack us in Canada. But I ask myself if it might not come to pass that our enemies will not be at all frightened by this bravado.[47]

The next day the news at court was that the American dispute with England was 'absolutely accommodated'. The king had said this to several people. D'Argenson wished he could believe it, and was encouraged a week later when there was talk that mentioned details of a settlement. All this changed on 10 April when there was word that the dispute was 'anything but accommodated', and the next day the talk at court was about the possibility of a British attack on the ships that were being readied to carry the troops to New France when they put to sea.[48]

[47] D'Argenson, *Journal et mémoires*, VIII, 466–7.
[48] Ibid. pp. 467–8, 473, 475–6.

On 1 May Sir Benjamin Keene at Madrid, who conversed a good deal with the French delegation, observed to a friend: 'The case is, France has depended too far upon our pacific intentions, too far upon the state of the nation, the age of you know whom [George II], and many foreign circumstances, in all of which, God be thankt, they have been balked in their expectations.'[49] Keene was a man of considerable perspicacity and knew, thanks to letters from Robinson, that by mid-March French reliance on British pacific intentions had become illusory. It seems that Louis XV did not understand this. Operating without restraint by the king and council of state during the negotiation, Rouillé's ministry led the French monarchy into a war for which it had no strategic plan – a fact which its conduct during the coming months plainly revealed. The only precautions the French government had taken were to make ready six battalions to be sent to New France and a fleet of warships to carry them.

---

[49] Keene to Castres, 1 May 1755, Lodge, ed. *Private Correspondence*, p. 404.

CHAPTER 5

War without declaration: North America, 1755

The British military ventures of 1754 in North America had been colonial enterprises. In contrast, the three expeditions of 1755 were planned in London and led by British commanders. They were poised to move at the end of April and went forth almost simultaneously. This was the moment when general hostilities actually began although another year passed before war was declared. In reality the Anglo-French Seven Years War was an eight-year war, and the first year of undeclared war was very active both militarily and diplomatically; and proved pivotal.

One of the expeditions was purely naval. On 10 April the British cabinet decided that a squadron should be sent to the Gulf of St Lawrence to lie in wait for the French squadron known to be carrying the six-battalion reinforcements. On the 26th Vice-Admiral Edward Boscawen sailed from Plymouth on this mission. He arrived at the entrance to the Gulf on 3 June. His secret orders called for capturing or destroying the entire squadron. A second expedition was mainly a colonial effort: the troops were all raised in New England. They were gathered at Boston in late April, where they waited for arms to arrive from Britain. After setting forth in May with a small Royal Navy escort they began to disembark at their destination in the Bay of Fundy also on 3 June. Major Charles Lawrence of the British army (acting governor of Nova Scotia) had joined them at Annapolis Royal and taken command. Major General Edward Braddock headed the third expedition. He left Fort Cumberland near the northernmost reaches of the Potomac River on 30 April and proceeded westwards over the mountains with a force of British regulars and Virginia recruits toward Fort Duquesne, taking with him heavy guns that could easily have pounded the fort into submission.

At the entrance to the Gulf of St Lawrence three ships of Boscawen's squadron encountered a few of the warships bringing reinforcements from France. Two French ships, with 800 troops aboard, were captured, but ten others, carrying almost 80 per cent of the forces, got safely to Louisbourg or Quebec. The New Englanders quickly conquered the Acadian isthmus and soon dominated all of Nova Scotia. Braddock's expedition was an unmitigated disaster. His army was only eight miles short of its destination when it was practically annihilated in a surprise attack. Braddock himself was killed.

The best known of these expeditions is Braddock's, but Boscawen's naval mission was fundamentally more important. If France had lost the 3,650 regular troops and officers embarked for North America as well as the warships that carried them, the outlook at Versailles would have been bleak. Such a clear-cut British success would have compelled French ministers to recognize a truth that was so hard for them to admit – the immense difficulty of carrying on a war in North America under conditions of naval inferiority. Newcastle fervently hoped that early and decisive defeats at sea and in North America would persuade the French to negotiate, thus avoiding a war in Europe. The worst possibility for the British would be a meagre success such as the capture of only one or two of the French ships, and that was what happened. As Lord Hardwicke gloomily observed upon learning news of the outcome, 'We have done too much or too little.'[1] The British thus incurred the stigma of launching an aggressive attack in time of peace without gaining the strategic prize.

The French navy gambles and wins

From the beginning of January 1755 the French dockyards had worked feverishly to prepare a naval squadron to carry troops to North America. The ships were ready at Brest on 15 April and waited only for provisions and a fair wind. Fourteen ships of the line carried six battalions of the king's best soldiers and some key officers. Among the latter were the new governor-general, the marquis de Vaudreuil, an experienced Canadian whom we met in Chapter 3 and also a competent major general who had European experience in irregular forms of warfare, and Jean-Armand, baron de Dieskau. These large ships were accompanied by two frigates.

[1] Hardwicke to Newcastle, 14 July 1755, Corbett, I, 58.

Although French authorities would later claim that Boscawen's attack came as a surprise, they had been well aware that the British might choose to intercept the squadron, perhaps as it emerged from Brest. With this possibility in mind they assigned an additional six ships of the line and three frigates, fully armed, to accompany the departure. Vice-Admiral Jean-Baptiste Macnémara was ordered to shepherd the expedition 200 leagues (600 miles) into the Atlantic and then return to port; his orders were to shield it if attacked, but avoid battle if at all possible. The French understood that the Royal Navy's best chance for a comprehensive interception was to attack immediately, off Brest, but they also suspected that London would wish to avoid the diplomatic consequences of so blatant an action in European waters. In any case, Versailles knew that its best chance of winning its gamble was to embark the troops in fast ships of the line and count on evasion. In fact, eleven of the fourteen ships of the line sailed with reduced armament; they left behind their lower tier of heavy guns to make room for the troops and supplies.

Boscawen sailed from Spithead on 21 April, called briefly at Plymouth, and set out across the Atlantic on the 27th with eleven ships of the line and one frigate. Nineteen French ships of the line with five frigates came out of Brest on 3 May, at night with lights extinguished – a hazardous undertaking. Even so, the squadron was spotted and shadowed by British cruisers. Their report of the size and composition of the French fleet (which was in fact remarkably accurate) was rushed overland from Penzance to London where a startled Admiralty ordered six more of the line, under Admiral Francis Holburne, to reinforce Boscawen immediately. Holburne sailed on 11 May under orders to turn back if some of the French did, but word of Macnémara's return never reached him and he proceeded across the ocean.

Boscawen stayed ahead of the French and kept his ships together despite having to deal with fog and icebergs near the end of the voyage. Landfall came on 3 June, and the squadron lingered in the Cabot Strait in a position south-west of Cape Race, Newfoundland. The French expeditionary squadron, under the command of Emmanuel-August de Cahideuc, comte Du Bois de la Motte, made a quick passage but the ships did not manage to stay close together – luckily, as it proved. Near the entrance on 6 June the French admiral sighted Boscawen's squadron and withdrew the seven ships with him eastwards. Two mornings later as the fog slowly cleared a group of three French ships found themselves less than nine miles away from the more unified British squadron. They dashed westwards, but the *Dunkirk* (60 guns), commanded by Richard Howe, was nearby and happened to be a very good sailer in light breezes. By noon she overtook her quarry, the *Alcide*. This was a fully-armed 64-gun ship, and Captain Gilles Hocquart de Blincourt, the senior officer, ran out his guns and deliberately positioned her to shield the other two, which lacked their main armament. As the *Dunkirk* approached the *Alcide*, Hocquart called across the water to Captain Howe, asking whether the two nations were at peace or at war. Howe gave no reply until he was asked a third time, and then answered: 'At peace, at peace!' With a red pennant, signalling attack, flying from the mast of Boscawen's flagship, not far away, Howe then unleashed a full broadside. The guns, loaded with chain and bar shot as well as iron debris, were aimed high to take down the *Alcide*'s masts and spars and shred her sails. Deprived of motive power, she soon fell within range of Boscawen's flagship, the *Torbay* of 74 guns, which fired a single cannon. The message was clear: honour did not require more bloodshed. Captain Hocquart struck his colours, though he knew he would acquire thereby the dubious distinction of surrendering a French ship of war to the Royal Navy for a third time, twice in the preceding war. The engagement had lasted about ten minutes; on board the *Alcide* there were 54 men killed and about 50 wounded; the *Dunkirk* suffered 9 killed and 29 wounded.

Meanwhile the *Defiance* (64 guns) was slowly overtaking the *Lys*, ordinarily a 74 but now lacking her heavy battery. The *Defiance* stayed beyond musket range and also aimed at the masts and rigging. The *Lys* lost speed and came under the guns of the *Fougueux* (captured by the British in 1747). The French captain struck his colours quickly. The *Defiance* suffered no casualties, and the *Fougueux* very few. The third French ship of the group, the *Dauphin Royal*, lightly armed and carrying troops, was a superb sailer and escaped to Louisbourg. The next day the area was blanketed by heavy fog.

Boscawen's squadron still lay across the path of most of the French ships. Nevertheless, helped by storms and fog, by swiftness, and by sailing near rocky shores under poor visibility, they passed by unseen, some reaching Louisbourg, others veering northwards into the Gulf. By 13 June all French ships not captured were either in Louisbourg harbour or proceeding to Quebec. Boscawen did not know this and optimistically believed that more ships would fall into his hands. By 21 June, however, he could only hope to pick up stragglers; a cruiser had looked into Louisbourg and seen the masts of three ships of the line and two frigates, safely moored. The admiral was trying to convince himself that he had done well, but he realized that although 'the King, the Ministry and the majority of the people' would express approval, they would expect that 'I should have done more.'[2] The prediction was accurate.

He could still hope to capture the French ships as they attempted to return home. When Holburne's six ships arrived on the 21st, Boscawen divided his force into three squadrons of about seven ships each: one to watch Louisbourg, a second to patrol the Cabot Strait and range into the Gulf, and the third to refresh at Halifax. None of this succeeded. In late August, by a daring feat of navigation, superbly executed, Du Bois de la Motte's ships from Quebec made their way, two by two, north of Anticosti Island and out into the Atlantic via the Strait of Belle Isle – in other words, by the exceedingly dangerous passage north of Newfoundland. A month later, three ships of the line at Louisbourg escaped Holburne's blockade. Though detected and chased, they outran their pursuers, even the *Dunkirk*. In fact, all the French warships made it back to France except one, which encountered a 70-gun British man-of-war in the Bay of Biscay and in spite of having only 22 guns mounted put up a stiff and bloody fight before surrendering.

One reason why the French ships got away from North America is that sickness rendered most of the British ships unfit to patrol. A malignant fever, probably typhus brought from England, spread through the British fleet. The early summer weather in that latitude was extremely cold and recuperation was delayed. It is 'the severest weather I ever experienced', Boscawen wrote to his wife. 'The whole ship's company have chilblains on their hands and feet; my feet have not escaped.'[3] The flagship and many others would have to remain in harbour at Halifax for much longer than expected. That would leave to Holburne the task of patrolling the Gulf and he did not have enough ships to do it effectively.

Boscawen had not been provided with enough ships. Some naval historians have remarked that the Admiralty sent too strong a force, and in terms of firepower that was true. The cabinet had intelligence as early as February that most of the French ships bound for America were intended to carry troops and would not be carrying their heavy armament.[4] The admiral's mission was to achieve a comprehensive interception, and foggy weather required that he cover the entrance to the Gulf in depth. Holburne's six ships should therefore have been dispatched from the start,

[2] 'Boscawen's Letters to his Wife' (26 June 1755), Lloyd, ed. *Naval Miscellany IV*, p. 193.

[3] Ibid. (13 June 1755), p. 188.

[4] BL Add. 32,853, ff. 221–3.

along with more frigates. The Admiralty's failure in this regard strongly suggests that their Lordships did not grasp the situation. In this particular case it was easy to predict where the French ships were heading, so the challenge was to achieve a comprehensive interception in a climate where visibility at sea was often poor. There were captains in London who knew what the weather was like in those waters from their experience when guarding the Newfoundland fishery. There is no sign that Lord Anson and his colleagues at the Admiralty had consulted any of those captains. In fact, the Admiralty seems to have been confident of success.

Newcastle had ruled out an attack in European waters on diplomatic grounds in hopes of confining armed conflict to North America. He also believed that such an attack would provoke a storm of censure across Europe, ruinous to British diplomacy. Versailles would cry foul no matter where the attack was made, but Newcastle judged that all Europe would join the chorus if it occurred in European waters. Was he right in supposing this? The assessment by Joseph Yorke, British minister at The Hague, is interesting. Opinion in Holland, he wrote to his father in mid-February 1755, held that the French would soften their demands because of Britain's naval mobilization. On all sides, he said, the power of the Royal Navy was held in awe and people would expect it to be used to prevent the French from transporting reinforcements to North America. When he learned that the negotiations had apparently collapsed, he was completely mystified by Versailles's conduct: in a letter to his eldest brother he wrote: 'I cannot yet bring myself to imagine, that the [French] ministers . . . will venture to send out their Fleets, when they must be morally certain that they will be attack'd by a Superior force; that in that case they have a chance at least of having their Marine once more ruined.' And if it was true, as he had heard, that most of the French warships would not have their heavy guns mounted, it would be 'the greatest Folly in the French to venture them out of harbour, for provided we are but out [to sea in] time enough, and have those orders which I would give, it is as good as making us a present of their Fleet'. He made it clear that if the choice were his he would order an attack straightaway, in European waters. Everyone he talked to thought this would be done and, he added, 'the war won't be a jot more or less certain' if the attack were delayed. France was 'much more likely to persist' if she succeeded in conveying the military reinforcements across the Atlantic. By mid-June Joseph Yorke knew that an attack in European waters had not been ordered. His eldest brother was cautioning him not to criticize. There were 'numberless good reasons', he was told, for not beginning hostilities in Europe.[5] These reasons will be examined in the next chapter, where it will be seen that when the court of Versailles received the news of Boscawen's attack at the Gulf no one there knew what to do – their bafflement vindicating Newcastle – but it will also be seen that the British cabinet would decide that it could not afford to postpone hostilities in European waters for long.

Nova Scotia

When New England's soldiers landed at the isthmus near Fort Lawrence on 3 June 1755 the French commander at Fort Beauséjour was taken completely by surprise. Even Acadians living on the shores of the Bay of Fundy initially assumed that the ships they sighted were French. Practically no one expected so many men and transports to be mobilized so soon. In fact, General Braddock had been astonished to hear from Massachusetts Governor William Shirley when they met at Alexandria, Virginia in mid-April that 2,000 soldiers were already assembled for embarkation. Braddock's secret orders called for the expedition to Nova Scotia to be the last campaign of the year, not the first.

Here was an instance of what La Galissonière had worried about: an expedition that drew on American colonial troops, transport vessels and provisions. A handful of British officers and troops already based in Nova Scotia were added upon arrival. The circumstances were, to be sure, unusually favourable for speedy preparations. Massachusetts had become attuned to military recruiting, and in maritime New England transports could be readily hired. Prominent Boston merchants extended credit; for instance, Thomas Hancock, one of the supply contractors, placed a credit of £20,000 at the organizers' disposal. Behind the vigorous preparations lay the remarkable political abilities of Governor Shirley, whose enthusiasm for an attack on Acadia was ingrained. He had obtained the Massachusetts assembly's approval in mid-February.

To persuade the assemblymen he had pointed out the strategic importance of Nova Scotia to the security of New England and its fishery. He also reminded them of the financial benefit the colony had received from the large sum of cash recently paid by the British government in recompense of its costs relating to the capture of Louisbourg in the last war. He

[5] Yorke to Hardwicke, 14 Feb. 1755, BL Add. 35,356, ff. 289–90; to Philip, Lord Royston, 7 March, 4 and 22 April, 13 June 1755, BL Add. 35,364, ff. 39, 43–4, 45, 49.

knew that, ultimately, financial support, arms and ammunition for this expedition would also have to come from Britain and assured the legislators that this would occur. How could he be sure? When Lieutenant Colonel Robert Monckton was ordered to Boston from Nova Scotia by Charles Lawrence, the lieutenant-governor, in November 1754 to help the colony raise an army he brought a promise that any expenses not covered on the British army establishment would be charged to the budget for Nova Scotia. Parliament's willingness to vote the annual appropriation for Nova Scotia, including overruns, was by this time well established. This was truly an imperial war chest. Nothing like it had been available to Virginia.

When the New England troops landed at the isthmus they found the French remarkably unprepared. The commander at Fort Beauséjour, Louis Dupont du Chambon de Vergor, had done almost nothing. Preoccupied with lining his own pockets at government expense, he complacently relied on receiving reinforcement from Louisbourg or Quebec. Naturally, upon learning that troops were landing he sent couriers to those places for help, but timely aid from Quebec was out of the question, and by the time his message reached Louisbourg all sailings had been shut down by the presence of Boscawen's fleet. The defence of Fort Beauséjour would therefore rest on a garrison of fewer than 200 officers and men plus whatever support could be got from the Acadian militia and Micmac Indians.

All Frenchmen in Acadia, as in Canada, had to serve in the militia, and in theory Vergor could have called on the refugees displaced from peninsular Nova Scotia; among these were about 500 men of military age who no longer had farms to tend. But taking up arms against the British was a fearful proposition for them. They had been born within the limits of a British dominion; many had declared themselves neutrals by oath to British authorities. If they fought for the king of France and were captured, they could be judged traitors. They therefore insisted that they must be formally compelled to serve on pain of death. This was done, but they remained reluctant soldiers all the same and were inclined to desert if assigned to patrols.

Fort Beauséjour, built of earth and stone, was not large. If the British could bring their mortars within range, they could pound the huddled inhabitants to a pulp. The only hope was to employ raids and ambushes to disrupt the attackers' progress. The French attempted two raids and both failed. Despite the urgings of the abbé Le Loutre, the Acadians and especially the Micmacs were inclined to keep their distance from British

6-pounders. The French troops were not disposed to press an attack, so Monckton's men crossed the Missaquash River rather easily and experienced no serious opposition until they came within range of the fort's guns. They began bombarding the fort on 14 June, the same day that the French commander received word that no help would come from Louisbourg. This news quickly leaked out to the Acadians, who immediately asked Vergor to be allowed to leave and threatened desertion if permission were denied. Two days later a large mortar bomb exploded upon one of the few spaces within the fort thought to be well sheltered by earth and stone; six officers were among the dead. A staff meeting reached the decision to surrender.

The French asked for 48 hours to consider Monckton's terms. Though surprised by the suddenness of the capitulation, he had the presence of mind to give them only two, and by 7 p.m. Fort Beauséjour was in British hands. According to the terms the British would ship the 130 surviving French regulars to Louisbourg under a flag of truce; they were pledged not to fight for six months. Monckton pardoned the 350 Acadians still at the fort on the ground that they had been compelled to take up arms on pain of death. Soon after, Fort Gaspereau, on the north coast of the isthmus, surrendered without a shot, and the British swiftly established military control over most of the isthmus and all of peninsular Nova Scotia. All Acadians within those areas were at their mercy.

Lieutenant-governor Charles Lawrence had always been opposed to leniency. He did not trust the Acadians and hoped that Monckton would not offer those who surrendered at Beauséjour a chance to take an oath of allegiance: it would 'tye up our hands and disqualify us to extirpate them, should it be found (as I fancy it will) hereafter necessary'.[6] As for those domiciled in British-held land he soon decreed that they must now without delay take the unconditional oath with its assent to bear arms or else expect to be expelled from Nova Scotia. An Acadian delegation from the Minas Basin area soon appeared before the provincial council at Halifax to announce their refusal to take this oath. They were asked some searching questions. Had they suffered in any way under British governance – with respect to their lands, their freedom to trade and fish, or their exercise of the Catholic religion? Could they deny that when the French had power over them they were required to bear arms? Could they deny that their behaviour as neutrals had been one-sided? Could they think of a single instance when they had rendered an important service to the British?

[6] Lawrence to Monckton, 20 Jan. 1755, Faragher, *Great and Noble Scheme*, p. 299.

To all these questions they offered no reply. The council asked again if they would take the unqualified oath. When they declined they were given a day to think it over. The next day they still refused, whereupon they were informed that the government 'could no long look on them as Subjects of His Britannick Majesty, but as Subjects of the King of France, and as such they must hereafter be Treated'.[7]

The council extended this principle to all Acadians within the province of Nova Scotia. Anyone who refused the unconditional oath would not be given a later opportunity and was liable to removal from the province. This policy was reviewed at Halifax by Admiral Boscawen and his second in command on 15 July; they agreed with it. The Chief Justice of Nova Scotia, Jonathan Belcher, also approved the council's decision, and by this authority the lands and cattle of those who refused the oath would be declared forfeit. During the month of July members of Acadian communities throughout Nova Scotia petitioned to be allowed to continue under the former, more lenient form of oath; they persisted in refusing the unconditional oath.

The British authorities now had to consider what to do with them. Simple expulsion would result in their migrating to nearby French territory, especially to Île St Jean (Prince Edward Island), an outcome that French colonial authorities had long been trying to achieve. Shipping was becoming scarce under the pressure of hostilities, so transporting them across the Atlantic to France was deemed impractical. The council therefore decided to request shipping from Boston and to distribute them to British American seaboard colonies. Lawrence immediately sent orders to the army commanders in the various communities, instructing them to employ 'some stratagem to get the men both young and old (especially the heads of families) into your power and detain them till the transports [from the colonies] shall arrive'.[8] The round-up of the Acadians began in August. In order to disarm and assemble them for eventual deportation without creating serious disturbance the British officers routinely employed deception. The Acadians had no idea what was about to happen to them; the women, who were not confined, believed that only the men would be sent away. But in September and October everyone within reach was embarked; immediate families were generally kept together.

Charles Lawrence was undoubtedly the driving force behind the policy of comprehensive expulsion. Colonel John Winslow of Massachusetts

[7] Gipson, VI, 256.

[8] Quoted in Stanley, *New France*, p. 119; see also Gipson, VI, 264.

expected the Acadians captured in the French sector of the isthmus to be deported, but he realized that the vast majority of Acadians in Nova Scotia had simply stayed where they were. It would be a 'disagreeable business', he wrote to Shirley, 'to remove people from their ancient habitations' who had not participated in open violence and wondered if it was warranted, but he complied with the order. There was also a question of whether it was truly necessary. Admiral Boscawen gave his approval at a time when he was upset and worried by the fact that the French had out-manoeuvred him. With a large military force in Canada the French might choose to make war anywhere. Everyone including Lawrence was aware that the shipping costs of a general expulsion would be high. In addition, the British colonies to which they were sent would have to pay to look after them. More serious, however, was the probability that many would escape the round-up and, having lost the farms and villages to which they were so passionately bonded, would probably become enemy combatants. The government in London was aware of Lawrence's temper and inclinations. Upon learning of the capitulation of Fort Beauséjour in mid-August Robinson, the secretary of state, wrote a letter mentioning this very point. He cautioned the lieutenant-governor to be prudent in his conduct toward these 'Neutrals'. If they became alarmed there might be 'pernicious consequences' and he should consider 'how suddenly an Insurrection may follow from Despair, or what an additional Number of useful Subjects may be given, by their Flight, to the French King'.[9] As it happened, when the Acadians were gathered they showed how tame they were. There were no insurrections. They trusted the British officers to the very last. But it was also the case that over 1,500 Acadians escaped to Île St Jean or the 'Acadian coast' of what is now New Brunswick, and some of these soon participated in a guerrilla campaign against the British.

Westward communications across the Atlantic were slow – two months was common – and Lawrence did not receive Robinson's letter until after his brutal work was nearly completed. Although letters passing from Nova Scotia to England could arrive in about a month, he did not report what he had undertaken in July until mid-October. Thus he kept the London authorities in the dark until mid-November about such things as ordering transports from Boston, rounding up all Acadian families in Nova Scotia to be deported, and confiscating their lands and cattle to help pay for the shipping.

[9] Robinson to Lawrence, 13 Aug. 1755, Griffiths, *Acadian Deportation*, p. 111.

Almost 7,000 Acadians were shipped off by the British during the year 1755. Over 1,000 died en route to their destinations (in colonies from New England to Georgia) either by shipwreck or epidemic disease. When Île St Jean was captured by the British in 1758 its inhabitants, too, were removed. It is estimated that during the war as a whole, the British transported 11,000 Acadians. Their travails and eventual settlement in various locations – in 1765 some decided to go to Louisiana where 'Acadian' became 'Cajun' – form a subject that will be briefly touched on in the concluding chapter.

From a British viewpoint it was convenient and in many ways justified to lay the blame on Charles Lawrence. Unquestionably, he harboured an anti-Catholic bigotry that shaped his mistrust of the Acadians. Such bigotry was not unusual at the time – the Acadians who arrived in the American colonies would feel its effects – but it was unseemly in a British governor. Perhaps just as important, Lawrence had a malevolent temper. He had already earned the detestation of the German settlers, and later he would display such bullying, high-handed behaviour in the office of governor that even British colonists learned to hate him: in 1757 the Nova Scotia council took the extraordinary step of calling for his removal. It was indeed a sad moment for the Acadians and the reputation of British imperial government when, in 1753, the appointed governor, Peregrine Hopson, fell sick and had to resign, leaving Lawrence as lieutenant-governor in charge of the colony.

Yet it has to be recognized that no one in authority at the time, in Britain or British North America, condemned his decision to impose a comprehensive expulsion. When the lieutenant-governor's report finally reached Whitehall Sir Thomas Robinson may have been disappointed but no disapproval was expressed.[10] Lord Halifax at the Board of Trade was highly satisfied and Lawrence was soon promoted to the governorship. Popular politics in London may have played a role in this. When his report from Nova Scotia finally arrived Parliament had just convened after seven eventful months of hostilities that were stamped chiefly by failure; the opposition was in full cry, claiming that the administration had been irresolute as well as inefficient. It was not a good moment for anyone in government office to criticize the leader of a successful campaign on the ground that he had been too vigorous and severe, for the conquest of Nova Scotia was seen as a bright spot in an imperial war that was going badly.

[10] Griffiths (ibid. pp. 158–61) prints J.B. Brebner's careful account of London's response.

It was left to later generations to condemn the massive expulsion of the Acadians for what it was – an egregious and unnecessary act of inhumanity – so egregious that it blotted out the fact that before then the Acadians had been put under imperial pressure from both sides. French policy had aimed at frightening them into abandoning their farms in peninsular Nova Scotia in order to help meet the provisioning needs of Louisbourg. British policy had aimed at requiring them to commit to full allegiance to the British Crown, a dangerous thing for them to do when Le Loutre and his allies could so easily incite neighbouring Indians to attack them. To be sure, British plans that were favoured by Governor Shirley and the Board of Trade looked forward to inviting New England Protestants to settle on vacated Acadian lands, but that was not the pressing motive behind the policy of expulsion. Its motive was simply mistrust of Catholics with a view towards military security, regardless of how they had actually behaved. During the war the policy continued to be justified on this ground and no one looked too closely at its results. Second thoughts began to set in as soon as Canada was completely conquered, and by the end of the war the policy of uprooting Acadians from the region was discarded. After the war, when it was safe for New Englanders to settle, some Acadians returned to Nova Scotia, but they were not given back their lands; they served as labourers who were useful because they knew how to repair the ruined system of dykes. Eventually, the shamefulness of the expulsion was amply exposed, most evocatively by the American poet, Henry Wadsworth Longfellow, in his epic poem of 1847, *Evangeline, A Tale of Acadie.*

There have always been unanswered questions about the conduct of the Acadians in this crisis. Clearly, they convened as communities in July 1755 and made their decision collectively, and basically they all made the same decision. Why? There was of course a fundamental positive reason: although they were staunchly independent and insisted on neutrality with respect to military obligations, they were at heart Catholic and French, and the thought of breaking those bonds was distressing to them religiously and culturally (though the British did not require a religious break). Moreover, the future in 1755 was doubtful. Who would end up controlling Nova Scotia? Might not Le Loutre or some successor turn the Indians upon them? It appears that they had recently come to fear the French and the Indians more than they feared the British, who had threatened dispossession before but not implemented it. In fact, the British authorities had shown that they wanted them to stay in order to benefit from their agricultural production while denying it to the French. The

Acadians had avoided provocative action and believed they had shown consistently and unmistakably that their attachment was not to insurgency and war-making but to their farms and communities. For the British to remove them, they reasoned, would be not only cruel but contrary to British interests, and when the time came for them to embark they could hardly believe it was really happening. Even then, many assumed that only the men would be shipped off, or that if women and children were also to be expelled they would all go to French-held territory. To get them to go quietly aboard the ships the British officers deceived them on these points. They had wanted to trust the British. The expulsion was despicable because it was not just inhumane but dastardly.

Braddock and disaster

Major General Edward Braddock arrived at Wills Creek, near the northernmost bend of the Potomac River, on 10 May 1755. During the winter Virginians had built a fort there named Fort Cumberland. An army of over 2,000 men had assembled. The regiments from Ireland, the 44th and 48th, had added 40 per cent to their numbers by recruiting in Virginia and Maryland. Units of the Independent Companies of New York and South Carolina had joined. In addition there were 400 Virginia provincials. George Washington was along, serving as a volunteer aide-de-camp, and Benjamin Franklin journeyed west to visit the gathering army. This proved fortunate because the expedition was waiting impatiently and fruitlessly for the arrival of horses and wagons contracted in Virginia and Franklin quickly organized a successful emergency effort to hire teams and wagons in Pennsylvania. Braddock was impressed. One thing he did not have was Indians, or rather, he had only eight of them whose commitment to the British cause was long-standing. He dismissed the offer of the Delawares and others of the region to join, partly because they asked for guaranteed reserves of land in return for service, partly because they had their women with them, which generated trouble in the British camp, but on the whole because he saw them as an unnecessary complication.

On 30 May the 110-mile trek westwards began, following at first a crude existing road. Its grades were too steep for hauling the guns, however, and progress ceased. At this point a Royal Navy lieutenant who had been assigned to command a detachment of 30 seamen from Commodore Augustus Keppel's ship reconnoitered on his own and discovered an alternative route where the grades would be moderate and the distance only 2 miles longer. (Seamen skilled in block-and-tackle work commonly helped the British army with handling heavy guns ashore in many theatres of war.) It took only a week for the new road to be built, but when progress resumed the pace was slow and there was reason to think that French reinforcements might reach Fort Duquesne first. Braddock therefore split his force. A body of about 1,300 men marched forward with four 12-pounders, two 6-pounders and four howitzers, while 550 men were left to follow and bring up the bulk of the supplies. The decision to advance with a less encumbered force had been urged by Washington, and it was a wise move. These soldiers arrived at the Monongahela River at a point 10 miles from their destination with more than adequate strength and supplies to open a siege. In sum, a force of over 1,300 men with an artillery train had managed without benefit of river transport to penetrate 100 miles of wilderness, across mountain ranges and soggy meadows, in just over a month. Though some of the preliminary delays might have been avoided, it was nevertheless a commendable achievement.

Moreover, the march had been conducted with prudence. Scouts had ranged ahead. High ground and other commanding positions along the route had been occupied in advance. Although the French had dispatched a number of Indian raiding parties, none had found an opening; they had killed a few stragglers and massacred some undefended villagers, but the advancing army was secure. Prudence continued to be the watchword on the morning of 9 July when the army forded the Monongahela twice, at a point about half a mile below Turtle Creek. Recent lack of rainfall permitted the double fording, and thus a dangerous route via the defile of Turtle Creek was bypassed. The crossings were carefully planned and well covered. As the long file of redcoats recrossed under a bright noonday sun, and the lead columns snaked their way up a path hacked out on the east bank, moving smoothly onwards upon a good road into a wooded area, one can imagine the gorgeous contrast of colours thus imported to the wilderness. An eyewitness later told a group of visitors that a 'finer sight could not have been beheld, – the shining barrels of the muskets, the excellent order of the men, the cleanliness of their appearance' and music that 're-echoed through the mountains'.[11]

The vanguard was commanded by Lieutenant Colonel Thomas Gage of the 44th regiment. This body of 300 men included the forward scouts, among them the eight Indians, and an advance party of grenadiers. Next

[11] During a battlefield visit in summer 1776; 'Jasper Yeates and His Times', *The Pennsylvania Magazine of History and Biography*, 46 (1922), 213.

came 200 axemen for clearing the road, though on this segment they were not much needed. A space of 200 to 400 yards separated them from the main body under Braddock. Most of the 700 soldiers of that body (mainly British regulars but also some Virginians) were strung out on the road in columns arrayed on each side of the wagon train, but 200 were deployed in the woods on the flanks. A rearguard consisted of 100 Virginia provincials.

At about 1 p.m. shots rang out. What occurred was not really an ambush because the French were almost as surprised as the British. Coming forward fast, they had run headlong into the British scouts and grenadiers, who rushed back to Gage with the news. Gage's soldiers had time to organize and fire at least one concentrated volley, possibly two or three (accounts differ). The French commander scarcely had time to give an order before he was killed by a musket ball to the head.

The brave young captain of the *troupes de la marine* who was thus killed was Daniel Hyacinth Marie Lienard de Beaujeu. Born at Montreal in 1711, he had followed his father into the service. He had just taken over command of the fort from Contrecoeur, who stayed on because of the impending British attack. Fort Duquesne could not possibly withstand the artillery that Braddock was known to be bringing and the garrison was small. There were, however, about 800 Hurons, Abenakis and Ottawas in attendance. The only hope was to use them in a pre-emptive attack. On 8 July, after learning of Braddock's proximity, Beaujeu had gone to the Indian encampment and urged the warriors to join him in such an attack. The chiefs said that the idea was senseless – the British were too numerous – but they told him to come back the next morning. At daybreak he appeared and said he was resolved to attack with his 72 regulars and 146 Canadians whether the Indians joined him or not. The chiefs again refused, but when Beaujeu's force prepared to move on, a Huron chief, Athanase of Lorette, and an Ottawa leader named Pontiac, from Detroit, resolved to join. Soon there were 600 Indians filling their powder horns at the fort gate and joining the march. If Beaujeu had succeeded in persuading the Indians the day before, he could have attacked Braddock's army where he planned – either in the Turtle Creek defile or when it crossed the river. Instead, the two forces, at midday on 9 July, met in the woods.

This was actually a stroke of fortune for the French. The British officers, having moved beyond what they believed to be the last hazardous passage, were overconfident. After recrossing the river the army was entering a woodland of a particular character: within a half mile it became devoid of underbrush, thus providing excellent avenues for musket fire. The officers and troops were therefore blithely marching into an extremely dangerous situation, yet they had deployed no strength on their flanks nor considered a plan for answering an attack. As a precaution Gage should have directed a detachment to occupy a hill on the right. For the French and Indians the situation was the opposite: they knew exactly what to do. Swiftly the Indians moved down both flanks of the British force and began firing from behind trees. Beaujeu, if he lived long enough, might well have directed this move, for he was familiar with methods of wilderness combat – he entered the battle in Indian fashion, stripped to the waist with only a gorget for identification – yet it is something the Indians and Canadians would have done anyway. The result was that Gage's men were soon receiving deadly musket fire from three sides but were unable to see much to shoot at. The British officers, on horseback, were obvious targets. According to one report, 15 out of 18 officers of the van were killed or wounded, as well as half of the 300 men that composed it. The residue fell back towards the main body.

The general had heard the shots and ordered his guard forward. In accordance with standard tactical doctrine, the 200 men deployed in the woods on the flanks came in when they heard the sound of gunfire. Thus, the whole army except the rearguard ended up in a compressed mass along a short stretch of road, forming a target that required no marksmanship. Some of the Indians on the river side were firing from the lip of a shallow ravine; on the other side they occupied a small hill which sloped upwards from the road. The only move for which the British troops had solid training was to form a line and charge up the hill. If they could occupy it and spread out, they might be able to fight with a measure of advantage. Lieutenant Colonel Ralph Burton, commander of the general's guard, organized such a charge, but his line was speedily slaughtered and he fell wounded; a second attempt quickly turned around. Meanwhile, officers died in droves trying to get the men to form lines for disciplined action. Braddock himself had four horses shot from under him before he, too, was felled by a ball that smashed his arm and entered his lungs. Instead of forming lines the soldiers huddled together on the road and kept firing to no purpose, or worse, at puffs of smoke or anything that moved. Quite possibly the men who set out to occupy the hill received fire from four sides. A company of Virginians who had formed a firing line behind a fallen tree was decimated by friendly fire. After two hours of this the regulars had largely spent their ammunition. Thereupon, in Washington's words, they

broke and run as Sheep before Hounds, leav'g the Artillery,
Ammunition, Provisions, and Baggage and in short every thing a prey
to the Enemy; and when we endeavour'd to rally them in hopes of
regaining the ground and what we had left upon it, it was with as little
success as if we had attempted to have stop'd the wild Bears of the
Mountains.[12]

At the end of the day, about 800 of the 1,300-man force were dead or wounded; of the 86 officers, 63 were killed or wounded. For an eighteenth-century battle this was a very high level of casualties. The general was carried off and died four days later. Today, three railway lines run through the battleground in an industrial suburb of Pittsburgh named Braddock. The only open ground is a cemetery on the hill that Colonel Gage should have ordered to be occupied.

On certain points all accounts of the battle agree: the officers were clearly brave, the Virginia provincials fought well and took heavy casualties (one company lost every officer down to corporal), and the British regulars panicked. In the aftermath, defeat was commonly blamed on the panic of these regimental troops, as if no more needed to be said. That they were ripe for panic seems probable; they had heard stories of Indian savagery, and the constant war-whooping during the battle was, to say the least, unsettling. As a surviving officer remarked three weeks later, 'The yell of the Indians is fresh on my ear, and the terrific sound will haunt me till the hour of my dissolution.'[13] Yet the accounts do not suggest that the British troops panicked straightaway. To be sure, the van fell back in disorder, but this did not occur immediately – only after very heavy casualties were sustained, especially among its officers. The sense of panic seems to have set in when the retreating van and the axemen collided with the main body, that is, when the army became a crowd. As Burton and others realized, they needed to form lines, move to the side, and occupy more ground – the hill on the right was the best bet – but the situation may not have afforded enough open space for viable lines to be formed. Moreover, even if the hill had been taken, methods for coordinating a perimeter defence in the woods would have needed to be improvised. The only other option was an immediate retreat to a defensible position or at least to more open ground where their massed firepower could be employed

---

[12] Washington to Dinwiddie, 18 July 1755, Abbot, ed. *Papers of George Washington*, I, 339–40.
[13] Quoted in Parkman, *Montcalm and Wolfe*, p. 128.

effectively. Retreat was evidently not considered, probably because the wagons could not be easily turned around. But it might have at least served to stop the regulars from firing, which was doing more harm than good. Washington reported, '[I]t is conjectured (I believe with much truth) that two thirds . . . receiv'd their shott from our own cowardly Regulars who gather'd themselves into a body contrary to orders 10 or 12 deep, wou'd then level, Fire and shoot down the Men before them.'[14] Clearly, panic played a key role in this battle.

But it was not the cause of defeat. Eighteenth-century military men were well aware that soldiers were likely to panic if they lost unit cohesion or lacked a tactical focus. The desperate situation in which the men found themselves was created by three serious blunders on the part of the senior commanders: failure to protect the flanks (done properly before 9 July); failure to suspend the standing order to have the flanking parties come in; and Braddock's decision when shots were heard to keep the main body moving forward. Once the crowding together occurred, the chances of extrication without serious losses were slim. At that moment more than courage was needed: without methods of communication and liaison for managing a sizeable force in woodland fighting, the price of confusion was bound to be high.

For decades afterwards, opinions were expressed on the issue of American (frontier) tactics versus European. Yet this large force with its artillery train could not possibly adopt a purely 'irregular' or frontier style; rather, its duty was to be properly prepared to defend against that style of warfare. Although Braddock should have acquired more Indians for scouting, the lack of Indians did not cause his defeat. He and his officers understood that they would be marching blind unless the vanguard and its advance scouts discovered the enemy. But in fact the van did discover the enemy; in this respect the army's arrangements were successful. The problem was that the British officers had no plan for dealing with the situation that suddenly arose whereas the Indians and Canadians knew exactly what to do. Many officers of the van were killed – one may think of that as an ambush. Still, it does not appear that any of them were equipped in advance with a feasible tactical response. As for Braddock, directly in command of the main body, he needed to be patient – to send ahead for information (as he did) but not to move ahead as he did (a serious error); instead he needed to form lines. Yet had he or any of his officers conceived

[14] Washington to Dinwiddie, 18 July 1755, Abbot, ed. *Papers of George Washington*, I, 340.

of how infantry lines might be effectively arrayed in a wooded landscape? It seems that an order to form a line was the only tactical manoeuvre that the British regulars could be counted on to perform, and it needed to be done right away rather than under fire. In the final analysis, the disaster occurred because Braddock and his officers did not realize how dangerous this apparently benign woodland terrain was and had no idea how to defend against the kind of attack it invited.

The surviving British officers were understandably disgusted with the troops' behaviour, and many of them chose 'to put the blame, un-reservedly, upon that poor dumb ox, the British private soldier'. These officers had an interest in turning attention away from the omissions and errors of the general and his staff. By October the high command in London evidently had at hand information revealing the true causes of failure but found it politically expedient to let the defeat be attributed to the panic of the troops.[15] Certainly, as Washington remarked, those men panicked, while, as seems fairly clear, the Virginians did not. But those men had not been trained in what they must do under those circumstances.

Was Braddock a bad choice for commander-in-chief? Opinions expressed before the battle are the only ones worth attention, and they varied. Governor Dinwiddie thought him 'a very fine officer, and a sensi-ble, considerate gentleman', but young William Shirley, son of the gover-nor of Massachusetts, who was Braddock's secretary, had a very different view; on 23 May he wrote to a friend, 'We have a General most judi-ciously chosen for being disqualified for the Service he is employed in, in almost every respect.'[16] Joseph Yorke, Lord Hardwicke's youngest son, had originally followed an active army career and had known Braddock for fifteen years; he informed his father: Braddock 'would have been the last Man in the Army I should have chose for that Command'.[17] The gen-eral was not a bad administrator, but was somewhat unintelligent, quite prejudiced and inclined to be dismissive of advice. Everyone had agreed he would be brave in combat. Moreover, Braddock was disposed to think well of his troops, and they of him, and it is unlikely that, had he lived, he would have allowed the soldiers to bear most of the blame for the defeat.

Despite Braddock's serious limitations, the unexpected loss of his leadership had serious consequences. Most immediate was the fact that

---

[15] Pargellis, 'Braddock's Defeat', 266–9. A few officers did challenge this explanation, both privately and publicly.
[16] Kopperman, *Braddock*, p. 94.
[17] Yorke to Hardwicke, 20 May 1755, BL Add. 35,356, fo. 315.

Colonel Thomas Dunbar, far to the rear with the supplies, inherited the top command. His response to the defeat was to destroy most of the supply train lest it fall into enemy hands and to march the surviving troops back to Fort Cumberland. There he might have paused to send out scouts and assess the situation. Instead, notwithstanding Governor Dinwiddie's pleas and offers of assistance, he immediately resolved to take the army all the way to Philadelphia to go into winter quarters – in August! It seems certain that Braddock would not have done this. Just before he died he had said, 'We shall better know how to deal with them another time.' He would certainly have realized that a complete withdrawal from the frontier would have contravened his orders from London, which specified that the three Independent Companies now in Virginia, sustained by provincial troops, were intended to protect friendly Indians as well as frontier settlements. Such protection was now more necessary than ever because the British had built a road over the mountains which enemy forces and raiding parties might use.

As far as Dunbar was concerned there was to be no 'next time', an attitude that might be forgiven a lowly, fearful private soldier but not a colonel in command. When he left Fort Cumberland on 2 August he did not even keep a promise to leave behind one of the Independent Companies. Dinwiddie, upon hearing reports of Dunbar's intentions, remarked: 'He appears to have determined to leave our frontiers as defenceless as possible.'[18] The remark was made in anger, but it was the sad truth. Under Dunbar, the British regular army added shame to defeat, and for the settlers and neutral Indians of Virginia's north-west frontier as well as those in central Pennsylvania the consequences were disastrous.

The Delaware tribe immediately sensed danger. Although Braddock had rebuffed their offer to help, most had remained neutral. Now, however, neutrality was not an option and verbal pledges in the midst of hostile tribes would not suffice; they must choose sides and demonstrate the choice. In mid-August a delegation went to Philadelphia with the message that if the English would 'give them their Hatchett they would make use of it . . . against the French'.[19] They were asking for firearms and powder. Governor Robert Hunter Morris, knowing that the Quaker-dominated legislature had a principled objection to providing weapons of war to anybody, took no action except to forward their proposal to the Onondaga council of the Iroquois. The disappointed Delaware chiefs well

[18] Freeman, *George Washington*, II, 105.
[19] Quoted in Jennings, *Empire of Fortune*, p. 165.

knew, as Morris surely knew, that the council would not act. So they took the French side and authorized their young warriors to join in raiding English settlements.

These were the months that gave the 'French and Indian War' its American name. Farms and communities were ravaged and settlers murdered as far east as just 80 miles from Philadelphia. As refugees fled eastwards telling their tales of slaughter, mutilation and destruction, it became impossible even for Pennsylvania's Quaker assembly to ignore the mayhem; money was released for sending arms and ammunition to the frontier. Still, Quaker leaders could not believe that the 'affections' of the Indians could have become 'so alienated' as to bring them to such violent acts unless they had been mistreated. The Delawares and Shawnees had certainly been mistreated in preceding decades – displaced from their eastern lands by deceptive purchase agreements – but at this moment they were thinking of their defenceless situation in the face of raging swarms of invading Indians out of the north-west, teamed with the French. The intimidation of regional Indians and ravaging of English settlements was a matter of French policy, prescribed by the governor-general. Depredations and massacres in central and northern Pennsylvania continued for many months before the Quaker majority in the legislature gave up their belief that Indians would remain friendly if treated fairly. Sadly, during those months frightened settlers would all too readily strike out at local Indians who were, and wished to remain, friendly.[20] The bloody consequences of Braddock's defeat and Dunbar's shameful departure were all too evident.

The northern frontier of Virginia was also ravaged, especially the Shenandoah Valley. Governor Dinwiddie tried to mount a defence. It had to be improvised because the sudden withdrawal of British forces had taken him by surprise. He pleaded with George Washington to take command, but the Virginia colonel declined, insisting that he must be allowed to choose his officers; otherwise, he said, he risked failure and dishonour. Yet volunteer regimental captains and lieutenants appointed by the governor were necessary for successful recruiting. In a compromise, Dinwiddie allowed Washington to appoint his field officers but not the rest. The new commander-in-chief of Virginia's forces, only 23 years old, set up his headquarters at Winchester. Recruiting was slow and frontier farms and hamlets continued to be destroyed, their inhabitants killed. But Virginia

[20] Jennings, *Empire of Fortune*, pp. 165–8, 189–96; Ralph L. Ketcham, 'Conscience, War, and Politics in Pennsylvania, 1755–1757' *WMQ* ser. 3, 20 (1963), 420–1.

had made a start that would in due course limit, though very unevenly, the scope of French and Indian raiding. For almost three years there would be no help from the regular British army. Governor Shirley, who succeeded Braddock as commander-in-chief, ordered Dunbar's forces to Albany.

Campaigns in northern New York

After securing the Ohio River, the 'next service . . . of the greatest importance' according to Braddock's secret orders was 'the dislodging the French from the Forts they now have at the Falls and passes of the Niagara'. The orders also called for the British to make themselves 'masters of the Lake Ontario'. The governors of New England and New York were to see to the construction of warships on the lake shore. If all this were done, the line of communication from Canada to the forts on the Ohio would be cut and they would become untenable.

It might seem, therefore, that the decision to send Braddock to the Ohio from Virginia was superfluous, a strategically wasteful diversion of effort. Yet the case for attacking Niagara first was in fact weak. Since the French had a good claim to be there, the move would have been clearly aggressive and certain to provoke war. Moreover, the British ministers had wanted their military response to French encroachments to be rapid. Did they realize how onerous and time-consuming the task of getting an army into position for assaulting Niagara was bound to be? Even Governor Shirley, though in North America, did not grasp the level of difficulty. There was no possible way in which Niagara could have been speedily attacked, whereas Braddock's force arrived within a few miles of Fort Duquesne in early July with siege equipment, well before French rein-forcements could reach the place. Apart from a follow-on assault by Braddock (if he had been successful) the only possible route to Niagara was via Lake Ontario, departing from Oswego, and Oswego was not easy to reach.

The Hudson River from New York to Albany was navigable by sail, and there was a good wagon road from Albany to the Mohawk River at Schenectady (18 miles), where bateaux could readily proceed 80 miles west to the Great Carrying Place (Rome, New York) except for a mile long portage around Little Falls. The remaining 65 miles, however, were troublesome. Only the 20-mile voyage across Lake Oneida was easy, and the last tumble down the rapids of the Oswego River, which descends 400 feet in 15 miles, required experienced bateaumen. Near the bottom was a 16-foot waterfall which necessitated a portage. Hundreds of bateaux

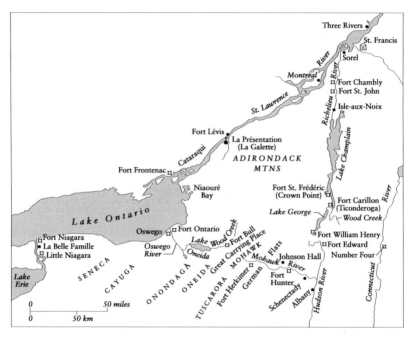

MAP 2 *Northern New York*

were needed, plus horses and manpower for the portages. The eastern Iroquois nations, Oneidas and Mohawks, were willing to provide some assistance, but not much could be expected at Oswego from the local Onondagas. In summer weather canoes and bateaux could safely traverse Lake Ontario from Oswego to Niagara, a distance of 150 miles, and shelter could be found along the south shore. Nevertheless, lake warships would be needed straightaway because the French had armed sloops stationed at Fort Frontenac that could make short work of any troop-carrying bateaux.

Shirley, a Massachusetts major general as well as governor, was in charge of the Niagara expedition. He sent shipwrights from Boston to Oswego to build the lake warships and tried to hire every available bateauman in the Mohawk-Albany region. The former arrived in early June and, using local labour and soldiers, began felling trees and starting construction. The two largest vessels, named *Ontario* and *Oswego*, were to be decked and would carry eight 4-pounders plus numerous swivel guns. Although Shirley's regiment reached Schenectady in mid-June, two months were required to move them and their equipment to Oswego. Shirley did not reach Albany until early July and did not arrive at Oswego until 18 August. When the artillery and remaining troops arrived on

2 September, the assembled army numbered about 2,500. The officers came from Britain; the soldiers were recruited in New England for two reactivated regular regiments. They were without army experience. The warships were not ready until mid-month. Ordnance was hurried aboard them but incessant rains slowed progress and it was nearly the end of September when the expedition was finally ready, at which point those Indians who had agreed to accompany it began to leave, saying that the season was too late. Even then, an expected supply of provisions had not yet arrived because the Oswego River, swollen by the rains, was too dangerous for bateaux. Shirley's staff all agreed with Captain John Bradstreet – a valuable officer of the regular British army born in Nova Scotia – who had been at Oswego since May, that bateaux manned by soldiers could not now be risked upon the lake waters, already turbulent from storms. On 27 September Shirley acknowledged that Niagara could not be attempted until the following spring; in the meantime a fort must be built and barracks erected for the defence of Oswego.

In any case, a force of 2,500 was not nearly enough. Bradstreet had detailed information from local Iroquois regarding the numbers of troops that the French had been sending across Lake Ontario from Fort Frontenac to Niagara all summer. There was an even more troubling point: if the bulk of the army went to Niagara, Oswego, lacking a defensible fort, could not withstand a French assault, which could be easily launched across water from Fort Frontenac, only 50 miles north. Though the British officers did not know it, the French were already preparing such an attack. Clearly, in this region the French enjoyed the advantage of interior lines of communication with routes that were not only shorter but involved fewer obstacles to water transport (except in the depths of winter). This obvious point seems to have exercised no influence on the planners of British strategy, whether they were in England or America.

Most accounts of Shirley's failure emphasize political and military jealousy. The implication has been that all might have gone well if lieutenant-governor James De Lancey of New York had not mistrusted and undermined the efforts of the governor of Massachusetts, or if William Johnson, resident in Iroquois country and officially charged with Indian affairs, had not criticized Shirley for mishandling these sensitive relationships, or if Johnson and Shirley had not been competing to hire the same limited number of horses, bateaux, bateaumen, and so on. For there were, in fact, two offensive military expeditions planned. Johnson was directed to proceed northwards from Albany to neutralize Fort St Frédéric at Crown Point. Clearly, the expedition to Niagara should have been promptly cancelled because it could not possibly be readied in time. This decision should have become all the more obvious once it was realized that Braddock had failed (the news reached Shirley in early August). For even if Niagara were taken, it could not be held without Braddock's support. In retrospect, the degree of strategic and logistical ignorance and overconfidence was astounding.

Because water routes gave the French a great advantage, the real British challenge in northern New York was to provide an effective defence. If the French were to invade the region south of Lake George, Albany would be at hazard and the supply line to Oswego cut. Such an invasion was not hard to mount in the Lake Champlain corridor. The most obvious route was via Lake George (named thus by Johnson 'not only in honor of His Majesty, but to ascertain his undoubted dominion here'). The water connection at this incomparably beautiful lake's north end was not navigable; the water spilled down to Lake Champlain by a 3-mile river featuring extensive, violent, impassable rapids and waterfalls. Indians called the place Ticonderoga; the French called it Carillon, because the tumbling water made the sound of bells. But a steep portage road was in place.

The British did not even have a fort at the northern bend of the Hudson River. With the assistance of General Phineas Lyman of the Connecticut provincials, one was built and named Fort Edward. Johnson, who had been at Onondaga (near modern-day Syracuse, New York) trying without success to gain broader cooperation from the Iroquois Confederacy, arrived there in mid-August. He was soon joined by over 300 Indians, mostly Mohawks.

Johnson had followed an unusual course of life. Born in Ireland (Co. Meath) in 1715, he was the nephew of Admiral Sir Peter Warren who, while a captain stationed at Boston in the late 1730s, had begun to buy land along the Mohawk River. Warren paid for Johnson's passage from Ireland in 1738 to serve as his agent, to supervise settlement as well as trade with the Indians. Johnson proved himself adept in business, and he dwelt among the Indians. When his first wife died he married a young Mohawk woman. He was a natural leader. By the early 1750s his influence among the Iroquois, and particularly the Mohawk nation, was well known in New York political circles. All the same, Mohawk co-operation in 1755 was not only based on personal connection; it was also based on efforts to curtail raiding from the north.

A road from Fort Edward to Lake George was being improved; with Mohawk warriors in company Johnson considered it safe to press on immediately with 1,200 soldiers to the lake, where Captain William Eyre, a British army engineer, helped choose a campsite. At the south end of Lake George it lay between two swamps and featured some high ground overlooking the road coming from Fort Edward.

At Montreal, Governor-General Vaudreuil received intelligence of Johnson's activities, and by early August also had in hand a copy of Braddock's true orders, found on the Monongahela battlefield. They indicated a British intention to occupy Crown Point. He thereupon redirected his field general, baron de Dieskau, who had just arrived on a ship that evaded Boscawen, from Lake Ontario where he was preparing to attack Oswego, to Lake Champlain. Dieskau chose to go on the offensive. Leaving detachments of regular soldiers and Canadians at Crown Point and Ticonderoga, he took 216 French regulars, 684 Canadians and 600 Indians by bateau through the southern stem of Lake Champlain and up a creek to South Bay. They were travelling light with only four days' provisions and raced quickly southwards along a secluded path, reaching the road from Fort Edward at a point 3 miles north of it late in the day on 7 September. The fort's garrison was at that moment quite weak, but Dieskau's Indians refused to proceed, asserting that they would not attack a fort that lay within English territory (as by the watershed principle the place plainly was). The next morning Dieskau, having learned from captured wagon drivers that Johnson had 2,000 men in a camp at Lake George, turned northwards up the road.

Johnson was not to be taken by surprise. The evening of 7 September his Mohawk scouts brought an accurate report of the size and movement of the French invaders, and therefore on the morning of the 8th he ordered Colonel Ephraim Williams of the Massachusetts provincials to march with 1,000 troops and many Mohawk warriors southwards to rescue Fort Edward. Despite having Indians in company, who were commanded by Johnson's close friend and father-in-law, Theyanoguin or 'King Hendrick' (he was 66 and had been to England twice), they failed to deploy scouts on their flanks. Dieskau got word of their approach and set up an ambush. While his regulars blocked the road, his Canadians and Indians positioned themselves in the woods in a U-shaped deployment. Williams's men suffered severely, and the casualties would have been heavier if shouts and shots had not prematurely sprung the ambush; it is likely that these were early warnings from Laurentian Iroquois to warn their brethren to withdraw. An immediate burst of musketry ensued, however, and Theyanoguin's horse was shot; in due course Theyanoguin was killed. Colonel Williams was killed by a bullet that struck his head as he climbed upon a boulder to survey the situation. Nevertheless, most of the Massachusetts provincials and Mohawks retreated through the woods towards Lake George in an orderly manner, firing upon the road and thereby slowing the enemy's pursuit of the fleeing main body.

The men at the camp by the lake heard the sounds of musketry coming ever closer. They feverishly prepared their defences. Trees were hurriedly felled, a line of logs was established as a breastwork, and wagons and bateaux were turned on their sides for a barricade. The adjacent high ground was occupied by men with muskets. Noise and confusion abounded as the retreating soldiers flung themselves into the camp; the last to come in were carrying wounded men. All in all 1,700 provincials plus surviving Indians were awaiting the onslaught. Equally important, Captain Eyre had four guns in position, loaded with grapeshot.

Dieskau's force, arriving around noon, could have overwhelmed the defences by an immediate, massive, full-scale charge, as he well knew, but his Indians desired a consultation. Storming a position defended by cannon was not their mode of fighting, and their French leader, Legardeur de Saint-Pierre (the officer with whom George Washington had conversed at Fort Le Boeuf), had just been killed at the ambush site. It appears that Dieskau thought he could encourage the Indians by the example of his grenadiers, but when they marched forward in their brilliant white uniforms, firing in platoons in the disciplined manner of European warfare, they were decimated by grapeshot and musketry. The Indians and many Canadians melted away, but the French regulars turned to attack the high ground. About this time, however, Dieskau received two bullets in the leg, one in the knee rendering him unable to move. The attack faltered and the troops began to turn back. The general urged a renewed assault – no longer possible – and his second-in-command tried to get him carried to the rear. A Canadian who tried to lift Dieskau was killed instantly by a bullet, however, and at the general's request further attempts were abandoned. When he was taken prisoner someone fired a pistol and injured his bladder.

Johnson was wounded in the thigh, but Lyman and Eyre remained unscathed and directed the fighting. When it ended Johnson did not order a pursuit. Perhaps he should have.[21] The invaders had been on the move

---

[21] Vaudreuil, in his report of the battle (*NYCD*, X, 322–3), claimed that a pursuit could have easily annihilated the French force, but such a pursuit was far more problematic than he realized; his account of the aftermath of the battle is quite different from British accounts.

since 3 September and were tired. When some Canadians stopped to rest while Indians took scalps at the scene of the ambush they were surprised by 200 men under Captain William McGinnis, coming northwards, who inflicted numerous casualties while suffering few (though McGinnis died of wounds). This late afternoon encounter on 8 September balanced the casualty numbers for the day. Only about 120 died on each side in the Battle of Lake George, but the number of officers killed on both sides was very considerable.

Dieskau's capture was symbolic of a British victory. The Mohawks wanted to revenge the loss of Theyanoguin and asked Johnson to hand him over, but Johnson refused and made sure that Dieskau was guarded closely, treated courteously, and looked after by the surgeon. He was given gentle and competent care at Albany – administered by the widow of a slain provincial officer. Dieskau expressed his gratitude openly.[22] His words did not serve the propaganda needs of the French government which had been trying for many months to portray American colonial officers as barbarous. (For whatever reason, Versailles would not respond to a British offer in 1758 to send him home on parole.) Dieskau had been rash and had misjudged how his Indians could be expected to fight but, though 55, he was the sort of man who could learn and adapt. His capture cost Canada a potentially valuable field commander.

A high-level meeting in Albany on 17 November resulted in a letter urging Johnson to occupy Ticonderoga before winter set in. Suffering miserably from his wound and 'an Inflammation in the side of the head', he lacked the will to press on. He also knew that the French could establish themselves at Ticonderoga with more ease and security than his forces could and that French troops were already encamped there. In fact, they were constructing the breastworks, storehouses and barracks of Fort Carillon. Instead of advancing Johnson chose to improve the defences at the south end of Lake George. Eyre seconded this decision and laid out Fort William Henry on higher ground not far from the existing camp. Johnson asked to resign and revert to his superintendency of the Indians. After negotiating the assignment of provincial forces for winter garrisons – about 700 men for each fort, practically none of whom wanted to stay – he was permitted to lay down his military command.

All the British failures of 1755 were offensive failures. The only successful offensive operation occurred in Nova Scotia where troops and supplies could be brought by ship from Boston. The planners in London

---

[22] See *Papers of Sir William Johnson*, II, 183–5, 280–1.

seemed to have no idea that Nova Scotia could be quickly attacked and secured. In the North American interior the only successful campaign was Johnson's, who had cautiously given priority to defence. Whether it was widely known in Britain that Johnson had been cautious, the administration desperately wished to report a military victory, and the news of the successful encounter at Lake George reached London just before Parliament opened. Johnson was deemed a hero, made a baronet, and granted a royal bounty of £5,000 – a sum upon which a man could live handsomely for life, whether in England or America. The prospects of success in North America for the coming year, however, were not bright.

CHAPTER 6

Indecision in Europe: May to December 1755

When the report of what had happened at the entrance to the Gulf of St Lawrence reached Lord Hardwicke on 14 July 1755, he remarked: '*Voilà*, the war begun!' He supposed that the war would now be extended to Europe. Lord Anson, who had sent him the report, expected unrestricted war at sea to erupt immediately. Not all members of the Regency Council (the executive authority when the monarch was abroad) shared this view, and the issue was debated at an urgent high-level policy meeting held in London a week later. The immediate practical question was whether the home fleet should be restrained or allowed to begin acting aggressively right away. Anson thought the whole discussion irrelevant. In a private letter to the fleet's commander, Admiral Sir Edward Hawke, he wrote: 'I make not the least doubt but the French will declare a war, and that you will hear of their having taken our ships, and that our Channel will be full of their privateers.'[1] This prediction was utterly mistaken. Six months were to elapse before the French committed hostilities on land or sea, and France did not actually declare war until 16 June 1756, almost a year later.

During the second half of 1755 decision-making at Versailles was paralysed. There was not even a tentative plan for war, or any naval plan for retaliation. Thoughts about what should be done militarily in Europe remained diffuse. Versailles's response to Boscawen's attack consisted of an anti-British propaganda campaign accompanied by diplomatic efforts to ensure good relations with European powers. There was still talk of a possible peace settlement. This turmoil featuring false optimism and prolonged indecision at the French court will be examined (to the extent that the scant evidence allows) at the end of this chapter.

[1] Anson to Hawke, 22 July 1755, in Mackay, ed., *Hawke Papers*, p. 125.

For its part, the British government had many difficult decisions to make. All British statesmen agreed that war was practically certain, but because France was refraining from hostilities and responding to Boscawen's attack with nothing more than expressions of outrage, it was not easy to justify aggressive action. More immediately there was the question of the war at sea. Could Britain afford to keep her navy hand-cuffed while France, remaining pacific and refusing to declare war, brought her merchant ships safely back to home ports? A possible solution was for Britain to declare war anyway. This would not have been wise: European powers would certainly conclude that the British were aggressors and, more important, it made no sense to bring on a European war when the southern Netherlands and Hanover were in jeopardy. As will be seen shortly, by the time the news of Boscawen's attack arrived in London the situation in the Netherlands was beyond remedy. Newcastle believed, however, that Hanover might be defended if he were given time to make arrangements. He wished to avoid anything that might goad the French into declaring war and therefore tried his best to persuade his colleagues that hostilities in European waters should be delayed.

The seizure of French shipping, 1755

The high-level British debate over using the navy began in June. A Channel squadron was then ready for sea with Hawke in command, and the public wanted the fleet to be active. In addition to political considerations there were strategic ones: French trade was about to come in from both the East and West Indies, and its safe arrival would benefit French finances and naval mobilization. Yet the 'numberless good reasons' that had deterred the ministers from ordering an attack on the squadron that carried troops to Canada on its emergence from Brest were still cogent, and if Hawke's squadron were at sea, he might encounter French ships of war. If that happened and Hawke held orders that forbade him to engage, the popular uproar would be deafening, especially because he was known to be an admiral of proven courage and fighting ability.[2] Before long, London learned that the Brest squadron had indeed gone to sea, under Rear-Admiral Hilarion-Josselin, comte du Guay-Trouin; it was probably heading for Cadiz both to cover incoming French trade and to show the flag to Spain. Newcastle, seconded by Hardwicke and with Anson's

[2] Hardwicke discussed the problem with Anson and wrote to Newcastle on 8 June 1755, BL Add. 32,855, fo. 442. See also 30 June, BL Add. 32,856, ff. 394–5, 399.

approval, decided to keep Hawke in port in order to avoid a risk of hostilities in European waters. The squadron was still at Spithead when the news of Boscawen's encounter at the Gulf arrived on 14 July.

The ministers now considered it politically impossible to keep Hawke from going to sea. Though his orders were not yet decided upon, he was instructed to sail immediately; the orders could be conveyed to the flagship at St Helens or Torbay. The Regency Council, to which the king (in Hanover) had specifically delegated at its request the power to decide Hawke's orders, was urgently summoned. The Duke of Cumberland argued for seizing all French trade. Anson was similarly inclined but saw no point in arguing because he believed the French would soon declare war. Newcastle and Hardwicke preferred to wait, and at length a compromise was reached. The orders, dated 22 July 1755, directed Hawke to cruise off the west coast of France to protect trade and to intercept any 'French squadron, or French men of war of the line of battle' he met with and bring them to Plymouth or Portsmouth.[3] By confining him to attacking ships of the line which were likely to be found in squadrons, the general war, if it came, would at least be ignited by a substantial encounter. Hawke sailed on 24 July and after taking on beer in Plymouth Sound headed for Cape Finisterre.

Du Guay had departed from Brest many weeks before, on 4 June; he sailed to Lisbon, then Cadiz, exchanging diplomatic courtesies in both ports. At Cadiz he was warned by a dispatch rushed from Versailles by courier that hostilities had erupted at the Gulf of St Lawrence and that a British squadron stronger than his might be at sea. There were new orders which continued to emphasize protection of trade but also allowed him to attack British men-of-war if his force had clear superiority. On leaving Cadiz (2 August) he sailed westwards before heading north in hopes of avoiding interception by a British squadron. While proceeding north he captured the frigate *Blandford*. From 15 to 31 August the French admiral lingered in a position 200 miles west of Cape Finisterre in the latitude of Bordeaux where he could welcome and warn incoming French vessels of the danger of possible capture. On 1 September he took advantage of a strong north-westerly gale and sped straight towards home, arriving at the entrance to Brest on the 3rd, a voyage of 450 miles in three days. Hawke's squadron was waiting about 60 miles north of Du Guay's track and did not see his ships pass by.

---

[3] Printed in Mackay, ed. *Hawke Papers*, pp. 122–4; the names of thirteen Regency Council signatories are included.

On 6 August the Admiralty sent orders to Hawke whereby the Regency Council authorized him to attack not only every French warship he encountered but merchantmen as well. Three weeks later the escalation at sea was as complete as it could be without a declaration of war when Royal Navy ships everywhere, not just those under Hawke's command, were allowed to do the same. The ships were ordered 'to take by every Means in their Power, all French ships & vessels, as well Men of War & Privatiers as Merchantmen that they shall meet with' and send them into a convenient port. They were 'to be particularly careful not to molest or detain any ships or vessels belonging to the King of Spain or his subjects, or any other State except the French'. The arrested ships were to be kept at a British port 'without Embezzlement, until his Majesty's Pleasure shall be known'.[4] Hawke did not receive this order until 23 August, but Du Guay, by giving warning to French merchant ships at sea undoubtedly saved some from capture.

Arresting French shipping and conveying it to British ports served to deprive France not only of ships which might be used as troop transports but also of seamen, the scarcest naval resource. Old castles near the south-coast ports were hurriedly fitted out as prisons. News of French ships and crews being brought in was promptly reported in the British press. Not only was the French government aware of these captures, it publicized them, trumpeting a sense of national outrage at these 'piracies' (*pirateries*) to its people and to foreign courts.

Strictly speaking, the British government avoided piracy. The formula was that the ships, cargoes and crews were being detained. Making them prizes would have been tantamount to a declaration of war. To ensure control, the government permitted only ships of the Royal Navy to participate – privateers were not authorized. Theoretically, all ships and property would be returned in the event of a peaceful accommodation with France, and the seamen, treated as prisoners of war, would be repatriated. It was recognized that a declaration of war by either side would cause the ships, cargoes and seamen to be permanently lost to France. The French court accepted the ongoing humiliation and forbade retaliation. When it learned of Du Guay's taking of the *Blandford* it quickly ruled the capture to be a mistake, apologized and made restoration. Obviously, France was determined to avoid any act that might be regarded as provoking a war.

On 23 September Hawke at last learned that Du Guay had got safely into port and he resolved to end his cruise. Many of his ships were by now

[4] Admiralty minute, 27 Aug. 1755, TNA Adm. 3/64.

foul and slow, having languished at Spithead most of the summer; more important, the beer was spoiled, the water bad and men were falling ill at an alarming rate. The Admiralty deplored his bringing the entire squadron to Spithead on the 29th. Anson wished that he had left some ships on station because there was now practically no coverage of the Western Approaches or Brest at all, but the First Lord did not realize that every ship in the squadron had become sickly. Indeed, as Anson feared, Du Bois de la Motte did in fact arrive from across the Atlantic soon after Hawke left his station.

Hawke's successor, with fresh ships, was not ready to sail until 14 October. As it happened, only one of the incoming French warships was intercepted, and when it is remembered that all nine of Du Guay's ships also got in safely, it must be concluded that the campaign against French warships – the principal mission outlined in Hawke's orders – was a total failure. Despite their inferior naval force the French had done well: Du Guay had occupied the Admiralty's and Hawke's attention, then eluded interception, and Du Bois de la Motte's ships got into Brest unopposed.

Could anything have been done to prevent these British naval failures? If an early attack in European waters had been authorized, perhaps. But that strategy had been rejected, and it was necessary to hear from Boscawen. Hawke's squadron, ready and waiting, was sent to sea as soon as word from across the Atlantic arrived, but Hawke did not have much time to search for Du Guay. As for his remaining at sea longer, the only way it could have been done, considering how sickly his crews became, was for the Admiralty to have reduced the size of the cruising squadron to allow for shuttling ships to Plymouth for refreshment. Instead of fifteen or sixteen of the line, twelve would have sufficed since Du Guay, as the Admiralty knew, had only nine. There was a slight chance that Du Bois's ships would join Du Guay's, a possibility that French naval planners had considered but decided not to order because it was impractical. In any case, Du Bois would not have wanted to engage in battle because nearly all his ships lacked their heavy guns, a fact the Admiralty also knew. As it happened, the Admiralty did plan to send out ships to relieve some of Hawke's, but the arrangements were made too late. When Hawke came in there was no relief squadron ready to sail.

The squadron that put to sea on 14 October plied the waters west of Ushant (the island off Brittany's western tip) for a month in a season of windy, cold, punishing weather. It was during this period that most of the French vessels and seamen were arrested and conveyed to British ports.

The admiral in command did his duty efficiently and without complaint, and did not elect to come in until terrible weather in mid-November 'almost crippled all the ships'. By then the Admiralty had already sent out an order for him to return. Lord Anson cannot have failed to be pleased by his dogged performance. The admiral's name was John Byng.

The Royal Navy arrested and detained a total of over 300 French vessels and 6,000 seamen before the end of 1755. Although the effort to intercept and defeat French naval squadrons was an utter failure, the seizing of French merchant ships and their seamen was a significant success. Of course, it was far from heroic; the surprised French vessels were helpless, their crews stunned. Understandably, Versailles deemed these seizures piracy and orchestrated a virulent and quite successful (in France) anti-British propaganda campaign. But otherwise the French government did nothing. Its submissive inactivity was excused in the name of peace but the policy was also consistent with hopes of recovering the captured vessels and crews by negotiation. Reluctant to defend their shipping in the face of superior British naval power, the French ministers persisted in simply declaring the seizures illegitimate. Unchecked, the Royal Navy continued to take French ships and crews. Of course, as the months passed the idea that these were temporary detentions lost credibility. Still, to everyone's amazement the French avoided hostilities, authorized no reprisals and refused to declare war.

Many members of the Regency Council had agreed with Newcastle in July that hostilities at sea should be delayed. Others emphatically had not. They judged that war was coming anyway and that Britain should therefore employ naval advantage as soon as possible, and they were backed by a popular clamour for naval action. As we have seen, the Regency Council hesitated. Accusations of pusillanimity are misplaced, however. Newcastle had a good reason for wanting to wait – he needed time to try to work out a means of defending Hanover – but the strategic and political arguments for using the navy to detain French shipping were compelling. A month after the 6 August order was issued the ambassador, Keene, at Madrid received word that Hawke's ships had been ordered to take every French vessel they encountered. He was glad to hear it. To his friend and ambassadorial colleague in Lisbon he remarked: 'We should be the dupes of more moderation, for the French are only waiting the return of the trading vessels they have abroad, and consequently more wealth for their subjects and more sailors for the public, more means to distress us'.[5]

---

[5] Keene to Castres, 5 Sept. 1755, Lodge, ed. *Private Correspondence*, p. 425.

The Netherlands and Hanover

Newcastle reopened discussions with Vienna in late 1754 when hostilities in America pointed to a possibility of war. The Netherlands Barrier needed more troops; the Austrian force numbered a mere 12,000, half of them positioned in Luxembourg. Vienna asked once again that commercial restrictions in the provinces be moderated but delayed an answer about more troops until March 1755. They then offered to bring their force in the Netherlands up to 25,000, but only if the Dutch supplied 12,000 and the British 10,000 plus 18,000 German mercenaries. They also wanted Britain to fashion a subsidy treaty with Russia that would place 60,000 Russian troops near Prussia's eastern border, to deter Frederick. Newcastle was not averse to a Russian subsidy treaty, and the cabinet was now inclined to support it, but considered Vienna's other troop demands excessive. The British counter-offer of 28 April 1755 proposed 8,000 Hessians, 6,000 Saxon and Bavarian mercenaries (which would require renewal of subsidy treaties that were near expiration), but no British troops. Whereas Vienna was stipulating that Britain should supply on the British payroll a total of 38,000 men, London was offering 14,000. The cabinet justified its limited offer by pointing out that Britain would also be paying a substantial subsidy to Russia. If the court of Vienna declined to accept this offer, Britain's minister at Vienna, Robert Keith, was instructed to say that the refusal would be taken as signifying that the Austrians were not serious about maintaining their alliance.

It was a remarkably stiff response and the empress-queen was much annoyed. Although she dropped the demand that some troops should come from the British Isles, she added a new stipulation: no Austrian troops would be sent until Britain's subsidy treaty with Russia was actually signed. Upon hearing this, George II, who had strongly favoured good relations with Vienna, was furious, and not without reason because the Austrians must have known that Russia was certain to agree to accept a British subsidy and that there was no time to waste (by now it was the end of May): the Maritime Powers (England and the Dutch Republic) needed to know immediately whether the Austrians really meant to leave the territory undefended. Keith was ordered to insist on the immediate dispatch of at least 30,000 Austrian troops to the Netherlands. The last message was solely for form's sake because the parties had become angry and were clearly moving away from each other.

Newcastle did not wish to acknowledge the basic incompatibility. He clung to a belief that the 'Old System' remained viable and kept pointing to the fact that Austria and Britain (mainly because of Hanover), continued to share a common anxiety and antipathy towards Prussia. The trouble with this line of reasoning was that Hanover's safety had been but one concern of the 'Old System' and not a major one, notwithstanding what George I and George II as electors of Hanover wished to think. The 'Old System' as Britain conceived of it had been focused principally on containing French power and defending the Netherlands. The Austrians, with their attention on Silesia and Prussia, now considered these goals to be of secondary importance. It was this fundamental difference of goals that undermined Anglo-Austrian relations. Even Lord Hardwicke, who always had his eye on the strategic importance of the Netherlands, became reluctantly convinced by late May that the Austrians were not going to assist in defending the region. Their original plan, he observed, was designed to be 'very burdensome to England', but now they were putting restrictions on their earlier offer. The latest proposal, he conjectured, was meant to be refused: 'They will send 20,000 men into the Netherlands provided certain things are done which they know will never be done.'[6]

Hardwicke's outlook was undoubtedly tinged by remembrance that Newcastle had not followed his advice in 1749 but was reinforced by recent developments in Dutch policy. Holdernesse, the secretary of state, after a gloomy visit to Brussels went to The Hague for discussions. He found that even the Anglophiles among the Dutch leaders were frozen with fear, and reluctant to augment their army even for home defence without a firm, substantial, timely commitment of troops from Vienna. Knowing this was unlikely, the Dutch soon pulled back their garrisons and artillery to their border leaving only one Barrier fortress, Namur, defended. By the end of May the States of Holland made a decision to avoid provoking France: they resolved to delay military augmentation and submissively planned to ask Versailles whether France intended to invade. Hardwicke knew that the Dutch had reason to be timid, and he felt sure that the British Parliament would not support a heavy commitment to defend the Barrier unless Maria Theresa showed herself willing to make a stand there. It was now clear that she would not; her argument was that she dared not send her army so far away because the Prussians, who could mobilize quickly, were capable of invading her nearby provinces before the Russians could act. Thus, as war became imminent the defence of the Austrian Netherlands was abandoned by all three of its guarantors.

[6] Horn, *Sir Charles Hanbury Williams and European Diplomacy*, p. 200.

That Austria should do so little was not surprising. The amazing fact is that Britain did not respond by playing a larger role, for as Joseph Yorke remarked in April – and every British statesman knew – the Low Countries 'are tremendous in the Hands of our Enemies'.[7] The difficulty and expense to Britain that a French battle fleet based in the estuary of the Schedlt would create has already been pointed out.[8] Moreover, French occupation of the Austrian Netherlands was bound to terrify the Dutch by placing them under threat of imminent invasion; they would do France's bidding. Yet Britain's vital interest lay in keeping the Dutch allied, or at least genuinely neutral. Occupation of the territory would also facilitate a French military thrust towards Hanover. Finally, as the French were well aware, the Austrian Netherlands constituted the most valuable counter to be used in future peace negotiations for redeeming colonies that might be lost to British conquest.

France's decision not to enter the Netherlands must be deemed equally amazing. Since the territory could have been conquered with ease – the Barrier fortresses being dilapidated and troops woefully lacking – the French could have walked in, using forces already under arms. It would have been much less expensive, difficult and problematical than trying to occupy Hanover. Moreover, France's enemy at this time was unquestionably Britain, and as France's chief fear was loss of her colonies to British capture, her best move was to take hold of the Low Countries, the part of Europe that Britain was most anxious to keep out of French hands. The truth of this had been amply demonstrated by the 1748 peace treaty.

In every Anglo-French war between 1689 and 1815 involving military campaigns on the continent (only the war of 1778–83 involved no European campaigns) the southern Netherlands, whether ruled by Spain or Austria, were a scene of action, often a major battleground.[9] This was not the case in the 1756–63 war. There would be no fighting in the southern Netherlands, and France did not occupy the region. In strategic terms it was still as much the prime object of French policy in 1755 as ever, yet on this occasion when it could have been conquered almost without a fight, Versailles held back. The prize lay on a silver platter, but was not

[7] To his brother, Philip Yorke, Lord Royston, 22 April 1755, BL Add. 35,364, fo. 45.
[8] See Chapter 1.
[9] The Netherlands and the Low Countries (*Pays Bas*) are terms that can include both the northern provinces of the Dutch Republic and the southern Netherlands, but statesmen of the time commonly meant both terms to refer only to the southern Netherlands.

picked up. An intriguing feature of the Anglo-French Seven Years War is a geopolitical choice that was not made.

To be sure, there was the awkward question of disturbing peaceful relations with Austria. Just after the news from the Gulf of St Lawrence arrived at the French court, Newcastle's informant wrote: 'I am assured that they will commence in the Pays Bas [Low Countries]. The only difficulty is to find a good pretence for breaking with the Empress, as she hath given no cause [for having her possessions attacked, but] . . . I believe that will soon be got over by this Court, when they find their Interest in it.'[10] There were indeed many sorts of offers that Versailles could have made to persuade Vienna to acquiesce, especially because the Austrians now had other concerns more important to them than the Netherlands.

Newcastle had believed all along that France would not be the disturber of the peace of Europe. Others, astute men who knew how tempting France's military opportunity in the Low Countries was, were filled with anxiety. By midsummer the cabinet resigned itself to the possibility that France would invade the region, and Newcastle, though a chronic worrier, did not seem to think about it much – as if he knew that France would not attack there. Did he have grounds for supposing this? The surviving intelligence reports amongst his papers and Joseph Yorke's letters from The Hague which reported Versailles gossip were, at best, contradictory on this point. Did he receive intelligence of which no record has survived? This is unlikely because he appears to have kept every paper he saw. One must conclude that his policy was so intensively focused on the safety of Hanover that it continued to be dominated by fear of Prussia. This fear, fully shared by George II, underlay Newcastle's belief that Prussia, not France, would be the first to break the peace on the continent. There is reason to prefer the latter explanation because his policy gave priority to restraining Prussia. By mid-August there were hints that France might not seize the opportunity. Hearing these hints at The Hague, Joseph Yorke remarked to his father, 'It would be very fortunate indeed if we could avoid engaging in a Flanders War, which is ruinous to us, & the cheapest to France.'[11] Britain's good fortune prevailed, thanks to Louis XV. It seems that Newcastle's instincts were correct.

When George II and his ministers in Hanover, led by the Münchhausen brothers, realized that discussions between London and Vienna were fruitless, they made a last, desperate effort and drew up a defensive alliance

[10] 23 July 1755, BL Add. 32,857, fo. 418.
[11] Yorke to Hardwicke, 19 Aug. 1755, BL Add. 35,356, fos. 352–3.

plan.[12] It was constructed with an eye on Austrian cooperation. This 'general plan' was forwarded to London by the secretary of state, the Earl of Holdernesse, who was with the king. It counted on a Russian force to keep Prussia under threat; an allied army in Germany for the defence of Hanover, Saxony and various German states under the protection of the empress-queen; and another army for defending the Netherlands. A large number of troops – Austrian, Polish, Hanoverian and others from small German states – would provide the sinews. Britain was expected to con-tribute troops or else money to hire Germans as substitutes.[13] Newcastle immediately sent a copy of the plan to Hardwicke. The Lord Chancellor's reaction, penned on 14 July, was unequivocal:

I cannot help saying that the contents of their Plan alarm'd me much. So extensive & expensive a Plan in Germany is big with a thousand objections & difficulties. Besides, in the view of a General Plan, it seems to be beginning at the wrong end; for instead of defending the Low Countries, its great object seems to be making War in Germany, which can only be meant against the King of Prussia.[14]

By chance, Hardwicke was interrupted in the midst of writing by the arrival of a letter from Lord Anson. It was the report of Boscawen's attack. The Lord Chancellor was now certain that war with France could not be avoided; a plan that appeared to focus on 'making War in Germany' was even more plainly unacceptable.

Twelve days later another plan arrived from Hanover, this one modified to include a possibility of peaceful cooperation with Prussia. In great haste Newcastle forwarded the second large packet of documents to Hardwicke on the 26th. The latter apologized for his delay in replying; he had stayed 'up 'til one in the morning' reading the materials and think-ing out his response, whereupon, he admitted, 'I did not feel well enough to hold my head down to the Bureau'. On this latest 'Hanover Plan' one of his comments was: 'Who can answer what Terms of assistance [for

---

[12] George II had two sets of ministers, British and Hanoverian. British diplomatic exchanges with Austria and, soon, Prussia at this time were being carried on mainly from Hanover because the king was there. When the king was at Hanover a British secretary of state almost always accompanied him, and it was his duty to keep London informed.

[13] A summation of the plan may be found in Waddington, *Louis XV et le renverse-ment*, pp. 141–2.

[14] Hardwicke to Newcastle, 14 July 55, BL Add. 32857, fo. 91.

defending Hanover] the King may certainly depend upon from England? Nobody can', partly because it is 'further proof of what we originally saw, that it is a more German scheme.'[15] The House of Commons was therefore unlikely to support it. Hardwicke recognized, however, that this second plan appeared to be better aimed at preserving peace.

What was being offered from Hanover was a plan for continental commitment – for an extensive system of alliances that would defend both Hanover and the Netherlands, but also join Britain to the cause of Austria. Holdernesse expected Newcastle to support the second plan and it is reasonable to suppose that he would have liked to do so. He could not, however, persuade his colleagues who, whatever they may have thought of the plan's merits, saw no chance of its being supported in Parliament. By the end of July he saw he had no choice but to 'abandon the Continent'. It is reported that his great rival on the Regency Council, the Duke of Cumberland, upon hearing him say that he 'was [now] for a naval war and thought of no provision for a war on the continent' laughed with scorn – which was fair enough, but Cumberland thereupon remarked that 'it was because he could get nobody to take his money'.[16] This remark is sometimes cited as penetrating, but the reality was that Newcastle had acknowledged what his colleagues were telling him – that he could not hope to *obtain* money from Parliament to support a general plan of European alliances that was so obviously focused on protecting Hanover.

On 30 July 1755 Newcastle, Hardwicke, Robinson and Lord Granville, the leading policymakers, met in London and clearly affirmed their opinion of 'the Impracticality of Entering, in our present Circumstances into a General Plan' for the continent. At the same time, however, they promised something else: they agreed that 'all proper Assistance should be given for the Defence of His Majesty's German Dominions, if they should be now attack'd which Assistance should be confin'd simply to that Object'. A minute expressing the decisions was sent to Holdernesse at Hanover. In a covering letter Newcastle anxiously declared that he was not departing from his long-held principles but merely suspending them because of the current impracticability. Of the consternation that London's decision would cause at Hanover he was already aware, since he had just received a letter from Holdernesse, who had perceived the drift of London's thinking and was shuddering 'at the thought of abandoning

---

[15] Hardwicke to Newcastle, 26 July 1755, ibid. ff. 395–7.
[16] Carswell and Dralle, eds, *Political Journal of . . . Dodington*, p. 312.

the *Continent system*'.[17] The generalized promise to defend Hanover would seem empty and feeble compared with George II's idea of what was needed. When the text of the 30 July minute reached Holdernesse he would not find the courage to show it to George II. Newcastle sympathized, but his blunt reply admitted of no further argument: 'You need not plead with me for the Continent. . . . When you have been Twenty Four Hours in England, you will be of Our Mind. In short, there is, there *can* be no Reasoning upon it – *It is impossible*.'[18]

In this same letter Newcastle advised Holdernesse that any subsidy treaties made in Hanover for the defence of the Electorate should be 'enter'd into by the King, as Elector'. If such treaties were written in a manner that required submission to the British Parliament they would in the London ministers' estimation 'meet with the Greatest Opposition'. Newcastle was already pursuing a subsidy treaty with Russia, and the ministers worried about whether the House of Commons would accept it.

The draft treaty that was presented by the British envoy at St Petersburg offered Russia £100,000 per year for the upkeep of 50,000 troops stationed near Prussia's eastern border. If it proved necessary to requisition troops for active campaigning, Russia would make more men available and Britain would pay an additional £400,000. The posture would be defensive: Russia would pledge to keep its troops out of German lands until some power made an offensive move in Germany. Hanover would thus be made safe. In its final form the treaty included a stipulation that neither party could discuss a peace agreement with the 'common enemy' (presumably Prussia) without informing the other. It was signed on 30 September 1755. Russian ministers were bribed, as was usual in these matters, but the reason why it was not difficult to obtain the Empress Elizabeth's acceptance was that she really wanted the British subsidy, and so did Grand Chancellor Bestuzchev. What Elizabeth had in mind – she detested Frederick – was an opportunity to attack him and seize the eastern portion of Prussia. Bestuzchev was naturally pleased with the £10,000 bribe that London promised him, but he was genuinely eager to see Russian military forces play an influential role in European politics and, like the empress, was hostile to Prussia. The cost to Britain was high, but for the protection of Hanover at this juncture the ministers agreed with Newcastle that this Russian subsidy treaty was necessary.

---

[17] Holdernesse to Newcastle, 30 July 1755, BL Add. 32,857, fes. 495–6, 446.
[18] Newcastle to Holdernesse, 6 Aug. 1755, BL Add. 32,858, fo. 7.

Since the measure was transparently designed to protect Hanover, parliamentary approval was far from assured. Some strong arguments stood in its favour, however. Morally there was a national obligation. If in the coming war France or Prussia seized George II's German Dominions for the purpose of obtaining leverage over Britain, those territories would suffer through no fault of their own but merely because their ruler happened to be king of England. Also, the Electorate of Hanover was not entirely without intrinsic value: it covered the entrances of the Weser and Elbe rivers, important trade conduits into central Germany. In addition, the German Dominions and their affiliates such as Hesse-Cassel were the main suppliers of mercenary soldiers in case Britain needed to hire them. Lastly, Newcastle could present the Russian subsidy treaty as a means of preserving peace – he honestly believed it was – and the proponents of a maritime war could not deny that peace on the continent would be highly desirable. Notwithstanding these arguments, the Russian subsidy would not be easily approved.

There was another question: would the activation of a Russian army preserve peace? During the summer Newcastle became worried about this, although he did not seem to realize how eager Elizabeth and Bestuzchev were to attack Prussia. Frederick, however, was wondering uneasily about what the British and Russians were discussing and had opened a line of communication with George II and Holdernesse by a circuitous channel; the British could hope that secret conversations might lead to a pledge from him not to molest the Electorate of Hanover. This introduced a glaring complication since Britain would have to tell the Russians, who clearly considered Prussia to be the 'common enemy', that the king was talking about peace with Prussia. Perhaps Newcastle did not realize how upset the Russians would be to learn that Prussia was not to be considered an enemy. Still, he happily welcomed such conversations with Prussia, for if they succeeded his arrangements really would operate to guarantee peace in Europe, or so he thought. Hardwicke, however, was uneasy about the whole business and wrote to him at the end of July:

I am anxious about that [Russian] Treaty in our present circumstances. I don't see how we can do without or with it. When it is finished it will be made the foundation of further Schemes on the Continent, of which the whole Expence will be thrown upon England. How this can be accepted I know not; and yet if it should become necessary to make a Requisition [i.e. the £500,000 in case the troops were called upon to march], it will be thought a prodigious Burden for the defence of Hanover merely.

[Moreover,] . . . I fear for the practicability. The King of Prussia may lie by, and yet France may send such a Force that way [towards Hanover] as may strike so much Terror that the King [George II] may insist on the Requisition being made. On the other hand, may not the Czarina be revolted or disgusted when she hears that such a private Bargain is struck up with the King of Prussia; for she certainly . . . [expects that] £500,000 p.a. will come into her Coffers.[19]

As events would reveal, these were highly relevant questions. William Pitt was thinking along similar lines.

Pitt and the Russian subsidy

During the third week of August 1755 numerous reports came to London from afar: the Acadian isthmus conquered; Braddock's army destroyed; Spain more likely than ever to remain neutral (as will be seen shortly); the Russian subsidy treaty going forward; and, to Newcastle's immense relief, word from Hanover that the king of Prussia appeared to be serious about opening discussions. The domestic political outlook was brightening thanks to strong public approval of removing restraints on detaining French shipping. The immediate question, however, was whether the House of Commons would vote in favour of the Russian subsidy treaty. Parliament was scheduled to reconvene in mid-November.

Effective government leadership in the House of Commons would be needed, and there was nothing of the kind. Newcastle's decision, after the death of his half-brother in 1754, to govern without a strong leader in the House might be practicable in quiet times but not when a war was looming. There were two men, both already affiliated with the administration, who might provide strong leadership in the House. One was Henry Fox, secretary at war, who had been elevated to the cabinet in December 1754 and was given a place on the Regency Council in April 1755. He was an able debater and especially effective in personal negotiations. He was also the Duke of Cumberland's political lieutenant. If Fox became leader of the House of Commons as well as a secretary of state, an office that he would undoubtedly demand, he would be placed in regular, direct contact with the king – a factor that always worried Newcastle. Neither Newcastle nor Hardwicke wanted to see Cumberland's influence increased, and Hardwicke's distrust of Fox was profound.

[19] Hardwicke to Newcastle, 28 July 1755, BL Add. 32857, fo. 397; also printed in Horn, *Sir Charles Hanbury Williams and European Diplomacy*, p. 203.

The other man was William Pitt. He was paymaster of the forces, not a position of cabinet rank, and would certainly expect to be elevated. His rhetorical skill could sway the House to an extent unequalled by anyone in his time. He was not entrenched in opposition. In recent years he had cooperated usefully and amicably with Henry Pelham, who quietly shared with Pitt a dislike of Newcastle's fondness for continental diplomatic entanglement. After Pelham's death Pitt resolved to cooperate with Newcastle though it was painful for him. His restraint had been dictated by a hope that at some future moment the government would need him. In 1755 the moment came. It was obvious that if he were not now rewarded he would react dangerously, and his talent was such that he might single-handedly persuade the Commons to vote down Newcastle's Russian subsidy treaty.

There were three very considerable hindrances to bringing Pitt to high office. First, George II loathed him, mainly because he had fulminated against the Hanoverian bias of British policy in the preceding war, something the king would never forgive or forget. Secondly, if Pitt continued to hold the same views, how could he support Newcastle's foreign policy and, more immediately, the proposed subsidy treaty? Pitt knew that Newcastle always hoped for a situation that would invite a continental commitment and was determined to prevent it. The third hindrance was personal: Newcastle was profoundly afraid of Pitt.

There was no chance of employing both Pitt and Fox. Recently they had been allies, but Pitt had felt deeply wounded when Fox had accepted promotion to membership of the cabinet and Regency Council. Believing himself betrayed, Pitt broke away very publicly, and never acted in alliance with Fox again in his life.

Notwithstanding the formidable obstacles, Newcastle and Hardwicke initially decided to approach Pitt. A preliminary conversation between Pitt and Hardwicke's eldest son led to a meeting of Pitt and Hardwicke on 9 August 1755. The Lord Chancellor reported the conversation to Newcastle immediately. Pitt, he surmised, undoubtedly wished to become a secretary of state though he did not insist on it straightaway, and his manner was remarkably congenial. Pitt said that nothing was possible unless the king and Newcastle were willing to welcome his presence and participation. Hardwicke agreed that this was fundamental. The conversation moved on to 'measures'. Pitt, as expected, emphasized the 'maritime and American war'. He granted that ministers were obliged to defend 'the King's German dominions, if attacked on account of that English cause', but 'argued strongly against the practicability of it', partly because so many troops would be needed. His main worry was that the subsidy treaties (there was also a treaty pending with Hesse-Cassel for Hessian troops) would serve as 'a chain and connection' that 'would end in a general plan for the Continent, which this Country could not possibly support'. What, then, could be done for Hanover if occupied by the Prussians or the French? Pitt answered that it could be recovered at the end of a successful maritime war by exchange, and a handsome compensation could then be paid to the king as Elector and to his Hanoverian subjects. Hardwicke considered this idea absurd and told Pitt that he 'could not suppose he was serious in it'. Pitt retreated: he said he would think further and consult with his friends.[20]

The conversation was promising enough to warrant a meeting of Pitt and Newcastle, something for which the latter prepared himself carefully by consulting Hardwicke. Newcastle did not look upon the meeting with 'much *glee*'. It occurred on 3 September and lasted more than two hours. Again Pitt declared that 'the King's countenance was more to him than any other consideration' but now insisted on having an *office of advice*, saying 'that he would support the measures which he *himself* had advised, but would not, like a lawyer, talk from a *brief*'. He was willing to share power with Newcastle as, it now appeared obvious, a secretary of state. In replying to the duke's long letter Hardwicke cut through to

a point on which your Grace and I have frequently talked together:
'Whether you can think it right, or bring yourself to declare to him,
that you really wish him in the Secretary's office, and will in earnest
recommend him to the King on that foot.' 'Tis my opinion, though I
may be mistaken, that if you would think fit to do that, he would close
and take his active part *immediately, even without any present promise*
or declaration from his Majesty. But without this, he persuades himself,
or is persuaded, that nothing is sincere at bottom, and that the intention
is to have the use of his talents without gratifying his ambition.

Hardwicke then very pointedly put Newcastle on the spot: 'Your own heart can only dictate to you whether you should do it or not', but 'without it, all further meetings . . . with this gentleman will be in vain.'[21]

Newcastle could not bring himself to do it. He feared Pitt too much and did not want to accept the reality, pointed out by the Lord Chancellor more than once, that any leader of the House of Commons 'if he be a man

[20] Yorke, *Hardwicke*, II, 230–3.
[21] Ibid. II, 237–49.

of reputation and ability' was bound to attain more power than Newcastle seemed prepared to give. It is to be noticed, however, that neither Hardwicke nor Newcastle supposed that George II would actually refuse to accept Pitt as a secretary of state if they both insisted on having him.

The question of whether Pitt would have been willing to support the Russian subsidy is interesting. He was willing to allow the treaty with Hesse-Cassel which, he said, involved the king's honour, but not the Russian treaty. Of course, he was holding out for promotion to secretary of state, a consideration that has obscured the fact that Pitt's objection to it had substance. He believed that the Russian army's presence on Prussia's border might provoke war, not keep peace, and that Britain would be involved in ways unlikely to prove beneficial; his assessment was, in fact, not far from Hardwicke's. But Hardwicke and Newcastle knew two things by the end of August that Pitt did not know. They knew that the cabinet on 30 July had explicitly rejected any general plan for the continent. They were fully aware that if Pitt were informed of this decision, it might help them reach an agreement, but they felt they could not tell him, probably because George II would be furious if they did. Even less, and for sound diplomatic reasons, could they dare to tell him that private talks with Prussia might result in a removal of the war menace posed by the Russian subsidy, for at this stage there was no reason to be confident that the talks would achieve that object. How soon Pitt learned of these developments is unclear, but before he knew of them it was reasonable for him to suppose that the Russian subsidy would unsettle European affairs and probably lead to war on the continent.

Shortly after the king returned from Hanover in mid-September the offer was made to Henry Fox and he accepted. That master politician immediately set about his task. Combining promises and patronage, he built a strong majority. The evening before Parliament opened there was an informal meeting of members of the House of Commons, summoned by Fox; it was attended by 287 members, an unprecedented number for this sort of gathering. The contents of the King's Speech and the Address upon it, both already drafted for the government by Hardwicke, were conveyed to them. Pitt and his close allies stayed away from the meeting.

Pitt knew that if he spoke against the subsidy treaties it would be in a losing cause, but he also knew that the debates would be grand occasions, anticipated with excitement. For the opening debate on 13 November over the wording of the Address in answer to the King's Speech a dozen or more speakers were readied on each side; it lasted from two in the afternoon to five the next morning. Pitt spoke for an hour and a half, not beginning until one in the morning. He did not disappoint the expectations of his audience; it was magnificent – a superb display of his trained eloquence and rhetorical alertness. He dwelt upon what kind of war Britain should fight. It must be, he said, a war to help 'the people of America', and the navy would be the most important instrument. Then he turned to the issue at hand, the subsidy treaties. He asked:

Are these treaties English measures? Are they preventive measures? Are they not measures of aggression? Will they not provoke Prussia, and light up a general war? . . . If this is a preventive measure, it was only preventive of somebody's exit.

The last thrust, directed against Newcastle, was just the sort of personal shaft that lent so much excitement to Pitt's speeches.[22] Pitt's line of criticism of the treaties was simultaneously delivered in the House of Lords with complete congruence as to substance by his brother-in-law, Richard Grenville, Earl Temple.

Historians have acknowledged the dexterity of Pitt's performance on this occasion (attested to by all who heard it), but few have taken the speech's argument seriously. It has been said that in view of his warm support for a Prussian subsidy two years later, Pitt's opposition to subsidy treaties in 1755 was feigned. This superficial comparison ignores the difference between wartime and peacetime subsidies plus the fact that a number of respected statesmen, as well as the public at large, objected to peacetime subsidy treaties. Henry Pelham had been among these. Not only could the presumed military support end up vanishing when war loomed, but also such treaties, which were in effect alliances, could lead to entanglement in continental contests that might have little to do with the nation's interests and much to do with Hanoverian interests. Pitt's apprehension during the second half of 1755 was concerned with entanglement, as he made clear in his conversations with Hardwicke and Newcastle as well as his speech of 13 November. And he believed that it was just as logical to suppose that the Russian subsidy would throw Prussia into solidarity with France and generate a war as it was to imagine that it would preserve peace. To the Hessian subsidy his objection was that it was designed to help defend Hanover which, though it might be thought an obligation under the circumstances, was militarily impractical. 'Hanover',

---

[22] Horace Walpole, the famous letter-writer, wrote as fast as he could to record this debate, and his is the only good source (*Memoirs of King George II*, II, 69–72). He did not like Pitt, but that did not dampen his admiration for the performance.

Pitt said on 13 November, 'is the only spot you have left to fight upon', yet was formed by nature as 'an open defenceless country'.[23] In any event, Britain would be drawn into a disadvantageous continental war that was likely to expand in scope and expense.

Although Pitt was manoeuvring for high office, that does not mean that his apprehensions about the nature of the approaching war were insincere, fabricated or inconsistent. In the early 1740s he had spoken vehemently about the way in which Hanoverian concerns diverted resources away from British interests. (He had declaimed on this subject often to excess – 'that horrid electorate', he once called Hanover.) In the later 1740s and early 1750s Newcastle, somewhat dependent on Pelham, had used parliamentary majorities to restrain George II's continental inclinations. But Newcastle was now alone as dominant minister: was he still disposed to resist the king on this matter? Pitt had observed Newcastle's preference for continental involvements over the years since 1748 but had been quiet; he had accepted the duke's patronage. Moreover, the peacetime commitments actually made had been minimal, thanks to the restraining influences of Hardwicke and Pelham. In the summer of 1755, however, Pelham was dead, war was imminent and the Russian subsidy treaty could evolve into a major commitment. If Pitt were now to become Newcastle's spokesman in the House of Commons without also having an influence on the formulation of policy, he would be obliged to speak in favour of something he had always opposed, a substantial continental commitment for the sake of Hanover. Nothing could have been more distasteful, inconsistent and dishonourable to him. He therefore had to insist on an 'office of advice'. Such was his suspicion of Newcastle's being in command of policy that he would have wondered whether the minute of 30 July renouncing continental commitment (even if he had been informed of it) would long remain binding. In short, because he was determined to prevent the approaching war from acquiring a continental accent, he needed to be placed where his advice could carry weight. Nothing short of a secretaryship with the king's and Newcastle's approbation would do.

The discomfort with which the Regency Council made its decisions in the latter half of July and early August 1755 reveal a government in distress over a great issue of policy: whether Britain should risk becoming a key partner in a general land war on the continent. Though ignorant of the London inner circle's decisions and of the secret talks in Germany with

---

[23] 13 Nov., 15 Dec. 1755, Williams, *Life*, I, 269, 276.

Prussian representatives – and who then knew what would result from the latter? – Pitt could nevertheless readily grasp how much was at stake.

In the event, when the vote of 14 November was taken on whether the particular words of the Address, 'defend his Majesty's dominions', were meant to include the king's 'German Dominions', the result was not even close: 310–106 in favour of including the 'German Dominions'. This gave a strong preliminary indication that the treaties would be approved, and after further debates they were, in mid-December. Henry Fox was warmly congratulated; indeed he had achieved Newcastle's goal superbly, and was promptly installed as a secretary of state. Pitt and George Grenville, another office-holder who spoke in opposition, were dismissed from their employments.

Newcastle had made the more comfortable choice in elevating Fox and clearly gained what he immediately needed. But in the long run it was a poor choice – in ways that might have been foreseen. Fox was an able man, but would he remain loyal? Hardwicke was apprehensive. He was sure that Cumberland's influence needed to be curbed, not enhanced. Above all, he simply did not like Fox and did not trust him – something Newcastle could not have failed to observe. It has been suggested that the dislike stemmed from Hardwicke's anger at being slighted by Fox in a speech three years earlier, but the Lord Chancellor's ability to school his emotions when it really mattered was of an unusually high order. His mistrust had deeper causes: he doubted Fox's integrity. Newcastle himself worried about Fox's loyalty, but then, at times he worried about everyone's loyalty save Hardwicke's. The question remained, however: would Fox stand loyal in the inevitable moments of wartime adversity? Within a year Newcastle would know the answer, and it would force him out of office.

The decision to dismiss Pitt had a long-lasting effect. Pitt was hugely ambitious and conceited enough to believe that only he could save the nation in its hour of peril. By 1755 he had waited eight years for the moment when he was truly needed. Finding himself rejected regardless, he felt it deeply and knew without doubt that Newcastle had done it. He never got over it. During the war they would come together to govern and generally cooperate to good effect, but the underlying mistrust generated in 1755 never went away, and at a few critical junctures Newcastle would provide further cause for mistrust. Pitt was not blameless; he was a very difficult colleague, but the underlying mistrust, too often aroused by Newcastle's all-too-visible personal weaknesses, resulted in uneasy and corrosive relations, especially during the war's closing years. None of this characterized Pitt's relations with Hardwicke.

Paralysis at Versailles

France was in no condition to start a war in 1755, not least because of internal strife. A serious constitutional crisis generated by a struggle between the Church hierarchy and its opponents remained alive. At this time Jacques Barbier, a Paris lawyer, devoted most of the pages of his political diary to it. The contest originated when the Church's higher clergy reopened the old and sensitive question of strict orthodoxy of belief, and introduced a method of enforcement by which persons receiving the sacraments could only receive them from a doctrinally approved priest; anyone who could not produce a certificate from an approved priest was assumed to be a Jansenist. (Within French Catholicism, Jansenism had not consistently been deemed heretical, but its religious ideas tended to question absolutism.) The practice of denying sacraments was part of a campaign led by the archbishop of Paris to root out Jansenism. This particular campaign had begun in March 1752 and soon aroused the parlement of Paris, many of its members being religious moderates, more than a few of them Jansenists. Louis XV found no easy way to tame the parlement and other institutions which joined the contest. He forced members of the parlement of Paris into exile for many months before relenting. Although he imposed a 'Law of Silence' in September 1754, thereby attempting to smother public disputation, the issue festered and danger of a resurgence lingered on. Confrontations continued throughout 1755 with the parlement still bent on asserting its prerogatives, a condition that would not make it easy to get new taxes registered.

On the plus side, however, the monarchy's finances seemed adequate in 1755. In 1749 Machault, when controller general, had introduced the *vingtième*, a broad-based tax of 5 per cent on incomes. He insisted on bringing the assessments up to date; this was not a popular proceeding, but it produced a much needed revenue. Although the clergy successfully resisted paying it – the ecclesiastics had never had a royal tax imposed upon them and were united in opposition – the *vingtième* of 1749 was something that had always been lacking in the monarchy's financial repertoire, a peacetime levy to reduce post-war indebtedness. After some delay the usual 'voluntary' contribution by the clergy was agreed upon. When it became necessary to mobilize naval squadrons additional money was found by familiar expedients. One was a variant of the old practice of *venalité*: royal office-holders were obliged to lend considerable sums to the government or else risk forfeiting their places. More important, the French economy was prospering and interest rates were low, so it was not hard for the government to borrow.

As noted earlier, Newcastle knew that the French would try hard to win over Spain, that they would cry up the dangers of British colonial and naval aggression and appeal to Bourbon solidarity. Sir Benjamin Keene at Madrid was the first ambassador abroad to whom Newcastle and Robinson gave a detailed account of the negotiations, in order to counter a French version. Emmanuel-Félicité de Dufort, duc de Duras, the new French ambassador at Madrid, understood perfectly his mission and its huge importance; he did, in fact, present a version of the negotiation that portrayed Versailles as ready to accommodate and London as intransigent.

On the whole, however, he felt excluded. While Keene enjoyed frequent and long conversations with General Wall, Duras was treated as someone of no account. He believed that Ferdinand VI privately favoured France. The king, however, although only 42 years old, suffered from mental illness and occasionally departed from rationality without much warning. It was the queen who was the steadier source of authority, and Duras employed his duchess to try to influence her. To no avail: Queen Barbara of Braganza was Portuguese; she disliked the French. She was also a cousin of Maria Theresa's and grateful to the British ambassador, Keene, for helping to terminate, three years before, a long-standing source of conflict between Spain and Austria over Italian possessions. When the news of Boscawen's attack arrived on 26 July, however, the duc de Duras thought he saw his opportunity. He circumvented the ministers by applying for an audience with the king and queen.

It was granted on 29 July. Combining the French king's righteous outrage over Boscawen's attack with a recent report of a raid on a Spanish fort in Florida by British colonists and Indians, Duras fulminated against the British. This was to be expected. But he also criticized General Wall for his singular prejudice 'in favour of a nation that was forever the enemy of our illustrious House'. He added that Keene, the ambassador, had too much influence on the Spanish government. In this open and dignified forum it was one thing to appeal to the Bourbon connection, but quite another to criticize Spain's leading minister and his friendship with the British ambassador. To top it all, Duras declared that the whole system at the court of Madrid was such that the true opinions of the Spanish nation never reached the ears of the sovereign. Obviously, this reflected badly on all the ministers of state (who were present) and was resented by King Ferdinand and his wife.

The French ambassador evidently had no idea how much he had offended his listeners. The next day Keene, fully informed by his friends, made the most of it in a conversation with Wall, dwelling especially on the habitual French presumption that the Bourbon connection ('notre illustre maison') should control policy at Madrid. As Keene understood, this was a perpetual source of annoyance because French advisers tended to criticize Spanish royal administration in ways that implied French superiority and could not disguise their nation's self-interested motives. Keene was also aware that, for all their frailties, this particular king and queen were devoted to peace and the neutral policy of independence. The formal response the Spanish monarchy gave Duras was mildly worded but devastating to French hopes. The gist of it was that Madrid did not want to make too much of the Bourbon connection because the effect would be to provoke other nations' jealousy; Spain's policy was to pursue peace and avoid war.

Duras could not later pretend that he had not said what he had said because he had recorded it in writing and sent a copy to Rouillé. Versailles would have found out anyway because the Spanish ambassador at Versailles reported Madrid's displeasure. Keene, for his part, knew straightaway how offended the king and queen and their ministers were by Duras's performance and, though he liked the man personally, reported the whole story with elation to Robinson, the secretary of state, in a letter of 30 July 1755, not waiting for the Spanish court's formal response which came on 6 August. Only Duras seemed surprised by what happened. On 13 August Rouillé sent him a letter of recall, saying, 'it seems to me that you have only one choice, which is to ask to return, as something you have wanted to do for a long time'. Upon receipt of this letter Duras was smitten by 'a cholick that kept him from seeing company several days'.[24] He left Madrid in October.

Meanwhile in London, when news of Boscawen's attack arrived, Mirepoix soon packed his bags and departed. What would France now do? George Bubb Dodington, a supple and shrewd politician, observed: 'The sole question is whether France will submit to purchase the getting home her trade and sailors, and having the winter to tamper with Spain, at the expense of a little reputation in tamely suffering an insult, for a while.'[25] Shortly thereafter the British government decided to begin arresting French shipping. France did not get 'her trade and sailors' home without

[24] Waddington, *Louis XV et le renversement*, p. 123.
[25] 22 July 1755, Carswell and Dralle, eds, *Political Journal of . . . Dodington*, p. 312.

losses. As for 'the winter to tamper with Spain', Duras's experience suggested that success would be unlikely. Although talk about bringing Spain into alliance persisted at Versailles, in reality the effort was minimal and for quite a while there was no French ambassador at Madrid.

There was a flurry of French council of state meetings in the wake of the news of Boscawen's attack. The navy was urged to get ships ready for sea; orders were given to repair the fortifications at Dunkirk; the army was ordered to add recruits. These were sensible measures, but limited; there was still no plan for war. In fact, the king asked well-informed statesmen to offer strategic ideas for the council of state's consideration. The responses disclosed a profound division of opinion. Some men presented a case for a maritime and colonial war while others, like Adrien-Maurice, duc de Noailles, argued that although it was indeed necessary to oppose England's monopolizing of maritime trade, France was bound to lose a naval war, especially without Spain in alliance. He was strongly opposed, however, to engaging in a European land war and believed that an attack on the Netherlands would produce one; perhaps, he suggested, a mobilization of the French army near the border might soften British intransigence. It was probably the discussion of this proposal that prompted the Austrian ambassador to warn Vienna in early August that France intended to attack the Netherlands.[26]

Most members of the council of state favoured such an attack, but no commitment to action, or even to continental alliance-building, was made. On 30 August 1755 the Austrian ambassador made a secret proposal through Pompadour and Bernis, a favourite of hers, for closer relations, but Louis XV, though he welcomed the proposal, also knew that his ministers and the military high command were largely anti-Austrian. The result was hesitation. Perhaps the king of Prussia would take action; Versailles hinted to him that it would be a good moment for Prussia to invade Hanover. But he declined, expressing a fear that if he attacked to the west, Austria and Russia would attack him from the south and east. In any case, Frederick II had no wish to serve as France's sword in Hanover. His French alliance had never been more than one of convenience and was punctuated by resentments. The French, for their part, did not forget that Frederick had abruptly stopped fighting in the previous war, twice, and after 1748 they considered him an uncooperative ally

[26] See Camille Rousset, *Correspondence de Louis XV et du Maréchal de Noailles*, 2 vols (Paris, 1865), II, 396–409. The ambassador's warning was sent on 10 Aug.; J. Black, *From Louis XIV to Napoleon* (London, 1999), p. 106.

when he refused to commit Prussia to an elaborate system of northern alliances which they supposed to be beneficial. When Frederick declined to invade Hanover, the French behaved as if they had little interest in continuing the alliance.

What Frederick needed to know was whether France would engage militarily on the continent. He wished to see signs of action. In April he had told the French minister at Berlin that if he were the king of France, he would immediately march a corps into Westphalia to threaten Hanover and thus put pressure on the British government to make concessions. In early August he recommended that France demand guarantees from Vienna which, if refused, would provide an excuse for invading the Netherlands. Thereupon France should negotiate with Denmark and invade Hanover with her cooperation.[27] When he learned that the Royal Navy was seizing French ships with no other response from the French government than expressions of outrage, his contempt was boundless. He had not the slightest doubt that the British were determined upon war and could scarcely believe that the French ministers did not recognize this: 'they act like children who think they won't be seen if they keep their hands before their faces. I fear this ministry will become the laughing-stock of Europe.'[28] Both the advice and the sarcasm were conveyed in letters the king wrote to his envoy at Versailles, Baron Knyphausen. Nearly all these letters were intercepted and undoubtedly provoked royal rage at Versailles. But they also indicated that Frederick was becoming impatient.

The Prussian alliance was due to expire in May 1756 and the French government seemed not to care. The duc de Nivernais, a man of impressive rank and abilities, was given the mission of renewing the alliance, but there was no sense of urgency. He did not set out for Berlin until late December. All this time Rouillé offered vapid reassurances to Knyphausen but provided nothing substantive. The French foreign minister had heard rumours of secret discussions between Frederick II's representatives and George II's in Hanover, but was happy to accept Frederick's reassurances. Frederick decided to take action in late November 1755 when he received word that the Anglo-Russian subsidy convention had been signed. The Russian army, chronically a source of worry, was therefore going to receive British money to enable it to march, and he was sure that it would

[27] The plan sent to Knyphausen on 9 Aug. 1755 is outlined in Waddington, *Louis XV et le renversement*, pp. 174–6.

[28] Quoted in James B. Perkins, *France under Louis XV* (Boston and New York, 1898), p. 19.

march against him, in alliance with Austria. He immediately sought an arrangement with Britain. Hoping that the British could restrain the Russians, he pledged not only to avoid attacking Hanover but also to help defend it. (This negotiation would result in the Anglo-Prussian Convention of Westminster signed on 16 January 1756.) Frederick did not inform Versailles of this step; in fact, he kept the matter secret even from Knyphausen. He thus took the risk of offending the king of France. His motive in maintaining the secrecy of his pact with Britain has long been a matter for debate, but one point seems clear: seeing Versailles's reluctance to seize obvious military and diplomatic opportunities, the king of Prussia concluded that France had no intention of becoming engaged in Europe in her war with Britain that he believed was certain to come. Rouillé, for his part, thought he was keeping French diplomatic options open, but, perhaps under the influence of Pompadour, he was losing Prussia.

Louis XV, and Rouillé too, showed signs of continuing to hope that the British might back down. Secret emissaries were sent to London in the autumn of 1755, but they were not given anything new to offer. Versailles merely wanted to keep a channel open in case Newcastle and his colleagues decided to pay more attention to Britain's diplomatic and military vulnerability on the continent. Although Versailles could have unleashed French cruisers upon British trade in well-justified retaliation, this would have been deemed an act of war and the British would gain an advantage – being then able to keep the ships, cargoes and crews that they had already captured.

The French government anxiously waited to see a copy of the King's Speech upon the opening of Parliament and to hear reports of the parliamentary debates on the Address. If Parliament proved unwilling to vote the subsidies Newcastle wanted for bolstering the defence of Hanover, Britain might, Rouillé hoped, reopen negotiations. When it became clear in early December that Parliament would indeed approve the subsidies, Rouillé recognized that war with Great Britain was inevitable. Near the end of the month Versailles dispatched an ultimatum to London requesting release of all captured French vessels and stipulating that a refusal would be regarded as a declaration of war. It was not expected that Britain would comply. At the same time generals were appointed to coastal commands – the duc de Belleisle on the Atlantic and in the Channel, Louis-François-Armand de Plessis, duc de Richelieu on the Mediterranean.[29]

---

[29] Ilchester, *Henry Fox*, I, 302–3.

In sum, during the year 1755, while the British were busy sweeping up French shipping, mobilizing their navy and seeking to protect Hanover by diplomacy, the French government did almost nothing except voice complaints to the world about aggressive British conduct. No helpful answer to Vienna's enquiry was given; the Netherlands were left untouched; there was not much of an effort to mobilize a larger army or navy; no attempt was made to reassure the king of Prussia; although a new ambassador was appointed, there seemed to be no urgency about reclaiming influence at Madrid. And in North America the hope of avoiding war was not backed by concessions. The French government was in the grip of confusion and indecision.

During this time the king of Prussia, a man of action with a military force at the ready, believed he was coming under threat. In London, Newcastle and his colleagues were under pressure from Parliament and the public, and had no choice but to allow war at sea and in America to begin. They worried about the Netherlands and Hanover, but could not find a diplomatic means of ensuring the safety of either.

CHAPTER 7

French triumphs, British blunders, 1756

The Duke of Newcastle wished to discover the French war plan. When the new year opened he passed on to his colleague, the Duke of Devonshire, the gist of what was being reported from Versailles:

They [the French] say they cannot support the War both at Sea and at Land, and therefore they do not at present intend to carry the war upon the Continent, where they may be embarrassed with other Powers, not at Liberty to make Peace when they please, and have no Means of resisting the Efforts we shall make at Sea and in America; their Marine be destroy'd, and their Trade ruin'd . . . The French say positively, they shall have Fifty Ships of the Line ready this Month or the next, and 170 of all sorts, of which, I think, above One hundred and twenty of the Line, in a short time. . . . I hope, and believe, that this is not practicable, but as they now determine to turn their whole Attention to their Marine, upon which they will expend this year above Three Millions Sterling, they will soon most certainly have a most formidable Fleet.[1]

In fact, the French did not have 50 ships of the line ready by the end of February 1756; even by 1 June they had only 28, plus 5 of 50 guns.[2] The idea that they could have 120 available 'in a short time' was chimerical. In any case, Newcastle should have been happy to hear that the French intended to build up their navy rather than prepare their army for continental warfare.

---

[1] Newcastle to Devonshire, 1 Jan. 1756, BL Add. 32,862, fo. 6.
[2] Dull, *French Navy*, p. 265.

France's initial war plan

France's first step was to send two squadrons to the West Indies. The governor at Martinique, on his own initiative when he learned of Boscawen's attack, had already secured possession of nearby St Lucia in September 1755. In late January 1756 the 74-gun *Prudent* with two frigates left Rochefort and upon arrival in the eastern Caribbean surprised and captured the 64-gun *Warwick*. A somewhat larger squadron went to Saint-Domingue. In both cases the squadrons were ordered to escort the trade back to France, but they did a better job of taking prizes than protecting homeward-bound shipping.

A second step was to send additional reinforcements to Canada. Undoubtedly the Royal Navy would now try to intercept them upon departure. Machault, the naval minister, opted for a strategy of evasion. A squadron of six ships, three of the line, was prepared at Brest without delay. Although heavy cannon were in short supply, the three of the line did not need them because they were to sail *en flûte*, that is without their lower tier of guns to make room for two battalions of 520 men each. The other three were fast frigates. On board each was a high-ranking field officer. Louis Joseph Gorzon de Saint-Véran, marquis de Montcalm was Dieskau's replacement. Embarked in the other frigates were François Gaston, chevalier de Lévis-Leran, and François Charles, chevalier de Bourlamaque. These men would play important roles in the defence of Canada. Heavy losses were assumed, but the risk had to be taken because the force of regulars sent out the previous year had been reduced by sickness. The six warships were ready to sail from Brest on 29 March, and when the wind turned favourable a week later they got clear, unsighted and unscathed.

These transatlantic measures were of a defensive nature. But no one at the French court wanted a long war, and all agreed that a defensive maritime and colonial strategy was bound to invite a long and almost certainly losing contest that French finances could not sustain. An offensive success was desirable, the object being to persuade the British to seek an early peace. The trouble was that Versailles still wished to avoid land war in Europe and any attack upon Britain or its possessions required use of the sea. Given British naval superiority, the choices were to launch either a sneak attack across the Channel or an expedition where temporary command of the sea would be sufficient to allow success.

Regarding the latter, the British-held island of Minorca in the Mediterranean was the most promising objective. It was only 180 miles from the great French naval base at Toulon; the island's peacetime squadron based at Port Mahon was very small, and so was the squadron at Gibraltar. Troop transports, readily available at Marseilles, could reach Minorca in a week – in two days if winds were favourable – while the estimated time required for a battle squadron to arrive from England was five to six weeks. On grounds of feasibility Minorca was the obvious choice, and the duc de Richelieu argued strongly in favour of the operation. Machault, naval minister, and Marc-Pierre de Voyer de Paulmy, comte d'Argenson, minister of war, as well as Marshal Belleisle agreed. But everything would depend upon preventing the British from taking alarm, for if a strong British squadron came out to the Mediterranean promptly, the expedition would have to be called off.

It was impossible to hide the intense effort required to mobilize a large squadron at Toulon, but on the other hand there was no strategic reason for the British to think that it would be employed in a Mediterranean venture instead of going to the West Indies or perhaps providing augmentation of the Atlantic fleet at Brest or Rochefort. The task of moving the troops of the landing force to the south coast was another matter; secrecy and dissimulation were essential, and the best method was to threaten an invasion of the British Isles.

On 26 January Newcastle's informer at Versailles wrote: Belleisle 'told a friend of mine . . . that the Invasion must be attempted tho' they were to lose all the Troops and Vessels sent on the Expedition'. The French government was said to be 'blinded by rage' and ready to accept the sacrifice.[3] Orders were given to assemble 65,000 troops on the Channel coast. Another source mentioned that flat-bottomed boats might be able to sneak boats carrying troops across on a dark, calm night, and it was reported that suitable boats were being built inland to be floated down the Seine to the coast. There was also a report in mid-February that Belleisle was seeking 600 transports. Another report arrived six days later which said: 'Few of the officers and engineers of experience that are nominated to be of the expedition like it; but, for encouragement to them and the soldiers, it is given out by the Ministry that, by the precautions taken, they are sure of landing safe, and that by this stroke they shall destroy their rival.' The same report repeated that the French ministers were resolved to carry out 'the plan that was presented them for invading Great Britain and Ireland'.[4]

[3] BL Add. 32,862, intelligence, fo. 220; Bunge to Höpken (intercepted), 6 Feb. 1756, ff. 383–6; intelligence, 9 Feb. 1756, fo. 402.
[4] Intelligence, quoted in Richmond, ed. *Loss of Minorca*, pp. 163–5.

A few thousand troops were indeed marched to the Channel coast, but no plan with 'precautions' for landing them safely in the British Isles has ever come to light nor has any draft of orders for the purpose. Knowing that what was said at court would somehow become known in England, the French government was deliberately generating a false picture. Some discerning Frenchmen suspected as much. When the marquis d'Argenson, brother of the minister of war, learned that thousands of troops were being marched to the coast, he assumed that it was merely a display, though an extremely expensive one, to induce the English to make fools of themselves.[5] In the memoirs of Charles Philippe d'Albert, duc de Luynes, who was kept well informed on naval matters by his correspondents at the ports, one finds no mention of preparations for an invasion of the British Isles. Instead, the letters spoke of ships being readied to carry troops and military supplies across the Atlantic, many of which did in fact depart.[6] Belleisle was said to have requested 600 transports – word of this came to London in mid-February – but few were available, not least because 300 ships lay captive in British ports. On 23 January Joseph Yorke had remarked to his father: 'France turns her whole thoughts at present to the sea Coast. . . . [We should] keep a good look out; [but] . . . I see nothing to alarm us greatly, for till I see a quantity of Transports assembled fit for embarking Troops, the March of their whole Army to the Sea side is a demonstration which must cost them Money, and can't hurt us.'[7] It is impossible to believe that an attempt on the British Isles was actually intended. French military planners were long familiar with the strategy of a pretended invasion, and it met the needs of the current situation perfectly.

Meanwhile at Toulon, despite disheartening interruptions for want of money, the dockyard was making good progress on the warships. La Galissonière was appointed to command them. When he arrived on 2 March there was still plenty to do and he spent all day every day in the yard, pen in hand. His persistence and dedication to the service would be rewarded with success, but getting the squadron manned was a truly daunting problem. As on the Atlantic seaboard, French mariners on the Mediterranean coast were registered by the *inscription maritime* and when needed were called to the navy by 'classes', the idea being that they would take turns serving the king. But seamen registered on the Mediterranean

[5] D'Argenson, *Journal et mémoires* (cited in Chapter 4), IX, 217, 2 March 1756.
[6] Luynes, *Mémoires*, XIV, 414–5, 462–3; XV, 29–31.
[7] Yorke to Hardwicke, 23 Jan. 1756, BL Add. 35,357, fo. 5.

coast exhibited an aversion for naval service in wartime that was almost visceral, to a degree not seen in the Atlantic ports. One reason was that British captures in the Mediterranean were fewer and the trade of Marseilles was not greatly curtailed, so commercial demand at high wages persisted during time of war. Moreover, a French seaman might escape naval service by finding employment in Italy. Some were in fact Italian and therefore exempt from the registry. When commissioners at Toulon issued the naval call-up early in 1756 most of the seamen at Marseilles and along the coast went into hiding. With his squadron mustering only a quarter of its total complement La Galissonière estimated that though it could be refitted and stowed for sea by the end of March, it would not be properly manned until the end of April. On that schedule the Royal Navy would have too much time to come to Minorca's rescue. He decided to change the stingy rule whereby French sailors earned only half the navy's regular rate of pay until the ship actually put to sea; he offered full pay from the moment they came aboard at the anchorage. This helped some-what, but a degree of coercion was indispensable.

The duc de Richelieu arrived to command the expedition on 27 March. He was a remarkable man. As grand-nephew of the famous cardinal his rank by birth was very high, yet he had attained his standing and reputa-tion in affairs of state by exemplary service. Sixty years old, he had had a long military career and it seems that he was in the thick of every great battle of recent decades – fearless under fire and, though sometimes rash, intelligently decisive. His self-confidence was joined to a ready wit and warm sense of humour, making him a natural leader. It may be to his credit that madame de Pompadour detested him, and not because of his relentless womanizing but because she realized that he was not afraid of her power. With Saxe dead Richelieu was the best senior field general available. He was clearly vigorous and alert when he took up the com-mand, and his rank, manner and reputation gave him ample power to get things done. The expeditionary army's preparedness was already well advanced when he arrived, but its provisions were not yet aboard the transports. Richelieu saw to their being loaded within eight days.

Embarkation began on 4 April, and on the 8th the fleet and convoy were ready to sail. Twelve ships of the line and 173 transports carried 25 battalions which formed an army of almost 15,000 men. Very soon after leaving port the ships were hit by a storm, but on the 10th they left the shelter of the isles of Hyères and by 17 April were at anchor near Ciudadela at the west end of Minorca. A great invasion fleet is an uncom-mon sight and a wonder to behold, then and now. The 250-man British garrison at the fort commanding the harbour of Ciudadela quickly fled to join the main garrison in St Philip's Castle at the other end of the island. The people of Minorca were not sorry to see British rule challenged and gathered along the shore to watch. News of the fleet's arrival also brought crowds to the eastern extremities of adjacent Majorca, to gaze 20 miles in the distance at a sea covered with ships. The disembarkation of troops, supplies and siege guns began the next afternoon and continued through the night under the illumination of a bonfire. Thus, with skill, efficiency and determination the French launched a major offensive operation across water far in advance of interference from the Royal Navy. Quarrels between the army and navy had been kept to a minimum, and the poisonous rivalry within the navy of pen and sword had been quashed, quite possibly thanks to La Galissonière's leadership. It was a situation where delay was absolutely unacceptable.

The French assault on Minorca was a blow delivered from the sea, and as such extremely wounding and embarrassing to the British government. It was very likely to cause political chaos in London and perhaps a decision for peace. Also, Versailles had thoughts of offering Minorca (conquered by the British from Spain in 1708) to Madrid in return for an active Spanish alliance. If Spain refused this bargain, France would still have a useful counter for exchange at the peace table. Moreover, the conquest was likely to be very popular in France; it could help solidify public opinion behind the war in a way that a continental campaign could not, at a time when the monarchy lay under the stress of an intractable struggle with the parlement of Paris. But Louis XV and some of his ministers were also thinking about the continent.

France and the Diplomatic Revolution

Regardless of whether France chose to pursue a solely maritime and colonial strategy or envisioned a military thrust at Hanover, it would be important to secure the Dutch Republic as a friendly neutral. The Republic was a place where money and supplies could be readily obtained, but more important was the consideration that France, expecting her own merchant marine to be stifled, could make use of Dutch shipping. Neutral Dutch ships happened to enjoy an extraordinary claim to immunity from British seizure. An Anglo-Dutch treaty of 1674, still in force, gave them the right to carry French goods, even naval stores, at all times. Of course, the British under current circumstances might find an excuse for not adhering to a treaty that was 75 years old. The task of French diplomacy early in 1756, therefore, was to secure a cooperative neutrality with the Dutch government in a way that would allow Dutch shipowners to feel secure from British arrest for carrying French goods.

Diplomatically the Dutch Republic was in a very awkward position: the Barrier was weak and the French army formidable, so neutrality was the obvious choice, but the Republic was allied with England by a mutual defence treaty of 1678 which was reaffirmed in 1716. One of its provisions obligated the Dutch to mobilize 6,000 troops for the defence of England if France revealed an intention to mount an invasion of the British Isles. During the winter of 1755–6 the British government wanted to know whether the Dutch would agree to send the 6,000 troops. The Dutch leaders delayed giving an answer, waiting to see what the French would say. The French proposed neutrality, but the Dutch, for the sake of durable security, wished to receive two guarantees: one that the Austrian Netherlands would remain inviolate; the other that France would not invade the British Isles. Rouillé reacted strongly and told his envoy, Louis-Auguste-Augustin, comte d'Affry, 'to make it clear that the French would never promise to keep out of the Low Countries' and that the Dutch as neutrals 'could hardly expect to limit the French King's right to wage war where and how he chose'.[8] He followed this stern rebuke with a memorandum, drawn up in mid-February, which declared that because England was clearly the aggressor in this war, existing Anglo-Dutch defensive treaties were inoperative. The leader of the States General, Pieter Steyn, became alarmed and advised the French to lower the tone, and also to let the 6,000 troops go to England, arguing that by fulfilling this obligation the Dutch could then legitimately refuse any other assistance to its old ally.

Joseph Yorke, at The Hague, began to see a crucial advantage to Britain (no doubt pointed out to him by some Dutch friends) if the Dutch were to refuse to send the 6,000 troops. If they reneged on this key requirement of the 1678 treaty, it would then be 'unreasonable to expect that the King [of England] on his side, should be tied up to the execution of the Marine Treaty of 1674'. He added, with a touch of exaggeration:

At this very instant the Dutch furnish everything to our Enemies, and by the freedom of their Flag carry on all their Trade in their Bottoms, not only to distant Parts, but likewise from Port to Port . . . Add to this that France can, I am confident, never procure ships sufficient for a descent in England but from the Dutch.

[8] Rouillé's letter to D'Affry of 25 Jan. 1756 as summarized by Carter in *Dutch Republic*, p. 58.

Yorke thought that the French would come to regret their threatening attitude if, as a result, the British government was able to reach an agreement with the States General that would restrict the ways in which the French could employ Dutch shipping.[9]

Newcastle was already beginning to give up hope of receiving Dutch troops – rightly, because it was unlikely that the Dutch could assemble 6,000 men worth having – and was considering the idea of bringing over Hanoverians instead. Even though British transports had been dispatched to Helvoetsluys, they returned home empty. Obtaining an agreement to make certain cargoes impermissible would not be easy for the British to achieve, but the menacing declarations issued by Rouillé served to counterbalance some of London's initial mistakes and gave Yorke an opportunity to negotiate a compromise. Still, the French had secured Dutch neutrality, and they could hope that Swedish and Danish ships would also be allowed to carry Baltic naval stores to France unless Britain chose to confront the diplomatic complexities of trying to prevent it. Rouillé's blustering about the Austrian Netherlands would prove to be as pointless as it was thoughtless because the French court would soon find it expedient to grant the inviolability of the Netherlands after all, for a reason to which we now turn.

In late January 1756 news that the Anglo-Prussian convention of Westminster had been signed reached Versailles and struck like a bombshell. Baron Knyphausen met Rouillé and laid out Frederick's case, the main point being that the anticipated mobilization of the Russian army put Prussia in a desperate situation. Frederick II, seeing no hint of any help from France – in fact, Nivernais, the new French ambassador, confirmed that France's current arrangements were aimed at waging 'la guerre sur mer' – felt that he must take immediate action. The king of Prussia insisted, justifiably, that he had not formed an alliance with Britain. Neutrality and peace were the objects of the convention, he said, and he offered to renew the Franco-Prussian treaty that was to expire in June. He further argued that the convention of Westminster in reality helped to secure French objectives: peace in Germany with the Russian army kept out, and the Netherlands kept available for French occupation. As Knyphausen reminded Rouillé, the convention applied only to German lands; Frederick had pointedly required the British to leave the Netherlands out of it.

---

[9] Yorke to Newcastle, 16 March 1756, BL Add 32,863, ff. 301–8.

In his early conversations with Knyphausen Rouillé maintained a calm demeanour. He did mention Hanover. Although France had no current plan to invade Hanover, he said, she would be humiliated if she found herself blocked from doing so by this convention in the event of her maritime enterprises failing to succeed. He brushed aside the point that France could choose to occupy the Netherlands.

When Knyphausen met Rouillé a week later, 2 February, the foreign minister's tone suddenly became heated and his declarations passionate. Nothing seemed to matter except that Prussia had signed an agreement with France's sole enemy without a word of warning. It was deceitful, and renewal of the Franco-Prussian alliance was therefore not to be thought of. Two days later the council of state met and decided that Nivernais should be told to plead ill health and leave Berlin. A firm decision not to renew the alliance was made, but the French ambassador did not realize this and saw merit in keeping the negotiation going. At the same time Frederick was doing everything possible to please him. When Versailles learned at the end of the month that he had decided to stay, an unmistakable order went out requiring him to leave.

Some members of the council of state, together with Nivernais, agreed that the convention was not harmful to French interests. But, taking their cue from the king, people at Versailles showed anger. Undoubtedly, Frederick took a chance by not consulting the French. His explanation for secrecy and speed in concluding the convention was that the inevitable delays caused by careful scrutiny, reflection, advices and objections would have put Prussia in danger.

Frederick's failure to consult Versailles was only one cause of anger and resentment that enveloped the French court. Others were more important. The king of Prussia was entering into an agreement with France's only avowed enemy. Moreover, he was in effect dictating to the French king which countries he was allowed and not allowed to attack. Rouillé insinuated that there were secret articles attached to the convention, a claim that Frederick vehemently (and honestly) denied. That Prussia had not actually formed an alliance with Britain – there were no provisions for mutual defence in the convention of Westminster – was ignored, as was Frederick's expressed wish to renew his alliance with France. Given the emotional atmosphere, it is easy to see why this happened, but the French government was also ignoring, with less excuse, Prussia's predicament. Essentially, Louis XV considered himself betrayed and was happy to have this as an excuse to end France's alliance with Prussia. Personal feeling was unquestionably a factor – Frederick had carelessly voiced insults concerning the French court and Pompadour – but there was also pride: to the French king it was insufferable that an upstart monarch – the way he thought about the king of Prussia – should behave as if he, rather than Louis of France, was to be arbiter of sovereign affairs in Germany.

Knyphausen soon noticed that a small circle of French ministers were holding private conferences with George Adam, count von Starhemberg, the Austrian ambassador. By the end of February reports received in Berlin from Vienna as well as from Knyphausen strongly indicated that secret negotiations were under way. Frederick worried. He besought his envoy in London to make sure that Russia would not be allowed to attack him and told Knyphausen to remind people at Versailles about the drawbacks of siding with the Austrians. Not everyone in France, he said, was 'so destitute of good sense that they could neither penetrate the designs that the court of Vienna would like to conceal nor perceive that France has no need at all of a barrier in Flanders to give security to her possessions there'.[10] He was right: the anxieties regarding the Netherlands frontier were the other way round. When Frederick heard reports that the French would guarantee the neutrality of the Low Countries he could not understand how they could bring themselves to do a thing so plainly incompatible with their interests. But he also heard that Versailles was boiling with rage against him.

The surge of anger at Versailles gave Vienna its opportunity. Count von Kaunitz, Maria Theresa's foreign minister, seized it. The secret committee that had been selected the previous autumn to discuss Austria's overtures – Machault, Rouillé, Séchelles, Saint-Florintin and Bernis – began meeting again in early February. There were difficulties, however. The French asked the Austrians to help prevent Russian troops from entering Germany, which the Austrians refused to do. Would the empress-queen object to a French occupation of Hanover? That remained unclear. Most important, the French, though they had decided not to renew their treaty with Prussia, were not disposed to go to war. Therefore, when Starhemberg informed Bernis of Kaunitz's 'grand plan', which envisioned French cooperation in a war to dismember Prussia (all that would be required from Paris was money), those on the secret committee who heard about it became nervous; they feared a long and costly war on the continent in which Austria would gain too much ascendancy.

The court of Versailles therefore considered an offensive alliance with the Austrians to be out of the question. In March, Maria Theresa thought

[10] Frederick to Knyphausen, 27 March 1756, *Politische Correspondenz*, XII, 225–6.

that the most she could hope for was a simple convention of neutrality. Starhemberg pushed for a defensive alliance. France's hesitation, he said, made the empress-queen so apprehensive that she no longer regarded a convention of neutrality to be adequate. Pompadour hated Frederick II as fervently as the king did and was warmly in favour of close relations with Austria. Understanding this, Bernis spent four hours privately briefing the king in favour of a defensive alliance. But such a step needed to be decided in a meeting of the council of state. It was scheduled immediately.

Accordingly, half a dozen great men of the kingdom met on 19 April. It happened by chance to be the same day that the troops were disembarking at Minorca. The king was present, listening and not saying a word, but everyone in the room knew that he had made up his mind in favour of the Austrian request. Nevertheless, some objections were expressed and at a critical moment Bernis pulled from his papers a letter from Starhemberg which made mention of a dispatch just arrived from Vienna hinting that the empress-queen was contemplating discussions with Great Britain. Thereupon the council voted unanimously in favour of a defensive treaty with Austria, and ten days later, on 1 May 1756, the Treaty of Versailles was signed.

The most important step in bringing about the famous 'Diplomatic Revolution' was thus accomplished. A century or more of opposition between Austria and France was ended, and this *renversement des alliances* would endure until the French Revolution. Actually, there were two documents: a convention of neutrality and a defensive treaty. Certain features were of particular importance to the Seven Years War: (1) France broke irrevocably with Prussia; (2) France pledged that she would leave the Austrian Netherlands undisturbed; and (3) for mutual defence each party promised to provide 24,000 troops, or subsidy money for obtaining and maintaining that number in case one or the other were attacked. The treaty excluded attacks by Britain; in other words, Austria would have no obligation to help France in an Anglo-French war.

Some at Versailles welcomed the treaty. Like Voltaire when he heard about it, they lauded the termination of France's age-old enmity with Austria and the prospect of a durable peace in Europe. Pompadour gloried in it. Aided by her protégé Bernis, she had been the vital link: 'it is certain that it is to her that we owe everything', Starhemberg wrote to Kaunitz.[11] The military men at court, as Knyphausen informed Frederick, were disgusted by the treaty since opportunities for advancement and

[11] Quoted by Nolhac, *Madame de Pompadour*, p. 154.

fortune would evaporate if, as was claimed, Europe would be accorded lasting peace. The consensus at Versailles was indeed that France had secured peace on the continent and could focus her war effort on the navy and colonies.

The court of Vienna had an entirely different view. After the signing, Starhemberg and Kaunitz exchanged secret letters that radiated triumph. They were plainly contemplating war. A great obstacle had been surmounted; France by this momentous reversal of policy had placed herself firmly in the Austrian camp. They knew that the Empress Elizabeth of Russia was eager for war against Prussia and that Austria might therefore have a good opportunity to recover Silesia. French subsidy money was much wanted, however, and they hoped to find a way to tempt Prussia to attack the Habsburg dominions so that the defensive treaty would be invoked.

This treaty of Versailles of 1 May 1756, although defensive, was nevertheless extremely one-sided in geopolitical terms. The Habsburg dominions included countless territories and borders. France, in contrast, was well consolidated and had nothing to fear. British attacks were excluded from the treaty; the Dutch were fearful and supine; the Austrian Netherlands, far from constituting a threat to France, felt threatened; France's long-standing Italian contentions were settled; and the British by their initiatives were making it clear that they had no intention of using Hanover as a locus for waging a diversionary war. The only conceivable threat to France on the continent was from Prussia, but Prussian eyes were nervously and correctly fixed upon Russia and Austria. Since Germany was neutralized by the convention of Westminster, the only power France had to worry about was Austria, and all the signals from Vienna indicated that Austria was anxious to avoid hostilities with France. To be sure, the treaty guaranteed that there would be no continental war at a time when France's resources would be needed against Britain. Yet this was not a guarantee without dangers because it was bound to frighten the king of Prussia. Whether Vienna liked it or not, Versailles could have insisted upon maintaining relations with Prussia while agreeing to a convention of neutrality with Austria. Professor Walter Dorn's judgement still stands: 'France on the eve of the Seven Years' War was not compelled to choose between Austria and Prussia.'[12]

Of course, the Austrians might have shunned a convention of neutrality, but would France's situation then have been worse than the situation

---

[12] Dorn, *Competition*, p. 307.

created by the treaty? Anyone could see that Frederick II would feel threatened – that the treaty would certainly make him uneasy. But it was defensive, and Louis XV, Pompadour and Bernis may have thought it inconceivable that Frederick would attack the empress-queen's dominions knowing that he would then have to contend with the combined forces of France, Austria and probably Russia. Nevertheless, they must have been aware that Austria and Russia might welcome a war against Prussia, a point that Frederick had tried to get them to understand. As a guarantor of peace on the continent the treaty was not without risks, and if the Habsburg empire were to be attacked, France would be required to assist Austria for Austria's sake, not her own.

In agreeing to this treaty the council of state acted precipitately for a second time in two months: first in February, when the members agreed not to renew the treaty with Prussia, and now in the meeting of 19 April, when they were stampeded by an unverified threat from Vienna suggesting that Austria might resume its affiliation with Great Britain, a turnabout that any French statesman should have considered impossible. In both instances the decisions appear to have been influenced by Louis XV personally, and it was very difficult for members of the council to oppose his wishes. In this meeting of 19 April four men were bold enough to speak out, but the king's presence, along with awareness of Bernis's dependence on Pompadour, was felt all around the table. And then, when Bernis produced the letter from Vienna everyone had an excuse to yield to the king's inclination.

Although the defensive treaty of Versailles was presented publicly as a means of ensuring continental peace, it cannot be supposed that French statesmen gave no thought to the possibility of war. Bernis knew about Kaunitz's 'grand plan' for an offensive war against Prussia, and everyone recognized that France might in due course decide that it was necessary to conquer Hanover in order to offset losses overseas. If armed conflict on the continent were to erupt, Louis XV would not wish to stand aside: the proud royal tradition – the king of France as 'arbiter of Europe' – was not likely to be ignored, especially if the designated victim was the king of Prussia, whom Louis reviled. Behind the scenes were the military men at court – used to fighting against Austria – but would they not welcome a war against Hanover or Prussia if their royal master so desired? Might not such a war actually benefit France? On 20 April Starhemberg penned a letter to Pompadour in which he summarized some objections to the defensive alliance that had been agreed upon in the previous day's meeting of the council (Bernis had informed him). He mentioned the point that it seemed to impose a heavy burden on France without giving any advantage in return. But he added an assurance: the powerful assistance that France could count on from Austria 'in the course of a land war, [would] enable her to claim the upper hand'.[13] If the marquise could be told such things, it cannot be supposed that the advantages of a quick, easy, victorious war on the continent were beyond the thinking of the French king and his ministers at this time.

Louis XV did not wish to be the one to ignite a war in Europe – Newcastle was right about this – but he might be tempted to join a war ostensibly for the defence of Austria which would punish Frederick and lead to an easy occupation of Hanover. It should be mentioned that when the duc de Noailles offered his opinion on strategy in July 1755 he began by making a strong case for invading the Netherlands, but followed it up by an argument against this move on the ground that it would bring on a 'general war'. He thought that a land war in Europe would prove extremely injurious to France. It will, he wrote, 'absorb everything, and the outcome will be to leave the English more powerful than they have ever been'.[14]

We do not know Noailles's opinion of the commitments being made to Austria; old and feeble, he resigned in March 1756. But he had been among those who were much concerned about British naval and commercial dominance, and he deplored the idea of general war in Europe. Everyone knew that if France were to risk engagement in such a war, the quickest and most effective way of using her army to force Britain to the peace table was, after giving warning to Vienna and offering compensations, to occupy the Netherlands. The opportunity had never before been so militarily inviting, and the Austrians were fixated on recovering Silesia from Prussia. French diplomacy could have overcome the difficulties. All in all, if Louis XV was willing to think of a land war, his rejection of an invasion of the Low Countries and acceptance of a treaty guaranteeing the security of the Habsburg dominions from attack was a geopolitical and military mistake of the first magnitude.

Admiral Byng and the French conquest of Minorca

By 21 April 1756, 14,000 French troops were ashore at Ciudadela, Minorca. The distance by road across the island to Port Mahon was

---

[13] Flassan, *Histoire générale*, VI, 48–9.
[14] Noailles's memoirs to the king are printed in Rousset, *Correspondance de Louis XV et du Maréchal de Noailles* (cited on p. 165), II, 396–411.

35 miles and the British army had destroyed four bridges. Though these were soon repaired, very few carts or horses were available to transport supplies. Some of the guns and ordnance stores were carried round the coast to the port of Fornells, still 20 miles away from Mahon; a great deal of material was laboriously drawn overland by oxen which had been intended for food. The army camped on a plateau above Mahon; tents could not easily be anchored on the rock surface, bedding was badly needed and the island's supply of straw was minimal. The chief artillery officer informed the duc de Richelieu that 200 days would be needed to establish a proper depot. Richelieu ignored this and decided to get on with the siege as soon as possible.

St Philip's Castle commanded the narrow entrance to Port Mahon. The fortress was situated on a high plateau of triangular shape with water on two sides. Richelieu and his staff quickly realized how hard it would be to approach it, much harder than the planners at Versailles had supposed, not least because the trenches would have to be carved into rock. The first mortar battery was not ready to fire until 9 May and had to stop firing the next day when a cannonade from the fortress demolished the mounts and inflicted casualties. All digging of trenches and construction of batteries had to be done in darkness, so the citadel did most of its firing at night. In the beginning the besiegers were at a huge disadvantage as the fortress gunners could concentrate on just a few batteries. To many of Richelieu's officers the difficulties and slow progress foretold ultimate failure, but he remained optimistic.

The army's immediate fear was that La Galissonière, who was under explicit orders from Machault, the naval minister, to give priority to the preservation of his ships, might leave the area. On 14 May Richelieu received a letter from Machault warning that a squadron under Admiral Boscawen was said to be ordered to join Byng's. Should this occur the French squadron would have to return to the safety of Toulon. Greatly alarmed, Richelieu wrote an earnest reply. He pointed out that it would be very difficult for Byng to surprise the French admiral in a way that could block his retreat to Toulon. Besides, he observed, it appears that 'the forces solely under admiral Byng will not suffice, and that it is the junction of Boscawen with Byng that alone would put it beyond M. de la Galissonnière's power to measure his forces against theirs'. A naval withdrawal would therefore not be necessary, at least not before the end of the month in view of Boscawen's reported departure date. Richelieu admitted that the progress of the siege was slow and remarked that the place appeared formidable. But the main point, which he underlined, was that a premature retreat of the fleet would deprive him of additional troops, munitions and artillery pieces that were scheduled to be shipped from the mainland.[15] Four days later thirteen British ships of the line were sighted off Majorca. They came sooner than expected, the French supposing that Byng's squadron had left England on 14 April when they had actually sailed on the 6th.

That Byng's squadron arrived earlier than the French expected was paradoxical because in Britain a heated controversy was soon generated by the question of why it was sent so late. Was there a failure of intelligence, action, or both? By 2 March the British government had received from more than one source reports of the accelerated preparation of twelve ships of the line at Toulon and also the marching of thousands of troops to the coast of Provence. The intelligence came by way of British consuls at Genoa and Bern, and also by merchants' letters from Marseilles. The first report to mention Minorca as the objective (received 11 February) did so tentatively, but during the next three weeks specific information arrived. On 6 March a warning came from Keene, the ambassador at Madrid, that Minorca was to be attacked, and two days later Newcastle received intelligence from Versailles saying that a courier had been sent to Madrid offering a conquered Minorca, gratis, to the 'Crown of Spain . . . to induce the Spanish Ministry to enter into the War'.[16]

He immediately alerted Lord Anson, who convened a meeting of the Admiralty Board the same afternoon and selected ten ships of the line. The next morning Admiral John Byng was chosen for the command. The cabinet met and formally confirmed that 'as strong a squadron as can be spared from hence' was to be sent to the Mediterranean. Byng arrived at Portsmouth on the 21st and found the ships not fully manned, something to be expected, but he also found, to his justifiable annoyance, that the Admiralty was giving priority to ships assigned to other services. Finally, on 1 April an Admiralty order for him to put to sea helped him to get his ships manned. Within the week he was heading down the Channel, and on 2 May the squadron reached Gibraltar.

With a clearer perception Newcastle might have acted on the intelligence reports six days sooner, and with suitable Admiralty cooperation Byng might have had his ships manned and ready a week earlier. Even so, and even if Byng had wasted no time at Gibraltar, he would still not have

---

[15] Richelieu to Machault, 14 May 1756, Cisternes, *Campagne de Minorque*, pp. 162–3.

[16] Intelligence, 22 Feb. 1756, read 8 March, BL Add. 32,863, fo. 59.

reached Minorca before the French army completed its disembarkation. Once that happened the means of preventing a conquest depended upon the strength of the British squadron. Ideally, it should have been strong enough to defeat the Toulon squadron even if some of its ships were detached to harass French supply vessels coming from the mainland.

The question of strength had been left to Anson. He judged ten ships of the line to be the most he could spare; one 60-gun ship and two of 50 guns would be added in the Mediterranean from Commodore George Edgecumbe's squadron. Since recent reports had consistently reckoned the Toulon squadron at twelve ships, some of which were known to be large and heavily gunned, Anson was providing neither superiority nor a margin for mishaps, whether caused by storms or combat. Shortly after Byng departed, further intelligence came to London which revealed beyond doubt that the French were mobilizing a large-scale military expedition against Minorca, yet no additional ships were ordered to the Mediterranean. French apprehension that Boscawen might reinforce Byng stemmed from their knowledge that he had sailed down the Channel with ten of the line at the end of April. Boscawen's orders, however, were to take over the Western Squadron from Hawke; nothing was said to him about the Mediterranean. On 6 May, when news arrived from Paris that the French had actually landed on Minorca, the cabinet became alarmed. Henry Fox and the Duke of Cumberland 'proposed sending Orders imme- diately to Adml. Boscawen to detach part of his Fleet', but this was not done. Anson, thinking that such a detachment would weaken the Western Squadron too much, 'chose rather to send three or four large ships from hence', meaning Portsmouth. He also told the cabinet that Boscawen might not be at the rendezvous, so there was a danger of delay in getting word to him.[17] The trouble was that another two weeks would pass before the four from Portsmouth were ready to sail. Whereas in early March invasion fears had influenced the decision to send only ten ships, now, in late April and early May, when the French intention to attack Minorca was known with certainty, the delay was primarily due to Anson's wish to maintain a strong Western Squadron.

The admiral to whom Minorca's rescue was entrusted was the fifth surviving son of an able and vigorous admiral, George Byng, 1st Viscount Torrington. As a boy embarked in his father's squadron during the victorious battle of Cape Passaro in 1718 he witnessed combat, but never

[17] Fox to Newcastle, 7 May 1756; Newcastle to Fox, 8 May, BL Add. 32,864, ff. 478–83.

again. The father's naval influence was unmatched, and as a young captain John Byng enjoyed a sheltered career. He commanded a squadron off Scotland during the '45 rebellion and then served as a rear-admiral stationed in the Mediterranean in 1747–8. On the Riviera his lack of initiative enabled the Spanish to establish a safe route to Italy, and his letters revealed an instinctive defeatism. Anyone who bothered to look at the Admiralty file could have discovered this. But there were very few senior admirals from whom to choose, and Byng had recently displayed a stoic sense of duty when he endured harsh cruising conditions off Ushant in autumn 1755.

If ever an admiral needed firm guidance before setting out, it was Byng, but he was not asked to visit the Admiralty and received no guidance. Regarding Minorca his orders of 30 March simply said: '[I]f you find any attack made upon that island by the French, you are to use all possible means in your power for its relief.' Cluttered as his orders were with other contingencies, it is obvious that Byng understood that his mission was to save Minorca. In fact, after opening the orders at Spithead he wrote a letter to the Admiralty in which he commented on the island's importance (he had often been stationed there in the 1730s); he also mentioned that he would do all in his power to frustrate an enemy attempt upon it, but added, ominously, that he would consider himself 'most fortunate' if he were to succeed.[18]

Byng's defeatism was again on display when he reached Gibraltar. He had been ordered to take about 700 soldiers from Gibraltar to strengthen the garrison at Minorca and the army commander, Lieutenant General Thomas Fowke, was ordered to release them, but he and his staff argued that St Philip's could not possibly hold out – it would be throwing the men away – and also claimed that, in any case, French batteries would prevent them from being inserted into the fortress. Knowing that Byng carried an explicit order, Fowke offered to let him take the troops anyway, but Byng accepted his arguments and departed without them.[19] In his letter to the Admiralty of 4 May explaining this decision Byng echoed Fowke's opinion that Minorca must be given up as lost and care taken that Gibraltar not be lost as well.

That letter would eventually have fatal consequences for him. When it reached London on 31 May George II threw it on the floor, saying: 'This

[18] Dudley Pope prints Byng's 30 March instructions (*At Twelve*, pp. 344–6); Byng's response to the Admiralty is quoted in Tunstall, *Admiral Byng*, p. 53.

[19] The explicit order was given in an addendum issued 31 March (ibid. p. 66).

man will not fight.'[20] The king's ministers were distraught and angry. Although they realized that they should have sent reinforcements to Minorca sooner, their reaction was understandable: British military experts had long been confident that extensive works undertaken after the island's capture from Spain in 1708 had rendered St Philip's capable of withstanding a siege long enough to enable a superior British fleet to arrive to threaten the enemy's position and supply lines – if the garrison possessed enough men. By sailing from Gibraltar without the troops Byng had diminished its means of resistance. Furthermore, his idea that Gibraltar might be in imminent danger was ridiculous; all of France's Mediterranean forces were committed on Minorca, and in any case Gibraltar could be defended by sending the Western Squadron. Given the fact that the French had landed on Minorca, the question of whether Gibraltar was in imme-diate danger was not one for General Fowke and Admiral Byng to decide.

When he approached Minorca Byng detached three frigates to exchange messages with the fortress commander. Unfortunately, the lead frigate became becalmed in the lee of the island and the officers of the garrison, having deliberated too long over what to tell the admiral, sent out a boat too late to reach it before it sailed away in response to a signal from Byng to rejoin the squadron immediately. The French battle squadron had just appeared on the horizon.

The next morning, 20 May, the squadrons prepared for battle. As the two fleets approached head on, a shift of wind direction gave Byng's squadron the upwind advantage. Byng had grouped his thirteen ships in two divisions, casting the 50-gun *Deptford* aside. His tactical plan called for each ship to reverse course one after another starting with the rearmost, and as a result his flagship became third from the rear – not a good position for exercising command. He intended to close gradually with the enemy on an angled line of approach, but the ships that ended up in the lead under Rear-Admiral Temple West approached the enemy sooner than expected. Byng had no choice but to hoist the signal to engage, and, seeing the signal, the ships of his van became involved in furi-ous combat. Meanwhile, Byng's flagship was over 2 miles distant from the French line – far out of range – but he maintained his deliberate, angled approach. The risk of an accident up ahead was ever present, and that is what happened: the *Intrepid* (64 guns), last ship of West's division, spun out of control when her fore-topmast was brought down. Byng's division

[20] Tunstall, *Admiral Byng*, p. 153.

should have passed her on the side nearer the enemy, but the captains were hesitant and at first backed their sails to avoid collisions. Byng in the *Ramillies* (90 guns), four ships behind the *Intrepid*, gave no guidance. Arthur Gardiner, captain of the *Ramillies*, suggested that they turn the flagship downwind; the ships adjacent, he pointed out, would imitate the move and thus the division would quickly get into action. To this suggestion Byng responded by remarking that Admiral Mathews had been cashiered for doing that very thing – that is, breaking the line in order to close with the enemy. But the circumstances were utterly different. When Thomas Mathews steered down upon the enemy in 1744 his action opened the engagement whereas in the present case West's division was already engaged, fighting at close quarters, taking punishment and getting no support from Byng's division. No court-martial would have censured Byng for coming to their support as quickly as possible. (Actually, the court-martial of 1746 – on which Byng himself had sat – did not find Mathews guilty for the reason Byng claimed; his recollection was faulty.) Although the logbook of the *Ramillies* recorded that she began firing at 3 p.m., not long after the van became engaged, French battle narratives and testimony from numerous British eyewitnesses agreed that she opened fire too soon, and that by the time she got within effective range it was nearly 5 p.m. Soon afterwards, the French admiral signalled withdrawal and turned away.

La Galissonière conducted his squadron expertly. While awaiting Byng's arrival he had practised signals and manoeuvres, and the results showed it. His ships had fewer guns but they were of heavier calibre. His disadvantage lay in rate of fire, for his crews could not match the skilled efficiency of the British in reloading. During the action the ships of his van moved forward as they engaged and fell away after a couple of broadsides before re-engaging, a practice that may have been planned in advance since it tended to reduce the British advantage. The *Foudroyant* (80 guns), La Galissonière's flagship, and *Téméraire* (74 guns), both carrying 42-pounders, poured destruction upon the British van and centre. Byng's defenders later emphasized the greater total weight of the French squadron's broadsides and they had a point, but the French were never made to feel the massive firepower of Byng's flagship, the three-tiered *Ramillies*, and if she had promptly closed on the French rear, La Galissonière's tactics might have been frustrated. As it was, when the *Ramillies* finally got close the French admiral broke off the action. The number of casualties in the last five ships of the British line, which included the flagship, was zero. Nearly all the British casualties were sustained in the van division:

43 killed, including 2 captains, and 168 wounded; the French total was about the same: 38 killed, 175 wounded.

The masts and rigging of the *Intrepid* could not be quickly repaired and the *Portland* (50 guns) was leaking badly; the other damaged ships were ready for service in two days. La Galissonière's squadron also had to repair damage and Byng claimed victory because the French had quit the battle. But Byng made no attempt to carry out his mission: he did not communicate with the beleaguered fortress, let alone try to reinforce the garrison by landing the army officers, soldiers and marines who were aboard his ships. Instead, he summoned a council of war and offered five questions, their implications being, first, that nothing the British fleet could do would raise the siege even 'if there were no French fleet cruising off Minorca', and secondly, that the fleet should not be risked because it was vital to the defence of Gibraltar. Was no one among the 18 officers (5 army, 13 navy) present at that meeting on 24 May 1756 capable of imagining how a strategy of harassing the French army's supply lines might seriously disturb the besieging army? Did the army officers, some of whom had spent time in St Philip's Castle, believe that reinforcing the garrison was not possible? It seems that no one said a word, then or afterwards.[21] This was a shameful case of officers being all too ready to follow the lead of an admiral who had framed questions in a way that enabled him to avoid facing the enemy a second time.

The squadron thereupon headed for Gibraltar and arrived after a very slow passage on 19 June. Rear-Admiral Thomas Brodrick had arrived four days earlier with four ships of the line and one of 50 guns. Byng's ships needed to take on water, but despite the ample reinforcement he had no thought of hurrying back to Minorca and allowed the holding of a court-martial to waste time. The ships were still at Gibraltar when the 50-gun *Antelope* arrived on 3 July carrying Admiral Hawke and other officers of rank with orders to replace Byng, West and Fowke.

The garrison commander at St Philip's was Major General William Blakeney, of English extraction from County Limerick. He was a career soldier without family influence and his promotion to the rank of colonel did not come until he was 65 when he was made brigadier and sent to New York to train the American contingent that participated in the 1741 siege of Cartagena. He distinguished himself there despite the expedition's failure. Even more impressive was his stout resistance at Stirling Castle

[21] On the council of war see Pope, *At Twelve*, p. 351; Tunstall, *Admiral Byng*, pp. 131–40.

during the '45 Rebellion. The latter achievement secured his promotion to lieutenant general in 1747. With that promotion came the appointment as lieutenant-governor of the island of Minorca. Humane and loved by his men, living with his regiment almost his entire career, dependent on his salary, he represented the eighteenth-century British army at its best – and was just the sort of man who could be asked to spend many years commanding a distant outpost. But in 1756 he was 84 years old and, though of sound mind, not well able to move about.

The great citadel that he commanded possessed many advantages in addition to its favourable position. Provisions, water and ammunition were plentiful; there was ample protected space in underground caverns; numerous walled redoubts commanding the approaches were connected by underground passages to the castle. The fortress's firepower – 240 cannon plus 81 mortars and plenty of ammunition – would have remained greatly superior to the French even if half its ordnance became unserviceable. The garrison consisted of four regiments, all under strength, totalling just under 3,000 men. Richelieu himself judged that at full strength the place would have been impregnable. Perhaps more serious was Blakeney's lack of officers. Forty were absent on leave; the next ranking officer to him was a lieutenant colonel and there were only a few subalterns. The missing officers had been ready to come out to their posts in February but the navy had not been required to provide a ship to bring them. On board Byng's squadron – sailing away to Gibraltar – were the 4 regimental colonels, the governor, many officers returning from leave, 19 new subalterns, and over 250 recruits and marines, all of whom were meant to join the garrison.

Could they, in fact, have been inserted into the fortress? One other attribute of St Philip's was its protected access to the sea. Months later when he was testifying at Byng's court-martial, Blakeney averred that men could have been got in. On this point he was sharply cross-examined by Byng personally, who asked him: 'Do you apprehend that troops could have been landed . . . safely from the fire of the enemy?' To which Blakeney replied: 'I have served sixty-three Years, and I never knew yet any Enterprise undertaken without some Danger, and this might have been effected with as little Danger as I ever knew.' The exchange made a great stir and did Byng no good. Historians have tended to doubt Blakeney's opinion, but in fact the French had no way of reaching, nor any effective means of firing upon the landing places under the walls of St Charles fort at the point or inside St Stephen's cove, from both of which access to the castle was easily available. Throughout the siege the

British held St Charles fort as well as the Marlborough redoubt which lay across the cove from the fortress. There were, it must be said, French batteries capable of ranging upon the seaward approach to these places, but only at a distance, and as Blakeney pointed out, the boats would go in at night.[22] No British warship came within sight of the castle after the sea battle, however.

Disturbing as the squadron's disappearance over the horizon was, the garrison doggedly fought on. On 30 May Richelieu had a total of 38 cannon and 17 mortars on the island; he awaited 10 more cannon and 4 mortars from Marseilles and Perpignan. By 8 June the French had erected ten batteries mounting 41 cannon and 18 mortars, but two of the batteries were blasted out of service that night. At times it seemed that fire from the fortress was slackening, but then it would resume with great intensity. The enemy, Richelieu reported on 18 June, defends with 'stubbornness and courage'. His own gunners were forced to economize on powder and shot until a resupply from the mainland reached the batteries on 22 June. Letters sent home by French officers confirmed the slow progress and were generally despondent. According to information that reached The Hague the marshal himself was far from confident of success. As Joseph Yorke reported to his sister:

[H]e confesses neither he nor any of his engineers had any notion of the place, that it is one of the strongest in Europe; that he hopes, however, when he has got everything he wants from France, that he shall be able to reduce it, since Monr de la Galissonnière has been able to keep his station, which has enabled him to receive his stores and provisions from Provence.[23]

In fact, Richelieu concluded that he could not reduce it, at least not before a strong British squadron was likely to arrive, so he resolved to take the castle by storm. The plan was a massive assault employing nearly the whole army in simultaneous attacks on all sides; the attack on the south-eastern side bordering the sea featured grenadiers arriving in boats.

The signal was given at 10 p.m. on 27 June. The troops rushing forward towards the Queen redoubt took heavy casualties, but they succeeded in scaling the walls, which rose 22 feet above the rock base, by driving bayonets into masonry crevices for steps and helping each other

[22] Blakeney's and Robert Byrd's testimony, *The Trial of the Honourable Admiral John Byng* (London, 1757), pp. 33–8, 49–52. See also Tunstall, *Admiral Byng*, pp. 217–18.
[23] Yorke to Lady Anson, 6 July 1756, Yorke, *Hardwicke*, II, 304.

climb. Once over the parapet some of them entered a connecting tunnel where they happened to surprise and capture Lieutenant Colonel Charles Jefferies who was coming to assess the situation. Besides the Queen, two other redoubts on the north-western side were seized, though at great cost (the British successfully exploded two mines inflicting heavy casualties). In all other sectors the assaults were repulsed. Near the foot of St Charles fort the defenders were waiting at the waterside in the dark: the first boat carrying the grenadiers to shore was met with murderous musket fire; both French officers were killed and the other boats turned back. The French failed to capture either St Charles fort or the Marlborough redoubt. In the attack the French lost 8 officers and 204 soldiers killed, plus 50 officers and 412 soldiers wounded, compared with British casualties of 23 killed, 30 wounded and 12 missing. The fortress remained well armed, well enough provisioned and defensible; the ability of the French to remain in the Queen redoubt was uncertain.

During the entire siege including the final attack the British had suffered 71 killed, 304 wounded and 10 dead of sickness. Total French casualties numbered over 1,000, plus 800 men sick, a number that was increasing. Richelieu realized that the arrival of a strong British squadron could confine his large army to the island indefinitely, without means of resupply. Immediately, on the morning of 28 June he proposed a cessation of arms. A council of war summoned by Blakeney accepted Richelieu's terms, which were generous and included French conveyance of the entire garrison to Gibraltar. In hindsight it seems clear that the garrison should not have capitulated, but the men were dreadfully sleep-deprived and wondering if relief would ever arrive. If there had been a few more officers and Colonel Jefferies had not been captured, the decision might have gone the other way.

Three weeks later Admiral Hawke arrived off Mahon with seventeen ships of the line. La Galissonière fled to Toulon as soon as he learned that a battle fleet was approaching; only one of the five additional ships of the line that the naval minister at Versailles had promised him materialized. A shortage of guns prevented the others from being properly armed for combat.

The French conquest of Minorca had little strategic significance. If Spain had been willing to accept the island in return for going to war against Britain, the strategic impact would have been tremendous, but the Spanish government turned the offer down. Of course the naval base of Port Mahon with its well-fortified harbour was a loss, but it was no longer as important as in the preceding war. At that time a Spanish army had been fighting in Italy against an Austrian army, and the Royal Navy had assisted the Austrians by interdicting supplies sent from Spain. A British battle squadron based on Minorca was essential for supporting these operations. The treaty of Aranjuez (1752) had changed the picture: Italy was no longer a theatre of war. Upon hearing the news of the capitulation Newcastle, in a frenzy, told his colleagues that Minorca must be retaken, but cooler heads prevailed and in fact the British government never made any attempt to do so throughout the war. (The island would be returned to Britain at the peace table.) To some extent the loss of Port Mahon made it harder to protect British Mediterranean trade, but the Royal Navy did not withdraw from that sea. They would use Gibraltar as a base and also rely on the willingness of merchants in various Mediterranean ports to accept British bills of exchange in return for provisions and repair services. All in all, the French ended up maintaining a sizeable garrison on the island to little purpose. Anson's inclination to give low priority to Minorca had therefore made sense considered in strategic terms. The political consequences of its loss were, however, enormous.

Critics focused not only on the administration's slow response to intelligence but also on the number of ships sent out. Writing to Pitt on 7 June George Grenville asked: '[W]hat can be the excuse for sending a force which at the utmost is scarcely equal to the enemy upon so important and decisive expedition?'[24] Reading reports of the sea battle, Joseph Yorke wrote to his brother that he was 'convinced, from the force of La Galissonière's 74 gun ships, that he was much an overmatch for Byng', adding that 'if Mr Byng had had another 90 gun ship, he would have beat the French fleet out of the sea'.[25] Yorke was implicitly criticizing his sister's husband, Anson. In deciding not to detach three or four ships from the Western Squadron (which was much stronger than what the French could put to sea from Brest) when intelligence revealed beyond doubt Minorca's imminent danger, the First Lord made a mistake.

Byng's abandonment of Minorca confirmed George II's prediction that the man would not fight. Joseph Yorke had at first defended Byng, but when he heard about the slow progress of the French siege and its dependence on resupply from the mainland, and noted that Byng had failed to open 'communication with the Castle and left the sea to the Enemy', he lost all respect. Henry Fox had predicted what Byng would do. When news arrived via French sources that a sea battle had been fought without

---

[24] *Chatham Correspondence*, I, 163.

[25] Yorke to Philip, Lord Royston, 15 June, 2 July 1756, Yorke, *Hardwicke*, II, 297.

a British victory, he wrote: 'I doubt not, our first news will be that Byng is returned to Gibraltar, and that a council of war says he did wisely. The consternation, anger and shame of everybody here on this occasion is extreme.'[26] This was the moment when the cabinet resolved to supersede all the participating generals and admirals without waiting for Byng's official report. When they learned shortly thereafter that Fox's prediction was entirely accurate, their views of the admiral's character and conduct became fixed. Soon after Byng arrived at Spithead on 26 July he was arrested and confined – ostensibly to protect him from the mob, but it was done with harsh intent.

Minorca's loss came as a complete shock to the public. Island bases under British naval protection were assumed to be invincible. Politics in Britain became unsightly. Newcastle realized that the cabinet and Anson had not done all that they should have done, but tried to place the entire blame on Byng, and Byng, even before receiving notice of his recall, let the ministers know that he blamed them. In a letter justifying his decision to retire to Gibraltar after the sea battle, he cited the inadequacy of his squadron. The dispute would fester for many months because a court-martial could not be convened until numerous officers called on to testify came home from their Mediterranean service. (That trial and its result, fatal to Byng, will be considered in the next chapter in its proper chrono-logical and political setting.) In the meantime accusations and pamphlets proliferated. The public blamed both Byng and the administration; they burned the former in effigy while demanding that the ministers resign.

Why, if there was so little strategic benefit, did the French choose to capture Minorca? No record of how the decision was made exists, but it seems that the French government, realizing that war was inevitable and still thinking in terms of a maritime contest, was looking for a practicable means of scoring an early victory. All other possibilities, including an invasion of the British Isles, were thwarted by British naval superiority in the Channel and the Atlantic. It could be hoped that Spain would accept a gift of the island and join the French war effort, but that was unlikely. More certain was the island's value in an exchange at the peace table.

Another likely benefit for the French monarchy was gaining popular support for the war. This was clearly achieved. The Minorca triumph gave encouragement to an intensively anti-British 'new patriotism'. The con-quest was celebrated in print, on stage and in song. Boscawen's capture of the *Alcide* and the *Lys* and the 'piratical' attacks on French merchant

---

[26] Fox to Devonshire, 3 June 1756, Ilchester, *Henry Fox*, I, 330.

ships were avenged. Carthage – the name French authors found for Britain on this occasion – was humbled. The *Observateur hollandois* even went so far as to declare that Europe had been deceived about the strength of the Royal Navy: its ship lists, it was claimed, were a sham, containing countless vessels unfit for sea. Although the editor of the *Observateur hollandois* received a government subvention, there can be no doubt that the triumphant enthusiasm was genuine. The Anglo-French Seven Years War was now officially begun: a British declaration on 17 May upon the news that the French army had landed on Minorca was answered by a French declaration on 16 June. The war began with enthusiastic popular support – a somewhat unusual occurrence for the French monarchy.

The king did not follow the popular path, however. At the end of August the victorious duc de Richelieu, welcomed joyously by the people of Paris, was received coldly at Versailles. The reason was partly personal – Pompadour's dislike of him was known – but there was a deeper current developing: Louis XV and his inner circle were secretly contemplating the possibilities of war in Germany. Versailles would soon decide to pursue success on the continent and would thereby turn its attention and the bulk of French resources away from the direct confrontation with Britain that was the focus of public enthusiasm.

Some French ministers had mentioned a political argument for attacking Minorca. They supposed that the conquest would create political turmoil in Britain, which it certainly did. This, however, was a case of not being careful about what one wished for. As will be seen shortly, public furore in Britain would lead to demands for a parliamentary investigation, and these would, in turn, open the way for William Pitt to become director of the British war effort. The political effect of the conquest of Minorca was to install in Britain a great war leader whose influence over matters of strategy and preparation would in due course cause France to lose many of her overseas possessions.

Oswego destroyed

By January 1756 the marquis de Vaudreuil, governor-general of New France, had been thinking about Oswego (Chouaguen), the British base on Lake Ontario, for many months. He knew that the British had intended to launch an attack on Niagara from Oswego the year before; he did not doubt that they would attempt it again, or else attack Fort Frontenac (Kingston) to the north. Vaudreuil judged that he could attack first. He knew that Oswego could not be speedily reinforced because of its position at the end of a long and arduous passage from Albany. Moreover, friendly Indians controlled the eastern shore of Lake Ontario, and Niaouré Bay (near Watertown, New York) could serve as a French marshalling point, only 40 miles from the objective.

He began by ordering raids on Oswego's supply line. Lieutenant Gaspard Joseph Chaussegros de Léry of the *troupes de la marine* led a winter expedition of Canadians and Indians from La Présentation (Ogdensburg, New York) to the Oneida Carry (Rome, New York), the place where British supplies were hauled a mile overland from the Mohawk River to the headwaters of Wood Creek. Two forts were there; the one at the Wood Creek acquired the name Fort Bull. On 27 March after overcoming the extreme hardships of a 14-day, 150-mile winter march through the western Adirondack wilderness, De Léry surprised and annihilated Fort Bull. The place exploded when fire reached a powder store. The raiders killed 30 men and took 35 prisoners while suffering only 3 killed (1 Canadian and 2 Indians) and 6 wounded.

The winter garrison at Oswego was literally starving to death; the daily ration fell to 2 ounces of salt pork and 8 ounces of bread. By March more than 50 of about 1,000 soldiers were dead, and the rest could scarcely stand up. The commander was preparing to leave when a volunteer party which had left Fort Bull before the raid brought food. They had rolled barrels and pulled the bateaux the length of frozen Lake Oneida. There was no further relief until Captain Bradstreet came down the Oswego River with a large convoy of bateaux on 16 May. He brought a second convoy on 1 July. Upon returning he was ambushed on 3 July at a point 8 miles up the Oswego River by a force of 450 Canadians, 180 French regulars and 100 Indians under Coulon de Villiers, the officer who had compelled Washington's surrender at Fort Necessity. John (originally Jean-Baptiste) Bradstreet was born in Nova Scotia, the son of a British army officer and an Acadian woman of property, and understood wilderness combat. Heavily outnumbered, he occupied an island and gave his armed bateaumen time to cross the river. Then he counter-attacked some of the enemy who had crossed the river and drove them from a wooded swamp back into the water where they were exposed to his musket fire. Neither commander's casualty report can be trusted, but the number on each side was probably close to a hundred. Although the French force retired, Indians lurked in the vicinity of Oswego picking off stray individuals for scalps and falling upon parties of woodcutters.

Only slowly did the men at Oswego regain their health and strength during the spring of 1756. Still, there were not enough of them for the necessary tasks, even with a reinforcement of 200 provincials from New Jersey. The soldiers were employed mainly as workmen, but guards were needed because of lurking Indians. Thanks to Bradstreet's energy and bravery most supplies got through, but axes, spades and other tools lost in the raid on Fort Bull were sorely missed. The main effort at Oswego was focused on building armed vessels. The purpose was now defensive, to prevent the French from bringing cannon. None of the wooden-palisaded forts at Oswego could withstand cannon fire. By 22 July, although four of these vessels were afloat, not enough guns, ammunition, rigging and sails had arrived to fit them for service. The French still had two strong warships plus other armed vessels at Fort Frontenac. Emphasis therefore shifted to the three forts. The strongest, Fort Ontario, lay on the eastern side of the river but it could be readily dominated from higher ground.[27] The other structures, Fort Oswego and Fort George on the western side, were flimsy and incomplete.

Under the command of the marquis de Montcalm the French were accumulating an assault force in Niaouré Bay. Coming from Sackett's Harbour in their bateaux by night and hiding inshore by day, they landed a mile east of Fort Ontario on 10 August. The British, unable to place lookouts on the lake's eastern shore because of the hostile Indians, were completely taken by surprise. The attackers, 1,323 *troupes de terre* from France, 137 *troupes de la marine*, 1,327 Canadian militia and 260 Indians, outnumbered the defenders 3,100 to 1,100, and the woods were dominated by unfriendly Indians. The British got no help from the local Iroquois; William Johnson had talked confidently but almost no one came. Nothing could be done to disturb the French and Canadians as they built a log road for bringing up the artillery.

Seeing French batteries established only a hundred yards away from Fort Ontario, the commanding officer at Oswego, Lieutenant Colonel James Mercer, moved everyone to Fort George on the west side of the river. At dawn the next day, 14 August, he could see guns arrayed on the high ground next to Fort Ontario. His own guns were facing the other way, and if turned around, most of them would have no parapet for shielding, but Mercer bravely repositioned them and commenced firing anyway. Upstream, hundreds of French soldiers were crossing to the west side. Not far away from Fort George was a stockade, Fort Oswego.

---

[27] Fort Ontario has been preserved as a historic site in its nineteenth-century form, an expanded and rather impressive stone edifice very different from the wooden square of 1756.

Though its works were incomplete and its garrison small, it put up stiff resistance but had no chance of holding out, so its garrison was transferred to Fort George. At nine in the morning Mercer was beheaded by a cannonball fired from across the river. An hour later the second-in-command signalled for a ceasefire. Montcalm's terms required all combatants to submit as prisoners of war. Civilian traders and workers together with their property were to be released and 'no injury' was to be 'done them'. In the event Montcalm was unable to keep his word because when the Indians had been recruited they had been promised plunder and scalps. The result was a slaughter of the wounded and many others who allegedly tried to escape. The French version of the signed capitulation was later edited to obscure the promise of 'no injury'. Montcalm reported that to bring the mayhem to a halt yet 'preserve . . . the affection of the Indian Nationals' he spent 'eight to ten thousand livres' to buy them off.[28] Besides taking 1,600 prisoners the French captured 2 warships, 200 boats and bateaux, 55 guns, 14 mortars, 5 howitzers, a great deal of ammunition and ample quantities of provisions. They destroyed everything else before departing.

By this raid French supremacy on Lake Ontario was assured: Niagara was safe; the lifeline to the west could not be obstructed. The swiftness of the success, which cost fewer than thirty casualties, enabled the French to move troops and captured provisions quickly to Lake Champlain, and consequently a planned British offensive against Crown Point had to be called off. Moreover, the decisive annihilation of the British presence at Oswego had a significant effect on the regional Indians. Formal Iroquois neutrality temporarily lost its hold, as countless warriors, witnessing the dramatic tilt of power, openly sided with the French.

Major General Shirley's responsibility for the loss of Oswego was considerable. He did not appear to understand how difficult it was to provide for its defence. He had placed the entire business for providing supplies at Oswego in the hands of Peter Van Brugh Livingston and Lewis Morris, Jr. of New York under one great contract, and left the task of on-site supervision to a 29-year-old personal secretary who lacked authority and expertise for matching supplies to needs. The contractors did not plan for nearly enough wagons, horses, bateaux and bateaumen. Provisions were already becoming scarce at Oswego by the end of August 1755 and not enough food was sent during the autumn. In late November Shirley left Albany for Boston and became preoccupied by his duties as governor of

---

[28] Jennings, *Empire of Fortune*, pp. 295–6.

Massachusetts. In late January 1756 he realized that numerous bateaumen must be hired, but only in mid-March did he take the important and positive step that was so much needed of bypassing his contractors and appointing Bradstreet to command 2,000 bateaumen to take supplies to Oswego. Shirley, who thought he was preparing to conquer Fort Frontenac in 1756, not only failed to make timely provision for his own logistical needs but also failed to understand how much better the enemy was at solving these kinds of problems.

The officers of the *troupes de la marine* were, as noted earlier, experts in wilderness campaigning. They had a realistic grasp of what could and could not be accomplished logistically; they understood the strengths and weaknesses of wooden fortifications; they knew the waterways and how the seasons affected them; they never neglected scouting and intelligence gathering, and knew how to recruit Indians who could accomplish these vital tasks. Thanks to their knowledge and experience, the assault on Oswego was well planned and expertly carried out. Although Montcalm had initially tried to resist their advice, judging that the attack on Oswego had little chance of success, he soon yielded and gave the necessary orders. Fortunately for the French cause, he knew he must yield. His orders issued at Versailles made very clear that in all circumstances he must conform to the instructions of 'the governor general who controls everything and orders everything for military operations'.[29] Montcalm personally disdained the Canadians, and would in due course try to impose his own ideas, but in the spring of 1756 Canadian expertise dominated decisions. The officers of the *troupes de la marine* had a decisive influence on the strategy and the preparations.

Viewing the larger picture, it is obvious that the geography of the interior strongly favoured the French. Shirley seemed not to understand this. At Oswego in late September 1755, with the place already suffering from food shortages, he drew up a plan that envisioned not just raiding and destroying Fort Frontenac in the coming year, but holding it. Shirley was aware that French forces would inevitably come upriver from Montreal to relieve Frontenac but somehow supposed that they would be at a disadvantage, through a process of reasoning that can only be labelled fantastic.[30] Vaudreuil, in contrast, saw that geography and military

[29] MacLeod, 'The Canadians against the French', 147.
[30] Shirley to Secretary of State Robinson, 28 Sept. 1755, Lincoln, ed. *Correspondence of William Shirley*, II, 294–5.

readiness gave him substantial advantages, but had no thought of retaining Oswego. With control of the St Lawrence River, he needed only to dominate Lake Ontario and Lake Champlain to keep British forces at arm's length. His logical strategy was to raid, plunder, spoil and withdraw, not to invade and conquer. Canada's relatively small population and limited resources dictated this strategy.

The garrisons of the western forts were accordingly kept small, and the forts on the upper Ohio were an exception to this policy. They were established because orders from Versailles had made them necessary (though officials in Paris wished to deny this). Canadian losses to sickness in the effort to establish them were, as we have seen, dreadful, and the forts were predictably difficult to support. Spoilage and theft of provisions en route by Indians was commonplace; bateaux were constantly in need of repair; horses, wagons and men at the portages became worn out. The permanent garrisons of the three forts had to be limited to a total of 500 men, and they were instructed to plant vegetables and try to feed themselves locally. Vaudreuil was right about Oswego. Its destruction was a necessary safeguard for the upper Ohio forts as well as Fort Niagara, but trying to hold it would have required more resources than Canada could afford.

Shirley was an energetic man of ability who was congenitally optimistic. When he supervised preparations for the successful expedition to the Bay of Fundy he was dealing with resources to be transported by sea from the well-developed city of Boston. He had no understanding of the difficulties of campaigning in the interior. He held the position of commander-in-chief only because of Braddock's death, and he had shown there were compelling military reasons for replacing him. It fell to Sir Charles Hardy, a rear-admiral who had recently accepted the governorship of New York, to explain to the authorities in London not only why Oswego was lost but also why the proposed attack on Crown Point had not been carried out. Most of the British and American troops had been kept south of Lake George for the purpose, yet no attack was launched. Hardy's letter of 27 November 1755 dwelt on logistical chaos: supplies arrived before troops and vice versa, and there were not enough wagons and teams to carry both supplies and bateaux overland to Lake George. Since the forces in northern New York could not be supported by local provisioning, he said, better management was essential. Hardy was disturbed by Shirley's ignorance of military affairs. At Albany, he had heard him talk grandly about matters he did not understand. Hardy did not see 'any prospect of Success, without some more able & experienc'd General

... at the head'.[31] This letter went to Lord Halifax and was in hand during a London meeting of 19 January 1756.

The new commander-in-chief was the Duke of Cumberland's choice: John Campbell, 4th Earl of Loudoun. Two other senior officers were created major generals to assist him, James Abercromby and Daniel Webb. Six months were to pass, however, before the war in North America received effective direction because Lord Loudoun did not land in New York to take up his command until 22 July. The problem was not slow passage. Loudoun left Spithead in a frigate on 20 May, and an Atlantic voyage of two months from east to west was about average. The problem lay in the British government.

There were three basic causes of delay. First, the government wanted to give its new commander-in-chief in America amplified powers, and it took time for the ministers to agree on formulas that would be legally justified and politically tolerated in the colonies. Secondly, the Duke of Cumberland entertained the idea of having the regular troops do all the fighting. He assigned two more regiments to North American service, the 35th and 42nd, both of which needed time to build up their ranks. The larger numbers would require more transports than were originally requested. Further means were adopted for increasing the force of regulars by an innovative establishment, the Royal American Regiment (more about them shortly). Thirdly, preparations involved the War Office, Admiralty, Ordnance and Treasury as well as the cabinet. Newcastle was not the sort of man who could coordinate departments or instil a sense of urgency. Besides, in the face of transport shortages he was more concerned with bringing Dutch or German troops to England to defend against invasion than with the war in North America.

When Cumberland and Fox realized that the preparations were taking far too long they decided that Abercromby and Webb should sail forthwith. Webb reached New York on 7 June, Abercromby on the 16th, both arriving in packet vessels. Webb, essentially an administrator, was dreadfully unfitted for military command and seemed to realize it, but came with orders superseding Shirley. Having delivered these, he did nothing constructive and waited for Abercromby, and then they both waited for Loudoun. In effect, although the campaigning season was imminent, neither of the subordinates was disposed to make any commitments. Because Loudoun was known to be a favourite of Cumberland's any big

[31] Governor Hardy to Halifax, 27 Nov. 1755, Pargellis, ed. *Military Affairs*, pp. 149–53.

decision they made that displeased him could be career-ending. The Duke of Cumberland and Henry Fox should have foreseen this problem.

Finding recruits for the 35th and 42nd regiments was not Loudoun's job, and although he needed to be consulted about establishing the Royal Americans, those arrangements were completed by early April. Transports and provisions were a concern but to be dealt with by others. Granted, he could not sail until his powers as commander-in-chief were defined and orders sealed, but this complex task was completed by 17 March. Somehow it took seven more weeks for the War Office to produce his supplementary instructions. If Loudoun had sailed for America in early April, he probably would have reached New York at about the same time as his subordinate generals, but Cumberland preferred to keep him in London to assist with the administrative arrangements.

The two subordinate generals reached Albany on 25 June with ample time to send their own subalterns to Oswego to report on the situation, but it was only when Bradstreet appeared on 12 July with clear and abundant evidence that the French were poised to attack Oswego that Abercromby and Webb took action. They could also read a report from Patrick Mackellar, an engineer whose recent survey of the forts described their vulnerability. In a council of war on the 16th Abercromby ordered the 44th Regiment to march 'forthwith . . . to Reinforce that Garrison, and put the works in a posture of defence'.[32] But wagons and money as well as a sense of urgency were lacking, and although Lord Loudoun arrived in Albany on 29 July, the regiment did not go forward until 12 August. Even then, Loudoun's orders conveyed no hint of an emergency, as Webb was given some routine tasks to accomplish along the way. On the 12th Oswego was already under attack, and after hearing that the place had surrendered Webb advanced no further than Fort Bull. Deciding to turn back, he ordered the fort to be burnt. The British army had been left for two months under thoroughly incompetent generalship.

In the aftermath of this military debacle, Abercromby threw all the blame on Shirley, asserting, on the whole falsely, that he had failed to pass on vital information about Oswego's defences. Abercromby could have learned about the situation for himself, but neither he nor Webb nor Loudoun perceived the French advantages that placed Oswego in imminent danger. Shirley protested vehemently when Loudoun repeated Abercromby's accusations, but the one man who could have supported Shirley's case effectively, Bradstreet, chose to keep quiet. Observing the

---

[32] Godfrey, *Pursuit of Profit*, p. 82.

merciless character of Loudoun's takeover, he gave priority to his own future in the British army.

So extreme were the accusations against Shirley that the Duke of Cumberland wanted him brought home a prisoner. Hardwicke talked him out of it, but Shirley was soon deprived of the governorship of Massachusetts. The military justifications for his recall as commander-in-chief have been historically overshadowed by disputes concerning politics – his quarrel with Sir William Johnson about his meddling in Indian affairs and the hostile connivance of a New York political faction against him. Yet the loss of Oswego came as a shock to everyone, and the blame fell on Shirley. The Duke of Cumberland and the generals he assigned to America needed to mask their own failures, and could easily use him as a scapegoat. The disaster at Oswego was fundamentally due to Cumberland's overly ambitious offensive scheme, but, ironically, Shirley had enthusiastically supported the scheme and seriously misjudged its requirements. His replacement as commander-in-chief was therefore necessary, but that the architect of victory in Nova Scotia who had lost two sons in the campaigning – one killed under Braddock, the other succumbing to pneumonia at Oswego – should have his governorship taken away was inherently unjust and inappropriate. It also deprived the British cause in America of a leader who had a genius for generating enthusiasm and gathering recruits.

British and American armies

Oswego was neglected partly because almost everyone at Albany was focusing, as Shirley had been, on preparations for an offensive against Crown Point. The assault force was to be composed of 8,000 New England and New York provincial troops; 6,000 had in fact arrived. Thus the campaign on the New York frontier in 1756 was well supplied with provincials, but not with regulars. Britain did not send many regular troops to North America early in the war simply because the kingdom did not have enough of them. Unlike France and other continental powers, Britain had a very small peacetime army, and finding recruits to enlarge it was very difficult. Officer candidates were plentiful; younger sons of the aristocracy were often eager for army commissions, as were volunteers who came from the 'middling classes', but very few men were willing to serve in the ranks. England's population was a third of that of France. Conscription was constitutionally forbidden, and practically all young men could find employment at better wages than the army paid. Enlistment was long term. The British soldier existed in a world apart, very often literally, because regiments could be sent overseas and stationed there for years. Anyone who agreed to enlist had to be either avid for adventure or desperate to escape miserable and alarming circumstances (such as being condemned in a magistrate's court), or else cajoled and made drunk out of his mind by recruiting sergeants. Given England's relatively developed economy, it is not surprising that Ireland and Scotland were the most likely sources of able-bodied recruits. The 42nd, the Black Watch, sent to America in May 1756, was recruited in Scotland. The 35th was recruited in England, but of poor quality by Loudoun's estimate.

Piecemeal recruiting could maintain regimental numbers, but any sudden need to defend the British Isles against invasion posed a problem of a different order. When the Dutch failed to honour their obligation to send 6,000 troops the cabinet saw no alternative but to hire 8,000 Hanoverians and transport them to England. William Pitt, who had served briefly as a junior cavalry officer, regarded this recourse to German mercenaries for home defence as shameful, dangerous (because of sailing delays) and expensive. Most members of Parliament agreed with him. A bill for creating a rejuvenated militia, strongly supported by Pitt, passed the House of Commons in May 1756. One argument in its favour was that a homeland militia would enable more regular troops to be released for service abroad. Nevertheless, the administration opposed the bill in the House of Lords.

A notable speech against it was delivered by Lord Hardwicke and is of general interest. Although he agreed that England should have a militia for home defence, he wanted it to be under royal authority. He also wanted it to be a smaller militia than the bill's proposed 60,000 men. So large a number, he said, would affect the character of English society and under-mine England's unique source of prosperity and power: 'For my own part, I never was more convinced of any proposition in my life than of this, that a nation of merchants, manufacturers, artisans, and husbandmen, defended by an army, is vastly preferable to a nation of soldiers.' A large militia would lead to Englishmen behaving like ex-soldiers, sharing 'a love of idleness, of sports, and at last of plunder'. Hardwicke elaborated:

[I]t is to this progressive change in your people, from arms to industry, that your commerce, your colonies, and consequently your riches, are owing.

What is the object of the present war? The preservation of that commerce, and of those colonies. If you turn the bulk of your common

people into soldiers, what will become of all these? You may indeed
stand upon your guard, with arms in your hands; but, in a course
of years, I fear you will have little in value left worth guarding; an
untrading, unmanufacturing, unimproved, impoverished country.[33]

In the bill that eventually became law the size of the militia was cut
by half.

Hardwicke was not opposed to the regular army (his youngest son
Joseph was an officer), but one argument against a large militia was that
it would leave too few men to be recruited by regular regiments, which,
unlike militia units, could be ordered abroad. But, clearly, Hardwicke had
most in mind a balance of military needs against the value of a productive
workforce. The kingdom's greatest advantage in warfare, he realized,
stemmed from its superior economic and financial condition, which was
sustained by manufacturing and commerce. Superior financial capability
was the result, and it supported a great navy, subsidies for allies, mercenaries to be hired and ample stocks of munitions and supplies.

During the Seven Years War the British army would eventually succeed
in recruiting, training up and deploying high calibre British infantrymen
and cavalrymen, most of the best infantrymen coming from Scotland and
Ireland – but none came quickly, and never in ample numbers. As we have
seen, in 1754 the Duke of Cumberland had proposed a bold offensive
plan which the cabinet accepted, but the British Isles provided only two
undermanned regiments from Ireland to support its execution. In 1755
when the cabinet learned that the French had largely evaded Boscawen's
attempted interception and landed 3,000 regulars in North America, there
was no thought of trying to match them. The Newcastle administration's
reluctance to send troops to America under fear of invasion continued
to hold sway even after the government learned of the near annihilation
of Braddock's army. Finally, two regiments were ordered to America in
spring 1756, almost as an afterthought. On 11 May George Grenville
reminded the House of Commons: 'Braddock had been defeated in July
[1755]; not a man was sent thither till within the last fortnight.'[34] It is
little wonder that Britain's regular force in America in 1756 was not
numerous.

[33] Speech in the House of Lords, 24 May 1756, *Parl. Hist.*, XV, 733–6. This is one of
the few parliamentary speeches of the period of which an accurate transcript exists,
not of the exact words Hardwicke uttered but of the words he intended, because he
prepared a written version for publication.
[34] Walpole, *Memoirs of King George II*, II, 146.

Basically there were two British armies in America, regular and colonial – the latter called provincials. All regular officers were career men,
and they were all British with the exception of the officers of the 60th
Regiment, a unique institution that was specially created for service in
America. This regiment, called the Royal Americans, consisted of four
battalions; its creation was proposed by foreign (Protestant) officers. Two
of these in particular, who were well experienced in the military profession and would prove to be very capable military leaders, Lieutenant
Colonels Frederick Haldimand and Henry Bouquet, both Swiss, came into
British service by this channel. It was expected that most of the Royal
American Regiment's recruits would be found in America. In fact, all regular regiments that came across the Atlantic were expected to top up their
numbers by drawing upon the population of British colonial America
because raising recruits in Britain was so difficult. Lord Loudoun, like
most British officers who served in North America, looked upon American
provincial soldiers as 'execrable', but he was bent on recruiting Americans
to complete regular regiments, for it was his aim to fight the French with
forces trained and led by British officers.

The recruiting methods used by regular regiments in America were
similar to those used in Britain – getting the prospect drunk and sometimes employing trickery – but in America, particularly Pennsylvania and
Maryland, there was a category of young men (many of them Germans)
who might easily be tempted: indentured servants. The servant received
only food, clothing and lodging from his master who had bought his
indenture (which covered costs of passage from Europe), usually from a
ship's captain. The British army's offer of an enlistment bonus and the
prospect of regular pay was relatively attractive. Enlistments, however,
deprived masters of labour during the remaining period of bonded service
– often four or five years for males in their twenties. Naturally, masters
considered the army's proceedings outrageous. The Pennsylvania assembly ruled the recruiting of indentured servants to be illegal, and there were
rioting mobs in which property owners took part. Local officials often
supported the mobs, but the London government directed royal governors
to allow servants to be recruited. It was not a new problem, as Parliament
was aware, and in January 1756 in hopes of facilitating recruiting in
America an act was passed requiring the army to pay a proportion of the
master's costs according to the years remaining to be served on the indenture. The master's loss was not fully recompensed.

The provincial forces, constituting the other army in America, were
created by the legislature of each colony and recruited for a particular

period of service, usually nine months to a year. They were not militia, though in times of urgency militiamen could be drafted into provincial regiments. A provincial soldier served under officers drawn from his colony of residence, but for the planned attack on Crown Point, General John Winslow of Massachusetts was appointed commander-in-chief of all New England provincials, and New York provincials recognized his authority.

Provincial and regular units had usually been serving under completely separate commands, and the attack on Crown Point was to be carried out by the purely provincial army under Winslow. This arrangement led to a serious quarrel when General Abercromby reached Albany. On 15 July as Winslow was beginning to move his 6,000 men north to begin the attack he was recalled to Albany by Abercomby, who asked why provincials should not be joined with regular troops and their officers. Winslow's response was blunt: the result would be 'universal desertion among the Provincials, because they were raised to serve solely under the command of their own Officers'. The proposal would therefore violate the terms under which they had volunteered. Abercromby and his staff realized that it was too late to change the order of battle for an imminent operation so they agreed to let it go forward as planned. Two weeks later, however, when Lord Loudoun reached Albany he reacted with rage. He denounced the arrangement, met with Shirley, promptly blamed the problem on him, and then called Winslow back to Albany, demanding that the provincials must act in conjunction with regulars and under a British commander. Contrary to what Loudoun reported to the War Office, Shirley supported Loudoun's claim that a British general should take over command of the operation on the ground that the war effort came first. Winslow agreed to place himself under Loudoun's command, and the latter agreed not to assign regular officers to provincial units. Apparently, the minds of Loudoun and his fellow generals at Albany had been mainly focused on something other than the situation of Oswego.

Winslow's recalcitrance and wariness was aggravated by his experience in Nova Scotia of existing British army rules which allowed provincial generals and colonels to rank no higher than senior captains of the regular army. According to those rules provincial troops came too readily under the harsh disciplinary practices of regular officers; also, the men would not fail to notice their own officers' loss of authority. Shirley had been able to mix some provincials with regulars at Oswego by persuading regular officers to leave provincial officers in charge of their units. Despite recent new rules that gave a lessened advantage in rank to regular officers, provincial officers remained wary. On this occasion Loudoun understood the practical necessity of compromising, but he was not content, and when news of the surrender of Oswego gave him a good excuse to cancel the Crown Point operation, he quickly did so. But he realized that he greatly needed the provincials. He positioned them in the region north of Albany in case the French chose to attack; his regular regiments were depleted and the troops that arrived from the British Isles during the summer scarcely matched the number lost at Oswego.

Lord Loudoun was in some respects a good choice to be commander-in-chief. A Scotsman from Ayrshire, he was an experienced military professional and skilful administrator, educated and hard-working. He talked to people candidly yet courteously and made a good impression when he arrived in New York. While appearing to be an adroit politician he lacked, however, the political flexibility that the job required. His mind was dominated by powerful prejudices: military necessity must override civil law; political assemblies, especially the more popular variety prevalent in the American colonies, were a menace. Such attitudes were common in the British army. Its officer corps was beholden to the king; for it was an army of the Crown and at this time happened to be ruled, with George II's permission, by his second son, the Duke of Cumberland. Lord Loudoun's authoritarian ideas were perfectly in accord with those of the duke. The terms of Loudoun's commission had been shaped by Halifax, Cumberland and Fox; as commander-in-chief he was provided with comprehensive authority: colonial governors were directed to assist him. But the terms left unclear the issue of whether he could obtain colonial assistance by force.[35]

Lord Loudoun generally restrained himself when conversing with Winslow and other colonial leaders, and poured his anger and frustration into private letters to the Duke of Cumberland. In those letters his expressions of contempt for American colonial society were extreme: merchants and tradesmen were 'naturally Avaricious'; politicians were corrupt; law and order was lax. He continually remarked on the lack of subservience that, to his dismay, he found everywhere in America. The people

have assumed to themselves what they call Rights and Privileges, totally unknown in the Mother Country, and are made use of for no purpose but to screen them from giving any Aid, of any sort, for carrying on the Service, and refusing us Quarters.

[35] Pargellis, *Lord Loudoun*, pp. 57–60.

Whatever rights they might think they enjoyed as English subjects, Loudoun was sure they had an exaggerated view of them. This was the cause of delays in military preparations. He deplored colonial legislatures and viewed royal governors as dangerously subservient to them. Something, he warned, would have to be done about it. His authoritarian attitude was particularly evident when it came to quartering troops. In England troops could be quartered in public houses, but Loudoun claimed that English law allowed the army to impose quartering on private houses as well (it was permitted in Scotland but not England). He openly threatened – in Albany, Boston, Philadelphia – that quartering would be imposed on private residents by force of arms.[36]

Loudoun was understandably annoyed by colonial failure to provide quarters for the newly arrived regulars; before long local authorities solved the problem by finding suitable structures for barracks. That a measure of force was necessary in order to meet the military need for wagons, teams and vital supplies was undeniable, but he and other British officers should have understood, if only from the British army's past experience in Europe, that the workable formula was to join an ultimate threat of commandeering to a reasonably attractive offer, as Benjamin Franklin had done when he obtained wagons and teams for Braddock.[37] Lord Loudoun, however, instinctively began with summary demands and threats.

Loudoun's authoritarian attitude, contemptuous towards American colonists, seriously undermined his effectiveness as commander-in-chief. It would be a mistake, however, to overlook his contribution to winning the war. His assiduous administrative efforts significantly advanced British military capability and competence in North America. Even colonial leaders who were annoyed by his dictatorial habits, presumption of superiority, and inclination to marginalize the colonial contribution to the war effort could appreciate that he was putting the British colonies in a condition to defeat the French. His greatest contribution was in the realm of logistics. The New England colonies had shown that they could raise troops, but lacked the organization and resources for maintaining them on distant frontiers. Loudoun quickly concluded that the army's provisioning and transport had to be handled by strongly financed London contractors who would place a partner on location in America. This method was costly but proved reliable. Nevertheless, a decade later when the pre-revolutionary

[36] Pargellis, ed. *Military Affairs*, esp. pp. 225, 230, 251, 269–73.
[37] Rogers, *Empire and Liberty*, pp. 52–3.

disturbances erupted, Americans would remember the man's arrogance, which symbolized the attitudes of so many British army officers. They did not forget his contempt for them and his threat to use muskets and bayonets to gain his point about quartering in contravention of an explicit provision of the English Bill of Rights of 1689.

Provincial troops quickly learned to fear service under British officers. Captain Eyre of the Royal Engineers put it mildly when he said that provincial soldiers seemed 'not to be fond of red Coats'.[38] Harsh discipline was the main reason, but there was also the nearly universal regular officers' presumption of their troops' superiority in combat – very annoying when, as yet, the regulars in America had done nothing to establish it. Braddock's force annihilated; Dunbar's shameful and injurious retreat to Philadelphia; the loss of Oswego – all this could be contrasted with successes in Nova Scotia and at Lake George, which the colonists viewed with considerable justification as achieved by provincial forces. The numbers recruited by British regular regiments in America fell by half in 1757. This was unfortunate because the war in North America needed an army that could be trained and kept in service for years rather than months. Nevertheless, it was mainly Winslow's provincials who supplied the labour needed to carry out Captain Eyre's plan to strengthen Fort William Henry. When the work was mostly done, however, they disbanded. The fort was garrisoned for the winter by 400 regulars; there were 500 at Fort Edward.

In addition, 500 rangers remained in the area. French success at Oswego had discouraged the Mohawks from serving the British in the vital tasks of scouting and intelligence-gathering. The rangers, mostly recruited from sparsely settled regions of New Hampshire and New York, were an indispensable substitute. Since they were needed all year long they were placed on the regular army payroll. At first, these unruly men lacked sufficient military skill and discipline, but an outstanding leader emerged, Captain Robert Rogers of the New Hampshire provincials. It was Sir William Johnson who learned of his merit and put him in charge of the ranger companies.

The French, of course, had a huge advantage in scouting, which was increased when word of Oswego's destruction and plunder spread among Indians in the north and west. Many came to Ticonderoga looking for scalps and captives (the French offered rewards for producing prisoners who could be questioned). Montcalm, however, did not plan a winter

---

[38] Pargellis, ed. *Military Affairs*, p. 170.

attack and did not even order bateaux to be built for an offensive in the spring. Remaining at Ticonderoga until 26 October, he employed his soldiers in strengthening Fort Carillon and enabling its winter garrison to be sustained.[39]

Lord Loudoun did not underestimate the fighting capabilities of his opponents. He feared a winter attack. He realized how hazardous and demanding the task of retaking Oswego would be, and how little benefit could be derived from doing so.[40] He quickly grasped that the crucial Albany area was at risk unless Fort Edward and Fort William Henry were properly defended and the waterways and roads serving them secured. He saw that campaigning in northern New York was bound to employ large numbers of soldiers and that the logistical challenges were formidable; it was therefore best, he advised London, to have the British army acquire its own horses and wagons rather than depend upon colonial contractors. If Shirley had possessed influence that could recruit New England provincials, Loudoun possessed influence that could bring more money from Britain. Finally, he realized that the colony of Pennsylvania, the best recruiting ground for regular regiments, felt badly let down by Dunbar's retreat and Shirley's strategic priorities. Shirley had told the governors of Pennsylvania and Virginia that they must take care of themselves, but the task of protecting frontier communities from Indian raiding was daunting, in fact nearly impossible. Loudoun was unable to help these colonies in the near term, but he would not forget them.

[39] Bougainville's journal, Hamilton, ed. *Adventure in the Wilderness*, pp. 33–63.
[40] Loudoun to Cumberland, Albany, 2 Oct. 1756, Pargellis, ed. *Military Affairs*, pp. 237–8.

CHAPTER 8

France's new war plan, 1756–57

The two pivotal events of the year 1757 were the installation of William Pitt as leading minister of the British government and French implementation of a new plan of grand strategy. Pitt's desire to direct the British war effort was intense, and he proved in fact to be a great war minister. It will be seen that the Earl of Hardwicke played a key role in enabling him to rise. As for the new French war plan, it amounted to a 'changing of the Sea War into a Land War' and as such alarmed the British cabinet.[1] The ministers correctly surmised that France's primary objective was to occupy Hanover, and they had every reason to think that France would succeed.

At the same time, very few British successes would occur at sea or in North America during 1757. Nothing seemed to go well. On 6 October Lord Anson would sadly remark to his father-in-law: 'I just come from Council, heartily tired with the reflection that not one event from the beginning of the war has come before us, that has not been unfortunate.'[2] Britain was losing the maritime and colonial war while at the same time nothing, it appeared, could be done to prevent George II's dominions in Germany from being overwhelmed.

Pitt attains his goal

After Newcastle rejected him in autumn 1755 Pitt tried but could not find a means of embarrassing the administration. His mistrust of any British diplomatic involvement in Germany had carried him to excess in the

---

[1] 'Our Ministers are very sensible of the necessity of changing a Sea War into a Land War'; intelligence from Versailles, 24 April 1756, BL Add. 32,864, fo. 393.
[2] Anson to Hardwicke, 6 Oct. 1757, Yorke, *Hardwicke*, III, 186.

winter debates of 1755–6, and he deserved to have his condemnation of
the agreement with Prussia thrown back in his face less than a year later.
In early May 1756 when the possibility of losing Minorca loomed, Pitt
blamed Newcastle. For one thing, he said, the cabinet did not take collective
responsibility. 'I don't call this an Administration', Pitt told the House of
Commons, 'They shift and shuffle the charge from one to another: says
one, I am not General; the Treasury says, I am not Admiral; the Admiralty
says, I am not Minister. From such an unaccording assemblage of separate
and distinct powers with no system, a nullity results.'³ This was close to a
description of what had happened. He blamed the ministry for mobilizing
the navy too late, but he also made some absurd accusations, insinuating,
for instance, that the tardiness and inadequacy were deliberate, as if the
government had wished to risk losing Minorca so that it could achieve an
early peace by bargaining away future conquests in America for its return.
Such harangues made him appear ridiculous, and it was just as well for his
sake that on 27 May 1756 Parliament went into recess. Soon after this, news
arrived indicating that Minorca's loss was almost certain; Pitt was keenly
aware of the political importance, privately remarking to Grenville that it
was 'a selfish consolation, but a sensible one, to think that we [two] share
only in the common ruin, and not in the guilt of having left us [Britain]
exposed to the natural and necessary consequences of [an] administration
without ability or virtue'.⁴

On 14 July, upon news of the capitulation of St Philip's Castle, the
public furore reached a crescendo. In the City of London, Fox observed, the
'rage of people, and of considerate people, for the loss of Minorca increases
hourly'; he noted that Newcastle was the minister most blamed. The duke
was mobbed in his coach at Greenwich, the coachman being urged by the
crowd to drive him straight to the Tower. Popular street songs proposed 'to
the block with Newcastle, and the yard-arm with Byng'.⁵ Although Byng
was burnt in effigy all over England, it did not mean that the administration,
in which Fox was a secretary of state, would be excused.

It would be Fox's duty to speak in defence of the administration in
the House of Commons and he hated the thought of it. He believed, not
without justice, that Newcastle and Anson had made strategic mistakes
that he would not have made. Yet when he served as secretary of war he

³ Walpole, *Memoirs of King George II*, II, 142–3.
⁴ Pitt to Grenville, 5 June 1756, *Grenville Papers*, I, 165.
⁵ Ilchester, *Henry Fox*, I, 335; and Thomas Potter to George Grenville, 11 Sept. 1756, *Grenville Papers*, I, 173.

had failed to insist that a frigate should be assigned to carry the garrison's absent officers out to Minorca, and his role in editing Byng's dispatch for publication in a manner that omitted certain passages, thus giving Byng's supporters a handle for crying foul, had become publicly known. He knew all too well how venomous a House of Commons inquiry into a naval failure could be, for in 1745 he had taken a prominent role in attacking Admiral Mathews during a similar inquiry. His only hope of assistance would have been the debating skill of William Murray, the Attorney-General, but Murray claimed the recently vacated office of Lord Chief Justice and was awarded it, and also a peerage as Earl of Mansfield. So Fox would be left as the only prominent representative of the ministry in the Commons. He foresaw that all the odium would fall upon him when Parliament reassembled.

The combination of Minorca's loss and Fox's trepidation destroyed the Newcastle administration. It was rare for a single event to produce such a result, but Minorca's loss was such an event. On 13 October Fox submitted a letter of resignation. He said he was willing to make way for Pitt, who now stood aloof from the political turmoil, to be a secretary of state. Newcastle and Hardwicke believed this to be a ploy; they supposed that Fox felt certain that the king would reject Pitt and was seeking to secure his own position. George II, however, was incensed when he learned that his principal spokesman in the House of Commons proposed to resign just as Parliament was about to convene. He viewed it as a betrayal. Seeing how angry the king was, Newcastle went to him and suggested that either Pitt must be installed in high office or Fox must be allowed more power than could be considered wise. The king answered, 'Mr Pitt won't come'; besides, he 'won't do my German business'. Newcastle replied that Pitt was the only man in opposition who had the ability to do it. The king then said he would first talk to Fox, which he did, but without success. When Newcastle went to the king the next day, 15 October, he found him still angry with Fox. George II allowed him 'to have Mr Pitt sounded'. At the same time, he raised an important question: 'Suppose Pitt will not serve with you?' The duke replied, 'Then, sir, I must go.' Anticipating that Fox would also receive royal permission to sound out Pitt, Newcastle urged Hardwicke to meet with Pitt immediately to ask whether he would join the cabinet as a secretary of state. Their conversation took place on 19 October and lasted three and a half hours. Pitt's answer, Hardwicke reported, was 'an absolute *final negative*'.[6]

---

[6] The correspondence is printed in Yorke, *Hardwicke*, II, 321–6.

Pitt thereupon surprised everyone by conveying to the king a plan for a cabinet. It covered nearly all the important offices; the names of Newcastle and Fox were notably absent. Learning that Pitt had offered a plan and supposing his final negative to be not quite absolute, Hardwicke arranged another conversation. Pitt told him that there must be a parliamentary inquiry into the failures at Minorca and in America (news of the destruction of Oswego had recently arrived), and that a militia bill must be brought forward. In addition he stated that he was 'to have such powers as belonged to his station [as secretary of state], to be in the first concert and concoction of measures, and to be at liberty to propose to His Majesty himself anything that occurred to him for his service originally, and without going through the channel of any other minister'. Hardwicke's response suggested that these points might be found acceptable.

But then Pitt reiterated that 'it was impossible for him to serve with the Duke of Newcastle'. He gave as his reason the fact that 'all these mistakes in the conduct of the war had been committed, and all these ill successes had happened, whilst his Grace was first Minister, and the nation was . . . to the last degree incensed against him'. The Lord Chancellor expostulated, but to no avail.[7] (The insistence on excluding Newcastle was the essential reason why he considered Pitt's position to be a *'final negative'*.) After consulting friends Newcastle decided that his only recourse was to resign, and informed the king of his intention to do so on 26 October. Hardwicke resigned with him, thereby retiring from his long career as Lord Chancellor.

Events now moved rapidly. The king sent for Fox the next day and gave him a *carte blanche* to form a ministry. Fox wanted Pitt to join with him and talked with him, but was rebuffed. Fox then met with Cumberland and began, as Hardwicke remarked, 'negotiating round the compass' with all sorts of politicians in hopes of cobbling together a ministry.[8] On the 30th the king turned to the Duke of Devonshire, a high-ranking, trusted Whig peer friendly to Fox but without political ambitions, and asked him to try to get Pitt to join Fox. Devonshire met Pitt the same day. Pitt refused to collaborate with Fox but said something that was to be important: he would not press the inquiry to the point of criminal censure and punishment; his aim would be to uncover the neglect

[7] Hardwicke's memorandum of the 24 Oct. conversation and letter to Joseph Yorke, 31 Oct. 1756, Yorke, *Hardwicke*, II, 278, 331.
[8] Ibid. II, 333.

and incapacity that warranted removal of the ministers from office, something that was now being accomplished by their resignations. Fox, urged
on by the king and Cumberland, persisted in efforts to put together a
ministry. When it looked as if he might succeed, the Earl of Bute entered
the picture. He was political leader of Leicester House, the court of the
young Prince of Wales (the future George III), which was presided over
by the prince's widowed mother; it was a place where everyone loathed
and feared the Duke of Cumberland. Bute threw his support behind Pitt.
By 3 November Devonshire was sure that any administration organized
by Fox could not last a week, and therefore, with the king's permission,
travelled 12 miles to Hayes where Pitt was laid up with gout to offer him
practically everything that he asked.

Thus was born the Pitt–Devonshire administration. Devonshire was to
be First Lord of the Treasury; Pitt's ally Henry Bilson Legge as Chancellor
of the Exchequer would direct Treasury policy; and Pitt as Secretary of
State for the Southern Department would, as everyone acknowledged,
exercise overall direction of the war and foreign policy. Newcastle, Fox,
Hardwicke and Anson were out. The extent of the change was astonishing
– the great men of politics all dismissed. 'There must be', thought Lord
Chesterfield as he viewed what had happened, 'a *dessous des cartes*
which, when one does not know, one can only think at random and talk
absurdly.'[9]

If there was a hidden element – a 'hole card' – it concerned the inquiry
and Pitt's assurance to Devonshire that he would not press for censures and
punishments. The leading men of the Newcastle administration took the
danger they were in very seriously, and because the scope of the inquiry
as described by Pitt was to include failures in America, Cumberland and
Fox would be prime targets. If there were to be no censures and punishments, the logic of Pitt's refusal to join with Fox became evident, for if
Fox, whom the king and Cumberland strongly favoured, was not excluded
from the new cabinet, Pitt's power would be minimal. Fox understood
what Pitt must be thinking: 'he sees, in that case, that the moment the
enquiry is over I am as much master as if he was at the Board of Trade
instead of Secretary of State'; in terms of power to influence affairs Pitt
would in reality 'be but Paymaster again'.[10] Hardwicke, for his part,
was not much frightened for himself – the king and Pitt greatly respected
him – but he was worried for his son-in-law, Anson. As he wrote to Joe:

[9] Quoted in Clark, *Dynamics of Change*, p. 295.
[10] Ibid. p. 288.

'[T]he affairs of the Admiralty consist of so many branches, and admit of such variety of opinions, that nobody knows how far enquiries may be carried. Ill success will be worked up into mistakes, mistakes into neglects, and neglects into crimes.'[11] When Pitt told Cumberland that his 'inquiry' goals were limited (information that was undoubtedly conveyed to Newcastle and Hardwicke) it became easier for everyone who had held power to accept the Pitt–Devonshire administration.

The loss of Minorca had shaken the Newcastle administration to its foundations, and the threat of a parliamentary inquiry into the causes enabled Pitt to achieve his goal of becoming the director of war policy. With patience and daring he had held course and won his gamble. He came 'as a *conqueror*', independent – something Newcastle had always dreaded. Allegedly, Pitt had remarked: 'I know that I can save this country, and that no one else can.'[12] The stratospheric self-confidence, indeed arrogance, of the remark has been ridiculed, but it captures a crucial difference between him and Henry Fox.

Yet what, in fact, had he won but a wagon-load of troubles? Laid up with gout he confided to a friend: 'I find it still difficult to use my pen. . . . I am, in all senses, unfit for the work I am going to set my feeble hand to. . . . Be the event what it may, as soon as I can crawl I will embark, perhaps on board a wreck; and trust I shall have your honest and kind wishes for a fair wind and favourable seas.'[13] The political seas were not favourable. Beyond his connection through marriage with the Grenvilles, Pitt had almost no followers. Parliamentary patronage remained under the control of Newcastle, a fact blatantly confirmed by the duke's crowded levees where attendance, far from declining after the duke's exit from office, sometimes equalled that of the king's levees at court. To be sure, Pitt could initially count on support from Leicester House, and even from Tories, those 'country gentlemen' in the House of Commons who were staunchly anti-Hanoverian (and inveterately opposed to Newcastle). But Tories could not be considered a parliamentary foundation; they lacked numbers and reliability.

Although the Great Commoner, as the press now referred to him, came into office as he wished, independent and unfettered, his lack of a parliamentary following left him without loyal colleagues of experience, competence and character to fill key offices. Devonshire was a partner of

---

[11] Yorke, *Hardwicke*, II, 334.

[12] Williams, *Life*, I, 285.

[13] Pitt to Charles Lyttelton, from Hayes, 19 Nov. 1756, Black, *Pitt the Elder*, p. 128.

convenience, not a friend; Legge, who had opposed Newcastle's subsidies in 1755, could speak for the Treasury in the House of Commons, but his loyalty to Pitt was uncertain. The one truly close and supportive political ally was his brother-in-law Richard Grenville, Earl Temple. Unwisely, Pitt placed Temple at the head of the Admiralty, where his insolent behaviour made him disliked by everyone. Granted, Temple was bold and talented enough to speak effectively in the House of Lords, but George II did not want him in his sight and resented Pitt for placing him in an office where conversation was occasionally necessary. In any case, the king, coerced into accepting Pitt, was very unhappy, and behind the scenes stood the king's son, Cumberland, eager to get rid of the new secretary of state. Fox was, as usual, his instrument. On 4 December a publication called *The Test*, written by a 'creature' of Fox's, began to spread its venom.

Newcastle and Hardwicke, however, were prepared to give Pitt time – perhaps to let him self-destruct but also because they wished to leave the door open for future cooperation. Two days after the article in *The Test* appeared Hardwicke called on Pitt to offer congratulations and used the fact that they were both insulted 'in the same paper' to establish friendly informality; he wanted to talk candidly and privately. He and Newcastle, Hardwicke said, had no intention of mounting an opposition, adding, however, that nothing could drive them into joining Fox 'but violence in pushing enquiries and censures'. Pitt was reassuring: he said that he would never have anything to do with Fox and that although he could not publicly retreat from demanding an inquiry, he had no desire to pursue censures and punishments; he treated the inquiry as 'a slight thing'. Hardwicke asked whether he had made commitments to the Tories that would interfere with his obligations to the king. Pitt answered by saying that he was supported by the country gentlemen without any conditions, to which Hardwicke, smiling, responded with a question: 'How long do you compute it will last on that foot?' It was a scarcely veiled suggestion that Pitt might wish to reach out to Newcastle, but the new secretary of state brushed it aside.[14]

Horace Walpole predicted that Pitt would not last six months. It was a reasonable prediction and proved correct. But this fact should not be taken to indicate that Pitt's political strategy had been foolish. His goal was to attain the directing power and for that he needed to keep his independence intact. If he were beholden to Newcastle, or Fox and Cumberland, he would have no real command of policy – of 'measures',

[14] Hardwicke to Newcastle, 6 Dec. 1756, Yorke, *Hardwicke*, II, 375–7.

to use the language of the time. He would merely be the government's leader in the House of Commons, valued as such but subservient, and vulnerable to dismissal when the uproar over Minorca died down. In that situation he might not even last six months. Instead, he placed his future hopes on conducting the war with success. Of course, like anyone taking charge of a bad situation, he faced the risk of being sacked before his measures could bear fruit.

Nevertheless, he knew he could use his position to define strategic priorities. The King's Speech on 2 December 1756, which Pitt wrote, stated that the 'Succour and Preservation of *America*' was 'a main Object'. It also called for a firm defence against invasion and recommended the formation of a 'National Militia'. In the debate that followed Pitt said that the navy was not strong enough and would have to be speedily enlarged. His measures would be expensive, he admitted, but the House of Commons in its wisdom would 'prefer more vigorous Efforts (though attended with large Expense) to a less effectual, and therefore less frugal, Plan of War'.[15] He meant what he said and went on to obtain parliamentary approval for a global effort: a substantial army was to be sent to North America, lesser forces to the West Indies and India. When Hardwicke got wind of all this through Newcastle, he replied: 'Here is a great deal of extensive and expensive work cut out for the new Ministry, more I am sure than we could have gone through under the weight from bad successes and their opposition.'[16] A few days later Pitt persuaded the cabinet to send 8,000 troops to America, and soon the House of Commons was asked to approve the full 4 shillings in the pound Land Tax, which it did without murmur. Obviously, Pitt had Parliament's support for these measures. In the ensuing weeks he spent most of his time and energy on preparing a large expedition to capture Louisbourg.[17]

Lord Barrington, secretary at war, a holdover from the previous administration, contrived to suppose that Pitt's programme amounted to no great change. But the Newcastle administration had sent very few troops to America since hostilities began, and it was obvious that Pitt truly intended that America should become the main object. He plainly planned to conquer America in America. The King's Speech mentioned a plan for the continent, but Newcastle could see that Pitt would, in fact, prefer to pay almost no attention to Europe. If an opportunity for resuming office

[15] *Proceedings and Debates*, I, 180.

[16] Hardwicke to Newcastle, 21 Dec. 1756, Yorke, *Hardwicke*, II, 379.

[17] Williams (*Life*, I, 314–16) provides a chronology of Pitt's actions in this period.

alongside Pitt were to arise, Newcastle told Hardwicke, Pitt's 'measures must alter much, before we can join in earnest with him'.[18]

War begins on the continent

Newcastle was referring to Pitt's apparent indifference to the continent. A major war in central Europe had erupted when, in late August 1756, the Prussian army had marched into Saxony. Why did Germany, supposedly protected from hostilities by the defensive treaties of Westminster and Versailles, become so promptly the scene of war?

The key fact was that Prussia was dangerously isolated by the Austro-French treaty of Versailles of 1 May 1756. When Newcastle learned of the treaty's existence on 8 June he hoped that war might be avoided but also wondered whether Britain would be compelled to elevate the convention of Westminster into a Prussian alliance. Shocked and puzzled by the startling news from Paris, he begged Lord Hardwicke to come to London immediately, and also sent a long letter to Joseph Yorke at The Hague. Of Hardwicke's advice on this occasion there is no record, but his son's response was unequivocal. It was now absolutely clear, he wrote, that Austria had earlier 'determined to abandon us unless we fought for Silesia, when we should be fighting for America'. Therefore, 'We must unite with Prussia . . . Wavering between the two systems, or building upon a renewal of the old one at this time, would be fatal to us.' Britain must therefore be prepared to make Prussia 'the great Power of Germany, in opposition to France and French Measures'. Newcastle did not want to hear this. He clung to a hope that Austria could be persuaded to keep peace and looked to strengthening the British subsidy alliance with Russia. Perhaps, he supposed, St Petersburg could be persuaded to designate France 'the common enemy', though both sides had initially assumed it to be Prussia.[19]

There was no chance that the Empress Elizabeth would accept this change. She was determined to attack Prussia. In March 1756 a high-level meeting in St Petersburg decided upon mobilization for war. Frederick II had not at first perceived danger from Russia; he was inclined to suppose that the Russian court could be swayed by British bribes. He knew that the two empresses would be eager to attack him but believed he 'had

---

[18] On 9 Jan. 1757, Clark, *Dynamics of Change*, pp. 320–1.
[19] Newcastle to Hardwicke, 12 June 1757; Yorke to Newcastle, 18 June, BL Add. 32,865 ff. 277–8, 339–41.

nothing to fear from Vienna or Petersburg' unless their 'evil wishes were made real by foreign pecuniary aid'. The treaty of 1 May 1756 introduced a new danger, however, and he therefore began to worry that France might be able to match 'the large subsidies that England accords Russia'. He asked Knyphausen to find out.[20] From London he was receiving optimistic reports about its negotiation at St Petersburg. Newcastle considered the dispatches of his ambassador there to be credible, but the ambassador was being duped and Newcastle was consequently misinforming Frederick II. The king of Prussia repeatedly asked Andrew Mitchell, the British minister at Berlin, 'Are you sure of the Russians?' As he worried about Russia's growing belligerence, Frederick mistakenly assumed that Vienna was prompting it, but in fact the efforts at persuasion were operating the other way round, and when Maria Theresa realized that the Russians were well advanced towards launching an attack she sent an urgent message asking them to wait. More time, she said, was needed to make sure of French approval, on which subsidy money would depend. Also the Austrian army was not yet ready.

On 18 June Frederick suddenly awoke to the reality of the Russian threat. Mitchell reported that his courier from St Petersburg had just seen abundant evidence of military preparations on the road. The same day Frederick received intelligence that the Austrians were moving artillery into Bohemia in the direction of Silesia and placing more troops in those regions. These were defensive measures, but he saw them as threats and ordered an extensive mobilization. London was still falsely telling him about hopeful progress at St Petersburg. Frederick politely asked Mitchell to tell his government that further negotiation with Russia was pointless.

Although he had heard that Russian military preparations had slackened, Frederick adopted a plan in mid-July: he would use the advantage of his quickly mobilized army to defeat the Austrians before they could mount an adequate defence and would then deal with the Russians separately. (He assumed, incorrectly, that the Russians had paused because of mobilization difficulties.) By the end of July, despite objections raised by his foreign minister, he was resolved upon attacking. Mitchell also raised objections. Both men pointed out that by doing so he would be taking on not only the Austrians and Russians but also the French, who were certain to honour their obligations under the treaty of Versailles. Mitchell suggested that he should at least make sure that the Austrians truly

---

[20] Letters to Knyphausen at Paris, 16 Feb., 12 June 1756, *Politische Correspondenz* (cited in Chapter 7) XII, pp. 120, 400–1.

intended to make war against him. In consequence, Frederick II sent an emissary to Maria Theresa to ask her why she was putting troops in motion and tell her that he was prepared to pledge to stand down if she gave her word not to attack him either in 1756 or 1757. He also accused her of forming an offensive military alliance with Russia, which was technically not true, but she was certainly conspiring with Russia with a view towards war. What mattered to Frederick was that she did not accept his offer. He knew that in France there was no sign of logistical preparation for enabling an army to march deep into Germany. By waiting until the end of August and taking time to communicate with Vienna, Frederick could show sensitivity to Britain's desire for continental peace and also be sure that a French army would not arrive in Bohemia before the campaigning season ended.

The initial success of Prussia's attack, launched on 29 August 1756, was impressive. Marching through Saxony yielded huge strategic advantages. Frederick was prepared to fight the Saxon army if it confronted him, and to bypass it if it did not. Moving swiftly with over 100,000 men he occupied Dresden within ten days. The Saxon army had left the city undefended and taken up a fortified position on the Elbe river at Pirna. Bypassing Pirna and employing the Elbe as his supply link to Bohemia, Frederick took 28,000 men through the mountains. He met an Austrian army on the Bohemian (Czech) side at Lobositz. The battle fought there on 1 October 1756 was by no means an easy victory for the Prussians. Although Austria's armed forces were only partially mobilized, the 34,000 men who fought against him were better trained than he expected; their defensive manoeuvres were superbly directed by Field Marshal Maxmilian von Browne, whose father had been born in Ireland. The Austrians inflicted heavy casualties before withdrawing in defeat. Frederick returned to Pirna and received the surrender of Saxony's army on 14 October. He would ruthlessly exploit Saxony as an economic resource for the rest of the war, drawing on it for as much as one-third of Prussia's material costs. At this point the armies went into winter quarters.

Frederick's decision to launch a war in which he engaged the three greatest land powers of Europe was a huge gamble. He hoped to fight them one at a time and defeat each quickly, an optimistic plan that could be justified – if at all for such a horrendous undertaking – only by the fact that Prussia was in a truly desperate situation. Whether Frederick created that situation by his precipitate signing of the convention of Westminster is a matter for argument, but there is no doubt that Louis XV left him dangerously isolated. The Russians were clearly planning to attack

Prussia in 1756; the Austrians asked them to delay but never suggested a cancellation. So, in reality Frederick had only two choices: to give Silesia back to the empress-queen by immediate negotiation and with no assurance that the two empresses would stand down, or to attack.

Pre-emptive strikes that initiate wars are never viewed favourably, and this one had the practical disadvantage of triggering the Austro-French defensive alliance. Before concluding that Frederick made a colossal error of judgement, however, one must understand that Austria and Russia were determined to attack him the following spring, so war was inevitable – or, rather, the only conceivable preventive would have been French denial of subsidy money for Austria (which was to be passed on to the Russians, who would have dire need of it). And this raises the question whether, if Prussia had not launched its attack, France would have been willing to support the offensive war that the two empresses were planning for the following spring.

The question is intriguing. Louis XV was aware of Austria's plans for an 'enterprise' against Prussia. He might have chosen to tell the Austrians, as the French public was told, that France's policy was peace and that therefore neither money nor troops would be furnished to support such a project. He did the opposite. As soon as the ink was dry on the treaty of 1 May 1756, which was defensive, Louis XV indicated support for an offensive war by suggesting that Austria might wish to reward France for participating in one: the empress-queen might consider ceding the Netherlands to Louis's son-in-law, Philip of Parma. Her response was that she would consider this if France were to make no objection to a dismemberment of Prussia, and would pay the cost of an army of 50,000 to be raised in German states in addition to the cash subsidy specified in the treaty of Versailles. Throughout these negotiations the French court never advised the Austrians to abandon their 'enterprise' or lower the temperature. After she learned of Prussia's mobilization Maria Theresa asked the French to guarantee payment of a subsidy to her so that she could immediately promise some of the money to St Petersburg; at this time she was frantically urging Russia to put an army in readiness. The French response was encouraging. The Austrian ambassador was permitted to tell Vienna that there was nothing to worry about: 'His Most Christian Majesty [the king of France] will reimburse Their Imperial Majesties all of the advances which They should make on this occasion.'[21] This was written three days

---

[21] Starhemberg to Kaunitz, 26 Aug. 1756, Batzel, 'Austria and the First Three Treaties', p. 186.

before Frederick launched his attack. Thus, Versailles not only allowed but supported Vienna's project for a continental war (though the Austrians wished it had not come so soon).

France's new war plan

When news that the Prussians had actually launched an attack reached Paris the French government reinforced its support, informing the Austrians that France was prepared to give more to help than the terms of the defensive treaty required. This was very welcome news in Vienna, but within three weeks Maria Theresa began to suspect that the French were planning their own major offensive, probably against Hanover. 'In no way', she wrote to her ambassador at Versailles, 'do We consider a French attack on the Hanoverian Lands as a beneficial undertaking.' France should 'shun a Land-war', she advised, and 'expend its greatest strength on Maritime affairs'.[22] She repeated this advice on 10 October, emphasizing the import-ance of leaving Hanover alone. General Louis le Tellier, comte d'Estrées, was sent to Vienna to coordinate military plans, and it was only when he revealed the gist of his instructions in mid-November that the Austrians realized that the French were determined to send an army of 85,000 men into Germany. This army would be joined by 18,000 German troops in French pay. The main force would march from the Rhine to the Weser, cross it, and press on to besiege the Prussian fortress of Magdeburg. It would proceed by way of Hanover.

Both Kaunitz and Maria Theresa protested vehemently against this plan. The employment of so large an army, they said, was inappropriate, and it indicated an attack on Hanover, an electorate of the empire under the empress-queen's protection. Moreover, the French monarchy was formally committed to preserving the integrity of the empire. The Hanoverians were disposed to remain neutral, and an attack upon them might generate a Protestant coalition against Catholic Vienna. They also presented military arguments: the French army might have to confront a Hanoverian army which could check its progress toward Magdeburg; this would result in no help for Austria against Prussia. Even if the Hanoverians were defeated in battle, they might remain a threat to the French army's flank as it conducted operations against the Prussians. Finally, an attack on Hanover would probably bring Prussia closer to Britain with the strong possibility that British money would then be sent to support the common enemy,

[22] Maria Theresa to Starhemberg, 19 Sept. 1756, ibid. p. 214.

the Prussians. Her conclusion was to insist on Hanover's neutrality. A smaller number of troops sent directly against the Prussians was what she wanted.[23] Since Prussia was the principal enemy (in her eyes) France should avoid distractions, and she clearly meant military distractions.

But for the French government, at war with Britain, Hanover was not a distraction; it was the main point. Occupation of King George II's German Dominions was seen as a way of forcing the British government to an early peace. Foreign minister Rouillé had often remarked that Hanover might be seized as a counter in a peace negotiation to offset France's colonial losses, and although such losses had not yet in fact occurred, the conquest of Hanover now became the basis of French grand strategy. This was France's new war plan.

In surveying these developments one sees that France had a choice. She might have chosen a limited, auxiliary role in Europe, which was all the existing treaty of Versailles required, while concentrating on defence of her colonies overseas – a choice that was actually preferred by the Austrians. Instead, France chose a massive military thrust into Germany against Hanover. This choice – a French continental commitment, as it were – involved two complications, however. One concerned strategic goals. Although both the French and the Austrians understood that France was under an obligation to assist against Prussia, the French treated this obligation as secondary. Kaunitz, of course, viewed it as primary. Looking ahead to the spring of 1757 and desiring immediate military support, he wanted the 24,000 troops pledged by the defensive treaty to march to Bohemia without delay. He told d'Estrées that he 'regarded as nothing the 100,000 Frenchmen who will act against Hanover'.[24] But the French government postponed dispatch of the 24,000, using approaching winter weather as an excuse. The second complication will be considered in a moment.

The Austrians were willing to accept d'Estrées's plan if the 70,000 French troops that he proposed were committed to a direct attack on the Prussian duchy of Magdeburg. Kaunitz pointed out that the French army did not need to pass through Hanover to reach that objective and said he could easily arrange an alternative route. A direct attack on Magdeburg by the French army would be risky, however, unless Hanover, on its flank, remained neutral. From February to April the Austrians steadily urged the French to allow Hanover's neutrality, but Versailles

---

[23] Ibid. pp. 250–1.
[24] D'Estrées to Rouillé, 6 Jan. 1757, Waddington, *Guerre*, I, 102.

was completely unreceptive. Marshal Belleisle's requirements for agreeing to it were that George II must not only permit the French army to march through Hanover but also take responsibility for provisioning it and even for facilitating its passage by making sure bridges and roads were in good order. As the old marshal and his colleagues must have known, such terms were unacceptable in London. Whatever George II as Elector of Hanover might have desired privately, he could not, as king of England, agree to a proposal that would pave the way for Britain's enemy to attack her only possible ally.

While d'Estrées was at Vienna, political life in Paris was in turmoil. The quarrel in the parlement over religion would not go away, but another issue contributed to crisis in the latter half of 1756: taxation. After the French declaration of war the king introduced a second *vingtième* (a somewhat broad-based tax). The parlement of Paris refused to register it, as well as other new levies, unless the king agreed to consultation. Louis's response was high-handed: 'I alone', he said, 'am able to know the extent and the object of the expenses that circumstances render indispensable.'[25] Starhemberg, the Austrian ambassador, feared that a constitutional crisis might destroy France's usefulness as an ally and wished that the king and his circle of advisers would find a path to accommodation; he observed that the public appeared to side with the parlement. But Louis resorted to a *lit de justice*, invoking the full power of royal authority. By December 1756 the king was extremely unpopular, and fully aware of it. In fact, he and Pompadour feared a conspiracy of French Protestants supposedly in league with members of the parlement. On 5 January 1757 a frightening incident changed the atmosphere. A man named Robert-François Damiens thrust a knife into Louis XV's side as he was about to board his carriage. Damiens evidently acted alone, but some insiders at court believed him to be connected with a Protestant conspiracy. The knife did not find a vital organ and Louis recovered. Suddenly the public felt sympathy for their king, and the trial, torture and dismemberment of the would-be assassin (in public view) offered a distraction from the ominous constitutional confrontation.

Of more immediate importance to the war was an action that stemmed from the failed assassination. By 1 February Machault, the naval minister, and the comte d'Argenson, the war minister, were dismissed. Just at the time France was planning a major military campaign, two competent, hardworking administrators in vital departments of state were discarded.

[25] Ibid. I, 127.

Their fall was unrelated to performance in office. Machault who, like many others at court, had surmised that the king would die and Pompadour would therefore be swiftly exiled, made the mistake of showing indifference towards her. D'Argenson had never been her ally. After Louis XV recovered Pompadour persuaded him to dismiss both of them. Their replacements were François-Marie de Peyrenc de Moras and Antoine-René de Voyer d'Argenson, marquis de Paulmy. Moras was already overloaded by the office of controller-general of finance, and Paulmy, d'Argenson's nephew, was inexperienced and incapable of imposing any authority. The consequence of these dismissals went beyond the loss of administrative efficiency: Machault opposed the policy of a heavy military commitment in Germany, and d'Argenson had not been friendly toward Austria. Pompadour and her protégé, Bernis, gained more influence than ever, and so did the Austrian ambassador, Starhemberg.

Perhaps the second treaty of Versailles with Austria dated 1 May 1757 (exactly a year after the first) might have taken the form it did anyway, but Bernis and Pompadour were key facilitators and she probably influenced its terms. By this treaty France undertook to commit 105,000 French troops to the war in Germany plus an annual subsidy of 12 million florins to Vienna, these commitments to continue until Austria's war ended satisfactorily – satisfaction defined essentially as Prussia's surrender of Silesia. Although Austria, in return, would cede some key possessions in the Netherlands to the king's son-in-law, these transfers would only occur after Prussia's defeat. Historians have been at a loss to explain this extraordinarily one-sided agreement. Not only did Austria stand to gain much more from ultimate victory than France, but also there was the fact that unless Maria Theresa got what she wanted France would get nothing. And for this France assumed an enormous military and financial burden. Thus France formally exchanged its auxiliary and defensive role in the European war for a principal role, undertaking a huge commitment, apparently for the sake of Austrian goals. It is notorious that the Bourbon monarchs did not care to be bothered by estimates of cost, but, as Richard Waddington observed more than a century ago, 'the levity [légèreté] with which they put in play all the resources of France' was remarkable.[26]

What drove Louis XV's ministers to accept these terms and this burden? Since France did not need Austria, but at this moment Austria desperately needed France, there can be no obvious answer. Undoubtedly Versailles counted on a short war, so the potential cost might have seemed irrelevant.

[26] Ibid. I, 156.

Yet it should not be forgotten that Louis XV was sensitive to considerations of legitimacy in international relations – one reason he detested Frederick, who clearly was not. In this case the treaty negotiations had dragged on for many months and the French army was poised to launch its great offensive, which appeared to require an immediate attack on Wesel, the king of Prussia's fortress on the Rhine. Louis XV, much as he despised Frederick II, knew that the latter had never attacked or threatened France, and one accomplishment of the second treaty of Versailles was a justification of offensive action against Prussia. But Louis XV also knew that he had no justification for invading Hanover. This was the second complication (as mentioned above), and Maria Theresa continually called it to his attention. During the treaty negotiations Louis had earnestly sought her imperial permission to invade Hanover, and in early March she relented. Her excuse was that the British cabinet had asked Parliament to consider a subsidy for Prussia, her bitter enemy; this, she said, enabled her to see herself 'placed before God and the World with full justice to return like for like to the Crown of England'.[27] In this way she informed the French that she would not object to the invasion of Hanover. It seems possible, then, that the generous terms of the second treaty of Versailles resulted not just from overconfidence and Pompadour's influence on policy – she was passionately attached to the Austrian cause – but also from a wish to dampen Austrian complaints about France's diplomatically unwarranted attack on Hanover.

The second complication was thus overcome by this new treaty, but the first complication, the difference in priorities, remained a fundamental flaw in the Austro-French alliance. It would lead to harmful military consequences. If everyone at Versailles had been firmly agreed that the main objective was to occupy Hanover, the consequences might have been less serious, but Louis XV and Pompadour felt a strong obligation to meet the commitments made to Austria. As it happened, this sense of obligation would undermine the execution of France's new war plan.

The trial of Admiral Byng

Pitt was not oblivious to the upheaval on the continent. The King's Speech of 2 December 1756 spoke of the 'unhappy and unnatural Union' that had formed in Europe, producing a 'new and dangerous Crisis', but

---

[27] Maria Theresa to Starhemberg, 5 March 1757, Batzel, 'Austria and the First Three Treaties', p. 290.

his mind, as we have seen, was on plans for North America. Soon, however, a major, inevitable distraction intervened. On 28 December 1756 the court-martial of Admiral John Byng convened on board HMS *St George* in Portsmouth harbour. It heard testimony for four weeks, and was followed by an uproar over Byng's punishment. The political storm over Minorca's loss reached a second peak of intensity.

The charges brought before the court amounted to two questions: Had Byng done his utmost to relieve or assist the garrison at Minorca? Had he done his utmost during the sea battle? Regarding the first, the admiral had made no real effort to learn General Blakeney's opinion about the prospects of holding out or how the fleet might help. Byng had ordered the frigates he initially sent to the castle to return when the French squadron appeared on the horizon, and after the battle had made no further attempt to establish communications. During the court-martial he argued that it would have been impossible to land anyone at the fortress. As we have seen, General Blakeney refuted this and also pointed out how sorely needed the absent officers were.[28] The court found that since the officers 'on board the fleet belonging to the garrison . . . [were] much wanted, the Admiral ought to have put them on board one of the frigates he sent ahead, in order to have been landed, if found practicable', and should have allowed the frigate to endeavour 'to land them, notwithstanding he did see the enemy's fleet'.[29] Byng did not send a ship to communicate with St Philip's after the battle. He was 'certain almost', he told the court, that his damaged squadron was no match for the enemy. A defeat would have exposed Gibraltar, a place, he argued, 'equally recommended to my protection' (a literal but senseless reading of his orders). The court found that he should have returned to the castle with his squadron after the battle, tried to open communications, and 'used every means in his power for its relief, before he returned to Gibraltar'.[30]

The court did not presume to determine whether Minorca could have been saved by landing the absentee officers, but the members knew that if the garrison had held out for three more weeks, Hawke's arrival with a strong fleet would certainly have placed Richelieu's army in a very difficult situation. Byng's excusing his failure to assist the garrison by arguing that the squadron was too weak constituted an implicit acknowledgement that he had failed to 'do his utmost to relieve St Philip's castle' in order

[28] See Chapter 7.
[29] Resolution 7, Beatson, *Naval and Military Memoirs*, III, 133.
[30] Byng's written defence and Resolution 32, ibid. III, 130, 135.

to avoid risk. He considered it prudence, and if this had been the only charge, he probably would have been cashiered (dismissed from the service without pay).

The Articles of War, however, were mainly concerned with conduct during a sea battle, and most of the testimony was related to this. Incontrovertible evidence showed that Byng's division had lagged behind and scarcely suffered at all while captains and crews in the hotly engaged van were getting killed. The court saw that early in the battle the admiral had allowed the van to become separated and ruled that thereafter he 'retarded the rear division . . . from closing with and engaging the enemy'. Byng had argued that the forward progress of his rear division had been frustrated by mishaps beyond his control. The members of the court, all of them experienced sea officers, were well aware that naval battles could go awry and that the prescribed rules of the Fighting Instructions were often hard to apply. It was the admiral's failure to take remedial action that suggested negligence, for it was obvious that Byng did not act to bring his ship into battle until quite late; he had rejected the suggestion of his flag captain to turn downwind towards the enemy. The court found him guilty of the charge that

he did withdraw or keep back, and did not do his utmost to take, seize, and destroy the ships of the French King, which it was his duty to have engaged, and to assist such of his Majesty's ships as were engaged in fight with the French ships, which it was his duty to have assisted.

The court thereby concluded that, however much the Fighting Instructions may have stressed maintaining the line of battle, it was the duty of an admiral to do all he could to assist ships of his squadron that were already engaged.[31]

The language of the charge that he had kept back and did not do his utmost to assist ships of his squadron that were 'engaged in fight' was closely modelled on the 12th Article of War, which called for a mandatory death penalty if such misconduct stemmed from cowardice, negligence or disaffection. The court judged Byng innocent of disaffection and cowardice (there was testimony that he had remained cool and self-possessed on the quarterdeck), but found him guilty of negligence. In drawing up the sentence, however, the court did not use the word – deliberately, it may be inferred, because before pronouncing a sentence they asked the Admiralty if they might inflict a lesser penalty. When a

---

[31] Resolutions 19 and Conclusion, ibid. III, 134–7.

negative answer was returned the court transmitted the death sentence, but attached a letter asking the Admiralty 'in the most earnest manner to recommend him to His Majesty's clemency'. Every member of the court signed that letter. It raised the point (suggested by the admiral in his written defence) that the 12th Article, 'which admits of no mitigation, even if the crime should be committed by an error in judgement only', was too severe.[32] The members did not actually say that they had condemned him for making 'an error in judgement'; they were offering a hypothetical argument to protest against a law that deemed negligence a capital crime.

The sentence was read on 27 January 1757. Byng did not expect the death penalty and the court obviously did not want to pronounce it. Some members, most notably the presiding officer, Admiral Thomas Smith, immediately appealed to their friends to try to get the punishment mitigated. The Admiralty's duty was to notify the king, and the Board faced a stark choice: to recommend mercy, or to obtain permission to issue a warrant for the admiral's execution. The Board played for time by sending a memorial stating that the sentence, having not used the word 'negligence', required legal clarification. George II was furious but was persuaded to appoint a panel of twelve eminent judges, who found, unanimously, that the sentence was legal.

At this point Parliament became involved. On 23 February a motion was made in the House of Commons for inquiring into the 12th Article and the court's application of it. In the course of the debate a need for strict naval discipline was mentioned, which prompted Pitt to say that 'for his own part . . . he wished for mercy for he thought more good would accrue to the discipline of the navy' in this case from it rather than from strict justice.[33] Fox had tenaciously opposed mitigation of punishment throughout these debates and strongly differed, but both men agreed that Parliament should not meddle with the king's prerogative to pardon. Pitt called upon the king and pleaded for mercy. The First Lord of the Admiralty, Earl Temple, after being asked by seven members of the court-martial to intercede, also went to the king with the same plea. George II was obdurate, and Temple's manner of protesting did not help the cause: the First Lord approached his Majesty almost nose to nose to deliver an insult.

[32] Quoted in Tunstall, *Admiral Byng*, pp. 246–7.
[33] Quoted in Clark, *Dynamics of Change*, p. 330.

Byng was an MP, as were some members of the court-martial. Captain Augustus Keppel, a member of both the court-martial and the House of Commons, pushed for a bill that would release members of the court from their oath of secrecy so that they might explain their reasons for advocating mercy. Attendance in the Commons was by now huge – between 400 and 500 – and there could be no doubt that the majority did not want Byng put to death. The next morning Pitt went to George II and informed him of this fact, but the king rebuffed him, saying: 'Sir, *you* have taught me to look for the sense of my subjects in another place than in the House of Commons.'[34] The king was referring to Pitt's reputation as the voice of the people, and that voice was loudly demanding the death penalty.

Because the execution was scheduled for the following Monday the House met in special session that Saturday afternoon (26 February), and Pitt got the king to agree to a two-week postponement; the royal message to Parliament stated, however, that His Majesty was determined to 'let the law take its course' unless an examination of those who wished to be freed from their oaths should show that the admiral was 'unjustly condemned'. A bill that would free members of the court-martial from their oaths passed the Commons and went to the House of Lords where each member of the court was questioned separately whether he knew of some matter bearing on the justice of the sentence that he would wish to reveal if released from his oath. They could offer nothing more than their opinion that the death penalty was too severe. Since only Keppel and one other officer said they desired the bill to pass, the Lords rejected it. Byng's fate was sealed. He was executed by firing squad on the quarterdeck of HMS *Monarch* at Portsmouth on 14 March 1757. Though his sense of bitterness was extreme, he faced death with stoic bravery.

In his written defence Byng had claimed that a 'national prejudice' had been propagated against him and that false information had been given out 'with . . . uniform malicious intention'. The malicious persons he had in mind were the leading ministers of the Newcastle administration, and it is obvious that they had indeed sought to make him a scapegoat, well knowing that they could be criticized for reacting to Minorca's danger too late with too small a naval force. The public did blame the administration and, as we have seen, the administration disintegrated. Yet the public also blamed Byng.

The results of the court-martial had been eagerly awaited. It was presided over by one of the most humane, best loved and personally

[34] Walpole, *Memoirs of King George II*, II, 223.

respected admirals of the era. In the month of January daily reports of testimony were rushed from Portsmouth to London and published in newspapers. (The reporting was accurate – almost identical to the official record published soon after the trial.) Byng's performance as exhibited in print was hard to defend, and when the court's findings were announced there was no groundswell of indignation in the admiral's favour.

As for Byng's fellow officers, they had long before gained enough information to despise his conduct. Admiral Boscawen was deeply upset. 'Everybody knew the French were arming against that place long before he was ordered,' he wrote to his wife, 'so that if he is to blame, he is not the only person to be blamed.' But he blamed Byng too; the man consistently failed in his duty. He stayed at Gibraltar too long, assumed the situation at Minorca was hopeless, and failed to bring his flagship into the thick of the battle. 'My love, you cannot think how much this misfortune has afflicted me. What a scandal to the Navy, that they should be premeditated cowards that have been so long bred to arms.'[35] Although Byng had some defenders in the officer corps, notably Captain Augustus Hervey who was totally partial to him and helped organize his defence, most were shocked by his cautious, craven conduct. Still, not many favoured his execution. The professional view was that discipline did not require such severity, though some members of Parliament and pamphleteers said it did (thus giving rise, no doubt, to Voltaire's famous remark that in England it was deemed necessary to kill an admiral from time to time '*pour encourager les autres*').

The moral unacceptability of executing Admiral Byng has reverberated down the centuries. Malicious intent has been imputed to anyone who did not make an attempt to prevent it, and the outcome has been attributed to political calculations. Horace Walpole famously promoted such a viewpoint.[36] To be sure, the deadly charge had been drawn up by Lord Anson's Admiralty Board, but the court-martial was appointed after Anson left office and the appeal to save Byng's life was heard by a different board. It is true that the king, aware of the popular demand that *somebody* should be severely punished, did not wish to expose his son, Cumberland, and the ex-ministers to public wrath by issuing a simple pardon, but it is also true

[35] 'Boscawen's Letters to his Wife', 3 and 23 June 1756, Lloyd, ed. *Naval Miscellany* (cited in Chapter 5), IV, 218, 228.
[36] Walpole, *Memoirs of King George II*, II, 198–207, 209–13, 216–44. Walpole, who had attended the House of Commons proceedings assiduously, provides the most thorough account of them; he fervently supported Byng.

that George II was convinced that Byng was a coward. He said so to Lord Temple. Undoubtedly he recalled his own vehement reaction to Byng's defeatist letter from Gibraltar – 'This man will not fight.' – a prediction that appeared to be confirmed a mere three days later when news arrived from Paris that the admiral had failed to win the sea battle.

The king was not alone in perceiving cowardice. When Admiral Smith wrote to Lord Lyttelton begging him to use his influence in the cause of mercy Lyttelton replied:

I will only observe to you, that his not having shewn any symptoms of fear, when he was in scarce any danger, will not be sufficient to acquit him of cowardice in the sense of the law. His not going into danger, *when he ought to have done so, is that criminal* negligence *which the law has made capital.*

The law might be too severe, he added, but neither Smith nor the court presented sufficient reasons for overturning it.[37] The court was unable or unwilling to explain away evidence that displayed a consistent pattern of timidity and defeatism, and it is not surprising that although many people regretted the severity of the sentence, there was no great stir of public protest at the time it was carried out.

Pitt, George II and Germany

Lord Hardwicke had marvelled at the 'extensive and expensive' plans for the navy and North America projected by Pitt when he took office, but wondered whether the new administration would do anything to assist Prussia. Frederick the Great, in winter quarters, realizing that in the coming spring his forces could be overwhelmed, was asking for help from Britain. Hardwicke judged that without British assistance he would 'be forced to make his separate peace with the Courts of Vienna and Versailles', and added, 'and then where are we?'[38]

Pitt was disposed to assist Prussia. Despite his prior rhetoric about avoiding engagement in Europe, he could see the value of a militarily strong and capable continental ally, and Prussia met the requirements. Besides, if one ignored his diplomatic suggestions (most of them unwise), Frederick's

---

[37] George, Baron Lyttelton to Admiral Smith, 31 Jan. 1757 (Lyttelton's emphasis), Phillimore, ed., *Memoirs and Correspondence of . . . Lord Lyttelton*, II, 588. Smith, born out of wedlock but brought up by the family, was Lyttelton's half-brother.
[38] Hardwicke to Newcastle, 12 Dec. 1756, Yorke, *Hardwicke*, II, 379–80.

proposals were reasonable: establish an allied army in Westphalia to give the French pause, and conduct diversionary raids on the coast of France. George II and his Hanoverian ministers were already thinking of mobilizing 27,000 German troops to act as an Army of Observation. This figure counted the 8,000 Hanoverian soldiers in England who were ordered back to their homeland; 6,000 Hessians would be added. When the Hanoverian ministers mobilized these soldiers they were merely hoping to make the French understand that an attack might encounter opposition.

Nearly all British statesmen, whether in or out of office, wanted Britain to form an alliance with Prussia. Many saw this as the best way to defend Hanover while at the same time frustrating the French. Even Newcastle, long hesitant, swung round completely to supporting a Prussian alliance. On 25 January 1757 he wrote a private letter to G.A. Münchhausen, the leading minister at Hanover, telling him emphatically that it was the only realistic course of action. But the Hanoverian ministers made it clear that they were opposed to military cooperation with Prussia and George II agreed with them. If Frederick II had been in a position to commit troops to the defence of Prussia's isolated possessions near the Rhine, the British ministers might have been able to persuade George II that Hanover's true interest lay in aligning with Prussia. But when asked to commit 10,000 troops to the Westphalian front Frederick gave a vague reply, knowing that he must concentrate on defeating Austria and Russia.

George II's principal concern was to prevent Hanover from being pillaged. He wished to keep it neutral. Cooperation with Prussia would antagonize Maria Theresa and thus ruin any chance of this. The long-standing rules governing the constitutional relationship between the Electorate of Hanover and the Kingdom of Great Britain did not permit the British ministers to put pressure on George II with respect to Hanoverian matters. Therefore they could not forbid him to allow his Hanoverian ministers to discuss neutrality with Vienna, and their envoy at Vienna was already talking about it. If the envoy were to meet with success, the British ministers believed that Frederick would react by seeking a separate peace with France.

A British administration's only instrument of persuasion in this situation was money. Pitt could see that if George II was to overcome the defeatist attitude of his Hanoverian ministers he had to be given a subsidy. Pitt worked out an agreement with him and on 17 February presented it to the House of Commons. A grant of £200,000 was to be given simply 'to his Majesty'. In moving for its approval Pitt managed to give the impression that the money was designed to assist Prussia rather than Hanover, the latter being unpopular with many of his followers, as it had been with him. He pointed out the net cost would only be £100,000 because it was no longer necessary to pay the £100,000 subsidy to Russia. Aware that he was bound to be criticized for inconsistency, he asked those who would be startled by his new-found enthusiasm for supporting war in Germany to save their criticism for another day. He justified his decision by dwelling on Prussia, and by claiming that he 'never was against granting moderate sums of money to the support of a continent war as long as we did not squander it away by millions'[39] – an assertion that was hardly truthful. Nevertheless, the occasion was a triumph of speech-making and political craftsmanship. Not a peep of protest was heard, even from the Tories, and George II was thus given £200,000 to help pay for the Army of Observation.

If Pitt earned any gratitude from the king by this measure, it was decisively undercut by Henry Fox and the Duke of Cumberland. Fox had let the king know in early January that 'whenever it was proper, to drive out those gentlemen' he was ready to assist.[40] With tabloid impertinence *The Test* ridiculed everything the Pitt–Devonshire administration did and failed to do. When Pitt's appeal for a royal pardon of Byng caused his popularity to waver the king asked Newcastle whether he would be willing to form an administration alongside Fox. The duke answered that the time was not ripe: the Minorca inquiry first needed to be gone through and the year's supplies (parliamentary funding) for the war voted. Privately, Fox wished to exclude Hardwicke – otherwise, Fox calculated, he would be '*the* Minister' – but even without knowing this Newcastle was inclined to hold back.

Notwithstanding Newcastle's refusal, Fox and Cumberland urged George II to make a change. Hardwicke had predicted that the king would wait until the House of Commons voted the supplies, which was done in March. Near the end of the month George II as Elector of Hanover appointed Cumberland to be commander-in-chief of the Army of Observation and drew up his orders. Shortly before Cumberland was scheduled to depart for Germany he announced that he would not go if Pitt remained in office. The king knew that dismissing Pitt would cause an uproar, so he first dismissed Temple, hoping that Pitt would resign. Pitt declined to do so and the king dismissed him the next day, 6 April 1757.

---

[39] Clark, *Dynamics of Change*, p. 328.
[40] Newcastle reporting what he had heard to Hardwicke, ibid. p. 319.

The result was a political disaster. For the next three months there would be what Horace Walpole called an 'interministerium'. Although Fox and Cumberland surmised correctly that Newcastle was eager to return to office, Hardwicke persuaded him not to do it, arguing that if he joined Fox he would not be serving the king as he wished to think, but serving Cumberland. Since the crisis had been 'precipitated without reason or common sense', Hardwicke observed, the only explanation was that the king was in thrall to Cumberland.[41] Stock prices fell. Addresses of protest flooded Westminster, and 'for some weeks it rained gold boxes', as Horace Walpole remarked; the boxes conveyed the freedom of a dozen English cities to Pitt and also to Henry Bilson Legge who had resigned upon Pitt's dismissal. To be sure, the outpouring was orchestrated by Pitt's supporters, but it was not hard to do so: Pitt's popularity surged, along with a wave of revulsion against Fox and Cumberland. Noting that some members of Parliament were going off to their houses in the country at this time to avoid being solicited by Fox and his adherents, one who stayed behind wittily remarked to a friend: 'I begin to be afraid of walking the streets lest the press-gang for Ministers should seize me and force me into office.'[42]

The House of Commons inquiry into the loss of Minorca could not be scheduled before Byng's court-martial ended; no one wanted to see the Admiralty's authority undermined by requiring officers to answer Parliament's questions before they testified at a court-martial, as had happened twelve years earlier. The inquiry commenced on 19 April and lasted until 3 May. Byng having been executed, the focus was on the ex-ministers. In the end they went unpunished; findings and resolutions consistently approved by majorities forgave their mistakes. There was momentary danger for Anson. The last of the resolutions stated that 'no greater number of ships of war could be sent into the Mediterranean than were sent on the 6th April 1756'. Evidently, many members found this hard to swallow and an amendment was proposed stating the opposite. It was defeated 195 to 115, but the margin was close enough to suggest that it would not be wise to pursue a vote that would have implied full exoneration. Thus, as Horace Walpole acidly commented, 'the late Cabinet, to their great disappointment, were forced to sit down contented, without

---

[41] Hardwicke to Newcastle, 9 April 1757, Yorke, *Hardwicke*, II, 390.
[42] Sir Henry Erskine to George Grenville, 1 April 1757, *Grenville Papers*, I, 191; also Clark, *Dynamics of Change*, p. 359.

receiving the thanks of the House of Commons for the loss of Minorca'.[43] The sarcasm was appropriate because it was obvious that Pitt was adhering to his commitment not to push for a prosecution.

Yet in other respects the inquiry did not deserve Walpole's derision. Despite bushels of papers and boring recitals of data, more than 300 members attended to vote on the resolutions. The inquiry did what Pitt said it would do: it placed facts before the public (Walpole's claim that key facts had been withheld was probably not correct). Granted, the defence set forth its case in better order than the prosecution did; its materials had been prepared quietly over many months under the direction of Lord Hardwicke. Nevertheless, the published evidence when closely examined revealed the ex-ministers' failures. Although members of the 'late Cabinet' were not condemned by formal resolutions, their neglect was made visible.

Pitt, in reasonably good health, enjoyed exile at Hayes, while George II was miserable. With the inquiry over, the king hoped to persuade Newcastle to return to office, but his preference for Fox and Cumberland was too obvious. Newcastle therefore decided that he must side with Pitt and the party at Leicester House (which he normally detested) and remain temporarily aloof. Moreover, because the king had got rid of Pitt and was happy he had done it Newcastle knew that any arrangement which included the Great Commoner would be rejected. Weeks passed fruitlessly. Eventually, on 19 May, Newcastle and Hardwicke met with Pitt, but the result was discouraging. The offices that Pitt demanded for himself and his friends pointed towards solid control of the House of Commons and therefore to his domination of the government.

George II and Fox were glad to hear that Pitt was unyielding, seeing it as an indication that Newcastle would soon have to accommodate himself to their plans. Newcastle proposed instead a tentative plan of his own: he would act as sole minister, adding key persons as occasion offered. On hearing of this Hardwicke was greatly alarmed and told him it was a bad idea, an 'incomplete broken plan' that would bring nothing but degradation. Above all, it failed to surmount the basic difficulty which still rested 'where it was found to be in October last', namely finding someone other than Pitt or Fox to fill up 'the great void in . . . the House of Commons'.[44] Newcastle proceeded anyway, but he got cold feet when George II told him that Fox (who feared being set aside) must be

---

[43] Walpole, *Memoirs of King George II*, II, 254.
[44] Hardwicke to Newcastle, 1 June 1757, Yorke, *Hardwicke*, II, 396–7.

appointed to the Paymastership right away by royal authority and not by
Newcastle's recommendation. The king continued to find ways to ignore
the fact that Fox was more unpopular than ever, not only with the public
but with politicians who were considering their careers.

On 6 June Newcastle, Hardwicke, Pitt and Bute met together. Bute's
decision to attend stemmed from a realization that the king seemed
fully prepared to proceed with a 'Fox–Cumberland' ministry. Pitt now
moderated his demands. Newcastle went to the king the next day, telling
him he would not serve with Fox and that if he were to serve at all he,
Newcastle, would have to bring in his 'enemy', Pitt. George II 'dismissed
him in wrath'. When the House of Commons reassembled after a week's
recess on 10 June the members sat a whole hour in silence; there was
nothing for them to do. Two months had now passed under a caretaker
administration without leadership. In an emotional interview with Fox
the king begged to be saved from becoming 'a slave for life' to Pitt and
Newcastle. Thus compelled to construct a ministry Fox tried not to be
discouraged by the many refusals. Finally he put together a plan. The
climax came at the court at Kensington on 11 June when Fox was waiting on the king to receive the seal as Chancellor of the Exchequer; his
companions were with him in the anteroom. Formalities required Lord
Mansfield to enter the closet first to deliver a seal of office. The king,
having second thoughts, asked Mansfield's private opinion of Fox's
arrangements, and Mansfield, knowing that Fox must deal with a House
of Commons that would be extremely hostile to him, said frankly that
such a ministry would face immediate ruin. George II believed him and
ordered him to speak to Hardwicke and Newcastle about renewing talks
with Pitt. The rest was denouement.

Mansfield quickly turned over the mission of go-between to Hardwicke.
The retired Lord Chancellor's capacity for political finesse was now tested
to the full. The process began with a 'very disagreeable and painful' royal
audience. There were numerous meetings with Pitt and more audiences.
By 18 June the plan was settled: Pitt, Secretary of State for the Southern
Department; Holdernesse for the Northern (as before); Newcastle, First
Lord of the Treasury; Legge, Chancellor of the Exchequer; Barrington (as
the king desired) to continue as secretary at war; Anson, First Lord of the
Admiralty; Fox, Paymaster of the Forces.

The restoration of Anson was achieved fortuitously but with Hardwicke's
cunning intervention. Pitt thought that Anson bore heavy responsibility
for the loss of Minorca and did not want him heading the Admiralty. He

realized, however, that Temple was unacceptable since the king could not bear to be near him. When Hardwicke informed the king that Pitt's suggestion for First Lord of the Admiralty was Legge (who had been a junior lord of the Admiralty in the previous war), George II raised objections, and Hardwicke used the moment to ask whether Anson might be suitable, adding that he was 'far from knowing what the other persons would say to it'. The king quickly answered, 'I shall like it extremely.' Hardwicke reported this to Pitt and Bute as if the king had suggested it, a proceeding he described to his son-in-law as 'some honest dexterity'. Pitt assented, but of the many compromises he made the restoring of Anson was the least popular with the Tories and the City of London.[45]

This was the government that carried Great Britain to victory in the Seven Years War, yet at the time, 29 June 1757, Pitt came into office with deep misgivings, not because he doubted Britain's capacity to win the war, but because he wondered whether he would be allowed to try. The king plainly did not like him. Although Fox said he was satisfied, he remained an enemy who was not necessarily out of the picture and would probably return in strength if Cumberland were to achieve success in Germany. Pitt also knew that the king and Newcastle would press him to make commitments on the continent. Since his Tory supporters would react badly to such measures, his assent to them would amount to exchanging his popular base for dependence on Newcastle's, and he did not trust Newcastle. He remarked to Hardwicke, whom he did trust, that the final compromise amounted to 'a mutilated, enfeebled, half-formed system'. Hardwicke disagreed totally: 'I am persuaded it will come out a complete, strong and well-cemented one to which your wisdom, temper and perfect union with the Duke of Newcastle will give durableness.'[46] These were fine, flattering words – strangely optimistic about Pitt's temper – and as for 'perfect union', how could Pitt put out of his mind the turmoil of betrayal and intrigue that had preceded his restoration to office?[47] But the old man's prediction proved basically correct.

[45] Hardwicke to Anson, 18 June 1757, Yorke, *Hardwicke*, II, 403–5; Clark, *Dynamics of Change*, p. 444.

[46] Pitt to Hardwicke, 22 June 1757 and Hardwicke to Pitt, 25 June, Yorke, *Hardwicke*, II, 407, 409.

[47] The machinations during the twelve weeks appear even more unsightly when all the details are viewed, for which see Clark, *Dynamics of Change*, pp. 354–447.

The French invasion of Germany

During the winter of 1756–7 a large French army was assembling near the lower Rhine. Frederick II ordered his garrison at Wesel to be evacuated in March; the cannon were sent downriver to the Netherlands for shipment to a Prussian Baltic port. French troops had already taken possession of the great fortress when d'Estrées, recently elevated to the status of marshal, assumed command of the army in late April 1757. It appears that his instructions were to march directly eastwards, cross the River Weser into Hanover, occupy Brunswick as well, and then proceed to the Prussian fortress of Magdeburg.

Because of lack of fodder he could not begin his march across Westphalia until 21 May. The Prussians had carried off as much as they could, the new grass had not yet emerged, and, as always, there were not enough wagons. It did not help that the army was encumbered by the presence of 46 lieutenant generals and 65 other senior officers of the elite nobility plus princes of the blood – almost all superfluous. For the nobility the camp was a place to be seen, perhaps to find advancement. Each of these officers was allotted twenty or thirty horses. No other army of the time except possibly the Russian allowed so many elite super-numeraries to be in attendance or to be given such lavish allowances. Many of them spent their time criticizing d'Estrées in letters to friends and relatives at court. The commander-in-chief felt constrained about criticizing them, however, because some had very influential connections and he was already on bad terms with Paulmy. By 4 June d'Estrées's army numbered 61,000 and two weeks later he was at Bielefeld.[48] But provisioning arrangements for a further advance were not yet in place and Westphalia was not capable of supplying the huge army's needs. Provisions were more easily available in Hesse-Cassel and a portion of the army went there, but in Westphalia the progress was very slow. All the while, Marshal Belleisle was urging him to speed up, to be less methodical. In late June Versailles practically ordered d'Estrées to bring the Duke of Cumberland's army to battle.

Cumberland's voyage to Stade, at the mouth of the Elbe, took only six days. The Army of Observation of which he took command was soon joined by the 8,000 Hanoverian troops that had been in England. His orders were to monitor the French advance but not engage. He retreated across the Weser and concentrated his main force at Hameln on the east

[48] Waddington, *Guerre*, I, 405, 414.

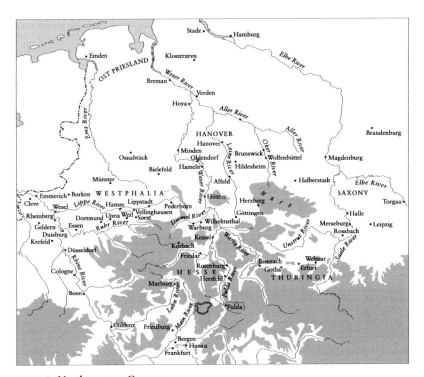

MAP 3 *North-western Germany*

bank. Near this place at a village named Hastenbeck, 130 miles from the Rhine, the two armies came to grips on 24 July. The battle lasted three days. Cumberland's total force numbered 47,000 or less, and when a large French reinforcement came up on the third day he wisely broke off, but he had chosen his terrain well and his soldiers fought admirably. In fact, d'Estrées was not sure he had won – his army suffered almost twice as many casualties (2,300 versus 1,400) – and the Hanoverians and Hessians did not think they had been beaten.[49] It was reported that they wished to make another stand, a plausible report since they were defending their Protestant homelands against occupation by an age-old enemy. But this was not done; Cumberland chose instead to retreat rapidly northwards, opening up a large gap between himself and the French.

The court of Versailles had already appointed the duc de Richelieu to take over the command. The Austrians had complained that d'Estrées

[49] Savory, *His Britannic Majesty's Army*, p. 38.

was not advancing fast enough, and Joseph Pâris Duverney, the *grand munitionnaire* responsible for provisioning the army, had been angered by d'Estrées's complaints of provisions shortages. (Duverney belonged to an inner circle that directed the war effort.) The people of Paris heard the joyful news of a successful battle at the same time as they heard that the victorious general was being replaced, and d'Estrées became a popular hero. Richelieu arrived on 3 August. A week later a detachment entered the city of Hanover unopposed. Hesse-Cassel had already been occupied, and Brunswick would soon capitulate. After resting a few days the main French force moved north.

In mid-August Cumberland proposed a suspension of arms. Richelieu replied that he must be joking, adding: 'My orders are to destroy the Electorate.'[50] Nevertheless, he did not follow closely upon Cumberland's heels, mainly because his army was experiencing the same shortages that had hampered his predecessor. Duverney urged him to push Cumberland out of Verden and Bremen without delay, saying at one point that the shortages must be imaginary. You 'cannot lack for subsistence', he wrote to Richelieu. 'I have the relevant figures before me, and these figures are more reliable than all the reasoning in the world.'[51] Reports from the field were trumped by office records – but before long Duverney was more understanding, especially after hearing that Richelieu was in possession of both Verden and Bremen, the latter on 29 August. The Army of Observation retreated towards Stade where provisions were limited and there were no transports for embarking the troops. Surprisingly, at this point Richelieu changed his mind and invited Cumberland to negotiate – an offer much welcomed by the latter. The resulting convention, arranged through the good offices of Denmark, was signed by Cumberland on 8 September and by Richelieu at Klosterzeven on the 10th. The terms restricted the Hanoverian army to Stade and the territory east of the Elbe, sent the Hessians home, and permitted the French army to remain in areas it occupied, which by this time included most of Hanover.

Richelieu's step took almost everyone by surprise, especially at Versailles which had not authorized him to enter into negotiations. But his motives were practical. He calculated that further operations in the northern extremities of Hanover would take too much time and use up provisions, and also feared that his opponent might be reinforced from Britain by sea.

[50] The king passed this on to Newcastle, Yorke, *Hardwicke*, III, 172.
[51] Duverney to Richelieu, 14 Aug. 1757, Kennett, *French Armies*, p. 102.

Besides, such operations would carry his army away from the direction it needed to go. His orders called for him to establish a base at Halberstadt (30 miles from Magdeburg in territory belonging to Prussia), which was south-east of his current location, and then, if possible, to go to the Elbe to threaten the Prussians. The convention of Klosterzeven afforded security to the troops left behind in Hanover. Duverney wanted Richelieu to establish winter quarters at Halberstadt because its environs afforded provisions in abundance compared to what could be obtained in the Electorate of Hanover.

Almost immediately after signing the convention Richelieu received word that a French army to the south might be in danger. This was a force commanded by Charles de Rohan, prince de Soubise. Versailles's decision to dispatch it – a second French military thrust into Germany – came in the wake of dreadful news from Bohemia. Thanks to a brilliant plan devised by two of Frederick's generals a large Prussian army had suddenly penetrated to the gates of Prague. In a great battle outside the city on 6 May 1757 Frederick defeated the Austrians. Louis XV, hearing that Prague was under siege and that capitulation by the inhabitants who would soon be starving was expected, felt that French strategy with its concentration on Hanover, to which the Austrians had strenuously objected, was failing his ally in a moment of crisis. On 26 May the king emphatically declared to his council of state that an army must go directly to the assistance of the empress-queen. It took time for this army under Soubise's command to be assembled, especially because it was to be joined to an 'Imperial army', that is, a force recruited from a myriad of principalities, large and small, of the Habsburg empire.

By the time Soubise's troops were ready to cross the Rhine (30 July) Versailles had known for a month that the rescue mission was no longer desperately required, since news reached Paris on 28 June that the Austrians had beaten Frederick decisively in the battle of Kolin (18 June), 40 miles east of Prague. Field Marshal Leopold von Daun showed himself on that day to be a far wiser general than Frederick the Great. The slaughter of Prussian soldiers was horrendous: 13,000 killed, two-thirds of them Frederick's best infantrymen. He was forced to withdraw from Bohemia. The question now was whether the Prussian army could recover soon enough to avoid being overwhelmed by its many opponents. Louis XV and Pompadour were eager to help Austria drive the Prussians out of Saxony. Rouillé, who had objected to Soubise's operation as wasteful and not in the interest of France, was replaced. The new foreign minister was Bernis.

During August, Soubise's force of 22,000 Frenchmen (8,000 of which had come from d'Estrées) proceeded eastwards and was joined by 11,000 of the Imperial army, commanded by Joseph Friedrich von Saxe-Hilburghausen. The latter was constituted commander-in-chief, but Soubise, with Belleisle's support, insisted on making all decisions governing the French force. There was no real military coordination between the two commanders nor, despite Versailles's earnest appeals, with the Austrian army. If the combined army wished to expel the Prussians from Leipzig and Dresden, the only Austrian contribution on which they could count for assistance was two cavalry units. When on 25 August this combined army approached Erfurt, 70 miles west of Leipzig, Frederick decided to confront it. The rapid Prussian thrust, especially by the cavalry, created mayhem. Soubise pulled back and called for help.

Richelieu responded to the call by telling Soubise that he would hurry to Halberstadt, where his troops would be only 30 miles from the Elbe. Frederick had anticipated Richelieu's move and sent a detachment of 7,000 men under an able general, Ferdinand, duke of Brunswick, to hamper it. Richelieu's 40,000 men were slowed down by the Prussian detachment and did not reach Halberstadt until 28 August. Sixty-five miles south of Halberstadt, Frederick, in mid-September, halted his pursuit of the combined army at Gotha and withdrew across the River Saale into Saxony.

Observers in London and Versailles expected Richelieu to assist an attack by the combined army on the Prussians, but in fact he decided to remain at Halberstadt where he could rest his troops and also make Frederick worry about his right flank. Richelieu's long march – 120 miles from Verden, 80 from the city of Hanover – had been exhausting. The men had been in the field for five months. Their boots were worn out, their health and discipline deteriorating. Harsh weather soon announced itself. By 1 October there was snow in the mountains; high winds were preventing the troops from sleeping at night and blowing tents away.[52] Richelieu judged that his tired army had accomplished its main mission: it had subdued Hanover and was well positioned to attack Prussia the following spring. Every officer at Halberstadt – even the Austrian military attaché – agreed that the army was incapable of further operations.

Duverney wanted Richelieu to choose Halberstadt for winter quarters, partly, no doubt, because the area belonged to the king of Prussia. The

---

[52] Reported by the comte de Gisors to his father, Marshal Belleisle, in a private letter, Waddington, *Guerre*, I, 553.

general granted that it afforded abundant provisions, but pointed out that the town's fortifications were minimal and easily approached, and the Prussian stronghold of Magdeburg was not far away. If Frederick were to force a battle, Richelieu argued, the advantage would lie with the Prussians who were more skilful in open-field manoeuvres; and if either side needed to retreat, the Prussian force could fall back on the fortress of Magdeburg whereas he had only Wolfenbüttel with an inadequate stock of provisions.[53] He was so worried about being attacked that he proposed to Frederick a truce until spring, which Frederick seemed willing to consider – at this point he could not even shield Berlin – but Versailles disapproved. Clearly, Richelieu was apprehensive. He would be wintering amid a hostile population deep inside Germany (Halberstadt was 200 miles from the Rhine) with Prussian forces only 30 miles away. He did not need Duverney's reminder that the country he was in was not Flanders. Letters went back and forth on the subject of winter quarters. Richelieu wanted to pull back to the Oker river and leave only light troops at Halberstadt, who would ensure that the inhabitants furnished provisions.

Richelieu realized that he must detach troops for Soubise's army (a personal letter had come from Pompadour). He had protested and delayed, but on the 5th knew he must send 12,000 men. Every general is inclined to avoid releasing troops to another's command, but in this case Richelieu had strong reasons for protesting. His troops were exhausted; his army, he reported, was 'lost, without power to recover for next spring when we need it, if it does not enter winter quarters promptly'. He wondered whether Soubise understood this. Writing to the younger general, he told him 'not to lose sight of the importance of conserving this army and of having one next spring', and added a historical reminder: 'Give thought to all the care that M. marshal de Saxe took at the end of campaigns.' He also wondered what Soubise might choose to do with the reinforcement. Would he press forward and risk a battle? Even if the troops were in a condition to fight and win, the season was late and the fruits of victory would not be easily secured. He urged Soubise to avoid a confrontation with the king of Prussia, since, given Frederick's reputation, it would involve 'much to risk, much to lose and nothing to gain'.[54] After he dispatched twenty battalions and eighteen squadrons he wrote to Duverney: 'I have done it to avoid all bothersome quarrels, and

[53] Ibid. I, 551.
[54] Richelieu to Duverney, 3 Oct. 1757, and to Soubise, same date, Waddington, *Guerre*, I, 543, 553.

to obey the king who desires it; but it is not possible to commit, in my opinion, a greater military blunder [*sottise militaire*].'[55] With his army thus weakened, Richelieu moved his main force to the Oker and Aller rivers for winter quarters.

A Hanoverian policy

By the second article of the convention of Westminster England was pledged to cooperate with Prussia in resisting foreign military incursions into Germany. Observing the ominous build-up of the French army on the lower Rhine in February 1757, Pitt, as we have seen, asked Parliament to grant £200,000 to George II to support the Army of Observation, which could be used both to defend Hanover and to protect Prussia from attack on her north-western border. He justified this proposal as a treaty obligation to Prussia, but it could also be viewed as contributing to the defeat of France. Joseph Yorke made the case in strong terms when the disappointing news of the Prussian defeat at Kolin arrived:

I am far from despairing upon it. I . . . think that as an Englishman our chief object is to give some diversion to France and that the king of Prussia by this war he has undertook employs the force that would be otherwise employ'd against us. The French will spend this year a great deal more than twenty Millions sterling, and it must be our Interest to keep them up to that Expence as much as possible, which can only be done by supporting the war in Germany.

To his father he argued that the diversion was worth keeping alive 'whether *beat or beaten*'.[56] Hardwicke and Newcastle while out of office had supported since January a policy of strengthening the Prussian alliance. Pitt agreed. When the campaigning season began everyone hoped to see a strong show of resistance by the Army of Observation; it might preserve Hanover and would certainly encourage Frederick II, but the Duke of Cumberland clearly did not do this. The French plan of war was thus allowed to go forward with minimal obstruction, and there was nothing the British ministers could do about it because policy in Germany was not in their hands. George II controlled it, and his goals were different.

---

[55] Richelieu to Duverney, 11 Oct. 1757, *Correspondance*, I, 247.
[56] Yorke to Newcastle, 5 July 1757, BL Add. 32,872 ff. 90–1; same date to Hardwicke, Yorke, *Hardwicke*, II, 411.

Members of the Pitt–Newcastle administration could not work out what was going on. Why, the ministers wondered, after Hastenbeck was Cumberland taking his army north towards Bremen and Stade instead of east towards Magdeburg (a few miles closer) where it could find greater safety by joining with the Prussians and be in a better position to inhibit French ravaging in southern Hanover? Joseph Yorke could not provide an explanation. His father considered the track of Cumberland's army a 'mystery' and lamented more than once that the London ministers were told so little. On 2 August when news of Hastenbeck arrived and Newcastle had asked Hardwicke for advice on what he should say to the king, the latter remarked: 'The opinions of the King's English servants seem to me to be asked as if you were to ask the opinion of your lawyer or physician, without fully stating your case to them.' He reminded Newcastle that he was not 'yet authentically informed' about anything pertaining to the battle or the circumstances of the army – or of course its commander's orders.[57]

Cumberland's instructions, dated 30 March 1757, had not been shown to any British minister. Written in German, signed by George II and counter-signed by the Hanoverian envoy in London, Philip Münchhausen, their intent was to keep Hanover from becoming a battleground and to avoid cooperation with Prussia. If the French army stayed south of Hanover, it was to be allowed to pass into central Germany without opposition – in other words, allowed to proceed undisturbed to attack the Prussians. If French troops invaded Hanover, Cumberland was not to carry his resistance to an extreme. He was advised 'to keep a retreat towards Stade open and free', where the Army of Observation was to retire and maintain itself. In all this George II was pursuing the policy preferred by his Hanoverian ministers.[58]

Fox wrote to Cumberland asking whether he desired British troops. The response: it would be 'inappropriate'. This answer from the Captain General of the British army who had first-hand knowledge of its personnel and knew he needed every competent soldier he could get, appears logical only when it is understood that George II wished to keep the task of defending Hanover entirely under his and Hanoverian direction. If British troops had been attached to the Army of Observation a different set of instructions, with input from Pitt, would have been required, and Pitt

[57] Hardwicke to Newcastle, 7 Aug. 1757, Yorke, *Hardwicke*, III, 164–5.
[58] For Cumberland's instructions see Charteris, *William Augustus, Duke of Cumberland*, pp. 252–5; and Dann, *Hanover and Great Britain*, pp. 112–13.

would have reacted vehemently to the idea of allowing the French army to proceed untouched to the Prussian border. Perhaps one reason why George II wanted Pitt dismissed was that he might, as a secretary of state, find reasons to demand to see Cumberland's orders.

Upon receiving the news of Hastenbeck the king, seeing that Hanover was bound to be overrun, quickly made up his mind to seek a separate peace for the Electorate. When Newcastle asked him about the bad effect this would have on the king of Prussia he replied that he 'could do nothing more for him' and would tell him so, but would not object if the British ministers wished to offer him something. Newcastle then spoke with Granville, Holdernesse and Pitt. All agreed that it was too late to send troops to Cumberland's army, and also agreed that the constitutional stipulations of the Hanoverian Succession disabled them from intervening; they could not block the king's plan for a separate peace because the British government had not formally offered Hanover any assistance (though informally it had provided George II as Elector of Hanover with a good deal of money). Pitt focused on the king of Prussia and said 'that *we* [British ministers] should forthwith send him . . . large offers of money in order to engage him . . . not to make peace, or at least not to give him a pretence to say that he is abandoned by England'. Hardwicke agreed, but was despondent: with Hanover neutral (but undoubtedly coming under French control) he was sure that Prussia could not avoid seeking peace. In his judgement the war on the continent was over, and he hoped there might be 'tentatives' leading to a general peace that would include Britain and France.[59] The terms, he realized, were bound to favour France.

George II hurriedly sent his son full powers to treat with Richelieu if he could. Pitt, however, was against this. He proposed that a further grant of £100,000 should be made to the king to help meet the expenses of Cumberland's army and also a grant to the landgrave of Hesse-Cassel whose territory was already under partial French occupation. On 5 September the cabinet resolved to ship provisions, forage and ammunition to the castle at Stade.

The British ministers all agreed that a separate Hanoverian peace was a bad idea. Hardwicke pointed out that it would not even achieve the king's obvious purpose of trying to save the Electorate from the ravages of the French army, since everyone was aware that the French intended to subsist their army on Hanoverian resources. In any case, a separate peace

[59] Newcastle to Hardwicke, 3 Aug. 1757; Hardwicke to Newcastle, 4 Aug., Yorke, *Hardwicke*, III, 160–5; BL Add. 32,872, fo. 442.

was dishonourable, as the king's invaluable confidante Amalie Wallmoden, Countess of Yarmouth, bravely told him. Nevertheless, George II authorized Hanover's envoy at Vienna to pursue it. He was so intent on avoiding Austrian displeasure that he would not allow his name to be attached to a single word of encouragement for the king of Prussia.

Like his cabinet colleagues Pitt had no knowledge of Cumberland's instructions, but when he heard on 9 September that a Hanoverian envoy was actively seeking a separate peace at Vienna and that the king was refusing to allow any word of royal encouragement to be sent to Prussia, he declared it to be a notorious 'breach of faith'. The English ministers must 'for the sake of their own honour, disculpate themselves', he said, and Holdernesse must write immediately to Mitchell 'giving the strongest assurances of support from England to the King of Prussia'. Pitt insisted that Hanoverian negotiations at Vienna be broken off, and he brushed aside the constitutional objection to giving advice about Hanoverian policy. 'For it is impossible', he said, 'for the ministers to serve on this foot.' Newcastle agreed.[60] With Pitt leading the way the ministers resolved that they must announce a British commitment to Prussia. Justification for interference in the king's Hanoverian policy was found in the fact the British government was directly paying for the Hessian contingent of the Army of Observation. This was a technical excuse, of course. The truly motivating consideration was the absurdity of George II's hopes, for there was no chance that Austria would agree to allow peaceful neutrality for Hanover; the empress-queen would happily do it if she could gain French approval, but that would be denied. Clearly, the ministers were determined to take over the direction of policy in Germany.

News of the convention of Klosterzeven reached London a week later. George II had authorized his son to accept a dispersal of his army and to pledge that if Hanover were granted neutrality, he would adhere to it as long as the war lasted. His hope was that the French would not occupy the Electorate. But the convention of Klosterzeven permitted them to remain, and when he saw this he flew into a rage. Since he had ignored the warnings of his British ministers that France's conquering army would undoubtedly insist on occupation, he now blamed Cumberland for allowing it to happen as if instructions had been disobeyed. He vehemently and openly denounced his son, and soon sent a letter of recall containing expressions unbearable for a military commander to read. Cumberland quickly sailed to England.

[60] Newcastle to Hardwicke, 10 Sept. 1757, Yorke, *Hardwicke*, III, 173.

Upon his appearance at court on the evening of 11 October George II greeted him by saying, 'Here is my son who has ruined me and disgraced himself.' Cumberland defended himself by mentioning orders he had been given and messages he had received, but this only made the king angry. After the brief and stormy interview ended, Cumberland quietly asked Lady Yarmouth to inform his father that he wished to quit all his employments including that of captain general; he was determined to sever all connection with the British army and retire to private life. Fox could not dissuade him. Hardwicke cautioned Newcastle not to be too hard on him – a commander who had been urged by the king to reach an accommodation under extremely adverse military circumstances. Pitt, too, defended Cumberland against the king's diatribes, reminding him that he had granted his son 'very full powers'.[61] It was a gentleman's act of justice to an arch-rival. For reasons of state, as the duke undoubtedly understood, the blame was bound to fall on him lest all Europe blame the sovereign of Great Britain.

Cumberland's treatment was quite unfair, yet not entirely so, for he had retreated too hastily, his harassment of the French after Hastenbeck had been too feeble, and his agreement to terms too prompt. Such conduct may have accorded with his father's private wishes but was contrary to British interests. For there could be only two reasons why the victorious French commander would suddenly agree to a suspension of arms and allow a beaten army to retire without completely surrendering. Either he judged his own army to be under supply difficulties and therefore too weak to keep up the pressure or he wished to hurry away to support the direct military advance against the Prussians that was in progress south of him. Newcastle and Hardwicke were sure that Richelieu's motive was the latter: 'For there could be no other reason for it', Hardwicke wrote, 'but what your Grace assigns, the enabling the Marshal to detach a considerable reinforcement to that Prince [Soubise]. How disgraceful will this appear in the eyes of the whole world?'[62]

It was indeed disgraceful. A way had to be found to persuade the king to compel his Hanoverian ministers to cooperate with Prussia. Fortunately, George II was at last asking advice from his British ministers; he specifically requested Hardwicke's. The first step was taken in a

[61] Sherrard, *Lord Chatham*, p. 242.
[62] Hardwicke to Newcastle, 19 Sept. 1757, Yorke, *Hardwicke*, III, 182. Newcastle's letter of 18 Sept. to Hardwicke upon the news of Klosterzeven shows how astute the duke could sometimes be when analysing a situation (III, 178–9).

cabinet meeting of 7 October where the ministers resolved to inform George II that if he, as Elector of Hanover, were to annul the convention of Klosterzeven, the British Treasury would supply the entire 'pay and charge' of the Army of Observation. But this would be done only after the troops became an active force; the payment was to start 'the day that they shall recommence the operations of war against the forces of France, in concert with the King of Prussia'.[63] George II accepted. The legality of breaking the convention was not a problem because Richelieu had technically violated it by ordering the Hessian contingent to be disarmed. Over the objections of the Hanoverian ministers, who still hoped for neutrality, the Army of Observation was ordered to duty, and the king was persuaded to allow the troops to join the Prussians if they could.

British policy in Germany was now in the cabinet's hands, but the outlook in October 1757 was dire. Although supplies were shipped to Stade, it was not clear that a Hanoverian army could or would be reconstituted; in fact, and thanks to Klosterzeven, it appeared that Richelieu's troops were free to join Soubise's in attacking Frederick. To the king of Prussia the British government could offer nothing but messages of encouragement and promises of financial assistance that would probably arrive too late.

Louisbourg and Lake George

While the British ministers were trying to cope with the consequences of Klosterzeven, dispatches from the commanding general and admiral in Nova Scotia were crossing the Atlantic announcing that they had called off the attempt on Louisbourg. Pitt had looked to its capture as a highly visible overseas conquest which would hearten the public and solidify support for his newborn administration, but the attack was not carried out.

He had tried hard to make it succeed. Back in January he had complained to the Duke of Devonshire about slowness of recruiting troops for America, which he blamed on limitations that Cumberland as captain general was imposing. He was frustrated by poor coordination between departments. Contrary winds in the Channel then compounded the delays so that the transports for carrying 6,000 troops from Cork, accompanied by fourteen ships of the line under Admiral Holburne, did not leave Ireland until 8 May, almost two months later than planned. The southerly

---

[63] Quoted in Dann, *Hanover and Great Britain*, p. 116.

route via Madeira was supposed to yield favouring winds, but the voyage was slow and the fleet did not reach Halifax until 9 July.

Lord Loudoun, after leaving 2,300 regulars and 5,500 provincials on the northern frontier, gathered 5,000 regulars at the port of New York in good time. They were expected to sail to Halifax in early June but were forced to wait when it was learned that a French squadron from the West Indies was on its way north. Sir Charles Hardy (now reactivated and promoted to rear-admiral) sent out frigates to scout, and after it was learned that the path was clear the transports sailed with only a small escort, arriving on 30 June. To their surprise Loudoun and Hardy found that the fleet and transports from the British Isles had not yet arrived.

Although they did not know it, eighteen French ships of the line were in Louisbourg harbour. If some of them had been cruising off Halifax, many of the transports from New York might have been captured. The French admiral had to consider, however, that a cruising squadron could be surprised by the unpredictable arrival of the enemy's battle fleet from England. Besides, his orders were to defend Louisbourg and preserve his ships.

Louisbourg was a fortress city built of stone between 1718 to 1738.[64] Three objects justified the expense: protection of the fishery; a harbour for trade, merchant shipping and privateering; and a naval base which could help defend Canada. In peacetime the fishery was the main concern. It brought greater profits to France than the fur trade and served to train expert seamen. In wartime Louisbourg's chief importance arose from its geographical position. It was not actually a 'bulwark' protecting Canada because ships going up the St Lawrence River could easily slip past. Nevertheless, because its fortified harbour enabled a battle squadron to be based near the entrance to the Gulf, any enemy expedition that went upriver might find its lifeline threatened. Loudoun's preferred plan proposed to bypass Louisbourg and go directly to Quebec, but it was risky and Pitt wanted no more 'misfortunes' in North America.

When Pitt returned to office at the end of June he received disturbing intelligence that a squadron under Joseph de Beauffremont which had left France for the West Indies in January was heading northwards. It thus appeared that the British naval squadron might be outnumbered, so he immediately asked Anson to send four more ships of the line to Holburne. They could hardly arrive on time, and, once again, the French navy had

---

[64] It has been attractively restored in the manner of Colonial Williamsburg, though not so extensively.

been deployed with greater imagination and cleverness than the British. Once again, as in the case of Minorca, the British Admiralty underestimated the likely opposing force and failed to provide fleet preponderance. This time, however, the fault did not lie with Anson, or with Pitt. While they were out of office word reached the Admiralty that four ships from Toulon had evaded the small squadron based at Gibraltar and sailed westwards. Since the British intention to attack Louisbourg or Quebec could not be disguised, it had to be presumed that the French would try to concentrate a naval force at Louisbourg and that Beauffremont would be heading north for the summer, but after receiving the report from Gibraltar on 28 April the Admiralty dispatched only three more of the line to Halifax. Worse, the Admiralty was unaware that Du Bois de la Motte departed from Brest on 3 May with nine ships of the line. There had been a lapse in the Western Squadron's coverage – not uncommon, but the failure to keep a frigate or two off Brest to report the departure of ships that were known to be fitting out was inexcusable. Those nine ships formed the crucial component that foiled the attack on Louisbourg. All in all, between late May and 20 June, five ships from Saint-Domingue, four from Toulon and nine from Brest found their way to Louisbourg – eighteen ships of the line, three of 80 guns and five of 74.

During the weeks following his arrival at Halifax, Holburne was prevented by contrary winds and heavy fog from sending a frigate north to count the ships in Louisbourg harbour. Fragments of information suggested, however, that the French were there in strength, and on 4 August intelligence from a captured vessel confirmed this. Holburne and Loudoun were already worrying about the calendar: even if a landing were successful, three weeks would be required to get the siege equipment ashore and brought within range of the fortress. The operation might therefore extend into late September when it would become hazardous for the fleet to remain offshore. The most compelling argument for cancelling the operation, however, was the size of the French squadron, not because it might come out and challenge a British squadron that was approximately its equal – that was unlikely – but because British warships dared not enter the harbour against so great an opposing force. In addition to the French fleet's firepower its sailors, totalling about 13,000, were available to assist the garrison, and of course the British could not stay long enough to starve it into submission (Louisbourg had, in fact, been well supplied with provisions). Holburne recommended cancelling the attempt and Loudoun quickly agreed. Most of the 12,000-man army at Halifax sailed back to New York.

Eastbound voyages in the North Atlantic were generally swift and the letters reporting the decision reached London in four weeks, on 30 August. The ministers were shocked, and Pitt entertained a suspicion of treachery. Hardwicke read the packet of letters with a lawyer's eye and concluded that Lord Loudoun 'might be a very good colonel but was absolutely unfit for command'. Why, he asked, did they lose 'almost a Month at Halifax in doing nothing, except repairing a mast or two?' He continued: 'In short, it seems to me that they all proceed upon the *Byng principle*, – that nothing is to be undertaken where there is risk or danger . . . Not an officer or a soldier was to be landed at Mahon because there would be danger in it. So now of Louisburg.'[65] When he wrote this Hardwicke was not aware of the size of the French fleet in Louisbourg harbour. The decision made by the general and the admiral was correct. A costly failure was likely.

Holburne was determined, however, to make the French pay a price for bringing a large fleet to America. He blockaded Louisbourg on 23 August. But a month later his cruising squadron was hit by a hurricane. The storm's intensity peaked at night, and a south-west wind pushed the squadron towards the rocky shore. The wind shifted to the south-east just in time to avoid a complete disaster, but by morning's light on 25 September the admiral could count only seven ships that still had all their masts. One ship had been driven ashore and two-thirds of its crew somehow survived to become French prisoners. The French ships, in harbour, also suffered but only three were disabled.

Du Bois de la Motte might have sailed out to seize some crippled British ships, but his orders were defensive and his crews sickly. Seven of Holburne's ships stayed to winter at Halifax; the rest got home safely after making minor repairs. The French admiral, waiting to get one last ship repaired did not sail until 30 October. The Admiralty directed the Western Squadron to intercept him, but his ships made it safely into Brest on 23 November with a loss of only two frigates.

Seeing Loudoun's departure from the New York frontier, Montcalm went on the offensive. He knew that 5,000 British regular troops had been withdrawn for the expedition to Louisbourg, so in July his men laboriously hauled twenty-two guns, two howitzers, and two mortars up the portage road at Ticonderoga to Lake George (its level 225 feet above Lake Champlain's). Each artillery piece, some of them captured from

[65] Hardwicke to Newcastle, 5 Sept. 1757, BL Add. 32,873, fo. 469; Yorke, *Hardwicke*, III, 171.

Braddock's army and at Oswego, was placed aboard two bateaux lashed together. Three-quarters of Canada's military force was gathered for the operation; 2,600 French regulars, and 3,100 Canadian militia and *troupes de la marine*. Montcalm was joined by other leading French and Canadian officers: Lévis, Bourlamaque, Rigaud, Marin, Langlade and Longueuil. In addition, there were almost 1,700 Indians, an unprecedented number to accompany a military operation. About 800 had come from mission villages and 900 from the wild and distant north-west. Montcalm's objective was Fort William Henry. This operation was not a small affair and its preparations should have been discovered, but the French had the surrounding area blanketed with Indians, who frightened off British scouts.

By the early days of July the British garrison learned from escaped prisoners and deserters that a French attack was being prepared. There was an urgent need to discover its size and forwardness, but scouting parties failed to get close enough to find out. On 23 July Colonel John Parker with 300 men in whaleboats, mostly New Jersey provincials, rowed north on Lake George to take prisoners and gain information. He had no idea of the danger. Utterly exposed to detection, his flotilla was swarmed upon by Indians in canoes. Only about a third of the men managed to escape by fleeing to a far shore and running through the woods. Upon receiving their harrowing report Major General Daniel Webb, the acting commander-in-chief, came north to Lake George to consult with Fort William Henry's commander, Lieutenant Colonel Monro of the 35th regiment. Monro's garrison consisted of 1,500 regulars, but some were recently recruited in America and untested. Webb provided him with 1,000 more men – 122 Royal Americans, the rest provincials. Returning to Fort Edward, Webb wrote an urgent letter on 30 July to the governor of New York asking him to dispatch militiamen immediately; similar letters went to the New England governors.

The French attacking force numbered over 3,800 plus Indians. There were not enough bateaux to permit everyone to advance upon the lake, so a 40-mile march by 2,600 men under Lévis through difficult terrain along the western shore was necessary. It took three days, and the arrival of canoes and bateaux at the south end was timed accordingly. On the morning of 2 August, sentries at Fort William Henry looking out upon the lake saw a spectacular and terrifying sight: hundreds of canoes approaching them in a line abreast that extended from shore to shore.

Only 500 men could be fitted inside the fort; the remaining 2,000, mostly provincials, defended a camp 700 yards to the east on high ground fortified by timber ramparts. Montcalm courteously suggested surrender, but Monro, expecting reinforcement, refused. The siege began the next day. The fort itself resisted well, and the camp was competently and bravely defended by its provincials, refuting Lord Loudoun's dismissive opinions in both instances. Although shells from the enemy's howitzers took a considerable toll, the main problem for the fort's garrison was the overheating of its guns: the iron ones burst or split; altogether eleven of twenty-one became useless. Monro's urgent appeals to Fort Edward for guns and men got no reply – or, rather, Webb's reply of 4 August was intercepted by the French, held by Montcalm for three days, and then presented to Monro with a renewed suggestion that he surrender. As the French commander could not fail to notice, the letter was extremely disheartening.

Evidently, General Webb believed a captured Canadian's word that the attacking force numbered 11,000. His letter explained that delays in mobilizing militia forces made it impossible to send assistance and advised Monro to 'make the best terms' he could.[66] For this decision Webb has been unfairly pilloried. The number of provincials available at Fort Edward on 4 August is unclear, yet it is certain that there were too few to resist the French attack, and most were inexperienced. If the relief force were annihilated in an ambush, Fort Edward would be lost and the French could easily move down the Hudson to raid and burn Albany.

By the morning of 8 August the French had built a forward siege battery. French casualties had been very light, and the British regulars had lost only 20 killed and 27 wounded, but Monro and his officers, despairing of reinforcement, decided that evening to discuss terms of capitulation. The terms Montcalm offered were generous and were accepted. British and American survivors, 2,300 in all, were to march the next morning to Fort Edward with their possessions including firearms, but without ammunition. They would be escorted by French and Canadian officers. They would remain on parole not to bear arms for eighteen months. Montcalm would look after the sick and wounded and send them along when recovered. In return British America was to return all French prisoners within three months. Montcalm's army would of course seize all serviceable ordnance, ammunition and provisions.

Indians hovered about as the march of the prisoners commenced, and mayhem soon erupted. Indians slaughtered many of the sick and wounded, and threatened women and children, whom no one had arranged to protect. They then fell upon the rear of the column to take scalps. Some British and

---

[66] Steele, *Betrayals*, p. 103.

American soldiers broke and ran despite the dangers that lurked in the woods. The massacre lasted less than five minutes, but Indians continued to seize prisoners until Montcalm and his officers stepped in to stop it. Montcalm promised the Indians that he would recompense them if they gave up their prisoners. In the coming months Canadian authorities made a genuine effort to recover those who were taken away.

French officers blamed the massacre on the ungovernable savagery of the wild tribesmen from the upper Great Lakes and lamented the presence of so many of them. No doubt, the recruiting calls for these men from the *pays d'en haut* had yielded greater numbers than expected – reports of success at Oswego evidently enticed them – but it is clear that Montcalm desired their presence. After capturing and scalping Parker's men many of them wished to go home, but Montcalm called a meeting and urged them to stay. As he realized, their great numbers, if properly coordinated by experienced men like Marin, Langlade and Longueil, gave him absolute dominance over communications in the region. They had prevented the British and Americans from viewing his preparations, and thanks to them Fort William Henry was scarcely able to communicate with Fort Edward.

The trouble was that the Indians, especially those from the western Great Lakes, had come to plunder, to take scalps as badges of manhood and prowess, and to seize prisoners for service or ransom. Surrender terms that allowed defeated soldiers to march away with their belongings astonished them. They considered this arrangement absurd, and when they saw it actually being put into practice, they felt deprived of what they came for. Perhaps Montcalm did not expect their reaction, but it can hardly have been unforeseen by the Canadian officers who were present.

Considering the great size of the French attack force and the way the preparations were kept secret, it would have been difficult for the British to save Fort William Henry. Nevertheless, Lord Loudoun was seriously negligent. Granted, he was preoccupied by the task of preparing the campaign against Louisbourg, and of course after he sailed from New York in mid-June there was nothing he could do. Yet he remained the commander-in-chief in North America, responsible for the New York frontier, and he knew better than anyone that it might be in jeopardy, for one of his principal arguments in favour of a direct attack on Quebec, bypassing Louisbourg, had been that it would draw French forces away from the New York border.

In the light of Pitt's rejection of this strategy, what measures did Loudoun adopt for the defence of northern New York? In the spring, realizing that the number of troops on the frontier might be insufficient, he informed the governors of New York and New England to keep militiamen 'in readiness to march at an hour's warning'. The militia would therefore not be activated until needed, a method that saved expense. The obvious question was whether a militia force could be mobilized in time to march to the point of attack. Timely knowledge of French preparations and prompt action by the theatre commander would be essential. Loudoun knew that Webb was slow-witted and suffering from illness. Sir Charles Hardy had watched him at close quarters and mentioned to Loudoun that he could 'neither read nor write a page without its making his head turn round so that he did not know what he was doing'.[67] The other major general in America was James Abercromby, who was more intelligent and energetic, but Loudoun decided to take him to Louisbourg.

A lapse in Loudoun's strategic thinking is also to be noticed. Montcalm and his officers were bound to find out that Louisbourg was the expedition's initial objective. They could confidently estimate how long it would take a British force after capturing Louisbourg to reorganize its supplies and equipment, re-embark, enter the Gulf, and accomplish the tedious passage upriver to Quebec, 800 miles in all. When a British assault force entered the Gulf a report would be sent Montcalm who could order his troops from Lake George 300 miles downstream to Quebec in plenty of time. Loudoun should have realized this and given Webb practical advice on how to organize a defence of the frontier, but instead he seized upon an unverified bit of intelligence. It was a report from Montreal that the French were 'now drawing their whole Force to Quebec, for the Defence of their Capital'. In his last letter to Webb, apparently dashed off on 20 June while his ship was heading out to sea from New York, he suggested that Webb might think about attacking the French! The letter said nothing about precautions Webb should take in case the intelligence proved false.[68]

Just one day after Connecticut authorities received Webb's urgent summons, their militiamen began heading for Fort Edward, more than half of them on horseback.[69] As early as 12 August, 4,200 were at Fort Edward with more arriving daily as New York and Massachusetts also

---

[67] Qutoed in Pargellis, *Lord Loudoun*, p. 234.

[68] The letter is printed in Pargellis, ed. *Military Affairs*, pp. 370–2.

[69] Harold E. Selesky, *War and Society in Colonial Connecticut* (New Haven, 1990), pp. 109–10.

answered the call. Fort William Henry had capitulated, but the militiamen contributed to the safety of Fort Edward: Montcalm gave it as one reason why he chose not to proceed further south. Yet he was also worried about the harvest and released his Canadians from active service almost immediately after the surrender so that they could return to their farms. His regulars stayed a week to destroy the fort. Everyone at Fort Edward saw the vivid orange glow of the bonfire of destruction 15 miles to the north which confirmed that the French were pulling back.

The British were fortunate. Far away at Halifax when he heard of the surrender at Lake George, Sir Charles Hardy feared that the entire area would have to be evacuated, 'and we must content ourselves with Albany for a Frontear, if the Progress of the Enemy can be stopped there'.[70] But a looming food shortage in Canada combined with caution on the part of Montcalm had limited the damage. Webb was able to send the militiamen home. In Britain the events at Fort William Henry had little impact. Word of its loss and of the massacre reached London six weeks after the bad news about Louisbourg came from Halifax, but when it was realized that the French had not pushed further south the strategic consequences were considered tolerable. Indeed, the next year the British would undertake an assault on Fort Carillon as if the demolition of Fort William Henry made little difference, though the destruction of its boats and bateaux would in fact cause delays.

Among American colonists and British army personnel in America, however, the massacre was keenly remembered; it was taken as proof that the French were countenancing Indian savagery. The proof was far less clear than people at the time thought, but the episode has echoed down the years in American and Canadian history, partly thanks to James Fenimore Cooper's classic novel, *The Last of the Mohicans: A Narrative in 1757* (1824). Only in the early twentieth century did it begin to slip from public memory. For a long time the commonly accepted number of deaths in the massacre was 1,500, but the most careful and recent estimate puts the figure between 70 and 184.[71]

---

[70] Hardy to Loudoun, 24 Aug. 1757, Pargellis, ed. *Military Affairs*, p. 397.

[71] This includes only those permanently lost (dead or never ransomed) as a result of the post-capitulation massacre; it excludes British and American losses from Parker's fatal expedition and during the siege. Final provincial casualties, greatest among the New Jersey contingent, are especially difficult to trace because quite a few of the missing were returned by the French. See Steele, *Betrayals*, pp. 133–44.

The Rochefort expedition

When the Pitt–Newcastle administration was on the point of entering office Newcastle wrote to Hardwicke, 'Mr Pitt must seriously think of Foreign Affairs in a different manner from what he has hitherto done, or the K. of Prussia will make his separate Peace; and we shall lose the Electorate this year, and God knows *what* the next.'[72] The immediate occasion for this comment was Frederick's request for a naval squadron to be sent to the Baltic, and the duke was aware that Pitt was not inclined to agree to it. At first glance, his reluctance is surprising. Clearly, he was anxious to keep Prussia in the war and also understood that naval assistance was a popularly acceptable way to help a beleaguered ally, as opposed to the highly unpopular step of committing British troops. Britain, as Pitt knew, had regularly used its navy in past wars to assist continental allies. Yet he refused to send a squadron to the Baltic.

He gave his reasons in two long letters to Andrew Mitchell, British minister to the king of Prussia. These were written by the Northern secretary of state, Holdernesse, but undoubtedly dictated by Pitt. In the second letter Pitt conveyed his understanding of a fundamental principle of British grand strategy:

I am convinced that you will agree with Me in one Principle, that we must be Merchants while we are Soldiers; that our Trade depends upon a proper Exertion of our Maritime Strength; that Trade and Maritime Force depend upon each other; and that the Riches, which are the true Resources of this Country, depend chiefly upon its Commerce.

Pitt followed this up with a promise to deliver some of these 'true Resources' to support Prussia's war effort. Monetary assistance, he warned, was the only type that Prussia could expect. As for naval assistance, Britain's warships were fully engaged in 'defending the British Dominions' and 'protecting the Trade', and would also be employed in covering 'a Number of Land Forces considerable enough to alarm the Coasts of France' to make the French think of protecting their shores and not just campaigning in Germany. The king of Prussia, Pitt argued rather dubiously, would 'find more Relief from these Operations, which may be performed with safety to the King's British Dominions, than from the uncertain and precarious Efforts of a Baltick Squadron'. He even claimed that 'distant Operations in America' were 'of at least as much

---

[72] To Hardwicke, 26 June 1757, BL Add. 32,871, fo. 407.

Consequence' as other operations in securing Prussia's ultimate goal, 'a safe and honourable peace'.[73]

The king of Prussia was upset by this letter, and by the first letter too, which had set forth the grounds for refusing to send a battle fleet to the Baltic. Frederick II wanted this fleet in order to make it harder for Russia to land troops and supplies on Prussia's north coast. Whether men-of-war could operate effectively in the shallow coastal waters was doubtful, but there was certainly the risk of an armed confrontation between Russia and Britain. All British statesmen wished to avoid this, for Russia supplied Britain with naval stores and was by far the best source of hemp. There was also a danger that neutral Denmark, which possessed ships of the line and was already annoyed by British efforts to deny her merchant ships the right to carry goods for France, might join Sweden, an ally of France, against Britain. Consequently, a British Baltic fleet would have to be large enough to overawe three potential naval enemies. It is strange that Newcastle, supposedly expert in diplomacy, seemed to set aside these considerations, but Pitt did not.

Before the disastrous battle of Kolin, Frederick, always lavish with strategic advice, had recommended raids on the French coast as a means of restraining French military commitments in Germany. Pitt used this as an excuse for planning an amphibious raid on Rochefort dockyard. On 14 July he obtained the cabinet's approval for this secret expedition. Sixteen ships of the line and twelve frigates were to escort sixty-five transports carrying ten battalions (over 8,000 troops) to Basque Roads. The troops would be rowed ashore and then proceed a few miles overland to the dockyard; they would burn the ships, storehouses and works, then re-embark. In strategic terms the moment was perfect. Most of France's active navy was overseas, mainly at Louisbourg.

Newcastle had assented to the cabinet's decision, but he wanted the troops to join Cumberland instead. Aware that cancelling a seaborne operation 'in order to send the Troops to the Duke's Army' would be highly unpopular, he hoped that the expedition might be 'thought hazardous and almost impracticable by the Generals (as it certainly is, and, as I am informed by my Lord Anson, both [Admirals] Hawke and Knowles think it)'. He tried to persuade military experts to oppose it.[74] Sir John

---

[73] Holdernesse to Mitchell, 17 July 1757, BL Add. 6,815, ff. 34–43. See also Doran, *Andrew Mitchell and Anglo-Prussian Diplomatic Relations*, pp. 144–50.

[74] Hardwicke to Newcastle, 22 July 1757; Newcastle to Hardwicke, 25 July; BL Add. 32,872, ff. 300–1, 320–1.

Mordaunt, the general appointed to command the expeditionary army, was, in fact, extremely sceptical and raised numerous questions. Anson and Sir Edward Hawke, the admiral selected to command the supporting fleet, exhibited their usual caution about the prospects. But Sir John Ligonier, the cabinet's senior military adviser in the absence of Cumberland, answered the doubters' questions with firmness and sound advice, and preparations were pushed forward quickly and efficiently.

The preparations could not be concealed, but the destination was a well-kept secret and the French had no idea where the blow would fall. It could occur anywhere in the Channel or Bay of Biscay. Moreover, French defence had to rely on land forces because so much of the navy was across the Atlantic. There were twenty ships of the line at Brest, but shortages of stores and seamen allowed only ten to be made ready – far too few to confront the British squadron. The expedition left Spithead on 8 September. Word of its departure provoked alarm along the entire French coast.

By 22 September, though delayed by adverse winds, the sizeable armada was anchored in Basque Roads. The first objective was the small, fortified island of Aix in the midst of the roadstead. Ships generally avoided gunnery contests with stone forts, but coastal defence batteries were seldom manned by experienced gunners. On the 23rd the *Magnamine* led the approach to the little island with just three men on the open deck: Captain Richard Howe, a pilot named Joseph Thierry (a Huguenot) and the helmsman. When the fort opened fire the 74-gun ship made no reply until she was 50 yards away. She then unleashed a devastating broadside, and she was soon joined by the *Barfleur*. The fort's defenders stopped firing almost immediately as the gunners took cover and lay down. After 45 minutes the commandant surrendered, despite little damage and few casualties among his 600 men.

That afternoon Colonel James Wolfe, quartermaster for the expeditionary force, climbed atop the fort's highest bastion. Six miles to the north-east he could see the coastal village of Châtelaillon. To the east lay the point and fort of Fouras which guarded the entrance of the Charente River. In the distance beyond, 12 miles up the winding river, stood the naval dockyard. Learning of the surrender of Île d'Aix, the inhabitants of Rochefort expected the enemy to be soon upon them; buildings, timber and stores as well as the thirteen warships under construction and repair or moored in the river would probably be set afire. The town itself seemed in danger (but the expedition's orders did not call for its destruction).

That night and early the next morning Rear-Admiral Brodrick with three navy captains rowed close to shore to survey the terrain, and when

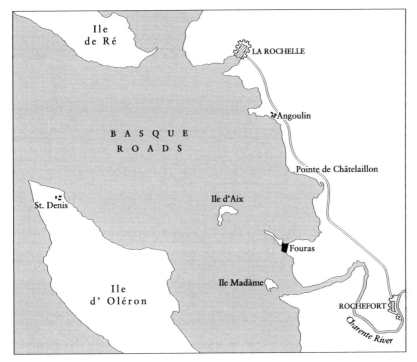

MAP 4 *Basque Roads and Rochefort*

Hawke read their report the next day he agreed that the small bay next to Châtelaillon was the best landing place. From there the troops could move along a good road through open country to the dockyard, 11 miles away. Hawke had already worked out a detailed landing plan in which he assumed it was 'more than probable' that the troops would 'only be opposed by Militia which may easily be dispersed'.[75] Shallow water would require the transports to lie a mile and a half off the beach but the seamen could row that distance without undue strain. Two battalions of marines would be responsible for securing the beach. A potential hazard that was *not* present thanks to the sheltered roadstead was the possibility that a strong gale from the west might force the fleet for its safety to leave the anchorage while the troops were ashore.

Upon receiving Hawke's recommendation Mordaunt exercised the right specified in his instructions to call a council of war. It convened the next

[75] Mackay, *Admiral Hawke*, p. 169.

morning, the 25th. The generals and admirals agreed that a landing was possible, but then the generals (Mordaunt supported by Generals Henry Seymour Conway and Edward Cornwallis) wondered whether the town could be entered by escalade if the ditch surrounding its walls was flooded. The council summoned Lieutenant Colonel Robert Clerk, an engineer who had viewed the place in 1754 and had been a key consultant for the expedition's planning. He could not assure them that the ditch remained as dry as it had been three years before. They also worried that numerous soldiers might be lurking behind the dunes where the landing would occur. They asked Hawke if he could guarantee re-embarkation a few days after landing in case it suddenly became necessary, to which he answered that he could unless the wind came strong from seaward and stirred up a heavy surf. The meeting lasted all day, the only conclusion being that the town could not be taken by escalade. The possibility that the town wall might have gaps – in fact it did – was not considered. Hawke had already ordered the transports to stand nearer to shore with boats in readiness, but the order to proceed was never given because the generals spent the entire day in a conference discussing reasons why they should not land the troops.

It seems clear that they had made up their minds before they reached Basque Roads not to carry out the landing. No other explanation of their conduct is possible, for nothing had interfered with, nor did new information cast doubt upon, the feasibility of the plan. Actual conditions – a mild land breeze, spring tides and clear moonlit nights – were unusually favourable. The only unforeseen factor was the length of the boat journey, but it was for the navy to decide whether it was a serious problem. It was learned much later that the generals' fears of the unknown were groundless: the ditch was dry; Rochefort's amateur defenders were filled with dread and despair; the scattered soldiers visible along the shore were mostly untrained militiamen, fewer than 4,000 in number. (There is a story, probably apocryphal, that the French area commander kept dressing them in different regimental uniforms to make a show of strength.) For two days conditions remained ideal for landing the troops as the weather held, but the generals wasted them studying alternatives.

Hawke was furious. At a second council of war on the 28th he bluntly stated that the troops should attempt *something* and the generals must decide what it should be; he would 'readily assent to any resolution they should come to, and assist them to the utmost of his power'. He and the three other naval officers then walked out. This ultimatum had an effect, and a night assault on the fort at Fouras was planned, but the generals learned that wind and tide would allow only half the force to be landed in one push and gave this as their reason for abandoning the project. The next day Hawke informed the army commanders in writing that if they had 'no further military operation to propose', he intended to take the fleet to England.

The fleet was back at Spithead by 7 October and not one soldier had got his boots wet. The British public erupted in anger. At first, Pitt was inclined to accept the popular conspiracy theory for this fiasco. Newcastle reported, '[He] is outrageous upon it; is not angry with the officers, but imputes it to a prevailing opinion that neither the King nor the Duke [of Cumberland] wished success to this expedition, treated it as a chimera of Mr Pitt's, which must miscarry, in order to show that the only practicable thing to be done was to employ our whole force in *a German war*.'[76]

Although Newcastle and Hardwicke had originally preferred that choice, Hardwicke, after he read the reports of the councils of war, shared Pitt's anger: 'It puts an end to all one's Patience. The Land-officers seem to me to have copied Lord Loudoun's Precedent . . . In short, the whole appears to me to proceed upon the *Byng-principle*, that nothing is to be attempted where there is any Danger or Hazard. . . . The accumulation of Reasons in the first Council of War is no more than was known and deliberated upon, before they sailed.' (He had attended those meetings.) In fact, he observed, the prospects had turned out to be more favourable than had been expected because the French were so obviously unprepared.[77] Newcastle joined Hardwicke, Hawke and Anson in taking Pitt's side. He heard that some people – had he not been one of them? – had insinuated that 'the Expedition was Chimerical and Impracticable, and the Production of *a Hotheaded Minister*. This is industriously given out, [but] . . . here Mr Pitt will stand his ground. And he is greatly supported in it, both as to the practicability and Infinite Consequence of the Expedition, by Sir Edward Hawke and My Lord Anson, and I own, I think with great Reason.'[78]

The claim of 'Infinite Consequence' might seem puzzling because the project not only failed to accord with Newcastle's previous opinion but also runs contrary to the common historical verdict which has been that the expedition was useless from the beginning since it could not be launched in time to draw French troops away from Germany. This latter point was

[76] Newcastle to Hardwicke, 8 Oct. 1757, Yorke, *Hardwicke*, III, 187.
[77] Hardwicke to Newcastle, 9 Oct. 1757, BL Add. 32,874, fo. 489.
[78] Newcastle to Hardwicke, 15 Oct. 1757, BL Add. 32,875, fo. 124.

true. Although some French forces near the Channel were temporarily detained, and Swiss guards were pulled from their comfortable duty at Versailles and urgently marched to the Loire to go downriver in barges (they arrived after the British left), no troops were withdrawn from Germany. The valid justification of the expedition was in fact naval. There were only two royal dockyards on the French Atlantic coast, and Rochefort was one of them. Hardwicke commented: 'I always thought, the only sensible principle of the Secret Expedition was to gain an opportunity of destroying the Docks and Magazines, and the Men of War, in the Port of Rochfort [*sic*], which the French would not give you a Chance to do by meeting you fairly at Sea. This was an important Object.' His assessment was confirmed by the information that came in from France. It revealed how great a blow materially and morally a successful raid on the dockyard would have been. Joseph Yorke at The Hague wrote to his sister, '[A]ll our Enemies provoke me every day by saying it could not have failed, and that all the Magazines, etc. at Rochefort were at our disposal, if our People had chose to give themselves the trouble of taking them.'[79]

Pitt soon discarded his notion that the king and Cumberland were to blame and switched to another conspiracy theory: he attributed 'the Behaviour of the Land Officers . . . to a formed Design in great Part of the Army against Him'. Either he or Sir John Mordaunt, he told Newcastle, 'must be tried'. Hardwicke agreed that there must be an inquiry. How to undertake it was a problem, however.

Regardless of whether there was a 'formed Design', senior army officers would inevitably try to shield their brethren from punishment. George II knew this. 'The King says, and rightly,' Newcastle reported, '. . . [if we] refer it to a Court Martial, or Board of General Officers, they will do as they did in Genl. Fowke's case, and then things will be worse than ever. . . . The Officers concerned are all Men of Great Quality, Rank, and Distinction, and of Extreme good Characters.'[80] Mordaunt's father had been a lieutenant general and his brother was the Earl of Peterborough; Conway was the Earl of Hertford's brother and a groom of the bedchamber; Cornwallis's father was a peer and his wife a daughter of Viscount Townshend. Although aristocrats dominated the officer corps of every army of Europe, the problem had an openly political aspect in Britain. Practically every senior army officer was related to a family member or a

---

[79] Hardwicke to Newcastle, 9 Oct. 1757, BL Add. 32,874, fo. 489; Yorke to Lady Anson, 21 Oct., BL Add. 35,389, fo. 28.

[80] Newcastle to Hardwicke, 15 Oct. 1757, BL Add. 32,875, fo. 124.

patron in the House of Lords, and many sat in the House of Commons (where army officers outnumbered navy by about three to one); Mordaunt, Conway and Cornwallis were all members. Hardwicke had already mentioned the problem to Newcastle: They 'are Men of Families, and have great and extensive alliances. I could add one thing more, that the *Clan of Inactives* is, this year, a numerous Clan; and they will all join to support and excuse one another. Upon the whole this Clan is so great, that I think it is to give over warring: I reflect upon nobody, but I see nothing is done in any quarter.'[81]

Mordaunt requested a board of inquiry into the conduct of both the land and sea officers. Hardwicke, after consulting with Mansfield and Anson, told Newcastle that it was a bad idea, not least because army officers would be judging naval, and in any case it would be difficult to find officers willing to accept the assignment. Also, such a board would inevitably be drawn into evaluating the whole scheme, and if Mordaunt and his fellow generals had decided against landing 'not upon any material new Incidents, but upon their judging a thing *wrong* that the King and Ministers judged *right*', their offence constituted a strong breach of orders and the excusing of it would be intolerable. 'I own', Hardwicke continued, 'I could well approve the King's breaking some of them (perhaps one would be sufficient) without an enquiry, by his own authority. . . . If the case be as it is represented . . . Cromwell would have sent them to the Tower, immediately upon their landing, as he did Penn and Venables.'[82] The ministers did not want an inquiry in the House of Commons – it would create further political turmoil – so a board of three high-ranking generals was appointed to inquire into the causes of the expedition's failure. This actually proved useful (the detailed report was published) and it did not excuse Mordaunt. Its most important findings were that no evidence existed then or since of 'a Body of Troops or Batteries on the Shore, sufficient to have prevented' an attempted landing, and that Rochefort's 'posture of defence' did not change after 'the Expedition was first resolved on in England'.[83]

Before the report was published numerous letters came from France which suggested that the raid would have succeeded. The conduct of Mordaunt and his colleagues appeared all the more inexcusable, yet it

[81] Hardwicke to Newcastle, 9 Oct. 1757, BL Add. 32,874, ff. 489–90.
[82] Hardwicke to Newcastle, 24 Oct. 1757, BL Add. 32,875, fo. 255. He was referring to an event that occurred a hundred years before.
[83] *Report of the General Officers*, p. 58.

seemed equally apparent that they would escape punishment. Pitt was incensed. He did not fail to note the contrast between discipline in the navy and the army. Admiral Byng had been shot, he reminded Newcastle, but the generals who had shied away from their duty at Rochefort 'are *about.* [They stand] behind the Kings Chair at the Opera.'[84] In December in a thunderous speech to Parliament he said that 'nothing could be well, till the Army was subjected to the civil power'.[85] But when Mordaunt was tried by a court-martial the generals and colonels observed that his orders did not absolutely require him to attempt a landing. Thus a necessary flexibility of orders was used to acquit him. This, however, was not the end of it. Pitt with the cooperation of Newcastle and Hardwicke would find a way to minimize the possibility that operational commands would be given to army officers who might be inclined to favour 'the Byng principle'.[86]

[84] Memorandum, 28 Nov. 1757, BL Add. 32,997, fo. 297.
[85] 14 Dec. 1757, Walpole, *Memoirs of King George II*, III, 3.
[86] See Chapter 10.

CHAPTER 9

The tide turns, 1758

On 5 January 1758 Lord Hardwicke, while attending a family gathering at Anson's home, began writing a long letter to his son Joe at The Hague. Six weeks earlier, in close consultation with Pitt, he had composed the King's Speech, delivered to Parliament on 1 December 1757. It spoke of the 'late signal success in Germany' – a victorious battle that Frederick the Great had fought at Rossbach – which had 'given a happy turn to affairs'. Parliament was urged to consider offering appropriate support for the king of Prussia. The speech did not ignore the 'disappointments' of British arms, but looked forward with 'firm confidence' to a future vindication of 'the spirit of bravery of this nation'. At Christmastime Hardwicke had received a letter from Joe reporting news of a second Prussian victory, this one in Silesia. Joe had commented that the outlook was brightening, but on 5 January his father did not share his optimism. He began with a pessimistic assessment of the king of Prussia's situation. Even with the help of British money, Hardwicke asked, how could he 'keep up, for any length of time, a force sufficient to encounter the three great Powers of Europe united against him?' It seemed impossible. Besides, the Army of Observation remained in disarray. But the old lawyer was most upset by the lack of achievement upon and across the sea. He continued:

Turn your Eyes to the Ocean and to the other side of the Globe. These we have taken for our proper Department, and what have we done in it? Even when I ask myself this Question alone in my Closet, I [blush] for my Countrymen. At sea no one Expedition or Project has succeeded against the Enemy's Fleets or Places, nor have our Cruizers met with any of their squadrons. Vast Equipments and prodigious Expences ending in nothing but disappointment to our Measures, Disgrace to

our Army, and Loss of our Honour. Officers instead of executing, have
employed themselves in [trying] their Orders, and seem to have made
it a Rule in the art military that nothing is to be attempted where there
is Danger or Risque. If, with some [persons] at home, this should be
a Merit and Recommendation instead of Demerit, what will become
of such a Service? If I could see hopes of wiping out these stains in
our Reputation, that is the only thing that would make me look with
patience on the Prospect of continuing the war; for it would be an
eternal Reproach to this Country, once so famous for their military
virtue both at sea and land, that History should tell Posterity that
the War of 1755 ended without any one . . . [success] performed by
Great Britain.

The king of Prussia, he added, might contrive to win a few more battles
before becoming completely worn down, but what good would it do?[1]

In fact, however, there were developments pointing toward a brighter
future. Prussia's two victories in the final weeks of 1757 were not only
signal successes but destined to have important consequences. The first,
at Rossbach, would lead to a dramatic military turnaround in Germany
and a severe degradation of French military capability. The second, at
Leuthen in Silesia, would bring devastation to the Austrian army. Within
a few months a firm British alliance with Prussia would be signed. On
the oceans the Royal Navy was, at last, about to acquire overpowering
superiority. On 'the other side of the Globe' British arms had already
achieved a momentous success in India. In North America (which Hardwicke
probably meant by 'the other side') conditions of warfare were changing
in Britain's favour, and an altered method of selecting operational commanders was about to be introduced that would enable a recovery of
Britain's military reputation. (The changes affecting North America will
be considered in the next chapter.)

Finally, a growing imbalance of financial capability would soon become
obvious. Pitt's war plans could not be implemented without copious
amounts of money. He called for a larger navy, more regular troops,
more provincial forces in America, and subsidies to support allied armies
on the continent. His sense of urgency inspired the House of Commons

---

[1] Hardwicke to Joseph Yorke, 5, 10 Jan. 1758, BL Add. 35,357, ff. 221–5. The son's
letters from The Hague have survived, but practically all of those addressed
to him have disappeared. This letter, a rare exception, survives as a rough draft in
Hardwicke's compact hand and is almost illegible. Words appearing in brackets are
my best guess.

to vote the funds. The estimated total for 1758 was £10,486,457, a third greater than the 1757 figure. Newcastle at the Treasury was staggered by the anticipated expense. Nevertheless, despite his complaints, he was aware that the funds could be easily borrowed, for he had to admit: 'There is plenty of money in the City at present, and a great inclination to lend it.'[2] This proved to be true. Four million pounds were instantly subscribed for a fifteen-year loan at $3^1/_2$ per cent, a rate not much higher than what was usual in peacetime. In contrast, the French army and navy would become victims of serious money shortages. The French government chose to shy away from introducing new taxes and instead raised money by expedients. So long as it could envision a short war this was acceptable, but a major military disaster in Germany took the prospect of a short war away.

The French army in Germany: defeat and disaster

At the time when the duc de Richelieu urged the prince de Soubise to end the campaign and think of winter quarters, he urged him not to risk an engagement with Frederick's army, pointing out that nothing permanent could be gained by a victory so late in the year. To the war minister, Paulmy, he wrote: 'I persist in thinking that there is nothing good to be done that would justify the risks that would be run.' Yet he strongly suspected that when Soubise received the 12,000-man reinforcement he would not heed this advice, nor would the leadership at Versailles restrain him. Richelieu sensed that the court did not really believe his troops were immediately in need of winter quarters. 'I am worried to death', he commented to Duverney, 'that the necessity of it is not enough felt, and that the Court of Vienna drags us along.'[3]

The Austrians were indeed urging the French to keep the campaign going. They were proposing that Richelieu should threaten the Prussians along the Elbe and Saale rivers. They wanted Soubise and the Imperial army to expel them from Leipzig and Dresden. They did not, however, plan to assist by concentrating an army of their own in the area; their eyes were on Silesia. If Richelieu and Soubise did decide to press on, a 15,000-man Austrian force positioned somewhat east of Saxony was scheduled to join the effort, but only then. As matters stood, the Austrian contribution

---

[2] Newcastle to John Page, 26 Nov. 1757, BL Add. 32,876, fo. 137.
[3] Richelieu to Paulmy, 6 Oct. 1757, Waddington, *Guerre*, I, 556; to Duverney, 3 Oct. 1757, ibid. 543.

was two cavalry units loaned to the Imperial army. Paulmy and Bernis protested. Since French troops had marched a very long way to get to the scene of action, the Austrians should make good use of them instead of campaigning in Silesia. Paulmy reminded Vienna through the new French ambassador, comte de Stainville (soon to become duc de Choiseul), that Richelieu could not be counted on to advance. As for Soubise's recently augmented army, Paulmy said that he hoped that it would 'force the king of Prussia to go back across the Saale' but would not attempt to go further this year unless it could rely on the presence of an Austrian force of 30,000 men.[4] The Austrians were unmoved, and the opportunity for an allied concentration against Frederick in Saxony was missed. Annoyed perhaps because the French had insisted on invading Hanover, the Austrians chose to pursue their own priority of conquering Silesia.

During October Soubise was in direct communication with Stainville, who forwarded Vienna's calls for action to him. He was also receiving letters from his close friend Pompadour, who is known to have wished that he could win a victory that would earn a marshal's baton. More immediately he was being prompted to move forward by Hilburghausen, also in direct contact with Vienna. He did not follow the commander-in-chief all the way to the Salle, but stayed not far from him. For his own part, Soubise wished to be optimistic. He managed to believe that Frederick's army was weak and in retreat. He told Stainville, 'we shall take solid and assured positions on the Saale, and we will be masters of Saxony without running any risk'. To Paulmy he remarked that it would be shameful, after receiving reinforcements, to draw back and do nothing.[5]

The combined army under Hilburghausen permitted Frederick to cross the river unopposed while it consolidated for action. Near the village of Rossbach, when Soubise brought his forces down from high ground under the mistaken impression that the Prussian army was retreating, Frederick saw his opportunity. He positioned his artillery on a patch of elevated ground and hid his cavalry behind another slope while arraying his infantry lines in a V-formation. The French infantry foolishly attacked them in broad and compact columns and were devastated by Prussian artillery and musketry. When the troops broke and ran Prussian cavalry slaughtered them. It was a relatively short battle, but the imbalance of casualties was astonishing: Frederick had an army of 22,000; it killed,

---

[4] Paulmy to Stainville, 17 Oct. 1757, ibid. I, 545–6.
[5] Soubise to Stainville, 24 Oct. 1757, ibid. I, 611–12; to Paulmy, 2 Nov. 1757, p. 616.

wounded or captured 10,000 opponents, who had numbered 34,000 (about half of the casualties were prisoners including 11 generals), while the Prussians lost a total of 550 dead or wounded. Rossbach was Prussia's most lopsided victory of the war and perhaps the most humiliating military defeat suffered by France in the eighteenth century. In retreat the combined army split. The Imperial force fragmented, while Soubise's troops headed north-west towards Hesse and would not stop though Frederick was not in pursuit. The men took to widespread marauding and many deserted. Claude Louis, comte de Saint-Germain, an able and respected general, could not control them.

Despite strong advice from Richelieu and Duverney not to risk an encounter with Frederick's army, Soubise had done it. The last instructions he received from the war minister before the battle told him to avoid putting his army at hazard but did not rule out a 'prudent' engagement.[6] In broad context the ultimate responsibility for the debacle must rest with the king and Pompadour. They had called for Soubise's army to be strengthened with troops from Richelieu's. They wished not only to bring glory to French arms but also to please Vienna, even as Vienna was resolutely employing its main army elsewhere. The decision to reinforce Soubise's army was truly a *sottise militaire* – an encouragement to engage an experienced opponent under circumstances that were far from promising. The king and his mistress were playing with fire. Other battles during the war would see greater numbers killed or captured, but Rossbach was truly decisive. It opened the way to a catastrophic overthrow of French arms in Germany.

Five days after the battle Frederick took a moment to answer a request made by Andrew Mitchell. The British government had been asking whether he could appoint a Prussian general to be commander-in-chief of the Army of Observation. He chose Ferdinand of Brunswick, brother of the reigning duke. Ferdinand was willing to accept the appointment but insisted that in matters of strategy he must have a free hand, and on larger questions of policy he said he would be answerable only to the king of England. This was exactly what the British ministers wanted and in due course he was informed that he should communicate directly with a British secretary of state. Although the officers and soldiers of this army were all German, almost its entire cost was to be borne by the British Treasury, and it acquired a new name: His Britannic Majesty's Army in

---

[6] Paulmy to Soubise, 23 Oct. 1757, ibid. I, 613.

Germany. Pitt soon insisted that any Hanoverian minister who continued to seek neutrality should be dismissed.[7]

Ferdinand headed north immediately to take up his command, arriving at Hamburg on 23 November 1757. The landgrave of Hesse-Cassel had learned of the appointment a week earlier and immediately countermanded an earlier order, prompted by the convention of Klosterzeven, for the Hessian troops to come home. The duke of Brunswick's men who were marching home in keeping with the convention were intercepted by a body of Hanoverian troops and turned around. Thus, remnants of the former Army of Observation were already concentrating by the time Ferdinand was on the scene. Although he could muster only 8,000 healthy soldiers, he judged that he must attack to avoid being confined to an unproductive area near the coast and perhaps lose access to the port of Stade. He tried to cross the Aller river near Celle in mid-December, but the French destroyed all the bridges and he had to withdraw.

Richelieu happened to be pulling out of Halberstadt when he heard the news of Rossbach. His aim was to firm up the occupation of Hanover for the winter. After repelling Ferdinand's attempt to cross the Aller, his best option was to counter-attack because the small enemy force was bound to become stronger among friendly inhabitants and would acquire money and supplies by sea from Britain. But Richelieu did not think his malnourished and demoralized troops were capable of it. His reluctance appears to have been a mistake, yet it is unlikely that Ferdinand would have made a stand and difficult to see how French troops could have long remained in the northern sector where provisions and forage were scarce. Richelieu's army, numbering 75,000, but reduced to fewer than 60,000 by sickness and other losses, was spread widely, the greater part of it in winter quarters along the Aller from Verden to the Oker and in a line from Minden to Brunswick, each stretch extending about 60 miles; there were detachments in the ports of Bremen and Emden.[8] As Ferdinand waited in the vicinity of Lüneburg to restore the health of his troops, receive money from Britain, and look for promised reinforcements from Frederick II, the French army's ability to winter safely in Hanover was becoming problematic. It was situated in the midst of a hostile population and cantoned over a wide area. Food and shelter were growing scarce,

---

[7] Newcastle's notes of a conversation with Pitt, 16 Feb. 1758, BL Add. 32,997, ff. 342–3.

[8] A report dated 12 Jan. 1758 provides personnel figures, Waddington, *Guerre*, I, 683.

and local officials, having heard about Rossbach and the rebirth of the Hanoverian army, were becoming resistant to cooperation.

Sensing Versailles's loss of confidence in him, which undermined his authority over subordinates, Richelieu tendered his resignation in January, and it was promptly accepted. He left Hanover on 8 February 1758, ten days before his replacement arrived. The new commander-in-chief was a favourite of Pompadour's, Louis de Bourbon-Condé, comte de Clermont, a prince of the blood who was also a lavishly rewarded man of the church. He had chosen to follow a military career, however, and had studied and served accordingly.

Versailles remained confident of the army's superiority and security, and was planning to send 24,000 troops to Bohemia under Soubise early in the spring. At first Clermont shared this confidence, but when he arrived in Hanover on 18 February he found corruption, poor leadership (a quarter of the officers had taken leave), misery and demoralization. The army was living day to day – no money, its credit sunk, men and horses falling ill, and practically nothing done to fortify key locations.

Just as Clermont was trying to get his bearings Ferdinand struck. Bolstered by cavalry loaned by Frederick, he brought forward 35,000 men with artillery. Verden had not been made defensible and was evacuated on 20 February without care being taken to destroy the bridge over the Aller. At nearby Hoya the French tried to prepare a strong defence. This time, although the bridge (over the Weser) was barred and then burnt, the garrison was surprised from the rear; it was outwitted by Hanoverians who crossed the river on boats and rafts at a point further north while their comrades fired on the town from across the river. The cavalry assigned to patrol the area failed to report the enemy's presence on the western side. Hoya's surrender on the 24th cost the French 700 casualties. Also lost were considerable stores of food and fodder, supplies that helped Ferdinand's winter campaign to keep up the pressure.

The French now had to withdraw from their eastern cantonments in Brunswick and Hanover. Despite efforts to carry away supplies and burn depots the evacuations were done hurriedly, and Ferdinand's forces captured significant amounts. Clermont intended to use the Weser as his line of defence and called for the main army to assemble at Hameln, near Minden. But the unexpected loss of Hoya was unsettling. The comte de Saint-Germain, afraid of being surrounded, evacuated Bremen, marching his substantial garrison to Osnabrück. When Ferdinand's forces gathered to besiege Minden on 5 March Clermont decided to make a stand, but snow and ice rendered reinforcement of the town difficult, and although he had promised the garrison's commander that support would be coming, he never gave the required orders. Minden surrendered on 14 March. The terms were shameful; they protected the officers and their baggage while allowing 3,400 troops to be made prisoners.

Meanwhile, Clermont decided that the line of the Weser could not be held. Saint-Germain had sent him advice resembling Richelieu's advice to Soubise, namely that the army was in such miserable condition that nothing worthwhile could be accomplished until it recovered.[9] Both French generals were oppressed by fears that Ferdinand's forces were close by and ready to strike almost anywhere; they also worried about sudden thrusts by Prussian cavalry. In reality Ferdinand's operations were being slowed by seasonal flooding, but Clermont imagined that the siege of Minden might be a ploy to hold his attention while the Hanoverian army with Prussian cavalry raced behind him and took control of the Lippe river and other routes westwards. He urged the remnants of Soubise's force to evacuate Hesse and soon decided, despite pleas from the king and Pompadour, that his own army must retreat to the Rhine. By the end of March this was done. Clermont established headquarters at Wesel, but within a few days most of the troops crossed to the west side for safe winter quarters. In a period of just six weeks the great army abandoned Brunswick, Hanover and Westphalia. Thousands of sick soldiers were left behind. Ferdinand's expertly conducted winter campaign has received little historical notice, yet it was, as Sir Reginald Savory has remarked, 'a triumph of will-power, improvisation, and endurance . . . without equal'.[10] But it was also a triumph over an exhausted and disorganized opponent.

At this point the opposing generals rested their armies, but there was a skirmish at Emden. A small British squadron under Commodore Charles Holmes had been off the coast all winter, and on 18 March two frigates in the Ems estuary got past the defending batteries. The next day Emden's garrison (2,500 French, 1,100 Austrians) began to withdraw. The British sailors pursued with an armed cutter, intercepted two of the boats, and took some prisoners. When news that they had gained control of Emden reached England the cabinet had to decide whether British troops should be dispatched to hold it. Since the port's usefulness for supplying Ferdinand was obvious, 2,200 were soon sent. These were the first British troops to serve in Germany in this war.

[9] Saint-Germain to Clermont, 4 March 1758, Waddington, *Guerre*, II, 29–30.
[10] Savory, *His Britannic Majesty's Army*, p. 66.

Why had everything gone wrong so disastrously for the French army? Versailles tended to blame Richelieu. The army's lack of food and its indiscipline were said to be his fault. It was true that he had kept for himself some large payments that the citizens of Hanover and Brunswick made to gain protection from marauding. Regulations held that such money was to be turned over to the monarchy's agents who would then give the commander a share. He thus set a bad example which was readily imitated by other officers, and money that might have bought provisions was diverted. Without doubt Richelieu greedily enriched himself in Hanover, and at Versailles it was convenient to make him a scapegoat for the failure of the whole campaign. The story that the soldiers called him '*le bon Père la Maraude*' was circulated at the time of his removal from command.[11]

Nevertheless, the idea that Richelieu's greedy conduct was the chief reason for the army's distress is not to be believed. The troops had been healthy enough to march rapidly to Halberstadt, and all the officers were agreed that this march (in cold, rainy weather) was the main cause of their exhaustion, sickness and low morale. Duverney had insisted that food and forage should be obtained by local impositions and that the troops should continue to find their provisions by this method, while Richelieu and his officers protested that impositions did not work. They wanted contractors employed so that provisions came to the troops, not the other way round. The use of contractors increased costs and Duverney was anxious to save money, but as all military men knew, the line separating impositions and marauding was easily crossed.[12]

Versailles's emphasis on corruption and marauding obscured a key fact: although there were considerable supplies of food in depots (though not forage), these places were not made safe. The army in Germany, dispersed as it was, required fortified places of refuge in case of attack. Richelieu had emphasized the need for security and gave it as a reason for going into winter quarters promptly. Plans existed for fortifying certain strong points, but they were not carried out. This may have been partly the general's fault; perhaps he failed to exert enough pressure on subordinates, but in any case both money to hire workers and time were lacking. To say the least, the French army was not prepared for Ferdinand's winter offensive.

[11] Barbier, *Journal*, VII, 16–17.
[12] See especially Rousset, *Gisors*, pp. 268–9, 273.

Richelieu should not have left Hanover before his replacement arrived, but the court should not have so eagerly accepted his offer to resign. It was a terrible moment to replace an experienced general who had become familiar with his army's problems and surroundings with an inexperienced one who, though intelligent and well meaning, arrived with no idea of the situation and had no time to learn how to deal with it. During the entire retreat there was only one battle, at Hoya, and that might not have gone so badly for the French if the local cavalry unit had followed some basic rules of reconnaissance such as taking care to make surveys from high ground and reporting immediately the enemy's presence.

In reality, Clermont faced a management problem. His army was widely dispersed, so communications were as vital as they were difficult. He was in the midst of a hostile population, so risks had to be run to gain intelligence of the enemy's movements. He ended up groping in the dark. Should he have made a stand at Minden? Winter campaigning required specialized knowledge, and in any case, everyone around him seemed to agree that his sickly, weary and disorganized troops could not prevail against Prince Ferdinand's, who were healthier and better supplied. The French army's fundamental problem was the inadequacy of its administrative arrangements for campaigning in Germany, in any season. Almost from the beginning it was ill supplied, and when Ferdinand's counter-offensive caused depots to be lost, no assistance came from France, not even money.

Viewing the situation from Versailles and Vienna, critics wondered whether Richelieu, if he had pushed his men forward to the Saale instead of lingering at Halberstadt, could have enabled the combined army to succeed against the Prussians and thereby obviated the need for a strong defensive posture in winter quarters. To be sure, if Saxony had come under allied control, security would have been easier to arrange, but without Austria's cooperation that goal was out of reach. Richelieu's assessment of the risks and rewards appears valid: only a crushing victory over the Prussians could have guaranteed safe winter quarters to an exhausted French army.

Until the end of February very few at Versailles considered the French army's situation to be serious. There was much greater concern over the plight of the Austrian army. At first, its offensive in Silesia had been highly successful. But eight days after Rossbach, Frederick pushed eastwards, and on 5 December his army of 40,000 met 50,000 Austrians at Leuthen (10 miles west of Breslau). Prussian quickness defeated an incompetently commanded Austrian army. The Prussians lost 6,300 dead or wounded, but the Austrians lost 10,000 dead or wounded plus 12,000 taken prisoner. This great battle, which was made possible by Frederick's victory at Rossbach, produced a complete reversal of Austria's success in Silesia, as the Austrian garrison at Breslau numbering 17,000 surrendered soon afterwards. Thereupon the Austrians suffered, like the French, grievous losses during a long winter retreat. By the time the retreating remnants of the empress-queen's army were secure in Bohemia the losses may have amounted to a half, perhaps three-quarters, of its manpower.

Bernis was shocked by the news from Vienna. Unlike others at court, he suspected that the French army, like the Austrian, was in serious trouble and doubted that it could remain in its German winter quarters. On 6 January he therefore urged Stainville to try to convince Kaunitz that the war must stop; he stated his view of the situation succinctly: 'The Empress without an army, and the French between the king of Prussia and the Hanoverians, without subsistence.' In any case, he warned, France would have to cut back her contribution to the alliance. A week later he sent a military plan for the coming year; it revealed how little he was prepared to assist the Austrians if Maria Theresa wished to continue fighting: the only troops France would send her would be German and Swiss mercenaries. As for the French 'army of Hanover', part of it would be assigned to protect French coasts against English raids; the rest would be formed into corps of observation on the Weser and Rhine. Kaunitz and Maria Theresa did indeed wish to continue the war. She believed that Prussia was a danger to European security as well as her empire, and told Stainville that she would fight on regardless. She hoped that France would not abandon Hanover and would also prepare to launch a new campaign in support of the alliance.[13]

When Stainville's dispatch reached Versailles Bernis asked for a meeting of the council of state. Louis XV attended (on 8 February) and his words were decisive. It was agreed that Maria Theresa would be supported to the hilt: 'the king is resolved', the message to Vienna stated, 'to make war, not only this campaign with all his forces, but also to continue it so long as the safety of his allies and the interests of the alliance require it.'[14] All subsidies would be fully paid, and an army of 24,000 troops would be dispatched to Bohemia as soon as possible. An order soon went to Clermont directing him to detach 10,000 men to serve in that army.

---

[13] Bernis to Stainville, 6 Jan., 14 Jan., 7 April 1758, Waddington, *Guerre*, I, 732, 735; II, 423.
[14] 9 Feb. 1758, ibid. I, 742–4.

Within a fortnight, however, Versailles learned the truth about the condition of Clermont's army. All letters coming from it (Newcastle's informant at the French court reported to London) 'are filled with Lamentations of the epidemic Distemper that reigns among the Troops, and sweeps off great Numbers. It is computed that above 10,500 have died from the lst December to the 10th February.' There were 22,000 in hospitals; some regiments had fewer than half their men.[15] By mid-March, Marshal Belleisle, who had just replaced Paulmy as war minister, was admitting to Clermont that the only choice was to withdraw to the Rhine.[16] On 6 January Bernis had written that the 'grand project' that seemed infallible in the early days of September was now just 'a beautiful dream'. By the end of March the dream was completely shattered. The army that had conquered Hanover was ruined. Louis XV would soon be compelled to recognize that he could not keep his promise to send 24,000 troops to Bohemia.

War in India: Bengal

Near the end of September 1757 Lord Hardwicke received a personal letter from Calcutta written by Robert Clive. It reported two British successes in Bengal: recovery of Calcutta and capture of the nearby French base at Chandernagore. Six weeks later when responding he remarked, 'I wish I could in return send you an account of any success of our military operations in this part of the world, equal to what you have obliged us with.' He congratulated Clive on his 'signal victory' over superior numbers at Chandernagore and noted the 'assistance of so able a sea-officer as Admiral Watson, who I find from your narrative as well as from others, did his part extremely well'.[17] In his gloomy letter of 5 January 1758, however, Hardwicke made no mention of this 'signal victory', though Pitt had noted it in the King's Speech, calling Clive 'that Heaven-born general'. At that time Hardwicke had his eye on chances for peace, and he probably did not realize what the reported success in Bengal implied. Besides, one never knew in London or Paris whether a positive achievement

---

[15] Intelligence, 22 Feb. 1758, BL Add. 32,878, fo. 7.

[16] Belleisle to Clermont, 15 March 1758, Waddington, *Guerre*, II, 41–2. An estimated 16,000 men were lost during the retreat (II, 47).

[17] Hardwicke to Clive, 11 Nov. 1757, Yorke, *Hardwicke*, III, 195–6. Clive's letter was dated 23 Feb. 1757.

in India might soon be overturned – might already have been overturned – by subsequent developments.

The war in India had its own rhythm. Oscillations of hostilities and quietude, and of success and failure, on the Asian subcontinent were quite out of step with events in Europe and North America. These oscillations were occasioned primarily by changing political circumstances of Indian states – new rulers, altered alliances, surging military ambitions – and the fact that contending princes were often inclined to seek military assistance from the European East India companies. Company governors on the spot, seeing opportunities, were strongly tempted to act. Their directors in London and Paris could not keep current with changing political and military circumstances, for not only was it difficult for the governors to convey the complexities but also there was an insuperable problem of slow communications.

The outbound voyage from Portsmouth to Madras (Chennai), the principal trading establishment of the English East India Company on the Coromandel Coast, generally required four and a half to six months. Return voyages rarely took less than six months, eight or nine when winds did not cooperate. In 1755 an artilleryman aboard an East India Company ship reached Bombay six and a half months after leaving the English Channel, the ship stopping at the Cape Verde Islands and Madagascar for water and fresh provisions; he reckoned the distance by log at well over 15,000 miles.[18] Much shorter routes passed by land through France to Marseilles or across Germany and Austria to Venice, then by sea to Aleppo, overland to Basra, and through the Persian Gulf to Bombay. For important dispatches the shorter routes were used, but the arrangements, which depended upon trusted merchants, were complicated. In the Seven Years War, with France and Austria hostile, the British could seldom use an overland route.[19]

The great feat in Bengal accomplished by Lieutenant Colonel Robert Clive of the English East India Company and Admiral Charles Watson illustrates the point that the war in India had its own rhythm. This striking success could not have occurred if there had not been at the right moment a British naval squadron on the coast of India when the French had none. The squadron, four ships of the line and two sloops of war,

[18] Whitworth, ed. *Gunner at Large*, p. 93.
[19] Holden Furber, 'The Overland Route to India in the Seventeenth and Eighteenth Centuries' in Rosane Rocher, ed. *Private Fortunes and Company Profits in the India Trade in the 18th Century* (Aldershot, 1997), esp. pp. 116–22.

had sailed from England on 24 March 1754 under circumstances already described.[20] By the time it arrived at Madras the local governors had arranged a truce, so the squadron soon sailed for Bombay where it could be cleaned and refitted. Three companies of British army troops along with some artillerymen had gone out to Bombay. From there they could march inland to try to counter Charles Bussy's influence in the Deccan, which the East India Company wanted done, particularly because that very skilled strategist and diplomat had gained exclusive trading concessions on the east coast north of the Carnatic. The plan was to use company troops joined to the 700 regular army troops to support a Maratha campaign against Bussy and his allies. The Bombay Council decided not to go ahead with it, however, because if the articles of a negotiated peace signed in Madras were confirmed in London, the expedition would have to be called off. The Marathas, preparing for a campaign, would then feel deceived and might take out their resentment on Bombay. The Bombay Council had an alternative plan, namely to resume a campaign against Kanhoji Angria, the 'pirate king' of the western coast, who, like his father before him, had preyed upon the trade of all nations, especially the British. His base was at Gheria, 200 miles to the south. In February 1756 a British expedition with Watson commanding the navy and Clive the army sailed there and was speedily successful. Afterwards the admiral took his squadron to Madras, arriving at the end of May. Clive went with him. Thus, for reasons that had nothing to do with Bengal, a Royal Navy squadron happened to be at Madras along with 700 British regulars and Lieutenant Colonel Clive when word arrived that Calcutta was under threat.

The threat came, not from the French, but from the new nawab of Bengal who was eager to confirm his mastery of the region. His elderly predecessor, who had established stable government after a desperate struggle to keep the Marathas away, had been aware of the successes of British and French troops in the Carnatic and Deccan and was uneasy, but did not wish to disturb the prosperity and revenue that the European trading stations produced. The principal establishments were concentrated in the Hughli river, which had its origins not far from his capital city of Murshidabad. The two largest trading centres, Calcutta and Chandernagore, featured fortified citadels garrisoned by European troops.

The old nawab died in mid-April 1756. His 22-year old successor known as Siraj-ud-daula was far less cautious and greatly resented the

---

[20] Above, Chapter 3.

British. They were abusing their special trading privileges to the detriment of his revenues. More disturbingly, they had permitted a close associate of an obvious rival to find refuge in Calcutta. Soon after coming to power the young nawab announced to the governors at Calcutta and Chandernagore that they must dismantle fortifications on which they had recently begun work. The reply from the French at Chandernagore was tactful and possibly truthful: they were merely repairing a bastion damaged by lightning. The British justified their action by claiming, not entirely truthfully, that they were doing no more than enhancing the river defences of Fort William because an Anglo-French war was likely to be declared in Europe. This reply made the nawab furious; he asserted that he was the sovereign authority and bore sole responsibility for the defence of all establishments in his territory.

At Calcutta an incompetent governor, Roger Drake, treated the nawab's emissaries with discourtesy. He acted as though Fort William could not possibly be conquered by an Indian army and doubted that the nawab would actually make the attempt. His confidence rested solely on arrogance. His garrison was small and ill-trained (about 500 men counting town militia), the town could be easily overrun, and once that occurred the fort could be quite easily attacked. On 16 June 1756 the nawab's army, numbering more than 30,000, appeared. Predictably the town was quickly occupied, and in just four days Fort William capitulated. While the siege was in progress women and children and, shamefully, Governor Drake took refuge in nearby ships, none of which stayed near enough to evacuate the defenders who remained. The refugees went to Fulta near the river's mouth, and there they learned from stragglers that on the night of the surrender many of the British who had remained were crammed into a small, almost windowless room called the Black Hole which served as a military prison. When the door was opened the next morning only twenty-three remained alive; in the airless heat forty died of suffocation. Although it is unlikely that Suraj-ud-daula knew about the deadly incarceration, it became notorious that Calcutta had not only been sacked but subjected to an atrocity. An exaggerated estimate of the number of victims became accepted truth in British accounts.

Prior to his attack on Calcutta the nawab had asked the nearby French and Dutch to join him. They had answered that their military resources were too feeble, a half-truth at best. Although the removal of their chief competitor was welcome, they feared that the same sort of violence might in due course be turned upon them, and they were also keenly aware of something the nawab failed to consider – that the British had a fleet of warships at Madras together with a body of troops and would almost certainly retaliate.

The councillors and officers at Madras learned that Calcutta was over-run on 16 August. They had been planning an expedition to the Deccan from the south, and although this idea was quickly abandoned, it took time to arrange the rescue of Calcutta. The presence of a regular army regiment complicated matters because its colonel, John Aldercron, refused to accept direction from the Madras Council. He was therefore replaced, whereupon he insisted on removal of royal artillery and stores from the transports. Laboriously, East India Company artillery had to be substituted. His refusal to release any of his troops was overcome by Admiral Watson who persuaded him to allow three companies (about 250 men) to go aboard the warships as marines. The expedition did not leave Madras until mid-October, a terrible time of year because the monsoonal wind was contrary. After a long and frustrating drift to the east the fleet finally reached the mouth of the Hughli river on 8 December.

Colonel Aldercron's failure to cooperate was in one respect fortunate because it allowed the troops to be commanded by Clive. A Shropshire lad, son of a lawyer, he showed a penchant for fighting and bullying as a boy, but was sent to good schools and eventually learned accounting. He was intelligent as well as courageous, and had a genius for balancing caution and decisiveness. Military experience in the struggle against the French in the Carnatic sharpened his skills. In 1752 Margaret Maskelyne, whose brother had a position at Madras, came out to India. She married Clive in February 1753 and they soon embarked to go home. In England with his military reputation established by his successes against Dupleix, Clive forged political connections (among them Henry Fox and Lord Hardwicke) and tried to enter Parliament. Ranked a lieutenant colonel in the East India Company's service and appointed governor of Fort St David, he returned to India with Margaret in 1755. When the emergency in Bengal arose the Madras Council were thoroughly familiar with his military ability and knew that the directors in London also had confidence in him as a field commander, so they had no trouble deciding that he should be commander-in-chief of the expeditionary army. At 31 he was about to become one of the most famous military and political figures in British history.

When the squadron arrived at Fulta, a low-lying malarial village, half the refugees from Calcutta had died. Not all the ships arrived: HMS *Cumberland* (66 guns) had to turn back and the *Marlborough*, a com-pany ship with guns and ordnance stores aboard, was delayed. Watson and Clive resolved to head upriver without them. On 27 December with skilled native pilots and 700 troops and artillerymen embarked, the ships got under way, the 1,200 sepoys of the Madras army marching along the shore. Only one of the river forts offered opposition, but when its defenders realized they might be cut off they fled. Fort William's garrison also departed. Calcutta was occupied on 2 January 1757 without a fight, except for a quarrel that erupted when the admiral appointed a regular army captain to take command of the fort. This provoked a fierce reaction from Clive, as it reinforced his perception that the forces of the Crown were too readily prepared to make the company's army subservient. The dispute was mediated by navy Captain Thomas Latham of the *Tyger* (60 guns) who was married to Margaret's best friend, the solution being to have the admiral come ashore, assume command of the fort, and hand the keys over immediately to the restored Calcutta Council.

The sight of the ruined, burnt-out city gave intense meaning to the Madras Council's conception of the mission: 'The mere retaking of Calcutta' would be insufficient. All the company's settlements, trading factories and former privileges must be restored, and 'ample reparation made . . . for the loss . . . lately sustained; otherwise we are of opinion it would have been better nothing had been attempted, than to have added the heavy charge of this armament to the former loss'. And, of course, the company's trade would have to be secured from 'future insults and exactions'.[21] These results could not be obtained without military action. Expecting the nawab to assemble an army, Clive immediately declared war on him in the name of the company; Watson did so in the name of King George. Two small warships went 40 miles upriver to the fortified town of Hughli and used their guns to make a breach in walls though which Captain Eyre Coote's men could enter. They burnt the town and then went on to burn a large granary 3 miles to the north.

The progress of the nawab's army could not, however, be stopped. On 3 February, an estimated 40,000 men including 18,000 cavalry camped on the outskirts of Calcutta. Clive sent two emissaries to inquire as to the nawab's purpose. They spoke with officials who answered that it was a convenient place to camp, informed them they would learn more in the morning and invited them to stay the night. They chose to escape and reported to Clive at 11 p.m. whereupon he resolved to attack immediately. He required 600 sailors to help with the field guns and ammunition, so it was almost dawn when the little army of 470 troops, 800 sepoys, and

---

[21] Quoted in Edwardes, *Battle of Plassey*, p. 78.

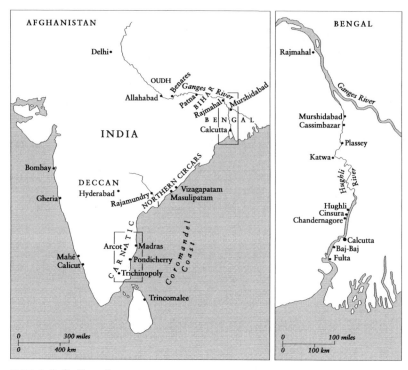

MAP 5 *India/Bengal*

600 sailors set off to attack the nawab's headquarters. Groping in the morning fog they lost their way and blundered into the heart of the enemy camp. By firing in all directions and fending off two cavalry attacks with grapeshot they survived, but when the fog lifted they were in great danger and hurried forward to find entry to the city just in time. All in all, it was a desperate affair and for such a small force casualties were high: 27 British soldiers killed, 70 wounded; 12 sailors killed, 12 wounded; 18 sepoys killed, 35 wounded. A candid assessment must conclude that Clive lost this battle. But the next day there came word from the nawab that he wished to negotiate. Although he was by no means defeated he had lost over 1,000 men and some key officers. It was his army's first real encounter with British arms and his generals were evidently shaken by the suddenness and boldness of Clive's attack. On 9 February 1757 a treaty was signed in which he met most of the British demands except for adequate compensation of losses incurred when he took Calcutta.

To this point the contest in Bengal was solely between the nawab and the British. It could not remain that way because a French military force lay at Chandernagore, just 20 miles above Calcutta. There was an ever-present danger that the nawab might enlist French military cooperation, repudiate the treaty and attack. The situation featured a diplomatic triangle loaded with perplexities and was fraught with insecurity all round.

The French were the weakest of the participants. Their situation was perilous. Although Fort d'Orleans at Chandernagore was well built, the garrison was small, ships in the river were few and weak, and no outside help was likely to come, Bussy being engaged in the Deccan. Governor Pierre Renault had immediately dispatched a proposal of neutrality to Watson when word came that his squadron had arrived in the Hughli river. In refusing, the admiral suggested that the French should ally with the British instead. To this the governor returned no answer. In any case, a letter soon reached him from his superior, the governor at Pondicherry, prohibiting an alliance with the British against the nawab. Renault and his council expected Siraj-ud-daula to ask for such an alliance and dreaded it. They feared that the nawab would not or could not follow through to victory yet a refusal would annoy him, and if he did happen to gain success he might then seize all French trading stations in Bengal or at least demand tribute at an extortionate level. Seeing no good choice the officials at Chandernagore followed the advice from Pondicherry, namely to adhere to neutrality while improving the fortifications. Work on the latter was speeded up when it was learned in January (overland from Europe through the Persian Gulf and Surat) that the Anglo-French war had been declared.

The nawab was certainly intent on gaining the French as an ally. He was confident that with French help he could defeat the British and break the treaty of 9 February. He could then hope to drive the British from Calcutta, though this would probably not be feasible until after the navy departed. He offered the French all the privileges that he had given the British by treaty, but they would not commit to an alliance. Afraid to act alone, all the nawab could do was tell the British that if they attacked Chandernagore, he would come to its defence.

The Select Committee at Calcutta was officially responsible for British policy decisions, but both Watson and Clive were in direct communication with the nawab's court. At first the admiral and the colonel disagreed about policy, and, interestingly, it was Clive – later recognized as the man responsible for planting British dominion in India – who exhibited worried restraint. Convinced that a French combination with the nawab could not be militarily withstood, he preferred a policy of trusting in the treaty of 9 February and establishing neutrality with the French. Watson had opposed that treaty, arguing that the nawab needed first to be 'well threshed'. Once it was signed, however, the admiral insisted that the peace had to be honoured: the British must not make war on the French without the nawab's consent. Yet at the same time he objected to contracting a treaty of neutrality with the French and refused to sign one that French representatives and the Select Committee had just negotiated. His argument was that the council at Chandernagore did not have the power to make such a treaty; it would have to be approved at Pondicherry, and during the inevitable three-month communications delay the British would be officially pledged to inaction while the French could consult their needs and interests.[22] Clive and the Select Committee believed, however, that if the admiral were to reject a treaty which the French negotiated in good faith, they would soon ally with the nawab. Chandernagore must be attacked before that happened, they told the admiral. But he would not allow this. He seemed oblivious to the danger.

The difference in views ultimately stemmed from a difference in viewpoint. Watson mistrusted the nawab and believed in the power of his warships. He believed that the French feared them and presumed that the nawab's generals were equally afraid. (When the nawab's officers came to the *Kent* with presents to celebrate the 9 February treaty, he had given them a tour of the lower deck with its 32-pounders and they were clearly impressed.) He seems to have understood that his squadron possessed complete and unchallengeable command of the river – that the British advantage lay not just in firepower but also in communications. Clive was aware that the French feared the men-of-war, but was not sure whether the nawab was of the same mind. If the French in their anxiety were to join the nawab against him, he considered his chances of military success 'precarious'. Moreover, he argued, 'our future operations against the Nabob' would chiefly depend 'upon the land forces, and the officers of such forces must certainly be the best judges of what can be effected by land'. As to the future he was right, but with regard to Chandernagore he was wrong. The error, however, was understandable because never in

[22] The full text of Watson's letter to the Select Committee of 3 March 1757 may be found in Hill, ed. *Bengal in 1756–1757*, II, 268–70. Each presidency of the English East India Company – Bombay, Madras, Bengal – was independent, so Calcutta's commitment did not require approval by higher authority, whereas Pondicherry's authority was supreme in the French company's case, so Chandernagore's commitment while morally binding was not officially so.

previous wars had powerful ships of the line come up the river like this; there was no experience of it.

Soon the admiral came round to the view that it was imperative to launch an attack on Chandernagore. On the same day that Clive was questioning Watson's judgement, the admiral wrote a letter to the nawab which criticized his backwardness in carrying out the 9 February treaty and noted the assistance with men and money that he was reportedly providing to the French. Patience, he wrote, was at an end, and it was now time 'to speak *plain*'. Watson gave the nawab ten days to meet his treaty obligations. If this were not done, he wrote, 'I will kindle such a flame in your country, as all the water in the Ganges shall not be able to extinguish.' Three days later Clive also wrote to the nawab, more courteously, but he expressed Watson's argument that a neutrality agreement with the French could not be relied upon. His purpose in writing was to obtain the nawab's permission to attack Chandernagore.[23]

An external development provided an opening that gave Clive a measure of confidence that permission would be granted. Siraj-ud-daula wrote to Calcutta reporting news that an Afghan invader who had sacked Delhi, Ahmed Khan Abdali, was heading for Bengal. Thoroughly alarmed, he asked for British military help, offering to pay for the troops. Watson was the first to reply, and he pointed out that the British could not safely proceed on such a mission if the French remained behind them at Chandernagore. Clive of course agreed, and on 8 March he headed upriver under pretence of getting ready to assist the nawab. Meanwhile, William Watts, the British company's representative at Cassimbazar, near the nawab's court, cleverly and with suitable bribes to the staff, elicited a letter containing words that the admiral and Clive chose to interpret as granting permission to attack the French. At about the time this letter reached Watson a packet from London arrived, at long last, with an official copy of the declaration of war and a letter from the Admiralty directing 'all officers under the King to distress the enemy as far as it is in their power'. It was an order that Watson wished to obey. Thus the Anglo-French Seven Years War began in Bengal.

As in many far-flung localities during this war, the French would fight bravely without receiving assistance from the home country. Chandernagore had 700 defenders, consisting of 360 soldiers and sailors, 170 townsmen and 167 sepoys. An additional 2,000 native infantry sent by order of the nawab to support the defence fled during the opening

---

[23] The above quotations are in letters of 4 and 7 March 1757, ibid. II, 271–5.

skirmish on 14 March (the official who provided them had been bribed). Although the French quickly withdrew troops from their outworks, Clive proceeded cautiously. Not until 19 March did he erect batteries, and these were immediately nullified by the fort's guns. On its land sides Fort d'Orleans was more defensible than Fort William, but on the river side it was vulnerable. Clive knew that Watson's ships would be coming upriver as soon as the tides permitted. Governor Renault had understood the danger and caused four to six ships to be sunk to block their passage.

Arriving in sight of the fort on the 19th, Watson sent a boat the next day under flag of truce to demand surrender. The lieutenant in charge was able to see where the sunken vessels lay and detected a path through. Sailors cut away a chained boom, and early in the morning of the 23rd the *Tyger* led the way. Before dawn Clive's men had captured the battery that was supposed to fire upon the narrow channel. The *Tyger* passed through and anchored opposite the north-west bastion at a distance of less than 100 yards. Rear-Admiral George Pocock had just come on board. He had been aboard the *Cumberland* which finally reached the Hughli two days before and heard that the squadron was heading for action. Sailors rowed the admiral's barge day and night to speed him upriver. The *Kent* (70 guns) with Admiral Watson aboard passed through the channel but failed to achieve its intended location because the fort's guns, well directed by the captain of a French East Indiaman, killed or wounded the men in charge of anchoring; consequently the cable ran out unchecked and, the tide having turned, she drifted down to a position near the south-east bastion. There was thus no room for the third ship, the 50-gun *Salisbury*, to join the battle. The fort's gunners did not flinch despite being fired on from land as well as the river (Clive had positioned batteries to harass them from the flanks), but the firepower of the ships' broadsides could not be withstood. The French guns, five 24-pounders at each bastion, were blasted off their mounts and the ramparts became covered with dead and wounded. After slightly more than two hours of fierce cannonading by the men-of-war, the French flew the white flag and proposed terms of capitulation.

It was a naval victory. Watson's inclination to exclude Clive from signing the surrender terms was militarily and politically reprehensible, and was properly overridden by his fellow naval officers, who recognized that the land force had cooperated expertly. But it was certainly true that the navy bore the brunt of the casualties: the *Tyger* had 13 killed and 56 wounded, Pocock, cut by splinters, among the latter; the *Kent* lost 19 killed and 74 wounded. Every commissioned officer on board her except a lieutenant and Admiral Watson was killed or wounded. The troops ashore under Clive suffered only 1 killed and 10 wounded. No reliable record of French casualties has come to light. By the terms of capitulation the garrison officers were released on parole; the civilians and sepoys were allowed to go and to carry away their possessions; the soldiers and sailors, however, were deemed prisoners and transported to Madras, although about 40 escaped.

The loss of Chandernagore was, as Clive commented, 'an unexpressible blow to the French Company'.[24] The conquerors found little treasure (the money had been exhausted by expenditure on preparing defences), but they acquired enough military and naval stores to compensate for what was lost at Calcutta. Dupleix when he was governor of Chandernagore in the 1730s had greatly enhanced its trade, and the place had become, as Calcutta was for the British, the most profitable French trading centre in India. In sum, the French company not only lost a key source of wealth, but also its maritime base in Bengal, and everywhere in India French arms lost prestige.[25]

Still, the British position in Bengal was not secure, nor had French influence been completely eliminated. The 40 escapees joined 60 other Frenchmen under Jean Law at Cassimbazar, the trading centre used by all nations near the nawab's court at Murshidabad. Although Siraj-ud-daula wrote letters congratulating Watson and Clive on their military feat, he also wrote to Bussy in hopes of persuading him to come to help him drive the British out. But he was very fearful; he proposed to dam the Hughli's flow from the Ganges so that low water would keep British ships from coming further upriver. Clive asked the nawab to deliver all Frenchmen over to the British. His argument was that, since Britain and France were officially at war, this was necessary for a stable and mutually beneficial peace in Bengal. The nawab did not hand them over but did tell them to depart; they withdrew up the Ganges, remaining, however, within reach of summons.

Clive was much annoyed, but his decision to forsake the nawab stemmed from a different cause: Siraj-ud-daula was in serious danger of being over-thrown. The stories of his impulsive sadism might be exaggerated, but there could be no doubt that he had frightened and alienated too many important people – top officials, Hindu merchants, and, not least, the Hindu banking house of Jagat Seth. This family handled the nawab's

---

[24] Clive to Select Committee, Fort St George, 30 March 1757, ibid. II, 307.

[25] Edwardes, *Battle of Plassey*, p. 116.

revenue, commanded the coinage of Bengal, and financed a vast amount of trade not only in Bengal but elsewhere in northern India. The Seths had been horrified by the nawab's attack on Calcutta. His subsequent actions, hesitant and contradictory, revealed his weakness and incapacity. He was showered with competing advice and had few men he could trust to see that orders were carried out. Jean Law remarked that the Seths 'managed so well that they undid in the evening all that I had effected in the morning'.[26] A conspiracy had been afoot for weeks. After receiving urgent reports from William Watts, the British representative at the nawab's court, the Select Committee at Calcutta held a meeting on 1 May and decided that they must side with the 'revolution'. The substituted nawab, they learned, was to be Mir Jafar, an experienced general and paymaster of the nawab's army. Throughout May and early June, with Watson's acquiescence, Clive and the Select Committee followed a path of deceit and dissimulation. The affair culminated in a clash of armies on a field of battle at Plassey, which occurred precisely three months after Chandernagore surrendered.

As the nawab's army assembled, 750 British troops plus 150 artillerymen began moving northwards by boat while 2,100 sepoys marched. Plassey, only 25 miles from Murshidabad, was 85 miles above Calcutta, and warships could scarcely reach half way. Chandernagore could be temporarily garrisoned by sailors expert in gunnery. The question was whether the conspiracy would hold firm, and the key man was Mir Jafar whose troops, Clive hoped, would join the battle to come. Mir Jafar never actually gave his word that he would do this and Clive understandably yearned for reassurance. Like some of his officers he wished to be cautious, but any turning back would give the nawab an appearance of a triumph, so he resolved to go ahead. He crossed the river to Plassey, committing his army without knowing whether Mir Jafar would actually support him.

On the morning of 23 June 1757, standing on the roof of a hunting lodge, Clive could observe the enemy army as it spread out over the plain. The scene was spectacular, with beautifully draped elephants, some wearing armour, and countless oxen pulling platforms on which large cannon were mounted. The enemy numbered perhaps 35,000 foot and 15,000 horse, so it appeared that his 3,000 men might have to face 50,000. He remarked to an aide that they might have to fight as best they could during the day and then raid or retreat by night. An initial exchange

[26] Quoted by ibid., p. 110.

of cannon fire in which a body of escaped gunners from Chandernagore fired with considerable accuracy caused the British troops to fall back and take shelter in a grove of trees. Luckily, around noon a thunderstorm erupted and the deluge soaked the powder of the nawab's artillery. The British had shielded theirs with tarpaulins and were thus able to surprise an enemy cavalry charge and turn it back, mortally wounding the nawab's best general. Of the 50,000 men Clive had seen that morning the majority were under the command of Mir Jafar and colleagues who were party to the conspiracy. Arrayed in a long arc to Clive's right, they stood immobile throughout the day, watching the combatants. Siraj-ud-daula begged Mir Jafar to come to talk to him; in the afternoon he did, and gave advice: the nawab should break off the battle and recall his troops. Against the protest of his officers the nawab gave the order. French gunners fired from a redoubt in hopes of halting the British advance, but Clive's army moved forward, its artillery wreaking havoc on the retreating soldiers and oxen. By 5 p.m. the battle was over. Siraj-ud-daula fled in disguise but was captured and killed within a few days.

In view of the minimal casualties suffered by the British side – 11 British killed, 24 wounded; 13 sepoys killed, 21 wounded – it is sometimes remarked that Plassey was a staged demonstration, not a real battle. It certainly seemed like a real battle to Clive and his officers, who went into it with justifiable anxiety. Granted, Mir Jafar stood inactive, but they could not be sure of his intentions and had to fight without him. They had no knowledge of the pernicious advice he gave the nawab, nor did a message from him pledging support arrive until after the battle was over. Had Clive's army been forced to retreat it might have suffered severely. If that had happened, the warships could defend Calcutta, but the situation in Bengal would have been unsettled and dangerous. Plassey was in fact a battle, but it has gone down in history as a *decisive* battle, and undeniably what made it decisive was the conspiracy. At the end of the day Siraj-ud-daula was not only beaten on the battlefield but had nowhere to turn. Thus, Mir Jafar was installed as nawab of Bengal. Although the British had neither initiated nor matured the conspiracy, everyone knew, as Mir Jafar did, that British troops and sepoys had fought the battle and were his guarantors.

For the company Clive succeeded in obtaining by treaty with Mir Jafar compensation for all British losses and military expenses. For himself he gained by its terms an immense reward; his military colleagues were also amply served. A grant of £500,000 was distributed to the navy and army, and it was said that each British soldier and sailor received

£2,000 – for them a fortune if they lived to enjoy it. (James Wood later wrote down a list of 22 artillery officers who had gone to India with him in 1755, noting that all had died except for himself and one other.[27]) News of the victory at Plassey and installation of Mir Jafar did not reach London until many months later, in February 1758. Even then, war news from India was given relatively little publicity in Britain; battles won and riches said to be seized were reported in newspapers, but little else. Not until the war was near its end did there begin to be an understanding of how much Chandernagore and Plassey implied strategically and politically.

The long-term effect of the British success in Bengal was to secure for the English East India Company a very wealthy region while substantially excluding the French from it. The Bengal economy was underpinned by immense rice production, and the region was the principal source of silk and inexpensive cotton cloth, products which were not only shipped to Britain but also traded inland and to ports in the Indian Ocean as well as, quite importantly, to China. Sixty per cent of the British company's trade would become centred in Bengal. The treaty with Mir Jafar also gave the company possession of the southern environs of Calcutta. In 1760 Clive would forcibly acquire the revenues of more sizeable areas. Future security was seen to depend upon an ever larger company army which required an enlarged territorial revenue to pay for it.

Clive therefore appears to have accomplished what Dupleix had hoped to achieve in the Carnatic, and it was commonly supposed by French colonial historians of a century ago that if only Dupleix had been allowed to proceed, the Carnatic could have been similarly secured and made profitable. In important ways, however, the situation of Bengal was different. The region generated more surplus wealth than the Carnatic, and its revenue was more systematically collected.[28] It was also easier to defend from invasion thanks to its geographical position, for unlike the Carnatic, Bengal could only be attacked on one side unless by water, and it suited British capabilities and priorities to guard the sea approaches and command the waterways. Although the fact was not immediately realized in London or Paris, the secure possession of Bengal swung the balance of power in India decisively in favour of the British. A war involving larger Anglo-French forces was about to begin in the Carnatic

---

[27] Whitworth, ed. *Gunner at Large*, p. 72.
[28] Marshall, *Making and Unmaking of Empires*, pp. 140–1, 147–8, 152, 156.

and, as will be seen in a later chapter, while the French were running out of money in that contest Madras would receive much needed infusions of cash from Calcutta.

Achieving naval superiority

'Of one thing you may be sure,' Joseph Yorke wrote to his brother when hostilities threatened in early April 1755, 'that the French Nation in general is violently against the War, and dreads the superiority of the British Navy.'[29] Yet in the near term the French navy achieved a remarkable record of success. Du Guay evaded Hawke in summer 1755. Du Bois de la Motte with large squadrons twice evaded the British on homeward-bound voyages from America. La Galissonière defeated Byng off Minorca in May 1756. Louisbourg was saved in 1757 because a large number of French ships of the line made it safely across the Atlantic and achieved a concentration. The same year half a dozen French warships reached Africa and the West Indies, all but one returning safely.[30] The Royal Navy's only significant achievement was the arrest, before war was declared, of numerous unsuspecting French merchant vessels. Lord Hardwicke certainly had a point when, after noting (see beginning of this chapter) that 'we have taken for our proper Department' the maritime and colonial sphere, he then asked, 'what have we done in it?'

To be sure, diplomatic restraints limited British opportunities for success in 1755, Byng was worse than inept and strategic mistakes were made. Yet in some instances – at the Gulf of St Lawrence, the Straits, and perhaps even off Minorca – better results might have been achieved if more ships had been employed. In retrospect it is clear that Anson should not have kept the Western Squadron so numerous as he did in spring 1756, but apart from that single mistake the problem was that there were simply too few ships available to meet the needs. By early 1758 the problem was essentially solved, as the British fleet achieved something close to full mobilization. This came three years after the beginning of wartime expansion. Why did it take so long?

The intractable problem was to get ships manned. All eighteenth-century navies experienced serious manning difficulties. Spain built beautiful big ships but had trouble finding seamen for them. The French navy had a mobilization advantage over the British because a registry had been instituted

[29] Joseph to Philip Yorke (Lord Royston), 4 April 1755, BL Add. 35,364, fo. 43.
[30] Dull, *French Navy*, p. 82.

in the time of Louis XIV by which merchant seamen, apportioned into 'classes', were obliged to serve. The Royal Navy had no such system, Parliament having refused to allow one to be instituted. A few skilled seamen volunteered for the navy, and generally they enlisted to serve under particular captains with a view towards becoming petty officers, but when war loomed most trained seamen realized that the merchants would soon pay high wartime wages while the navy's rates stayed at peacetime levels. Impressment, the strong-arm system that aroused indignation and revulsion, was therefore used to bring seamen into the service. Most were impressed afloat; incoming merchant vessels were stopped and the men removed (trustworthy substitutes being placed aboard to carry the vessel into port). Trading vessels came home gradually, however, and when they did their crews often tried to escape. Manning upon mobilization was dreadfully slow. It was the Royal Navy's Achilles heel.

The problem was aggravated by disease. Scurvy is the most famous of sea diseases. The death toll from tropical fevers is also well known, but upon mobilization typhus was the disease most to be dreaded. Lice transmitted it all too readily among men who were crowded together in a tender after being impressed. The germ would then spread through the ships' companies to which the new men were assigned.

The British navy gradually solved its manning problem. Just before the Seven Years War there were about 58,000 British seamen in employment of which 17,000 were in the navy. By the war's middle years the total was over 115,000 (about 75,000 in the navy). How could this be? For one thing, the restriction of the Navigation Acts prohibiting foreigners from serving in merchant vessels was relaxed in wartime. Most important, however, was the navy's own role in building up the seafaring population: it recruited large numbers of volunteer landsmen and made seamen out of most of them. To be sure, ships newly placed in commission needed a body of experienced seamen, and captains were desperate to acquire them; without them a ship could not be safely navigated. But once this initial need was satisfied the skilled seamen on board a ship at sea could train many more. Desertion was a problem, but since the deserters generally found their way into British merchant ships they continued to serve the nation's maritime needs.

The French navy's registry system enabled its Atlantic squadrons to be manned quickly in 1755, but from then on there were difficulties because fundamentally the realm did not possess enough seamen. French merchant tonnage had grown along with France's increased Atlantic commerce, but crew sizes did not increase in proportion to tonnage because the ships were larger. Around 1750 the total number of French seamen remained what it had been at the beginning of the century – about 60,000. The British capture and detention of over 4,000 seamen in 1755 was deliberately calculated to aggravate the French navy's manning problem. Captures of French merchant vessels and privateers continued thereafter, and by the end of 1757 at least 10,000, perhaps 12,000, French seamen were in British prisons.

A terrible misfortune added to the French navy's difficulties. Admiral Du Bois de la Motte managed to return from Louisbourg in late 1757 with the loss of only one ship, but the ships had left Brest with a virulent germ aboard and the contagion spread; the men were especially vulnerable to sickness in cold northern waters, and on the return voyage some ships had scarcely enough healthy men to handle sails. Scurvy contributed to the losses, but there is no question that the dreadful epidemic originated in France. Of approximately 11,700 seamen who sailed on the ships that came together at Louisbourg only 6,200 were still alive in the spring of 1758. Moreover, when the survivors disembarked at Brest they spread the germ to the inhabitants. As many as 10,000 additional people of the town and surrounding country were reported to have died. As word of the epidemic at Brest reached the French Channel ports during the winter of 1757–8 men became terrified of naval service. The ships had returned, but the ability to find men for them was seriously impaired. It was a human and naval catastrophe.[31]

By 1758 some French privateers but very few merchant ships were venturing into the Atlantic. Fishing off Newfoundland was shut down, and French warships began to spend less time at sea. They worried about being captured by the British. In the Mediterranean, losses to British capture were fewer and disease was less of a factor, but the number of French seamen in the region was inherently small, and the Minorca expedition had used almost everyone available. Although those men survived, they knew that wartime merchant-marine wages were three times the naval level, and because France's Mediterranean trade was not so greatly threatened by British cruisers as its Atlantic trade, commercial competition for seamen's services was strong. Unsurprisingly, naval manning difficulties at Toulon continued to be severe: warships sailed late, short of complement and lacking experienced seamen.

Thanks mainly to the epidemic the French navy became incapable of manning its Atlantic fleet at the very moment when the British navy

---

[31] Le Goff, 'Problèmes de recrutement', 226; Pritchard, *Louis XV's Navy*, pp. 83–4.

approached full strength. The situation was made worse by a British modification of policy regarding naval prisoners of war: unskilled men, boys and cripples were selected for exchange while experienced seamen were kept. (The number held prisoner who would be returned to France when the war ended was close to 25,000, and an additional 8,500 died in captivity.) In August 1758 Marshal Belleisle observed after seeing the figures, 'We cannot at this moment fit out 14 ships of the line, though we have 63; and it is because we have neither sailors nor money.'[32] Belleisle's figure of 63 was fairly accurate. Clearly, by this stage the French navy's chief problem was not a shortage of ships, but of seamen.

In fact, the French navy began the war with a respectable number of ships. Few had expected this. People were aware that for half a century the story of the French navy had been one of decline. In 1690 France had possessed the strongest navy in the world, but after 1694 Louis XIV, with his treasury half-empty, judged his great battle fleet to be a useless luxury compared to the needs of his army and allowed it to waste away. Medium-sized and smaller men-of-war were kept in repair and employed against British trade as well as assigned to convoy duty, but after 1710 very few warships of any kind were built and by 1720 the French navy reached its nadir. Rebuilding efforts during the next two decades of peace were sporadic and meagre. It was not until 1740, with war breaking out all round, that naval construction was resumed. In the early 1740s France was not officially at war with Britain and her naval recovery was undisturbed, but neutrality ended in 1744 and the recovery was ruined. The victories of Anson and Hawke in 1747 when the French lost a total of 11 ships above 50 guns, most of which were quite new, did the greatest damage. The remaining ships included many that were old, worn out, and not worth repairing, so in 1748 the naval minister, Jean-Frédéric Phélypeaux, comte de Maurepas, accepted reality and prudently got rid of 16 of the line. Fewer than 30 of the line remained, though there were 19 useful frigates.[33]

At this point Maurepas persuaded Louis XV to initiate an aggressive building programme, and under the naval ministers who succeeded him it became reality. Eight to ten ships of the line were launched per year until funding was curtailed in 1753, but in 1755 construction was resumed and continued through 1757. The effort testified to Versailles's newfound concern for the maritime sphere, and it contributed to the

---

[32] Quoted in Chaussinand-Nogaret, *Choiseul*, p. 72.

[33] Meyer and Acerra, *Histoire*, pp. 101–2; Pritchard, *Louis XV's Navy*, p. 136.

French navy's success in the opening years of the war. In June 1756 when war was declared the French navy could count 62 ships of the line and 38 frigates in reasonably good condition. The number of ships of the line amounted to about 70 per cent of the British total of 89 – an impressive achievement.

British policy allowed this to happen. If the peacetime renewal of the French fleet after 1748 is worthy of remark, the failure of the Royal Navy to keep pace is even more so (though the fact has been largely ignored). Earlier in the century, in the peacetime decades after 1714, the British navy's ship strength (active and reserve) had been generally maintained at about 85 per cent of the prior wartime level even though the French navy posed no threat. But after the peace of 1748, when the French were industriously building new ships, the British response was meagre. The young Earl of Sandwich, First Lord of the Admiralty from 1749 to 1751, requested an estimate for Extraordinary Repairs (which could cover new construction), but it was refused because Henry Pelham, firmly in charge of Treasury policy, placed emphasis on restoring public finances. When Anson became First Lord in 1751 he acquiesced in Pelham's policy and only 5 new ships of the line were completed between 1751 and 1754. During the five-year period from 1749 to 1754 only 13 ships of the line were built and 24 repaired, a total of 37, whereas during the same period the French built or rebuilt 38. Thus, on the matter of maintaining warship numbers during time of peace the reality turns the traditional view on its head: it was after 1748, not after 1714, that the British navy gave up its overwhelming preponderance.

On paper the British figures for 1749 had looked satisfactory: 92 ships of 60 to 90 guns were listed. Of these, however, only 33 were in a condition to be fitted for sea. The other 65 per cent included some that had been worn out by cruising in hard weather and some that were weakened by service in the West Indies. But many were victims of premature rot. This was especially true of those built in the 1730s, a decade that featured remarkably warm weather and frost-free winters. As a result, 'winter-felled' timber did not season in the normal manner, and the average life of a ship (until it required an extensive repair or replacement) launched in that decade fell to nine or ten years from a normal level of twelve to sixteen. To the dockyard officers in 1749 the rapid deterioration of the ships must have been alarming and mystifying, yet what was to be done? If the navy were to build ships whose life expectancy was only nine or ten years, it would be making a poor investment. Pelham and Newcastle were probably unaware that quite a few of the navy's listed ships were silently rotting away. Since the public lists showed the British navy to be vastly superior to its rivals, the truth remained hidden from view.

Clearly, there was wisdom in not building ships too soon. Most of the listed ships were worthy of repair (among them were nine recently captured French ships of the line), and the dockyards could restore them. The policy of gradual restoration was risky, however, since there might be a sudden need to put the navy on a war footing. In March 1755 there were at least fifty ships of 60 guns or more in good condition, so it would seem that the navy possessed as many as could possibly be manned during the first year of a war, but forty-three of these were already in commission and there were not many in reserve.

In the latter half of 1755 the Admiralty ordered seven new 74-gun ships to be built, four in the dockyards, three in private builders' yards. Nine more of 60 to 74 guns were ordered in 1756, six of them assigned to private yards. Whereas the French navy built all ships of the line and most frigates in royal dockyards, some private yards in England were capable of building warships of any size up to 74 guns. Britain's royal dockyards could therefore concentrate in wartime on refitting the active fleet. But it took a while for this private shipbuilding capacity to build up the fleet. Only three of the sixteen new ships mentioned above were launched before the end of 1757 and only seven by June 1758. On average, two and a half years passed before the six 74-gun ships ordered in 1755 were launched.[34]

The British naval mobilization crisis in 1756 is commonly attributed to manning difficulties, and undoubtedly manning was the main problem, but it would have helped if more ships had been repaired and commissioned sooner. Until captains and lieutenants could be appointed the process of manning could not begin effectively. The navy tried to complete ships that were under construction quickly, but shipwrights (men for whom the navy and the private builders competed) were in short supply. The shipwrights at Chatham saw their opportunity and struck for higher pay. Pitt was right when he criticized the Newcastle administration for not requesting a larger naval budget when Parliament met in autumn 1754 since, as he said, it was then known that the French had 'attacked Mr. Washington'.[35]

---

[34] These figures are based on tables in Brian Lavery, *The Ship of the Line, Volume I: The Development of the Battlefleet 1650–1850* (London, 1983), pp. 174–7.

[35] Speech of 2 Dec. 1755, *Parl. Hist.*, XV, 601.

In June 1757 the active British fleet counted 76 ships of the line and 20 of 50 guns, while the French figures were 38 and 3, but the British preponderance was not great enough because to accomplish its tasks the Royal Navy required a fleet two and a half to three times larger than its opponent. The French navy's practice was evasion, and its ships were designed for it – somewhat narrower and often faster than British ships. French warships generally carried lofty masts and were therefore more likely to lose them and suffer hull stress in a storm, but if undamaged they escaped. The French navy's best class, the 74s, carried guns handily on two decks. It had very few three-deckers whereas British battle squadrons had at least one. French squadron commanders in the Seven Years War were cautioned against engaging in battle whenever possible. To the Lords of the Admiralty the speed of French ships combined with the strategy of avoidance caused immense frustration. They had looked for a great battle similar to those fought in 1747, but instead the Western Squadron had to carry on a wearying and wearing task of cruising offshore with no enemy warships in sight.

One of the most important reasons why the British navy needed so many more ships than the French was its obligation to protect trade. It will be noted in the next chapter that French naval ministers in the Seven Years War decided not to provide convoy escorts for trade. The British navy, however, treated convoying as essential: merchant wealth supported war finance, and merchant losses led to war-weariness. British newspapers regularly published news about convoys, arrivals, privateering encounters and captures. Merchants often pleaded their case for convoy protection at the Admiralty Office. In the war's opening years outbound convoys were shepherded to the open Atlantic by ships of the line; convoys carrying troops and munitions were similarly escorted. But when Britain finally achieved overwhelming naval superiority, merchant convoys no longer needed strong escorts, and even military expeditions did not always require strong naval protection.

Overwhelming superiority was attained by the spring of 1758. In June the British navy had 82 ships of 60 to 100 guns, 24 of 50 guns, 120 frigates and sloops of war and 70,000 seamen in active service. These figures equalled the highest levels of the preceding war. (In 1759 and 1760 more ships and 85,000 men would be in sea pay.) That same month of 1758 the French navy had only 22 of the line and 3 of 50 guns in active service.[36] Moreover, sea power's advantage became cumulative.

---

[36] Figures based on lists in Dull, *French Navy*, pp. 262–71.

With this level of superiority it became feasible to inaugurate very close surveillance of Brest and of the Biscayan coasts, rendering all naval and maritime activity by the French hazardous. And as France's ability to fit out and man large battle squadrons diminished, the size of the British Western Squadron could be accordingly reduced and the ships assigned to other missions.

French naval ministers realized that their severe manning problem rendered ship construction largely irrelevant. As it happened there was no longer any money to build new ships anyway because Versailles spent it on the army in Germany. Although 34 million livres were allocated to the navy in 1758, only 14 million were actually received and much of that sum was devoted to paying debts incurred the previous year. For the rest of the war French naval administration was hampered by financial stringency: sailors and dockyard workers as well as contractors for stores and provisions went without payment for months on end.

Undoubtedly, if the navy had been better supported financially, the French could have made the maritime war more troublesome to the British, but getting skilled seamen would have remained a problem. Yet no amount of money could have raised the French navy's performance to the British level. A strong navy consisted of much more than ships. For half a century the British navy had been developing an impressive shore establishment while the French navy had not. The British navy's victualling service, drastically reformed after 1700, became remarkably competent; the French navy continued to rely on contractors. French dockyards were not well equipped for keeping cruising squadrons in repair – in 1756 France had four dry docks, Britain sixteen – a weakness that was obscured by a policy of minimal cruising. Possessing no royal facilities overseas, the French navy depended on private or foreign repair services. The British navy had three yards in the Caribbean and one in the Mediterranean at Gibraltar (after Port Mahon was lost), and could use the East India Company's well-equipped yard at Bombay, which even had a dry dock. The French navy suffered from a shortage of cannon in the first three years of the war. The domestic iron industry was not fit to cope with the challenge; hundreds of flawed guns delivered by incapable contractors were rejected, and some had to be borrowed from fortifications. The problem was partly sidestepped by sending a number of warships to North America *en flûte*, but shortages persisted until 1759.

In both navies the commissioned officers were not easily governed, but in the British case the Board of Admiralty – there was no equivalent in France – played the key role in promotions, discipline and selection of squadron commanders. In the French case there was only the naval (and colonial) minister, and his authority over the French officer corps was weak. This corps was an aristocracy of birth and naval connection, and because few naval operations had been conducted during the period of peace after 1714, patronage was not sufficiently moderated by operational experience. The situation was not much improved by the wartime expansion of the 1740s because, although the navy acquired quite a few highly competent officers at that time, they often came from merchant and privateering backgrounds and were therefore consigned to a separate category; they were referred to as *officiers bleus*, to distinguish them from higher born and well-connected officers, the *rouges*. It was very difficult for the naval minister to deal with proud officers like the *rouges*. When he criticized their performance or conduct they might seek direct intervention by an admiral or by an influential friend at court. British sea officers also looked to senior naval officers and sometimes political patrons for protection and favours, but they could never doubt that the Admiralty was the focus of authority in matters of discipline. In France, although the naval minister exercised his authority in the name of the king, officers rather easily appealed over his head. Consequently, it was up to the king to punish a well-connected or high-ranking officer, and Louis XV did not want the job.

Once the small cadre of capable, healthy and willing old admirals handed down from the wars of Louis XIV was exhausted, it was not easy for the naval minister to find suitable leaders with sea experience to command fleets and squadrons. *Officiers bleus* were barred from achieving high rank regardless of demonstrated skill and courage. Nevertheless, the corps of *rouges* included a number of talented, intelligent and courageous officers, sensitive to honour and reputation, who performed quite brilliantly. And while some ageing admirals showed all too plainly that they were no longer fit to command, others, like the elderly Du Bois de la Motte, were a credit to the service.

In Britain, a secretary of state in consultation with the cabinet made the major strategic decisions after receiving advice from the First Lord of the Admiralty. Appointments to key naval commands were invariably recommended by the Admiralty, a system quite different from that of the British army. Since the Admiralty secretary was in direct correspondence with sea officers of all ranks, his office accumulated a vast fund of naval and maritime knowledge. For the French navy the only high authorities were the naval minister and the king. One naval minister, Machault, generally acted with admirable insight and cogency, and in the early years of the war the available ships were astutely deployed, but after his dismissal there came a succession of appointees whose stay in office was brief. They endeavoured to learn, but their tenure was vulnerable and they inevitably lacked the combination of reputation and experience which could equip them to turn away impractical proposals. Strategic planning involving the navy was therefore subject to hazards of ignorance and incoherence. From 1758 onwards the French navy suffered not only from material inferiority but also inept direction.

Raids on the French Channel coast

Since Britain enjoyed naval superiority and had some troops available in 1758 it seemed obvious to the king of Prussia that British troops should be sent to Prince Ferdinand's army. Andrew Mitchell's letters to London in early 1758 repeatedly expressed the king of Prussia's desire to see this done. Ferdinand fought against the French, not the Austrians or Russians, did so very effectively, and reported directly to the British government. Britain could hardly hope for a more useful ally on the continent. But Pitt tried to avoid sending him troops. He realized that he had to allow some to be sent to garrison Emden in late March, but he asked for 'proper Assurances . . . that no future Demand in Relation to English troops, would be founded' upon it.[37]

Strategically this was perverse, but Hardwicke had understood Pitt's motives. As he told Newcastle:

It will probably be suggested by some here that it [the request for troops] has proceeded from the Insinuations, or advice, of the Hanover Ministers to the King of Prussia. I fear our new Friends [Pitt and his close associates] have promis'd the Country-Gentlemen that no such thing shall be; and that may be part of the Terms of their agreeing to give the Money. . . . [If the issue were to create] a Breach in this administration, it would do more hurt to the King of Prussia and weaken the King's cause in Germany more than 10,000 men may do it good. The whole Supply for Germany may possibly depend upon it.[38]

In other words, the problem was political. People would not fail to notice that British troops in north-western Germany would be fighting to defend

---

[37] Holdernesse's conversation with Pitt reported to Newcastle, 27 March 1758, BL Add. 32,878, ff. 383–4.

[38] Hardwicke to Newcastle, 29 Jan. 1758, BL Add. 32,877, fo. 276.

Hanover, and this was bound to anger Pitt's core supporters.[39] In late January he dispatched a furious attack on Mitchell, saying that the envoy had provoked the king of Prussia's requests. It was entirely unfair, but it was a way to put a stop to the troop requests without criticizing Frederick. It was also a warning to Newcastle, who had openly favoured the dispatch of British troops. Pitt's political position mattered. As Hardwicke observed, it was more important to ensure continuing appropriations to sustain Ferdinand's army, which had to be voted by Parliament annually, than to send a contingent of British troops.

There was also the question of an annual subsidy for Prussia. At a cabinet meeting of 23 February attended by Pitt, Newcastle, Hardwicke and Holdernesse, a clear-cut decision was reached to tell Frederick that neither a Baltic squadron nor British troops would be sent, and that he must quickly declare whether he was willing to accept a subsidy so that a parliamentary vote could be obtained for it. Frederick had not wanted to ask for a subsidy. He wanted a free hand to open negotiations for peace whenever it suited him. Undoubtedly he had peace with France in mind – he had in fact made gestures in that direction – and it was exactly what the British cabinet did not wish to see. But his resources were running low and he accepted. On 11 April 1758 a treaty forming a solid Anglo-Prussian alliance was signed which provided a subsidy of £670,000 per year. The only proviso was that the kings of Great Britain and Prussia must both consent to any decision for peace. Maria Theresa had feared that British money might be transmitted to her enemy, and now it was going to happen, on a regular basis.

Pitt was determined to pursue a strategy of coastal raiding. The raids were to be timed to coincide with an offensive by Ferdinand. At the end of March Pitt got the cabinet to agree to appoint three high-ranking generals – Sir John Ligonier, Charles, 3rd Duke of Marlborough and Lord George Sackville – as a committee to decide upon the objective and draw up plans. In mid-April troops were ordered to gather on the Isle of Wight. Marlborough and Sackville were to command the army, and Commodore Richard Howe to lead the naval force, which consisted mainly of frigates. Hawke, believing he had been disfavoured (Anson had failed to communicate to him the nature of Commodore Howe's command), angrily struck his flag, and to prevent this mistaken personal reaction from causing delay the First Lord himself took over command of the Channel fleet. Its task was to make sure that the Brest squadron did not interfere.

[39] He was right; see Peters, *Pitt and Popularity*, pp. 118–22.

This was not a small expedition. Howe's ships carried 6,000 seamen; the expeditionary army numbered almost 14,000 including engineers and artillerymen; 1,000 cavalry were to be transported and landed. Flat-bottomed boats that could land 50 troops at a time were specially designed and hurriedly built; they were quite large but could be slung aboard the transports. The objective was the fortified port city of St Malo, one of France's principal privateering bases. This old city, built of wooden structures was mostly located on an island and was ringed by formidable stone ramparts. The expedition carried mortars capable of launching red-hot cannon balls as well as explosive shells. If St Malo, fearing destruction by fire, were to surrender, the French would have to devote a strong land force to its recovery. On 1 June the fleet headed across the Channel, and five days later it reached Cancale Bay east of St Malo; immediately after arrival army officers went ashore and examined the landing area. It was a good location. The beach lay at the bottom of cliffs, but there were four passages to high ground and frigates could anchor close enough inshore (one propped itself up on the mud) for their guns to bear. Naval gunfire soon forced a small French battery above the beach at La Houle to be abandoned, and the troops were landed without a shot fired at them. A quarter of the soldiers were then employed in building a strong perimeter defence of the landing area. After the town of Cancale was given up without a fight the bulk of the army marched westwards to the outskirts of St Malo, and 2,000 men were quickly dispatched to attack Saint Servan which lay just south of the city. There they burnt 2 frigates under construction, 20 privateers in harbour, and 70 other vessels as well as ships' stores and warehouses. The British could not, however, deliver the planned threat to St Malo itself. Because the terrain and roads from Cancale were unexpectedly bad Marlborough decided that the heavy guns and mortars could not be brought to the scene. On the 10th, believing that strong enemy forces were converging on him, he resolved to leave, and by 12 June re-embarkation was completed. There had been practically no losses of any kind. Marlborough's anxieties were, in fact, unfounded. French troops were not approaching, and his own force was superior to anything in the vicinity.[40]

As will be seen shortly, the premature withdrawal was extremely upsetting to Pitt and the king because the timing of the operation had been coordinated with a planned offensive by Ferdinand. When the fleet

---

[40] There was no sign that more than a battalion or two had come near the area. Corbett's thoughts on this question are cogent (I, 279-80).

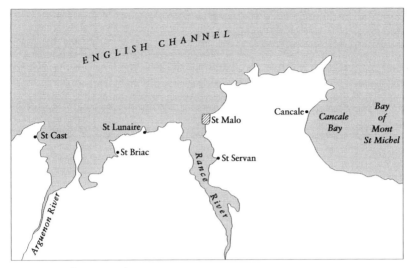

MAP 6 *Raids on St Malo*

returned to Spithead on 30 July Pitt was eager to see another effort launched, but the troops were disembarked to restore their health, and at this point the expeditionary force lost its two generals since both were granted their requests to go to Germany. The new commander was Lieutenant General Thomas Bligh, 74 years old, appointed after other senior officers refused. (Obviously, Pitt did not yet have the support he wanted from the army.) Howe remained in command of the naval support squadron. A force numbering about 11,000 men including cavalry and artillerymen sailed on 1 August. Its destination was Cherbourg, a fishing and privateering port that the French had long thought of fortifying but never really did.

The objective and the landing site were well chosen. On 7 August, leaving a bomb vessel to launch mortar fire on the town as a diversion, Howe anchored off a beach 5 miles to the west. As boats of the first wave advanced, Howe's warships cannonaded the shoreline, much in the manner of modern amphibious landings. Of the 8,000 French defenders only 2,000 were present in the landing area. Their resistance was ineffective and they were quickly overwhelmed. In fact, they suffered more casualties than the British. The French commander, the comte de Raymond, retreated with his entire force to Valognes, 13 miles to the south-east. (He was quickly replaced, subsequently court-martialled, and dismissed from the army.) Bligh's men marched to Cherbourg unopposed and received the town's surrender on 8 August. There was a good deal of marauding but also some well-focused destruction: guns and ordnance stores were seized, and vessels were captured or burnt. Engineers and artillerymen tried to outdo each other when demolishing the fortifications, a rivalry that was not without acrimony. Even under new commanders the French troops could not be persuaded to counter-attack, and in truth the British position, situated as it was at the extremity of the Cotentin peninsula, was easy to defend. So long as the transports were able to hold their anchorage there was no need for the army to leave until such time as the French could produce a superior force. In any case, Bligh's army, having suffered very few casualties, re-embarked on 15 and 16 August. All in all, it had been a highly successful raid and was praised by press and public in Britain.

Bligh and Howe knew that they were expected to conduct another raid, but strong winds forced the fleet to take shelter on the English coast. When the commanders put to sea again it was without adequate planning or instruction. Pitt, who had been closely involved in planning the raiding strategy hitherto, was negligent in this instance, and so was Ligonier. Howe seems to have thought that an attempt on St Malo from the west would succeed, and Bligh's staff wanted to do something impressive. Returning to St Malo was a bad idea, however. The city was on guard, and the supposition that troops could cross the River Rance (where a large tidal power-generation facility stands today) was wildly erroneous. Besides, the defenders had moored a frigate and five privateers at the river's entrance. Howe's men put the army ashore at St Lunaire, unopposed, on 4 September. It was quickly discovered that there was no attainable objective of any value. When a north-west wind blew hard on the 6th, Howe's anchorage became unsafe and he moved a few miles westwards to shelter in the bay of St Cast. Fortunately the beach at St Cast was suitable for re-embarking troops, guns and horses, and was not far away. Bligh's task was now clear. He needed to send engineering and artillery units ahead to make the beach defensible for re-embarkation and to get his army there as quickly as possible.

What he and his aides were thinking is a matter of dispute. Possibly they considered giving battle; the mission might then be accounted a successful diversion. Only at a location near St Cast could this be considered a sane strategy, yet Bligh's army was slow to move and when preparing to cross the small Arguenon river allowed itself to be delayed by local volunteers with muskets. The contrast between Bligh's unhurried performance and the conduct of the conduct of Emmanuel-Armand de

Vignerod du Plessis de Richelieu, duc d'Aiguillon, who commanded the Breton coast defence, could not have been greater. When word reached d'Aiguillon, then near Brest, that British troops were ashore he immediately ordered half the military force stationed there to go east by forced marches. The troops reached a position fifteen miles southwest of St Cast in three days. Meanwhile, the battalion at St Mal. plus a number of other Breton-based units hurried to the scene. At 10.30 in the morning of 11 September French troops came into view from Howe's warships, which immediately poured cannon and mortar fire upon them, but d'Aubigny seeing that most of the British force had already been got safely off in boats, ordered a lunge at the beach. French musketry pelted the boats as they continued to bring troops off, while British grenadier guards on the beach repelled attackers despite their lack of prepared defensive positions. Pounded from high ground by French field guns and thinned by musket fire, the British rearguard took heavy casualties before surrendering. It was a clear victory for the French, and considering how rapidly troops and artillery had come from Brest, a well-deserved one. According to an official count the British lost about 800 men, half of them prisoners. On the French side about 400 were killed or wounded. Thus, an expedition undertaken without careful planning and without a competent army commander overshadowed the first two successes. Pitt abandoned the strategy of raiding. The event was triumphantly celebrated in Paris; in French historical memory it became established that the British army lost 4,000 men at St Cast.

France in distress

In April 1758 George II wrote to Prince Ferdinand (letters drafted by Pitt) urging him to put pressure on Clermont's army. The general responded that his troops needed time for rest and recuperation, but hinted that he might attempt something big and suggested that the British should think of preparing an expedition to threaten France's coast near Dunkirk. This would make the French hesitate to send reinforcements to the Rhine. A landing near Dunkirk was not feasible. As we have seen, the British selected St Malo. The planners expected that the raiding force could remain long enough to provoke a significant French military response, but Marlborough failed to stay. In fact, he departed just when Ferdinand had committed his army to a hazardous offensive on the west side of the Rhine, so Pitt and George II had a very good reason to deplore Marlborough's premature departure. They knew that Ferdinand was being let down.

When Ferdinand of Brunswick crossed the Rhine near the Dutch border he took the French completely by surprise. In great secrecy and under false pretences his engineers had obtained in the Dutch Republic boats and equipment to construct a boat-bridge. On the night of 1 June at a point that was slightly over the border in Dutch territory 6,000 of his men got across, and more followed within two days. Preparations had been beautifully disguised by scheduling a formal review of the whole army near Münster the day before, ostensibly to muster the troops of His Britannic Majesty's Army in Germany prior to payment by the British Treasury. In this deceptive manner it was assembled and organized to march. When he received news of the crossing on 5 June, Marshal Belleisle ordered Soubise, who had started heading for Bohemia, to go north to threaten Ferdinand's flank from the east side of the river and urged Clermont to counter-attack the bridgehead. Clermont retreated instead.

In an urgent dispatch to Marlborough, Pitt reminded him of his orders and insisted that some further attempt should be made, preferably on the coast of Normandy. Although the fleet paraded along that coast, no landing occurred. And then Pitt did something that amazed his colleagues. On 17 June he proposed that 6,000 British troops, including 12 cavalry squadrons, should be sent to Ferdinand. Clearly, he admired the general's boldness and skill, and he knew that the British people were responding warmly to reports that the French were being pushed back. He may also have felt that his expeditionary force in the Channel had not kept his side of a bargain.

The French commander-in-chief was by nature hesitant and it did not help that he was being deluged by letters from Versailles. Pompadour's were a nuisance. The letters to Clermont from Belleisle contained good military advice but crossed with his own and the delays were harmful. Because Paris was 250 miles away courier transit took at least two days each way. It was a moment when Louis XV ought to have gone to the army as his forebears had done, with Belleisle at his side, but both men remained at Versailles. Although the French army in the area outnumbered the enemy by about two to one, Clermont was apprehensive about counter-attacking and ended up fighting a defensive battle at Kreveld on 23 June 1758.

The French chose their ground well, but Hanoverian and Prussian cavalry found points for penetrating which Ferdinand's infantry and artillery exploited. At the end of a long afternoon the French were forced to withdraw, which they did in an orderly manner, but they lost 5,200 killed or wounded while the Hanoverians lost 1,800; in addition 3,000

French were taken prisoner. Among the French dead was the comte de Gisors, Belleisle's only son. Alarm and despondency reigned at Versailles; it was aggravated by dismaying celebrations in Paris where the public hoped that the defeat would force a peace. Undaunted, Belleisle made the right moves. He ordered Soubise to divert to Hesse-Cassel in order to put pressure on Ferdinand's rear in Westphalia. Clermont, who had lost confidence in himself, was replaced by Louis-George-Erasme, marquis de Contades, an experienced but cautious military man. The new commander-in-chief was not without means to make Ferdinand's recrossing of the Rhine hazardous but nevertheless failed to do so. On 9 August, just south of Wesel which was still in French hands, the entire Hanoverian army retreated over a boat-bridge without loss. Shortly afterwards it was joined by British troops and cavalry which came by way of the North Sea.

The victory at Krefeld was celebrated in England with bell-ringing and bonfires, so public opinion was, for the moment, not a problem, and Pitt's long-standing anxiety that George II might try to replace Ferdinand with the Duke of Cumberland drained away. He decided to raise the total number of British troops for His Britannic Majesty's Army in Germany to 9,000.

As ordered by Belleisle, Soubise marched his army through Hesse to threaten Hanover, and Ferdinand was forced to meet the challenge. He took up a position between Soubise and Contades, the latter moving slowly eastward along the Lippe. In October Soubise won a battle which brought him a marshal's baton, but retired to winter quarters in the southern sector of Hesse. Lack of provisions and forage prompted Contades to withdraw back across the Rhine, while Ferdinand was able to winter his army in Westphalia near Münster. Thus France's 1758 campaigning season ended. The army had begun to improve its capabilities under Belleisle's administration, and its strength would always be greater than Ferdinand's notwithstanding the British reinforcements, but serious logistical problems would persist whenever it tried to maintain itself deep in Germany.[41]

Throughout 1758 the abbé Bernis saw the war as one that France could only lose. The army might be recovering, but the monarchy's finances were under severe strain. Recent attempts to raise funds by issuing annuities were complete failures. Despite Louis XV's February resolve to give full support to Austria, Bernis continued to urge peace. Unable to persuade him, Bernis hoped to persuade Vienna. He asked Stainville to suggest to

---

[41] The basic logistical problems are pointed out in Scott, 'Hanover', pp. 293–4.

Maria Theresa that she begin a negotiation by offering to confirm Prussia's possession of Silesia in exchange for liberation of Saxony.

Bernis was wasting his breath. The Austrian army, with new recruits coming from all over the Habsburg dominions, made a remarkable recovery in 1758, and it was employed with great wisdom by Marshal Daun, whose skilful night-time manoeuvring compelled Frederick to lift his siege of Olmütz. This achievement in Moravia on 30 June was seconded by an Austrian ambush of a vital Prussian supply convoy; about 4,000 wagons were destroyed. Soon Frederick was forced to go north to confront the Russians, who had marched to the River Oder. By September Daun was at the gates of Dresden, joined by an Imperial army, but Soubise was still in Hesse. After the bloody battle of Zorndorf on 25 August, in which Frederick launched an unwise attack that cost him heavy losses, the Russians left the Oder, and Frederick was able to rescue Dresden. In the final battle of the season, at Hochkirch in mid-October, Daun once again outwitted Frederick, but the Austrian general nevertheless retired from Saxony to winter his army in Bohemia. All in all, Austria had recovered brilliantly and was certainly not going to quit the war, and the Russians had demonstrated that their army was a formidable opponent.

Compared to the Austrian, the French military record in the months after Krefeld was anaemic. When Bernis heard about Daun's rescue of Olmütz he emphasized to Stainville that France's situation remained, and would remain, unaltered:

The nation is in despair. Whatever success the empress may have, we have lost our cause, since our navy is gone; and so, if we wish to support the maritime war, it will be necessary to give up the other war totally. The navy owes one hundred million. There are no more sailors in the kingdom. . . . The stroke has failed, and one must never run after lost money. We have no army; we have no generals; we shall have still less by continuing the war, because this army will lack everything, and it makes war in a country wretched of itself [Westphalia] and ruined by both sides. The physical theatre of the war will not change. It can no longer be hoped that our military glory can recover without money and without the well-being of the troops and officers.[42]

---

[42] Bernis to Stainville, 4 Sept. 1758, Masson, ed. *Mémoires et Lettres de . . . Bernis*, II, 266–7.

The foreign minister's description, though exaggerated, was perceptive. Stainville may have agreed with it but was also receiving letters from Pompadour, who supported the Austrian desire to continue fighting, and it was by her influence that he was made duc de Choiseul and brought back to Versailles. Although Pompadour still liked Bernis, abandonment of the Austrian alliance would have brought her down. Bernis welcomed the idea that he would be sharing authority with Choiseul, but in early December he was dismissed and Choiseul became foreign minister.

While in Vienna, Choiseul had been thoroughly involved in Bernis's effort to extricate France from the onerous terms of the second treaty of Versailles. He had an interview with Maria Theresa and informed her that if Austria wished to continue the war, a new treaty would be necessary in which French assistance would be sharply curtailed. Kaunitz was furious: France had hardly fulfilled any of her treaty obligations and now proposed to nullify them. But, unlike Bernis, Choiseul was not asking for peace. The ambassador was, in fact, playing a double game, formally conveying the advices of Bernis while bending to opinions that the king and Pompadour were sending him in private letters. Kaunitz soon realized that Choiseul, unlike Bernis, was in favour of maintaining the alliance although he was also determined to reduce the subsidy. And indeed, upon returning to Paris to serve as foreign minister, Choiseul continued to insist that the Austrians must accept a reduction. He also showed that he was perfectly suited to the task of imposing it on them. Using a blend of duplicity and bluster (Starhemberg found him insufferable to deal with) he obtained Vienna's acceptance of a third treaty of Versailles that essentially abrogated the second. Louis's claim to the Netherlands for his nephew was given up, France's monetary obligations to Austria were materially lessened, and France was no longer required to keep fighting until Austria recovered Silesia and Glatz. France promised to deploy a 100,000-man army in Germany but it was understood that she would not send troops against the Prussians. Continuation of subsidy money for Vienna, and also for Sweden, Denmark and selected German principalities was affirmed. There were actually two treaties, one of them secret; both were accepted in March 1758 but backdated to 31 December 1757.

The cost of the 100,000-man army and the subsidies, when added to naval and colonial expenses, vastly exceeded the French monarchy's ability to pay, a fact that it was hard for the king and his mistress to accept since they judged France to be a rich country. They talked blithely of procuring funds sufficient to continue the war for several more years in order to achieve a satisfactory peace.[43] But their personal views were not in accordance with what Choiseul told the Austrians. He presented a bleak report of France's financial condition. Kaunitz's reaction was to doubt that Versailles was making a genuine effort. What excuse (he posed this question to Starhemberg) did the monarch of France, ruler of a much richer country than Austria, have for failing to raise funds?

A modern historian would answer by pointing out the deep flaws in Old Regime France's financial arrangements, flaws that played a major role in toppling the Bourbon monarchy 31 years later. There were, however, specific causes of the financial distress that loomed in 1758. At the fundamental level the problem was woefully insufficient revenues. In the preceding war the government had promptly raised taxes to meet wartime expenses, so the accumulating war debt did not become excessive. In the Seven Years War this was not done.

At first, it appeared that it would be done. Upon the eruption of hostilities in 1755 the parlement of Paris agreed to register new loans and to allow an increase of indirect taxes to meet the interest payments. After the declaration of war in June 1756 the government proposed that a peacetime *vingtième* (a 5 per cent tax on income and property) that was introduced in 1749 to begin paying off war debt should be extended for ten years, and in addition asked for a second *vingtième*. In recent years royal relations with the *parlementaires* had been rubbed raw by the controversy over withholding sacraments, as noted earlier, so it was not surprising that the parlement of Paris objected strenuously to the second *vingtième*. There were heated debates. (This institution lacked the power that the British House of Commons wielded in matters of finance, but it did possess a right to register new taxes, and unless they were registered they could not be legally collected.) For whatever reason, Louis XV adopted a hard line. He cut short the protest and moved quickly to a *lit de justice*, thus bypassing ancient formalities. The parlement of Paris did not meekly submit, however, and in mid-December 1756 the king issued edicts to discipline the members who had disobeyed. The monarchy obtained registration of its second *vingtième* by means of the *lit de justice*, but it had used that power impatiently, as if to declare that a French king at war should not be expected to consult parlement. As we have seen, Louis told a delegation that he alone could be the judge of necessary royal

[43] In their letters to Maria Theresa and Stainville (Choiseul) at Vienna, Waddington, *Guerre*, II, 434–5.

expenditures.[44] In other words, royal budgetary needs were to be decreed, not discussed.

After this episode Louis XV avoided dealing with the parlement of Paris. The war was carried on by delayed bill payments and other expedients, instead of long-term loans financed by new taxes. No doubt the king expected an early occupation of Hanover and rapid defeat of Prussia to bring a quick end to the war, but when disaster befell the French army in Germany and introduced the prospect of a long war, this financial policy became dangerous. Bernis realized that something had to be done. He tried to obtain the cooperation of the parlement of Paris by consulting with its leadership. He was working towards a rapprochement (against the wishes of the king and Pompadour) when he was dismissed on 9 November 1758.

Much of the growing cost of the war was now being financed by bills and notes whose holders had a right to expect reasonably prompt payment. But delayed payment became the rule, and suppliers inflated their prices not only to compensate for higher wartime costs but also to reflect steeper discount rates on the bills they received in payment. The government reacted to the inflated prices by supposing them to be unwarranted and appointed commissioners to scrutinize the bills. From April 1758 onwards, rumours spread through money markets that bills drawn for the navy and colonies, already being paid late, might not be paid at all. The general uneasiness about government credit affected the operations of the great financier, Jean Pâris de Monmartel (Pâris Duverney's brother). Monmartel, who supplied money to the army and for subsidies to allies, was having great difficulty raising money. He knew how deficient the monarchy's revenues were and, seeing his own fortune at risk, he wished to stop lending. This man's ability to raise cash and obtain credit for the government was indispensable to the monarchy's ability to continue the war. Monmartel's age, poor health, and growing reluctance to serve the government was one reason why Bernis considered peace essential. In fact, Monmartel was strongly urging him to end the war. To all appearances the only action anyone at Versailles could think of was to investigate and disappoint the creditors. The French monarchy was heading towards a financial black hole.

As foreign minister, the duc de Choiseul was not required to become involved in the problems of finance, and he avoided them. He could not, however, avoid the fundamental issues of grand strategy, and here he

[44] See above, p. 227.

faced a political and personal dilemma. Louis XV was determined to uphold his standing in Europe, and was aware that if he now abandoned the effort to occupy Hanover, all Europe would perceive the measure of his weakness. Belleisle as war minister agreed, and Pompadour was determined to support the Austrian alliance. Choiseul had to recognize their priorities, but he worried about the war with Britain. Before he left Vienna he told Maria Theresa that France could 'no longer close her eyes to her exhaustion and to her own true interests; she is not able to give up two hundred millions which her maritime commerce had provided France, which allowed her to maintain a great army and to pay subsidies to her allies'.[45] In other words, trade and colonies were essential to French capabilities as a great power; thought must be given to their recovery and preservation.

Yet Choiseul was unable to answer the question that Bernis had asked repeatedly: How would France find money to restore the navy? As a practical matter – taking into account the king's and Pompadour's wishes – his policy had to consist of maintaining the Austrian alliance at reduced expense and pursuing the conquest of Hanover in hopes that it would bring Britain to the peace table. Thought might be given to the vulnerability of the colonies, but without a navy little could be done to help them. They would have to defend themselves as best they could.

---

[45] His memorandum of an interview with Maria Theresa, quoted by Batzel, 'Austria and the First Three Treaties' (cited in Chapter 8), p. 499. I have altered Batzel's translation of 'abandon' to 'give up'.

CHAPTER 10

The Atlantic and North America, 1758

By the spring of 1758 the Royal Navy was easily able to over-match the French at Louisbourg because of its overwhelming superiority. But superiority measured in numbers, tonnage and guns could not guarantee 'command of the sea', which embraces two goals: reasonably safe communications for one's own strategic and commercial purposes, and denial of use of the sea to the enemy.

In the Seven Years War, security for British expeditions and commerce was fundamentally guaranteed by the Western Squadron. By its presence off the French coast this strong squadron deterred the French from form-ing attack squadrons. Fifty years before, such squadrons (often organized as privateering enterprises which leased French navy ships) had posed a serious problem. Now, the Royal Navy's cruisers had the upper hand. (Ninety per cent of bounty money paid for capturing or destroying enemy cruisers and privateers in the Seven Years War went to officers and crews of the Royal Navy; very little was earned by British privateers.[1]) Thus the navy protected British shipping, not just by escorting convoys, but also by reducing the number and strength of French predators at sea.

The navy was not nearly so effective in denying France the use of the sea. Warships, from Brest or from ports in the Bay of Biscay, generally escaped. The Western Squadron was often able to delay their sailing, some-times to the point of forcing an expedition to wait so long for a favourable wind that its mission was entirely frustrated. But sailings could seldom be prevented. This was especially true regarding warships, but even merchant ships, if reasonably fast, were able to get to sea safely. In other words, there was no effective blockade: the British navy could inhibit but not

---

[1] Based on navy office 'Head Money' vouchers, analysed by Michell in 'British Prize-taking'.

prevent the French from carrying troops and supplies to India, the West Indies or North America. Notwithstanding its attainment of superiority in early 1758 the British navy could not even prevent desperately needed French provisions from reaching Quebec.

Nevertheless, in 1758 the war in North America turned in Britain's favour, just as it did in Europe. This chapter will mention certain basic changes that gave advantage to the British and Americans over the French and Canadians. Among them was an alteration of Indian allegiance away from active support of the French, a trend which, though not plainly visible, was of great importance. In addition, thanks to steps taken by Pitt, Hardwicke and Newcastle, there was, as will be seen, an improvement in the quality of military leadership in North America. The record in 1758 was not perfect. Regular army forces, although they conducted a successful siege at Louisbourg, misconducted an assault at Ticonderoga. Provincial troops, ably commanded by a British general and his Swiss second-in-command, would be the mainstay of a logistically challenging offensive in Pennsylvania. A provincial force, led by a regular army colonel, John Bradstreet, would carry out a daring and successful raid on Fort Frontenac. The idea that the military victories in North America in this war were all achieved by regular troops is false. Provincial troops were important in combat as well as support roles. A big change was that from 1758 forwards the British regular officers did a better job.

Sea power and shipping

Applied to the Seven Years War the phrase 'British blockade' is misleading. French warships and merchant vessels often reached open sea by waiting for a strong wind from an easterly quarter. Ordinarily it was that simple. If, however, a large merchant convoy was involved, the odds changed. Gathering a hundred ships or more took time and could not be kept secret, so the Western Squadron would be alerted, and such a convoy inevitably sailed at a slow pace. Even so, interception was not guaranteed. Sir Edward Hawke's success in the second battle of Cape Finisterre (October 1747) resulted from a feint: he paraded his squadron off the north coast of Spain and thereafter deduced the convoy's probable course. The interception was called by the British the Second Battle of Cape Finisterre – misleadingly because it occurred far to the north of that cape. Mindful that the French naval squadrons had twice suffered grievously when assigned to escort convoys in 1747, Machault, the naval minister in 1756, abandoned the practice. Merchants at the ports protested, but in fact their ships were almost always able to get to sea in small groups unscathed. A favouring wind and an alteration in course after dark did the trick.

Yet despite their success in getting ships to sea, within two years French merchants stopped sending ships to the West Indies because losses became unacceptable. The reason was that numerous captures occurred in Caribbean and American waters (often made by American colonial privateers), and also on the return voyage, especially near Europe's landfalls. There were simply too many British cruisers and privateers patrolling the seas. Bordeaux lost a total of 140 ships during the war, not counting its 96 merchant ships taken in 1755 when the victims thought they were safe. There were 103 departures from Bordeaux in 1756, but the number dropped to 38 in 1757, and 4 in 1758.[2] La Rochelle merchants kept hoping for success, but results were disastrous: 45 of their 57 ships that sailed in 1757 were lost; in 1758 they lost 34 of 39.[3] The merchants of Nantes, where the slave trade was dominant, quickly decided not to send out any ships at all. Their voyages were triangular – first to Africa to acquire slaves, then to the Caribbean to sell them, then home with plantation goods. In wartime this was far too hazardous. The number of British captures reached a peak of 390 in 1757 – 252 made by privateers, 132 by the Royal Navy, and 4 unspecified; of the total, 202 ships were condemned as prizes.[4] Taken as a whole, French commerce with the West Indies fell by the end of 1758 to a value less than a quarter of the pre-war figure, and in 1759–60 it was almost non-existent. Privateering was a possible alternative, and some Bayonne merchants took it up, but to make a profit one needed not only a fast well-armed ship and large crew but also luck when bringing a prize vessel to port for condemnation. That vessel, often a slow sailer, stood a good chance of being recaptured.

Initially, Machault planned to deploy small offshore squadrons to greet incoming ships and see them safely to port, but these squadrons never materialized. In 1757 when the Bordeaux chamber of commerce asked for one he refused, as did his successor Moras. Such a squadron was bound to get the attention of the British navy and suffer accordingly. The Bordeaux merchants on their own initiative armed a strong privateer to chase the enemy away from the entrance of the Gironde estuary, but by

[2] F. Crouzet, in Pariset, ed. *Bordeaux au XVIIIe Siècle*, pp. 290–1.

[3] Charles Frostin, 'Les colons de Saint-Domingue et la métropole' *Revue historique* 237 (April–June 1967), 396, citing a thesis by H. Robert.

[4] Michell, 'British Prize-taking'.

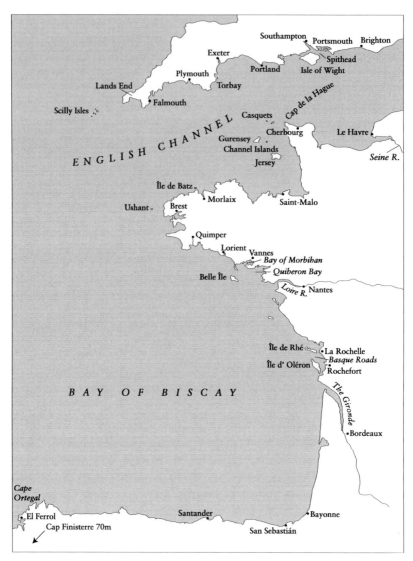

MAP 7 *English Channel and French Atlantic coasts*

summer 1758 it dared not operate because enemy frigates lurked nearby. Fifty years earlier, in the war of the Spanish Succession, French privateering captains commanded powerful squadrons that were often strong enough to overwhelm their British naval opponents. In the Seven Years War such a strategy was impossible. Any French squadron cruising offshore was bound to be overmatched by the Western Squadron.

Knowing how dependent the French West Indian islands were on food and wine from France, and seeing the reluctance of the merchants to undertake voyages without naval escort, Machault proposed in early 1756 to throw open the trade to neutral shipping. Colonial governors and plantation owners were happy about this, but merchants in France hated it, and the chambers of commerce at Bordeaux, La Rochelle, Nantes and Rouen held back from issuing the authorizing passports (which would undoubtedly be taken up by the Dutch, their despised competitors). Having claimed that there was no need for neutral assistance, Bordeaux merchants, joined by those at La Rochelle, felt they must back up words with deeds. The effort, as we have just seen, cost them dearly. Although they continued to oppose the admission of neutral carriers into their trade monopoly, the minister kept on insisting, and by the autumn of 1757 practically no one doubted that neutral shipping was the only remedy for serving the islands. As a result, Dutch and Danish vessels busily carried provisions to the French West Indian colonies and brought sugar, coffee and indigo to Europe. The British were therefore face to face with the problem of neutral carriers.

When a belligerent power attempts to deprive an opponent of money and materials by seizing its ships and cargoes this problem invariably arises. A delicate balance between strict enforcement and diplomatic harm must be struck, especially if the neutral country might be provoked into active alliance with the enemy. On what legal grounds could the British curtail neutral carriage of French goods? The solution was found by focusing on a commonplace of mercantilist policy. Foreign vessels were forbidden to enter French ports and load cargoes in peacetime. To allow it in wartime French officials had to issue special passports. This provided Lord Hardwicke with a handle. He observed:

All nations shut out foreigners from trading to their American colonies and so things stood at the time of making the Treaty of 1674. . . . The question is whether we shall suffer them [the Dutch] to trade thither in time of war without seizure, when the French themselves will not suffer them to trade thither in time of peace.[5]

In other words, if French authorities forbade foreign vessels to trade with their colonies in peacetime, why should the British government freely allow them to remove the restriction in wartime? This question became the basis of the 'Rule of the War of 1756'. The rule declared, essentially,

[5] Memorandum to Joseph Yorke, 17 Sept. 1756, Yorke, *Hardwicke*, II, 312–14.

that a foreign ship having gained French official permission to load cargo in a French or French colonial port was deemed a French ship by adoption. It followed that both the ship and its cargo could be condemned in a British prize court. Approved by the cabinet and authorized by the High Court of Admiralty, the text was transmitted to The Hague on 29 August 1758 and then to the other capitals of Europe.

There remained another problem, however. The Dutch and the Danes possessed colonies of their own in the West Indies. Except for Dutch Surinam, these produced very little, but some were situated to serve as trans-shipment points for French trade, especially the tiny Dutch island of St Eustatius, which was close to Guadeloupe. It was obvious that the sudden growth of traffic at these islands in 1757 stemmed from shipments of French goods. In response the British developed the doctrine of 'Continuous Voyage'. Its justification was found in standing regulations that forbade foreign ships to carry French colonial produce. (Under 'Continuous Voyage', however, only the cargo, not the ship, could be condemned as prize.) These innovations crafted by the British government in the Seven Years War continued to serve as reference points in debates over belligerent and neutral rights for decades, even centuries, to come.

During the rest of the war the Dutch and Danish authorities had to accept the Rule of the War of 1756, though the Dutch government did not say so publicly. The doctrine of 'Continuous Voyage', which allowed cargoes from St Eustatius and Curaçao to be condemned, took Dutch merchants and insurers by surprise, however, and expressions of outrage erupted. The consternation caused by the new rules coincided with a furore aroused by reckless arrests of innocent neutral ships and crews in the Channel by British privateers. The number of detained neutral vessels also surged in 1758; less than 10 per cent of these were detained by Royal Navy cruisers.[6] Most were eventually set free, but detention was often prolonged, and there was talk in Holland of providing naval escorts. Joseph Yorke told his father that something had to be done.

In late December 1758 Pitt took action. He directed the release of some Surinam ships and pledged to shorten the detention process. Moreover, he realized that British privateers were too numerous and the smaller ones were unruly. By requiring a substantial bond to be paid when a privateer received its commission, so that damages could be recovered if it were to seize an innocent vessel, fewer privateers would be authorized. The new regulations would be unpopular with some of his political supporters, but

[6] Michell, 'British Prize-taking'.

would make manning the navy easier, and Pitt used the manning problem to justify the measure. Since, for both the Danes and the Dutch, the greatest grievance was unwarranted arrest and the threat of prolonged detention (a threat that some British privateers used to extort money), the bill enacted as 32 George II c. 25 had good effects. Abuses by privateers could never be completely eliminated, but the British government now took the problem seriously.

The new rules covering neutral trade with the French West Indies provided clarity and predictability. It is interesting, however, that the Spanish were not held to the same strict rules that were imposed on the Dutch and the Danes. It was feared that Spain, if provoked, would actively assist France and penalize British commerce. Another reason was that Spanish ships, though they traded with Saint-Domingue (as did Irish, British and American colonial vessels), did not commonly trade with Martinique and Guadeloupe. In any case, it was impossible to interdict trading with Saint-Domingue significantly. Another consideration was that British strategists did not contemplate capturing that colony. Martinique and Guadeloupe, however, were targeted for eventual conquest, and the determination to cut off all shipments to and from these islands stemmed partly from a desire to weaken the resources and morale of the French colonists who would be called upon to defend them against a British invasion. Although St Eustatius remained in business, the relief it provided to the French was sharply reduced under the new rules. At times Martinique was dreadfully short of food, and it survived mainly because its privateers captured vessels carrying British provisions.

The annihilation of commerce between the home country and the West Indies caused severe economic distress in France's port cities. Closing down this commerce, which had fuelled a highly profitable re-export trade to northern Europe, was a considerable British achievement, but, one may ask, did it have a significant war-winning effect? Although measurement is impossible, it undoubtedly caused the French monarchy's revenues to suffer from loss of import duties. Perhaps more significant was the curtailment of the port merchants' profitable returns, on which the navy's treasurers often relied for cash and credit. Nevertheless, if Britain's crushing of France's trade in plantation goods had been a separate naval endeavour, its trouble and expense could probably not have been justified as a war measure.

But it was not a separate endeavour. The capture of French merchant ships trading to the West Indies had side effects which served military purposes. It deprived France of seamen, who were made prisoners of war.

It gave British captains and ships' companies, hoping for prize money, an incentive to stay at sea. Given the attraction of prize money and the ultimate protection afforded by the Western Squadron, British cruisers and privateers had strong reasons for going to sea while their French opposites had strong reasons for avoiding it. The resulting imbalance in the number of cruisers and privateers at sea was what stacked the odds so heavily against the safe return of French merchant ships.

The curtailment of shipments of naval stores and timber to French dockyards was clearly a military objective. These commodities were, in modern terms, 'strategic materials'. Russia and the Scandinavian countries were the places of origin, and geography dictated that British interception of ships destined for France from those countries was bound to be easy. The French understood from the outset that they could not employ their own shipping in this service. The Dutch, long accustomed to Baltic voyages, were happy to assist. After some ill-judged diplomacy Versailles realized that Dutch neutrality was advantageous to France and soon asked the Dutch to observe an 'exact neutrality', adding that they should insist on their right by the treaty of 1674 with England to carry naval stores to France.[7]

In the summer of 1756 British cruisers stopped a convoy of Dutch ships off Dover; many were found to be carrying naval stores destined for France. The materials were clearly not of French origin nor were they shipped from French or French colonial ports, so they did not come under the Rule of the War of 1756 and doctrine of 'Continuous Voyage'. Dutch merchants were allowed to ship naval stores to France, but Swedish and Danish merchants were not. The British government initially allowed their shipments to pass, but this leniency was soon withdrawn. Pitch, tar and masts carried by Swedish vessels to France were declared to be contraband of war and subject to seizure along with the ships carrying them. Danish shippers were given the same warning. Both countries reacted bitterly. They drafted a convention of armed neutrality, resolving to employ their navies to escort shipments to France. They supposed that the British would not risk a naval confrontation which might bring on war. The French encouraged the convention of armed neutrality by offering subsidies to Sweden and Denmark, and hoped that the Dutch would join it. Luckily for the British, disunity wrecked the scheme: the Swedes moved from neutrality to active war against Prussia, and the Danes, wishing to preserve the lucrative wartime traffic of carrying non-contraband commodities, became cautious.

[7] Above, Chapter 7.

Notwithstanding the treaty of 1674 Newcastle and Hardwicke were adamantly opposed to permitting the Dutch to transport naval stores, masts and timber to the enemy. Hardwicke observed: 'This is assisting France more effectually than if they were allies to them in the war.' In a memorandum of September 1756 in answer to his son's urgent letters from The Hague requesting guidance Hardwicke decided on reflection that the naval stores problem was likely to be negotiable – actually easier to resolve than the problem of forbidding neutral carriage of French West Indian trade.[8] And despite French diplomatic efforts to prevent it the Dutch did in fact prefer to negotiate with respect to naval stores, and the British government chose to compromise. It adopted a policy of arresting Dutch ships, buying the naval stores found in their cargoes, paying some freight charges, and then setting the ships free. Danish and Swedish shipments of timber, masts, hemp and tar were dealt with in the same manner. The French were thereby deprived of the stores, and the neutral merchants escaped with marginal losses. It was imagined that the British navy would buy the materials, but they seldom met navy standards and were sold in London to commercial buyers.

Did the curtailment of Baltic shipments hobble the French navy? Small masts could be obtained in the Pyrenees, and in any case supplies were adequate because demand from merchant shipowners was minimal. Large masts were a different matter; most came from Norway and Russia. By 1757, Toulon, despite acquiring some from Mediterranean sources, was woefully short of them. Rochefort had received a considerable supply of large northern masts before the declaration of war, but practically none arrived in the months afterwards. Of two Dutch vessels carrying masts for Brest in early 1756 one was captured. The general shortage of large masts might have become a prominent problem if the number of active French ships of the line had not been reduced for other reasons.

Hull timber and plank came mostly from France's domestic forests. It was floated down the great rivers and held in storage at depots near their mouths to await transport by coastal shipping to the yards. In the middle years of the war British cruisers and privateers began to operate close inshore. Even the short passage from the big depot on Île d'Indret (at the mouth of the Loire) to Lorient was not safe. The voyage from Le Havre to Brest was even more hazardous. Shortages of particular shapes and sizes of timber at Brest was one reason why construction was halted in 1758. Basically, timber could not be carried overland to Brest: the roads were

[8] Hardwicke to Yorke, 17 Sept. 1756, Yorke, *Hardwicke*, II, 312–14.

bad and the cost was prohibitive; it was estimated that even if all went well, it would take three months to carry enough timber to Brest to construct one large man of war. Shortages of seamen and money were the main reasons why the French government allowed the navy to decline in 1758; shortages of materials were a nuisance but not decisive.

The British navy's most egregious failure in the earlier years of the war – apart from allowing the loss of Minorca – was its inability to prevent reinforcements and supplies from reaching Louisbourg and Canada. We have seen that troop reinforcements got through in 1755 and 1756. Food was a crucial commodity, a fact known to experts in London by late 1756, and the Admiralty knew that the best season for sailing to French North America was winter and early spring. Yet during the first five months of 1757 the Royal Navy's watch on the French coast was skimpy. Half a dozen ships cruised off Cape Finisterre in March and early April 1757 under Admiral Brodrick, but only three, under Commodore Francis Geary, cruised the Bay of Biscay. They managed to capture the *Victoire*, a new 26-gun privateering frigate bound from Bayonne to Louisbourg (its rigging was storm-damaged) and also two large armed merchantmen from Bordeaux bound for Quebec, carrying ammunition, flour and salt pork plus 242 officers and soldiers. Deplorably, the Western Squadron's cruising off Brest in this period was discontinuous, one result being that the French were able to send ample supplies and food to Louisbourg (as well as ships of the line which bolstered its defence). The following year, 1758, when Canada was desperate for food, nearly all the ships that sailed in the spring from Bordeaux for Quebec arrived safely, and in 1759 a vital supply convoy accomplished the outbound voyage to Quebec with almost no losses.

Since the British supposedly regarded North America as the main theatre of war one would think that intercepting these shipments would have been a British naval priority. It appears, however, that the French were more determined to send supplies to Canada than the British Admiralty was to prevent it. Far from neglecting their obligation to sustain Canada's defence, the French made extraordinary efforts to send supplies, especially provisions. The government had to assume the responsibility, however. Pre-war exports to French North America, stimulated by defence preparations, had boomed, but by the end of 1757 merchants who had sent ships to Canada (nearly all from La Rochelle, Bayonne and Bordeaux) had given up. Naval ministers told them that it was their patriotic duty to ship food, munitions and replacement recruits to Quebec, but they refused to take the risks. The prospect of profit from high prices was more than offset by high insurance premiums, difficulty in finding seamen and ship losses. If the wartime dispatch of supplies to Canada had been left to these merchants, nothing would have been done.

Somehow, naval ministers had to find willing shipowners. Very few neutral shippers would attempt a voyage to Quebec in wartime; they supposed, correctly, that their excuses would be ignored by the British and their ships seized. Among French shippers who stepped forward the most prominent were Abraham and David Gradis, and Pierre-François Goossens, the former of Portuguese Jewish background, the latter of a Huguenot family that had emigrated to Holland. Abraham Gradis was already involved in the business of shipping food and merchandise to Canada. A close study of his wartime participation reveals how risky the business was. In 1757 he undertook to convey 800 recruits plus provisions and military stores to Quebec. Two ships, though strongly armed, were captured off Brittany; but six others reached their destination safely. Of these, however, only two got back to Bordeaux unscathed, one of which had carried British prisoners to Plymouth under a flag of truce. Two others were captured; another may have been shipwrecked. The last, a private frigate named the *Robuste*, got into Rochefort after fighting off repeated attacks by British cruisers. (The heavily damaged *Robuste* was repaired and purchased by the French navy; her brave captain was commissioned a lieutenant.) In 1758, Gradis sent fourteen ships to Quebec. Nearly all were armed, each carrying 8 to 20 guns. Along with others they left the Gironde estuary in three groups of about a dozen each, escorted by three privately-owned frigates. One of the vessels was captured near the Gulf of St Lawrence and another shipwrecked, but the rest reached Quebec; so did most of the ships that some French privateers agreed to load with cargo. The return voyages, however, were disastrous. Thirteen of Gradis's fourteen ships were either captured or shipwrecked; five were taken while en route to Saint-Domingue, and six on the return voyage to Europe. According to Dutch newspaper reports, Channel Island privateers accomplished most of the captures. A French list shows that of the ships sailing for Canada in 1757 and 1758 (total departures unknown) seventy-three were captured, twenty-six of them from Bordeaux.[9]

[9] The details are in Maupassant, *Un grand armateur de Bordeaux*, pp. 59–77. Maupassant's account included ships hired by Gradis, which may account for the discrepancy with the listing in J.F. Bosher, *Business and Religion*, pp. 474–5. The summary of records of ships seized may be found in Bosher, 'Guerre et activités de la marine marchande au Canada 1743–1763' in *État, Marine et Société* (Paris, 1995), p. 67.

Clearly, losses upon return made the effort to help sustain Canada extremely costly. The government was pledged to cover part of the merchants' losses, but would it pay? Certainly not right away. In fact, delayed payment forced Gradis to give up. Having lost so many ships, he was in dire need of money to carry on. He journeyed to Paris to obtain a partial payment, but a new minister of marine coldly turned him down, whereupon he decided not to join the effort to supply Canada in 1759. In fact, the monarchy would soon renege on agreements already made. The Fontanieu Commission, appointed to inquire into how the naval debt had reached so high a level, would decree in May 1759 that the freight rate to New France paid by the government was to be reduced from the contracted 350 or 400 livres per ton to 190 livres, the peacetime level – as if high wages for crews and high insurance premiums plus strong odds of losing the ships were of no account. Eventually the French government would prosecute, on grounds of corruption, quite a number of merchants who had been involved in supplying Canada.[10] Although it is true that the French monarchy tried hard and rather successfully to supply Canada in the early years of the war, it is also true that it evaded much of its obligation to pay those who had taken the risks.

West Africa

Pitt was persuaded by a Quaker merchant, Thomas Cumming, to seize the settlement of Saint-Louis on an island in the mouth of the Senegal River. The purpose was to take over the 'gum trade' from the French. Gum arabic was used in many manufacturing processes, especially silk finishing and calico printing, and its chief European source was no longer the Middle East but Senegal. Thus the motivation accorded with the traditional mercantilist goal of transferring trade from a rival to oneself. This was quite unusual in the Seven Years War when most conquests were sought to acquire territory or to gain counters at the peace table. Cumming was by no means an imposter; he had important friends among the Arab rulers of the region and had seen the place with his own eyes. Interviewed by the Board of Trade, he obviously knew what he was talking about, and it happened that Anson favoured the project; he had served for a year or more on the African coast as a young captain.

The expedition with 200 marines and four warships, the largest of 64 guns, sailed from Plymouth on 9 March 1758. After arrival on

[10] Bosher, *Business and Religion*, pp. 352, 507.

23 April careful soundings were made on the ever-shifting bar across the river's entrance, and the sloop *Swan*, helped by a gust of wind, managed to get past it. The French position depended entirely on the bar for its defence. The fort at Saint-Louis, 13 miles upriver, was built of clay, and on 2 May as soon as marines and sailors dragged artillery ashore representatives came forth with articles of capitulation. The only British casualties – about 30 killed – occurred two months later during a foolish mission to challenge a local emir.

It was decided to make an attempt on the little island of Gorée off Cap Vert, 100 miles down the coast, but because the ships took soundings upon arrival the French had time to prepare a defence and the attack was driven off. Word of the success at the Senegal River and the failure at Gorée reached London during the summer, whereupon Pitt assigned to West Africa four companies of foot that had been readied for Jamaica. In September four ships of the line plus a 50-gun ship, three frigates and two bomb vessels were ordered to make preparations, Captain Augustus Keppel being put in command. Keppel had sailed with Anson on the round-the-world voyage of the early 1740s, had served briefly on the coast of Africa, and performed bravely and effectively in Basque Roads the preceding autumn. The squadron left Spithead on 22 October 1758 and went to Kinsale to embark the rest of the troops, amounting to 700 in all. Each warship and transport carried one of the newly designed flat-bottomed boats. After being held up in Ireland by bad weather until 11 November, the squadron encountered fierce thunderstorms on its way southwards. On the night of the 29th the 50-gun *Litchfield* ran ashore on the Moroccan coast at a location 115 miles east of the navigator's dead-reckoning estimates. It was the most tragic instance of this war arising from the inability to ascertain longitude at sea, a long-standing problem that was solved within the next eight years. When the *Litchfield* broke apart 130 men perished but 220 survived to be made captive by the Moors, eventually to be ransomed.

During the last leg of the southward voyage Commodore Keppel briefed the captains and colonels on his plan. Like Wolfe, he had concluded after the failure at Rochefort that an amphibious assault must be launched without delay. Careful planning was essential. Each boat was assigned a designated body of soldiers and given a particular destination ashore; every ship was given a precise station; appropriate signals were specified. After sighting Gorée on 28 December the squadron anchored in the bay of Dakar and prepared to launch an early morning attack. Everything went according to plan, except that a frigate and bomb vessel closed the range too quickly and came under fire from a French fort on high ground before the *Nassau* (64 guns) *Dunkirk* (60 guns) and *Torbay* (74 guns) reached their stations and provided counter-battery cover. Also, the bomb vessel, overcharging its mortars, was sending its shells clean over the narrow island; Keppel had to advise the second bomb vessel to avoid the mistake. It was soon obvious that the guns of the two forts were no match for the ships' heavy broadsides. The French hoisted a flag of truce and firing ceased. The commandant asked for honours of war. Keppel assumed that this was a ploy to gain time, replied that he would fire one shot over the island as a warning, and then resume the bombardment. A rapid and concentrated fire from all the ships' guns as well as the mortars soon produced the desired capitulation. The British suffered 16 killed, the French 30. The 300 Frenchmen of the garrison would be transported to France for prisoner exchange, the black soldiers released. Since the British regular troops never landed, Keppel denied them a share of the prize money, but Pitt would wisely overrule that decision.

Although Gorée was a minor operation and has been almost forgotten historically, it showed that intelligent preparation and quick action could bring success in a seaborne attack. Commodore Keppel's performance was certainly remembered by Pitt and Anson. He would later be given command of the naval forces in the amphibious operations against Belle-Île-en-Mer and Havana.

Changing conditions of warfare in North America

In September 1757, after success at Fort William Henry and arrival of news that Louisbourg was safe, the chevalier de Lévis was full of optimism, but he was mistaken.[11] The task of defending Canada was about to become more difficult. Guns and stocks of ammunition were adequate, partly because of captures from the British, but shortage of food was a serious problem. It affected almost every aspect of Canada's defence. The military planners at Versailles realized that there was no point in sending more troops to Canada unless food could also be sent, and they also knew that shipments from France had become hazardous and costly.

Even in peacetime a good harvest was needed for Canadian agriculture to meet the needs of the population. The season for growing grain and pasturing livestock was short. Furthermore, manpower that might have been applied to bringing more land under cultivation, especially in the

---

[11] Lévis's letter to Paris of 7 Sept. 1757 is summarized by Gipson (VII, 171–2).

potentially productive land west of Montreal, was employed in the fur trade. In wartime the difficulties multiplied. Canada's amazing military prowess (given its small population) was itself part of the problem: mobilizing the *habitants* and holding them in service for many months put a great burden on women, children and old people, and inevitably reduced the family farm's output. This war posed especially troublesome problems on the demand side, since *troupes de terre* from France came in unprecedented numbers. Also, Indians serving in conjunction with the army had to be fed, and in addition there were refugees from the Acadian isthmus.

Canadians had to hope for fair, warm weather in summer 1757 and did not get it. The army's winter (1756–7) demands created a dearth of corn for seed in the spring, and then it rained continually in July and August. The harvest was one of the worst ever experienced. Customarily when bad weather reduced the harvest, Canada relied on transatlantic grain and provisions shipments. Louisbourg was well supplied from France in 1757, but the interior was not. Although about fifty ships reached Quebec, only seventeen carried provisions, and since officials in France lacked timely information, follow-up shipments, even if they managed to evade British cruisers, were unlikely to arrive before the river froze. Thus it happened that during the long, cold winter of 1757–8 Quebec suffered a severe famine. Rations for the civilian population were minuscule. Nothing arrived from France until May. For the British, food was not a problem, thanks to the agricultural productivity of the British colonies and to the better organized methods of purchase and distribution for the armed forces that Lord Loudoun had introduced.

A second restraint on Canadian military operations was the diminishing level of Indian support. Very few western Indians came eastwards to assist the army in 1758. Those warriors who had come in 1757 had unknowingly carried smallpox back to their villages, with devastating consequences. Montcalm, notwithstanding his lamentations about savage Indian behaviour, tried to recruit Indians in 1758, but the numbers were disappointing.[12] There were also fewer volunteers from mission villages, and Canada's resident Iroquois were refusing to participate in offensive operations in New York beyond a certain point. The refusal appears to have stemmed from an event in mid-November 1757 when Vaudreuil sent a small force composed of Canadians and Indians to the Mohawk River. At German Flats the settlers chose not to seek refuge in nearby Fort Herkimer and offered no resistance, but they were nevertheless taken

[12] Steele, *Betrayals*, pp. 131–2.

captive and some were killed. Iroquois principles of neutrality prohibited participation in French raiding east of Lake Oneida, and here was an attack on unarmed civilians on the Mohawk River. The following March at a general meeting at Onondaga which included Iroquois delegates from Canada as well as New York it was resolved that the neutrality principles must be firmly upheld. Recent French military successes had inclined many Canadian Iroquois to ignore the neutrality restrictions, but this meeting marked a turning point. Montcalm would find not only that the western Indians would not come to Carillon in 1758 but also that fewer would come from Laurentian villages than in the year before. (The Iroquois leadership in Canada, however, permitted warriors to go to the Pennsylvania and Virginia frontiers as raiders.) All in all, a reduction of Indian support was far more serious for the French than for the British because by 1758 the British had been forced to recognize that, much as they wanted to recruit Indian scouts, they could not even count on obtaining Mohawks. So they had been compelled to try to train rangers.

Britain's biggest military problem was to find recruits. Pitt, like Loudoun, wanted to see more regulars in America, but, as we have seen, recruiting was difficult. He therefore made a bold decision to bring Scottish Highlanders into the British army for service overseas; these were men who had sided with the Jacobite Rebellion only ten years before. Lord Hardwicke disliked the idea, for in his eyes the Highlanders were incorrigible rebels. But their performance in North America proved him wrong and Pitt right. As for recruiting in the colonies, enlistments in regular units fell off sharply in 1757.

The remedy was to augment provincial forces. Existing procedures for raising provincial soldiers, however, were based on quotas and demands made by the commander-in-chief, a method that had produced quarrels and complexities which made everybody in the colonies mad, wasted Lord Loudoun's time, and aggravated his ill-tempered attitude towards the colonists. In a decision of December 1757 Pitt swept all this away. He addressed requests for provincial forces directly to the colonial governments and promised that the British Treasury would reimburse the entire cost of their pay, arms and provisioning. As one historian has commented, 'Lord Loudoun's niggling insistence on control and compliance had been sand in the gears of colonial cooperation. Pitt's appreciation of the matchless lubricating qualities of money and autonomy . . . guaranteed an enthusiastic American response.'[13] At the same time Pitt altered an army

[13] Fred Anderson, *A People's Army: Massachusetts Soldiers and Society in the Seven Years' War* (Chapel Hill, NC and London, 1984), p. 14.

regulation that had placed British army officers of low rank, who were often inexperienced, above provincial colonels, an arrangement that affected the morale not only of provincial officers but also of the rank and file.[14] It has been suggested that the consequence of all these measures was an over-abundance of provincials and resulting inefficiency. Operations, it has been argued, were delayed because the provincials could not be quickly mobilized and deployed.[15] To be sure, there were delays, yet in all major campaigns in the American interior British generals chose not to begin an offensive without them. Felling trees, building roads, tending wagons, protecting supply lines, garrisoning and so on were tasks mainly performed by provincials. And, in fact, given the opportunity to fight (which occurred in two key campaigns of 1758) they fought well. In drawing up his new arrangements Pitt relied on conversations with Admiral (and former New York governor) Sir Charles Hardy, who went back to England from Halifax in late 1757 with a detachment of storm-shattered ships. He also received information and advice from the acting governor of Massachusetts, Thomas Pownall.

Pitt's changes were designed to encourage the colonists rather than berate them, and for that reason alone it was advisable to replace Lord Loudoun. Pitt had known that the general was inclined to be quarrelsome, not only when dealing with colonial representatives but also with officers under his command. In talking with Hardy the secretary of state must have taken notice of Loudoun's mishandling of the defence of the New York frontier. There was a political consideration as well. When word arrived that the attempt on Louisbourg had been cancelled Pitt angrily announced that Loudoun would be recalled, but he did not carry this out. Before long, however, he found out that Loudoun had conveyed his ideas about the coming year's American campaign in a private letter to the Duke of Cumberland without sharing them with him as secretary of state. Loudoun was close to Cumberland, and Pitt always worried about a possible revival of the duke's influence over the army. On 30 December 1757, when he sent off his long letters to the governors in North America informing them of the new military arrangements, he recalled Lord Loudoun.

[14] Kimball, *Correspondence of Pitt with America*, I, 136–43.
[15] This argument was vigorously propounded by Stanley Pargellis; see *Lord Loudoun*, pp. 353–6. His later assessment (in *Military Affairs*, pp. xiv–xix) is penetrating and better balanced. For the impracticality of Loudoun's method of obtaining soldiers in America see Anderson, *Crucible of War*, pp. 227–31.

The question of finding a replacement for the commander-in-chief in America raised the general problem of how to get more reliable field commanders appointed in all theatres. Pitt had reason to feel that his plans were being ruined by poor selections, and in one of his more extreme instances of paranoia he went so far as to imagine that Loudoun and Cumberland had actually wanted the Louisbourg expedition to fail so that he would be politically undermined. But he was quite sane when he remarked to Newcastle that it was essential for the army to support an administration's objectives. Newcastle replied that the problem 'had been long felt before this time', implying that nothing could be done about it. To which Pitt firmly answered that 'proper Officers' must be found for important commands.[16]

By tradition British army appointments were at the king's disposal. George II had delegated the execution of this power to Cumberland. In mid-October 1757, the duke had just resigned, and the king informed Newcastle that he would personally resume the task of supervising the army and also hinted that he wished to mend the breach with his son. Thus it appeared that there would be no real change. Pitt wanted General Sir John Ligonier to be given powers of authority similar to Cumberland's as captain general. A Huguenot who emigrated to Ireland at the age of 18 and soon joined the British army, Ligonier was an ideal candidate in every way except his age (77) though he was still alert and vigorous. Cultivated (a fellow of the Royal Society), affable, judicious and expert in his profession, he was trusted and respected throughout the army, and by the king and cabinet too. He had attended cabinet meetings while Cumberland was absent. But George II refused to appoint him captain general.

Coincidentally, the return of the Rochefort expedition empty-handed and without excuse had made Lord Hardwicke furious, and as we saw in the preceding chapter he and Newcastle were frustrated by the problem of how to discipline the generals. But there was also the question of what sort of generals were being appointed, and, begging not to be quoted to anyone ('these are very delicate subjects to put opinions upon into writing'), he vented his scorn to Newcastle:

The scene is really too ridiculous. It is true that 'the officers concerned are men of great quality, rank and distinction'; but if that objection should finally prevail [to shield them from punishment], men of quality ought not to be let into the army, for it will ruin the service. Indeed,

---

[16] Newcastle to Hardwicke, 3 Sept. 1757, BL Add. 32,873, fo. 433.

I have for some time thought that the army was too full of them,
and that the public would be better served by having more soldiers
of fortune, and perhaps some foreigners of service and experience,
if that restriction could be opened. I don't wonder that Mr Pitt is
very anxious about this.[17]

Newcastle initially shied away from addressing George II on the subject, but Hardwicke told him that he must – that Pitt was right about this: 'for if . . . the generalship is supposed to remain in the King, I see plainly where it will soon centre behind the curtain, and that will be the worst of all . . . [because] the Duke will have the whole army in his power without being responsible.'[18] Newcastle conferred again with the king and persuaded him to promote Ligonier to field marshal and appoint him Commander-in-Chief of His Majesty's Forces; also to make him an Irish peer.

Though not named captain general, Ligonier functioned as such, and from this time forward made the recommendations for the key commands and promotions. Obtaining this power for Ligonier was one of Pitt's most important contributions to military success in the Seven Years War. He did it with Hardwicke's solid support and Newcastle's help in the royal closet, for which he was effusively grateful. At the time he wrote his gloomy letter of 5 January Hardwicke could not be sure whether the king would be steadfast in supporting the new system. The answer came ten days later. After a conversation with Ligonier, George II struck the three generals who had served on the Rochefort expedition from the list of employable officers. Ligonier's pre-eminent influence over key army appointments would last until George II's death.

The new commander-in-chief for North America was Jeffrey Amherst. Son of a lawyer in Kent, he got his start in the army by the Duke of Dorset's patronage and was therefore closely associated from boyhood with Lord George Sackville, the duke's third son. Ligonier remembered Amherst's service as his aide-de-camp in the 1740s. He was reaching far down the hierarchy – numerous officers were senior to Amherst – and despite 22 years of service the 41-year-old colonel's resumé included practically no front-line combat experience. But Ligonier knew him to be intelligent, thoughtful and careful – a man who would not make rash mistakes. George II was strongly opposed to the choice; Newcastle and Lady Yarmouth had to use all their powers of persuasion to gain the

---

[17] Hardwicke to Newcastle, 16 Oct. 1757, Yorke, *Hardwicke*, III, 189–90.
[18] Ibid. III, 190.

king's grudging acceptance. To serve as brigadiers in North America Ligonier selected James Wolfe and John Forbes. None of the three was an aristocrat by birth (but Wolfe's father was a lieutenant general). Unlike George II, Pitt welcomed Ligonier's choices.

Amherst and Wolfe were assigned to the renewed expedition against Louisbourg, and Forbes, already in America, would be ordered to move against Fort Duquesne. That left Abercromby on the New York frontier – a more able man than Webb but not experienced as a field commander. From 1758 onwards the commanders of British troops in North America were more competent than before, and unlike Montcalm and Vaudreuil they were generally disposed to work together in harmony.

The conquest of Louisbourg

Of the British operations planned for North America in 1758 the attempt on Louisbourg was the one that absolutely had to succeed. A second failure there would be politically dreadful and would delay a seaborne attack on Quebec. Timely preparation, numbers to be employed, and selection of leaders for the expedition were elements that Pitt could try to control and he took an active interest in all three.

The expeditionary army was to number no fewer than 14,000. Three regiments had wintered in Nova Scotia, about 2,000 men; 2,500 more would come from the British Isles, and the rest would be drawn from regiments already in New England, New York and Pennsylvania – all regulars except for 500 rangers. The transports from Philadelphia, New York and Boston would sail to Halifax in lightly escorted convoys, a proceeding that would have been considered too dangerous if the French navy had not become so weak. To make sure that there were enough transports at New York and the other colonial ports Pitt ordered, on 30 December 1757, that ships hired in Britain should cross the Atlantic, and the army and its supplies did in fact arrive in time. While the troops waited at Halifax, light infantry units were selected and drilled; boat-landing exercises were conducted; carts with very large wheels were constructed for carrying siege ordnance over rough and swampy terrain; frames for wooden blockhouses were prefabricated.

The only person to arrive late – actually, just in time – was the military commander, Major General Jeffrey Amherst. Because Amherst had to be summoned from deep in Germany, where as a colonel he was responsible for the commissariat that supplied Hessian mercenaries, there was reason to worry about whether he would reach Halifax in time, so Pitt had given an order to the fleet commander and the three brigadier generals appointed to the operation to start without him if necessary. On 15 March 1758 Amherst was able to sail from England in the 74-gun *Dublin*. She was specially assigned to take him to Halifax but en route happened to meet with a richly-laden French East Indiaman, and after capturing it Captain George Bridges Rodney detoured to take the prize into Vigo. Thereafter the *Dublin* encountered adverse winds and fog, arriving off Halifax on 29 May just as the armada bound for Louisbourg was coming out of harbour. Amherst immediately went aboard the flagship by boat.

The naval force was impressive. Seven ships of the line, one of 50 guns, and two frigates had wintered at Halifax. The main force – nine of the line and many frigates with very few transports in company – departed from Spithead on 23 February. Stops at both Madeira and the Canary Islands were needed because the trade winds faltered, but when the fleet finally reached Halifax on 28 May almost everyone aboard was in good health. The admirals in command, Boscawen and Hardy, were both capable men and had prior experience of the seas off Cape Breton. All in all, the naval force consisted of fourteen frigates and twenty-three of the line, twenty-one of which proceeded to Louisbourg.

Given these numbers, the French could not possibly have reproduced the parity by which they had saved Louisbourg the year before. Nevertheless, despite severe manning difficulties Mauchalt and Moras had done the best they could. The *Magnifique* (74 guns) made a winter crossing but found the harbour blocked by ice. Buffeted by storms with almost her entire crew sick, she returned to Europe. The *Prudent* (74 guns) and other warships *en flûte*, which were carrying provisions and munitions, sailed from Brest on 9 March and gained the harbour safely, but they were horribly sickly: of the *Prudent*'s crew on departure of about 650 men 150 died en route and 300 were sent to the hospital upon arrival. On 4 April the *Entreprenant* (74 guns), accompanied by three 64-gun ships *en flûte* carrying supplies and a regiment of foreign volunteers plus one frigate, made an amazingly quick passage from Brest (just three and a half weeks) and was able, thanks to fog, to evade the British squadron which had wintered at Halifax and was then cruising off Louisbourg under Hardy's command. Apart from two ships of 50 guns and two frigates these were the only ships that got into the harbour. One ship sailing singly from Brest was captured by British men-of-war, and another was shipwrecked.

The naval ministry had intended to send reinforcements from Basque Roads, but the British navy disrupted the preparations. The previous autumn Sir Edward Hawke, as he was preparing to leave the roadstead to return from the abortive Rochefort expedition, wrote a letter to Anson in which he described Basque Roads as a 'much finer' anchorage than the British charts described. It was so large and spacious that 'the whole fleet of England might lie upon occasion with great safety; and now that we are acquainted with it,' he wrote, 'it is in our power, with a superior force, to prevent the enemy from making up their fleets here'.[19] In March 1758 Hawke was at sea, and after picking up intelligence that a convoy was assembling in Basque Roads, he stormed into the roadstead on a following wind with eight of the line and four frigates. The French were loading and arming four of the line and two frigates off the Île d'Aix, and there were forty merchantmen preparing for departure. Surprise was total. Overboard went the warships' guns. Anchors were cut away as the ships fled to shallow water. Low tide the next morning, 5 April, revealed men-of-war and merchant ships heeled over in the mud. As the tide rose boats came out to pull the warships into the Charente River. Hawke felt the frustration of having no fireships or bomb vessels with him, but his boats were able to cut away the buoys by which the French had marked the locations of their guns and anchors. He also landed twenty marines to destroy the batteries on Aix for the second time in six months.

Upon departure on 7 April Hawke gained intelligence of fifteen supply ships at Bordeaux that were expecting to join the convoy in Basque Roads. As he wrote, 'the present circumstances of their settlements [overseas] may oblige them to sail without convoy [and therefore] I have left out . . . [two of the line and four frigates] to cruise upon them, which I hope their Lordships will approve of'.[20] He placed Augustus Keppel in charge of this detachment, and several vessels from Bordeaux were in fact captured. While Keppel's ships lingered, the French at Basque Roads were afraid to resume loading and arming, and in fact the principal convoy intended to reinforce Louisbourg never sailed.

Four French warships (only one of which carried all its guns) under the command of the comte du Chaffault did sail from Basque Roads on 2 May carrying a reinforcement of 700 troops. Arriving off Cape Breton on the 29th, du Chaffault had a three-day opportunity to try to enter Louisbourg harbour before the British invasion armada arrived. Choosing not to risk interception by Hardy's ships, he went to St Ann's Bay, 50 miles north-west of Louisbourg, landed the troops, and proceeded to Quebec. Hawke's decision to go to Basque Roads allowed the *Entreprenant* and its companions

---

[19] Hawke to Anson, 30 Sept. 1757, Mackay, ed. *Hawke Papers*, p. 179.
[20] Hawke to Admiralty, 11 April 1758, ibid. pp. 200–1.

to get away from Brest, but, all in all, the combination of severe manning difficulties and British naval hindrance kept the size of the French naval force in Louisbourg harbour small. When the British assault force arrived on 2 June the French had only five ships of the line (three of them with reduced complements and no heavy guns) plus three frigates in harbour.

Events during the winter in the Mediterranean prevented a larger French naval force from getting to Louisbourg and also deprived that force of a better commander. The British squadron stationed at Gibraltar was much stronger than it had been a year earlier; there were, under Admiral Henry Osborne and Rear-Admiral Charles Saunders, eleven ships of the line plus an ample number of frigates. Jean-François Bertet de La Clue-Sabran sailed from Toulon with six of the line on 8 November 1757 with orders to cross the Atlantic. Learning the strength of Osborne's force at the Straits, he hesitated and put in at the neutral Mediterranean port of Cartagena where two more of the line from Toulon soon joined him. He expected a further reinforcement of three of the line, led by Admiral Duquesne. Osborne and Saunders received word of this reinforcement and decided to stand towards Cartagena with eight of the line and six frigates to prevent La Clue from gaining superiority. They calculated that they could win a race back to the Straits if the need arose. Their plan worked. When he arrived off Cartagena, Duquesne sent a signal to La Clue urging him to hurry out, but La Clue's ships were not ready. On 28 November a north-west wind pushed Duquesne's ships towards Osborne's and the French admiral ordered them to disperse. One soon surrendered; another found refuge under a Spanish shore battery and was left alone, the British not wishing to risk offending Spain. When the flagship *Foudroyant* (80 guns) headed for open sea the *Monmouth* chased and was able eventually to engage. Though heavily overmatched, the 64-gun *Monmouth* fought a running battle as evening gave way to night. She was commanded by Arthur Gardiner, who as captain of the *Ramillies* off Minorca had urged Byng to turn downwind to engage the very same flagship, at that time carrying La Galissonière. Captain Gardiner was soon killed and his first lieutenant took over. The *Foudroyant*'s masts and rigging suffered serious damage and she began to move sluggishly. At dawn she was hemmed in by two more British ships that had steered towards the sound of the guns during the night. Duquesne was forced to surrender and was made prisoner. When La Clue learned of the fate of this reinforcement he abandoned all thought of passing the Straits and went back to Toulon. If he had reached the Atlantic, it seems certain that most of his ships would have gone to the West Indies, but whether many of them would have gone on to Louisbourg, as five of Beauffremont's ships had done the year before, can only be guessed.

What seems certain is that the *Foudroyant* would have gone to Louisbourg to enable Duquesne – the same man who had established forts on the Ohio – to take command of the naval force there. Moras knew he needed a commander more competent and authoritative than Charry des Gouttes, captain of the *Prudent*, who had become senior naval officer at Louisbourg by happenstance.[21] When word reached Paris that Duquesne had been captured in the Mediterranean, Moras immediately ordered Charles, comte de Courbon-Blénac to sail to Louisbourg. He was empowered to take command of all forces there, sea and land, and directed to cross the ocean without stopping 'to make prize of any enemy ships' he might encounter (an order that calls to mind Rodney's conduct on a similar assignment). A full month passed, however, before he left Brest. After reaching Cape Breton his ship, the *Formidable*, spent most of her time looking for places to hide. On 9 June, Blénac had word that the whole British squadron was guarding Louisbourg, so an attempt to enter the harbour was out of the question. He soon returned to Brest.[22] It seems not to have occurred to him that he might go ashore somewhere and find his way overland to the fortress to take command of its defence.

The attention given above to the naval antecedents of the Louisbourg campaign is in accordance with their importance. Although the fortress city had sufficient provisions and ammunition to withstand a long siege, its hope of survival depended on two things. One was a fleet of armed and fully manned warships in harbour, not only to keep the British navy out, but also to harass British siege works within gun range and, above all, to supply added manpower ashore. Louisbourg had such a fleet in 1757. It did not in 1758 when only eight armed ships and fewer than 3,000 sailors were available. The other source of hope was the possibility of preventing the enemy from landing. Ultimate success in this regard was unlikely because the huge preponderance of British forces, land and sea (over 13,000 troops and officers, and about 12,500 sailors and marines), permitted simultaneous landing attempts in separated locations. The absence of a strong French naval force was therefore decisive.

---

[21] Sir Julian Corbett assumed (I, 255) that La Clue's squadron was destined for Louisbourg. Richard Pares (*War and Trade*, pp. 184, 279) challenged this assumption. Probably the *Foudroyant* and perhaps another warship would have gone straight to Louisbourg, the others to the West Indies. Caron, *Guerre incomprise*, pp. 279–80.

[22] Ibid. pp. 282–3, 310–11.

Nevertheless, securing a defensible foothold ashore in an amphibious operation is a notoriously hazardous proposition. The original plan, drawn up by the brigadiers and approved by Admiral Boscawen, called for a landing at Miré, 10 miles east of Louisbourg, but Amherst opted for the beaches of Gabarus Bay, 2–4 miles west of the citadel, despite their being the obvious choice and therefore strongly defended. After reconnoitring inshore Amherst drew up a revised plan. The assault force was to consist of three divisions, two of which would feint landings near Flat Point and White Point, while the third, on their left, would go ashore at a cove named La Cormorandière (now Kennington Cove). This division, under Wolfe, 31 years old, was composed of grenadiers drawn from each regiment, plus light infantry comprising the best marksmen, some New England rangers and a company of Highlanders. The troops of this division, numbering 3,300, would carry only two days' rations and were expected to move rapidly off the beach.

Fog and high surf delayed the order to land for five days. Finally, after midnight nearly 10,000 troops were quietly loaded into more than 300 boats. Amherst had left the flagship and was aboard one of the transports. At first light on 8 June the frigate *Kennington* and the *Halifax* bomb vessel bombarded the higher ground above the beach and soon the frigates off White Point opened fire while hundreds of navy oarsmen pulled toward shore. The French governor, Augustin de Drucour, had recognized that the enemy would probably choose La Cormorandière: the beach's slope was gradual and the ground behind rose only about 20 feet. Altogether the French had about 3,500 troops, including town militia. Drucour ordered 2,800 of the best men to positions outside the fortress to repel landings. Of these 1,000 were entrenched above the beach at La Cormorandière, many having two muskets at hand. Swivel guns were mounted on wooden posts. On the flanks stood batteries of 6-pounders, and one 24-pounder loaded with grapeshot. All were hidden by spruce branches, and the bombardment by the *Kennington* and *Halifax* hardly touched them.

The French held their fire until the boats got close to shore and then unleashed a volume so tremendous that Wolfe had to signal a retreat. The boats turned and spread out, according to standing instructions from Amherst. When those on the right came near the rocky promontory that defined the eastern extremity of the cove the men on board perceived a patch of sand between the rocks. It was scarcely 30 feet long but was sheltered from French bullets by a ridge. They headed for it. Observing this, Wolfe ordered his own boat to steer towards them and waved to all

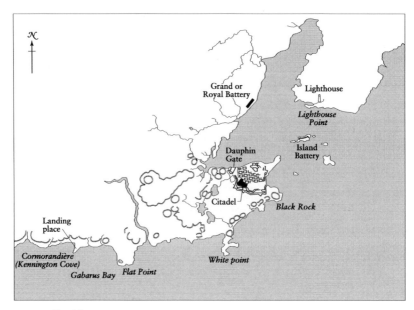

MAP 8 *Louisbourg*

boats to follow. At the sandy opening the troops jumped into the water, muskets held aloft, and climbed up the rocks.

Colonel St Julhien, who commanded the cove's defenders, could not see what was happening on his left, not only because of the ridge but also because the smoke from the *Kennington*'s guns, blowing on shore, obscured the movements of Wolfe's boats. Fifty to seventy armed French and Indians were positioned at the promontory and they attacked, but their attack was repulsed by the first British troops to climb the rocks; among these were Highlanders led by Major James Scott. He immediately ordered a bayonet charge upon a small battery that menaced them. By the time St Julhien received a well-founded report of what was happening and overcame his hesitations it was too late to organize a counter-attack. The British forces, ashore in strength, soon came storming over a ridge to attack his flank and rear. His men fled, fearing that their path back to the fortress would be cut off. News of their flight spread to the adjacent 900 defenders of the beach near Flat Point and they, too, retreated. Wolfe's men kept up a hot pursuit until coming within range of the fortress guns. When officers of the other assault divisions realized La Cormorandière's defenders had fled, they directed their boats to that beach and in a short time almost the entire invasion force was ashore. Begun at 4 a.m., the landing operation was completed by 6.

Wolfe, who was fond of tossing out extravagant pronouncements, later declared to a friend that it had not required any 'prodigious exertion of courage' to achieve the landing, but this conclusion did not accord with his opinion at the time.[23] Squeezing many boatloads of soldiers into that small stretch of sand among the rocks did require courage as well as skill. Men were crushed and boats stove in (about thirty-five soldiers and ten sailors drowned). Thereupon the troops had to climb, form up under fire and face down an attack. It was a dangerous undertaking, and its success stemmed from Wolfe's quick decision to commit his entire force as soon as the opportunity was revealed. Luck was undoubtedly a factor, as well as French mistakes: the defenders had failed to post watchmen and messengers on a high observation point above the promontory, as had been done when Louisbourg anticipated an attack the year before. Also, they fired on the boats too soon. If the troops had landed on the beach as planned, they would have been at the mercy of guns shrouded by cut foliage and protected by an abatis (a tangle of logs and branches) on the slope. Even a 'prodigious exertion of courage' would probably not have prevailed and losses would have been severe. Given time, however, British bomb vessels could have made a bonfire of the abatis.

Amherst and Boscawen were both convinced that the fortress was in good repair and would have to be blasted into submission by a formal siege requiring heavy ordnance. Bad weather hindered efforts to get everything ashore. Amherst, careful and methodical, decided to construct a good road across the swamps from the beach to the siege trenches. Preparations on the main front were therefore slow. Yet, during this time an opportunity for an indirect approach was exploited. After the successful landing, Drucour called in the troops that he had positioned to the east, instructing them to destroy the Grand and Lighthouse batteries. Amherst promptly ordered Wolfe to occupy those positions.

And so, in the early morning hours of 12 June with 1,220 men, 400 of them rangers in the lead, Wolfe advanced stealthily around the north side of the harbour. There was a dense fog and his men were neither heard nor seen by anyone aboard the French men-of-war. They found the guns at Lighthouse Point spiked, but the fleet's lighters and boats offshore soon landed British artillery, ammunition and provisions at nearby coves. Protected by the rangers from French and Indian raiding (the threat of which proved much less than expected), Wolfe established batteries near Lighthouse Point. On the night of 19 June cannon and mortar fire was

---

[23] Quoted by Hitsman and Bond, 'Assault Landing', 325.

directed at the French warships, which soon retreated to the western end of the harbour. Wolfe's artillery then demolished the Island Battery that guarded the harbour entrance on the opposite side. The way was thus cleared for elements of Boscawen's fleet to force their way into the harbour. If that happened, the fortress city would be lost, because it had practically no defences on the harbour side. Drucour suggested that two frigates and the 50-gun ship should be sunk in the harbour entrance. It was done, and the Island Battery was repaired and re-garrisoned.

The retreat of the French men-of-war made it easy for Wolfe to establish batteries along the harbour's northern perimeter on rising ground that overlooked it. His men built two behind the abandoned Grand (or Royal) Battery, and batteries were then built on the northern slopes at positions ever nearer the fortress; the guns and ammunition were brought from the coves near Lorembec. On 5 July a completed battery of six cannon and two mortars brought the city and the warships huddled near it within range of shell fire. Much of the battery construction work had been accomplished in hours of darkness, but the nights were short, and the transporting of materials and ordnance largely occurred in daylight. If, instead of retreating, French warships had moved close to the north shore in order to disturb the enemy working parties they would have slowed progress. The timidity of Commodore des Gouttes and his fellow officers at this moment of opportunity was disgraceful, because once the batteries on high ground were established, low-trajectory naval gunfire could not deal with them effectively. The one remaining frigate, the *Aréthuse*, commanded by Jean Vauquelin, a merchant and privateering captain from Dieppe (an *officier bleu* in the navy), moored his ship in the north-west corner of the harbour where, with a spotter in the maintop, he harassed Amherst's working parties on the main front, which were not on high ground.

Des Gouttes had been urged by his captains to ask permission to escape. Their argument was that once the British army had landed in force Louisbourg was lost and there was no point in losing the ships too. A successful departure was not impossible, since wind and fog might frustrate interception. More than once des Gouttes asked for permission to depart, but Drucour knew that abandoning the harbour to British naval occupation was tantamount to surrender and refused. Wolfe's advance battery of 5 July put all the ships in danger, however, and for safety most of their powder was landed. By the 6th the crews of all but one were also ashore; only a watch of twenty-five seamen with an officer remained aboard each. Vauquelin could no longer hold his position. He was directed to carry dispatches to France and slipped out on the night of the 15th without mishap.

Meanwhile, Amherst was steadily preparing the main siege front, with a deliberateness that would have been fatal if the mosquitoes round Louisbourg had carried malaria or yellow fever. A night sortie from the fortress captured two dozen British troops, but the main causes of delay were Amherst's slow methods, made even slower by his engineer's un-necessary measures as well as bad weather and the loss of a hundred New England carpenters to smallpox. Not until 18 July, when his batteries were established in a full semi-circle, did he unleash his onslaught. The garrison defended the fortress bravely, but disasters soon came in rapid succession.

On the afternoon of 21 July a shell from the nearest northern battery ignited some cartridges on board the *Célèbre* (64 guns). Sparks spread the fire downwind to the *Entreprenant*, and from her to the *Capricieux* (64 guns). The caretaker crews could not cope with the fires, and British artillery poured a withering barrage on the boats that tried to bring seamen to assist them. The loaded guns aboard the ships got hot and discharged unpredictably. The ships burnt all night and were totally consumed; only two remained. On the morning of the 22nd a shell caused the roof of the Citadel to catch fire; half of the impressive edifice was destroyed. Drucour tried to keep up the men's spirits, and the intrepid Madame Drucour came daily to the bastions and touched off guns firing upon the besiegers. Wolfe's detachment from the east penetrated within 200 yards of the Dauphin gate, and Amherst prepared an assault. But the next step was the navy's.

Boscawen gave his approval to a bold enterprise which effectively put an end to French resistance. On 25 July boats and pinnaces, moving piecemeal to avoid attracting attention, assembled amidst Hardy's squadron. With the help of fog they slipped quietly into the harbour that night and approached the French warships. When hailed by an officer on board the *Bienfaisant* (64 guns) a boat officer replied in French that he was coming from the town; in reply he was told to bring five or six men aboard. Soon there were two hundred. A party of sailors similarly boarded the *Prudent* (74 guns). She was aground and the raiders burnt her, but the *Bienfaisant* was towed away and eventually became a ship of the Royal Navy.

The next day Boscawen composed for Amherst's approval a letter urging the governor to surrender or else expect an immediate attack by land and sea. Drucour was already thinking about capitulation. He was aware that he had only three guns capable of ranging on the enemy still in service. The British, however, were demanding a complete surrender, and he sought better terms. But a representative of the townspeople persuaded him to reconsider: the troops were exhausted and the people had suffered severely from bombardment. Besides, there were no grounds for hope. Consequently, the entire garrison became prisoners of war. During the campaign approximately 400 French troops had died, and another 400 were wounded; British casualties were 195 killed and 363 wounded.

Bolder use of the French warships might have delayed the capitulation, but on the other hand, speedier progress by Amherst and his overly cautious engineer might have brought it sooner. Certainly, the cooperation of Boscawen and his ships' companies with Amherst and the army was exemplary, in marked contrast to that of des Gouttes's lack of cooperation with Drucour. Des Gouttes was later cashiered, but Blénac, who should have been in his place, enjoyed an uninterrupted career. After Louisbourg's capitulation its townspeople were shipped to France. The British then rounded up Cape Breton's villagers and had them conveyed, along with 3,500 Acadians on Île St Jean, to France as well. Thus, eradication of the Acadians continued.

There was not enough time to prepare a strike at Quebec. Nevertheless, when news of the fall of Louisbourg reached London on 18 August 1758 it provoked exultation, for it was the first prominent *British* victory of the war. Newcastle, who tended to focus on Europe, remarked that it was 'the greatest event, in all respects, and in all considerations, that could happen for this country'.[24] Perhaps not, but it was certainly timely.

Ticonderoga and Frontenac

In October 1757, after returning from Halifax, Lord Loudoun contemplated a winter thrust at Ticonderoga. Supplies and artillery were to be hauled upon frozen Lake George in sledges and carts. A massive snowfall nullified the plan. In mid-March 1758 Captain Robert Rogers with 180 rangers on snowshoes was seeking to surprise the French at Carillon when he was himself surprised by a larger scouting patrol. Rogers lost over half his men. On the Canadian side, Vaudreuil planned a large spring expedition of 3,000 troops under Lévis which would raid forts and settlements all the way to Schenectady; one purpose was to impress the Iroquois and bring them into alliance with the French. This expedition was cancelled when Montcalm learned of the size of the offensive that the British

[24] Newcastle to Devonshire, 31 Aug. 1758, BL Add. 32,883 fo. 193.

were preparing against Fort Carillon and Fort St Frédéric. He could not immediately reinforce the garrisons because of the prevailing famine. The vessels from France with provisions did not arrive until the latter half of May, but in fact the French generals would have plenty of time to prepare a defence.

Pitt, who ordered the offensive, had envisioned a provincial force numbering 12,000, but by the end of June only 6,000 arrived at the camp-ground near the ruins of Fort William Henry to join the 6,000 regulars, 500 rangers and 1,600 bateaumen. Although all boats and bateaux had been destroyed by the French the previous summer, 700 new ones built in the Albany area were ready by the end of April. Unfortunately, the provincials lacked muskets; the transports bringing them from England were encountering adverse winds and did not reach New York until 14 June. Indians were wanted for scouts, and General Abercromby, who had inherited the command on the New York frontier, pleaded fruitlessly with Johnson to provide them. But very few showed up on time. The offensive did not proceed in total ignorance, however. Abercromby's highly intelligent assistant, Brigadier General George Augustus, Viscount Howe, had sent out scouts during the winter and spring, and a sketch of the terrain at the north end of Lake George was developed.

On the morning of 5 July a flotilla of 900 bateaux and 135 whaleboats headed northwards upon the lake. In addition to the 6,000 regulars there were more than 6,000 provincials, their numbers increasing daily to 9,000. Boats covered the lake from shore to shore in a body 7 miles long. Helped by a following wind they advanced 25 miles before resting near Sabbath Day Point. They soon got under way again during the night and were ready to land at the north end of the lake the next morning, a move that surprised a 350-man French detachment that had marched to the north-west shore to observe. In danger of being cut off, the French retreated through thick woods. A body of British light infantry then pushed northwards on the western side of the narrowing lake, and a blind collision brought on a skirmish in which the French suffered the most casualties. The day's action was marred, however, by the loss of Lord Howe. As he came over a crest of rising ground while leading a body of light infantry towards the sounds of the skirmish a musket ball pierced his heart and lung, killing him instantly. His unwise bravery deprived the army of a respected leader whose intelligence and military acumen were to be greatly missed.

The next morning engineers replaced the pontoon bridge at the top end of La Chute river, and Bradstreet persuaded Abercromby to let him advance a strong scouting force along the portage road. The French had abandoned a breastwork that guarded its entrance. It was a good road and undefended, so the British were free to move heavy ordnance and supplies forward to the vicinity of the water-powered sawmills. The mills stood next to a waterfall which, coming after numerous rapids, descended to the level of Lake Champlain, 220 feet lower than Lake George.

The stone fort known to the French as Carillon and to the British as Ticonderoga stood (and stands, restored in a subsequently enlarged form) on a high promontory which commands the southern reaches of Lake Champlain. The fort was untenable, however, if an enemy managed to place artillery on the 'heights of Carillon', higher ground located a mile north-west of the fort. Montcalm's men worked feverishly to entrench this elevated ground; beginning at first light on the 7th, working all day, and carrying on by the illumination of bonfires after dark, officers joined soldiers with axes in hand. They cut large logs to create a jagged chain of breastworks along the outer crest of the heights. Sandbags were placed on top; slits were provided for musket fire, and swivel guns were mounted. Felled trees with their branches sharpened at the extremities were crowded in a tangle upon the slopes; this abatis extended out and down from the breastworks for a distance of 50 or more yards. The French engineers planned well and Montcalm assigned nearly all his manpower to the task. On the morning of the 8th, though some improvements were needed, the defences were ready. The troops rested with spare loaded muskets at hand. They had been reinforced just in time by 400 regulars hurriedly dispatched by Lévis.

The position was vulnerable, however, to enfilade by artillery. On the south bank of La Chute river where it widened to flow into Lake Champlain rose Rattlesnake mountain (now Mt Defiance). Guns placed part-way up its slope could range upon the camp behind the breastworks. On 7 July Abercromby's trusted young engineer, Lieutenant Matthew Clerk, selected a location for such a battery. It was not high up, but its fire could be adjusted by signals from spotters further up the mountain. A few 6-pounders had already been brought down the portage road to the sawmills, and Clerk asked for more. On the morning of the 8th carpenters hurriedly built two rafts to carry guns; each raft was to be towed down-river by ten whaleboats to a location hidden from the fort's line of sight by a projecting contour of land. Here the guns could be landed and hauled up the slope. Unfortunately, they were never landed. The chosen spot for bringing them ashore, though plainly visible from the slope above, was masked from the men in the boats by bulrushes. They passed it by and drifted too far downstream where they were seen from the fort and instantly drew cannon fire. Two boats were swamped and the crews turned back.

While these efforts were being made General Abercromby was holding a council of war. Montcalm's defences had just been reconnoitred that morning by Bradstreet and an engineer to verify a scouting report made the day before. The verdict was that the French defences were in an unfinished condition and did not present a serious obstacle. What the two men had seen, however, was a chain of loosely laid logs for shielding an outer guard positioned to give early warning to the men at work on the real defensive obstacles. This report misled the general into deciding to storm the defences before they were completed. The council of war ended quickly, the consensus being: 'We Must Attack Any Way, and not be losing time in talking or consulting how.'[25] Later on, Lieutenant Clerk, who had reported what he had seen of the defences the day before, was blamed for the mistaken assessment. But he was not at the meeting; he was on the slope of Mt Defiance waiting for guns to arrive. By the time he rejoined the general the orders to the attacking forces had gone out. If Abercromby later regretted that Clerk's guns were not ready at the time, he never mentioned it.

The formidable abatis surprised and dismayed the attackers. The plan was to attack swiftly and simultaneously, but the assault was ill-coordinated from the start. At about 12.30 p.m. the rangers clashed with a French advance guard and failed to continue on around to their assigned position on the left, thus leaving the New York regiment vulnerable to a similar disadvantageous skirmish. Colonel William Haviland of the 28th Regiment heard the sounds of musketry and ordered his regulars to attack. This premature move – other regiments were not yet formed up – was directly contrary to Abercromby's orders and should have been restrained by a brigadier. There was none: Lord Howe was dead, and Brigadier Thomas Gage who inherited the role of second-in-command from him was not present; no one knows to this day where he was during the battle and what he was doing. Abercromby had made no provision for someone in authority to take over the vital role of coordinating the assault, and his orders had made no allowance for difficulties; the regimental and company commanders were told, in effect, simply to keep advancing towards the French position. The enemy, as one officer wrote after the battle, had an 'abundance of time to mow us down like a field of corn, with their wall pieces and small arms, [we] being ordered to receive the enemy's fire, and march with shouldered arms until we came up close to their breastwork'.[26] The general arrived late, at 1.15 p.m. He made no attempt to halt the attack and regroup; instead he walked to high ground near the river to observe. He did not inform subordinates as to where he would be and issued no orders until the end of the afternoon. As a company commander later remarked, 'no General was heard of, no Aid de Camps seen, no instructions receiv'd'.[27]

With extraordinary bravery the men struggled to overcome the abatis. French sharpshooters at the breastworks picked them off, firing in some cases six rounds per minute, twice the normal rate because spare muskets were reloaded by others. For the British the best chance of success lay on the north side where the ground sloped more gradually, and there the Highlanders of the 42nd (Black Watch) Regiment pressed the attack. A few actually managed to surmount the breastwork, but Lévis was alert and shifted enough defenders to nullify the threat. When the order to withdraw came at about 5 p.m. the Highlanders did not hear, or at least did not obey; they retreated only when they ran out of ammunition. Of about 1,000 officers and men of the regiment 647 were recorded as killed, wounded or missing in the day's action (27 out of 37 officers), a measure of loss not equalled by any other regiment in North America during the war. In four days of combat at Ticonderoga the British regulars and provincials lost 1,967 of all ranks (killed, wounded or missing) out of 17,550 while the French lost 554 out of 4,236. Firing from behind trees on the wings where Abercromby's battle plan had placed them, provincials, rangers and light infantry inflicted most of the French casualties; they also covered the retreat.

The exhausted French knew how greatly outnumbered they were. They realized that artillery might be brought to bear upon them and expected the attack to be renewed, but the British retreated in a hurry. Bradstreet quelled disorder at the landing place and supervised the embarkation, but lots of provisions remained behind for the enemy's use. The boats and bateaux, speeded by a northerly wind, arrived at the camp at Fort William Henry by nightfall.

[26] Lt. William Grant of the Highlanders wrote on 17 Aug. 1758 a private letter containing one of the most detailed accounts of the battle to have survived; it is published by Westbrook, in 'Like roaring lions', 54–8.
[27] Capt. Charles Lee, in Colonel Eyre's regiment, to his sister, 16 Sept. 1758, quoted by McCulloch, in Graves, ed. *Fighting for Canada*, p. 68.

In the wake of this bloody defeat and precipitate withdrawal by Abercromby's greatly superior army, criticisms of the general by his officers abounded. In a self-justifying letter to a relative, written five weeks after he penned his brief and bland official dispatch of 12 July, the general showed how aware he was of the criticism. Why did he not wait until the artillery could be brought up? He said that 'it must have been a Work of several Days', citing how long it took the French to bring their ordnance along the portage road when they prepared their attack on Fort William Henry the previous year. Actually, the difficulty was not comparable because the French had to pull their guns uphill whereas the British advanced downhill. Besides, his claim that it would be 'a work of several Days' can only have referred to the entire siege train rather than a few guns and howitzers needed to enfilade the French position.

Abercromby blamed the inadequate scouting of 'Engineers, who . . . had seen the Ground & Works the preceding Night and that Morning' for his decision to storm the position.[28] His official dispatch implied that Lieutenant Clerk (whom he liked) was much to blame. According to the dispatch, the young lieutenant had viewed the enemy's entrenchments from across the river on the morning of the 8th, and, 'Upon his return and favourable Report of the practicability of carrying those Works, if attacked before they were finished, it was agreed to storm them that very Day.'[29] But in fact Clerk viewed the enemy's position on the 7th and was on Mt Defiance on the morning of the 8th hoping to establish a battery to bombard it, a fact Abercromby did not mention. The lieutenant was unable to respond because he was dead of wounds he suffered near the end of the battle. (Only within recent years has Clerk's progress toward establishing the battery that morning been brought to light.[30])

Given the misleading scouting reports, the belief that an immediate attack was necessary because the enemy was about to receive a strong reinforcement, and the enthusiasm of the council of war in urging it, the decision to go ahead was understandable. But even if no one wanted to wait for artillery, a proper survey of the terrain could have revealed the advantages of concentrating the attack on the British left, towards Lake Champlain, where conditions were more favourable. Above all, the

[28] Abercromby's letter to a Mr James Abercromby in Scotland, dated Lake George, 19 Aug. 1758, is printed by Westbrook, 'Like roaring lions', 71–7.
[29] Abercromby to Pitt, 12 July 1758, Kimball, *Correspondence of Pitt with America*, I, 299.
[30] By Westbrook, 'Like roaring lions', 85–7.

absence of command and control in the early stage of the battle when the formidable obstacles were discovered reflected serious incompetence in the general. It was bad luck to lose Lord Howe, but Abercromby failed to take steps to remedy it.

The precipitate withdrawal from Ticonderoga, shameful as it was, yielded one benefit. For many months Bradstreet had been hoping to raid Fort Frontenac, and now, with much of the summer remaining, and a defeated general who badly needed to register a success prepared to listen, he saw his opportunity. At a council of war held at Lake George on 13 July the issue was heatedly debated because Fort Frontenac was not mentioned in Pitt's plan. In the end, Bradstreet got the general's permission. It is to Abercromby's credit that he allowed the venture to go forward, and it was just as well that the raid was not mentioned in Pitt's strategic plan because its success depended entirely upon secrecy. Apprehensive that his encampments would be raided by French and Indians, the general kept his forces at Lake George and Fort Edward strong; he allotted the expedition only 27 artillerymen and 154 regulars plus 60 rangers. But he realized that Brigadier General John Stanwix's position at the Great Carrying Place (Rome, New York) would become less vulnerable if Fort Frontenac were neutralized. He sent secret orders to Stanwix to allow Bradstreet's force to go on to Fort Frontenac if there was no indication that French and Indians were likely to attack the Great Carrying Place. Having a garrison of about 2,000 and confident that there would be no such attack, Stanwix granted permission.

Bradstreet's force consisted overwhelmingly of provincials, almost 3,000 of them, of which 1,100 were New Yorkers. These, together with his handful of regulars and rangers and 60 Indians, he took up the Mohawk River, employing 300 bateaumen. On 10 August they reached the Great Carrying Place. Secrecy was maintained; the purpose was said to be to assist the rebuilding of forts along the Mohawk. The heavily laden bateaux were floated to Oneida Lake by damming Wood Creek at intervals. From thence they went downriver to Oswego where, without hesitation, the force of 3,100 was embarked on Lake Ontario. On 22 August the flotilla of 95 whaleboats and 123 bateaux headed northwards. They stayed near the eastern shore in case of sudden high winds or the appearance of French armed vessels. Late in the afternoon of the 25th they neared their objective: the point of land where the Cataraqui River joined the origins of the St Lawrence.

There stood Fort Frontenac. At anchor nearby were the nine armed vessels that Bradstreet so greatly feared. At the fort Major Pierre-Jacques

Payen de Noyan commanded a greatly reduced garrison; withdrawals had been made to help defend Carillon, so he had only 110 men. He did not choose to gamble by putting some of them aboard the armed vessels, five of which were not even rigged. The walls of his stone fort with four bastions were almost 14 feet high. The trouble was that only a dozen of its sixty guns could be manned. De Noyan desperately needed men. He learned that a British attack was probably coming only two or three days before it arrived and immediately sent a messenger to Vaudrueil at Montreal. When the message reached the governor on the 26th he instantly called out 1,500 militia, but they could not possibly get upriver in time, the 26th being the same day that Bradstreet's men were landing their guns. The French were caught completely off guard.

Four 12-pounders and four 8-inch howitzers were brought ashore, unopposed, at a location less than a mile from the fort. On the night of the 26th Bradstreet went forward to establish two batteries. One was placed just behind the crest of a rise of ground that lay only 150 yards from the fort's walls. Firing commenced during the night, but the truly effective bombardment began at dawn on the 27th. By 8 a.m. the commandant knew that he must surrender.

The French suffered few casualties (Bradstreet's force none), and the prisoners – soldiers and civilians numbering about 150 – were released to go to Montreal from whence an equivalent number of British prisoners was to be sent to Lake George. French material losses were extensive. The raiders took away two of the nine armed vessels (8 to 18 guns), loaded with provisions and Indian trade goods, and burnt the others. The trade goods, valued at 800,000 livres, were destined for the western outposts. 'The enemy have found at Frontenac', Vaudreuil reported, 'much food, trade goods, and artillery which were intended for the posts of the Ohio and Niagara.' One loaded vessel had been ready to depart for Niagara with provisions, and Vaudreuil feared that the garrison there would be destitute.[31] Before they departed on 28 August Bradstreet's men demolished the fort, spiked its guns, broke off their trunnions, set fire to the buildings, and burnt goods and provisions that they could not carry off. This meant that New France's Lake Ontario navy and its base was wiped out. The booty taken away was prodigious and Bradstreet decided to divide it evenly, the troops and bateaumen sharing equally with the officers. Not all lived to enjoy their riches, however, for at the end

[31] Vaudreuil to the naval minister, 2 Sept. 1758, Preston and Lamontagne, *Royal Fort Frontenac*, p. 264.

of September, Stanwix reported, nearly 1,000 camped at 'Oneida Station' were dead and dying. The 'Enterprize,' he said, 'was perform'd with so much expedition & fateague that few could well bear it.'[32] Yet he also said that its success had depended on its speed. Indeed, the raid on Fort Frontenac showed that a well-conceived operation employing a small army that moved rapidly on waterways could do wonders if kept secret. The raid also showed how seriously Canada lacked troops. Providing a stronger garrison for Fort Frontenac was primarily Vaudreuil's responsibility, but he had been reluctant to pull militiamen away from their farms during the harvest season at a time when no one expected such an attack. When Montcalm decided, not without reason, to concentrate his forces in the main corridor he left this important perimeter base defenceless.

Mountains and Indians: the road to Fort Duquesne

By early 1758 the ravaging of the Virginia and Pennsylvania frontiers had continued for two and a half years. After the British forces abandoned Pennsylvania in the wake of Braddock's defeat, Vaudreuil ordered raiding parties to be continually sent out from the upper Ohio forts; usually there was a French officer accompanying the Indians. So fearsome were these raiders, many from afar, that local Indians came to consider neutrality too dangerous and joined with them. Lord Loudoun recognized that something should be done and proposed a military expedition to capture Fort Duquesne. Although Pitt recalled him, plans for such an expedition were renewed.

The most efficient strategy for dealing with the French forts on the upper Ohio would have been to sever their communication with Canada by seizing Fort Frontenac and Fort Niagara. In early 1758, however, Oswego was still in ruins and Lake Ontario was under French control. The alternative was a direct attack on Fort Duquesne. In accordance with Pitt's plan, it was to be carried out by 5,000 provincials provided by Pennsylvania and Virginia, 1,200 Highlanders, four companies of the Royal American regiment, and a detachment of British artillery regulars – an army of about 7,000.

The store ships carrying tents, guns, ammunition and other military supplies from England were sent to Philadelphia, and the Highlanders and the body of Royal Americans, both of which had been in South Carolina,

---

[32] Stanwix to Abercromby, 29 Sept. 1758, ibid. p. 267.

were also ordered there. For economic reasons Philadelphia was the best choice. It was the leading commercial entrepôt of North America, and its hinterland, especially westwards towards Lancaster, was the continent's richest and most highly developed agricultural region. Livestock, provisions, horses and wagons were plentiful in south-eastern Pennsylvania.

From Philadelphia there was a well-established road by way of Lancaster to Carlisle (then a frontier town with a fort garrisoned by Pennsylvania troops), a total distance of 135 miles. West of Carlisle a 47-mile road passed through Shippensburg to Fort Loudon (not to be confused with Fort Loudoun in Winchester, Virginia); it needed work but was passable. From Fort Loudon to Fort Duquesne, if a direct route through Pennsylvania were to be attempted, there existed only foot and deer paths. A wagon road at least 150 miles long through dense forests, unmapped mountains, swamps and thickets of laurel would have to be created. An army advancing through the wooded Pennsylvania wilderness could count on clean water and some fresh pastures but no habitations. There are no east–west rivers in Pennsylvania. Provisions, except for driven cattle, and other supplies would have to be hauled.

The first mountain range, rising steeply behind Fort Loudon, is the Tuscarora. It extends on a north–south axis for many miles (the current Pennsylvania Turnpike tunnels through it). It could be avoided by turning southwards along a crude 27-mile road that already ran to Fort Frederick, Maryland, situated near Big Pool on the Potomac River. From there to Cumberland the Potomac is an east–west river. The original plan supposed that the expedition would proceed from the settled parts of Pennsylvania into Maryland and follow this route. The trouble was that the river was too shallow for reliable water traffic and no road from Fort Frederick to Fort Cumberland existed. A road on a river bank would have been ideal, but the government of Maryland was not disposed to build it.

The other choice required a northward journey from Fort Loudon for 10 miles to reach a pass over the Tuscarora range that was familiar to traders and provincial military forces. On the other side lay Fort Littleton, recently established, and further on lay Raystown (Bedford, Pennsylvania) where no town or fort existed, only a couple of buildings. This 50-mile horse path needed to be upgraded for wagon traffic, and west of Raystown, where nothing resembling a road existed and the mountain ranges became formidable, it was by no means clear that a suitable road could be built. The safest choice, therefore, would have been to build a road in the Potomac corridor and use Braddock's road from Fort Cumberland to the objective.

Brigadier General John Forbes was the expedition's commander. He had been strongly recommended by Sir John Ligonier and was already in America, colonel of the 17th Regiment of Foot. Born near Edinburgh in 1707, he had studied medicine but abandoned it for a military career. He was an experienced officer of proven ability and only 50 years old, but he happened to be in poor health. Luckily he had a remarkably competent second-in-command, Henry Bouquet. He was born in Switzerland in 1719 of Huguenot parents who had emigrated from France, had chosen a career as a mercenary soldier, and came into the British army as a colonel in the Royal American Regiment in 1756. Bouquet's analytical skill, administrative capacity and tough-mindedness were joined to a temperament and sense of courtesy that enabled him to get on with practically everybody. Forbes could not have wished for a more effective and reliable executive officer. His deputy quartermaster general was a very different matter. Sir John St Clair had been substituted for Pitt's choice, John Bradstreet, when General Abercromby granted Bradstreet's request to remain on the New York frontier – a wise decision because Bradstreet's experience with bateaux would have been wasted in Pennsylvania. Forbes tried to prevent the appointment of St Clair and considered it a misfortune; not without reason, as will be seen.

Forbes was in New York on 4 March 1758 when Pitt's letter of appointment arrived and soon journeyed to Philadelphia. Because the troops sailing from South Carolina and the store ships from England were not due to arrive until early June, he had to remain in Pennsylvania's capital, but used the time to gather support for the campaign. Although the Pennsylvania provincial regiments were slow to recruit, Virginia soon had 800 men ready under Colonel Washington, many of them now experienced in frontier warfare. In addition 600 Cherokees and Catawbas were present; they had come north in response to encouragements given them the year before, with Loudoun's approval, by southern officials. Washington's men needed arms and clothing, but were otherwise ready to go. The thinking at Winchester was along the lines of Loudoun's plan, that is, a strike at Fort Duquesne using Braddock's road.

Forbes was determined to avoid Braddock's mistakes and was contemplating a different plan. A serious reversal, he believed, would produce a worse effect on Indian attitudes than no campaign at all. He envisioned building a good road with depots and stockades spaced about every 40 miles. This would permit defensible fall-back positions (he got the idea from published French military manuals). Many provincials had to be recruited; some came armed with rifles but most with either broken firearms or none and few had any experience of wilderness warfare. The Highlanders also lacked any real experience of North American campaigning. The Royal Americans were better trained but needed to complete their numbers by recruiting (chiefly) young German immigrants. Forbes ordered Bouquet to select the ablest men and have them trained as rangers. But the great task was to build a road. His army would do very little fighting and a great deal of tree-felling and digging.

Hoping to retain the Cherokees, Forbes gave urgent orders to supply their needs. Primarily he wanted them for warding off attacks on his road builders; as he remarked, 'I have no troops up the Country.' Yet he also hoped that the Cherokee warriors might play a key fighting role in the campaign. Road building and troop movements were hurried up to give them the impression that a strong advance was about to get under way. They were not fooled, however, and before long, disgusted by the prospect of delay, nearly all of them went back to their homelands, to the relief of local settlers. In hindsight it is clear that Forbes's chosen strategy made it impossible to keep them, but a few did stay and proved useful in scouting against surprise attacks.

On 7 May when in Philadelphia, Forbes ordered a palisaded depot to be built at Raystown. It has never been clear why he made this decision or even whether he realized the degree of commitment it involved, for if he had not ruled out an advance via Fort Cumberland and Braddock's road, Raystown was very much out of the way. Forbes later claimed that Sir John St Clair was responsible for the choice, but he also said that he was 'advised by everyone to go by Raestown'.[33] Colonel John Armstrong of the Pennsylvania Regiment, an able man, may have been a key adviser: the route from Fort Loudon over the mountain via Fort Littleton was familiar to him because he was in charge of those forts.

Bouquet, who was in Lancaster while the road to Raystown was being built, did not actually see the result until 10 June. The next day he wrote:

We were deceived, my dear general, about the road I am taking. It is almost impassable from Loudoun [Fort Loudon] to Littleton. Of all the roads where it is possible for a wagon to go, this is the worst, and it cannot be repaired. It is of rock, partly solid, partly loose, and sharp stones. The rains have carried away all the earth . . . Our wagons are breaking down; our horses are losing their shoes. It is a wretched state of affairs.

[33] Forbes to Bouquet, 16 June 1758 and 23 July 1758, *Bouquet Papers*, II, 103, 264.

But he worried that there was not enough time to switch to a different route.[34]

Meanwhile, St Clair was entertaining thoughts of reviving the Potomac route. The idea was undoubtedly nourished by his conversations at Winchester with George Washington and some frontier guides there. Governor Horatio Sharpe of Maryland participated in the conversations, and he was now able to commit resources to the project. Bouquet headed south to meet with Sharpe and Washington on the Potomac. Fresh from his experience of the road to Raystown, he approved on 12 June Sharpe's suggestion that a road should be built through the Potomac corridor from Fort Frederick to Fort Cumberland. He could not confirm that the army originating in Pennsylvania would go that way – such an assertion would have exceeded his authority – but when reporting to Forbes he declared that the road via Fort Littleton to Raystown would inevitably be a 'breaker of wagons'. Reluctantly Forbes accepted the change, replying that the Maryland road 'ought to be set about immediately'. Bouquet ordered Washington to employ 300 Maryland troops that were with him to work from the Fort Cumberland end, while Sharpe got work started on the Fort Frederick end. If the final choice had been up to St Clair and Bouquet, the expedition would have used the Braddock road.

In early July, however, Forbes decided against building the Maryland road. Progress was too slow and there was not time, he thought. He was very angry with Sir John St Clair. He ordered a road to be cut from Raystown to Fort Cumberland, but its purpose was to open a direct line of communication with the Virginians, not to convey the main army to Fort Duquesne. Saying that it would be 'a great way about' if the campaign had to follow Braddock's road, Forbes urged Bouquet to make surveys in the mountainous region west of Raystown, 'particularly the Laurell Ridge that he [St Clair] says its impossible wee can pass'.[35]

Bouquet doubted that the direct route over the Pennsylvania mountains was a good idea. The road over Tuscarora Mountain to Raystown had turned out to be much worse than expected, and he was now hearing from some Pennsylvania experts that Laurel Hill would be an insurmountable barrier. Because Forbes was still back at Carlisle – seriously ill because of his intestinal disorder (the journey from Philadelphia nearly killed him) – and Bouquet had to supervise all the campaign's arrangements himself, he could not leave Raystown to see for himself, but he

[34] Bouquet to Forbes, 11 June 1758, ibid. II, 73.
[35] Forbes to Bouquet, 6 July 1758, ibid. 164.

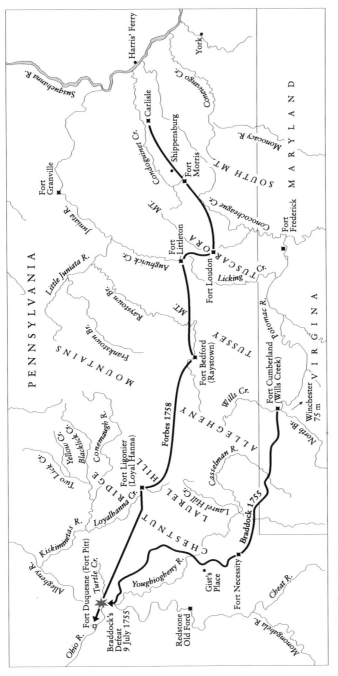

MAP 9 *Roads to Fort Duquesne*

quickly ordered out a number of surveying parties. The reports of these experienced wilderness guides were on the whole promising: Laurel Hill, which had been 'made a monster', appeared to be less daunting than Allegheny Mountain, which would have to be crossed first. The best news was that beyond Laurel Hill the succession of hills would be easy to cross. Still, it was not clear that a road suitable for wagons could be built, and Bouquet knew that the 'Virginia party', now alert to the proposed all-Pennsylvania route, were speaking out 'full force' against it. It was necessary therefore to be doubly cautious, Bouquet told Forbes on 21 July, so 'that we may answer their outcries convincingly in case of an accident, which they would not fail to attribute to the choice of a new route'.[36]

The chief spokesman of the 'Virginia party' was Washington. He was well aware that Virginia's political leaders would be extremely upset if the Braddock road were bypassed. A direct road over the mountains was exactly what Pennsylvania traders and settlers wanted, and Virginia traders and land developers (including himself potentially) would be losers. Yet his passion on this issue was not motivated simply by political and economic interest. He sincerely believed that trying to conquer the mountains was a dreadful mistake.

Bouquet addressed Washington carefully. Mentioning that Forbes would probably send 'a Body of Troops' by a road over Laurel Hill he asked: Would you 'desire to have your Regiment and Self employed immediately' or would you rather wait 'until the General is able to determine fully about the Roads?' Washington responded the next day (25 July), saying that he would cheerfully serve on any route, but took the occasion to observe that all the guides he knew doubted that a usable road over the mountains could be built, certainly nothing comparable to Braddock's. He offered to go to Raystown to have an hour's conference. Bouquet accurately conveyed Washington's information to Forbes, but emphasized the Virginia colonel's readiness 'to march from whatever direction you may determine'. He further suggested: 'Would you not find it apropos to see Colonel Washington here before you decide, and if our [surveying] parties continue to bring good news, persuade him to yield to the evidence?'[37] Unfortunately, this could not happen. Bouquet thought Forbes was at Fort Littleton, but the general was so ill that he had not yet left Carlisle. Instead, Bouquet arranged to meet Washington himself, expressing the

---

[36] Bouquet to Forbes, 21 July 1758, ibid. 251–2.

[37] Bouquet to Washington, 24 July, Washington to Bouquet, 25 July, Bouquet to Forbes, 26 July 1758, ibid. 268, 273, 278.

hope that they could discuss 'impartially the advantages and disadvant-ages' of each route. The meeting occurred halfway between Raystown and Fort Cumberland on 29 July. The result was unsatisfactory.

Upon his return to Fort Cumberland Washington wrote a very long letter, filled with geographical and logistical details. Why go to the trouble and expense, he asked, to cut a 100-mile road though inaccessible moun-tains when a good road 145 miles long already existed and could easily be reopened? If length were a problem, a road could still be built through the Potomac corridor from Fort Frederick; the extra distance from Carlisle to Fort Duquesne via Fort Cumberland by that method was only 19 miles (30 miles would have been closer to the truth). These were complex matters. On one point, however, his argument was blunt and clear: 'But supposing it was practicable to make a Road from Rays Town quite as good as General Braddock's, I ask if we have time to do it?' His own answer: 'Certainly not.' It would take too long and the army would have to winter in the mountains at a post nowhere near any town and difficult to supply in bad weather.[38]

Washington now made a serious personal mistake. He falsely assumed that Bouquet was the chief promoter of the mountain route (evidently Bouquet had not revealed his uncertainty in their conversation) and there-fore bypassed him by writing a letter to Colonel Francis Halkett, who was functioning as Forbes's aide-de-camp, that urged the general not to fol-low Bouquet's advice. Again Washington predicted that the army would end up spending the winter in the mountains in a very bad situation for resupply. This circumvention of Bouquet definitely earned Forbes's sub-sequent remark that Washington's 'Behaviour about the roads, was no ways like a Soldier'.[39] Whether he was engaged in some sort of conspiracy, as Forbes imagined, is dubious, but Forbes and Bouquet had reason to worry because if the expedition stalled, the Virginians would undoubtedly criticize their choice of route publicly.

There is no evidence that Bouquet ever forwarded Washington's long analytical letter to the general. He knew that Forbes had already made up his mind, and in any case he accepted Forbes's argument that it would be foolish not to give the shorter route a chance to succeed. On 3 August Bouquet received a clear direction from Halkett to go ahead, and by the time he responded to Washington on the 9th he could tell him that new

[38] Washington to Bouquet, 2 Aug. 1758, ibid. 298–303.
[39] Washington to Halkett, 2 Aug. 1758, Abbot, ed. *Papers of George Washington*, 5, 360–1; Forbes to Bouquet, 4 Sept. 1758, *Bouquet Papers*, II, 478.

reports confirmed the road's feasibility: 'I cannot . . . doubt', he concluded, 'that we shall all now go on hand in hand, and that the same
Zeal for the service that has hitherto been so distinguishing a part of your
character will carry you by Raes Town over the Allegheny Mountains to
Fort Du Quesne.'[40]

The month of August would witness an extraordinary effort to build
the road. Bouquet's arrangements were admirable: Allegheny Mountain
and Laurel Hill were to be worked on simultaneously, and 1,500 men
were to go forward with pack horses to Loyalhanna (Ligonier, Pennsylvania),
just beyond Laurel Hill, to construct a post and storehouse there. Sir John
St Clair, who was sent forward to supervise, called the road building
'most diabolical work'. It was accomplished by both Virginians and
Pennsylvanians – over 2,000 men wielding felling axes, pick axes, and
shovels. Cattle were driven forward to local pastures for food, and whiskey
was essential. Notwithstanding the mighty effort, however, the goal began
to appear unreachable. On 27 August Bouquet wrote to St Clair angrily
about his employing men to construct redoubts who were needed on
road work.

Yet the truly serious problem was a shortage of wagons and teams.
Many of the vehicles hired on long contract were now shattered; horses
had been overworked and underfed. The result, when it became obvious,
was to be seen not so much in the mountains as at Raystown where the
store of provisions was not being adequately replenished. Consequently,
at the beginning of September the expedition was halted for want of food,
fodder and wagons. The responsibility for this neglect was the quartermaster general's, but Bouquet should have realized that St Clair was away
in the mountains and that in any case he always needed to be watched.
'He is a very odd Man, and I am sorry it has been my fate to have any
Concerns with him', Forbes remarked,[41] yet the general had been too ill to
keep an eye on him.

Forbes had given hints that delay might not be a bad thing; some of the
Indians who helped the French were likely to go home in the autumn.
Bouquet responded vehemently and wrote a blunt letter to his chief. He
argued that the enemy would keep the Indians they still retained 'in the
rear to save provisions' but could gather them to oppose when the time
came, and notwithstanding an anticipation of a peace agreement, he
further argued, the Indians near the Forks 'would never dare to desert the

---

[40] Bouquet to Washington, 9 Aug. 1758, *Bouquet Papers*, II, 343.
[41] Forbes to Bouquet, 4 Sept. 1758, ibid. 477.

French if they did not see us prepared and ready to beat them'. The army was now 'bored and impatient'. Most important, 'England and America have eyes fixed on you.' Of three expeditions this year, Bouquet observed, one had failed (Ticonderoga) and another had succeeded (Louisbourg), 'but all have acted, and we are remaining inactive'. What should be done? 'Everything,' he said, 'depends on having wagons.' He urged Forbes to write a letter to Governor William Denny demanding help, which Forbes did on 9 September; he also wrote to acquaintances in the Pennsylvania legislature.[42] The unpleasant St Clair was dispatched to Philadelphia with authorization to use 'violent measures' if necessary.

By the third week of September, thanks to a combination of threats and agreeable contract terms, convoys of wagons carrying provisions were moving westwards to Raystown. Meanwhile Bouquet had gone forward to Loyalhanna. The weather turned rainy and the road was abominable. Judging that artillery could not possibly climb over Laurel Hill on it, he sought an alternative route and started anew. Rain interrupted the progress. On 15 October Forbes wrote to him, 'Your Description of the roads pierces me to the very soul.' For the first time the general openly worried that his choice might be a mistake, and fervently hoped for some dry weather. When wagon wheels sank in the mud, Forbes observed, they 'hurt the roads more in one hour than wee could repair in a week'.[43] As intermittent heavy rainfall continued both he and Bouquet envisioned failure, but Forbes said that no matter how they felt they must keep the army's spirits up, and although his abdominal pains were excruciating, he set out for Loyalhanna in a litter slung between two horses.

He arrived on 2 November. The rains diminished, but Bouquet worried about the onset of cold weather and the fact that the Pennsylvania provincials were officially not required to serve after 1 December. He proposed that the army should strike forward over the 45 remaining miles to the objective. Washington, who had just arrived at Loyalhanna, tried to talk him out of it, saying the risks far exceeded the possible gains, especially if the French with their Indians chose to attack. For the enemy knew the terrain, and even if the attackers were repulsed, British casualties would probably be heavy and the objective still too distant. The Indians would see Braddock's defeat replicated. On 11 November Forbes convened a council of war. It was agreed that the arguments against a thrust

[42] Bouquet to Forbes, 4 Sept., Forbes to Denny, 9 Sept. 1758, ibid. 471–2, 483–5.
[43] Bouquet to Forbes, 11 Sept., Forbes to Bouquet, 15, 25 Oct. 1758, ibid. 492, 551, 585.

forward outweighed those for it. Among the major considerations were wet weather and bad roads, which together put the provisioning of the army at hazard.[44] Thus, with winter approaching the expedition appeared to be stranded in the mountains. Washington was right after all: a reliable road had taken too long to build. His private letters to Williamsburg were despondent, but in the encampment he, finally and wisely, held his tongue.

Nevertheless, for all its difficulties the route had offered strategic advantages. The French found it hard to believe that the principal thrust would come over the mountains. They were busily preparing defensive positions and surveying points for ambush on the Braddock road, and Forbes had encouraged their assumption by directing Washington and his men to reopen that road part-way during August and September. This was one reason why the expedition was remarkably free of enemy harassment. Another reason was that Forbes and Bouquet took no chances: they insisted on continuous protective scouting (in which Indians often assisted) all along the route as well as troop escort for every convoy.

There were only three noteworthy encounters with the enemy, each spaced a month apart. The first may be termed a battle. It was brought on by a British officer, Major James Grant of the 77th (Highlander) Regiment. In early September Forbes had intelligence that a major French and Indian attack was likely to be launched before the Indians from the far west headed home. Bouquet was ordered to find out more and planned to send forward two 100-man patrols. Grant convinced him that one very large detachment would get better results, and on 9 September a body of 800 men set out, half of them regulars (300 Highlanders, 100 Royal Americans) and half provincials (175 Virginians, 100 Pennsylvanians, 100 Marylanders) plus two or three dozen Indians. The main object was to reconnoitre the ground on the way to the fort and try to discover the measure of the enemy's Indian support, but – a mistake, as it proved – Bouquet authorized Grant to attack the enemy if opportunity offered.

When Grant reached the vicinity of the fort there were no Indians out on patrol and his ambush arrangement produced no result. Thereafter he assembled 750 men on top of a hill overlooking the fort, undiscovered, and near midnight on the 13th he sent 200 provincials and 200 Highlanders under Major Andrew Lewis of the 1st Virginia regiment down the hill to attack Indian camps that were supposed to be there. They got lost and straggled back. Near dawn on the 14th, not far from the fort with 550 men, Grant felt frustrated because nothing had happened. A forward

[44] Ibid. 593–8.

detachment was allowed to set fire to a storehouse and he ordered his drummers to sound reveille. Both of these were done for no good reason except the hope of achieving something. Like angry bees French troops and Indians swarmed from the fort, formed small parties, and raced through the woods firing from behind trees at British and American troops in the open. The Highlanders' officers were easy targets, and many of the bewildered troops broke and ran. Hearing the shots, Major Lewis's officers persuaded him to leave a strong defensive position and come forward to help. (Grant's order to hold his position was not delivered.) The slaughter was terrible and would have been worse if 40 Virginians under Captain Thomas Bullett, assigned to guard the baggage, had not confronted and withstood the advance of the French and Indians. No fewer than 22 officers and 278 soldiers were killed or missing, the Highlanders suffering most; a few of the missing were taken prisoner, including Grant and Lewis. Only 525 survived to return to Loyalhanna, almost 100 of whom were wounded. The French lost 8 killed and 8 wounded.

In the aftermath it was clear, as it should have been from the outset, that the self-confident Scottish major was totally ignorant of the hazards of wilderness warfare and had too much disdain for provincial officers to accept any advice from them. Forbes had liked him but was furious, and was much annoyed with Bouquet for letting so many men go on such a mission without consulting him. It was contrary to his broad strategy and exactly what was not needed at this time. Forbes now made an assessment of the progress thus far, and revealed his strategic priorities as well as his opinion of Grant's conduct: the army 'secured in a good post well Guarded and Cautioned against surprize, our Roads almost Compleated [the rains had not yet come], Our provisions all upon wheels, and all this without any loss on our side', and the army in an advance position near the enemy and ready to come together and attack when opportunity offered. All this, he continued, was endangered by Major Grant's foray. Besides, there was a strong possibility of 'alienating and altering the disposition of the Indians, at this critical time' when they might be ready 'to embrace our alliance and protection'.[45]

A month later the security of the Loyalhanna post was tested by a French and Indian raid. A body of Illinois militiamen assisted by 100 local Indians, perhaps 600 men in all, came from the post to mount a night attack. Bouquet was not there when it happened, and direction of the defence fell to Lieutenant Colonel James Burd of the Pennsylvania

[45] Forbes to Bouquet, 23 Sept. 1758, ibid. 535–6.

provincials who, thanks to Bouquet's planning, had 1,500 men at his disposal. The attackers happened upon an advance guard the morning of 12 October and Burd, hearing the shots, sent some of his troops forward to meet them. His troops gradually fell back to the breastworks where, with cannon and small mortars, the garrison proved invincible. Although the defenders lost 5 officers and 62 soldiers, and the attackers made off with horses and cattle, the fact was that the enemy had tried to dislodge Forbes's army and failed. The French commandant understood this; so did the local Delawares and Shawnees.

The third encounter occurred on 12 November when Forbes was with the army at Loyalhanna. (By then it numbered about 2,600 men fit for service.) He ordered Washington and Lieutenant Colonel George Mercer, also of Virginia, each to take 500 men on a mission to surround an enemy party that was raiding horses which were grazing 3 miles away. The chief object was to take prisoners in order to gain intelligence of enemy strength. On the way back at nightfall Washington's detachment was fired upon, and returned fire. The attackers were Colonel Mercer's men, so it was a case of Virginians firing at each other. Two officers and thirty-five soldiers were killed before the leaders got it stopped. But the mission succeeded. One of Washington's prisoners was an Englishman who had lived in Lancaster but said he had been carried off by Indians. His questioners told him that his life was forfeit for taking up arms against his countrymen but that he could salvage it and receive a good deal of money if he reported accurately the situation at Fort Duquesne. He was also told that if his report proved false, he would suffer death in an 'extraordinary manner'. He reported that most of the Canadian troops had been sent away and that even the regional Indians had gone off to their villages. A captured Indian gave indications of agreement with this information.

It was exactly what Forbes needed to hear. Without hesitation he sent forward Virginians and Pennsylvanians under Colonels Washington and Armstrong as brigade commanders and supplied them with as many axes as could be found. Their men tirelessly hacked their way to a point about 12 miles from Fort Duquesne. The main army followed, with Forbes in his litter. On the night of the 24th they were startled and puzzled by the sound of loud explosions coming from west, and the next morning when they came in view of the fort they saw a smoking ruin. As the troops approached, the Highlanders confronted a hideous scene: the heads of their comrades mounted on posts, kilts attached below. In a rage they ran forward to exact vengeance, but the last of the French troops had left the day before.

The commandant, François-Marie Le Marchand de Lignery, had been confident in early September that he could hold out. Three hundred Canadians had reached him during the summer, and his garrison numbered about a thousand Frenchmen plus numerous Indians encamped nearby. He was sure that the enemy would advance on the Braddock road where his preparations would bring about their defeat. Soon there came the success against Major Grant's force, after which the Indians from the west returned to their homelands.

A month later, in mid-October, Lignery had to inform most of the nearby Indians that he must send them away to their villages. The reason was a shortage of provisions. Early in the year provisions came up the Ohio River from Illinois and later some came from Detroit via Lake Erie and Presqu'Isle, but the latter had stopped coming. Thanks to Bradstreet's pillaging of Fort Frontenac there could be no emergency supply from Canada. The outlook was grim. When the Illinois militiamen returned from their mid-October raid Lignery sent them home, and also sent many of his Canadians up the Allegheny River to the northern forts. Unless he did this, he wrote to Vaudreuil, he 'would have only had provisions to subsist for about 10 days'. The garrison was thus reduced to 300 troops, a third of which were sick. The raid that he sent out on 9 November was mainly accomplished by local Indians, and shortly afterwards even these suddenly became unavailable. An officer he sent to visit them returned to report that their villages were deserted and that none 'dared come to Fort Duquesne because the enemy was too numerous'.[46] But it was not until a scouting patrol returned on the 23rd with a report that the attacking army was only 15 miles away that Lignery resolved to abandon the fort. He sent most of the cannon downriver to Illinois and made preparations to burn and blow up the structures. After making sure the charges detonated the commandant with his remaining men rowed up the Allegheny River to Fort Machault.

In terms of geography Washington was right about the roads, but when all factors are considered Forbes was right. The more direct route suited his deliberate method of approach with fortified depots along the way; and Lignery proved unable to thwart him. The French would have much preferred to defend against an attack via the Braddock road.

Forbes's choice was also justified by political and economic advantages. There can be no doubt that he wished to please the Pennsylvanians.

[46] Lignery to Vaudreuil, 18 Oct. 1758, Waddington, *Guerre*, II, 407; Vaudreuil to the naval minister, 20 Jan. 1759, Stevens and Kent, eds. *Wilderness Chronicles*, p. 128.

When the Virginians accused him of falling under Pennsylvania influence they were right, and some Pennsylvanians had narrow and selfish goals similar to those that he reviled in the Virginians. But Pennsylvania, despite its pacifistic legislature, had made a strong effort to try to defend its interior settlements and had demonstrated an ability to recruit soldiers; moreover, Forbes very much wanted to draw on the province's plentiful food supplies, horses and wagons. Early in the preparations Bouquet was astonished to see him wring so much assistance out of the notoriously stingy Pennsylvania council and legislature. When the September provisioning crisis arose and wagons and teams were urgently needed, Pennsylvania's political and mercantile leaders were aware that the route the general had chosen was the one they desired, and their speedy response to the crisis demonstrated a willingness to deliver.

There was another reason why Forbes was eager to cooperate with the Pennsylvanians. They were best prepared to ameliorate the Indian problem. Forbes placed a high value on Indian assistance, and when the Cherokees went away he focused on trying to bring the Delawares and Shawnees to his side, or at least on convincing them to become neutral. Some Pennsylvanians were already developing this possibility. When he arrived in Philadelphia in April, Forbes became acquainted with a Quaker merchant, Israel Pemberton, whose pacifism coincided with his wish to trade with Indians and who was a friend and strong supporter of Teedyuscung, the eastern Delaware chief. There was a settlement of Delawares on the north-central frontier at Shamokin where the two great branches of the Susquehanna River join; the Pennsylvanians had built Fort Augusta there with adjacent dwellings for the Indians. Pemberton had information that some Delawares were hoping for peace, but none of them could do anything until they received an official offer. Two factors combined as one to prevent such an offer: the Iroquois connection and the Pennsylvania proprietors' party. The latter, for the sake of preserving their vast gains in eastern Pennsylvania under the iniquitous Walking Purchase of 1737, did not want to see the Iroquois, whose leaders had granted it, lose authority over the Delawares, who objected to it.

In mid-June, in a conference with Governor Denny and the council, Forbes seized the initiative and insisted that an official offer to Teedyuscung be made. Soon afterwards, two Delaware chiefs arrived at Shamokin from villages west of the Allegheny River and asked Teedyuscung about rumours of peace they had heard. He took them to Philadelphia, and after a private conference there was a public meeting at the State House (now

Independence Hall) on 11 and 12 July, attended by Governor Denny, the council, and 'a great number of the Inhabitants of the City'.[47] At this meeting the Indians pledged to turn the 'hatchets' given them by the French against the givers. But the pledge needed to be formalized, and Forbes, who had left Philadelphia for Carlisle, wrote to Abercromby seeking authority to conduct Indian diplomacy without waiting for Sir William Johnson to act (Johnson, not wanting to offend the Six Nations, had done nothing to help Forbes). To his credit, Abercromby granted the request and Johnson was circumvented.

The Pennsylvania governor did not wait for Abercromby's reply to send a representative to the Delawares in the western part of the province. The man chosen was Christian Frederick Post, a Moravian missionary dedicated to peace who had married a Delaware woman and learned her language. From his dwelling he journeyed under the protection of Pisquetomen and a small party of Indians to the villages along Beaver Creek and other places under French influence; on one occasion he delivered his message at a location across the river from Fort Duquesne. French officers tried to get him handed over or assassinated, but the Indians protected him. His message was to announce a forthcoming peace conference to be held in eastern Pennsylvania. At length the Indian leaders responded that they longed for peace and would be represented. After managing to evade French scouts sent to intercept them, Post and Pisquetomen got back to Shamokin on 8 September. From there the missionary went to see Forbes at Raystown while his companion set out for Easton. A very large congress would assemble there.

Pisquetomen's western delegation was vitally important to peace, but tiny. Even the eastern Delawares were heavily outnumbered at the congress by hundreds of Iroquois, among which there were representatives from all six nations. Clearly, the Iroquois now realized that they must not ignore what was happening, but so large a congress could not be gathered at short notice. It did not convene until 7 October and the formalities of the negotiation took almost three weeks. Governor Denny and the governor of New Jersey convened it and were present. The Pennsylvania authorities, in order to obtain peace on the Ohio, gave up all claim to lands of the Albany purchase that lay west of the Allegheny Mountains. Although acknowledgement of the ultimate authority of the Iroquois over Indian affairs in Pennsylvania was reaffirmed, the Ohio Indians were empowered to negotiate with provincial officials on their own. Knowing these things

[47] *Bouquet Papers*, II, 187–96.

Pisquetomen believed he could persuade his colleagues to stop fighting, and before the final ceremonies concluded he left Easton to head west, Post with him.

They found Forbes at Loyalhanna on 7 November. He sent them on to Beaver Creek with wampum belts to support the seriousness of their mission, and added a message of his own:

As I am now advancing, at the Head of a large Army, against his Majesty's Enemies, the French, on the Ohio, I must strongly recommend to you to send immediate Notice to any of your People who may be at the French fort, to return forthwith to your Towns; where you may sit by your Fires with your Wives and Children, quiet and undisturbed, and smoke your Pipes in safety. Let the French fight their own Battles, as they were the first Cause of the War.

The general's message also urged the chiefs to keep their young men back, since in case of an encounter his troops could not distinguish them from enemies, and blood would be tragically shed.[48] Pisquetomen and Post set out, putting themselves again in peril. At Kuskuskie on Beaver Creek where they met with assembled tribal leaders they found them to be painfully slow to make up their minds. On one hand the Indians feared – not without reason – that once the French were driven out the English would break their word and encroach upon their Ohio lands. On the other hand they were aware of the weakness of the French garrison and its lack of supplies as well as the proximity of Forbes's large army. The prospect of peace and trade goods was also tempting. A decisive moment came on the 20th when a young French officer came from the fort with a war belt and an invitation from Lignery to take part in a new attack. The Indians kicked the belt from fire to fire as if it were a snake, and at midnight the terrified Frenchman sent a messenger to the fort reporting that no help was to be expected from them.

Fort Duquesne's fall may be correctly attributed to a shortage of provisions which compelled Lignery to diminish the garrison and to effective diplomacy which at the crucial moment in November caused local Indians to deny assistance. Yet such an explanation would leave out the third indispensable factor: the presence of Forbes's army. Lignery made his decision to abandon the fort, and the Indians made theirs, in the knowledge that a strong and well-guarded attacking army was nearby. Forbes

[48] Quoted in Anderson, *Crucible of War*, pp. 279–80.

himself believed that the Indians' failure to dislodge the army at Loyalhanna played a role in their decision 'to act a neutral part'.[49]

Its presence was the result of what was perhaps the most remarkable and certainly most distinctive campaign of the Seven Years War in North America. Unlike other expeditions this one involved no water carriage. The supply line was extremely long, and the army was, in the context of wilderness warfare, quite large. Extensive and complex logistical measures had to be improvised. The heavy burden of road cutting fell upon the provincial soldiers, which was not unusual, but good relations with them were maintained. In private letters Forbes sometimes uttered the usual British army expressions of contempt for lower-level provincial officers and troops, but he reminded Bouquet to exert himself to keep 'the provincials, officers and soldiers in the best temper of mind possible', this after reading a letter from the defeated Abercromby in which he complained about his provincials. Bouquet replied that he had established harmony among the different corps and was intent on 'holding the balance even, encouraging these [provincials], and restraining the overbearing spirit of others, chiefly of your countrymen'.[50] How the general reacted to the last comment is not known, but he could choose to suppose that it pertained chiefly to Sir John St Clair. He made sure that there would be a supply of lead for those Pennsylvanians who came with rifles and moulds.

Forbes's concern for good relations with provincial regiments reflected his approach to Pennsylvania's political leaders. He was exactly the kind of man Pitt wanted – someone respectful yet forceful who could gain their cooperation and support. Pennsylvania politics, particularly with respect to dealings with the Indians, were distressingly complex, yet from the beginning Forbes managed to prevail without rancour. He may be faulted for his attitude towards the Virginians. Their dismay over the route was entirely predictable, yet he made no allowance for their disappointment and was all too ready to attribute their arguments merely to political interest. Yet Washington may also be faulted for his persistent grumbling after the issue had been decided. When at length they campaigned together, however, Forbes and Washington worked in harmony. The way was prepared for this by Henry Bouquet, who realized that Forbes was in the throes of terrible pain and bodily weakness, and prevented serious

---

[49] Forbes to Abercromby and Amherst, 26 Nov. 1758, James, ed. *Writings of General John Forbes*, p. 262.
[50] Forbes to Bouquet, 18 Aug., Bouquet to Forbes, 20 Aug. 1758, *Bouquet Papers*, II, 384, 397.

trouble from developing by treating Washington courteously and generously (yet without yielding an inch on the matter of the route). Bouquet
perceived the strength and sincerity of Washington's desire to serve, and
Forbes agreed with him in valuing the Virginia colonel's experience and
judgement on questions of wilderness combat.

Clearly, Forbes was extremely fortunate to have such a capable and
hard-working executive officer as Bouquet in the field. Given the general's
need to make arrangements while in Philadelphia and then his debilitating
sickness, the campaign could not possibly have been carried through successfully without Bouquet. Not only were the commander-in-chief and his
second-in-command intelligent and experienced professionals, they were
also men who had the character and patience to work with each other in
near-perfect and supportive harmony across a broad range of requirements
and through innumerable crises. Their degree of cooperation (and deft handling of the worse than useless quartermaster general) was remarkable.

Forbes deserves to be remembered not just for his doggedness and
personal good sense, but for his highly intelligent and flexible approach to
strategy and tactics. It is obvious that he had carefully studied Braddock's
disaster and Dunbar's compounding of it. Although he was anxious to
employ the Cherokees, he did not let the threatened loss of their services
alter his strategic plan. He would use light infantry and rangers instead.
'I have been long of your Opinion', he wrote to Bouquet, 'of equiping
Numbers of our men like the Savages . . . in this Country, wee must comply and learn the Art of Warr from Ennemy Indians or anything [sic] else
who have seen the Country and Warr carried on in itt.'[51] Forbes did not
devise his plans so that they might give the principal honour to British regular troops, and as it happened regulars did not play the prominent role
in the success. In fact, their one significant action, led by Major Grant,
endangered the mission. All in all, despite the difficulties and disappointments, Forbes stuck to his strategy and it worked. Luck struck a balance
for him: the prisoner's timely information made up for the unusually rainy
September and October.

The winter garrison he assigned to the captured fort was limited to
250 men which would be increased to 350 when barracks were finished
and a food supply was assured, but initially the place was quite defenceless. At Loyalhanna a garrison of 400 was maintained, but with a French
force not far upriver the true defence of the position at the Forks lay
in Indian good will. Forbes understood the situation and invited the

---

[51] Forbes to Bouquet, from Philadelphia, 27 June 1758, ibid. 136.

local chiefs to a conference. They arrived a bit late, just after he left for Philadelphia, but Bouquet met them. He promised that trade goods would soon come, gave them powder and lead for hunting, and urged them to spread the word about the peace. They found everything agreeable.[52] When Bouquet departed in mid-December Colonel Hugh Mercer of the Pennsylvania regiment took charge.

Forbes wrote a letter to Pitt reporting the success, asking leave to return to England to restore his health and informing the secretary of state that he had renamed Fort Duquesne Pittsburgh. He also named Loyalhanna, Fort Ligonier; and Raystown, Bedford.[53] He arrived in Philadelphia on 17 January 1759 and died there on 11 March. The Pennsylvania authorities gave him a state funeral and he was buried in the chancel of Christ Church. During most of the twentieth century Pittsburgh's baseball park was named Forbes Field, but almost no one outside the city, and maybe inside, knew who Forbes was.

It says something about the man's character that in his final days he devoted his dwindling energy to the goal of maintaining peace with the Indians on the frontier which he had pacified. He realized that the new commander-in-chief, Amherst, would be preoccupied with taking over command from Abercromby and therefore with matters concerning New York. In January, even before reaching Philadelphia, he urged Amherst to come there and arrange a meeting with the governors of Pennsylvania, Virginia and Maryland. Forbes foresaw that contending colonial interests and a competitive desire to control the Ohio territory might undermine peace with the Indians unless matters were put 'on some solid footing'. He was apprehensive that Amherst had wrong ideas about dealing with Indians. 'I agree with you', Forbes wrote, 'that they will incline to the Strongest . . . But this requires a long and serious Confab to discuss; only I beg in the mean time that you will not think triflingly of the Indians or their friendship, when I venture to assure you that twenty Indians are capable of laying half this province waste.'[54] It was the dying man's last letter to the commander-in-chief, who did not come to Philadelphia in time to engage in that 'long and serious Confab'.

[52] Bouquet's report of the meeting is printed in ibid. 621–4. Also printed (624–6) is a version given by a Delaware chief to Lignery at Fort Machault that differs significantly and contains statements that Bouquet was unlikely to have made.

[53] Forbes to Pitt, 27 Nov. 1758, completed in Philadelphia, Kimball, *Correspondence of Pitt with America*, I, 406–9.

[54] Forbes to Amherst, 26 Jan., 7 Feb. 1759, James, ed. *Writings of General John Forbes*, pp. 283, 289–90.

CHAPTER 11

The West Indies and North America, 1759

Upon taking office in late 1756 Pitt had doubled the size of the squadrons based at Antigua and Jamaica, each from about six ships to twelve, but his thoughts were focused on Louisbourg. When news of its conquest reached London in mid-August 1758 he immediately gave serious attention to the West Indies. The capture of Martinique might bring an early peace. In any case the island was so highly valued by the French that they would certainly be willing, when the time came, to exchange Minorca for it rather than ask for the return of Louisbourg. Although Pitt's principal concern was Canada, the Royal Navy now had ships and sailors enough for both a Caribbean expedition and a major operation against Quebec.

Martinique and Guadeloupe

A West Indian conquest at this time would be useful politically. The disaster at St Cast had stirred up sharp criticism. Pitt's dispatch of regiments to Germany had perturbed his anti-Hanoverian supporters. What better way could there be to calm them down than to launch a maritime operation against a prominent French plantation colony? The Duke of Newcastle disliked the idea, but his opinion was nullified by unexpected enthusiasm on the part of the king, who in Newcastle's hearing remarked to Pitt: 'we must conquer Martinique as a set-off to Minorca.'[1] When Anson came ashore in mid-September he showed his habitual reluctance to send ships overseas but assented because the cabinet had already gone forward with plans; he even commented that Martinique afforded a good landing

---

[1] Quoted in Williams, *Life*, I, 380.

beach. Because the strategy of raiding the French coast was set aside 6,000 regulars were available.

The general appointed to command, Peregrine Thomas Hopson (the same man who had governed Nova Scotia in 1753), was not Pitt's choice. He was a congenial and intelligent officer, but too old for this sort of mission. Knowing how important it was to conduct Caribbean campaigns in the winter months to avoid the worst ravages of tropical disease, Pitt was relentless in urging Hopson to depart. Seven ships of the line, one 50-gun ship, four frigates and four bomb vessels sailed with seventy-five transports on 12 November 1758. At Barbados on 3 January the warships came under the command of Commodore John Moore in the *Cambridge* (80 guns), the senior officer on station who had with him one 50-gun ship and three frigates.

The invasion force appeared off Fort Royal, Martinique on 15 January 1759, and by 8 a.m. the next morning the *Bristol* (64 guns) was in position 50 yards off Pointe de Negrès at the harbour entrance to batter the fort there. After an hour's bombardment the garrison fled, whereupon a party of marines from the ship occupied the fort. Seeing its capture, the crews of the batteries above the beach at Case Navire, a mile and a half to the north-west (modern Spoerken), withdrew. Later in the day, the army, under General John Barrington, second-in-command, went ashore in twelve flat-bottomed boats, unopposed. It camped in a position just above Pointe de Negrès and rested for the night. The next day the defending militiamen took full advantage of the terrain, and the advancing British troops encountered murderous musket fire from hills, woods, cane fields and rocky ravines.

It was essential to compel surrender of the citadel. It was situated on a high rock formation extending out into the bay. The garrison was not large – only 480 regulars – and required sailors from the ships and troops from other batteries to maximize its firepower. Five miles and three hills lay between the landing beach and the fortress. The first hill, called Morne Tartenson, was expertly defended by sharpshooting militiamen. Barrington and his engineers judged that even with the 300 slaves brought from Barbados and the assistance of sailors, it would be extremely difficult to haul heavy guns across the broken terrain to come within effective range of the fortress, and throughout the effort the men would be exposed to musket fire. Hauling water, so much needed by the sweating soldiers, was an almost equally daunting challenge. Hopson hoped to find a landing place nearer the objective, but none was practical. He proposed that ships and bomb vessels should enter the bay to bombard the citadel into

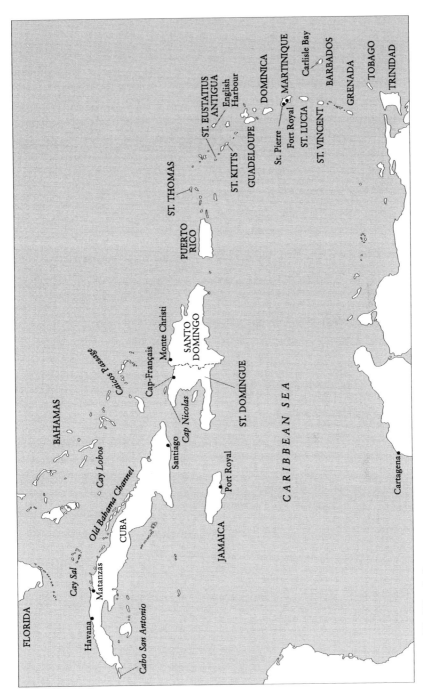

MAP 10 *The West Indies*

submission, but Moore's gunners doubted that the ships' broadsides could be effective against the elevated ramparts. In any case, the ships would need to tack in against the prevailing easterly wind and current, and thus would be exposed for many hours to the fort's cannon and mortars as well as heavy batteries elsewhere on the bay shore plus the guns of the *Florissant* (74) and a frigate, moored at the careenage.

A council of war estimated the difficulties and recommended abandonment. The withdrawal of the troops from the beach at Case Navire during the evening of 17 January was disguised by a clever ruse, some pieces of siege equipment having been brought ashore that afternoon. After the ships departed it was reported that most of the inhabitants had given up hope; they were short of provisions, demoralized and disaffected. But these reports were probably exaggerated and there was the undeniable fact that many of the militiamen were good marksmen.

The fleet sailed up the coast to the commercial capital, St Pierre. There the forts were less formidable and stood near the water. Only one ship of Moore's squadron, the *Rippon* (60 guns) moved in close to unleash its broadsides. The commodore did not order others to follow and failed to recall the *Rippon* before it sustained many casualties. Hopson and Moore could have destroyed the forts and captured the shipping in harbour, but their orders were to seize the island and they realized that even if St Pierre were occupied, it would probably not bring about a surrender of Fort Royal, so they sailed northwards to Guadeloupe.

The water near the south-western shoreline at Basse-Terre was deep. The citadel, Fort St Charles, stood near the shore and was vulnerable to naval gunfire. On the morning of 23 January 1759 Moore's ships of the line moved in. The three largest – *St George* (90 guns), *Cambridge* and *Norfolk* (74 guns) – fired on the citadel while three bomb vessels launched shells into it. The defenders returned fire but by early afternoon their efforts slackened and all was quiet by 5 p.m. Forty-seven British seamen and marines were killed in action. In the evening the ships and bomb vessels bombarded the adjacent town; stocks of gunpowder exploded and fires were started which lasted 36 hours, turning potentially valuable plunder to ashes. The inhabitants fled into the nearby hills, and the fortress's garrison joined them. British troops landed unopposed the next day.

Engineers informed Hopson that after some structural improvements the citadel could be armed with guns removed from shore batteries; with a garrison of only 500 it could thwart any land-based enemy attack. The navy and the bulk of the army could therefore proceed to other objectives. Everyone agreed that the terrain prohibited an attack on the enemy's mountain retreat at Dos d'Âne, and when the French governor, Charles François Nadau du Treil, refused terms it was necessary to adopt a new strategy. Hopson, who was very ill, failed to do this. Meanwhile soldiers were falling sick by the hundreds with dysentery. Over 2,000 were shipped off to nearby Antigua where, luckily, most of them gradually recovered. The number of effective troops was down to 3,300. Finally, in mid-February, Commodore Moore took the initiative and sent six ships – two of the line, one of 50 guns and two frigates – eastwards into the narrow bay that separates Basseterre and Grandeterre. After the squadron bombarded Fort Louis, adjacent to the town of Pointe-à-Pitre, Captain William Harman of the *Berwick* (64 guns) led an attack by sailors, marines and Highlanders. Although the landing was opposed and there were two dozen casualties, the operation was expertly carried out. The British now held a base from which they could launch offensive operations on either Grandeterre or Basseterre. General Hopson died of a fever on 27 February and the command devolved on Barrington. By 11 March he had joined Moore at Fort Louis. Even after generously granting Moore's request for 300 soldiers to fill out the ships' companies, he had about 1,200 regulars still healthy plus 350 volunteers along with 300 slaves from Antigua, Nevis and Montserrat.

Barrington's attack plan made use of the sea. A small force under Brigadier Byam Crump sailed eastwards to destroy the ports of Sainte Anne and Saint François. Closer to hand an amphibious assault was mounted on Gozier, thus ensuring the safety of Fort Louis. After obtaining information from local black guides and pilots, Barrington ordered Brigadier John Clavering to cross over to attack Basseterre's east shore. Assisted by the *Woolwich* (44 guns), some small cruisers and the bomb vessels, Clavering adapted his tactics to circumstances while keeping his moves unpredictable. In just nine days (12 to 21 April 1759) he progressed from Arnouville and Petit Bourg southward to Sainte Marie, routing the island's militiamen wherever they attempted to stand. Meanwhile, Crump went north across the isthmus to Baie Mahault and occupied the shore where the island's defenders were receiving military supplies carried by Dutch vessels from St Eustatius. To the south, Clavering's next objective would be the town of Capsterre and the region surrounding it where the richest sugar plantations of the island were spread out. Although the defending militia had better knowledge of the terrain, they were poorly trained and their commanders made many mistakes, while Clavering, though feeling his way, profited from the use of ships and boats and almost never put a foot wrong.

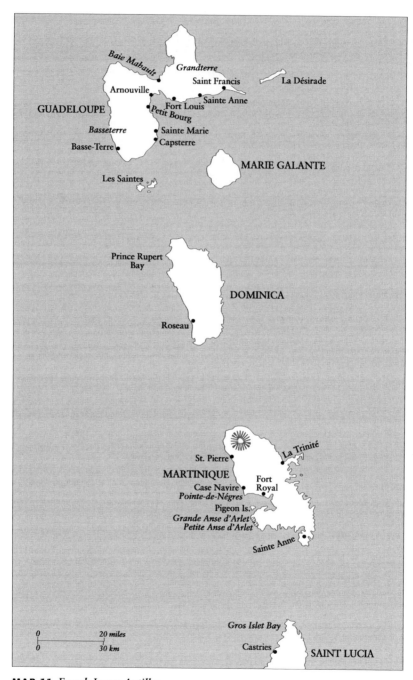

MAP 11 *French Lesser Antilles*

A deputation representing the principal residents came down from the refuge at Dos d'Âne to Sainte Marie on 21 April under a white flag. Clavering brought them to Barrington and by 1 May articles of capitulation were agreed to. The military and civil officers were accorded the honours of war but required to depart for Martinique; transportation would be provided for them, their families and servants. The inhabitants could stay or leave, the choice to be made within thirty days. They were allowed their religion and their system of government; internal taxes would continue, as would their property rights including the rights of absentees. Free blacks whom the British had taken prisoner were not to be enslaved, a provision that reduced the prize value of the conquest. Very welcome were the articles specifying that the island's produce could be exported to Great Britain and that the inhabitants were to enjoy commercial privileges as if they were British.

Barrington offered these generous terms because he knew that sickness among his troops was bound to intensify during the summer, and in fact the army, which suffered 59 killed and 149 wounded in action, would eventually lose a total of 800 to disease. He also had to consider the possibility that a hurricane would disrupt the achievement. The islanders had no trouble accepting the terms: their prospects were horrendous. As the leader of the deputation later commented: 'the women, the children, the slaves, and all of the resources of the island were exposed to the pillage and the fury of the soldier'.[2] Moreover, rescue appeared out of the question. Du Treil had received a letter from Governor François de Beauharnais at Martinique saying that no help would be coming.

In his letter Beauharnais reported that seven ships of the line plus one of 50 guns and three frigates had reached Martinique in mid-March under Maximin, comte de Bompar, but added that the admiral deemed his squadron to be overmatched and was refusing to come north.[3] The residents of Guadeloupe, who chronically mistrusted both the home government and the governor at Martinique, expected something like this, and Barrington's terms offered them not just a shield from personal and economic harm but their customary liberties and retention of property, and also a significant bonus: they could now export sugar to a profitable market.

---

[2] Quoted in Smelser, *Campaign for the Sugar Islands*, p. 139.
[3] It was only slightly overmatched in formal line strength. Bompar had brought seven of the line from France, and the *Florissant* made eight, but one of the ships from France came out with her heavy guns in the hold to maximize cargo space, and his men had not remounted them.

The story of Guadeloupe's conquest was not quite ended, however. Beauharnais knew that Commodore Moore had gone with his squadron to Prince Rupert Bay on the north-west coast of the island of Dominica, a place where the ships could find clean water and an absence of disease. Although Moore knew about Bompar's arrival, he considered himself well positioned to intercept any force that came north to Guadeloupe, because the bay was situated only 50 miles south of Fort Louis on about the same longitude. Moore was completely wrong. It was easy for ships from Martinique to come north on the windward side of Dominica and almost impossible for ships at Prince Rupert Bay to work eastwards to meet them. Wind and current were powerfully adverse. That the French might sail to windward of the island apparently did not occur to Moore, for he did not assign a ship to maintain a watch on that side. He relied too much, it appears, on his intercepted copy of Beauharnais's letter to du Treil which had said that no help would come. Beauharnais, however, collected some regular troops and volunteers and finally persuaded Bompar, who had done almost nothing for six weeks except await supplies, that an expedition could successfully evade the British squadron.

Bompar's squadron escorting eighteen transports rounded the south end of Martinique and easily kept to windward of Dominica, arriving at Sainte Anne on 27 April. Six hundred regulars and almost a thousand volunteers under Beauharnais's command were landed along with guns, mortars and 2,000 firearms to supply the inhabitants. When Beauharnais spoke with the commander of Grandterre's remaining forces, however, he learned that articles of capitulation were being signed and that no one on the island was disposed to reverse the decision. Without attempting to talk to du Treil he re-embarked his men and equipment. Moore did not get his squadron under way until 2 May, two days after the French left Sainte Anne, and was still fruitlessly trying to tack upwind on 6 May when Bompar and the transports were back in Fort Royal harbour.

The belated attempt to rescue Guadaloupe might have recovered Grandterre, but Moore's squadron could frustrate any French attempt to retake Basseterre, and the claim that disease would have forced the British to withdraw is not validated by Barrington's musters. Moreover, the residents knew that if they took up arms, their plantations would be burnt and their slaves stolen. One sees the wisdom of Barrington's generous terms. Moore was vehemently denounced by British planters and merchants for keeping his ships in Prince Rupert Bay while French privateers ravaged their shipping. If Beauharnais and Bompar had managed to reverse Barrington's success, Moore would surely have been court-martialled.

When news of the conquest reached Paris the government was incensed. Du Treil was court-martialled at Martinique by his political enemy, Beauharnais, found guilty of mismanagement and yielding unnecessarily, and sentenced to prison for life. He expected that this unfair verdict would be overturned when he returned to France, but Belleisle and Choiseul confirmed it and he was confined to a fortress. Twenty years later he was released and chose to spend his last years in Guadeloupe.

In London there was satisfaction. Experts knew that Guadeloupe was not only a richly productive island but also situated where its privateers could easily pounce on incoming British shipping. Joseph Yorke, who was upset by the Dutch government's refusal to prohibit vessels from carrying French plantation goods, saw another important benefit: the island's capture would 'do more to put a stop to the Dutch Contraband Trade, than all we can do with these Extraordinary Deputies'.[4] (He was referring to the negotiators appointed by the Dutch government. By 'extraordinary' he meant 'unreasonable'.) Everyone knew that the traffic between Guadeloupe and nearby St Eustatius was almost impossible to interrupt. British possession meant that Guadeloupe's products would be brought to Europe not by Dutch ships, but by British, and brought to Britain where they would pay customs revenue. And if the British sugar market happened to become oversupplied, British merchants would reap the profits of a re-export trade to continental Europe. Nearby Marie Galante was also captured at this time; its coffee production was impressive. The annual value of exports of the two islands under British occupation would amount to 72 per cent of the value of Jamaica's exports, and Jamaica was by far the largest British producer.[5] There was no question that the French would seek to recover Guadeloupe and Marie Galante at the peace table.

Niagara and Lake Champlain

General Amherst had wanted to lead the St Lawrence River attack on Quebec, but Pitt preferred to put his commander-in-chief at the centre of affairs in New York where he could deal with the colonial governors, for once again their legislatures were being asked to raise large numbers of troops. But Pitt also gave Amherst a military mission: he was to attack Canada from the New York frontier. Amherst was allowed to choose

[4] Yorke to Hardwicke, 19 June 1759, BL Add. 35,357, fo. 350.
[5] Based on figures in Pares, *War and Trade*, pp. 474, 481.

whether he wished to advance by the Lake George–Lake Champlain corridor or by Oswego and Lake Ontario.

Pitt's instructions mentioned Niagara, the capture of which would not only cut Canada off from the west and south but also challenge French efforts to recover dominance on Lake Ontario. The 'Utility and Importance of such an Enterprize' was obvious, Pitt wrote, but he made it clear that Niagara was not one of the 'great and main Objects of the Campaign'.[6] Amherst understood this, but decided nevertheless to attack Niagara.

The decision stemmed from an Iroquois initiative. Leaders of the Six Nations had mentioned to Sir William Johnson during the winter that he could probably count 'upon the greater Part if not the whole of them, to join His Majesty's Arms' for such a purpose, and in a formal meeting with Johnson of 21 April 1759 they pledged their support.[7] Thus, an opportunity was offered not only to capture a key French outpost but also to solidify Indian allegiance, and Amherst gave his approval. Knowing that preparations in the Mohawk valley and at Oswego could not be kept secret, he let it be thought that the objective was La Galette in the St Lawrence River.

Brigadier General John Prideaux, an able and experienced officer, was given the command. The 44th and 46th regular regiments along with a battalion of Royal Americans and a large body of New York provincials were to prepare to go up the Mohawk River. Four hundred muskets and carbines for arming Indians were collected. The force of about 3,500 men reached Oswego on 27 June. A thousand were ordered to remain there under Lieutenant Colonel Frederick Haldimand of the Royal American Regiment to begin work on a new fort to replace the ruined Fort Ontario. The others – 1,330 from the 44th and 46th, 200 Royal Americans and 720 New York provincials – were designated for Niagara. Joined to these 2,300 troops and 100 officers were 600 Iroquois warriors whom Johnson had directed to Oswego. The troops embarked on 1 July to begin their westward passage along the south shore of the lake.

Fort Niagara stands on the east side of the Niagara River where it meets Lake Ontario. The original structure of 1726–7 as built by the French was modest and the defensive perimeter was rudimentary (the idea was that the Seneca nation on whose land it was situated could regard it as non-threatening). After the arrival of troops from France in 1755 the

---

[6] Pitt to Amherst, 29 Dec. 1758, Kimball, ed. *Correspondence of Pitt with America*, I, 439–40.

[7] Dunnigan, *Siege – 1759*, p. 27.

place was transformed. Under the direction of Captain Pierre Pouchot of the Béarn regiment, an able officer who had engineering experience, it became the only fort in the American wilderness to be brought up to European standards. Stone barracks and storehouses that Pouchot erected still stand. Because the fort stood on triangular ground, two sides of which were bordered by the river and the lake, strong bastions fronted by ditches were needed only on the landward side. The guns had been Braddock's. The British knew about the guns, but, curiously, they had no idea that the fortifications had been made so strong.

After the raid on Fort Frontenac Vaudreuil was careful not to neglect Niagara. He sent 600 Canadians there for the winter, and Pouchot upon returning to serve as commandant in the spring of 1759 brought an additional 600 men, a quarter of them French regulars, the rest Canadian militia. Arriving at Fort Niagara on 30 April, Pouchot had plenty of time to prepare for an attack. But there was a complication. Since he knew that Vaudreuil wished to restore French sway in western Pennsylvania, Pouchot sent most of his troops, about 800, across Lake Erie to support a counter-offensive by Lignery. In hindsight this was a serious mistake, one that Montcalm did not fail to ridicule. But Pouchot knew that the planned offensive had a good chance of succeeding since it was to be joined by almost 900 Indians from the west; moreover, he did not make his decision until he was promised by Cayuga and Seneca envoys (on 28 May) that they would warn him of any developing British threats to Fort Niagara.

Could they have lied to him? To him this seemed incredible, because his relations with local Senecas when he was commandant at Niagara between 1755 and 1757 were warm and friendly. Perhaps the envoys who spoke with him did not know the truth and had been deliberately misinformed by their chiefs who certainly knew where the expeditionary force coming up the Mohawk River was heading. The French commandant, however, was disposed to trust the Indians' word and knew that the Iroquois intelligence network was excellent.

This did not mean that he blithely ignored the possibility of an attack. Two lake warships recently built near La Présentation (Ogdensburg, New York) had been ordered to keep surveillance on Oswego. The *Iroquoise* schooner called at Oswego in the latter part of June and sent a party of Indians ashore. Those scouts saw and learned nothing, despite the fact that Iroquois warriors were already beginning to gather; evidently, those who did not disappear into the woods gave false information. The other warship, the *Outauaise*, was under orders to cruise in the path of any

British whaleboats and bateaux that might be heading westwards, but it was disabled by a storm and had to limp back to the St Lawrence River. Consequently, Pouchot did not realize that an attack was coming until after the British landed at Four Mile Creek. The flotilla had put into small bays on the south shore each night and arrived undetected. Ironically, the *Iroquoise* was at Fort Niagara, its commander reporting that Oswego was quiet on the same afternoon, 6 July, when the British troops were disembarking. An accidental skirmish and sounds of a disciplined volley of musketry were Pouchot's first hints of danger. The Indians and the lake navy had failed him. The next morning he sent a courier to Lignery with an urgent order to bring back every man he could to Niagara.

Meanwhile there was action at Oswego. Four days after the Niagara expedition departed, Luc de la Corne (brother of the La Corne who had been at Fort Beauséjour) brought 1,500 Canadians and 100 Indians from La Présentation to raid Oswego. A detachment of pickets alerted the British camp, and while La Corne's men dallied Haldimand's 500 Royal Americans and 500 New Yorkers hurriedly fashioned a wall of provisions barrels. The Canadians were greeted with withering musketry and driven off into the woods. When they returned the next morning they faced, besides the muskets, three cannons loaded with grapeshot. Even their subsequent efforts to burn some bateaux were largely foiled and they soon rowed off. Because La Corne's raid was a failure it has seldom been noticed historically, but a British disaster at Oswego might have forced the recall of the Niagara expedition. General Amherst was habitually cautious about defending supply lines, and his decision to place 1,000 troops at Oswego under an able commander was wise.

Fort Niagara had forty serviceable cannons but lacked mortars. The garrison consisted of 149 *troupes de terre*, 183 *troupes de la marine*, 133 Canadian militia and 21 gunners; 70 troops drawn from the trading post a few miles up the Niagara River increased the total to about 560. Amazingly, there were only 11 commissioned officers, far too few, and despite the garrison's small size the stock of provisions was not plentiful. The fort itself was in good condition, but it lacked casemates for durable shelter and embrasures on the parapets. The *Iroquoise* was at hand, but it could rarely come within effective range of the besiegers.

Siege preparations progressed rapidly. The British cut their trenches mainly during the night; a guard against surprise sorties was provided by Iroquois warriors who lay silently on the ground. About 14 July, however, this form of protection was lost. On the 11th a pro-French Seneca leader left the fort with Pouchot's permission to talk to Senecas in the British camp; he brought back some delegates, blindfolded, and Pouchot exhorted them to adopt neutrality. When they returned to the British camp the leaders of the Six Nations held a meeting, the result of which was that about 800 of the 900 Indians that Sir William Johnson had recruited (300 had walked to Niagara) decided not to participate in the fighting. Although Johnson was present at the meeting, he did not speak out against the decision. Thus, although some Mohawks and a few others stayed loyal to the British and continued to assist, most of the Iroquois decided to stand aside while the white men fought it out. The Indians camped next to a place called La Belle Famille, about a mile south of the fort. Why did they remain nearby? They had nothing to lose, and if the British won, as seemed likely, they had Johnson's word that they might participate in pillaging the fort.

Meanwhile, mortars were brought within range. On the night of 13–14 July 300 bombs were lobbed at the fort; bursting in the air they detonated just above ground if the fuses were cut the right length. French guns had been active for days – 6,000 shots had been fired – because accepted doctrine called for blasting the besiegers' trenches early to prevent close approach. Pouchot was running out of 12-pound cannonballs. His opponent, Prideaux, paid cash rewards to men who found them and brought them to his gunners, who fired them back at the French. At this point no one in the fort had been killed, but fatigue was taking a heavy toll and the garrison's efforts were not preventing the British trenches from moving closer. As the range closed British sharpshooters began to pick off French gun crews. This worked both ways: a French musket ball killed Lieutenant Colonel John Johnston of the New York Regiment, a great loss since he was well liked and respected, and was the only officer with genuine competence in laying out the trenches and batteries. Also on the 20th, General Prideaux was killed when he accidently stepped in front of a cohorn (small mortar) as it was being discharged and was struck in the head by the shell. Command of the operation fell to Sir William Johnson, the next senior officer, who resolved to carry on Prideaux's and Johnston's programme. By the 22nd casualties on both sides began to increase and some of the fort's gun crews became reluctant to serve on the parapet despite the addition of earth-filled bags to serve as embrasures. At noon on the 23rd the final British battery, only 140 yards away, placed two 18-pounders in a position to open a breach. Soon the remaining active guns on the nearest French bastion were blasted off their carriages.

Yet on the same day the French were given cause for hope. That morning a party of Indians with a white flag came to the fort with a message from Captains Lignery and Charles-Philippe Aubry from Illinois that they had arrived with a large force – just ten days after the courier bearing Pouchot's emergency order reached Fort Machault (Venango, Pennsylvania). Although some western Indians had departed, at least 500 Indians came across Lake Erie and landed above Niagara Falls to augment the 800 Canadians.

Johnson learned from Iroquois scouts of the relief force's arrival on the 22nd. The next day he selected La Belle Famille as the place to make a stand; an intercepted message from Pouchot to Lignery on the 23rd confirmed him in this decision. He quickly dispatched 150 light infantry of 44th Regiment under Captain James De Lancey (son of the lieutenant-governor of New York), and by late afternoon De Lancey's men were building a southward-facing breastwork just east of the road that came from the falls portage. The following morning, 24 July, Johnson added another 300 troops, all but 50 of them regulars. Lieutenant Colonel Eyre Massey quickly completed arrangements for the defensive position. He placed his own men of the 46th Regiment across the road and extended his line eastwards to include part of the breastwork. On his right flank between the road and the river where the ground was higher he deployed two dozen grenadiers, expert with muskets. The defenders were positioned mostly among trees, yet they could not be surprised from the rear because behind them the terrain was open field. They were afforded clear lines of fire upon the approaching enemy because the undergrowth had been removed, probably because the twigs had been wanted by Pouchot's men for making gabions. On the morning of the 24th the British were ready.

Lignery and Aubry had had an interesting morning. A delegation of Iroquois leaders had talked with the Indians that had come with them and persuaded them to hold back until the battle was decided. Nevertheless, despite this loss of support the commanders decided that their 800 Canadians, most of them *troupes de la marine*, could overwhelm whatever British force might lie in their path. After 8 a.m. they began to march their men, formed up in a broad column, 12 men across the front, northwards on the road. In the lead were white-coated *troupes de la marine*. As the column approached La Belle Famille the pace quickened and the French came forward rapidly, pausing a few times to fire but without much effect. A light rain was falling. Massey had ordered his men to lie down and hold fire until ordered. It was not really an ambush since the Canadians knew the enemy was in front of them. Massey, though wounded by a musket ball, stood firm and waited until the attackers were 30 yards away, at which point he commanded his men to rise and commence firing. The seven volleys from 140 muskets were devastating. The grenadiers assisted by some men from the 44th who joined them poured a murderous fire on the Canadian left flank. The stunned column veered away to its right, but this pointed them towards De Lancey's breastwork. His men waited until they drew close and then unleashed a tremendous volley. Amidst the carnage and confusion, under fire on three sides, with Lignery, Aubry and other officers wounded, the troops turned back. As Massey's unit moved forward De Lancey's men of the 44th jumped over the breastwork to join them. Consequently, the officers were captured by British and American troops, and this saved their lives because as soon as the Iroquois spectators observed the retreat, they leapt to pursue and kept going all the way to the Niagara escarpment, taking prisoners, firearms and scalps as they went. The Indians who had come with Lignery and Aubry speedily departed. In the battle the British suffered 12 killed and 40 wounded; the French about 340 captured or killed, of which 23 were officers.

Thus, in less than an hour the force that came to relieve Fort Niagara was annihilated. How could Lignery, an officer experienced in wilderness warfare, have made such an error? He knew that British troops were waiting at La Belle Famille. Back on 10 June in a follow-up dispatch sent to Presqu'Isle, Pouchot had suggested to him that he might wish to come to the fort on the west side of the river. If Lignery had done this, the British could not have blocked his relief force from joining the garrison; the men could have crossed the river piecemeal under cover of the fort's guns. But Pouchot changed his advice on 23 July: in his message (a copy of which Johnson intercepted) he pointed out that the enemy was divided into three groups, and that Lignery, if he thought his force strong enough to attack one of these separated bodies, might overwhelm it and thus compel the British to abandon the siege. No doubt, Lignery was aware that Fort Niagara's provisions could not possibly feed 800 additional troops, and perhaps he worried about what the Iroquois would do if he chose to advance his men through the woods. What seems to have been decisive, however, was his wish for a clear victory that would lift the siege; also, he and Aubry believed that the British force waiting at La Belle Famille was weak. According to the latest report they had received, the British only had 150 men at La Belle Famille.[8] It seems to have been another instance of a common error: an intelligence report was allowed to overrule tactical prudence. In any case, Lignery's men met with a disaster similar to Braddock's though on a smaller scale.

[8] Pouchot, *Memoirs on the Late War*, p. 217.

It took a while for Pouchot to grasp what had occurred. The commandant did not believe the first report from a loyal Indian, but was shaken when Captain William Hervey under a flag of truce came to the fort a couple of hours later and essentially confirmed it. Still, it was only after sending an officer to Johnson, who let him see the wounded Lignery with a group of captured officers, that he realized that the fort must be surrendered. The terms were negotiated that evening. When Pouchot requested that the entire garrison be sent to Montreal on parole, Johnson reminded him that he was 'not master of the conditions'. All officers, some of which Johnson ransomed from his Iroquois allies at £160 per person, and all soldiers except 96 whom Johnson allowed the Iroquois to keep were then deemed prisoners of war. Mindful of what had happened at Fort William Henry, Pouchot and Johnson agreed on measures that would protect the prisoners from Indian attack. The terms signed on the morning of 25 July allowed them to march out of the fort bearing their arms, arms that they relinquished when they boarded the bateaux. Over 600 officers and troops under strong guard then traversed Lake Ontario and made an arduous passage down the Mohawk River towards New York.

General Amherst's preparations for the advance northwards to the heart of Canada were hampered by the late arrival of provincial regiments, a shortage of batteaumen despite Bradstreet's efforts, and heavy downpours of rain. He ordered a 60-yard clearance of trees along the road from Fort Edward to Lake George – a sensible proceeding but one of many defensive measures that slowed his progress. His 6,200 men did not assemble at Lake George until 21 June. (Nine days later the seaborne expedition against Quebec anchored within sight of its objective.) Amherst's army then spent an entire month repairing boats and bateaux and putting the artillery on rafts during which time a beginning was made on a new fort to replace Fort William Henry. Amherst wrote in his journal: 'As I can't cross the Lake till the Artillery and whale boats are ready I may as well keep on doing other things tending to the defence of this Fort, as I lose no time by it.'[9] This comment approximately summarizes the character of the whole campaign.

On 21 July when the army finally got under way on Lake George it moved briskly. The flotilla enjoyed a favouring wind – the troops rigged blankets as sails – and covered the 33 miles by evening; they slept on board (getting rained on) and landed at dawn. They brought guns – 6- and 12-pounders in bateaux – and by the end of the day had managed to bring

[9] Webster, *Journal of Jeffery Amherst*, p. 139 (17 July 1759).

up two of each calibre to the sawmill. Informed by scouts that the breast-works where such great slaughter had occurred the previous summer were unoccupied, the leading units moved quickly forward and spent the night there. Thus, in one day's march from the landing place Amherst's army arrived unscathed to a protected position within 1,000 yards of Fort Carillon's walls.

That night Brigadier Bourlamaque stole away to Crown Point with 3,000 men in boats and bateaux. The sudden burst of speed by the hitherto sluggish British attackers had taken him by surprise and that is why he failed to occupy the breastworks. On the 23rd the British advanced their siege trenches without being seriously hindered by the fort's guns. Bourlamaque had left behind a detachment of only 400 men with orders to destroy the fort. Late in the evening of the 26th when Amherst had finished placing his heavy artillery and mortars in position for a massive bombardment, a French deserter reported that everyone was leaving and the place was to be blown up. At about 11 p.m. explosions shook the ground and fires lit up the night sky. It took five days to put out the fires completely, but the fort could be repaired. Amherst renamed it Fort Ticonderoga.

Two days later he was informed that the French had three warships (two sloops and a schooner) at Crown Point. 'They depend', Amherst wrote, 'on my not getting my boats over and being forced to build some for Cannon, but I shall be ready sooner than they imagine.'[10] His troops landed unopposed at Crown Point on the evening of 4 August, Bourlamaque having demolished Fort St Frédéric and departed for Isle-au-Noix. This small island in the Richelieu River, about 8 miles north of the lake, had been selected earlier by Lévis, assisted by Pouchot, as the place to make a stand; 20 miles downriver to the north lay Fort St Jean from which there was a good road to Montreal. Assuming correctly that Bourlamaque's army would be well fortified at Isle-au-Noix and aware that it was quite far away from Crown Point (90 miles), Amherst decided that his assault force must be large and must travel upon the lake. A fierce storm on the 8th showed him that the 'boats with the Guns cant live in this Lake in bad weather', and the arrival of a French deserter on the 16th reminded him of the enemy's armed vessels.[11] He was indeed compelled to have some vessels 'for Cannon' built.

[10] Ibid. p. 148 (29 July 1759).
[11] Ibid. pp. 153–8.

He immediately sent for Captain Loring 'that we may prepare force enough to be superior to these Sloops'. Loring, a navy man, was already building an armed brig at Ticonderoga. It was now agreed that a radeau (very large raft) should be built to carry six 24-pounders. On 2 September word came from deserters that the French were adding a new 16-gun sloop to their lake fleet, and Amherst immediately directed Loring to build a ship to match. He also recruited some volunteer rangers along with some good swimmers for a mission to destroy the enemy's new war vessel by stealthily fixing combustibles to its hull at night. The attempt was bravely made, and the attackers survived, but the watch onboard heard a noise and was alerted, so the mission failed.

Although Amherst clearly understood that until the British built at least two armed vessels his offensive was stalled, he made a great mistake in failing to give urgent priority to the shipbuilding. There were quite a few ship carpenters in the ranks of the New England provincials, but the sawmill's production was vital. Three men quarrelled over who got its output: Loring, Bradstreet, who needed to build and repair bateaux, and Lieutenant Colonel Thomas Ord who was in charge of repairing Fort Ticonderoga. It did not help that the mechanisms of the water-powered saws repeatedly broke. Instead of giving priority to Loring and calling regularly at Ticonderoga to hurry his efforts, Amherst spent nearly all his time at Crown Point and settled the disputes by compromise.

A complacent assumption that the shipbuilding could not be carried on more quickly permitted another object to occupy his attention. Amherst was greatly impressed by Crown Point. His soldier's eye saw that a fort on its promontory could not be commanded from higher ground in any direction. He also saw that the adjacent land was excellent for farming and grazing. His journal reflects the spirit of a territorial imperialist. He envisioned settlement. He assumed that, whatever else happened, Britain would never give this position back at the peace table. Today one may readily see the great size of the fort by walking the length of its wall foundations, which overlook giant ditches. Amherst had at least 1,500 men at work on the fort while he awaited completion of the armed vessels.

It was not until 10 October that the brig, the *Duke of Cumberland*, joined the radeau, the *Ligonier* (84 feet long), at Crown Point. The sloop *Boscawen* arrived the next day and by afternoon the bateaux, troops and warships were under way northwards. As before, Amherst got his army moving swiftly forward once things were finally ready. On the 12th, about

45 miles north of Crown Point, Captain Loring's brig and the sloop encountered some French armed vessels. He chased them into a bay where three smaller ones were scuttled and abandoned. Amherst's flotilla, carrying 4,200 regulars and many pieces of artillery along with the radeau, had found security in a bay on the western shore.

The threat of the French armed vessels was gone, but it was now too late in the season. A severe storm churned up the lake and a freezing wind from the north followed. With his men huddled by their fires on shore Amherst was already of a mind to abandon the operation when a message came on 18 October that Quebec had fallen. Bourlamaque was therefore bound to be strongly reinforced. There was no point in continuing.

During November Amherst revealed his merit as a leader of men. He stayed on in miserably cold weather at Crown Point (watching provincial troops drift away) to see that the barracks were completed for a winter garrison (their stone ruins remain). He directed a road to be built from Crown Point to the Connecticut River at Number Four (Charlestown, New Hampshire). He waited until his people who had gone up the lake to float the scuttled French sloops of war brought them back successfully. He supervised an exchange of prisoners (Major James Grant came back this way). He displayed political wisdom in giving horses to the provincial commanders for their return journey. He then marched from Lake George to Albany in company with his troops. Actually, he stayed too long. The upper Hudson froze, and those troops who were heading south for winter quarters had to be disembarked and ordered to march; he saw to their provisioning arrangements. Finally, on 5 December he walked across the river to the east side and then walked all the way to New York, arriving on the 12th.

Historians have understandably focused on Amherst's slowness and on what he failed to accomplish. In England at the time, however, the capture of Ticonderoga and Crown Point were considered important achievements. Frontier residents of New York and New England knew that Crown Point had been the prime forward base for Indian raids upon their provinces. His decision to attack Niagara resulted in taking away Canada's chief link to the west and also, as will be seen, in frightening the French commanders at Quebec into sending away 800 troops at a critical moment. No doubt if the seaborne attack on Quebec had failed, Amherst would have received greater criticism both in England and North America, but it should not be forgotten that in contrast to his predecessors he had achieved solid gains without suffering any reverses.

Montcalm, Vaudreuil and the defence of Canada

Victory usually quells dissension, but the French victories at Oswego in 1756, Fort William Henry in 1757 and Carillon in 1758 provoked it. The underlying problem was mutual jealousy between the Canadians (*troupes de la marine* and militia) and the regulars who came from France (*troupes de terre*). In each case one side wished to claim credit for the victory while belittling the contribution and methods of the other.

In reality, the men of the ranks learned to get along. The French regulars learned to appreciate the toughness, expertise in wilderness warfare, and sense of independence of their Canadian opposites. Some would choose to stay in Canada after the British conquest, and many would marry Canadian women. For their part, Canadian militiamen tolerated the regular troops, though they sometimes had reason to consider them lazy. They recoiled, however, from the idea of serving under French officers (the comparison with British colonial America is apt). The dissension therefore was mainly a quarrel of officers, and the officers who came from France were at the heart of the problem; too often they bullied the Canadians. By the spring of 1757 the minister of war, having heard reports about their 'hauteur and harshness', reminded their commanding general that the Canadians must be well treated, not least because their expertise in dealing with Indians was indispensable. The minister of marine gave similar advice.[12]

These ministers cannot have been much surprised by such reports. When Versailles originally decided to send French regulars to Canada the possibility that their officers would antagonize the Canadians was admitted. The officer appointed to command them was therefore made clearly subordinate to Governor-General Vaudreuil, who was born in Canada. Although mutual consultation was expected, the decisions were ultimately Vaudreuil's as commander-in-chief, and it was the French general's duty to remain on good terms with him. Instructions along these lines were given in 1755 to baron Dieskau and his replacement, the marquis de Montcalm. The latter was carefully directed 'not only to avoid with care everything that might occasion the least altercation between himself and . . . Vaudreuil, but also to apply all his attention to establishing and maintaining the good relationship that is necessary between them'.[13]

[12] From the minister of war to Montcalm, 10 April 1757; naval and colonial minister to Montcalm, 27 May 1757; quoted by Michalon, in Delmas, ed. *Conflits*, pp. 106–7.
[13] Orders and instructions of 14 March 1756, quoted by Michalon, in Delmas, ed. *Conflits*, p. 92. See also Eccles, 'Montcalm', *DCB*, III, 459.

For this careful job description Montcalm was a perfect mismatch. Although the ministers at Versailles had been advised by an official in Canada that Vaudreuil, who was a rather good-natured man, would probably get along with someone who was also good-natured, they appointed a congenital complainer. As a child Montcalm was stubbornly resistant to edification, and in adulthood he was often peevish and petty. His father purchased a captaincy for him at 12, and during the war of Austrian Succession he sought and acquired considerable military experience. He was also fond of reading classical authors and learning modern languages. Social rank and a respectable war record led to permission to raise his own cavalry regiment in 1748. Yet despite his abilities and achievements he was unable to shake the habits of a closed military mind. He was 44 when he took up the command – proud, self-righteous, and used to getting his way. His professional outlook was rigid: his ideas about strategy and tactics generally followed standard French military prescriptions; in his mind, anything not done 'by the book' deserved to fail. These prescriptions were written of course for European warfare. It is likely that Dieskau would have willingly adapted to North American conditions once he had learned a lesson or two, but Montcalm did so with great reluctance. Perhaps most damaging of all, however, though the damage is not easy to pinpoint, was his sense of superiority as a French aristocrat, which led him to disrespect all Canadians. His mission, therefore, was to defend a people whom he held in contempt. He accepted it as a duty to the French king and brought to it, in the capacity of a field commander, a considerable measure of competence and dedication, but in his relations with Canadian officers he was instinctively uncooperative.

The comte d'Argenson, minister of war, selected him, and no one knows why. It was said that other senior officers were offered the command and refused it, which is not surprising when one remembers that at the time a large French army was about to launch a presumably glorious campaign in Germany. Whether the naval minister, Machault, had much to say about the choice is not known. There could be no proper interview because the decision had to be made in a hurry after it was learned that Dieskau had been captured – it was made in January 1756 – and Montcalm lived hundreds of miles away from Paris in Montpellier. He left Paris with his orders in mid-March and sailed from Brest on 3 April.

Vaudreuil, born in 1698, was the son of a governor-general. His military service had been with the *troupes de la marine*, and although he received a captain's commission in the navy, he never served at sea. He had formerly been governor-general of Louisiana and developed an extensive practical knowledge of Indian relations and wilderness warfare. Among recent governors-general of Canada (he took office at the beginning of 1755) his first-hand experience in these matters was unequalled. Montcalm considered Vaudreuil's birth and long residence in Canada to be defects. Vaudreuil was certainly not without faults; he was a bit slow of thought and too trusting, but there were good officers on whom he could and did rely for advice, and his personality was inclined towards cooperation. For example, he had a high opinion of Lévis, who had come to Canada at the same time as Montcalm to serve as second-in-command. Montcalm also thought highly of Lévis and was annoyed by the fact that he got along with the governor-general.

After the raid on Oswego in 1756 Montcalm, despite the striking success of this important operation and the ease with which it was accomplished, commented – this is scarcely believable – to the minister of war that if the decision had been his, he would not have tried it; it was too risky.[14] His preliminary caution had certainly annoyed Vaudreuil. A year later, Vaudreuil's orders regarding the Lake George offensive of August 1757 directed Montcalm to go on to Fort Edward if the siege of Fort William Henry was successful. As we saw, Montcalm decided against it, and this provoked more letters of complaint to Versailles. Montcalm soon penned a personal attack on the governor-general, and in due course Vaudreuil suggested that Montcalm should be replaced by Lévis.[15]

The paper-and-ink war was intensified by Montcalm in 1758 for no good reason. On 23 June he received his instructions from Vaudreuil. They called for him to defend Fort Carillon and gave him a good deal of flexibility, which should have made him content, but he characterized them in his journal as 'ridiculous, obscure, and captious' and wrote peevishly to Vaudreuil pointing out all sorts of mistakes. When Montcalm urgently asked for reinforcement at Carillon, Vaudreuil immediately cancelled Lévis's intended raid down the Mohawk and ordered him to take 400 regulars to Carillon as fast as he could. They arrived the night before the battle of 8 July and contributed significantly to the victory. In the immediate aftermath Vaudreuil congratulated Montcalm, and the latter praised the performance of the Canadians who had participated saying that he only wished he had had more of them, but good will quickly evaporated. Word soon reached Vaudreuil that Montcalm had not been satisfied with the hurried dispatch of the 400 regulars; he was

[14] Eccles, 'Montcalm' DCB, III, 459–60.

[15] Michalon, in Delmas, ed. Conflits, pp. 104–6.

saying that 2,000 available Canadians should have been sent at the same time. His officers were hinting that Vaudreuil had deliberately held them back. Soon Montcalm was changing his language about the battle performance of his Canadians, saying that they had been backward in carrying out orders (an opinion Lévis did not share). It seems that Montcalm was unable to rise above the level of his staff's gossip. Vaudreuil threw fuel on the fire by commenting to the naval minister that Montcalm's victory, however brilliant, was incomplete since there was no follow-up.[16] Naturally, Montcalm was furious when he learned that his remarkable victory was thus being diminished in an official dispatch.

Although the underlying causes of mutual resentment were personal, social and cultural, the two men disagreed about the correct strategy for defending Canada. Vaudreuil favoured a 'forward' strategy whereas Montcalm preferred a well-buttressed defensive posture and avoidance of risks. For instance, after the success at Carillon in 1758 Vaudreuil wanted Montcalm to send large detachments against enemy supply lines to the south. Montcalm wondered whether the governor-general realized how many thousands of troops Abercromby still had. Montcalm dared not risk a large concentration and confined his raiding to parties numbering 200 men or less, including Indians, which could rapidly retreat from danger.

Montcalm's ideas about strategy and tactics were often contrary to Vaudreuil's. He was always opposed to large-scale raids, especially when they relied heavily on Indian assistance, while Vaudreuil strongly favoured them. Who was right? Arguably, during the early years Vaudreuil was right. His strategy accorded well with La Galissonière's recommendations: it saved expense while frustrating British operations, and the larger enterprises enabled the French to capture and retrieve enemy guns, ammunition and stocks of food. This was the main reason why Vaudreuil wanted a large raiding force to penetrate southwards from Fort Carillon in 1758: 'You perceive, besides, Sir,' he wrote to Montcalm, 'that we can be sufficiently fortunate to enrich the Colony ... with whatever we shall oblige the enemy to abandon.'[17] In this year Canada was experiencing for the first time a shortage of ammunition. On 1 November Vaudreuil wrote urgently to the naval and colonial minister asking for an extra supply of gunpowder from France. In doing so he remarked, 'Were it not for the ammunition furnished me successively by the Beautiful river [Braddock's defeat, 1755], Chouagouin [Oswego, 1756], and Fort George [Fort William

---

[16] Ibid., pp. 109–17, quotation p. 110.
[17] Vaudreuil to Montcalm, 15 July 1758, *NYCD*, X, 759.

Henry, 1757], I should not have had enough either for attack or defence.'[18] Clearly, aggressive action on the frontiers had paid off, and captured supplies were wanted more than ever in 1758. The trouble was that by this time it had become dangerous and difficult to accomplish such feats. It is not clear that Vaudreuil understood this.

The causes of change were noted in the preceding chapter. First, enemy forces on the New York frontier were becoming too strong. Lévis's mission in spring 1758 as planned by Vaudreuil was, in Lévis's words, intended to 'prevent the reconstruction of Chouaguen' (Oswego) and to 'induce the Iroquois of the Five Nations to declare themselves; to make them act offensively with me against the English' on the Mohawk river 'as openly as circumstances will permit'. If the mission had proceeded, he might have encountered serious trouble. The British military establishment north and west of Albany was now formidable and it could move upon better roads; it therefore enjoyed good interior lines of communication. Also, the Iroquois were not likely to be cooperative – partly because of the increasing British military presence, but also because the New York Iroquois had learned of the Indian peace initiative that was afoot in Philadelphia. Montcalm himself had heard about it as early as mid-April. Vaudreuil persisted in thinking Iroquois allegiance could be commanded. Lévis correctly described the mission as 'delicate, important, political and military'.[19]

Thus, Vaudreuil's strategy was ceasing to be viable. In fact, Bradstreet's expedition against Fort Frontenac turned the tables. In the aftermath Vaudreuil explained that he had relied on recent assurances which the Iroquois had given to his emissary 'that the English were thinking at the time only of re-establishing Fort Bull'; furthermore, he did not think they would 'dare to enter the lake on which we had vessels'.[20] It raises a question: were the Iroquois in the vicinity of Lake Oneida deceived into thinking that Bradstreet and his body of troops had come upriver to Fort Bull merely to rebuild it, or did they get wind of the truth and choose not to report it to the French? The latter is more likely. Whatever the case, the surprising of Fort Niagara and successful defence of Oswego in 1759 provided clear evidence of how Iroquois support for the French had

[18] Vaudreuil to the naval minister, 1 Nov. 1758, ibid. X, 863.

[19] Lévis to Belleisle, 17 June 1758 (he used the traditional name, 'the Five Nations', but after the Tuscarora nation joined in 1722 people commonly used 'Six Nations'), Montcalm to Belleisle, 18 April 1758, ibid. X, 719, 696.

[20] Vaudreuil to Belleisle, 2 Sept. 1758, ibid. X, 822.

declined as the British military presence had increased. These developments not only made French raiding more hazardous but also undermined Canada's capacity to defend its perimeter outposts.

Montcalm was sure that Vaudreuil's efforts to retain distant posts and forts and try to retake Fort Duquesne were mistaken. His overarching strategic principle was to defend the Canadian core. This helped keep expenses down, communication lines short and command tight. It also accorded with tactical preference, which stressed the use of regular troops under strict obedience plus the security of defensive positions. His ideas represented a conservative interpretation of European military practices. Time and again when he expressed himself on these subjects he sounded not so much like a brave soldier, though he was undoubtedly brave in combat, as an operationally timid Old World general. In the weeks after his victory at Ticonderoga he was preoccupied by defence, keeping Lévis and quite a few Canadian troops in the vicinity for many weeks with very little to do.

On one strategic principle, however, he and Vaudreuil strongly agreed: the importance of naval superiority on Lake Champlain and Lake Ontario. As both men knew, these two lakes (apart from the St Lawrence River) provided the only means by which the enemy could bring its massed military power to bear on the Canadian heartland. They differed in their judgement of the military risks required to maintain naval superiority. In October 1758 Vaudreuil wanted to launch a surprise raid on Oswego. Montcalm objected that the enemy would be too strong. The two men also disagreed on where the French should base the Lake Ontario warships that were to be built in winter 1758–9 to replace those lost at Frontenac; Montcalm considered Frontenac too vulnerable and wanted to create a new base 50 miles down the St Lawrence River. Vaudreuil responded that if the British became firmly established at Oswego, they could only be watched from Frontenac or some place near it. As for Lake Champlain, Vaudreuil believed that with Ticonderoga and Crown Point in their possession the British 'would immediately construct a navy there that would soon be superior to ours'.[21] (We have seen the consequences of Amherst's failure to do this immediately.) The governor-general therefore insisted, when they were discussing plans for the 1759 campaign, that Ticonderoga should be held until an enemy force compelled its abandonment whereas Montcalm favoured an immediate withdrawal to a fortified position at the northern end of the lake. But he accepted Vaudreuil's

---

[21] Vaudreuil to naval minister, 1 Nov. 1758, ibid. X, 867. See also pp. 868–72.

proposal of a calculated withdrawal, and Bourlamaque's orders were drawn up accordingly.

Montcalm's conception of defence of the core, whether he realized it or not, meant that naval command of the lakes would probably be lost, and in this particular regard Vaudreuil's conception of strategy was sound. But otherwise Vaudreuil failed to perceive that changed conditions had not only reduced the odds for profitable raiding but also affected the feasibility of defending the distant perimeter. By 1758 Montcalm's approach to strategy was more realistic.

Without a strategy of raiding, however, Canada's survival depended on supplies from France. Vaudreuil recognized this quickly. In late August 1758 he sent Michel-Jean-Hugues Péan to Versailles to explain how desperately Canada needed assistance. After some delay Montcalm decided to send Louis-Antoine de Bougainville, who had come to America with him as his aide-de-camp (and would later gain fame as a naval officer for circumnavigating the globe). Bougainville departed on 11 November just before the river froze, had a stormy voyage, and barely escaped capture. Two emissaries were necessary, since each man was not only pleading for reinforcements and supplies but also trying to make sure that his side of the personal and strategic quarrel got a hearing – and to suggest the removal of the other man. Although he arrived first, Péan was completely outmanoeuvred. An official at Versailles linked to Montcalm reminded the authorities that Péan, an associate of Bigot, had made himself very rich in office. Since the new naval and colonial minister, Nicolas René Berryer, had quickly concluded from other sources that Canada was a sinkhole of inflated expense and corrupt skimming, he wanted nothing to do with Péan. In any case, Péan was utterly outclassed by Bougainville, a well-educated and socially gifted officer who enjoyed easy entry at the highest level. He conferred regularly with Berryer, Belleisle and Pompadour.

Nevertheless, Berryer was so apprehensive about the consequences of bad relations between Montcalm and Vaudreuil that he recommended a realistic though politically unworkable solution: Montcalm should be recalled and Lévis should replace him. This was promptly countermanded by a terse note penned upon the naval ministry's memorandum which said: 'After due reflection, this arrangement ought not to take place, M. de Montcalm being necessary in the present situation.' Without doubt it was a royal decision. In fact, Montcalm's powers were amplified, making him equal to Vaudreuil in administrative as well as military matters. There are indications that Belleisle was uneasy about what had happened. He warned Montcalm (and Berryer warned Vaudreuil) about the importance of harmony, and added: 'I have become responsible for you to the King.'[22]

Notwithstanding Canada's desperate needs, which the court of Versailles did not deny, the requests for material assistance were almost entirely refused. 'I am very sorry to have to inform you', Belleisle wrote to Montcalm, 'that you must not expect to receive any Military reinforcements [since they would only add to scarcity of provisions, and] . . . it would be much to be feared that they would be intercepted by the English on the passage.' Besides, he added, the only effect of sending more troops would be to inspire England to do the same. Reinforcement would therefore be limited to 400 recruits, and the navy would not be employed to carry them or shield transports. Only Bougainville's request for four frigates to assist Quebec's defence was approved; the ships were to be commanded by corsair captains. Berryer would engage merchants to send as much food and ammunition as possible, but, Belleisle told Montcalm, 'the rest depends on your wisdom and courage, and on the bravery of the troops'. What did Belleisle expect? He hoped to retain a foothold. 'However trifling the space you can preserve, it is of the utmost importance.' Berryer had provided the reason: the court of Versailles believed that conditions of peace would be very different if part of the territory were kept, even if it were small.[23]

Both Montcalm and Vaudreuil tended to dismiss the possibility that an invasion force might come up the St Lawrence River. Although both were extremely worried that the supplies they so desperately required would be intercepted by British warships at the river's mouth, neither believed that British ships of the line could overcome the navigational hazards of penetrating to Quebec. Montcalm had not been absolutely confident about this in 1757 and had surveyed the scene downriver; he recommended that a battery be built on the high promontory at Cap Tourmente where the deep channel lay near the north bank.[24] No order was given to build such a battery then or during the winter of 1758–9. The problem seems to have been shortage of provisions: Vaudreuil estimated that the construction would require 4,000 working men, and Canada could not provide the extra calories they would need.

[22] Memorandum, 28 Dec. 1758, Waddington, *Guerre*, III, 256; *NYCD*, X, 944.
[23] Belleisle to Montcalm, 19 Feb. 1759, *NYCD*, X, 944; Berryer to Vaudreuil, 3 Feb. 1758, Waddington, *Guerre*, III, 256.
[24] Casgrain, *Montcalm et Lévis*, I, 307.

The capture of Quebec

British preparations for the massive seaborne attack on Quebec began in earnest in mid-December 1758. Two months later there were two departures from Spithead. First, 4 ships of the line and 5 frigates under Rear Admiral Charles Holmes escorted 66 empty transports to New York. Pitt was making sure that ample shipping was available to carry troops to the marshalling base at Louisbourg. A few days later 10 of the line (but 2 were soon detached) and 3 bomb vessels under Vice Admiral Charles Saunders, accompanied by a small body of transports carrying ordnance stores and provisions, departed for Louisbourg. On board the flagship *Neptune* (90 guns) was James Wolfe, promoted to major general in America to serve as commander-in-chief of the expedition. The fact that the *Neptune* was a big ship did not prevent him from being seasick most of the way. Practically no troops were sent from the British Isles; the men were already in North America. Amherst, a careful administrator, made sure that the regiments designated to serve under Wolfe were marched on time to Boston and New York to embark for Halifax. Saunders's fleet had a rough passage but arrived off Louisbourg on 21 April 1759 where it found an impenetrable barrier of ice and diverted to Halifax.

Upon entering Halifax harbour on the 30 April Saunders was not happy to find Rear Admiral Philip Durell with his squadron of 8 of the line still there. Pitt had sent very clear orders to Durell that he was to take his ships to the Isle of Bic in the St Lawrence River as early as possible in order to prevent French supplies from reaching Quebec. Durell, however, decided to wait at Halifax until he heard that the river ice was breaking up, a strategically senseless idea. Granted, it had been an unusually long and very cold winter in Nova Scotia; frozen sails could scarcely be unfurled and some seamen lost their hands to frostbite. Durell sailed on 5 May with 5 ships of the line and 650 soldiers under Colonel Guy Carleton and reached Bic on 23 May. Realizing that he might have been neglectful he immediately proceeded upriver. Reaching Coudres on the 25th, he landed troops to occupy the island. Here he heard that 16 supply ships from Bordeaux had got in; they had been blocked by river ice for ten days and were escorted by only 3 frigates. He quickly proceeded on upriver to the Traverse, 25 miles from Quebec.

As a military objective Quebec presented two challenges: one was to get men-of-war and transports safely upriver in good time; the other was to defeat the defending army. From the tip of the Gaspé peninsula to Quebec the distance is 420 statute miles. The river was navigable by ships of considerable size the whole way. It is the greatest tidal river in the world and when winds were not favourable sailing vessels could make use of the tides. Since the powerful current of the St Lawrence (it empties all the Great Lakes) when amplified by an ebbing tide could only rarely be overcome by a favouring wind, timely anchoring was essential. Rocks and shoals, some treacherously hidden beneath the surface, are plentiful, yet for most of its length the river is very wide. Fog is a serious hazard, but the British were fortunate because in the spring of 1759 fog was infrequent and the attacking fleet received uncommon assistance from north-easterly winds.

The notoriously difficult and dangerous passage was the Traverse. Here it was necessary for ships to cross from the deep north channel to a south channel in order to pass by the Île d'Orléans. Durell promptly commenced a navigational survey of the Traverse, a step that would be immensely helpful. He had French-Canadian pilots with him, many of them lured to his ships by a display of false colours at Bic. Once they were aboard, he made them an offer they could hardly refuse: British pilot's wages if they agreed to help and were successful, and imprisonment or worse if they refused or failed. The existence of the Traverse and the hidden sandbanks that confined its channel were well known, but its outlines on Durell's French chart, which had been captured at Louisbourg, were not reliable. He directed three of the line with some smaller ships to proceed forward and take soundings, and thus from 9 to 11 June boats from British men-of-war were engaged in defining the Traverse. When the main fleet under Saunders began to arrive along with the transports from Louisbourg on the 27th everything was ready for them to proceed to Quebec. As the ships moved through the Traverse, boats of Durell's squadron were positioned on each side to mark the channel.

One of the ships sent ahead to conduct soundings was the *Pembroke* (60 guns), James Cook, Master. He was much involved in enabling the fleet to pass upriver safely. (His developing talent for this sort of work led to his being asked to stay on after the fall of Quebec for 2 years to create the first well-defined charts of Canadian maritime waters; his reputation as an expert hydrographer was thus established.) Conquering the Traverse was not an individual's achievement, nor was it primarily due to aid from the French pilots. It was rather a testament to the care and skill of many masters, mates, lieutenants and captains. They made it look easy. If there had been serious mishaps, all histories of the Quebec campaign of 1759 would dwell on them, but there were none and in most narratives the achievement is quickly passed over. It should therefore be pointed out that this mighty armada of 40 warships and 180 transports reached the basin of Quebec without a single ship, not even a transport, being lost; and among them were ships of the line much larger than any vessel that had ever been there before. On 27 June Wolfe landed most of his army near the western end of Île d'Orléans.

The marquis de Montcalm had passed a miserable winter, first in Montreal, which he truly hated, then in Quebec, where the residents were slowly starving. Four hundred women took to the streets in January to protest against a meagre ration which was similar in quantity to that given the winter before.

On the evidence of his diary and occasional letters to Bourlamaque and Lévis, Montcalm gave almost no thought to preventing an upriver attack. Bougainville, however, was concerned about it. In Paris he was presenting memoranda which mentioned numerous works to be undertaken; among them was a heavy battery on the high ground at Cap Tourmente. Yet even if Versailles had approved his proposals, with the river frozen nothing could arrive in time to answer a threat in 1759. In his heart Montcalm probably agreed with Vaudreuil that defence of the river was the home country's responsibility, not Canada's. He remained strangely silent on the subject.

Bougainville got back to Quebec on 13 May after his ship waited three weeks for the ice to break up. The good news was that twenty-two merchant ships, most of them from Bordeaux, also got in safely. Although ammunition would continue to be scarce, the dire provisions shortage was thus alleviated. But there was bad news. Official letters arriving with Bougainville warned that a large British force was on the way. This advice came just ten days before reports arrived of enemy warships already starting upriver.

The South Channel where most of the invasion fleet lay during the night of 27 June was not a secure anchorage. After the British troops were landed an extremely violent thunderstorm swept in from the west. Powerful gusts caused many ships to drag anchor and seven transports grounded, of which five were later recovered, but a number of flat-bottomed boats were permanently lost. During the next night conditions were perfect for an attack by fireships. Under a moderate south-west wind seven of these – decks crowded with barrels of gunpowder and pitch, grenades hung from the rigging, guns double-shotted – came downriver from the city. The manoeuvre called for the crews to venture as close as they dared before lighting fuses and jumping into boats. It was not the sort of thing that could be usefully practised ahead of time, and shortly after

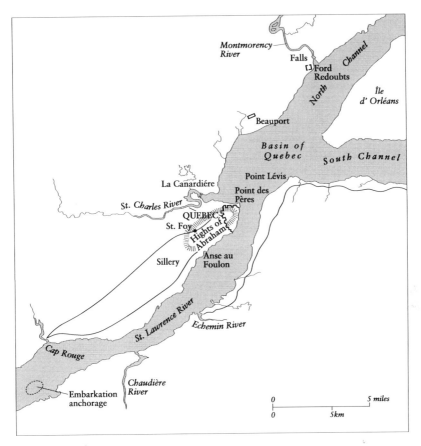

MAP 12 *Quebec*

midnight the officer in the lead vessel ignited too soon, when he was still 4 miles away from the westernmost ship of the British fleet. All but one of the other fireships did the same. The spectacular flames and booming explosions alarmed the British troops on Île d'Orléans, but British seamen rowed toward the burning vessels with grappling hooks in hand and methodically towed them ashore. The costly French effort was a fiasco.

The next morning, 29 June, Admiral Saunders sent a message to Wolfe recommending that Point Lévis should be occupied. The object was to secure a safe anchorage on the south side of the basin by preventing the enemy from building batteries on the high ground above the point. This commanding position appeared to be still unoccupied and unfortified. Which of the French generals was responsible for this neglect is not known, but one thing is clear: unlike the case of Cap Tourmente, there was no excuse. Wolfe approved Saunders's request immediately and the next day Brigadier Monckton landed on the south shore. There was skirmishing with a French detachment, but the big question was whether Montcalm and Vaudreuil would now send a strong force, assisted by Indians, to drive Monckton's four battalions off. On the 30th Montcalm proposed to do this, but a prisoner just taken told the French that Monckton's landing on the south shore was a feint to disguise a British attack on the north shore planned for that night, and he thereupon called everyone back to the north shore where they stood at arms all night to no purpose. If this is what happened – the story rests on a single French diary – one might ask why the French leadership was so readily disposed to accept the word of a single prisoner as the sole basis for deciding so fundamental a point of strategy. A likely answer is that Montcalm was fixated on keeping his army together and defending the north shore. It was a momentous decision. In early July the greater part of the men-of-war moved into the basin where a spacious anchorage would soon be securely defended by British batteries at Point Lévis. This achievement marks the end of the first phase of the operation.

The second phase stretches tediously over the months of July and August. Its dominant theme is Wolfe's frustration as he searched for a way to bring Montcalm's army to battle. Although his expeditionary army of 8,500 was outnumbered by Montcalm's 12,000, practically all of his troops were well-trained and experienced regulars, most of whom carried muskets of superior quality. Montcalm possessed five somewhat depleted battalions of experienced *troupes de terre* (about 2,000 men), 1,200 *troupes de la marine*, 1,200 sailors, 6,000 Canadian militia and 800 Indians. In addition, there was a city militia devoted entirely to its defence.[25] If the British were able to land on the north shore they could move west and cross the St Charles River and then ascend the gradual slope leading to the city's western side, where a low wall could be easily breached. Montcalm was fully aware of the need to fortify the north shore. On the suggestion of Lévis he extended the redoubts, trenches and breastworks as far east as the falls of Montmorency. It was a 12-mile front, with the village of Beauport at its centre. There he concentrated almost his entire force.

Working from maps, Wolfe had decided that this Beauport shore was the place to land, but when he walked to the western tip of Île d'Orléans on the evening of 27 June he was taken aback. He could see the endless line of redoubts and trenches on the rising ground above the beach.

<hr>

[25] Waddington, *Guerre*, III, 266–7.

Montcalm had no way of knowing that the British admiral would bring most of his remarkably strong fleet all the way up to Quebec; Saunders's decision to do this had surprised Wolfe, too. But the warships could be of no help against the Beauport shore where for its entire length the water was shallow: tidal flats extended far out into the basin. Training his spyglass to the left Wolfe saw the city of Quebec and its batteries. If the warships approached the city they could effectively bombard a portion of the Beauport shore, but they would be vulnerable targets for the city's heavy batteries. Were there alternatives? Further left, the river continued towards Montreal, but its north bank appeared totally inaccessible because it was lined by high cliffs as far as the eye could see.

The occupation of Point Lévis enabled the British to mount heavy batteries on the heights opposite Quebec. On 2 July Wolfe ascended a long path that led westwards and upwards to a position above Point de Pères. On this high ground he selected locations for the batteries. Standing near the edge of this high cliff the visitor today may be struck by how far away the city appears, but the actual distance is about a mile and Wolfe's artillery experts had no doubt that 13-inch mortars and heavy naval guns could range upon it. Did the French understand this? Montcalm's engineer knew that the lower town was at risk but thought that the upper town was safe. Before long, oxen were pulling ships' 32-pounders and other heavy ordnance up the path. The danger to the city was obvious, and on 11 July some worried citizens petitioned Vaudreuil to attack the battery. A mixed force composed of Canadian militia and citizen volunteers, including three hundred enthusiastic seminary students, crossed to the south shore during the night of the 12th. Their crossing was not detected by the British but they faced a 7-mile climb to the objective. An advance in darkness over broken terrain towards an enemy known to be well armed would have been hard to execute even with well-trained troops, and the commander, Jean-Daniel Dumas of the *troupe de la marine*, should have left the students behind to guard the boats. It was somewhat predictable that they would take alarm and end up shooting at their own forces. This happened. Only the accompanying Indians acted effectively; the others retreated in confusion. But there were almost no casualties and, in fact, the British never knew they were there. Aware of Vaudreuil's support for the venture Montcalm had allowed it to go forward, but evidently he took no responsibility for the arrangements.

The next night the British battery opened fire. By 4 August a citizen of Quebec estimated that 4,000 shells and 9,000 shot had been fired upon the city. New batteries were added so that by the end of August there were

29 pieces of heavy ordnance targeting the city. Mortar shells and incendiary carcasses did the most damage, and there were nights when fires fanned by strong breezes raged out of control. In due course nearly the whole lower town and much of the upper was destroyed.

As Wolfe anticipated, the bombardment could not induce a surrender: the citizens evacuated but remained defiant. Nor did it render the city vulnerable to a direct assault; the upper city's batteries remained largely undamaged, and British troops attacking the lower would have faced entrenchments in depth as well as devastating fire from above. All in all, the bombardment achieved no strategic purpose. It represented an instinct to hurt the defenders in whatever way possible; it made sure that the enormous firepower that the British managed to bring to the scene would inflict a terrible and enduring injury regardless of the final military outcome. But it was an ugly mode of war – even unwise, because if military success were achieved, the British would find that they had demolished the very buildings which might comfortably shelter them during a winter of occupation.

Admiral Saunders wanted to send some ships further upriver. On the night of 18–19 July, with a favouring wind and tide, the 50-gun *Sutherland*, two frigates, two sloops of war and two transports got through the narrow part of the river. French gunners saw them and fired furiously but fruitlessly, while enduring harassing fire from the British batteries above Point de Pères. Wolfe then surveyed locations where his troops might land on the north bank. Montcalm countered by ordering a new battery to be placed upriver from the city at Samar, a place where the river is narrower, and also took steps to defend landing sites that Wolfe would probably judge to be best. It soon became clear that trying to suppress French gunfire aimed at ships trying to go upriver, not bombardment of the city, was the true strategic value of the British batteries on the south shore. The trouble was that a prevailing summer wind from the west and south-west could not be overcome.

The campaigning season was wasting away and Wolfe was at a loss to discover a feasible way to attack. He did not share his deliberations with his brigadier generals. There were three: Robert Monckton, able and experienced, who had been in America since 1752 in Nova Scotia; James Murray, who had fought alongside Wolfe at Louisbourg; and George Townshend, eldest son of Viscount Townshend and member of Parliament for the county of Norfolk, who had followed an army career. He had helped Pitt push through the Militia bill, and when he wrote to Pitt requesting active military employment the request could hardly be refused. The first two were Wolfe's own choices but Townshend was imposed on him. What advice the brigadiers would have given at this stage can only be guessed, but they did not like the plan he adopted – a direct assault on the Beauport shore.

Already a British force from Île d'Orléans had crossed to the north shore east of the Montmorency Falls without opposition. Wolfe's plan was to attack the extremity of the French left using most of his army. Boats carrying Monckton's troops would come across the basin from Point Lévis, and Wolfe would accompany the grenadiers who embarked at Île d'Orléans, while Brigadier Townshend's forces east of the falls would come west by wading through the water below the falls. This part of the plan meant that the attack had to occur at or near low tide, and as a result the *Centurion* (60 guns) and two shallow-draft merchant ships mounting cannon were not able to get close enough to provide effective gunfire support. On the morning of 31 July when Monckton's men began to embark the French detected them. Montcalm sounded the alarm and concentrated his forces. The British boats steered at first toward the western segment of the French position as a feint, but the ploy failed when they were thwarted by underwater rocks upon turning eastwards. Montcalm had plenty of time to shift his strength to his left. There was no element of surprise.

The grenadiers landed first. Wolfe expected them to find shelter on the beach until joined by the others (there was a redoubt that the French quickly abandoned), but they proceeded to rush straightaway up the slope towards the enemy positions and were badly cut up by militia musketry. At about 5.30 p.m. a violent thunderstorm struck and the rain soaked everyone's powder on both sides. All firing stopped. It was actually a blessing for the British troops that nature terminated the operation, and Wolfe did the right thing: he quickly signalled a retreat, which the brigadiers conducted in an orderly manner. Wolfe counted 210 killed and 230 wounded, but the figures were probably higher. French casualties were light, almost all of them the result of cannonading by British batteries situated on a high cliff east of Montmorency Falls. Knowing that the British must attack him, Montcalm had steadfastly refused to be drawn into attacking them when they occupied that area. On this day his strategy of maintaining an entrenched concentration on the Beauport shore was fully vindicated. Certainly it made the best use of the Canadian militiamen, many of whom were very good marksmen.

In the aftermath Wolfe was much criticized, not just by his brigadiers, but by nearly everyone in the army, and his inclination to blame the failure on the impulsiveness of the grenadiers left a sour taste. He also grumbled about a backwardness of naval support, being ignorant perhaps of the navigational obstacles. The bright young colonel who had so freely dispensed ridicule when serving as a subordinate found that the role of commander was not so easy. He had enough presence of mind, however, to recognize that something different should be tried, and on 3 August he sent Brigadier Murray upriver with a large detachment to disrupt enemy supplies. Montcalm responded by augmenting the French force upriver to 1,000; he assigned Bougainville to command it.

On the 8th Murray, employing flat-bottomed boats, attempted a raid at Point-aux-Trembles, 22 miles above Quebec. It was effectively rebuffed by Bougainville's troops and cost the British 140 killed or wounded. Murray then put his army ashore on the south bank at St Antoine, and when local inhabitants sporadically fired at them he issued a warning that if they persisted he would destroy every farmhouse and church on the south shore. While at St Antoine he learned from a deserter that a large house at Deschambault, 40 miles above the city, contained military equipment, and on the 18th the boats moved upriver rapidly in darkness. This time surprise was complete and the storehouse was burned. Bougainville arrived just as the troops were leaving. Even with 100 mounted cavalry, it was very difficult to defend so extended a region. Perhaps Montcalm would have assigned more men to the task and placed them under a more experienced officer if he had not sent off Lévis with 800 troops to defend against the possibility of a British attack down the St Lawrence from Lake Ontario. This he did after news arrived on 9 August of the fall of Fort Niagara. Montcalm thereby deprived himself not only of 800 men but also of a fine general whose advice would have been valuable.

On the whole, however, Murray was unable to do much in the upper river because British river traffic was frequently attacked by enemy soldiers and seamen in boats, and floating batteries were deployed to ward off landings. The British needed more warships above Quebec. On the night of 11 August two tried to get through, but the wind died and they had to turn back. Thereafter the wind blew strongly from the west and south-west. Finally, on the night of 27 August it came from the east and the *Lowestoft* (44 guns) and the sloop, *Hunter*, got through, the *Hunter* suffering one killed and two wounded by French gunners on the Quebec heights.

Meanwhile, Wolfe maintained headquarters at the Montmorency camp. His relations with Townshend had become very unpleasant on 7 August when the latter hinted that Wolfe would be subjected to a parliamentary inquiry for failing to consult his brigadiers, and Townshend had strong enough political influence to make this threat credible. Unable to get at Montcalm's army, Wolfe gave orders to lay waste to villages that failed to cooperate. The *habitants* were caught between British demands on one hand and their obligation as potential militiamen to bear arms against the enemy on the other, a requirement that Montcalm was prepared to enforce by directing Indian violence against them. Whatever strategic excuse existed for intimidation of the inhabitants along the south shore above the city, there was no excuse for the British depredations down-river, and thanks to being assigned to this latter mission some companies of rangers and about 1,500 regulars would become unavailable when the main attack was eventually launched.

Although Wolfe was thwarted strategically, he was an officer who knew how to look after his troops; his daily orders saw to their welfare yet contained enough firmness on issues of importance to preserve security, discipline and respect. It was his practice to walk among the rank and file, in the camps across the water as well as those nearby, and when he did not appear word travelled that he was seriously ill. In fact, on 19 August he became so weak from a 'slow fever' that he was confined to a sickbed. The men were worried, and so were the brigadiers, who realized that nothing was being decided while only about a month of good weather remained.

Still terribly weak and confined to his little house at Montmorency, Wolfe dictated a letter on 25 August to his brigadiers. He realized that there must be some plan of action and suggested three options. All three envisioned an attack on Montcalm's army on the Beauport shore and none of them seemed feasible – even to Wolfe himself, it soon appeared. Perhaps he decided to consult his brigadiers because he felt too ill to think clearly. In any case, confined where he was he realized that he was out of touch with the general military and naval situation. Although it might give an outward appearance of weak leadership, he wisely invited his subordinates to offer suggestions. Receiving the letter, Townshend and Murray, on the 28th, went to Point Lévis and met with Monckton, whereupon all three went aboard the flagship, currently the *Stirling Castle* (64 guns). They met on board again the next day, and there is clear evidence that throughout their deliberations they were in consultation with Admiral Saunders and naval officers. Their conclusions were presented in a clearly written reply to Wolfe:

We [should] . . . bring the Troops to the South Shore, and . . . direct the Operations above the Town. When we establish ourselves on the North

Shore [above Quebec], the French General must fight us on our own
Terms: We shall be betwixt him and his provisions, and betwixt him
and their Army opposing General Amherst: If he gives us battle, and
we defeat him, Quebec and probably all Canada will be ours.[26]

On 1 September Wolfe gave the order to prepare to withdraw all forces
from Montmorency.

This order marks the beginning of the third and last phase of the siege.
On 3 September the troops abandoned the camp on the north shore without interference from Montcalm, bringing their artillery with them. The
army's focal point became Point Lévis, from which the troops marched
westwards along the south shore. Nature had played a role in initiating
this third phase. On the night of 27–28 August the steady south-westerly
wind of summer finally ceased and winds from the north and east became
predominant. Warships, transports and boats could now move swiftly
upriver past the French batteries.[27] By 5 September the British naval force
in the upper river consisted of the 50-gun *Sutherland*, three frigates
(*Lowestoft*, *Squirrel* and *Seahorse*), the sloop *Hunter* and four armed vessels.
These warships protected a dozen transports and numerous launches and
flat-bottomed boats. Quebec's supply line was seriously endangered, and
the three French frigates which had lain in safety 60 miles upriver were
ordered to prepare for combat (their crews had been helping to man the
city's batteries). But the British naval force above the city was now too
strong, and they never came into action.

French observers could see redcoats marching along the south bank in
great numbers and embarking in boats near the Etchemin River for conveyance to the warships and transports. Quite soon these ships had 3,600
troops on board. Since British ships could go upriver on the flood and
return on the ebb if they wished, Bougainville realized that his men would
have to march back and forth according to their movements. On 5 September he rode to Beauport and described the situation to Montcalm.
To guard 40 miles of shoreline he had about 150 Canadian volunteer
cavalry (very useful) and a total of 1,900 infantry, but 400 of these were
parcelled out at guard posts along the river. He would have liked to position 1,500 men at Cap Rouge, but occasional British threats on locations
further upriver made this impossible. Besides, Montcalm had advised him
to pay great attention to the more distant sector, as far as Deschambault,

---

[26] Quoted in Stacey, *Quebec, 1759*, p. 192.
[27] *Knox's Journal*, II, 56–73.

and Vaudreuil gave the same advice. To protect the sector near the city Montcalm ordered the 2nd battalion of the Guyenne regiment to camp on the Plains of Abraham, not far from the city wall. These troops did not remain there, however, because on 6 September he withdrew them to a position just east of the St Charles River where they could be readily used above or below the city. Whatever Bougainville may have felt privately, he did not protest at the move, which proved to be fateful, nor did Vaudreuil.

The brigadiers had envisioned an upriver landing between Pointe-aux-Trembles (near today's Neuville) and St Augustin, a stretch where the gradually rising ground of the north bank was accessible. Wolfe, who was healthy enough to come aboard the *Sutherland* on 6 September and direct operations, was prepared to agree and orders were drawn up. It then rained heavily for two days, giving Wolfe time to reconsider. On the 9th he surveyed the line of cliffs nearer the city, looking intently at the Anse au Foulon, a cove situated about one and a half miles from the city's western wall. The next day he brought Monckton, Townshend, his engineer Mackeller and Admiral Holmes with him. They were dressed in an odd assortment of clothing, hoping to disguise who they were (but a French officer at Sillery guessed correctly), and climbed up to high ground above the south shore. They noticed that tents for only about a hundred men were visible at the top of the cliff above the cove. The path that ascended to the top was apparently broken up and blocked, but a somewhat less vertical slope which could probably be climbed lay slightly to the right. Wolfe made his choice but did not confirm it in writing to his brigadier generals. Perhaps he did not want to argue with them, but his main concern was secrecy. Orders in writing tended quickly to become matters of gossip, and both sides were eager to capture stragglers and welcome deserters, for they were the principal sources of intelligence. Wolfe was keenly aware that his plan depended upon complete surprise. For this reason he did not state the objective in writing, even to the brigadiers, until 8.30 p.m. on the evening of the 12th, when directions for embarking the troops in the boats were already being issued.

Most analysts have concluded that it was a bad plan. A landing near Cap Rouge as recommended by the brigadiers would have been safer, it is said. Yet even if a feint had been made further upriver, such a landing would have met with stiff opposition from well-prepared defensive positions. Wolfe remembered how severely his men had been punished on 31 July and was aware of Murray's need to turn back on 8 August. Moreover, if the army did succeed in landing near Cap Rouge, it would face a difficult and hazardous march of at least 10 miles to Quebec's walls.

Wolfe's object was not to sit on Montcalm's supply line but to capture the city. There was no time to starve the place into submission before the season ended. At the Anse au Foulon he could not only avoid a long march but his attacking force, if successful, could be quickly augmented by the troops (almost a thousand) guarding Point Lévis. The daunting challenge of scaling the 160-foot cliff seemed worth the risk.

Everything depended on the stealth and speed of the approach. Did Wolfe know that he was selecting a night on which conditions would be absolutely ideal? He did not have much room for choice, but there can be no doubt that he consulted with naval experts who had calculated the tidal flows and was pleased by what he heard. He wanted the troops to land at first light, about 4 a.m. On the night of 12–13 September the tides were expected to carry the boats from the anchorage off St Nicholas (opposite and just above Cap Rouge) the 8.7 miles to the Anse au Foulon in two hours. Embarkation began at midnight and the signal for the boats to start moving was given at 2 a.m. on 13 September. Slowly at first and then rapidly with the accelerating ebb, the boats drifted silently down the river. Near the end they were making 5 knots, and some boats surged past the cove and came to shore a bit further down, but others arrived at the objective perfectly on schedule. The night was extraordinarily favourable in another way. A half-moon was rising ahead of them and it lit the line of cliffs for their guidance while at the same time there was no back-lighting on the water which would make them visible to enemy sentinels. Only when the boats came near Sillery did the moon, now more to the south, provide a glitter which made them visible from the north shore as they passed, and in fact they were spotted there by a sentinel standing near the water's edge who called out for them to identify themselves. An alert Highland officer replied in French, 'France', and cautioned the sentinel to be quiet because, he said again in French, these boats were carrying provisions to Quebec and were trying to sneak past the British warships. (That the French were intending to float a provisions convoy downriver that night was learned on board the *Hunter* from two deserters.) The story of the alert officer's ruse is attested by more than one source, but even if the sentinel had reported the incident immediately, the boats, moving very fast by then, were only 15–20 minutes from their destination.

Wolfe's plan avoided putting his whole army at risk. He wanted to make sure of getting a foothold on the high ground before committing it. The initiative that brought success came from 24 light infantry volunteers under Colonel William Howe – far more energetic here than he would be as an American Revolutionary War general. These men, many of them

Highlanders, managed to climb a steep slope that lay slightly to the east of the blocked path. The crest was 170 feet above the base and without trees and shrubs to grab they could not have done it. Once on top they hurried to the French post and routed the surprised defenders. Soon the path was cleared and the first echelon, 1,800 troops, ascended. Meanwhile, at 3 a.m. frigates and sloops of war carrying the second echelon of redcoats started downriver. The now empty boats at the Anse au Foulon were waiting to convey these troops ashore. By 8 a.m. the third echelon, the men who had come from Île d'Orléans and Point Lévis and were waiting on the opposite shore after a short march upriver, were being ferried across. Wolfe's attacking force now numbered about 4,500 men. The next task was to repair the path for bringing up field guns and ammunition; two brass 6-pounders were promptly hauled to the top. The army had acted with initiative and bravery, and the navy had carried out its exacting assignment to perfection. Wolfe immediately reconnoitred the terrain towards the city.

It has been commonly supposed that the plan succeeded only because of ample good luck. It was indeed fortunate that at the time when the British army and navy were finally in a position to attack, circumstances of moonlight and tide came together so marvellously. But, otherwise, was the achievement really due to luck rather than expert planning and execution? Wolfe did not stumble onto success accidentally: what occurred was what he foresaw if all went well. Of course, Montcalm's forces were not positioned to repulse the attack, but Wolfe knew this; he had ascertained that the French camp above the Anse au Foulon was small. If Montcalm had kept the Guyenne battalion on the Plains of Abraham, Wolfe would have detected an abundance of tents and let stand his earlier plan of attacking elsewhere. Montcalm, however, had removed that battalion to the St Charles River, while still counting on it to reply to an attack above the city. In reality, the French general had allowed for only two possibilities: the attack would occur either above Cap Rouge where Bougainville would quickly observe it and provide warning in plenty of time or it would be made somewhere below the city.

Montcalm's belief in the likelihood of an attack below the city was reinforced that night by the Royal Navy. Devising a plan to supplement Wolfe's, Admiral Saunders ordered his ships to make mock preparations for a landing aimed at the western part of the Beaufort shore. At sunset the warships unfurled their sails; marines embarked in boats; scouting boats went to work placing buoys off the beach; and signals were vigorously exchanged between Point Lévis and Île d'Orléans. After midnight broadsides swept the shoreline. At the same time heavy guns and mortars on the heights above Point de Pères began bombarding the city. Amid the noise and commotion French officers ordered the troops on the Beauport shore to their defensive posts, in which they would remain most of the night. They were dismissed to get some sleep at about the time Wolfe's men were climbing the cliff.[28] All this was fortunate for the British, but it was not accidental.

The French general's decision to concentrate his force needed to be supplemented by the placement of a trusted senior officer with scouts and mounted messengers west of the city's walls. When the first reports of British troops arriving on the Plains of Abraham came to headquarters, no one believed them and verification did not come until about 7 a.m. Not until then did Montcalm dispatch an urgent message to Bougainville telling him to hurry eastwards. In any case, his decision to engage in battle straightaway was probably incorrect. It is said by some that he had no choice, by others that he should have waited for Bougainville to join, or perhaps have taken up a defensive position at or near the city wall. Strong arguments for waiting have been pointed out. For an open field battle Montcalm's army (without reinforcement by Bougainville's men) was clearly inferior: many of his men, as he must have realized, did not match the quality of the well-trained redcoats, and their number was about the same, about 4,500 (though he probably did not know this). Strategically, there was the broad consideration that the British expedition had to worry about running out of time. Furthermore, although British sailors were already industriously hauling guns and ammunition up the path, it would not have been easy for them to keep 4,500 men supplied by this route. Canadians and Indians firing muskets from behind trees and shrubs were known to be very effective. On the whole, Montcalm's hurried decision helped the British cause, and it will be recalled that until this moment he had steadily avoided attacking.

Within 2 miles of the city's western wall Wolfe formed a very long line, two deep, extending all the way across the open plain. The chosen ground was fairly level, as if he wished to invite an attack. On the flanks, Townshend's troops on the left and Monckton's on the right came under musket fire from Canadians and Indians hidden by trees and underbrush. Wolfe ordered the troops to lie down. Meanwhile, Montcalm, on horseback, was positioning his men for the attack. The French columns moved forward at about 10 a.m. Montcalm had insisted on incorporating

[28] Casgrain, *Montcalm et Lévis*, II, 223–4; *Knox's Journal*, II, 93–4.

selected Canadian militiamen in French regular units, and because they did not reload their muskets with the same rhythm the front became ragged. The whole army advanced too rapidly and the lead units opened fire at too great a distance. When they approached the redcoats stood up and waited silently until the French were 40 yards away. In the British centre 1,000 muskets fired at once. To men aboard the ships in the river it sounded like an explosion. Each musket was double shotted and massive slaughter stopped the French advance instantly. The British reloaded and after taking a few paces forward to get clear of the smoke fired a second volley, upon which French troops who were still standing fled to the rear. Wolfe's men pursued with fixed bayonets.

The clash lasted only 15 minutes. Wolfe, active across the front, was hit three times – in the wrist, groin and chest. He kept going after receiving the first two wounds, but had to be carried to a sheltered place after the third where in a few minutes he died. Before dying he knew that his army had won and he urged a speedy pursuit to the St Charles bridge to cut off retreat. This was not done, partly because Canadian marksmen on the British left continued to exact a toll. The survivors of Montcalm's army reached the Beauport camp, from which they escaped to the north and west that night. Bougainville arrived after the battle with 1,100 men. He was met by Townshend (Monckton was badly wounded) with two battalions and two field guns, and compelled to retreat. Montcalm did not survive. While on his horse trying to rally his troops he was hit in the abdomen and died a painful death in the city the next day. On the day of battle the British suffered 58 killed, of all ranks, and 600 wounded. According to Vaudreuil's report French casualties were similar, but some observers thought that the actual figures were much greater, especially with respect to the number killed.

There were 6,000 people in the city of which 2,200 were combatants, mostly militiamen and sailors. Food was in short supply and the council of war that met to decide whether to capitulate was acutely conscious of this fact. No effort was made, however, to bring in the provisions left by the army at Beauport. It would have been uphill work. In any case, the inhabitants and garrison were demoralized. They did little to prepare a defence while the British were bringing siege guns on to the plain; by one officer's count there were, on 17 September, 60 guns and 58 howitzers ready to be positioned. At noon the same day, Saunders moved eight ships of the line close to the lower town.

Before departing to join Bougainville, Vaudreuil had suggested that a capitulation would probably be necessary, and at 3 p.m. the commandant hoisted a white flag. All of his proposed articles were accepted by Saunders and Townshend except the one requesting that the garrison be released and allowed to go to the French army's camp at Jacques Cartier. Quebec's leaders must have known that this would not be permitted. The admiral and general required all soldiers, marines and sailors to be sent to France. Lévis, who had made haste from the west, arrived on the 17th and was anxious to deny the enemy the use of the city during the winter. He persuaded Vaudreuil to allow a military effort to be made, but news of the capitulation put an end to it, and the British made no move to attack Jacques Cartier. Realizing that the terms were generous (they guaranteed the inhabitants their property, their religion and other protections), Townshend in his report to Pitt gave various reasons for allowing them. One of his reasons was vital: the conquerors needed time and tranquillity to prepare to winter a sizeable army at Quebec. No one in London was upset by the terms. The patriotic enthusiasm that greeted the news on 16 October drowned out all criticism, partly because the event was so unexpected; only two days before a disconsolate letter from Wolfe had arrived.

The capture of Quebec is the most famous of the British victories of 1759 and perhaps of the war, not least because of Wolfe's heroic death. But the achievement should be remembered as not only a military triumph but also a naval and navigational one. As Guy Frégault has written: 'It would be impossible to exaggerate the importance of the part played by the British navy in that operation.'[29] In Paris, when word of Montcalm's defeat arrived, the court was unable to soften the blow by its usual methods, and, as will be seen in the next chapter, the news had a much more consequential impact than its momentary stirring of popular anger and lamentation.

[29] Frégault, *Canada: The War of the Conquest*, p. 244.

CHAPTER 12

The British victory
at sea, 1759

When Berryer took over as naval minister on 1 November 1758 he fully supported his predecessor's plan to send eight ships of the line to Martinique, but could not persuade the king and council to agree. It was a moment when French policy was directionless: Bernis's attention was fixed on making peace, and Choiseul did not take office as foreign minister until December. The Toulon squadron, normally available for West Indian service, was slow to recover from its thwarted attempts to reach the Straits earlier in the year.

The most pressing problem, as Bernis had understood, was financial, and if he had remained in office, he would undoubtedly have continued to address it. But the duc de Choiseul, his replacement, was a military man turned diplomat, and was not disposed to become involved in state finances. Since the king and Pompadour showed little interest he could leave the problems to the controller-general of finances. (Holders of this office during Louis XV's reign were almost always secondary figures, unlike the case in Britain where the First Lord of the Treasury was usually considered the leading minister.) In any case, Choiseul could claim to be fully engaged in the delicate task of negotiating the third treaty of Versailles. Marshal Belleisle was planning another military thrust at Hanover, but little could be done to protect France's overseas possessions.

Under the circumstances it was desirable to end the war with Britain quickly. Pompadour and the king seemed determined to keep fighting, at least on the continent, not only for Austria's sake but also to uphold French influence in continental affairs. Observing the monarchy's dwindling naval and financial resources, Choiseul, who was fond of imaginative schemes, turned his mind to how allies might assist. Surveying the European scene he could see that the Dutch Republic was resolved to stay neutral and that little could be expected from Denmark. This left Sweden, Russia and, potentially, Spain. Within a year Spain would command the foreign minister's attention, but at the beginning of 1759 he focused on Sweden. In late January Choiseul asked his ambassador at Stockholm to persuade the Swedish government to provide warships and transports to convey an army of 10–12,000 troops – if not Swedish troops, then Russian – to land on Scotland's east coast. This would have been difficult for the British to prevent. The local defence force was thin; a naval squadron would be needed on the coast, and it could not be counted on to make an interception, the voyage from Göteborg requiring only two days on a good wind. This involvement of Swedish or Russian troops in Scotland was intended to support an evolving, elaborate plan for an invasion of Great Britain.

Invasion threat and blockade of Brest

The French plan to invade the British Isles in 1759 was not aimed at conquering and occupying but at alarming the British public and shaking the stock market. It was an article of faith in France that Great Britain's financial system was fragile and could easily collapse, forcing the government to seek peace. In 1745 rebellious Highlanders under Prince Charles Edward, the Jacobite Pretender, had marched south and provoked a panic. British troops had to be recalled from the continent to confront him. His defeat was followed by a rapid financial recovery in London. On that occasion a French army was not involved. This time Versailles planned to send over many thousands of troops. Since the great problem was to get them safely across the water, the plan involved three separate landings: one on the east coast of Scotland by Russians transported in Swedish ships, another by French troops to be landed in the Clyde estuary of Scotland's west coast, and the main effort by French troops landing on the south or east coast of England.

The troops landing on Scotland's west coast were to be joined by a rising of Scottish Jacobites, and Choiseul was in touch with them. He invited Charles Edward to a meeting on 7 February 1759 with Marshal Belleisle in attendance. This was serious business and it did not help that the prince – whose morale was thoroughly dissipated by this time – arrived late and drunk, thus confirming suspicions that he was not a man to be trusted with a demanding task of leadership. Dutch leaders got wind of the meeting and reminded the French of the Republic's long-standing treaty obligation to defend Hanoverian England if the Stuart Pretender were to land there. Choiseul responded that the French government was not supporting him (a half-truth) and failed to mention that a Jacobite rising was part of the plan.

Why did Versailles opt for this 'most chimerical and insane of enter-prises'?[1] When the Russian War Conference considered Choiseul's request for troops it judged the entire invasion scheme to be impractical and hope-less, and responded in late March with an emphatic negative.[2] Sweden temporized (a flat refusal would have hazarded payment of subsidy money owed by France), but both parties contending for control of the Swedish government shied away from risking war with Britain. It thus became obvious that no allied participation could be expected, but Choiseul was not deterred. Once again, the French government was tempted by a short-war solution to its problems, but unlike the invasion of Germany two years earlier, which had been undertaken confidently, this scheme was adopted in desperation. When Choiseul presented it to the council of state on 14 July 1759 he painted a dark picture of necessity: France's foreign commerce ruined; Canada soon to be lost; African settlements wiped out; the position in India not hopeful; all appeals to neutrals and allies to form a maritime league against England fruitless. As for success in Germany, it was likely to take too long. The only remedy, he said, was this admittedly chancy invasion plan drawn up by Marshal Belleisle. Since Choiseul was known to enjoy the confidence of Louis XV and Pompadour, and the experienced old marshal was prepared to commit thousands of troops to the enterprise, the council accepted it. To Bernstorff, the Danish minister, Choiseul wrote about it in extravagant style: all French troops not in Germany were to be directed against England, and 'if fifty thousand men should perish in a first expedition, the king has signed a resolution to send successively fifty thousand others and we shall not lose heart so long as we have men in France'.[3]

The landing in southern England was to include about 40,000 men – 60 battalions, 40 squadrons and 2,000 dragoons. The ideal port of embarka-tion would be Le Havre where 125 flat-bottomed boats large enough to carry both infantry and cavalry had already been built; they were equipped

---

[1] The words of a French naval historian over a century ago, Chabaud-Arnault, 'La marine française', 493.
[2] Lawrence Jay Oliva, *Misalliance: A Study of French Policy in Russia during the Seven Years' War* (New York, 1964), pp. 140–1.
[3] Choiseul to Bernstorff, 29 July 1759, in the Choiseul–Bernstorff *Correspondence* (cited in Chapter 13), p. 46.

with sails and were to be protected by *prames*, that is, floating batteries on a Swedish model. The troops would land in Hampshire and immediately raid Portsmouth dockyard. The advantage of Le Havre over Dunkirk was that the men and horses could be easily fed nearby and embarked very quickly, and thus the British might be taken by surprise. The expedition to the Clyde estuary called for 42 battalions and a regiment of dragoons. When joined by Jacobite volunteers they would march to Edinburgh to be reinforced, it was originally hoped, by Swedes or Russians. The expedition to western Scotland was to depart in September. The embarkation at Le Havre would occur two months later.

The plan met with criticism. Marshal Soubise thought Dunkirk a better point of departure because from there the landing site would be harder for the enemy to predict. Moreover, as Marshal d'Estrées warned in a memoir, British warships could easily keep station near the Isle of Wight and would pounce on a flotilla from Le Havre. He also predicted that British frigates would constantly cruise off the port to give early warning. When he wrote the memoir on 16 July he had undoubtedly heard about what had happened there two weeks before.

Captain George Bridges Rodney, now a rear admiral, had appeared off Le Havre with the *Deptford* (60 guns), three frigates and four bomb vessels. The bomb vessels were carefully manoeuvred in darkness by ships' officers (the pilots Rodney had been given were of no use) to positions close to a submerged sandbank, and at daybreak on 4 July the 10-inch and 13-inch mortars began launching their bombs and carcasses. By noon two more bomb vessels were in position, and over the next two days nearly 500 shells were fired into the town and upon the flat-bottomed boats along its adjacent beaches. The attack ended when hard usage caused the mortars to crack and the vessels to develop serious leaks. The attack shocked the French and caused damage, but they shifted boat construction upriver and built floating batteries. When Rodney returned at the end of August the bomb vessels could not safely moor within range. Nevertheless, d'Estrées's prediction that the British would continuously cruise off Le Havre was completely accurate. Rodney was so ordered. In all kinds of weather until the end of January 1760, well after the danger of invasion was past, his ships remained on station and prevented flat-bottomed boats from performing any service.

In August Belleisle shifted the proposed position of the main army from Normandy to Flanders. It would embark at Ostend, cross to the Blackwater near Malden, Essex, and from there strike westwards to London. As hope of Sweden's participation dimmed and confidence in effective Jacobite aid was lost, the French army destined for Scotland was increased to 20,000. These troops would go aboard transports in the bay of Morbihan on Brittany's south coast, access to which was available only through Quiberon Bay. In this form the invasion plan appeared to be settled.

From the beginning the French planners ruled out the idea of bringing the Brest squadron into the Channel to shield the flotilla's crossing. Choiseul told the council in mid-July (when Le Havre was still the planned point of departure): It is an 'opportune gale [*coup de vent saisi*] which will decide the enterprise, and our twelve *prames* are as good as ships of war. The idea of having the fleet would throw us into the difficulties of a combination that I regard as impossible'.[4] The Brest squadron would, instead, be ordered to Martinique! To escort transports from the Morbihan to the Clyde a squadron of moderate strength was assigned. After accomplishing this mission the squadron might proceed north about Scotland and head for Dunkirk. Would it then be ordered to escort transports from Ostend to the Essex coast? The surviving records do not say, nor is there evidence of any naval plan to shield this passage. Perhaps the crossing of the main army to England was silently being given up, though boats and some troops were left on the Flanders coast to occupy British attention. Preparations for the French invasion of Scotland clearly continued, however.

The admiral in command at Brest was Hubert de Brienne, comte de Conflans, who at 69 had a distinguished naval career behind him, so distinguished that he was given the honour, rare for a navy man, of being named a marshal of France. He had been left out of the planning. A difficult, proud, presumptuous man, his relations with the naval minister, Berryer, were saturated with mutual dislike. Belleisle, Choiseul and Berryer had deliberately kept Conflans in the dark. Instead they had consulted Captain Bigot de Morogues, founder of the naval academy, who was to command the naval escort from the Morbihan, and also the duc d'Aiguillon, who was the logical choice to command the expeditionary army. This was the Breton regional commander who had speeded the strong force to St Cast.

Bigot de Morogues proposed that a squadron of three ships of 74 guns and three of 64, plus two frigates and two corvettes should escort the transports to the Clyde. These would be detached from the Brest squadron, the

[4] Choiseul's memoir, quoted by P. Coquelle, 'Les Projects de Descente en Angleterre', *Revue d'histoire diplomatique* (1901), 613.

rest of which, he suggested, should be used to lure the powerful Western Squadron away from the convoy's path. The commander at Brest – presumably it would be Conflans – was to make sure his ships were seen, but at a distance, and should retreat if chased. 'This stratagem', Bigot de Morogues commented, 'is the only one that could succeed.' D'Aiguillon was called to Versailles to discuss the plan, but before leaving Brittany he spoke with Conflans at Brest to try to convince him of its merits. Conflans was adamantly opposed to dividing the fleet. Overruling his wishes, the ministry adopted the plan on 26 August and Louis XV wrote firmly to Conflans: 'I have ruled that my ships, *Magnifique, Juste, Superbe, Éveillé, Solitaire,* and *Brillant,* under the command of Sieur Bigot de Morogues, will be detached from my *armée navale* with some frigates and corvettes to go to join the fleet [of transports] in the road of Quiberon and escort it to [its] destination.'[5] The matter was settled – or so it seemed.

The British cabinet did not need accurate particulars to start preparing a defence. Rumours that the French were planning a descent circulated in late January, and soon reports came that the French dockyards were hard at work – activity that could not be disguised. The principal concern was naval, and on 19 February Pitt, Newcastle, Hardwicke, Ligonier, Granville and Holdernesse met with Anson. Of 100 ships of the line on active duty 59 were abroad, and of the 41 at home only 21 were ready for service. Anson believed that all 41 could be fitted out but doubted that they could be manned, the main cause being that the fleet had grown so fast: 12 new ships of the line had been launched during the past year and more than a dozen new frigates. In addition, 5 French ships of the line captured in 1758 were being taken into the Royal Navy, and 3 British-built 74-gun ships were due to be launched in March. Recruiting could not keep up. Although the navy mustered 71,000, a record level, 9,500 more men were needed. Rigorous measures were adopted, including an embargo on outbound shipping and impressment of seamen from the normally protected coastal trade. The restrictions that Pitt's legislation had placed on small privateers helped diminish total demand. By 9 May 7,500 more men were added to the ships at home.[6] The ministers also discussed troops for defence of the coasts. All regiments at home were ordered to add recruits if they could, and Pitt proposed employing the militia.

---

[5] D'Aiguillon to Belleisle, 2 Aug. 1759, the king to Conflans, 26 Aug. 1759, both quoted by Le Moing, *Bataille navale,* pp. 17–18.

[6] Lavery, *Ship of the Line* (cited in Chapter 9), pp. 176–8; Gradish, *Manning* (cited in Chapter 9), pp. 48–9; Middleton, *Bells,* pp. 109–11, 123.

Throughout the spring Newcastle fretted. He continued to receive reports of invasion preparations and urged Joseph Yorke to keep his ears open. Yorke was sceptical and wondered if the alarming intelligence was 'not sent over by the French on purpose', but promised to remain alert.[7] By May, Newcastle's intelligence from France strongly indicated that the threat was real. Urgent cabinet meetings were held. Pitt and Ligonier agreed that militiamen could be assigned the task of guarding prisoners of war so that regulars could be released for homeland defence. From counties which had been prompt in getting their militias organized 7,000 men were available; a royal proclamation of emergency was required to call them to duty and it was issued on 30 May. Orders were also given for 5,000 regulars to be camped on the Isle of Wight where transports were to stand ready to carry them to wherever they might be needed. Since public anxiety was bound to be heightened by the proclamation, it made sense to get the Western Squadron to sea right away.

In May, Choiseul sent a letter to his ambassador at Stockholm in which he conveyed information about the invasion plan as it then stood in hopes of persuading the Swedish government to make up its mind to participate. The letter was intercepted by a British agent. Reading the deciphered copy in early June, Newcastle felt a chill of anxiety but also a sense of personal satisfaction: as he had predicted, the French really did intend to invade. (At this time Jacques Barbier was recording in his journal that the prospective invasion was the talk of Paris.[8]) Ligonier assigned regular forces and militia to positions along the English south coast and some dragoons to Essex, but also paid attention to Scotland. The Admiralty ordered frigates and small warships to cluster in the narrows of the Channel, sent Rodney, as we have seen, to blast the flat-bottomed boats at Le Havre and watch the Normandy coast, and assigned frigates and hired privateers to cruise the north coast of Brittany.

Admiral Hawke, in command of a Western Squadron of twenty-five ships of the line plus assisting frigates, was ordered to be ready to take station off Brest. His instructions from the Admiralty urged him to intercept vessels carrying 'provisions and stores to Brest and Rochefort' as it 'must tend greatly to disconcert the enemy's measures'; he was to appoint 'smaller ships of the line and frigates' to accomplish this.[9] Brest has three exits. Hawke would quickly realize that the openings to the

---

[7] Yorke to Hardwicke, 20 March 1759, BL Add. 35,357, fo. 328.
[8] Barbier, *Journal*, VII, 164.
[9] The instructions are quoted in Mackay, *Admiral Hawke*, pp. 202–3.

north and south had to be monitored continuously by an inshore squadron; to this squadron he initially assigned two 64-gun ships and three strong frigates, plus a couple of smaller warships to relay messages. It was an unprecedented mission and the inshore cruisers would need fleet support, but keeping the whole squadron continuously at sea made no strategic sense when the French men-of-war were not ready to sail. Anson's initial orders suggested that Hawke should bring the squadron to Torbay or Plymouth periodically for provisions and refreshment. Near the end of May, however, Hawke's cruisers counted eleven large fully rigged ships in Brest harbour, and he resolved to keep the whole squadron on station, thinking it prudent not to let them come out. Aided by the inshore squadron's close surveillance the Western Squadron truly became a blockading squadron, and Hawke committed it to a continuous, durable, close blockade of Brest.

Ships of the inshore squadron carried orders that permitted them to manoeuvre singly when necessary; they could thus find safety in almost all weather conditions. In contrast, a battle fleet was quite unwieldy. Often it could not safely tack and was forced instead to wear, a procedure that occasioned extensive downwind drift, and because so much sea room was required the main fleet dared not remain close to the Breton peninsula, especially at night. If a strong westerly gale arose, the fleet had to steer for the Channel, and the best recourse was to attain Plymouth Sound or Torbay to avoid being blown too far eastwards. When this became necessary Brest was inevitably left unguarded, but a westerly gale that compelled the squadron to leave its station also prevented the French from getting out. As it happened, a series of storms kept the fleet in Torbay in mid-June, but from that time until early October when similar conditions again forced it to take refuge, Hawke was able to keep the Western Squadron off Brest.

In early July twenty large French men-of-war, fully rigged, were visible in the Brest roadstead, but they were scarcely manned. The soldiers and transports that were to go to Scotland had not yet gathered in the Morbihan. Although Hawke's arrangements succeeded in hindering shipments of supplies to Brest, the constant cruising resulted in frayed rigging, speed diminished by fouled hulls and, above all, crews incapacitated by scurvy. Nevertheless, Anson approved Hawke's decision to blockade Brest continuously and closely. There was a political factor: the cabinet knew how great would be the public clamour if any ships of the Brest fleet escaped.

In mid-July a meeting of leading ministers suggested that if Hawke were given more ships of the line, 'six of the line at a time' might be sent in to clean and refit by rotation.[10] It was important to ensure that the ships and crews would be in good condition when the time came to confront the French. Hawke was already sending two ships at a time to Plymouth every fortnight to clean hulls, replace damaged rigging, and presumably to refresh the crews. He soon found that this did not work; sending six at a time would certainly not work. The problem was that the crews were not really getting 'refreshment', by which he meant not only the beneficial effects of 'fresh provisions' (which generally meant fresh instead of salt meat) but also physical rest. The heavy burden of clearing a ship for dry dock and storing it for sea afterwards fell on the ship's company. If all this had to be done in ten days (since there were not enough extra ships to allow more time), 'the men', Hawke wrote, 'would be so harassed and fatigued that they would return to me in worse condition than they left me'. It came down to choosing between a thorough hull cleaning or refreshing the crews, and Hawke chose the latter. Let the ships, he advised Anson, be heeled and given a boot-topping – a procedure that required much less work – and then require every ship to come away from Plymouth with live bullocks and sheep aboard.[11]

Clearly, his principal concern was to keep the men healthy. Both he and the First Lord cannot have forgotten September 1755 when Hawke was determined to bring his sickly Western Squadron into port early and was criticized by Anson for doing so. The solution was to send fresh provisions to the squadron. On 19 July the Admiralty ordered the Victualling Board to ship bullocks and sheep to the rendezvous off Ushant. The immediate concern was to cure men who were sick, but Hawke suggested that everyone should have a share 'to prevent their falling down with scorbutic disorders'. The Admiralty agreed, and on 2 August it ordered that 'well men' should receive fresh meat by turns. Specially fitted vessels were assigned to the task, and the live animals were hoisted in slings aboard ships of the squadron in open sea. Forty years ago historians (including the present writer) thought that this mighty effort to send live animals out to the fleet was a misguided waste of time, effort and money except in so far as it improved the morale of the men, but in fact fresh

[10] Middleton, 'British Naval Strategy', 363.
[11] Mackay, ed. *Hawke Papers*, p. 260. Boot-topping: scraping and dressing near the waterline on a slight careen. Fatigue was thought to be a factor in the onset of scurvy.

meat does contain vitamin C. At about this time the Admiralty responded to a proposal from Captain Robert Pett, an alert member of the Victualling Board who had been sent to Plymouth to ensure efficiency; he suggested that the vessels going out to the squadron should also carry 'cabbages, turnips, carrots, potatoes, and onions'.

Thanks to Hawke's insistence, the Admiralty's resolute support, the Victualling Board's special arrangements, and a victualling commissioner's advice concerning fresh vegetables (inspired, it appears, by some shipboard surgeons), effective measures to prevent scurvy were instituted. Hawke's only complaint concerned beer. Strong-brewed 'sea beer' normally kept better than water. But Hawke's was spoiling within a week of being taken aboard. About this nothing much could be done: in the warm weather of July and August the brewery at Plymouth could not control the fermentation. Beer brought from the navy's eastern breweries supplied some of the need. All in all, except for one or two ships that could not rid themselves of an infectious disease, the health of the squadron despite its many months continuously at sea remained amazingly good. This was unprecedented.[12]

In mid-September French invasion preparations made progress. Sixty-eight transports from Nantes escorted by three frigates got into the bay of Morbihan on the 17th; British cruisers on Brittany's south coast were not properly positioned to prevent them. The close guard on entrances to Brest, however, was effective, sharply reducing the inflow of provisions and stores. In one instance, the cargoes of forty victualling vessels which came up the coast had to be carted overland from Quimper. By this time Hawke was assigning five ships of the line in addition to the frigates to the inshore squadron, and the augmentation certainly proved its worth when, between 17 and 20 September, two French ships of the line and one frigate attempted to escape. Three times they came through the Goulet from the roadstead and anchored in Cameret Bay where an escape in darkness seemed feasible, but the inshore squadron kept them from trying it. Watching the transports and frigates in the Morbihan was easy because Commodore Robert Duff's squadron (one of 64 guns, one of 60 and five of 50) could use the shelter of Quiberon Bay.

[12] Ibid. pp. 245, 254, 259. The demanding and successful measures to prevent scurvy in this blockading squadron deserve historical attention, especially because the Admiralty did not adopt them in the subsequent War of American Independence. In neither war did James Lind's experiment with lemon juice, published in 1753, affect the measures adopted.

On 10 October the Admiralty told Hawke that the moment was critical and that his task was to concentrate on Brest and the Morbihan, ignoring everything else. These orders were stimulated by intelligence reports but also reflected the level of anxiety in London. Hawke thought that the Admiralty was overdoing it. In his opinion Rochefort should be blockaded too, but his suggestion was rejected.

Even when a severe storm forced Hawke to take the fleet to Plymouth Sound on 13 October he remained confident and declared to the Admiralty, 'Their Lordships may depend upon there being little foundation for the present alarms.' Observing that the current state of anxiety in England was depressing prices on the stock exchange, he had written to his banker on 2 October suggesting that it was an opportune moment to buy. His banker disagreed, saying that stocks were expected to decline further.[13]

Lagos Bay and Quiberon Bay

Lord Anson did not neglect Toulon. Admiral Brodrick was ordered to blockade what was left of the French squadron. He was reinforced by six ships arriving from England on 16 May 1759 with Admiral Boscawen, whose just reward after so much hard service in northern waters was the Mediterranean command. With thirteen ships of the line, two of 50 guns, and a dozen frigates covering Toulon and Marseilles, Boscawen and Brodrick could and did frustrate French trade and privateering in the Mediterranean, but their main responsibility was to prevent the Toulon squadron from escaping through the Straits of Gibraltar. Boscawen had to pull back to Gibraltar in late July to refit, and Admiral Jean-François Bertet de La Clue-Sabran sailed on 5 August with twelve of the line and three frigates. The ships headed for the Straits with instructions to put into Cadiz and await further orders if they got through.

At Gibraltar, the British squadron had nearly completed refitting when just before 8 p.m. on 17 August a frigate came racing in from its cruising station east of Ceuta with a report that fifteen warships were entering the Straits. A signal for the squadron to get under way was seen 3 miles away from the terrace of the Spanish governor's house at San Roque where Boscawen and some other officers were dining. While they were hurrying back to the anchorage the ships' companies were feverishly hauling up yards and bending sails. By 10 p.m. seven ships were under way, led by Boscawen in the 90-gun *Namur*. It was a remarkable feat but not likely

---

[13] Ibid. esp. pp. 316–18; Mackay, *Admiral Hawke*, p. 231.

to bring success because La Clue's squadron, aided by a strong east wind, was well ahead. Off Cape Spartel at 2 a.m. on the 18th, La Clue decided to hold course to westwards because, he later explained, the wind was contrary for reaching Cadiz.[14] He assumed that the whole squadron would follow, but five of the line and three frigates apparently did not see where the lead ships were heading and turned north to Cadiz. Boscawen plunged westwards through the night with reefs out and top-gallant sails set. He was rewarded at dawn by the sight of sails ahead of him. La Clue knew that only seven of his fifteen ships were with him and, thinking the ships astern belonged to his squadron, paused to let them catch up. Only when his 'private signal' for identifying friend or foe was not correctly answered did he realize his mistake and press on, but the expertly handled British men-of-war closed the range.

At 2.30 p.m. Boscawen's lead ship opened fire on the lagging *Centaure* (74 guns), a poor sailer. When many ganged up on her Boscawen signalled some ships to hurry forward to cut off the enemy's escape. At four, the *Namur* overtook La Clue's flagship, the *Océan* (80 guns), and joined two others in engaging her, the cannonading lasting until seven. The *Namur* suffered few casualties but lost its mizzen mast and two topsail yards, so Boscawen had to transfer his flag to the *Newark* (80 guns). Meanwhile, Brodrick's ships were coming up, and it seemed that the *Centaure* was pummelled by every British ship that sailed past. Captain Sabran-Grammont maintained a brave and bloody fight for five hours before he struck; 200 of his men were killed or wounded. Darkness did not enable La Clue to get away because a British 50-gun ship, scouting ahead, was able to keep in touch with most of the remaining French men-of-war.

Their course was WNW, as La Clue was hoping to round Cape St Vincent. But the strong wind from the east died and was replaced by light, wavering breezes from the north and west. His best hope still lay in rounding the cape since the British squadron now stood between him and Cadiz. If the wind did not allow him to clear the cape, he could hope for immunity in Portuguese territorial waters. As the ships approached the coast on the morning of the 19th a land battery overlooking Lagos Bay fired a few warning shots at the British squadron, but that was all. In any case, Boscawen was not going to allow a predictable Portuguese diplomatic complaint to deter him from going after four trapped French ships of the line. In order to prevent the *Océan*'s capture La Clue drove

---

[14] La Clue's report to Berryer, Dec. 1759, Waddington, *Guerre*, III, 361.

his flagship onto the beach so hard that all the masts crashed forward. Wounded in both legs, the admiral was carried ashore. The *Redoubtable* (74 guns) also beached herself. The *Téméraire* (74 guns) and *Modeste* (64 guns) anchored near the shoreline and struck their colours. Resistance was brief because the crews were concerned to get ashore and avoid being taken prisoner. The British burned the two beached ships and took command of the other two. The eight French warships at Cadiz were blockaded by Brodrick and did not emerge until 2 January 1760, whereupon they sailed to Toulon. In sum, three ships were captured (all taken into the Royal Navy), two burnt and eight kept out of the 1759 campaign, the only exceptions being two of 74 guns that departed during the night of the 18th–19th and eventually reached Rochefort.

That the French planned to combine the Toulon and Brest squadrons was the belief of everyone in Britain at the time and also of most historians since, but evidence does not support it. La Clue and his captains all sailed from Toulon with orders to go to Cadiz if they got through the Straits. There La Clue was to receive a further order concerning the squadron's ultimate destination. The naval minister, Berryer, ordered the French consul at Cadiz to inform La Clue when he arrived that he should load a six months' supply of provisions and obtain money to pay three months' wages to the ships' companies; the consul was to handle the purchases. On 14 August Berryer wrote another letter to Cadiz, this one addressed to La Clue. It urged him to take aboard as much food and munitions as his ships could hold and mentioned that while this was being done a courier would come overland from Versailles with orders concerning the squadron's destination, not yet determined. But Berryer added, 'I confide to you (for you alone), that I have reason to think that it will be to go to Martinique' for a three-month deployment.[15] Of course, La Clue's failure to put into Cadiz rendered all this irrelevant. Only after he heard about the disaster at Lagos Bay did the naval minister order any of the Toulon ships to join Conflans; those at Cadiz received it, but they were blockaded.

Why during the night of the 17th and 18th La Clue decided not to go to Cadiz is an unsolved puzzle. A possible explanation is that the strong easterly wind pushed his ships as far as Cape Spartel sooner than he expected so that a tack northwards to Cadiz would increase the risk of his being intercepted. The trailing ships, unlike those with La Clue, probably changed course sooner. What is clear is that French strategists wished to delay their decision. Berryer wanted to help the West Indian colonies; the

[15] Costet, 'Une erreur historique', 639–40.

loss of Guadeloupe had shocked him, and he wished to use the Toulon squadron to bolster morale at Martinique.[16] He could not, however, simply go ahead and order it to be sent, for if Boscawen chose not to follow it across the Atlantic but came north instead, the British naval force opposing invasion would become even more formidable. A stop at Cadiz would enable the squadron to get money and provisions, and be in a position to go either to the West Indies or to Brest. Of course, it stood a good chance of being blockaded there, but in that case it would function, nevertheless, as a 'fleet in being', keeping Boscawen's squadron occupied. As an internal naval ministry memoir observed: 'It is absolutely the movement [*marche*] of the English squadrons which ought to determine that of M. de La Clue. If the English remain, they will have less assistance at home; if their ships return to England, M. de La Clue will come to reinforce M. le Maréchal de Conflans.'[17] By this reasoning La Clue's blockaded squadron at Cadiz could be seen as achieving an important strategic goal without risk of its destruction off Brest by Hawke. And if the invasion enterprise failed, as Berryer feared it would, the squadron would remain in a condition to go to the West Indies as he desired.

Returning from its refuge in Plymouth Sound, Hawke's fleet regained station off Brest on 19 October and soon made contact with Captain Augustus Hervey, commodore of the inshore squadron, who had ridden out

MAP 13 *Lagos Bay to Gibraltar*

[16] Boulle, 'The French Colonies', pp. 150–3.
[17] Costet, 'Une erreur historique', 642–3.

the storm. Hervey's ship was leaking badly, and Hervey was so weak that he had to be carried from gallery to gallery to see what was happening. Hawke ordered both the ship and her captain into port, sending a letter to the Admiralty that rightly praised his 'diligence, activity, intrepidity and judgement'.[18]

During Hawke's absence the Brest squadron had not stirred. Conflans had spent the month of September trying to overturn the king's order to detach six ships under Bigot de Morogues. He resented having no role in the planning and loathed the idea of his ships being shifted about by army commanders. On 3 October he addressed a counter-proposal to the naval minister: he would go to sea with his whole fleet and fight the British squadron unless its numbers were superior, then go to Quiberon Bay, destroy the small British squadron there, and proceed to escort the transports to Scotland. The king and his advisers yielded: Versailles sent instructions on 14 October that amounted to a carte blanche. Conflans was permitted to keep his entire squadron and to attack the enemy according to his judgement of circumstances. The only stipulation was that he should not lose sight of the basic purpose of the operation, which was to ensure the safety of the transports in the Morbihan and find a way to get them safely to Scotland.

Having got his way Conflans could not back out, but he soon began to think realistically about his chances of defeating the British squadron and carrying out the rest of the mission. He knew that his crews were untrained. The men of the Breton coastguard who had been pressed into the navy to complete the manning were largely peasant fishermen, and because British warships had been ready to pounce as soon as any of his ships emerged from the roadstead they lacked training in handling a large man-of-war at sea. The only positive development was the arrival of Bompar from the West Indies on 7 November. His ships were worn out, but some of his experienced men were recruited by promised bonuses. Still, Conflans expressed his worries in letters to d'Aiguillon and Berryer. He issued fighting instructions to his captains, but by the time he was ready to depart it was clear that he had made up his mind to avoid combat.

Bompar had got in during a furious north-west gale while Hawke's ships were desperately trying to stay north of Ushant. The British squadron

[18] Mackay, ed. *Hawke Papers*, p. 334. Hawke was well aware that Anson and Hervey were political enemies because of Minorca, and Hervey never moderated his animus even after the First Lord, recognizing his merits as a commander at sea, gave him important assignments.

reached Torbay without serious damage, but gales and adverse winds persisted a whole week, and a favouring wind did not arise until the 14th. This north-east wind also enabled the Brest fleet to sail. Twenty-one ships of the line and three frigates worked their way through the south passage and continued southwards before turning east. Hawke had been informed by an Admiralty letter of the 29th that Conflans had 'positive orders' to put to sea (another of Choiseul's letters to Stockholm had been intercepted and deciphered), and everything indicated that he would head for Quiberon Bay. That was indeed Conflans's destination, but late on the 16th a rising south-easterly wind pushed him 50 miles west.

Hawke assumed that the Brest squadron would sail at the same time as he did and estimated that it would enjoy a 200-mile lead. Yet he felt sure he could catch up. The south-easterly gale that pushed Conflans away from his destination also carried Hawke eastwards. Nevertheless, on the 19th the British squadron, probably because its crews were more skilled, was less than 30 miles behind as the two fleets converged on the intended landfall, Belle-Île-en-Mer. During the night the wind came strong from the south-west and pushed both of them rapidly towards the island.

Hawke's flagship was now the *Royal George*, a recently built ship of 100 guns and quite a good sailer for her size. (The *Ramillies* had begun to leak badly and left Torbay for Plymouth.) His fleet numbered twenty-three ships of the line of which two came from Boscawen's squadron. With two frigates out ahead, the battle squadron drove through the darkness under reefed topsails, pausing only in the hours before dawn to keep safely short of Belle-Île. Conflans sailed more cautiously. Having fallen to the south-west well beyond sight of land, he had no recent basis for estimating his longitude. His caution was sensible and, besides, he had no idea that the race would be close. His thoughts were focused on surprising Duff's squadron.

That squadron was in Quiberon Bay calmly loading provisions when the frigate *Vengeance* appeared on the afternoon of 19 November. Coming from her station off Lorient she had battled headwinds and braved the Teignouse passage, firing guns and flying the warning signal as she entered the bay. Duff's ships hurriedly cut their cables and exited by the same passage. The next morning they were about 6 miles west of Belle-Île when they saw the French fleet coming towards them. The little squadron of 50-gun ships split four and three, the former group, under Duff, heading north. Conflans ordered his ships to attack both groups, and with an early morning wind from the south and west Duff's group was in great danger because in heavy seas on a downwind chase large men-of-war generally had a sailing advantage. At 10 a.m., however, Duff saw a large body of ships which he knew must be Hawke's and turned towards them.[19] At first light Hawke had begun to move under full press of sail and was now bearing down fast because by this time the wind had shifted to WNW.

Conflans found it hard to believe that the British fleet could have arrived so soon. It was a moment of decision and there was very little time for the French admiral to think. Should he form up and fight? Or head for Basque Roads? Or take refuge in Quiberon Bay? He was well aware that his crews lacked experience. Spyglasses soon revealed that the enemy squadron was slightly larger in number than his and included three-deckers (four of them in fact). Sea and wind direction as well as geography gave Hawke's ships additional advantages in case of an engagement outside the bay. Conflans therefore rejected the first option. The second option seemed dishonourable; besides, Basque Roads was 120 miles away and his ships might not be able to outrun the British. He chose the third: it seemed most in keeping with his orders (the concern for the troop transports) and he could hope that Hawke and his captains would be deterred by their scant knowledge of the bay's navigational hazards.

Under the circumstances the choice was sensible, but Conflans believed he must place his flagship, the *Soleil Royal* (110 guns) at the head of his line so that, as he explained later, he could lead manoeuvres that might require improvisation. He thus removed himself from the centre, the proper station for directing combat, and stayed far away from the most likely point of initial engagement. Although he realized that his rear ships might be overtaken and signalled them to make more sail, he did not slow down to allow them to close up; the extended, loose line stretched back about 8 miles. In the early afternoon as the *Soleil Royal* rounded the Cardinals – the rocks at the western end of the broad entrance to the bay which provide the French name for the battle – the ships in the rear came under fire.

Hawke had devised and incorporated in his Fighting Instructions a signal whereby he could order particular chasing ships that were sailing fastest to form a line without pausing. In this manner seven British ships of the line engaged the French rear. The ships behind them passed on forward to come up with the enemy centre and van. The *Magnifique* (74 guns) and *Juste* (70 guns) were quickly put out of action and they retired to make repairs. The *Formidable* (80 guns), flagship of the rear division, suffered

[19] Private communication from Dr Ruddock Mackay.

terribly. Admiral Saint-André du Verger, though wounded, remained on the quarterdeck until killed; his brother, the ship's captain, was also killed. At about 4 p.m. she struck. The mayhem which began outside the bay continued on the way in. As the *Royal George* rounded the Cardinals at 3.55 p.m. the ship's master warned Hawke of the navigational hazards, to which he replied: You have done your duty; now 'lay me alongside the French admiral'. Perhaps these were not his exact words, but his orders to this effect are an established fact. He assumed that his ships could go anywhere the French went.

Conflans intended to moor his squadron in the north-west sector of the bay, just outside the landlocked bay of Morbihan in an impregnable array, but at about 3.30 p.m. there came a sharp northerly gust after which the wind settled at NW, blowing hard. Conflans was now unable to attain the north-west corner of the bay; he was forced to head NNE. The best way to keep the line unified while making this course change was to tack in succession. Although the *Soleil Royal* and some others tacked successfully in the tempestuous conditions, five of the trailing ships could not manage it and had to wear (stern to the wind). The consequences of their inability to tack were serious and irreversible. They ended up in the northern sector of the bay, while the flagship and six others which had been able to tack speeded approximately southwards. Conflans's situation was dire. He hoped to relieve his suffering rear division, originally composed of seven ships, but they had been badly beaten and some had withdrawn. Of the remaining two-thirds of his fleet he had only seven ships with him counting the flagship, and these were now in a line heading south, distancing themselves from the other six or seven in the northern sector.

Most sea battles of the eighteenth century were fought under moderate, sometimes calm, conditions. This one was fought in a violent storm with winds at 40 knots and blinding rain squalls.[20] Under such conditions it was not just the efficient rate of fire of which most British crews were capable that brought success, but a combination of firepower and seamanship. On that fateful afternoon two French ships sank: *Thésée* (74 guns) and *Superbe* (70 guns). Sinking as a result of combat in those days was unusual. The circumstances in which the *Superbe* went down will be described in a moment. The *Thésée*, commanded by the experienced Guy-François de Coëtnempren de Kersaint, suddenly began to go

[20] Dennis Wheeler, 'A Climatic Reconstruction of the Battle of Quiberon Bay, 20 November 1759' *Weather* 50, 7 (July 1995), 230–9.

under while engaging Keppel's *Torbay* (74 guns). Only twenty-two men survived, nine of them picked up by Keppel's boats despite the stormy seas. Undoubtedly the cause was water pouring in through open lower gunports. The same catastrophe had very nearly befallen the *Torbay* earlier in the afternoon, but she managed to turn upwind in time to keep water from flooding in. Other British ships had to make emergency turns upwind for the same reason.

When Hawke rounded the Cardinals he immediately caught sight of the imposing *Soleil Royal*. As he headed north to engage her, she was heading south. When the *Royal George* got near at about 4.30 p.m. the *Soleil Royal* wore towards the north-east and initiated an exchange of broadsides. Each ship in her train wore and fired broadsides, mostly inaccurate. Hawke conformed to the north-easterly course, thus making effective use of the *Royal George*'s firepower while in pursuit of the French admiral. He was engaging without support, but his flagship had three decks, 100 guns and an experienced crew. The fifth French ship in line, the *Superbe*, became engaged very closely, receiving two broadsides at pistol-shot range (not much more than ten yards). Upon receiving the second she suddenly rolled over and sank. Since she was to windward her lower gunports were bound to dip dangerously near the water and her captain knew this, but he needed his heaviest guns against so strong an opponent. There were no survivors. Perhaps a sloshing 'bathtub' effect caused by two great vessels so near each other contributed to her being swamped. Undoubtedly, Hawke's deadly broadsides delayed the crew's response to a flooding emergency. Both of the French ships that sank on this day were substantially manned by Breton fishermen, some villages losing almost their entire male population in a way not seen again until the First World War.

When darkness descended at 5 p.m. on 20 November 1759 Hawke signalled his squadron to break off and anchor. The battle had been fought during a very brief span of daylight, and some historians have speculated that given two more hours Conflans could have rallied his force and nullified the British victory. This idea is absurd. The French admiral's formation had become irretrievably dispersed and he had lost the *Thésée*, *Superbe*, *Formidable* (which surrendered) and *Héros* (74 guns). The last, although she had struck her colours, remained in French hands because a prize crew could not be sent in the tempestuous seas to take possession of her; but she was crippled and ran herself aground on the Four shoal to escape capture. In any case, Conflans's manoeuvres clearly indicated a wish to avoid battle. After turning away from Hawke to

MAP 14 *Quiberon Bay*

the north-east and towards Dumet island, he tacked counter-clockwise, thereby colliding with the ship behind him and one other. His new course was south, and he later stated that it was his intention to exit from the bay. But he had fallen too far to leeward. Overnight his pilots told him that the *Soleil Royal* would be unable to weather the Four shoal, and she anchored.

At daybreak on the 21st the only French ship that Conflans could see near him was the badly damaged *Héros*. During the night some of those with him had departed. Four of five sailed to Rochefort where they were joined by some survivors from the rear division. One joined the five ships of the line and four frigates which had remained with a disabled sixth in the north-eastern sector of Quiberon Bay near the entrance to the Vilaine river. Eight miles away from the flagship, these ships were further away from Conflans than the main body of Hawke's squadron, anchored just upwind of him in the direction of the Cardinals. Conflans saw that he had no chance of escaping; his choice was to go down fighting in the face of firepower massed against him or to run his flagship ashore to prevent her from falling into enemy hands; the *Soleil Royal* was an excellent ship, only ten years old. He chose the latter. Ordering the anchor cable cut he steered for the small, shallow harbour of Croisic and, as expected, she ran aground off the entrance. Hundreds of scarce sailors were thus saved to France. When a British ship approached the great flagship was set afire and reduced to ashes.

Not until the weather moderated on the 23rd could Hawke try to come to grips with the ships anchored near the Vilaine, but, seeing his intention, they threw guns and stores overboard and got into the river out of reach, except for the *Inflexible* (64 guns) which was wrecked on a shoal near the river entrance. All in all, the French lost seven ships of the line: one captured; two sunk during the battle, two burnt (the British burnt the *Héros* where she lay aground not far from the *Soleil Royal*), and two wrecked accidentally; in addition to the *Inflexible* the badly damaged *Juste* was wrecked when she tried to find safety in the Loire estuary and missed the channel. The total number of French sailors who died was about 2,500, half of them (1,240) aboard the *Thésée* and *Superbe*. The fierce storm permitted only 150 of the *Juste*'s 630 men to be rescued. The British lost two ships, both on the submerged Four shoal which neither captain knew was there, but their crews were largely saved. The total British loss of men was about 250. The ships of the line and frigates in the Vilaine were sealed in by British occupation of the bay, and the eight at Rochefort were blockaded by British men-of-war in Basque Roads.

The disaster that befell the French navy at Quiberon Bay had its origin in the decision to embark the troops in the Morbihan. If the Brest squadron's destination had been America it would have undoubtedly reached the open Atlantic before a British fleet at Torbay could catch it. And if the troop transports had sailed with the squadron from Brest, the expedition probably would have gained the open sea west of Ireland and might have succeeded in reaching Scotland. Afterwards, rumour-mongers attributed the separation of the French land and sea forces to professional jealousy and mutual dislike between Conflans and the duc d'Aiguillon, a false explanation that found its way into many historical accounts. The true reason was logistical: the expedition's planners knew that 20,000 troops awaiting embarkation plus 13,000 men of the ships' companies could not be fed at Brest. Even under normal circumstances the naval base depended on food supplies by sea, and the tight, continuous

British blockade that was particularly designed to prevent resupply allowed no room for thoughts about changing the plan.

Yet it was neither wise nor necessary to commit the entire Brest squadron to an enterprise that was likely to invite its interception and possible destruction. Given the Royal Navy's superiority and tenacity, and the strategic disadvantage of having to separate the site for embarking the troops from the Brest squadron, an asymmetrical solution to the problem was in order. Bigot de Morogues's scheme suited the circumstances far better; it made use of deception and limited the naval risk. If it had been adopted and executed, Hawke would have had to decide which squadron to confront. Perhaps if Conflans had not been bypassed in the planning, he might have accepted it and the main fleet would have been employed for diversion; if, on the other hand, he had refused to agree, there would have been legitimate grounds for removing him from command. But he had been bypassed, and as the situation developed Louis XV, it appears, could not bring himself to dismiss so distinguished an admiral. It is puzzling that the duc d'Aiguillon, an intelligent military strategist, did not protest against the decision to allow Conflans his choice. Instead, d'Aiguillon lapsed into a fatalistic mood, placing his hopes in the old marshal's character as a fighting admiral. The only hope of getting the convoy to its destination, he wrote to Belleisle, was to let Conflans do battle. If the battle were lost, at least the troops would not perish. And Conflans might conceivably succeed: for all his faults he was, d'Aiguillon declared, brave and ardent, and had a strong desire to distinguish himself; the officers of his flagship were intelligent and dedicated, and would give good advice; in combat the captains of the fleet, poor as their morale had become, would emulate the admiral's fighting spirit.[21]

By this time all Europe wondered whether Conflans would actually sail. The marquise de Pompadour wrote a note to d'Aiguillon saying that she passionately hoped that he would. After the battle she seems to have supposed – perhaps this was the dominant view at court – that the navy had not really fought: 'I am miserable', she wrote. 'Being defeated is only a misfortune; not fighting is a shame. . . . I am a thousand times more frightened of our humiliation than I would have been by the loss of the whole fleet.'[22]

---

[21] D'Aiguillon to Belleisle, 8 Oct. 1759, Marion, *La Bretagne*, pp. 104–5.

[22] Pompadour to d'Aiguillon, Christine Pevitt Algrant, *Madame de Pompadour: Mistress of France* (New York 2002), p. 255.

Superficially it would appear that 'the whole fleet' was not lost: only a third of the ships were sunk, wrecked or captured. Yet in practical terms the whole fleet was in effect lost, since as a consequence of the battle the remaining two-thirds were either tightly blockaded in the Vilaine River or bottled up in Rochefort by a British naval watch. The Brest fleet ceased to be a factor for the rest of the war. Quiberon Bay was truly a decisive battle.

In considering the causes of Hawke's tactical success and pondering the role of luck, one key point should not be forgotten. Although a shift of wind direction denied Conflans the anchorage he sought, the main reason why he could not find safety was that Hawke went after him without hesitation. If Conflans hoped that Hawke would not do this, he was dealing with precisely the wrong admiral. While it is true that the officers and seamen of the British fleet after so many arduous months at sea were hungry for their reward, Hawke's own credo was a critical factor. He had firmly believed for a long time – and this had repeatedly guided his actions in the past – that no opportunity for annihilating a French warship or squadron should ever be missed.

France defeated: the war lost

Word of Guadeloupe's capture had reached London in mid-June; Quebec in mid-October. 'Our bells are worn threadbare with ringing for victories', wrote Horace Walpole on the news of Quebec.[23] But the list of victories in 1759 was not yet complete. News of Quiberon Bay reached London at the end of November. Hawke was upset that so many French ships had eluded his grasp, but the British public was elated, not least because his victory ended the invasion threat. It was Quiberon Bay, not Quebec, that caused stocks to surge upwards on the London exchange.

These major successes were achieved by, or directly dependent upon, British sea power, but there was also a significant victory on the continent in 1759. The goal of the 100,000-man army that Choiseul and Belleisle kept in Germany was to occupy George II's German Dominions; helping Austria against Prussia was no longer an obligation. In June a large force under Contades began marching eastwards from the lower Rhine while another army, under the duc de Broglie, marched from the south through Hesse to join him. In late July they occupied the pivotal town of Minden.

[23] To George Montagu, 21 Oct. 1759, Lewis, ed. *Walpole Correspondence*, 9 (1941), p. 251.

Ferdinand of Brunswick realized that he would soon be seriously over-matched notwithstanding the 9,000 British troops now with him. Correctly assuming that Contades and Broglie would seek a victory – their combined forces in the field outnumbered his, 51,000 to 41,000 – Ferdinand positioned his troops during the night of 31 July to enable them to attack first. At the battle of Minden on 1 August 1759 the British fighting forces in Germany experienced their first major test. Marching forward boldly – a bit too boldly – the British infantry, with Hanoverians and Hessians adjacent, withstood three French cavalry assaults without breaking. The excellence of the British artillery units was also demonstrated.

Their performance stood in marked contrast to that of the cavalry under Lord George Sackville, senior commander of the British forces in Germany. At the height of the battle Ferdinand sent three messengers by different routes to Sackville with orders to advance to the left in order to support the infantry. Sackville had reason to believe that his cavalry would be ordered to move forward, not to his left where there was a wooded area. He had not assigned someone to reconnoitre the situation on the other side, nor did he know how the battle was developing. Because one messenger said the entire cavalry force (about 3,000, mostly British but some Hanoverian) was to advance and another messenger mentioned only the British cavalry, Sackville declared the orders to be inconsistent and confusing. A messenger persisted and urged him to advance to the left immediately, but Sackville had convinced himself that the proper move was forward and wasted precious minutes doing nothing. After this delay he passed the cavalry between the trees, but on the heath beyond he took time to dress his line with exactitude, exhibiting none of the sense of urgency felt by John Manners, Marquess of Granby, second-in-command. Shortly before this, the brave men of the infantry, assisted by alert field artillerymen, received three cavalry assaults without breaking. They then counter-attacked and routed the French infantry. The cavalry that might have pursued the French to destruction was not at hand. Afterwards, the Hanoverians and six regiments of British infantry celebrated (the battle of Minden continues to be honoured in their regimental traditions) while the cavalrymen bowed their heads in shame.

If the British cavalry had promptly pursued, the French army might have suffered a complete disaster. Even so, it retreated far to the south and evacuated Hesse. Finally, the French commissariat, now reformed, managed to assemble enough food and fodder to enable it to remain east of the Rhine. In the battle Ferdinand's army suffered about 2,700 killed or wounded, of which half were British infantrymen, while Contades and

Broglie lost over 10,000. Minden was a serious setback for the French army, and the consequences would have been worse if Broglie had not expertly rallied the retreating forces.

The French plan to occupy Hanover in 1759 was thereby thwarted, but it could be revived a year later. The naval situation, however, was a different matter. As a result of the battles at Lagos Bay and Quiberon Bay twelve ships of the line and a portion of the dwindling population of seamen were permanently lost. The Toulon squadron did not trouble the British navy again in this war. Moreover, the victory at Quiberon Bay enabled the British to impose a close blockade on Lorient and Rochefort. This was done with relatively little effort. As Hawke remarked in a letter to the Admiralty, 'Lying at anchor here [Quiberon Bay] and in Basque road, with frigates cruizing, will distress the enemy more effectually than keeping the sea, and at the same time be a great saving to the government in wear and tear of ships and their furniture.'[24] In other words, a steadily cruising Western Squadron was no longer needed. Admiral Boscawen, who relieved Hawke, continued this arrangement, and the French Atlantic coast was closely watched in winter and spring, something never done before.

The situation was one that Versailles did not wish to admit. Berryer, apparently under pressure from Louis XV, ordered the captains of the ships in the Vilaine River to sail to Brest, as if the British squadron anchored in Quiberon Bay and ready to pounce did not exist. On receiving this order the senior captain, Villars de la Brosse, held a meeting and all the captains agreed on the impossibility of carrying it out. Berryer viewed this response as an act of insubordination. Before long the senior captain was incarcerated in the chateau de Sammur, where he remained for almost two years.[25] Eventually, the ships in the Vilaine escaped, two by two, after waiting many months for the perfect combination of wind, tide and darkness; the last pair did not get safely out until November 1761.

The one French seaborne expedition of 1759 that succeeded in executing its mission was that of Captain François Thurot, a bold, successful corsair, 32 years old. He was authorized by Marshal Belleisle to take five frigates and a thousand troops under a brigadier to northern Ireland as a diversion. They sailed from Dunkirk on 15 October when a storm drove Commodore William Boys from his station. Winds pushed them to Sweden where Thurot replenished food and water. He then went

---

[24] Hawke to Admiralty, Quiberon Bay, 9 Dec. 1759, quoted in Marcus, *Quiberon Bay*, p. 166; see also Mackay, ed. *Hawke Papers*, p. 359.
[25] Le Moing, *Bataille navale*, pp. 93–5.

north about Scotland, captured livestock for fresh meat in the Hebrides, and eventually, on 21 February 1760, landed the troops at Carrickfergus in northern Ireland. After resisting two assaults the local defenders surrendered the dilapidated castle, whereupon Thurot marched to Belfast. Whether he might have forced the townspeople to surrender cannot be known because he offered to depart if they would supply provisions to his troops and sailors, and they agreed. Although the Admiralty ordered cruisers to the area, messages sent overland to Cork and Kinsale reached the frigate captains stationed there first. By the 28th three fast frigates under Commodore John Eliot intercepted Thurot's three frigates (all that remained with him) near the Isle of Man. Two frigates fled while Thurot fought on against overwhelming force and was killed. In the end all three French warships were captured.

Under the tightening British blockade could France still consider sending naval squadrons, troop reinforcements and supplies to her overseas colonies? The ships at Rochefort dared not move: upon indications of their being fitted out, the small British force watching in Basque Roads could be quickly strengthened by ships summoned from Quiberon Bay. Brest was different; a squadron could still escape on a strong easterly wind.

Nevertheless, there was very little chance of conveying supplies to Canada. The British presence at Quebec made a huge difference. Conceivably, in the early spring a French frigate or two might enter the St Lawrence River before the Royal Navy reappeared. (Except for two small cruisers the British fleet withdrew from the basin of Quebec to avoid damage by winter ice.) Yet Canada appeared to be doomed in any case. Large British forces were expected to push northwards from the New York frontier. In addition, the force at Quebec was poised to advance to Montreal by the efficient river route.

Berryer thought something might be done to defend the French West Indies. To the council of state in March 1760 he proposed sending a dozen ships of the line to Martinique and asked for money to prepare the expedition. Although he was counting on the ability of a squadron from Brest to escape the blockade, he was, nevertheless, not confident of success. The French navy, he informed his ministerial colleagues, was at a great disadvantage because, unlike the British, it was not in commission all year round; without that, he said:

all plans and expeditions are liable to fail. The reason is obvious; for when the French navy wants to make an expedition it is forced to let the world know it four or five months in advance; the English soon hear

of it, and are in a condition to prevent it by blockading the ports, and
in fact to frustrate any measures that may be taken.[26]

By 'frustrate any measures' he meant that, given the British navy's overwhelming superiority, any French squadron managing to escape to the
West Indies would be followed by a stronger opposing squadron. The
council of state acknowledged that permanent loss of Martinique would
be devastating to France and greatly beneficial to Britain, but Berryer's
proposal was turned down; the councillors said that there was not enough
money to pay for it. Lack of funds also prevented an augmentation of
naval and financial assistance to French forces in India.

Fundamentally, the monarchy's financial problems stemmed from the
enormous gap between revenue and wartime spending. The man charged
with assessing the situation and proposing solutions in 1759 was Étienne
de Silhouette, the new controller-general of finances who took office on
4 March. Today he would be classified as an academic. He had spent
a year in London studying the British system of finance, but, though 49,
had minimal political experience. He set about studying the situation in
depth, attempting to ascertain how bad it was and what might be done.
He realized that long-term loans and increased taxation were both necessary, but his first steps were to limit some pension payments and raise
money by selling shares in the united tax farms. He did try to issue some
long-term annuities despite the fact that a planned issue in the amount
of 60 million livres had brought in only 2 million the year before – a
public-offering disaster. Yet without a credible tax revenue for covering
the interest payments no one would subscribe to long-term loans, as
Silhouette quickly found out. After months of enquiry he presented a comprehensive report to the council of state, on 20 September. Looking ahead
to the year 1760 its calculations showed that the Crown could be sure of
collecting a revenue of only 140 million livres to cover a predicted total
expense of 357 million. Additional revenue was clearly necessary. Silhouette
judged that taxes could not be easily collected in rural areas, and his
proposed new levies were aimed chiefly at wealthy city-dwellers, notably
Parisians. The king and council of state approved the plan, but approval
was quickly withdrawn. Silhouette was, in effect, asking the state's most
powerful elites to take on most of the new tax burden, and the scheme was
blocked. He became instantly unpopular at court.

[26] Berryer's memorandum, quoted in Pares, 'American versus Continental Warfare
1739–63', 156–7.

Meanwhile, although the government was pressuring privileged groups and office-holders to make additional grants and loans, it was unable to cope with a frightening accumulation of contractors' bills and letters of exchange, payment on which was long overdue. Also overdue were cash payments on paper issues of revenue departments and financiers, the dates of maturity having been repeatedly passed over. By the time Silhouette assumed office all revenue for 1759 and part of 1760's had been spent, and there was nothing to cover approximately 200 million livres due on this paper.[27]

At the same time the problem was aggravated by a severe shortage of metallic money. Cash, usually in the form of silver coins, was always essential in time of war. Troops had to be paid in coin. Food and fodder locally purchased by the army also had to be paid for in hard money or at least with bills that the suppliers could count on cashing at low discount. The total expense could be reduced if the troops were encamped on an opponent's territory because threats and compulsion could be used to hold prices down; also, tribute (which was often justified as a cost of protection against marauding) could be collected. French generals were therefore expected to winter their troops, if possible, in Hanover, Hesse and Halberstadt. Even when this was possible, the French army in Germany had to be supported by money from home. In addition, subsidies to allies and payments for mercenary soldiers required money from France. Inevitably, coin drained out of the kingdom. Here was a case where the traditional mercantilist, or bullionist, concern to conserve a kingdom's precious metals was highly relevant, because an outflow of coin tended to reduce domestic currency circulation thus depressing economic activity. Austria did not experience this problem in the same degree. Its military operations occurred mainly within the Habsburg dominions, so the cash spent by its armies stayed largely within the empress's taxing and borrowing orbit.

The outflow of coin and bullion from France would not have been a serious problem if it had been compensated by an inflow generated by foreign trade. Before 1756 French overseas commerce had been a prodigious earner of hard-money surpluses, but by 1758, thanks largely to British sea power, this commerce was extinguished. For decades the treasurers of the navy and their agents had depended on the merchant wealth of ports near the dockyards for cash and credit. The practice became embedded in the latter days of Louis XIV's reign when the regional naval

---

[27] Félix, *Finances et politique*, p. 56.

treasurers had been encouraged by the monarchy – required really – to commit their personal wealth when necessity arose. The Seven Years War witnessed a very different situation. Large amounts of cash had been sent to Canada, while the stifling of seaborne trade meant that the port cities could no longer provide much cash and reliable credit for meeting naval needs and paying colonial bills of exchange. Wages owed to dockyard workers and seamen also went unpaid. To meet urgent needs Beaujon, Goossens and Company, a partnership half commercial, half governmental, was organized in 1758. This firm, interlinked with port merchants, drew money from Holland, some of it originating in Britain. It handled more than a third of naval spending in 1759.

As for the French army in Germany, cash and exchange credits for supporting it were obtained first from Amsterdam, then from Cologne. All was managed by Pâris de Monmartel (brother of Pâris Duverney who was in charge of army provisioning). When opponents' territory came to be occupied, sums collected as tribute were sent to a banking firm at Cologne and drawn upon by Monmartel. But when the army was compelled to retreat to the Rhine, tribute payments nearly ceased. The disaster that befell the French army in Germany in early 1758 was monetary as well as military.

In August 1758 Bernis remarked: 'No more commerce, consequently no more money, no more circulation. No navy, consequently no resources to resist England. The navy no longer has seamen, and its lack of money removes any hope of procuring them.' In September he observed, 'Circulation is totally cut off; silver no longer comes in from abroad and a great deal goes out. All proposals for paper [money] would lead to revolts in Paris.'[28] Although reliable figures do not exist, it is likely that the quantity of coin and bullion in France diminished somewhat during these financially desperate years of the war; to be sure, the great bulk remained within the realm, but it was generally unavailable for the government's purposes. Deposit banking existed only in Britain and the Dutch Republic at this time. Therefore, what counted in France was not so much the quantity of coin but the portion, usually created by commerce, which readily circulated; this, in turn, might support bills acceptable as cash. The situation may be contrasted to the British case. As noted earlier, the Duke of Newcastle was appalled when he realized the immense amount of public borrowing that would be required to support Pitt's

[28] Bernis to Stainville, 20 Aug., 4 Sept. 1758, Masson, ed. *Mémoires et Lettres de . . . Bernis*, II, 258–9, 266.

ambitious war plans for 1758, but he admitted that there was 'plenty of money' in London and 'a great inclination to lend it'.[29] The situation in France was the opposite. In his report to the king, Silhouette observed that outstanding bills were far too numerous in relation to metallic cash, and the parlement of Paris in its remonstrances declared that the main problem was the shortage of specie.[30]

This shortage combined with the reluctance of Frenchmen to lend to the government left only one recourse: external borrowing. The French monarchy was accustomed to making use of foreign money markets in wartime, often through the mediation of a well-connected banker. In 1758 the key man was Monmartel, 'his credit . . . being especially in Holland superior to that of the french Government'.[31] In August of that year Bernis remarked, 'It is inconceivable that the realm depends on one man alone.'[32] Yet continuance of the war thus seemed to be in Monmartel's hands, and he was growing weary and worried, fearful that his own fortune would be wiped out by the monarchy's dangerously overextended finances. He agreed to allow Jean-Joseph de Laborde, a Bayonne merchant, to replace him as court banker in April 1759. It may be noted that the monarchy's three prominent financiers at this point all had strong links to foreign sources: Laborde with Spain and Portugal; Goossens with Holland; Monmartel with all Europe.

Delayed payment of naval and colonial bills led providers of goods and services to compensate for the higher discount rate by raising their prices, which the ministers viewed as a form of fraud. Fearful rumours circulated that some colonial bills might not be honoured. When the monetary crisis struck it was not surprising that colonial credit was the first branch to collapse. The triggering event was Montcalm's lost battle on the Plains of Abraham, news of which reached Paris on 15 October. The effect was cataclysmic. No one would buy Canadian bills of exchange, and refusals quickly spread to all naval and colonial bills. Government paper in general was soon affected, as everyone demanded cash. On 26 October the government was compelled to suspend payments even on notes issued by the great revenue gathering institutions of the realm. Responding to

---

[29] See above, Chapter 9 opening.

[30] Félix, *Finances et politique*, p. 57, and a private communication from Prof. Félix.

[31] Information from a convicted Jacobite spy, July 1758, quoted in Price, *France and the Chesapeake*, p. 581.

[32] Bernis to Stainville, 11 Aug. 1758, Masson, ed. *Mémoires et Lettres de . . . Bernis*, II, 257.

the emergency, Louis XV ordered royal plate to be sent to the mint to be melted for silver coinage; some courtiers followed his example. The new coins were put to emergency uses but much more was needed, for this was a massive credit crisis. Choiseul begged Madrid to lend bullion and coin, but was refused.

Lacking means to cope with this 'violent crisis in French finances' – Berryer's description – the government turned to a policy of selective repudiation. Edicts were published announcing that bills drawn for the defence of Canada were to be set aside and reviewed for later payment. The market took this to mean never. The government adopted a policy of devoting all available cash to current and future expenses. In the wake of these proceedings Beaujon, Goossens and Company closed its doors on 14 November. Its bankruptcy happened to wipe out George Fitzgerald, a London tobacco merchant connected with the Royal Bank of Scotland, who was informed that because of the French king's recent edicts the company could 'neither accept or pay his Bills'. Indirectly he had been lending money to the French government.[33] Countless French suppliers to the navy were also bankrupted, the bills in their hands becoming for the foreseeable future worthless. French annuities tumbled on the Amsterdam exchange. Everywhere in France payments were either stopped or expected to be stopped. 'All this came like a clap of thunder; a general distrust ensued', wrote a merchant of St Malo to his partner at Cadiz. 'Everything is forbidden, credit stifled, Paris in a general consternation, the provinces too. Everyone is in a state of the most intense anxiety.'[34] Silhouette was dismissed. His hobby of making paper shadow portraits gave a handle for derision and his name entered the language.

At the end of October a British spy at Versailles, observing the 'surprise and sorrow' caused by the edicts, reported: 'I may truly say, we are in a violent crisis.' He concluded by remarking:

In the present situation of affairs, you may guess how the loss of Quebec has affected this court and nation. Never were ministers more surprised . . . they expected the news of the siege being raised. The general cry is Peace, as the only way there will be to avoid the common ruin we are threatened with by the continuance of such an unsuccessful war.[35]

---

[33] Price, *France and the Chesapeake*, pp. 583–4.
[34] Magon de la Balue, 5 Nov. 1759, Bosher, *Business and Religion*, p. 368.
[35] Intelligence from France, 29 Oct. 1759, BL Add. 32,897, ff. 465–7.

Many Frenchmen had feared for months that the government was on the brink of bankruptcy, and now it had arrived.

Many histories of the war have ignored this financial crisis. It is true that the monarchy kept the war going by exercising its absolute powers. It resorted to repudiations and forced loans, and made promises that would not be kept; and in due course it would obtain new taxes. But France's Seven Years War was never the same afterwards. The effort to achieve a military occupation of Hanover could be renewed, but success in Germany could not be supposed to balance French colonial losses, for those losses were bound to multiply since Versailles now gave up hope of reviving the navy. Proof of this is found in a budget decision. The allocation for the navy and colonies which had reached 77 million livres in 1759, its highest level of the war (though 27 million went toward building flat-bottomed boats and *prames*), was cut to 23 million in 1760, and much of this went to pay for naval expenses of the previous year.

Canada – what remained under French control – was left to save herself. The West Indian islands were also expected to defend themselves, and unflinching dedication was demanded. Berryer was incensed when he learned of Guadeloupe's surrender. His method of encouraging a spirit of resistance in future was to threaten the governors with severe punishment if they capitulated. In keeping with this approach Governor Nadau du Treil – after a court-martial that was hardly even-handed – was sent to prison for twenty years for yielding Guadeloupe. Nevertheless, Berryer was more inclined than others at Versailles to try to dispatch support to the islands. As we have seen, he wished to send a naval force to Martinique despite the hazards, but lack of funds caused the proposal to be rejected. Because France by the end of 1759 lacked enough money and seamen to enable her to assist the defence of her overseas possessions, and because even the conquest of Hanover could not be enough to compensate for increasing colonial losses, she had lost the war. The only question was, by how much, and the choices were to seek peace to prevent further losses or to keep the war going in hopes of attaining better terms by some new initiative, or some miracle.

CHAPTER 13

Britain conquers afar, disunity looms at home

Under a system of representative government public support for sustaining a war has often begun to erode in the third or fourth year of hostilities regardless of whether the war was being won or lost. At the end of 1759 Britain was definitely winning, and since people in general preferred peace they tended to agree with the Duke of Newcastle that it was time to begin negotiations. Yet there were strong arguments for keeping the war going. Because the French navy had been crushed and confined the prospects of further reducing French trade and seizing French colonies were excellent. Moreover, the nation's economy was in a remarkably prosperous condition, and while British foreign and domestic trade thrived, French foreign trade was practically annihilated. On the other side of the ledger was the rising expense. Supplies voted by Parliament had increased from £8.5 million in 1757 to £10.5 in 1758, £12.8 in 1759, and would be estimated at £15.5 million for 1760. Sums above the annual revenue of £8.5 million had to be borrowed.[1] Although there was little sign of serious financial difficulty (the reasons for this are considered in the concluding chapter), people worried about the national debt. This was a principal reason why the British public, on balance, favoured peace.

There was, however, another reason: the war in Germany. The level of spending required to support Prince Ferdinand's army was rising steeply. As for the Prussian alliance, it was now reckoned a liability. Frederick II's earlier military successes had led the British public to embrace him as 'the Protestant hero', but those days were gone. Frederick, fearing in June 1759 that he would be scarcely able to cope with the armies of Austria

---

[1] Williams, *Life*, II, 48.

and Russia, expressed to London a hope that Britain could arrange a peace. Pitt did not ignore his plight. As will be seen, he joined in issuing, in late November, an Anglo-Prussian Declaration proposing a general peace congress. The declaration was a genuine initiative, and for reasons deserving close examination – some of them relating to looming political disunity in the cabinet – Pitt would not have been displeased to see negotiating progress made towards a signing of peace preliminaries upon the close of the 1760 campaigning season. Everyone realized that he wished to complete the conquests in south India and Canada before agreeing to make peace.

Pitt was probably willing to welcome a peace negotiation during 1760, but the duc de Choiseul was not. Among France's leading ministers only Bertin, the new controller-general of finances, was openly willing to advocate winding down or ending the war. As for popular opinion, Choiseul did all he could to deny it any influence. In October 1759 when the king of Spain, who wished to see the war end quickly, suggested that the peacemaking process should be accompanied by a cessation of arms, Choiseul took alarm. 'You know the bent of this nation', he told his ambassador, 'she desires peace, and as soon as she were to see hostilities suspended, her hasty disposition would lead her to regard reconciliation as assured; the zeal which still remains to come to the aid of the state would be entirely chilled.' The result, he added, would be a humiliated and defeated France.[2] The parlements indicated a desire for peace, but the king rebuffed them. Choiseul seemed to change his mind after the stunning defeat at Quiberon Bay and the financial crisis. He told his ambassador at Madrid that peace was essential, citing the French 'nation's disgust [with the war] and the realm's real needs'.[3] Perhaps he really favoured peace, but he was not allowed to pursue it, probably because Pompadour and Marshal Belleisle thought the war should continue.

Choiseul's approach to peace, 1759–60

In the final months of his life Ferdinand VI of Spain was in the grip of extreme senility. Nothing of importance could be decided because he refused to speak with his ministers. The conduct of everyday affairs was in the hands of Ricardo Wall, who favoured neutrality and good relations with Britain. When Ferdinand died on 10 August 1759 the throne of

[2] Choiseul to d'Ossun, 19 Oct. 1759, Soulange-Bodin, *Diplomatie*, pp. 115–16.
[3] Choiseul to d'Ossun, 10 March 1760, ibid. p. 129.

Spain was inherited by his younger half-brother, who became Carlos III. He had ruled the kingdom of the Two Sicilies for 24 years. The French envoy at Naples, Pierre-Paul, marquis d'Ossun, had been a close confidant of Carlos's for over 5 years during which he nourished the anti-British attitude that he had long held. Upon learning of Ferdinand's death Carlos wrote from Naples, probably at d'Ossun's urging, to his minister for the Two Sicilies in London to offer his services as king of Spain as a mediator to end the Anglo-French war. At this time the duc de Choiseul was busily searching for intermediaries: he had approached Denmark and even Russia, and now learned that the king of Spain was willing. In a memoir drafted by Choiseul and delivered at Naples on 21 September 1759 the government of France readily accepted the king of Spain's offer. Thus began the brief history of Spanish mediation.

Under the influence of the duc de Choiseul, Spanish mediation was a peace initiative of a certain kind. Choiseul urged Carlos III to take a strong stance against Britain. The transatlantic situation, he said, had become seriously out of balance owing to French losses. Spain's imperial territories and trade were now at risk, he argued, unless British conquests in America were nullified. He recommended strong medicine. First, he wanted a reversion to the pre-war status quo: 'the equilibrium of possessions in America established by the treaty of Utrecht should not at all be altered'.[4] Secondly, Carlos should conduct an *armed* mediation so that if a belligerent party refused to subscribe to his proposals as mediator, he should declare war against that party. Carlos genuinely wanted to bring peace and in replying suggested to d'Ossun that Britain and France might first agree to an immediate cessation of arms, a proposal to which, as noted above, Choiseul reacted vehemently. Carlos dropped the idea, agreeing that there would be no cessation of arms and that his offer of mediation would be accompanied by a veiled threat of armed intervention. The British would have to make peace, he remarked to d'Ossun, 'or else they would compel me, however much against my wishes, to make war'.[5] In short, he acquiesced completely. Clearly, the duc de Choiseul's idea of mediation was to have Spain threaten war unless the British agreed to roll back their conquests in America.

When Carlos III's offer of mediation was delivered to Pitt he was cautious. He wanted Spain to remain neutral and did not wish to be discourteous. Realizing the delicacy of the situation, he decided to consult

[4] Waddington, *Guerre*, III, 433–4.
[5] D'Ossun to Choiseul, 7 Dec. 1759, quoted by Rashed, *Peace of Paris*, p. 38.

Hardwicke, who commented that 'Spain would be jealous of our retaining very considerable acquisitions in America' and that therefore its monarch was unlikely to be an impartial mediator. He was disposed, like Pitt, to resist the offer.[6] Pitt noticed in Carlos's offer of mediation a clause mentioning that the Spanish king 'could not regard with indifference' the impact of British conquests on 'the balance of power in America, as established by the peace of Utrecht'. The offer was delivered in London five days after news came of the French debacle at Quiberon Bay. It required a formal response, so Pitt convened a cabinet meeting. His draft of a reply was courteous, but mentioned that there was nothing in the treaty of Utrecht that established the principle of a balance of power in America. The reply also included a warning that the British nation was prepared to use military and naval conquests to prevent France from molesting British possessions in the future. Pitt did not reject the mediation out of hand but announced that he had an alternative plan: a general congress of all belligerents with a view towards peace. This response to Spain was 'highly approved' by the cabinet.[7]

Since June British ministers had been discussing the idea of a general congress. It had been suggested by Frederick II who saw Austrian and Russian military pressure building against him. After a blood-soaked loss to the Russians at Kunersdorf in mid-August, the result of which deprived Prussia of the resources of Saxony, Frederick's future looked very bleak. Pitt understood the seriousness of Prussia's situation and talked over the need for peace with the Prussian envoys in London. The result was an Anglo-Prussian Declaration proposing a general congress. It was issued at The Hague on 25 November 1759. Hardwicke was glad that it was announced before the 'covertly menacing' Spanish offer of mediation came to hand.[8] Although he was personally not eager for further conquests in America and much against keeping them all, his objections to Spanish mediation were firm.

The Anglo-Prussian Declaration was warmly welcomed in Europe, even by the French ambassador at The Hague, the comte d'Affry, who, according to Joseph Yorke, 'could not conceal his contentment'.[9] According to

[6] Hardwicke to Newcastle, 24 Oct. 1759, Yorke, Hardwicke, III, 241; also BL Add. 32,897, fo. 351.
[7] Rashed, Peace of Paris, p. 47; Thackeray, History, I, 461-3; TNA SP (F) 94/160, 13 Dec. 1759; Devonshire Diary, p. 33.
[8] Hardwicke to Newcastle, 5 Dec. 1759, BL Add. 32,899, fo. 301.
[9] Yorke to Newcastle, 29 Nov. 1759, BL Add. 32,899, fo. 171.

Newcastle's informant, it enjoyed the same happy reception at the French court: 'As what is now offered in the Declaration coincides with what the King, the Council, the Court, and the Nation in general desire, His Majesty will be very ready to concur in naming Plenipotentiaries to treat of Peace in concert with his allies.'[10] But it was not to be. The duc de Choiseul had been taken by surprise by the declaration and viewed it coldly. His response stated that a general congress was inappropriate because France's war with Britain was a particular one, distinct from the contest in Germany; an Anglo-French peace must therefore be negotiated separately.

Lord Hardwicke could not understand the reasoning. 'I really don't know what France means by the Separate Peace they talk of. Don't they mean that we should make up with them separately from the King of Prussia and the Landgrave of Hesse? I think they do, and they will support themselves in that posture by saying that they have no war declared against either of those Princes.' But, he continued, 'the King [George] can never treat separately from his Allies', and because the ministers at Versailles must be aware of this fact, what did they have in mind? He jotted down possibilities but concluded: 'In short, the Thing appears to me very dark.'[11] Three days later at the start of the new year he was somewhat better informed but still puzzled and wary. France, he supposed, would soon realize that Britain would insist on inclusion of the German war in any bilateral negotiation, and in order to end her maritime war with Britain, which she clearly wished to do, France might offer to abandon her efforts on the continent. In that case she would naturally expect a reciprocal engagement from Britain, which would require not only withdrawing troops from Prince Ferdinand's army and terminating British financial support of that army, but also cancelling the Prussian subsidy. Both steps would be popular in England, but strategically hazardous. Such an engagement, as Hardwicke bluntly put it to Newcastle, would be one that 'we should keep on our part, and they would not on theirs'. He continued:

Your Grace admits that there is great weight in Mr. Pitt's reasoning on this Subject; which I think is unanswerable. By delivering France from our Maritime War, we shall deliver them from their greatest Burden and Difficulties. If we should enter into mutual Engagements with France

[10]   Versailles intelligence, 8 Dec. 1759, BL Add. 32,899, fo. 374.
[11]   Hardwicke to Newcastle, 30 Dec. 1759, BL Add. 32,900, fo. 424.

not to intermeddle in the War in Germany, France would certainly still do it collusively, but you would not be able to come to Parliament for any Supplies for that purpose. There would be a plain treaty before them in contradiction to it.

He concluded that a bilateral agreement would entail great danger and that the general congress was best.

If the congress were to go forward, a related matter might come up. Commonly when there was agreement to convene such a congress calls for a cessation of arms soon followed. Would France ask for a cessation? Hardwicke thought not, but if she did Britain was in a position to allow it, considering 'Quebec is taken, Mon. Conflans Fleet beat, and the Remains of it skulking in their Ports'. He granted that Austria and France could use the time to recover strength, but so could Prussia.[12]

Arrangements for the general congress were blocked by Choiseul and the Austrians. The first thing the French minister did upon reading the Anglo-Prussian Declaration was to confer with Starhemberg. They both viewed it as a trap. In Vienna, Kaunitz reluctantly judged that the proposal could not be honourably refused and that Austria must pledge to send plenipotentiaries, but he insisted that there should be no suspension of arms: he calculated that deliberations would be prolonged and thus give Austria and Russia time to crush Prussia militarily. Choiseul had no qualms about spurning the proposed congress. France, Austria and Russia, he said, should issue a counter-declaration. This would cause a delay, which Kaunitz welcomed.

An opportunity arose at The Hague for separate informal talks between Britain and France. Clandestine meetings between Joseph Yorke and d'Affry began in December 1759. Initially, Choiseul informed d'Affry that the concerns of Hanover and the contest in north-western Germany could not be included, but eventually he withdrew this restriction. The question of including Prussia remained, however, and on this matter the French foreign minister was firm. As France was not formally at war with Prussia, he told d'Affry, she could not allow Prussian representatives at the table. The British tried to soften the issue. In early April 1760 Yorke told d'Affry that a formal statement was not necessary if France would grant the point that Prussian concerns were to be discussed. Choiseul replied by telling d'Affry that he was not even to mention Prussia.

---

[12] Hardwicke to Newcastle, 3 Jan. 1760, BL Add. 32,901, ff. 47–9.

Joseph Yorke was aware, thanks to his many sources, that hopes for peace at Versailles were high. He reported that 'the whole Opposition of France [to allowing an early peace] . . . is confined to the Duc de Choiseul . . . he is almost single in his opinion'.[13] But Choiseul had the support of the two people who mattered most, the king and Pompadour, and by May it was obvious to all that there would be no progress at The Hague.

By this time Frederick II had become so worried about probable defeat in the coming campaign that he decided to allow the British to negotiate on his behalf. Versailles received no such authorization from the Austrians. In fact, Kaunitz had exhibited so much anxiety about the separate Anglo-French negotiation that Choiseul sent him copies of all correspondence and memoranda relating to it. He even forwarded to Vienna the preliminary articles which he had drawn up to guide the king of Spain's mediation. Reading these articles, the Austrian minister noticed a suggestion that Britain and France, once at peace, could unite to force terms of a European settlement on their respective allies. Kaunitz erupted. He demanded that the article be rescinded and declared that if France made peace with Britain, she should not force her allies to make peace but on the contrary do everything possible to put them 'in a condition to be able to sustain and push the [continental] war with the greatest vigour'. Choiseul acquiesced immediately, and told Vienna that he hoped that France would be able to increase the level of her subsidy to Austria after making peace with England.[14] This secret promise, unknown to the British, was precisely what Hardwicke and Pitt had feared.

It had taken time for Carlos III to move from Naples to Madrid, where, after talking with Spanish advisers and reading London's courteous but questioning reply to his offer of mediation, he decided to abandon the mission. As Ricardo Wall told d'Ossun, insisting on it would not only prove fruitless but also invite bad relations with Britain and possibly war, and Spain was far from being ready for war.

One reason mediation was likely to prove fruitless was the content of the preliminary articles which Choiseul had dispatched to Madrid on 6 January. The document's details revealed how little the French minister was prepared to concede. Concerning North America, France would now

---

[13] Yorke to Newcastle, 1 April 1760, BL Add. 32,904 fo. 139. Newcastle's intelligence from Versailles dated 4 April 1760 confirmed this: 'the Joy that reigns throughout the Kingdom on the Hopes of an approaching Peace' (fo. 202).

[14] Kaunitz's memoir addressed to Choiseul, 30 Jan. 1760, and Choiseul's response of 15 Feb., Waddington, *Guerre*, III, 506–7.

accept the terms sent from London on 8 March 1755 that she had at that time refused; the vast Ohio territory was to become a demilitarized neutral zone and free passage on the lakes for both sides would be allowed. France would also give Minorca back to Britain. Otherwise, the articles envisioned a sweeping nullification of nearly all of Britain's wartime gains throughout the world. Britain would be required to return Cape Breton (though Louisbourg's fortifications could be demolished), the island of St Jean, and all territory that the British had conquered in Canada. Furthermore, Guadeloupe, Senegal and Gorée were all to be given back, and in India there was to be a reversion to the preliminary treaty terms of December 1754 that Godeheu had signed. The king of Spain would be permitted as mediator to adjust the North American terms.[15] But because France was no longer a naval power and showed little prospect of becoming one again, Carlos III and his ministers realized that the burden of limiting French losses in North America would fall entirely on Spain. Carlos immediately ordered forty ships of the line to be fitted for sea, but his advisers made him aware that the task of restoring Spain's navy, army and finances would be difficult and time-consuming, and in any case those ships must face the entire might of the British Atlantic and Mediterranean fleets.

Despite Carlos III's decision Choiseul kept up the pretence that Spanish mediation was going forward. From the beginning he had cited it as one reason why France could not participate in the general congress proposed by Britain and Prussia. Consistent with this argument, he included in the French, Austrian and Russian counter-declaration a statement that France had gladly accepted the Spanish king's mediation. He worded it in a way that implied the king of Spain's agreement to undertake it, and when Ricardo Wall read the document he protested. The king, he pointed out to d'Ossun, was not committed to serve as a mediator and the passage would therefore have to be eliminated. The alarmed French ambassador promptly informed Versailles, whereupon Choiseul insisted that Spanish mediation must continue to appear in the counter-declaration. Although d'Ossun got permission to allow it, the achievement was hollow because (as Wall told him) Madrid was determined to inform London that no attention should be paid to that clause. Spanish mediation therefore became no more than a diplomatic false front, a fact that Choiseul tacitly

---

[15] The articles concerning North America are printed in Pease, *Boundary Disputes*, pp. 267–74. For the other articles see Choiseul's letter of 27 Jan. 1760 in the Choiseul–Bernstorff *Correspondence*, pp. 119–24, and Dull, *French Navy*, pp. 164–5.

admitted when he allowed d'Affry on 31 March to let Joseph Yorke know privately that, notwithstanding what might be stated regarding mediation, France would not reject another way of treating for peace between France and England.[16]

From the outset Maria Theresa considered Choiseul's approach to peace useless. She told France's ambassador at Vienna straightaway that in her opinion the British would neither abandon the king of Prussia nor accept Spain's mediation.[17] When d'Affry informed Yorke that Spain's mediation was to be armed, Yorke could hardly believe his ears, commenting that he was sure that 'neither M. Pitt nor any English ministers would wish to have the appearance of giving in to the fear' of an intervention of that kind.[18] Choiseul believed, it must be supposed, that the British would be so anxious to avoid antagonizing Spain that they would accept mediation, and it was true that the British were very anxious to keep Spain neutral, but Joseph Yorke was not wrong.

When Choiseul learned in early February that the Spanish government had chosen to reject the path of mediation he wrote a long letter to d'Ossun. It was filled with gloomy predictions: Pitt has plans 'to conquer this year all French colonies in America . . . [except] Saint-Domingue. After conquering all of Canada, which will be quite easy . . . England will take Louisiana . . . She is working on an armament aimed directly at Martinique: lack of money prevents . . . [France] from sending what is necessary' for its defence. Moreover, British forces are preparing to dominate the Indian Ocean, cutting off communications with Pondicherry. Meanwhile Pitt will string out negotiations with Spain '*until we have lost everything we have*'. Then he will reject Spain's demands. He does not fear her forty ships, '*and, as we no longer have ships, colonies, or resources, we will not relieve the forces of the king of Spain and will be forced, whatever advantages we have on land, to cede to necessity and accept the most onerous and shameful peace conditions*'.[19] He concluded by urging the Spanish government to reconsider – to press an armed mediation upon the British. Ricardo Wall rebuffed this suggestion and advised the French to focus on conquering Hanover instead. Ten days

[16] Alfred Bourguet, *Études sur la politique étrangère du duc de Choiseul*, pp. 137, 146–7; Rashed, *Peace of Paris*, p. 52

[17] Choiseul-Praslin to Choiseul, 14 Dec. 1759, Waddington, *Guerre*, III, 493.

[18] Quoted in Bourguet, *Études sur la politique étrangère du duc de Choiseul*, p. 149.

[19] Choiseul to d'Ossun, 9 Feb. 1760, Bourguet, *Choiseul et l'alliance espagnole*, pp. 91–2 (emphasis Choiseul's).

later Choiseul repeated his urgent plea, and this time he brought forward without disguise the importance of the armed threat. The king of Spain, he said, should demand categorically that the British accept mediation, and if they were to refuse or evade, he should not hesitate to declare war in alliance with France. 'The evil is instant', he said. 'If it is left to spread, it can become irremediable.'[20] Evidently, Choiseul thought the Spanish would risk a declaration of war when France could provide neither naval nor financial resources to assist them. Carlos III wished he could call upon an army and navy strong enough to come to France's aid, but for Spain to comply with Choiseul's proposal at this time would have been suicidal.

War in India: the Coromandel Coast

After its declaration of war in June 1756 Versailles did not forget India. Realizing that the 1754 truce signed by the governors at Pondicherry and Madras could not possibly hold, the French government ordered two regular regiments to India. About half the force sailed from Lorient in December 1756 and reached Pondicherry the following September. The departure of the rest was delayed by a collision of two naval escorts when getting under way at Brest; the convoy did not sail until 3 May 1757. It consisted of ten company ships and only one ship of the line, the other two having been reassigned to the defence of Louisbourg. Instead of six battalions originally selected only four actually went to India. The ships made an extremely slow passage. They stopped at Rio de Janeiro to allow sick sailors to recover – evidently from the same destructive germ that Du Bois de la Motte's ships carried to Louisbourg – and did not reach Pondicherry until 28 April 1758, about a year after leaving France.

On board was the new military commander, Lieutenant General Thomas Arthur, comte de Lally, baron de Tollendal, a questionable choice. Born in France in 1702, son of an Irish Jacobite officer, he compiled a long and impressive record in the French army and was noted for his energy and bravery in combat, but knew nothing about warfare in India. There was already in India a military expert who also knew how to deal with Indian princes, Charles-Joseph Patissier de Bussy, but he was an officer of the French East India Company, not of the army, and since the troops now being ordered to India were regulars, the commander had to be drawn from the king's service. In any case, the directors of the company did not want Bussy in charge. He shared the outlook of Dupleix, whose political

[20] Choiseul to d'Ossun, 19 Feb. 1760, ibid. pp. 93–4.

and military alliances with Indian princes they blamed for all the company's ills. In their eyes Bussy's impressive achievements in forging and sustaining such alliances counted against him. When Lally was interviewed by company representatives he expressed a strong disdain for involvement in native politics and vowed that he would stand clear of them; his mission, he declared, was to expel the British from India. He therefore fitted the directors' job requirements perfectly, to a degree that led them to ignore other qualities necessary in a commander-in-chief. In vain the minister of war, d'Argenson, pleaded with company officials to accept a different general. Lally might be thought suitable in Paris, d'Argenson warned, but his fiery temper would sow dissension in India: when anything displeases him, the minister observed, he 'does not hold back what he feels and expresses it in terms not to be forgotten'. He predicted 'civil war' between Lally and company officials at Pondicherry.[21] Such an outcome was practically guaranteed by Lally's instructions: he was told to root out the corruption that prevailed among company functionaries there. The directors ignored d'Argenson's advice and reiterated their preference for Lally. The minister of war gave in.

By the end of the prolonged voyage Lally's abhorrence of wasting time was intense. As soon as he got ashore at Pondicherry he began organizing an attack on Cuddalore and Fort St David. The next day 500 regulars and 200 company troops began marching southwards. It was only a two-day march, but inadequate arrangements for provisioning caused the men to suffer terribly. As they approached Cuddalore sails appeared on the horizon. It was a British squadron composed of the ships under Admiral George Pocock which had come from Bengal, and four ships of the line from England via Bombay under Commodore Charles Steevens. From off Cuddalore the French squadron under Anne-Antoine, comte d'Aché de Serquigny, stood out to sea in anticipation of battle. Lally realized that if the French squadron were badly beaten, his plan to besiege Fort St David might have to be abandoned, but he went ahead with preparations while anxiously awaiting news of the outcome.

Pocock's line consisted of seven ships (two of 50 guns), all belonging to the Royal Navy and well armed. D'Aché's flagship, *Zodiaque* (74 guns) belonged to the navy, but the other seven in his line were East India Company ships. Since the French company's ships generally carried 50 to 60 guns (considerably stronger than British Indiamen), the two squadrons were of about equal strength. Pocock chased, and in the early afternoon

[21] Quoted in Hamont, *Lally-Tollendal*, pp. 65–6.

of 29 April 1758 he caught up. He positioned his flagship, the *Yarmouth* (64 guns), in the centre of his line as he closed with the *Zodiaque*, also in the centre. After the first broadside at 3.55 p.m. the action continued for two hours. The *Yarmouth* and the three ships of the British van received nearly all the enemy's fire because the *Cumberland*, sailing poorly, was slow to come up, and two others, recent arrivals from England, lagged behind for no apparent reason. The British might have been beaten if the entire French squadron had fought properly, but two of d'Aché's ships kept their distance. By the end the French suffered about 500 killed or wounded, the British 118; the difference was partly due to a higher British rate of fire but also to the British practice of aiming at hulls while the French aimed to take down masts, sails and rigging. After breaking off, d'Aché headed for the coast where, because of a damaged anchor cable, one of his ships went aground and was lost, although the crew was saved. Shifting to Pondicherry and Madras the squadrons repaired damages and landed the wounded.

At the walls of Fort St David, despite sun and sandstorms, the French dug trenches and constructed batteries; their guns and mortars began firing on 26 May. When Lally heard that d'Aché intended to remain at Pondicherry he was furious and hurried there to convince the council and the admiral that the ships must lie off Fort St David to prevent the British squadron from coming to the rescue. Pocock was in fact striving against the adverse wind to do this. D'Aché, whose first instinct in all dealings with the army and the company was to refuse to cooperate, acquiesced and took station. Fort St David had many guns but only about 400 soldiers to man the ramparts, of which 200 were sepoys. With the French squadron nearby, water running low (the best well had been hit), and the ramparts untenable, it surrendered on 2 June. In subsequent months the fort was methodically demolished.

The Lorraine regiment had come with the first convoy in September 1757. In April 1758 Lally arrived with his own 'regiment of Lally'. Each regiment numbered about 1,100 troops plus 50 artillerymen. About 800 European troops of the French company, not counting garrisons, were already in the Carnatic. This European field force of 3,100 men vastly outnumbered its British opponent, which was under 1,000. Because of this military preponderance the story of the three-year contest in south India inevitably focuses on the French and why they did not succeed.

The impressive size of Lally's army coupled with the capture of Fort St David attracted offers of affiliation from Indian princes and chieftains. He was not receptive. In fact, he would soon choose to terminate French influence in the Deccan by ordering Bussy to abandon his ally, the Mughal subadar Salabat Jang. This step was in conformity with his instructions from Paris, which expressly stated that he should not become involved in native politics and should limit his attention to 'commercial establishments on the coasts' and their environs.[22] He was left, however, with the problem of finding money.

In no other theatre of the war was money (silver rupees and gold pagodas) more essential to military success than in India. The country was populous and productive. In fact, practically everything necessary for carrying on a campaign except high-quality ordnance and ammunition could be bought or hired locally – food, teams, wagons, labourers, even native soldiers. Sepoys were recruited, and some were beginning to be established in units trained to fight under the overall direction of European officers (but this was before the era in which the British could recruit, pay and train large armies based on sepoys). Native cavalry were available in large numbers, though they preferred plundering to combat. When it came to cavalry the French had an advantage since they had a force of 300 Europeans while the British had less than 100. As for provisioning, sepoys bought their food from the bazaars which followed an army's advance. They were therefore absolutely dependent on their pay and ready to mutiny or desert if payment was seriously delayed. European troops, whether the king's or the company's, were fed by Indian contractors, usually organized by company personnel for private profit, who generally drew on local supplies.

For conducting the siege of Fort St David, Lally had possessed plenty of troops, but the task of transporting guns, mortars and ammunition to the scene had posed a problem. Heavy materials were best carried along the coast by water, but the threat posed by Pocock's squadron and the nearness of the objective (about 20 miles) dictated land transport. Pondicherry, however, was already short of money, so there was not enough to pay the hundreds of porters and bullock drivers who, unpaid and ill-treated, deserted in droves. Lally had taken matters into his own hands and abruptly pressed Pondicherry's residents into service, ignoring distinction of castes and causing a mass exodus of the Hindu population. The task had been accomplished, but only by provoking deep resentments. The problem of money remained.

---

[22] For the instructions, drawn up by the council of state, see Hamont, *Lally-Tolendal*, pp. 66–70, and Owen, 'Count Lally', 503.

How could it be that so early in the contest Pondicherry was short of money? Fundamentally, Paris was to blame. Campaigning costs and soldiers' pay were to be met by drawing on the company's funds at Pondicherry, the assumption being that the council had access to vast wealth, much of it ill-gotten. The first army commander to arrive, the chevalier de Soupire, shared this assumption and acted upon it: he accused Governor Duval de Leyrit and leading officials of stealing from the company. Undoubtedly, they had extracted private profit, as everyone who went to India did, but the turmoil of war was sharply diminishing company income from trade, and the regular revenues collected upon lands of the interior had been rendered less productive by threats of organized raiding. After he had been in India five months Soupire, although he did not exonerate company officials, who were very backward about lending money to support the army's operations, recognized the basic reality of the situation in a letter to the minister of war: 'If France does not send ten million [livres] per year, the entire expence of transporting the troops [to India] will be fruitless.'[23] One million livres had come out with him, and Lally brought 2 million, but all this was quickly expended to cover debts and current military expenses. Small caches of treasure were captured at Cuddalore and Fort St David, but officers and soldiers looked upon such takings as their rightful reward; therefore, nearly all of the plunder went to the captors, not the company's coffers.

After the conquest of Fort St David the French occupied the entire 400-mile Coromandel Coast except for a small Danish port and the Dutch ports of Sadras and Negapatam. They also dominated the 300-mile stretch of coastal lands to the north called the Northern Circars thanks to initiatives taken by de Leyrit and Bussy after the fall of Chandernagore. All that remained in British hands was Madras on the coast, and Trichinopoly and Arcot in the interior. Lally marked out Madras, capital of the British company in south India, as his primary objective; this accorded with his instructions. But at Madras there was Fort St George, a true stronghold. A lengthy siege would obviously be necessary, and it could become interminable unless the place were blockaded by the French squadron. D'Aché obstinately refused to assist, however. He knew he would have to confront Pocock and was reluctant to subject his crews to another bout of slaughter. Moreover, he had set his hopes on a cruise to intercept British

---

[23] Soupire to d'Argenson, 15 Feb. 1758, Waddington, *Guerre*, III, 382. Glimpses of Soupire's attitude and behaviour are found in *Private Diary of Ananda Ranga Pillai*, XI, 46–138.

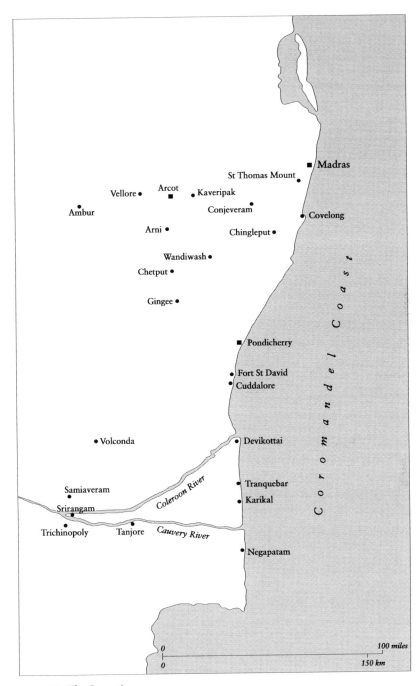

MAP 15 *The Carnatic*

and Indian traffic; the rich cargoes might yield prizes worth a fortune and also provide cash for the company's use in supporting Lally's operations. He sailed towards Ceylon (Sri Lanka) on 2 September.

Unable to overrule d'Aché's decision and knowing that he would need sea transport to carry ordnance and siege materials to Madras (90 miles north), Lally postponed the attack. This gave him an opportunity to raise money. Lally was persuaded by a Jesuit priest long familiar with regional affairs to go south to Tanjore (Thanjavur) and demand that the raja pay the bond by which in 1749 he had pledged a very large sum to Chanda Sahib. It appeared to be a quick and legitimate way to obtain a large sum.

For an expedition involving an overland march of at least 100 miles Lally would have been wise to engage native assistance, but this was against his principles. He once again set forth, on 19 June, with inadequate provisioning arrangements. His 1,600 Europeans ran short of food almost immediately, and their initial destination, the French-controlled port of Karikal, proved to have little on hand. While heading inland towards Tanjore the troops sacked a holy place, and instead of negotiating for provisions Lally demanded them and resorted to terror. Six priests he claimed to be spies were strapped to cannon muzzles and blown to pieces. This European adoption of native practice at its worst was not only shameful but also counter-productive. Word of the atrocity – witnessed by a crowd of Hindus – spread rapidly; the terrified local population dispersed, leaving Lally's army to gather food on its own.

When the army reached the outskirts of the city of Tanjore, Lally made his demand for payment, but the raja answered that he owed the debt to Chanda Sahib, not the French company. He offered a small amount but, aware of the French army's distress, was in no hurry to reach an agreement. Having only scant supplies of food and ammunition, Lally was trapped. He sent urgent letters to the council. Pondicherry was over 100 miles away and supplies would have to come by sea. The ships were already being loaded, but the process took time, and when the supplies arrived at Karikal they had to travel 40 miles inland. The commandant there lacked money and could not hire porters and escorts. Meanwhile the raja's cavalry were harassing Lally's troops night and day and interrupting carriage of local food. Preparations were being made to take the fort by storm when word came that Admiral Pocock was attacking Karikal. Lally summoned a council of war, and the majority favoured a march to Karikal over an attempt to take Tanjore. Knowing that the raja commanded thousands of soldiers and could mount a strong defence of the city even if its fort were captured, Lally agreed. When the weary, thirsty, hungry French troops arrived at Karikal on 18 August they saw Pocock's fleet offshore but a French flag flying at the fort; the British had not attacked. Lally and his officers had acted on a false report. From beginning to end the expedition was a fiasco. Robert Clive observed a decade later: 'Conquest in India at any Distance from the sea, could never have been effected without the Assistance of the Natives.'[24] Whether Lally ever understood this cannot be known because the rest of his campaigns took place not far from the sea. In any case, the money he received from the raja amounted to less than the expense of the expedition.

While Lally was attacking Tanjore a second naval battle was fought. Seven British ships engaged eight French at close range on the afternoon of 3 August 1758 off Negapatam. Pocock had his squadron tightly formed and its firepower was devastating. A shot from the *Yarmouth* disabled the *Zodiaque*'s rudder forcing her out of the line, and no sooner did she return than one of her lower-deck guns burst. The French squadron soon fled. Of its 600 casualties, the *Zodiaque* alone counted 33 killed and 151 dangerously wounded, almost as many as were killed or wounded in all the British ships: 31 and 166. Again, French gunners had aimed at sails and rigging, and Pocock's ships, much damaged aloft, were unable to chase. When d'Aché returned to Pondicherry to land wounded men and make repairs he had made up his mind not to face Pocock again. He announced that he would depart immediately for the French base at Mauritius (Île de France) in the Mascarene Islands. On 31 August Lally and the council pleaded with him to stay for at least another three weeks, but d'Aché was unshakeable. He put ashore 500 of his sailors and marines for the army's use and sailed away on 3 September.

Early conquest of Madras was undoubtedly the correct strategy. Lally could calculate that Pocock would leave the coast in mid-October to avoid the dangerous monsoon and probably not return from Bombay before early February. He would therefore have a limited period of three or four months which would include periods of adverse weather to make use of sea transport, carry out the siege, and compel surrender. While awaiting Pocock's departure Lally seized Arcot and moved to establish control of the hinterland west and south of Madras. It was what he should have begun doing instead of going to Tanjore. As Robert Orme commented, it 'presented a much easier conquest, and the chance of no inconsiderable revenue', some of it at the expense of Madras.[25] It would also have been

[24] Quoted in Bryant, 'Asymmetric Warfare', 433.
[25] Orme, *Military Transactions*, II, 317.

useful to capture the British-controlled outpost of Chingleput, which would later become a thorn in his side.

Wanting to assemble all available forces for an attack on Madras, he had called in Bussy from Hyderabad, asking him to bring most of his troops. He also called in Léon Moracin, the company's commandant at the port of Masulipatam in the Northern Circars. Thus, the Deccan and the coastal trading centres to the north were to be abandoned and put at risk. Bussy was shocked and distressed by these orders, especially because he had just succeeded in restoring Salabat Jang as Mughal subadar after a long struggle to overcome an adverse palace revolution. Salabat Jang and the Northern Circars coast could have helped the French raise money, but Lally preferred coercion over cooperation. As he remarked in a letter to Moracin: 'it matters little if your zemindars [sic] and avaldars refuse tribute, if I have an army with nothing else to do than to reduce them to obedience.'[26]

On the eve of the campaign to conquer Madras the treasury at Pondicherry was empty. In an emotional meeting Lally, Governor de Leyrit, and members of the council contributed their own funds. The army set out in early November but was halted halfway on the 12th by heavy rain and flooding. Two weeks later it was able to proceed and reached the outskirts of Madras on 12 December. There had not been time to lay siege to the fort at Chingleput, its garrison now strengthened to the level of 100 Europeans and 1,200 sepoys, with artillery both for the field and the fort, and provisions for three months. On 14 December French forces easily occupied the defenceless Black Town where the bulk of the Madras population lived, ordinarily over 50,000. Now the troops could subsist by plunder though at the expense of discipline. The initial looting was so wild and disorderly that it caught the attention of Governor George Pigot and Colonel Stringer Lawrence who, seeing an opportunity to fall upon a drunk and distracted enemy, ordered a sortie by 600 men under Lieutenant Colonel William Draper, recently arrived from England. The French soldiers rallied, however, and in the confused combat of streets and suburbs the British lost over 200 Europeans (killed, wounded or taken prisoner). The French lost only about 130, but this included two first-rate officers, one of which was Charles-Henri, comte d'Estaing (later to become a famous admiral) who was taken prisoner.

The walls of Fort St George enclosed 15 acres. Since 1756 the company had steadily employed 4,000 workers on improving the defences.

---

[26] Lally to Moracin, 11 June 1758, quoted in Dodwell, *Clive and Dupleix*, p. 179.

The eastern wall stood on the beach (shallow water kept warships beyond gunnery range); the other walls featured six bastions. The garrison numbered 1,750 Europeans. This figure included 100 marines put ashore by Pocock before he sailed for Bombay and 280 regulars of Draper's 64th regiment which had sailed for India in late 1757 and arrived in mid-September 1758. There was a trained body of sepoys serving with the garrison. For military assistance outside the walls Yusuf Khan, a trusted Indian ally, was summoned from the south. He arrived at Chingleput on 25 December with almost 1,000 cavalry and 800 infantry after ravaging villages in Pondicherry's hinterland. Governor Pigot promptly sent by night a small mounted detachment carrying bags of gold coins. Fort St George had provisions for three months, a great stock of powder and shot, and numerous guns in reserve to replace losses on the ramparts. Compared to other forts in India it was unusually strong, but it was not impregnable; the defenders would need to be alertly responsive. Chieftains and princes of south India did not think the place would survive. To deal with the emergency, command over regular as well as company forces was given to Governor Pigot, who was required to consult with Colonel Lawrence.

The Black Town's crowded buildings provided the French with shielding while they constructed their batteries, an important advantage, but the necessary siege ordnance and equipment was slow to arrive and bombardment of the citadel did not begin until 2 January 1759. In the early going the besiegers were occasionally hampered by shortages of guns and ammunition. They did not receive an ample supply until 17 January when two frigates which had sailed from Pondicherry over a month before were at last able to overcome the adverse wind and current. The bombardment took a heavy toll on the garrison, for the fort lacked strong casemates. On most days and nights five to ten men were killed, Europeans and sepoys. French mortar bombs were particularly effective. Notwithstanding steady night-time firing upon the trenches, the French zig-zag came within 50 yards, the saps closer. By 7 February a small breach was opened, but its approaches were easily commanded by guns on nearby bastions. When the French built a new battery to open a more suitable breach, the fort's gunnery, alert and accurate, prevented its use.

During the siege the forces based on Chingleput were active. Yusuf Khan's cavalry ravaged the Madras environs from which the French had been acquiring bullocks and food. On 7 February Major John Caillaud (of Huguenot background) reached the fortified town with additional forces that he had journeyed south to acquire. The success of his mission had been delayed by refusals of assistance from the raja of Tanjore, who believed that the French would succeed. Eventually, after covering 75 miles in three days he arrived. He brought the total available force at Chingleput to 2,200 native cavalry and 2,500 sepoys, but only 100 Europeans. Much of this force ventured forward to occupy Saint Thomas Mount, a defensible hill not far from Madras featuring fine houses and gardens. Lally, seeing his sources of food and fodder under threat, assigned a large force of 600 European infantry, 1,200 sepoys, 300 European cavalry and 500 native cavalry to attack it. In the assault of 9 February, although the French cavalry penetrated the Mount's outer defences, they were soon cut up by sepoy musketry from walls and hedges, and attacks were repeatedly repulsed.

The fruitless assault on the Mount aggravated Lally's shortages of food and ammunition. Because his army had greatly depended on plunder, which distracted officers and men from their duty, Lally was becoming frustrated and thoroughly disgusted. By 15 February half of his officers, including Bussy, had gone back to Pondicherry. The next day sails were seen on the horizon. They were British: two frigates escorting four Indiamen carrying the remaining six companies of Draper's regiment. That night, as the ships were guided to the anchorage by lights displayed at the fort, Lally's army hurriedly departed.

The siege of Madras was the decisive battle of the war for the Carnatic. Fort St George fired 26,500 rounds from cannon, 7,500 shells from mortars, expended 200,000 musket cartridges and 1,768 barrels of powder. Thirty-three British officers and 580 of the rank and file were killed, wounded or taken prisoner. Of the fort's sepoys 105 were killed, 217 wounded; another 440 deserted. French casualties were never counted. Sick and wounded were left behind for the British to care for. Lally cannot be blamed for seizing the moment to capture Madras and end the war quickly, even though he began with inadequate funds. The arrival of a frigate from Mauritius in December with 1 million livres had helped him carry on, but the money was quickly spent.

When the siege was over, Lally's European force still outnumbered the British despite the 600 men of Draper's regiment, and French preponderance in European cavalry, 300 to 100, would always keep the British wary. Both sides could hire plentiful native cavalrymen, but such horsemen were generally cautious, for if an Indian lost his horse he was likely to be destitute whereas a European could usually count on a remount supplied by the company. Like the British, the French recruited numerous sepoy infantry, some of whom were long in service and relatively reliable. Lally's problem was keeping them paid. The French army that withdrew from Madras was hungry and unpaid.

Although Lally had confidently declared that his army could extract all the tribute that it needed, this method, without a native prince or chieftain as intermediary, was inefficient. It wasted military effort and terrified the inhabitants; many stopped producing and fled, carrying away all that they could. After the effort at Madras the French still commanded more revenue districts in the Carnatic than the British did, especially in the country round Arcot, Wandiwash and Pondicherry, but the British began to send expeditions to take over control of these lands. Lally knew he must counter them, but he lacked campaigning money. He obtained 40,000 rupees by finding fault with a district collector's accounting and another 10,000 by promising the ruler of Vellore that he would restrain his troops from marauding on his lands. But this money was soon exhausted and he was then inclined to avoid combat, fearing that his ill-paid, ill-supplied troops would not fight.[27]

A source of funds from outside the Carnatic was to be cherished. The Northern Circars was such a source, but Lally threw it away, first by having ordered Bussy and Moracin to leave the Deccan, secondly by replacing them with an officer with no experience of warfare in India, the marquis de Conflans, and thirdly by wasting time in a quarrel with Bussy instead of sending him to rectify the mistake.

As soon as Bussy and Moracin withdrew, a local chieftain, Ananda Raz had occupied the northern port of Vizagapatam, raised a British flag, and immediately asked for military support from Madras and Calcutta. Madras, which was bracing for a siege, could offer nothing, but at Calcutta Clive overrode the Bengal Council's objections and in September 1758 ordered Lieutenant Colonel Francis Forde to sail with 500 Europeans and 2,000 sepoys to Vizagapatam. A bargain was eventually reached with Ananda Raz which required him to pay part of the campaigning costs. If the campaign were successful, he was to receive former French land revenues while the company would be given control of the ports. From Vizagapatam Forde marched south towards Rajahmundry, the old capital of the Northern Circars, and confronted Conflans at Condore on 7 December. The battle was decided when Conflans mistakenly attacked the 2nd Battalion of Bengal Sepoys, thinking them by their scarlet uniforms to be Europeans. As the French troops eagerly pushed them back Forde swung to attack their flank with his European troops. Initially masked by

[27] Orme, *Military Transactions*, pp. 496–8.

a cornfield Forde's men surprised and decimated their opponents; they were assisted by the musket fire of sepoys, who chased after the fleeing army. Three days later the British occupied Rajahmundry without opposition. Forde's next objective was the prosperous port of Masulipatam. He had to wait because Ananda Raz delayed paying the money he had pledged until he heard news of the outcome at Madras.

The walls of the fort at Masulipatam were of mud, but when the heavy ordnance arrived on the East India Company ship *Hardwicke* the task of dragging it to the batteries was tedious, and the troops became restless and demanded their money. The cash was on the way from Bengal but delayed by contrary winds. Forde asked the council at Madras to send money, saying: 'I now owe thirty thousand Rupees to the Seapoys, and twenty thousand prize money which I made use of for the subsistence of the troops.'[28] In the meantime, with carefully chosen words he pacified the soldiers. Hearing that Salabat Jang was approaching with a large native army, Maratha horsemen and a French detachment, Forde resolved to storm the fort. Though ammunition was running low, he ordered his artillerymen to double the tempo of firing to soften up the walls. According to his plan, on the night of 7 April two false attacks were made which employed about half the sepoys, each directed at a point distant from the main attack. This was carried out by 312 Europeans, 30 artillerymen, 30 volunteer sailors from the *Hardwicke* and 700 sepoys. The soldiers had to hack a sufficient opening in the wall while under fire and pass through. At first they took severe casualties, but once through, by employing a captured gun against the surprised garrison at a critical moment, they managed to take over the fort and compel a surrender. Five hundred Europeans were captured including Conflans, who, according to some witnesses, had stayed below during the action. Forde reported to Governor Pigot that 21 of his troops were killed and 60 wounded; of the seamen, 1 was killed and 6 wounded. He added:

my fifteen hundred Seapoys behaved very well . . . they mounted the Ramparts with the Europeans and behaved with great humanity after they had got in. I have lost great numbers of them both at the false and real attack; Captain Kallendar [Callender] is among the slain as is Moodenbeg my Commandant of Seapoys.[29]

---

[28] Forde to Madras Council, 19 March 1759, Forrest, *Life of Lord Clive*, II, 108.
[29] Ibid. II, 114–15.

The feat was deservedly called heroic, and it had a significant consequence: on 12 May 1759 Salabat Jang negotiated a treaty with Forde, signing over to the British territorial revenues that he had formerly assigned to Bussy.

In the wake of the battle of Condore, it was realized at Pondicherry that Masulipatam would probably come under attack. Everyone urged Lally to send Bussy to the rescue. To Lally's invitation Bussy responded by asking for assurance that his orders would allow him to re-establish relations with his long-standing ally, Salabat Jang (who in fact had been begging for him to come north). He asked for full powers and no interference, and reminded Lally that time was precious. But the commander-in-chief could not bring himself to grant Bussy's conditions, and after a fruitless and time-consuming exchange of letters (Bussy was at Arcot) finally gave the mission to Moracin. Sailing on 12 April and speeded by favouring winds, Moracin with a body of native troops arrived off Masulipatam on the 15th. The place had surrendered a week before.

Pondicherry was so drained of money after the failure at Madras that the government issued parchment rupees, something unheard of in 'this town formerly abounding in gold and silver, rich gems and diamonds'.[30] In early August 1759 Lally needed to counter British thrusts at Arcot and French-held revenue districts west of Conjeveram; he desperately sought money to launch a campaign. He squeezed what he could out of company officials and ordered resident native merchants to grant loans, locking the latter in dungeons when they did not produce the amounts assessed. (By now, most of them had transferred their savings to friends and relatives in the country.) When three such men insisted that they had no means of paying, Lally threatened to hang them, and on 4 September gallows were erected in a public place causing crowds to gather in angry protest. Truly, Pondicherry was in a state of 'civil war' between the general, backed by swords and bayonets, and everyone else. Lally promised that when the long-overdue squadron arrived, presumably with money, all would be resolved.

Seven months had passed since the dangerous monsoon season ended. When d'Aché reached Mauritius in early October 1758 he found that three ships of the line plus some company ships had recently arrived from France. They carried 3 million livres. He refused to send the money on. Only after vehement protests by the local governor was he persuaded

---

[30] Ranga Pillai, 20 Feb. 1759, *Private Diary of Ananda Ranga Pillai*, XI, 295–6. The diarist was a Tamil merchant who had served as chief dubash (liaison between the company and Indian businessmen and landlords) from 1747 to 1756.

to allow a frigate to carry 1 million to Pondicherry, which arrived in mid-December and helped sustain the siege of Madras. The Mascarene Islands could not possibly supply provisions for the many ships. It was necessary to send some of them to the Cape of Good Hope to buy from the Dutch. While awaiting their return d'Aché fitted out his fighting squadron with a full complement of guns. When he finally sailed in mid-July 1759 the squadron consisted of four royal ships of the line and seven of the company's, all well armed. Almost ten months had elapsed since he left Pondicherry.

Pocock had been lying in wait for a month and was watering his squadron at Trincomalee, Ceylon when, on 2 September, the company frigate *Revenge* raced in to report sighting the French ships. Pocock quickly got under way and chased, but lost touch in fickle weather. He headed immediately for Pondicherry and soon the French fleet appeared. A battle was inevitable. At 2.15 p.m. on 10 September the opposing vans engaged. Against eleven of the enemy Pocock had nine, but all were Royal Navy. The French squadron carried 740 cannon versus 536 British; 6,440 crewmen versus 4,000 British, but the British sailors and gunners were better trained. Fifth in line, Pocock matched the *Yarmouth*'s 64 guns against the *Zodiaque*'s 74, and the flagships and those in the van were soon exchanging fire at point-blank range. The rear divisions on both sides lagged behind and saw less action. Some French ships were temporarily driven out of the line by British broadsides, and some British ships were so badly damaged aloft that they could hardly steer. By 4 p.m. only five or six ships were still engaging heavily. A murderous blast of grapeshot swept the *Zodiaque*'s quarterdeck and wounded d'Aché in the thigh. He soon fainted from loss of blood, and because the flagship's captain had been killed a lieutenant assumed command. He steered away and the rest of the squadron followed. In this two-hour battle, even more sanguinary than the preceding ones, the British squadron suffered 570 killed or wounded, the French 880. Three of Pocock's ships had to be towed to Negapatam where he remained for ten days making repairs.

In the three battles off the Coromandel Coast the total number killed or wounded on British ships was 885, on French ships 1,980. These figures may be compared with an estimate of the total killed or wounded by gunnery action at Minorca, Lagos Bay and Quiberon Bay: 760 British and 1,420 French (excluding men drowned in ships that sank). In terms of casualties the naval battles on the Coromandel Coast were not a sideshow. George Pocock earned the knighthood that he was given upon his return to England.

The French squadron reached Pondicherry on 15 September and began putting stores and munitions ashore. D'Aché announced that he intended to return to the islands immediately. Lally and the company officials were appalled. The onset of the north-west monsoon was still a month away, and a precipitate departure, they said, would confirm the impression of a naval defeat. If, however, the squadron stayed, the fort could fire salutes, offer a Te Deum, and announce a victory. Their concern was 'to convince the Indians of our success'.[31] Native support was especially needed because the squadron brought less than 800,000 livres, almost half of it in the form of diamonds captured from a British Indiaman. Most of the 2 million from France that d'Aché had retained he had spent on provisioning and refitting the squadron. As it happened he could not be prevented from leaving Pondicherry on the 17th, but Lally, de Leyrit and the council dispatched a letter to him by a fast ship, providing a copy for each captain. Its blunt warning was that if Pondicherry were lost, they would blame the navy. The ship caught up with the squadron, and after thinking it over d'Aché decided to return to Pondicherry. But he remained only until 30 September. His sole concession was to disembark 450 sailors of inferior abilities.

After the failed attempt on Madras, Lally began to consider the value of alliances with native princes and chieftains. In April he had written about it to Bussy, who replied: I understand you to say that 'it is time to take advantage of the acquaintances that I have in the country', but Bussy then pointed out that the situation was no longer what it had been: 'the new face of affairs changes the attitudes of the chieftains'.[32] He meant that the French were no longer considered invincible. Bussy was apprehensive for a second reason: he doubted whether he would be permitted to make use of his familiar connections. Lally was bent on appointing a new nawab of Arcot without consulting Bussy's long-time ally, Salabat Jang, the subadar whose approval would confer legitimacy. Lally also wanted Bussy to lend the cause part of his personal fortune, but the latter had sent most of it home. A few months later Lally ordered Bussy to negotiate with Salabat's brother, Basalat Jang, who wished to usurp power for himself and appeared interested in cooperating with the French. But while Bussy was on his way north from Arcot to meet with Basalat, he heard news that spoiled his chances of success.

[31] Hamont, *Lally-Tolendal*, p. 221.
[32] Bussy to Lally, 24 April 1759, ibid. p. 183.

The French army had mutinied. Soldiers who had recently won a victory by repelling an ill-advised British attack on Wandiwash were aware that the squadron had come, and they presumed that enough money had been landed to provide for their pay, almost a year overdue. Seeing no sign of an intention to pay them, the troops of both regiments including all non-commissioned officers marched off on the morning of 17 October and pitched camp over a mile away. The mutiny was remarkably well organized: new officers were elected; an advisory council of senior soldiers was created; delegates were chosen to negotiate. At Pondicherry Lally convened an emergency council meeting, pledged his own money, pressed the councillors to send their plate to the mint, and dispatched a representative to address the mutineers. They shunned him, but listened to a second emissary, Colonel Crillon, an officer they trusted, who brought 50,000 rupees. Lally's proclamation promised ongoing payments and granted full amnesty.

When Bussy met with Basalat Jang on 10 November it was obvious that Basalat, who was as desperate for money as the French were, viewed the mutiny as proof that the French could not meet his needs. His interest in an alliance vanished. Bussy thereupon engaged for 2,000 sepoys from his old friends. He did not trust Marathas, but Lally arranged for 2,000 Maratha cavalry to be paid on a monthly basis. They set about ravaging British-held lands east of Arcot. As for his army of Europeans, Lally chose to divide it, partly because he feared another mutiny. He sent a large detachment southwards to defend French-dominated lands against possible attacks from British-held Trichinopoly.

He did not choose a good moment to do this. A year earlier in England a new regiment, the 84th, had been authorized and designated for service in India; numbering 1,000 men, it was originally intended to serve in Bengal. The troops sailed on 6 April 1759 and 300 of them reached Madras in only five months. The rest, escorted by four ships of the line and two frigates under Commodore Samuel Cornish, arrived off Negapatam on 19 October where they met Pocock, then on the way to Bombay for refit. Pocock carried a letter from the governor and council at Madras addressed to the regiment's commander, Lieutenant Colonel Eyre Coote, asking him to bring his troops there. Coote therefore went to Madras, disembarked 700 troops, and took overall command of the army. He soon marched, heading towards Arcot to drive off marauders. Because Lally had divided his forces Wandiwash was vulnerable, and on 30 November Coote captured it. Lally soon responded; he called upon Bussy to join him and prepared for a recapture.

Aside from the siege of Madras, the battle of Wandiwash, which commenced on the morning of 22 January 1760, was the only full-scale land battle of the entire contest for the Carnatic. The two armies fielded somewhat different assets but were about equal in strength. Essentially, the British won by overcoming the French cavalry advantage. At a critical early moment two field guns, alertly positioned and rapidly reloaded by a captain of the Royal Artillery, turned back a mass of onrushing Maratha cavalry, and when the Marathas failed to return to the attack the accompanying French cavalry withdrew. Lally ordered a bold infantry thrust at the British lines. In a column 12-men broad the Lorraine regiment rushed at the British centre and broke through, provoking a bloody encounter with bayonets, but the outcome was decided by British muskets on the flanks which tore into the French column and caused it to retreat. The French suffered a misfortune when a British artillery round hit an ammunition wagon located within a fortified position anchoring the left of their line. The explosion killed or wounded 80 French marines. Seeing them flee and sensing tactical disaster when a British contingent occupied the position, Bussy quickly rallied 50 men and bravely led them forward, but his horse was killed and he soon became a prisoner. At the battle's end shortly after 2 p.m. the French cavalry, 300 riders equipped with carbines, intervened to protect the retreat of the infantry. The French abandoned nearly all of their field cannon and 200 dead or dying soldiers. All told they lost nearly 600 men, 160 of which were taken prisoner. British losses were 63 Europeans killed, 124 wounded; 23 sepoys and native cavalrymen killed, 47 wounded.

It has often been claimed that Wandiwash was the 'decisive battle' that determined the fate of the Carnatic. Yet only a crushing French victory could have materially altered Lally's situation, and Coote, though only 33 years old, was too careful a general to allow it to happen. His battle arrangements and orders were consistently designed to avoid undue risks while watching for opportunities. Coote knew that time was on his side.

In the final analysis only three things could have saved Pondicherry: money from France; the Madras Council declining to bear the expense of capturing it; or peace in Europe. There was no chance of the first. Silhouette wrote to Lally: the company 'is exhausted in ships and money and it is to the country itself by your own success, that you must look to procure the means to sustain you and to continue operations . . . in a way glorious for the nation'.[33] The second was unlikely, thanks partly to

---

[33] Quoted in Pierre La Mazière, *Lally-Tollendal* (Paris, 1931), p. 123.

increased support from London (mainly in the form of troops and naval force), and partly to money from Bengal, where trade, especially trade with China, began to boom after being depressed in the year 1757. When Pocock sailed home in 1760 he joined at St Helena twenty-three East India Company ships, eleven from China; these ships which he escorted to England carried an unprecedented £18 million worth of goods. By contrast France's East India trade had collapsed. The third possibility, an early peace, was not going to happen because Versailles, guided by Choiseul and Pompadour, was unwilling to end the war promptly.

A year would pass before Pondicherry surrendered, but the features of Lally's predicament became quickly evident. In early February 1760 when Coote marched to Arcot to force its capitulation Lally moved to seize Chetput (18 miles west of Wandiwash). Before attacking, however, his Maratha horsemen demanded payment, and although he hurriedly raised money by selling some revenue rights, a report reached him that Rear Admiral Cornish was on his way from Bombay. For the safety of Pondicherry Lally abandoned his campaign, and from this time onwards he concentrated almost exclusively on its defence. Among the few outlying garrisons Karikal was especially vulnerable. Troops sailing from Madras landed on a beach near Karikal without opposition. Seamen brought ashore three 24-pounders and dragged them into position. The landing force was joined by troops marching from Trichinopoly. On 6 April, with the mechanism for raising a drawbridge damaged beyond repair, the commandant surrendered.

The British forces gradually closed the ring round Pondicherry, thus steadily diminishing the capital's sources of food and revenue. Lally arranged with Hyder Ali, the upstart ruler of Mysore, to bring 5,000 men. In late June they came, but the British disrupted their rice convoys, so they arrived without adequate provisions and soon resorted to indiscriminate plundering. By the time the Mysoreans departed in early August they may have done more harm than good. Relief by sea was cut off by a naval blockade maintained by Admiral Steevens, who had superseded Pocock as naval commander. Coote was patient and cautious, and Lally's sorties were fruitless.

Since Coote's troop numbers were growing (600 recruits arrived from England on 31 July, 614 more on 2 September) and the French were unable to halt his encroachment upon Pondicherry's environs, he saw no urgent need to begin a siege. In addition, British commanders were wary of a return by the French squadron. They did not know that a January typhoon had struck the Mascarene Islands, damaged ships and ruined agriculture. Not long afterwards d'Aché received word from Versailles advising him to stay where he was because the British were planning to attack the Mauritius base. He sent two frigates to Pondicherry with sealed dispatches informing Lally that the squadron would not be coming, a message that Lally kept secret. In September, as Madras prepared equipment for a siege, Governor Pigot informed Admiral Steevens that a continuing blockade was essential. If the navy were to leave during the monsoon season as had occurred in previous years, the French would find a way to bring provisions to Pondicherry by sea. Pigot urged him to remain despite the danger. It was an anxious decision, but Steevens and his captains agreed. It helped that there were now seventeen warships on station, and when October came with no sign of d'Aché's appearance, Steevens could send some of his ships to Trincomalee for refreshment and greater safety. The naval blockade was made absolute when British sailors rowing in complete darkness – their boats kept in line by ropes, their oar locks fitted with sheepskin – stealthily approached the two remaining French ships, overwhelmed the watch, battened the crews below decks, cut the anchor cables, and brought the ships away despite cannonading by the fort's guns. They were excellent frigates which were eventually added to the Royal Navy.

The layout of Pondicherry was unlike that of Madras. Both strongholds were next to the shore, but Pondicherry's extensive walls encompassed the entire town. Lally had plenty of cannon but not enough troops to man the perimeter walls. As always, he had very little money. The sepoys of the garrison as well as those with the army outside had to be paid, and when some of the latter were overheard plotting to desert they were rounded up and as an example to the others one of them was strapped to a cannon muzzle and killed. Within the walls Lally, who had alienated everyone, ruled by fear. Desperate for cash, he persisted with assessments that could not be collected even by threats of hanging. The inhabitants steadily departed. Pondicherry's non-military population, 22,000 in the time of Dupleix, fell to 3,000, and fell even further when the government asked most of them to leave in order to reserve food for the troops. At the end of November when the rains slackened Coote opened the siege from a thousand yards. But starvation was Pondicherry's key problem because the blockade by land and sea was relentless.

On the night of 1 January 1761, however, it was disrupted by a great storm, the eye passing directly over the roadstead. At 10 p.m. Steevens fired a gun signal ordering the squadron to cut cables and head for open sea, but the sound was lost in the tempest. The ships suffered terribly.

Four were totally dismasted; others were wrecked on the coast, and over 1,000 men drowned. The next morning Lally sent out messengers with an urgent circular letter announcing that the British fleet was destroyed and the blockade lifted; he promised rewards for all who would bring provisions. On 3 January, however, Steevens reappeared, and the next day he was joined by Cornish from Trincomalee with four ships of the line.

By this time Pondicherry was experiencing serious starvation. Lally proposed terms on the 15th, some of which Coote pronounced unacceptable, but the capitulation went forward anyway.[34] Coote had thoughts of leniency but was overruled by Governor Pigot, who declared that the captured city belonged to the company, and when army and navy officers joined in protest he backed up his claim by informing them that without their compliance the Madras Council would provide no more money for subsisting troops and prisoners. The company's standing orders specified that Pondicherry's fortifications and buildings should be completely demolished – in retribution for what had been done at Fort St David. The task took nine months.

Lally had assiduously and eagerly carried out the instructions given him in Paris, and had therefore avoided alliances with native princes until his situation was desperate and it was too late. Conveyed to England as a prisoner and released to go to France in December 1761, he found himself overwhelmed by false accusations that proliferated in print and stirred public opinion violently against him. In justifying his conduct he characteristically accused everyone who had opposed him in India, thus uniting in fear the company officials he had continually humiliated and insulted. Popularly dubbed 'the Irishman' and friendless, he was an ideal scapegoat for giving cover to the Parisian authorities who had issued his impracticable instructions. Choiseul, always content to see the blame for French losses overseas fall on someone not at Versailles, let the crowd have its way. Lally was committed to the Bastille on 5 November 1762. Eventually found guilty – absurdly – of treason, he was beheaded on 9 May 1766.

Pondicherry was given back to France by the treaty of 1763. It would be captured by the British three more times in the next forty years. Restored in 1816, it remained under French governance until the 1950s. In the years after 1763 it did not recover great commercial importance. The long, grinding process leading up to its surrender reduced the city to penury and starvation, discouraging and frightening off its merchants and

---

[34] Documents relating to the surrender are printed in Wylly, *Eyre Coote*, pp. 389–95.

bankers. It would be hard to find funds to rebuild its demolished walls. When the court of Versailles negotiated peace in 1762–3 its initial concern was to re-establish trading in the rich territory of Bengal.

The conquest of Canada, 1760

Snow fell heavily at Quebec during the winter of 1759–60, but there had been time to repair buildings to shelter citizens and occupying troops. All winter long, almost every day, the men of the garrison cut and hauled firewood, chiefly from near Ste-Foy, five miles away. Soldiers and citizens dragged sleighs, the latter sometimes harnessing dogs 'of the Newfoundland breed, naturally strong, and nearly in size to a well-grown sheep' to haul the loads.[35] Sickness among the British troops was a serious problem. Counting officers the garrison numbered 6,400 at the end of October. Few cattle were brought in for slaughter and there were practically no vegetables, so scurvy was common, yet for unknown reasons not one of the 570 women attached to the garrison died of illness and few became sick (the regular military diet was allowed them). By 24 March 1760 only 3,500 troops were fit for duty and 1,850 were reported sick. The army's clothing and bedding were grievously inadequate for the climate. Almost 700 men died and had to be temporarily buried in deep snow. By early April many sick men began to recover. One reason may be that they were served a broth prepared by soaking foliage cut from the tops of spruce trees in boiling water; a broth now known to contain vitamin C.

Despite the cold weather, Brigadier General James Murray, the governor and military commander, had done well. The garrison's morale was steady. Murray treated the citizens within the walls well and they remained peaceful. Nearby *habitants*, though urged by proclamations from the marquis de Vaudreuil not to cooperate with the British, rather to harass them, were kept quiet by British posts established at Ste-Foy and Old Lorette. Murray published threats that farmhouses would be burnt in localities where attacks on his men occurred; the credibility of these threats was perhaps the only positive result of the burning of villages during the 1759 campaign. Throughout the winter near Cap Rouge and on the fringes of British occupation on the lower river skirmishes with French and Canadian troops occurred, but these were of small consequence.

After Montcalm's death Vaudreuil gave command of all military forces to Lévis. Cooperation between the army, the governor and the population

---

[35] *Knox's Journal*, II, 319.

was excellent. French regulars, of which 3,900 remained, commonly wintered with families in farmhouses, and Canadian militiamen who served with the regulars were assigned where possible to a regiment wintering in their home region. Almost 8,000 Canadian militia answered the call to arms. Many were eager to defend their homeland, but in the background was Vaudreuil's announced penalty for refusal: death. Because the regulars quartered with *habitants* remained generally healthy the numerical strength of the defending army was much greater than that of the garrison at Quebec. Lévis's problems were of a material nature: good muskets, artillery, gunpowder and means of transport were scarce.

Lévis and Vaudreuil were well aware that General Amherst was preparing a massive attack from the south. They agreed that an early attempt to retake Quebec was the obvious strategy, because if the place remained in enemy hands, military assistance from France could not get through to them. They would have liked to launch a winter attack but could not obtain food for it. Instead, they prepared to push the army downriver towards Quebec as soon as the ice began to break up. This occurred on 20 April. The flotilla of bateaux accompanied by the two remaining small frigates plus four other armed vessels were at Pointe-aux-Trembles four days later. They dared not go further because the ice along the north shore remained thick and treacherous. Even so, there were mishaps in landing the supplies. As the men marched towards Ste-Foy through swamps the weather turned bitterly cold.

General Murray had known about the scope of Lévis's preparations for many days but it was only by a stroke of luck that he learned of the imminence of the attack. A French soldier whose bateau overturned saved himself on a slab of ice, and as it floated down river he cried out for help. The cries were heard in the middle of the night by the crew of the *Racehorse*, which sent a boat to the rescue. Upon hearing the man's story the sloop of war's captain had him carried in a hammock to the general who was awakened at 3 a.m. Four hours later Murray dispatched a sizeable force to bring outlying garrisons safely back to the city. All this occurred on the 27th and none too soon because shortly the French and Canadians were in sight of Ste-Foy.

Murray had two options. One was to devote his manpower to bringing every available gun to the city walls and to wait, but he chose a bolder course. Marching out early on the morning of 28 April with over 3,000 troops and only twenty-two guns, he placed most of his army on high ground adjacent to the Plains of Abraham with well-protected flanks. If the French chose to attack the position their losses would be enormous.

When, however, he observed them hurriedly trying to form their ranks for a possible battle, he thought he saw a moment of opportunity and ordered his men and guns forward. He thus threw away his position of great advantage, and a worse situation followed. As Lévis pulled his men back to avoid British artillery fire Murray's troops advanced enthusiastically after them. It was a dreadful mistake. For one thing, the artillery could not keep pace; guns and ammunition carts bogged down in snow and mud. For another, the advance of his left flank carried it to the edge of the woods at Sillery where Canadians lay in hiding with their muskets; the consequences were murderous. Soon after, Murray's right flank was shocked by a bayonet charge that was ordered by an elderly colonel of the Béarn regiment, and the integrity of the British line began to crumble. In the hurried retreat to the city all twenty-two guns were left behind. This action is known as the battle of Ste-Foy, fought not far west of the ground on which Wolfe had clashed with Montcalm. It lasted two hours and resulted in greater bloodshed than occurred in the famous battle fought seven months before. By official reports the British lost 259 killed and 839 wounded of 3,866 troops engaged, and the French had 193 killed and 640 wounded. Although the French suffered less in numbers, they lost some key officers.

Perhaps Lévis should have organized an immediate assault when the beaten army's morale was low. Murray soon rallied his men and redeemed his rash mistake by organizing a resolute and well-conducted defence of the city. He had already required the resident Canadians to leave. To make the 2,500 troops who were fit for duty more responsive he removed them from their familiar quarters to tents near the walls. In an exertion in which officers pulled with the rank and file, guns from the lower town were brought up to the western and northern walls. Lévis dared not attempt an escalade (though the ladders had been made) because the British with over 140 cannon on the ramparts had too much firepower. He knew that he must create a breach. His formal siege, however, took ten days to prepare: entrenchments on the rocky soil required great quantities of earth which the men laboriously brought forward. Intense cannonading from the city walls hampered work on the two French batteries, and not until 11 May were the French gunners able to open fire with their 12- and 18-pounders. They had only one 24-pounder and it blew up. Ammunition shortage compelled them to stretch out their bombardment. Obviously, relief from France was needed immediately, and two days before, a man-of-war had appeared in the basin of Quebec. It was British, but Lévis did not know this and kept up the siege; even if it were British he could hope that warships from France would soon come upriver to overpower it.

There was no chance of that. During the winter François Le Mercier, an artillery officer, had gone to Versailles with a desperate plea for help, and on 7 January he had submitted a memorandum stating the minimum requirements. The most pressing of these were: more troops, copious amounts of flour and salt pork, two dozen 24-pounders, and supplies of powder and shot. Five or six men-of-war, he added, were wanted not only to escort the convoy but to defend the basin against an arriving British squadron. He suggested that the convoy should be ready by the end of February and that the ships should risk passage through broken river ice. His conclusion, based on instructions from Vaudreuil and Lévis: peace would be best, but if the king did not wish to make peace, France must send ample support, or, failing that, allow the governor-general to achieve a reasonable capitulation.[36] In response Marshal Belleisle wrote to Lévis saying that Berryer would give orders to dispatch 'relief of every description in provisions, munitions of war and recruits' so that despite English advantages you 'will be able to dispute the ground with them, inch by inch' and perhaps 'arrest their progress'.[37]

Nothing of the sort happened. In fact, Belleisle provided only 400 recruits, and the minister of marine's contribution was pathetic. There was to be no naval escort. Instead, an expedition was arranged at Bordeaux by merchant *armateurs* led by Pierre Desclaux. Five merchant ships were prepared to carry troops, ammunition and provisions (mostly flour); they were to be escorted by a single privateering frigate, the *Machault* of 28 guns. They did not emerge from the Gironde estuary until 10 April, which was about the time they should have arrived in the Gulf of St Lawrence. The causes of delay were manifold. There were difficulties in gathering the troops, money from the receiver general was released too late, and the government's appropriation of funds did not extend to paying the ships' crews. Berryer was forced to declare that the cost of the *Machault*'s escort service was the responsibility of her owners. When the owners refused to provide money to pay the crew's wages, the seamen, already owed pay for many months, refused to sign on. The men stuck to their resolution even after the consortium of *armateurs* offered to let them have owner-ship of the frigate in lieu of wages. (The seamen believed, not without

---

[36] Le Mercier's memorandum, *NYCD*, X, 1065–8; Waddington, *Guerre*, IV, 333–4.

[37] Belleisle to Lévis, 9 Feb. 1760, *NYCD*, X, 1068–9; Gipson, VII, 436.

reason, that in due course they would be forced to give it back.) Thus, the drastically reduced naval budget of 1760 prevented the rescue force, feeble as it was, from sailing on time.

When the six ships finally got to sea they were immediately spotted by two British men-of-war. The frigate commander, Chenard Giraudais, gave the signal to scatter, and expertly enticed the British warships into a chase from which he eventually escaped. Three of the five merchantmen were captured, but the *Machault* luckily fell in with the two others and found open sea; they made a fast crossing, entering the Gulf on 15 May. There they learned that British warships were in the river ahead of them, so Giraudais headed for the Bay of Chaleurs and took refuge far up the Restigouche River in modern New Brunswick.

It would seem logical to suppose that the first British ships to reach the St Lawrence came from the squadron that had wintered at Halifax under Lord Colville, but this was not the case. The first ship to reach Quebec, the *Lowestoft* (28 guns), came from England; she had sailed with a small squadron escorting a convoy of store ships on 9 March. After becoming separated in bad weather she had headed for the rendezvous at Bic. Because Captain Joseph Deane and his officers had participated in the 1759 campaign they were acquainted with the navigational conditions and unhesitatingly made use of favourable winds to press on to Quebec. A week later, the escort commander, Commodore Robert Swanton in the *Vanguard* (70 guns), entered the river and followed the lead of the frigate *Diana*, which was also a veteran of the previous year's campaign. Easterly winds brought them from Bic to the basin in only two days and they arrived on the evening of 15 May. Lord Colville's squadron had put to sea from Halifax on 22 April but was beset by fog, contrary winds and ice, and did not arrive until the 18th.

On the morning of 16 May Commodore Swanton decided upon a bold initiative that had decisive consequences: he took his three warships immediately upriver past the city to engage the two French frigates which were anchored near Lévis's camp. Attempting to flee, one ran aground. The other joined the French transports at Cap Rouge, but because Swanton's ships were advancing fast the transports were ordered to be sunk. The remaining frigate fought a battle lasting two hours. Her captain, the brave and resourceful Vauquelin, veteran of the defence of Louisbourg, surrendered only when his ammunition was exhausted. Swanton's prompt action not only deprived Lévis of precious guns and ammunition, but also, and above all, cleared the way for General Murray to use the river for his advance to Montreal.

'I have ventured', Murray wrote to Pitt, 'to press Vessels for the conveyance of the Troops, an expedient which will render all my operations safe, quick & powerfull.'[38] His plan worked beautifully. With nine floating batteries and thirty-two sail, which included three small frigates, the army embarked at Quebec on 14 July. Some men had recovered their health rapidly in warmer weather and transports arrived from New York with supplies, but many men remained sick and, all told, only 2,400 of Murray's 5,500 men set forth. As they were conveyed upriver, rangers scouted ashore, and troops were frequently landed for fresh air and exercise when wind and tide were unfavourable to progress forwards. Occasionally, militiamen gathered to fire their muskets at the ships; the floating batteries went near shore and drove them off. Instructions for quick re-embarkation were followed when scouts reported an enemy concentration. The presence of warships influenced many *habitants* to take an oath of neutrality. Some of them bartered eggs, bread and butter for salt pork. By early August the fleet had passed Three Rivers and was working its way through the shallow, island-filled waters of Lake St Pierre. 'Their objective', Lévis wrote to Belleisle on the 7th, 'appears to be Montréal or Sorel, in order to effect a junction with Mr. Amherst. We have no means of stopping them.'[39]

Murray's army was untouchable because the troops did not have to land or stay ashore. The worst thing he could have done would have been to engage in a land battle before the other two armies that were converging on Montreal arrived. He had no need to hurry but nevertheless arrived first. At Sorel, where the Richelieu River joined the St Lawrence, Bourlamaque commanded a force composed chiefly of militia. Their solidarity vanished on 17 August when a reinforcement that had come from Louisbourg and proceeded upriver went ashore and set fire to houses. From this time onwards desertion, especially by militia, was a very serious problem for Lévis, but it was Murray's invulnerable presence only 50 miles from Montreal that most effectively constrained his capacity to confront the army under Amherst that would soon come downriver from the west.

The principal British army under Amherst's personal command embarked at Oswego on 10 August. A smaller force under Brigadier General William Haviland embarked at Crown Point. Given the huge preponderance of British forces, a three-pronged attack on Montreal made

[38] Murray to Pitt, 13 July 1760, *Knox's Journal*, II, 467.
[39] Lévis to Belleisle, 7 Aug. 1760, ibid. II, 485.

sense. But Amherst's decision to convey the largest force by the most roundabout and difficult route is at first glance puzzling. The plan required it to go up the Mohawk River and on to Oswego, go north on Lake Ontario to the St Lawrence River's entrance, and after overcoming a fort near modern-day Ogdensburg, New York, pass a series of rapids the lower parts of which were very dangerous. This route, measuring 580 miles from Albany, was twice the length of the direct route north via Lake Champlain, which posed no navigational hazards and included an existing road from St Jean on the Richelieu River to Montreal.

Amherst did not record the reasons for his choice at the time. One advantage of the Lake Ontario route was that it would prevent the French army from escaping westwards, but his strategy was probably shaped by three other considerations. First, he was not sure he could quickly achieve naval superiority on Lake Champlain whereas on Lake Ontario the British already possessed the two warships that had wintered at Niagara. Secondly, on the western route he could expect solid Iroquois support. Sir William Johnson informed him of this and Amherst gave him a large sum of money as a present to them to confirm it. Finally, the general was aware that opposing forces would face great difficulties and costs in mounting a defence upstream, whereas towards Lake Champlain they could operate with ease, especially if no threat from upstream existed, a fact that they could easily ascertain.

It was essential that the three armies should close in on Montreal simultaneously so that Lévis could not fight them singly. Amherst ordered Haviland to set out from Crown Point on the same day he would embark his army at Oswego. What he did not realize was how rapidly Murray could make progress up the St Lawrence. Most of Amherst's provincial troops arrived in Albany before the end of June, but progress in moving food, guns and ammunition to Oswego was slow, partly because many of Bradstreet's bateaumen had taken other employment. When Amherst arrived there on 9 July he noted with satisfaction that five row galleys, each capable of mounting a heavy gun, were under construction. He immediately sent 100 seamen to Niagara to make sure that the two warships there would come to him soon. When they arrived he rechristened one of them (on Johnson's suggestion) the *Onondaga* and invited Iroquois chiefs aboard for the ceremony, which included a nine-gun salute that impressed them greatly. Over 1,300 Indians with women and children had gathered at Oswego, 700 of them warriors.

On the appointed day the main army comprising 5,500 regulars and 4,500 provincials rowed north from Oswego. Guarded by Indians in canoes, the bateaux carrying artillery formed the column nearest shore where they could quickly seek shelter in case of high winds and waves, which did arise and caused a day's delay. By 16 August the army had passed through the Thousand Islands, and the next morning the five galleys, each mounting a 12-pounder, attacked the becalmed *Outauaise*, which, unable to bring its guns to bear, was compelled to surrender. The vessel was refitted and placed under British command. Amherst's forces now completely dominated the river except for a single defensive position, Fort Lévis, which was situated on a small island in mid-stream, 3 miles downriver from what is now Ogdensburg, New York. It was defended by 400 men under Captain Pouchot (the Niagara commandant had been returned in an exchange of prisoners) and might have been bypassed since bateaux could proceed close to either shore with very little molestation. But Amherst was determined to capture the place. Batteries established on islands and the nearest shoreline began to bombard the fort on 23 August. Amherst decided, however, to speed things up by sending his warships downstream to engage the fort with guns and musket-fire by trained marksmen. Each vessel intended to maintain its position by a stern anchor, but Pouchot's men loaded their guns with iron fragments and fired at the cables. They succeeded in severing two of them, and the ships fell away downriver. The *Onondaga* ran aground within range of the fort's guns and muskets. This was a serious mishap since she contained reserves of food and ammunition. The British army controlled the shoreline, however, and prevented the French from boarding her. Soon British cannon at the batteries wiped out all the fort's guns and on the 25th Pouchot capitulated.

Only the rapids remained between Amherst's army and Montreal. The initial series was easily navigated, but in the lower rapids called the Cascades over fifty boats and bateaux were lost with 84 lives despite guidance by Indian pilots. Wisely, most of the troops had been ordered to march around on land. On 6 September the army began to assemble on the western end of the large island on which Montreal is situated. From beginning to end the operation had enjoyed perfect protection by the Iroquois, not only by their scouting but also by their diplomacy: they had persuaded Laurentian villagers to adhere to an Iroquois decision to stop supporting the French cause.

When Amherst's army began its passage down the St Lawrence, Haviland's gunners were engaging the fortified position at Isle-aux-Noix. His army of 3,400 had left Crown Point on 11 August. Indian assistance was meagre, perhaps because British methods in this sector were violent:

Major Robert Rogers with companies of rangers had been sent ahead to raid French and Indian settlements near the Richelieu River. The Isle-aux-Noix garrison numbered about 1,100 and was commanded by Bougainville. Situated in the Richelieu river, the fort's guns commanded booms that blocked the channels on each side. Bougainville's strategy was passive. Evidently, the floating booms prevented him from sending forward his rideau and gunboats to harass Haviland's army when it landed on the east side of the river below the fort. During the siege a body of British regulars and rangers stealthily brought two light howitzers and a 6-pounder north-wards to a position from which they could fire upon the French vessels. With the advantage of surprise they captured the rideau and used its guns to scatter the gunboats, many of which were captured. Thus, Isle-aux-Noix was effectively cut off. Lévis had told Bougainville that he should fight to the last man, but a message from Vaudreuil which arrived on the 27th advised him to get away. That night most of his troops crept undetected across the swampy ground on the western side while fifty who stayed in the fort, many of them wounded men, maintained a noisy discharge of muskets. During the disorganized trek northwards many of the Canadians deserted. On 3 September Haviland received a message from Murray and in response sent Rogers north who, three days later, joined Murray on the south shore of the St Lawrence opposite Montreal. Thus, by 6 September all three armies had come together. Amherst had a right to congratulate himself: 'I believe never three Armys, setting out from different & very distant Parts from each other joyned in the Center, as was intended, better than we did.'[40]

Montreal was not a fortified city; its walls were designed merely to defend against Indian raids. The defenders, 2,400 regulars and 1,050 *troupes de la marine*, were not only heavily outnumbered by the British and provincial troops present, about 14,000, but also had few guns and little ammunition. The wooden city could easily be set on fire by bombardment. By this time nearly all Canadian militiamen, as they became aware of the mild treatment given to those who returned quietly to their homesteads, had chosen to desert. Vaudreuil and Bigot were forced to pledge their own credit to buy supplies because word had reached the Canadian people that their paper money no longer had French government backing. News that Iroquois warriors were accompanying Amherst's army had caused the Abenakis at Fort Chamblay on the Richelieu River to abandon the French.

[40] Webster, *The Journal of Jeffery Amherst*, p. 247.

Nevertheless, Lévis hoped to make a final desperate thrust against Haviland's army with the aid of loyal Indians. But when he summoned local chiefs to a meeting at nearby La Prairie on 4 September the proceedings were interrupted by an Indian delegate from upriver who announced that the villagers there had reached a peace agreement with the British. It had been brokered by Iroquois representatives. The chiefs departed and the attack was called off.

On the morning of the 7th Bougainville came to Amherst with a message from Vaudreuil. The latter had wished to delay proceedings until it could be known whether word of a peace in Europe had reached Quebec (Berryer had promised him that there would be peace by the beginning of August), but Amherst answered that Vaudreuil should be told, 'I was come to take Canada and I did not intend to take anything less.'[41] He invited the French governor to submit articles of capitulation. Fifty articles came back – obviously the document had been well thought out beforehand – and to everyone's surprise Amherst accepted most of them. He permitted the defeated people to keep their forms of local government and their Catholic religion; the priests would function in their parishes and the nuns in their religious establishments as usual. He agreed to allow every Frenchman, Canadian or Acadian, if Canada were to be kept under British rule, to choose whether to remain or go to France (Britain would provide transportation). They could not remain in Canada unless they acknowledged themselves to be subjects of the king of England, but they were not required to bear arms against the king of France. As for the French regulars and their officers, Amherst would not make them prisoners of war, but they must lay down their arms and agree not to serve during the present war. Lévis considered this treatment dishonourable and protested vehemently to Vaudreuil, but was overruled. The articles were signed on 8 September.

A few days later Amherst discussed with Vaudreuil in detail the territories encompassed by the surrender. Lakes Huron, Michigan and Superior were included. Amherst sent to Pitt a sketch map with a red line drawn by Vaudreuil that showed Canada's boundaries. This map would later prove useful when French peace negotiators sought to extend the scope of Louisiana with the aim of reducing the territory surrendered as Canada. To receive the submissions of the western forts Amherst sent troops led by Major Rogers and accompanied by George Croghan. With much truth he could write to Pitt upon preparing to leave for Crown

[41] Ibid. p. 246.

Point, 'I can assure you, Sir, this Country is as quiet & secure as any other Province of His Majesty's Dominions.'[42]

When Fort Lévis capitulated Amherst heard from Sir William Johnson that the Indians intended to ravage the place. He told Johnson that their entry to it must be forbidden, and Johnson, seeing the furore that this decree aroused, expressed anxiety that the Indians would leave the army. Amherst replied that while he wished to preserve their friendship, he would not allow horrible cruelties to be inflicted on the defeated garrison and would give the Indians gifts instead. Most of the Indians did then desert, leaving the army with just 170.[43] Amherst took for granted that French officers and soldiers had deliberately incited Indian violence against the people of the British colonies. He gave this as a reason for not allowing the French officers at Montreal an honourable surrender.

Yet he probably knew that Lévis had not been a principal actor in encouraging Indian mayhem, and when the French general came to him later and explained that the requirement not to serve in the present war would ruin his career, Amherst promised to write a letter to the secretary of state on his behalf. The British government granted Lévis his request; before long he served with distinction in Germany, and eventually he became both a marshal of France and a duke. Years later he and General Murray had occasion to do favours for each other and kept up a friendship. No doubt, by then the French general was aware that Murray, who stayed on as governor of Quebec after Canada surrendered, had favoured Amherst's policy of allowing the Canadians to keep most of their traditional laws, forms of governance, official language and religious institutions.

After reaching France, Vaudreuil received a letter from Berryer which told him that the king 'did not expect to hear so soon of the surrender of Montreal and the whole colony' and that, although he was 'perfectly aware of the state of Canada' and realized that capitulation was necessary, 'his Majesty was not the less surprised and ill pleased at the conditions, so little honorable, to which you submitted, especially after the representations made you by the Chevalier de Lévis'. Clearly, Versailles maintained its prejudice against the governor-general to the end, but Vaudreuil was deeply conscious of how greatly the people of Canada would have suffered if fighting had continued, and was also aware that the terms

---

[42] Amherst to Pitt, Quebec, 4 Oct. 1760, Kimball, ed. *Correspondence of Pitt with America*, II, 340–1.

[43] Waddington, *Guerre*, IV, 381.

were generous. This was evidently of no concern to the French court. In fact, Versailles was disposed to let the truth about Canada's long struggle to survive become obscured by an investigation of scandal which, as will be seen later, became known as the *affaire du Canada*. In this way the court of France managed to ignore the ingenious and exhausting effort that had been made to defend a colony to which it had virtually ceased to give military assistance. As Francis Parkman observed, 'The King himself, and not the servants whom he abandoned to their fate, was answerable for the loss of New France.'[44]

Pitt and the German war

In early February 1760 Horace Walpole remarked, 'The war was made for America, but the peace will be made for Germany; and whatever geographers may pretend, *Crown Point* lies somewhere in Westphalia.'[45] The prediction would prove to be inaccurate, but the remark elegantly summarizes how the situation appeared at the time. Intelligence indicated that France was preparing a military thrust aimed solely at Prince Ferdinand's army. (French generals were told categorically not to consider assisting Austria against Prussia.) The British government could not possibly deny him further military assistance, both in money and men.

For Newcastle the continent had never ceased to be the arena that truly mattered. The only seaborne venture in this war that he approved without complaint was the expedition proposed in September 1758 that ended up conquering Guadeloupe. In that instance he realized that unless an important French island were captured, the government might have to exchange Louisbourg – the conquest of which had just been joyously celebrated – for Minorca in a peace negotiation. The unpopularity of giving Louisbourg back to France in 1748 was still fresh in his mind. In all other cases he argued against maritime expeditions. It has been astutely observed that in 'spite of the common belief that Newcastle left the conduct of the war to Pitt, it is evident that he did nothing of the sort, but was for ever interfering or attempting to interfere in the hope of deflecting Pitt's strategy'.[46] Pitt had prevailed. Although he was prepared to spend money on the German war, he doggedly resisted sending British troops. They

---

[44] Parkman, *Montcalm and Wolfe*, pp. 525–6. Berryer's letter to Vaudreuil, 5 Dec. 1760, quoted p. 525.
[45] To Horace Mann, 6 Feb. 1760, Lewis, ed. *Walpole Correspondence*, V, 369.
[46] Observation by Sherrard in *Lord Chatham*, p. 276.

were always scarce and if sent to Germany they could never be got back. This was one reason why he had pushed for amphibious raids on the Channel coast – to keep the troops from going to Germany.

Pitt had allowed, even recommended, that British cavalry units should be sent to Ferdinand; they were not needed in transoceanic or coastal raiding operations. But in the spring of 1760 it was clear that infantry and artillery must be sent. In responding to Ferdinand's request for troops in December 1759 he had sidestepped by providing funds to recruit 7,000 Germans from Hanover, Hesse and Brunswick, but this would not suffice. He knew he must send British troops to the continent. How much he hated doing it was evident in his conduct. He attempted to divert public attention from the proceedings. One tactic was to put on a parliamentary show for the benefit of his independent supporters in the House of Commons: he paraded before them pleasing measures such as the Property Qualification bill. In cabinet discussions concerning how many troops should be sent to Germany he feigned indifference, as if none of it mattered to him.

Clearly he was upset, and not only because he disliked the strategic emphasis and entanglement that sending more troops implied, but also because of the impact on public support for the war and his political standing in the House of Commons. He could easily see that events on the continent would monopolize war news. To be sure, a complete conquest of Canada would be heralded, but its accomplishment was already built into public expectations. India was so far away that if anything good happened there, no one would know it for at least half a year. As for naval battles, there could be none because France was not putting squadrons to sea. Moreover, she was leaving her overseas possessions to fend for themselves. By default as well as proximity, the campaigning in Germany would be most in the public eye, and the German war was becoming increasingly unpopular. Even if Ferdinand were successful, the expense was great, and opposition politicians would claim that it was all being done for Hanover.

During the summer British troop strength in Germany increased from 10,000 to 22,000, yet Ferdinand remained on the defensive. Seeing this, Pitt could not control his frustration. He hoped for a victorious battle that would stir public enthusiasm. In mid-September he remarked to Newcastle that unless Ferdinand fought a battle he would not favour continuing British support of the German war another year. Hearing of this impatience, Hardwicke commented that it was unstatesmanlike, as it certainly was, since Ferdinand had about 80,000 troops against a French total of about 140,000 and could afford to accept a major battle only under the most promising circumstances. Besides, Pitt had never held the view that Britain's purpose in Germany was to win the war there, only to drain French resources. He was wringing his hands because he was aware of what the public was thinking. He had not adopted a policy of trying to win the war in Germany.

The French offensive's initial objective was to occupy Hesse. The generals realized that sufficient forage to sustain a thrust across Westphalia towards Hanover would not be available, whereas Ferdinand could maintain supplies via the Ems and Weser rivers. The main French army under the duc de Broglie pushed north and east from Frankfurt while a smaller army under Saint-Germain headed straight eastwards along the Ruhr. Despite a surprise attack on 31 July by British cavalry led personally by the Marquess of Granby and seconded by two rapidly deployed brigades of artillery, Ferdinand could not prevent the French from capturing the fortified city of Kassel. And because his army was positioned to the west Ferdinand could not stop the French from continuing on to Göttingen, which they occupied in September. They were thus poised to overrun Hanover and Brunswick. And yet the French went no further. Although Broglie's superior army remained in good health, food and forage at the front were lacking. The long supply lines from Frankfurt were harassed by Ferdinand's patrols; up to 25,000 French troops were needed to guard them, the local inhabitants being generally hostile.

Seeing the French offensive stalled, Ferdinand thought about retaking Kassel, but in this region he, too, faced a forage problem, there being 'no straw, hay, corn nor carts' on the only routes he could take towards the city. Yet he needed to deter Broglie from making a further advance into Brunswick and Hanover. He opted for a diversion. Making sure of his position on the Diemel River, he ordered a detachment of 20,000 to march westwards to the Rhine to lay siege to Wesel. His reasoning: 'If he [Broglie] decides to detach troops for the lower Rhine, I myself will detach more, and . . . this way I will succeed in disengaging Hesse and the country of Hanover, and perhaps also take the town of Wesel.'[47] The departure of this detachment on 23 September was accomplished quietly and the troops were far to the west before Broglie knew what had happened. He decided he could not act quickly enough to save Wesel. Marshal Belleisle,

---

[47] To Frederick of Prussia, 29 Sept. 1760, Savory, *His Britannic Majesty's Army*, p. 261.

however, wasted no time in dispatching over 10,000 troops from France to the lower Rhine.

To maintain secrecy Ferdinand had not informed the British cabinet of his plan to attack Wesel, but London had received word on 2 October that perhaps 15,000 troops were being ordered from France to the lower Rhine, and when Ferdinand's call for assistance came Pitt saw an opportunity. He would send no more British troops to Germany but instead mount a diversionary attack on the French coast. The king spoke in its favour and Pitt immediately asked the Admiralty to arrange transports for 10,000 men, but the expedition still required cabinet approval. Pitt proposed to capture the island of Belle-Île-en-Mer off the southern coast of Brittany. Hardwicke suggested a demonstration without a landing on the Flanders coast; he also proposed stationing an army on the Isle of Wight to tie French forces to coastguard duties. He rightly judged Belle-Île too far away to affect French deployments to the Rhine. Newcastle lobbied hard to persuade the experts in the war cabinet, Anson and Ligonier, to oppose Pitt's project. He gave many reasons but really wanted the troops sent to Ferdinand. When he saw forces marching near his country seat on their way to Portsmouth he thought: 'Would to God they were all now at Wesel.'[48]

At a cabinet meeting Pitt argued strenuously for an attack on Belle-Île. The best opposing argument was that it was too late in the season; this was a point that called for more information. At a second meeting, on 8 October, Captain Augustus Keppel, who was selected to command the naval force, was called in. Anson admitted that weather conditions would probably remain suitable into November and that if necessary the ships could find shelter in the lee of the island, but Keppel raised the question of whether the water off the landing beaches would be deep enough to allow ships' guns to come close and neutralize the defending batteries. Anson was directed to hurry a message off to Sir Edward Hawke who was at Quiberon Bay asking him to provide answers. After drawing up the directive Anson dictated a private letter to Hawke, asking him 'what prospect there may be of success'. He would be glad, he said, 'to be favoured with your private thoughts in a separate letter on this subject'. Receiving these letters, Hawke failed to put his private thoughts in a separate letter, and to make matters worse his letter quickly passed over the questions concerning Belle-Île and focused on how strategically

[48] Newcastle to Joseph Yorke, 10 Oct. 1760, Whitworth, *Ligonier*, p. 335; also Middleton, *Bells*, p. 167.

inferior the occupation of that island would be compared to his own idea of landing marines on the shores of Quiberon Bay; there they could harass the French and destroy the warships remaining in the Vilaine River. When his report reached the Admiralty on 24 October Anson compounded Hawke's mistake by taking it directly to the king without first showing it to Pitt. The king thereupon pronounced against an attack on the island. Pitt was furious: Hawke, he complained, had no business judging questions that were for ministers to decide. He also suspected '*that this seemed to be concerted*' – not exactly true, but Anson said nothing as Pitt angrily departed to talk with Lady Yarmouth. Hawke, he thought, should have emphasized the only reasonable objection to the Belle-Île operation – that it was too late in the year.[49]

Perhaps it had nothing to do with the stress of these confrontations, but George II died of a heart attack the next morning, 25 October 1760. As a result, the cabinet did not discuss the project until 11 November, on which occasion, to Newcastle's great disappointment, it was approved. Everyone recognized, however, that it should not be carried out in winter weather. Still, Pitt could take satisfaction in its being placed on the strategic agenda; this would keep the troops from going to Germany in the spring. Pitt had already made sure that the troops in North America would remain on the other side of the Atlantic. On learning that all of Canada was in British hands Newcastle had suggested bringing some of them home, but Pitt had his eye on using them for Caribbean conquests and a week later gave orders that some should be sent to capture the island of Dominica.[50]

Quite suddenly on 26 November Pitt mentioned to Newcastle that he thought peace was necessary, 'it being impossible to continue the war, and wished that his Grace and Lord Hardwicke would consult upon the method of attaining it'.[51] Pitt's remark, reported by Newcastle, startled Joseph Yorke: 'The most material part of your Grace's letter,' he wrote, 'a very interesting one indeed it is, relates to the dawning of peace from a quarter where it formerly seemed to meet with more difficulty.' In fact, Pitt even addressed the painful question of which overseas conquests might be kept or returned. Perhaps, he said to Newcastle, Britain might 'retain all Canada, Cape Breton and exclude the French from their Fishery on Newfoundland, and give up Guadeloupe and Gorée; or

[49] Mackay, *Admiral Hawke*, pp. 267–73.
[50] Newcastle to Hardwicke, 18 Oct. 1760, BL Add. 35,420 fo. 91.
[51] *Devonshire Diary*, p. 61.

retain Guadeloupe and Gorée with the exclusion of the French fishery on Newfoundland, and give up some part of Canada and confine ourselves to limits of the lakes'.[52]

Although Pitt had thought vaguely about peace in the spring, one may only guess why it was that in late November he suddenly considered it 'impossible to continue the war'. He could take satisfaction in the surrender of all Canada; this had been a primary war aim. Did he think the expense of the war was growing beyond Britain's ability to meet it? In early April when talks at The Hague seemed likely to fail Newcastle remarked that the nation 'could not carry on the war another year' at the current level of expenditure. Pitt 'flew into a violent passion', saying that this sort of talk would 'make peace impracticable and . . . encourage our enemy; that we might have difficulties but he knew we could carry on the war, and were one hundred times better able to do it than the French; that *we* did not want [i.e. need] peace'.[53] Pitt exaggerated of course, but was essentially right. Although the Bank of England had resorted to issuing £1 million in exchequer bills in February and would issue another £1.5 million in May, there seemed to be plenty of available money, for the interest rate stayed remarkably low and the new long-term loan subscription proceeded satisfactorily.[54] Pitt knew that the growing expense was unpopular, but it is likely that his interest in peace in late November was prompted mainly by worries about the German war.

Ferdinand of Brunswick's diversion to Wesel did not succeed. At Kloster Kamp, just west of the Rhine, French troops, some of them coming from France, defeated his detachment in a bloody battle fought on 16 October. Approximately 12,000 troops on each side were engaged. The Hanoverians and British suffered 1,600 killed or wounded, mainly British, the French almost double that number. Nevertheless, the French reserve force was large enough to compel the allies to withdraw. The consequence was that war in Germany would linger on, and with Hesse and Göttingen in French hands the French were well positioned for a spring offensive. Pitt could not avoid informing Parliament on 18 November that Prince Ferdinand would need substantial and continued support. His speech was not warmly received. Not only was there a rising tide of public and parliamentary opinion against continued participation in the German war, but it was

[52] Yorke to Newcastle, 2 Dec., Newcastle to Hardwicke, 3 Dec. 1760, Yorke, *Hardwicke*, III, 313–15.
[53] Newcastle to Hardwicke, 9 April 1760, Yorke, *Hardwicke*, III, 244.
[54] Middleton, *Bells*, pp. 153–4.

also the case that the young king, George III, shared the growing public aversion to it. On his accession he announced that he 'gloried in the name of Briton', which could be taken as indicating indifference to the fate of Hanover.

Pitt was also upset at this time about the attitude of Frederick II. The Prussian army was faltering under the weight of Austrian and Russian pressure. Since June Frederick had been asking the British cabinet to prepare an escape route through a negotiated peace. The Anglo-Prussian alliance, once an asset, was now a liability. On top of this, in late November and early December 1760 Frederick made himself very unpopular with all British statesmen. He had learned from his London envoys of the cabinet's growing interest in peace. Well aware that the alliance treaty contained an article binding each party to consult with the other before undertaking a negotiation, and also aware that France would insist on negotiating with Britain separately, he decided to make his ally pay a heavy price for the article's nullification. Although the British ministers recognized that after an Anglo-French peace Prussia, still at war with Austria and Russia, would need some support, Frederick's demands were tremendous. Prince Ferdinand's German troops, he stipulated, must be joined to the Prussian army and continue to be paid by the British Treasury. The £670,000 annual subsidy to Prussia must continue. All this would mean that Britain would be paying to support a Prussian war against Austria and Russia at very nearly the same level she was paying to defend Hanover against the French. Pitt gave no answer. He was deeply annoyed, and was determined not to let these inflated demands dictate British policy concerning peace.

The rising unpopularity of the war in Germany was supercharged by a remarkable pamphlet titled *Considerations on the Present German War*. The author, Israel Mauduit, began his argument unrealistically with a premise that the European power structure of a half-century earlier was still in existence. Then turning quickly to recent history, he asserted that when France first invaded Germany her prime purpose was to lure Britain into engaging the French army rather than to occupy Hanover. (As we have seen, this claim was false.) But when he turned to the situation as it stood in 1760 his arguments became powerfully convincing. Since the French no longer had a navy, he wrote, they had no choice but to do their fighting in Germany, but Britain could decide not to confront them there and choose instead to capture French West Indian islands unopposed. Undefended Hanover would thereby suffer French occupation, but could be redeemed at the war's end by offering to give back some captured

French islands. (The parallel with Pitt's arguments in 1755 is evident.) To capture such islands would be far less costly than further campaigning in Germany. In any case, the German war, he concluded, was a losing proposition. Campaigning in Germany cost the British Treasury more per soldier than it cost the French. There was no net benefit in terms of diverting French resources; in reality Britain was worse off. He supposed (dubiously) that the French monarchy's ordinary revenue could sustain the war in Germany for many years.[55]

Mauduit's arguments were of a kind that had worried Pitt all year long. *Considerations* sold over 5,000 copies, an astonishing number for a political pamphlet. Although pamphlets countering its arguments were published, its influence was enormous. As Pitt contemplated the year 1761 he saw Britain's land forces completely tied up in Germany and North America, and although he planned to make conquests in the West Indies using troops released from North America, he prudently decided that any large operation should wait until the worst season for tropical diseases and hurricanes had passed. Consequently, for many months people would see the German war and nothing else, and the French were likely to win it, being in a strong position in Hesse and Göttingen. Moreover, he sensed that under the new monarch his political situation was likely to become less secure. For all these reasons peace was not a bad idea.

The Pitt–Newcastle administration undermined

When he died George II was 76 years old. The new king was his grandson, a sheltered young man of 22 who remained entirely under the influence of his mother and his tutor, Lord Bute. They had inculcated in him an extreme sensitivity to any hint of a slight to his status as Prince of Wales and a hatred of all his grandfather's ministers. The spirit of Leicester House where Bute was the leading figure was inherently hostile to anyone who served the old king or worked alongside the Duke of Newcastle, whom they saw as the embodiment of everything detestable in politics. As for Pitt, Bute had hoped that he would reach out to the young prince and provide opportunities for him to share some of the glory of the successful war, but Pitt did not meet their expectations, especially after George II asked him not to inform the prince of cabinet affairs.

---

[55] Mauduit, *Considerations on the Present German War*, especially the last fifteen pages.

Pitt had laboured – he hated writing letters – to keep in friendly communication with Bute, but in the closing months of 1758 the effort became useless. In the wake of the St Cast debacle Bute supposed that General Bligh – a Leicester House favourite – was being singled out for dismissive treatment by George II and his ministers. It did no good for Pitt to point out in reply that Bligh's treatment was no worse than that of other generals whose expeditions had been failures. Bute then made some impossible demands, and in December 1758 boldly asked Pitt what would happen when the old king died, to which Pitt answered: 'everything should be done in concert with the Duke of Newcastle'. To this Bute replied categorically that in the new reign Newcastle 'could not be' a leading minister.[56] Pitt realized that if he said anything further on this subject, it would echo through Leicester House and then travel to the ears of Newcastle and the king. The result would be to undermine an administration which had many wartime goals yet to accomplish. The intercommunication between Bute and Pitt ceased. In summer 1759, young Prince George formally asked his grandfather to allow him to join the army, presumably in a high and honourable position. George II suggested a stiff negative reply, and Pitt tried to soften it but got no credit at Leicester House for his effort.

It was a month later that Lord George Sackville, who was a Leicester House favourite, was asked to leave the army because of his conduct at Minden. Prince Ferdinand had said publicly that he wished that he could have conveyed his battle orders to Granby, and Sackville, understandably upset, reacted by immediately trying to organize testimony from supporters. Ferdinand viewed the turmoil this caused among his officers as intolerable and wrote a letter to the secretaries of state saying that if Sackville were not recalled he would resign. London had already recalled him. Pitt did what he could to ease Sackville's distress; he allowed him to come home without threat of inquiry and did this in spite of popular outrage which was fully shared by George II. When the king summarily deprived Sackville of all his military employments the disgraced general sought Pitt's intervention. Pitt replied with an elaborately worded expression of heartfelt distress: the evidence, he explained, unfortunately left him at a loss to see how he could help. For Pitt the issue was not personal. Obviously it would be dangerous to send any signal to Ferdinand suggesting that Sackville was forgiven. To lose this able, dedicated, practically

---

[56] Sherrard, *Lord Chatham*, p. 306. For Bute's letter about Bligh (25 Sept. 1758) and Pitt's responses see Sedgwick, 'Letters from William Pitt to Lord Bute', pp. 162–6.

irreplaceable, commander-in-chief would be calamitous, and no one felt more strongly about this than Pitt. As could be expected, Lord Bute soon asked Pitt to intervene on Sackville's behalf. The secretary of state had no choice but to refuse, however much it might damage his relations with Leicester House.

To make matters worse Sackville requested a court-martial against himself, hoping to establish that his conduct at Minden had been justified. Friends cautioned him against it. The political circumstances were extremely adverse. Although Sackville was not a coward (the popular accusation), there was a case for judging him guilty of disaffection. After taking over command of the British forces in Germany from the deceased Marlborough he had said things to Prince Ferdinand that were bound to make the commander-in-chief uneasy, and had spoken openly to British officers in a manner bordering on insubordination. (In the naval service, it may be recalled, disaffection was a capital crime.) Convinced that he had been wronged, Sackville refused to allow his dismissal to go uncontested. No doubt, he counted on his social rank (his father was the Duke of Dorset), his reputation in Parliament, and an impressive range of political and military connections. During the trial, however, his egoism overwhelmed his intelligence. Allowed to speak, he exhibited an air of contemptuous superiority towards the dozen general officers who sat in judgment of him that dismayed everyone including his friends.

The trial lasted from 7 March to 5 April 1760 and dominated the news. Eighteen officers were brought to England from Germany. Sackville was charged with disobedience to the commander-in-chief's orders. The evidence included devastating testimony from all three messengers. The court found Sackville guilty of the charge, which carried the death penalty, but merely declared him unfit to serve in any military capacity. Infuriated by the lenient sentence, George II ordered that the court-martial's finding should be read publicly throughout the army, worldwide, so that officers might be 'convinced that neither High Birth nor Great Employment' could 'shelter offences of such a nature'.[57] During a pause on the banks of the upper St Lawrence Amherst ordered it to be read to his troops.

A few days after George III's accession Sackville went to court and was allowed in. Pitt was livid. He had warned Bute that 'Prince Ferdinand would be justly alarmed' by such a signal from the new monarch and might 'resign the command of the Army'. According to the Duke of

[57] Whitworth, *Ligonier*, pp. 320–4.

Devonshire, 'Pitt was so full of this subject that there was no getting him to talk upon any other.' Bute claimed that Sackville's coming to court was a surprise to him, and gave assurances that George III would not take Sackville's side. (Privately, however, Leicester House paid no attention to the evidence indicating the offender's guilt and in the course of time George III would see to it that Sackville was elevated to high office. Under the name Lord George Germain, which he took to receive an inheritance, he would serve in 1775 as the secretary of state responsible for directing the campaign to surpress, the American Revolution.) Devonshire supposed that the 'coldness' between Pitt and Bute began when Pitt refused 'to take some steps tending to save Lord George when he first came from abroad'.[58] Certainly the Sackville affair amplified Pitt's dislike, but, as noted above, the coldness began in late 1758.

At the end of April 1760, however, Lord Bute began to rethink the question of how matters might stand if the old king died. He decided to send a close friend who was an admirer of Pitt to talk with him. The aim was not merely to mend torn relations but also to propose a partnership in the new reign, 'tying the knot of union as tight as ever' in Bute's words. Pitt could see that Bute had in mind a government without Newcastle and Hardwicke, and this set him off. He compared his satisfaction in talking with Lady Yarmouth, 'a very fair and honest woman', against the obstruction he experienced from Leicester House. He condemned the 'imperious' instincts of Lord Bute; the two of them could never work well together, he said. He reiterated his old contention that as the minister responsible for 'measures' he would not take dictation, which was bound to occur in a partnership with Bute, who would have the king's backing. Pitt spoke his mind in a manner out of control, and the impact of the conversation when reported to Bute and the Prince of Wales was horrendous. Bute was reminded of how much he personally feared and disliked Pitt, and young George described England's most successful wartime statesman as 'the most ungrateful and . . . dishonorable of men' whom he could 'never bear to see . . . in any future Ministry'.[59] His opinion remained unaltered when his grandfather died.

When the moment actually came, however, Bute understood the need for patience, and he realized that in the near term Pitt was indispensable. On the very night of George II's death he called Pitt aside and told him

---

[58] *Devonshire Diary*, p. 51.

[59] See Namier, *England in the Age*, pp. 104–8. The mutual friend, who jotted down notes on the conversation, was Gilbert Elliot, a junior lord of the Admiralty.

that although he had been thinking of taking the helm at the Treasury (as Pitt had heard), he had given up the idea and would be merely 'a private man at the side of the King and give his best support to publick measures, that he approved of his system of the war and offer'd him his cordial and sincere friendship'. Pitt received these words with gracious courtesy, but sensing that Bute might be proposing a political alliance he mentioned that he 'approved of the Duke of Newcastle's being continued' as head of the Treasury.[60] Since Bute wished to exclude Newcastle and, despite his personal misgivings, wished to form an alliance with Pitt he was painfully disappointed.

Although Bute abandoned thoughts of the Treasury, he did not abandon the idea of ministerial office. Some of his friends urged him to avoid the risks and burdens, but George III wanted him to be a leading minister, and under the constitution the king could appoint anyone he wished. The only constraint was that his ministers must collectively command parliamentary majorities when vital issues arose, such as the voting of financial supplies. This would not be a problem if most current cabinet members were to remain in office: they could organize the necessary majorities. Newcastle was the key to this parliamentary power, and if the king wanted Bute in the cabinet, he would be wise to keep Newcastle at the Treasury. The duke, however, could choose to resign, and Hardwicke advised him to do so (and thus leave it to Bute to figure out how to cope), but this idea did not appeal to Newcastle or to his many friends in minor offices who might find themselves pitched out. After a week of hesitation he decided to stay.

Newcastle had no objection to seeing Bute appointed to a high ministerial office other than the Treasury. Bute was inexperienced but intelligent. He had the young king completely under his influence. He was definitely a 'royal favourite' and would wield enormous power whether he chose to join the cabinet or to exercise power covertly as 'minister behind the curtain'. To Newcastle, whose power lay in the sphere of distributing patronage and exercising personal influence, it did not make a great deal of difference which position Bute chose; either way the business would be accomplished by private communication. It was also possible to believe that government would be conducted more efficiently if the favourite acted in a position of visible responsibility. Hardwicke and Devonshire agreed.

[60] Ibid. pp. 120–1.

Pitt's situation was very different. His claim of responsibility 'for measures' was not mere rhetoric; from the beginning it had been a condition of his acceptance of office. So long as the war continued he would view the achievement of military success and an appropriate peace as personal duties. He also believed in cabinet government. Of course he wanted his own way, yet he felt obliged to consult with and gain the assent of the leading ministers, and, despite Newcastle's frequent opposition, the cabinet generally supported his proposals. In this sense 'cabinet government' had worked. When the inner circle of ministers reached a decision it was usually Newcastle who went to George II to secure royal consent, and he had admirably performed this duty in good faith regardless of his personal opinions. Pitt recognized the merit of it. Shortly after George III became king Pitt lamented its loss when he said to Newcastle: 'Formerly, my Lord, if I had not had an opportunity to see the King, if you told me that you would answer for the King's consent, that was enough; I was satisfied. Where is that satisfaction to be had now?'[61] Clearly, Pitt believed that with the royal favourite in cabinet office the whole system would change. The men at the council table would be conscious that their words could quickly travel to the monarch and that there was one member who could count absolutely on royal backing for his views. Discussions would take on a different character. Moreover, an unbiased delivery of ministerial decisions to the monarch could not be assumed. From Pitt's viewpoint there was a great deal to be lost if Lord Bute were to hold high office.

Did Newcastle, Hardwicke and Devonshire – the 'Whig triumvirate' – realize how strongly Pitt felt about all this and how much he wanted Newcastle to remain at the Treasury? With respect to the latter point Pitt made his position clear straightaway in a conference with Hardwicke on 29 October. Hardwicke reported to Newcastle that Pitt 'had most fully and expressly declared . . . to my Lord Bute . . . how sincerely he wished to continue to act with you, upon whom he could depend', that your differences of opinion about measures did not generate 'ill-humour'.[62] In January 1761 it became known to the leading ministers that Bute wanted a place in the cabinet. On the 20th Pitt bluntly told Newcastle that the nation would not suffer a favourite to be a minister, adding that in the case of Bute, '*he for one would never consent or lend a helping hand to make him one*'. On 9 February, during another long talk with Newcastle, Pitt went further and said that he 'would never have anything to do with

---

[61] Newcastle to Hardwicke, 3 Dec. 1760, Yorke, *Hardwicke*, III, 315.
[62] Hardwicke to Newcastle, 29 Oct. 1760, ibid. III, 308.

Lord Bute as a minister and that he would not go on if he could have no access to the King but through Lord Bute'.[63] The Sardinian ambassador, Francesco Giuseppe, conte di Viry (Count Viry), was continually sowing false reports that Pitt was aligning with Bute and scheming to undermine Newcastle and his friends, but there should have been no doubt in the duke's mind on this issue. For all his faults, Pitt was a man who honestly said what he meant, and Newcastle knew it.[64]

While Pitt's loyalty to Newcastle was firm, the latter's was in danger of being shaken. On 9 December, when Viry had come to Newcastle and proposed a close alliance with Bute, the duke was all too receptive. At the last minute he remembered that he should maintain good relations with Pitt and worriedly reported the conversation to Hardwicke, whose response was unequivocal. If, Hardwicke warned, he were seen to be drawing close to Bute, Pitt 'would undoubtedly fly out in the most violent manner; and what man has either your Grace or Lord B. to oppose him in the House of Commons?'[65] Over the years, as we have seen, Hardwicke often had occasion to issue this reminder.

Pitt had not said that he would resign if Bute came into high office, only that he would not work with or through him. The triumvirate supposed, correctly as it proved, that he was intent on remaining at the helm until the war was properly concluded. In fact, during this time of political turmoil he behaved more like a statesman than a politician. While everyone else at court schemed and gossiped about politics Pitt usually talked about foreign affairs. On 16 January the three Whig lords concluded that Lord Bute could be made a secretary of state without provoking Pitt's resignation. They agreed that the royal desire to give high office to Bute should not be opposed. Newcastle and Devonshire spoke of wishing to avoid 'confusion', their word for ineffective government.

At the same time they agreed that Pitt should be informed before the appointment was made. They judged that responsibility for doing this was not theirs since the initiative was coming (via Count Viry) from Bute and

[63] Devonshire recorded Newcastle's reports of these conversations in his diary; italicized emphasis is Devonshire's (*Devonshire Diary*, pp. 73, 81).

[64] Count Viry had an amazing talent for gaining the confidence of practically every highly placed British politician and clearly enjoyed serving as a conduit. However, unlike Lady Yarmouth he was not an honest broker. There is ample reason to think that throughout this period of political turmoil he consciously served Bute's goals, but Newcastle kept referring to him as 'my friend'.

[65] Quoted in Namier, *England in the Age*, p. 137.

the king. So they proposed that Bute should go to Pitt and let him know what they had decided. This was spineless. If they truly believed in their theory about less confused governance, someone, preferably Hardwicke, should have explained to Pitt why his objections to governing alongside Bute had to be overridden for the public good. Pitt would know of course that smooth governance was not their only concern; they were hoping to stand well with the new king. They all realized that a political earth-quake had occurred: a young man suspected of harbouring deep prejudices against them, prejudices that had been encouraged by his mother and Lord Bute, was now on the throne and might reign for decades. Their decision would make Pitt unhappy, but it was their duty as colleagues to inform him of it. As Devonshire remarked, 'it would not be honourable towards Mr. Pitt to take such a step without acquainting him first and having his concurrence'.[66]

In the event, Bute refused the mission. He would not even admit that he desired to become a secretary of state. He realized that the public would react badly if the king were simply to use his prerogative power to appoint a favourite to such an office, especially a man who had no claim to experience as a statesman and happened to be a Scotsman, an object of popular prejudice. Bute was therefore determined to have it appear that the Whig lords were the prime movers. (For this reason Viry had been pretending all along that the appointment was his own idea.) With Viry's deft assistance Bute succeeded in manoeuvring them into acting as instigators. He frightened Newcastle where he was most easily frightened, by having the king remove some of his closest allies from their situations. Viry played his part by telling Devonshire that Pitt might be getting the upper hand at court – pure fabrication. All this was done in conjunction with subtle hints that these difficulties would go away if the Whig lords would take the initiative and suggest to the king that Lord Bute should be made a secretary of state.

At the beginning of March the triumvirate concocted a plan whereby they would avoid the appearance of taking the initiative and at the same time make sure that Pitt was informed. Newcastle would go to the king and talk about the need for a better execution of business in general terms, and the king, getting the idea, was then to summon Devonshire and ask him to mention the possibility of Bute's appointment to Newcastle, Hardwicke and Pitt, wishing to 'know their thoughts upon it'. Viry short-circuited the plan by going quickly to Newcastle and urging him to go

[66] To Viry, 22 Jan. 1761, *Devonshire Diary*, p. 74.

to the king and recommend the appointment. When Newcastle answered that by doing this he might greatly upset Pitt, Viry answered that if he 'insisted too much upon the danger disobliging Mr. Pitt, it would fling them [Bute and the king] more into Mr. Pitt's hands than I would wish . . . In short [Newcastle recorded], I found that if I did not speak to the King, the whole was over; or possibly might be put into another channel.' Viry understood Newcastle's greatest weakness: against all reliable evidence the duke imagined that Pitt would join with Bute and push him out.

He went to the king as Viry suggested – and botched his mission. Instead of confining himself to general terms he allowed himself to be manoeuvred into directly recommending that Bute should be made a secretary of state. After the damage was done he had an afterthought and mentioned to George III that 'Mr. Pitt must not be offended . . . [being] absolutely necessary for the carrying on his service'. The king vaguely reassured him on the point, but a week later when the duke raised the issue of Pitt's importance with Bute in a private conversation the latter 'constantly objected to it', saying that Pitt's political influence was on the wane.[67] If Newcastle said anything in protest, he did not record it. His abandonment of Pitt was complete.

Why had Devonshire and Hardwicke allowed this to happen? Both were aware that Newcastle was hopelessly inept as a negotiator and would probably mishandle his interview with the king. Basil Williams's explanation, that they had finally grown so tired of Pitt's fulminations that they ceased caring, does not fit the known facts. After the death of George II Pitt did not speak harshly to any of them, though he openly and pointedly criticized Bute on one occasion. Perhaps Devonshire was influenced by Viry's (possibly inflated) account of Lord Temple's insufferable manner of conversing,[68] but Temple was known to be this way. Besides, up to this point Devonshire had never neglected to declare that Pitt must be consulted. Why did Hardwicke, who had consistently advised Newcastle to avoid alienating Pitt whenever possible, fail to act at this critical juncture? One explanation is that he felt old and tired; after George II died he told Newcastle that he no longer had the stomach for political battles at court, especially among a new set of courtiers. Hardwicke also had a selfish motive: he did not want to prejudice Bute and the new king against his sons, three of whom were well launched on careers in government.

[67] The quotations in this and the preceding paragraph (from Newcastle's papers) are all from Namier, *England in the Age*, pp. 164–6.
[68] 19 Feb. 1761, *Devonshire Diary*, p. 83.

None of the three Whig lords took the trouble afterwards to go to Pitt, ill at Hayes, and tell him what had been done. No doubt, they felt in their shame that there was nothing they could say to him. The task was left to Bute who travelled to Hayes on 12 March and heard Pitt's calm acquiescence: if it was his Majesty's wish, he said, so be it, but then Pitt asked, 'pray, my Lord, what say the King's other Ministers to it?' – a question that Bute fended off.[69]

These transactions destroyed the spirit of the Pitt–Newcastle administration. Despite the inevitable disagreements there had been an underlying trust based on good faith, and that was now corroded. Bute's elevation to secretary of state was unavoidable. Pitt knew he would have to accept it, but the way it was done gave him reason to think that he could no longer be sure of the support of the Whig lords, and he needed them more than ever now that cabinet meetings were attended by new people of influence, like the Duke of Bedford, who were asked by George III to join the deliberations. Bute would exacerbate disunity and mistrust by playing Pitt off against Newcastle, often going out of his way to make the duke feel powerless. In any case, Newcastle, always filled with anxieties, was having his own difficulty in adjusting to the changes. For decades he had enjoyed a trusted relationship with the monarch, a relationship that was the ultimate source of his power, and this power now belonged to Bute. Pitt was not the sort to feel powerless but revealed his sense of insecurity in small ways. Always highly strung, he became more so; it affected his health and spirit, and would in due course upset his mental balance. His troubled mind would never forget that Newcastle had weakly and without informing him allowed the royal favourite to attain high office – in a manner indicating that this was done at the request of the Whig lords. Twenty months later Pitt's resentment of this betrayal would play a role in the politics that allowed parliamentary approval of the peace terms.

More immediately, as royal patronage came increasingly under Bute's control he could contemplate supplanting Newcastle, but any attempt to get rid of Pitt in wartime might provoke a political storm. George III hated both men, but Bute restrained the young king's impulses, and everything on the surface looked as if his gaining the secretaryship had produced no change in the administration. Yet the cabinet was now vulnerable to serious dissension.

[69] Namier, *England in the Age*, pp. 166–7.

CHAPTER 14

The chance of peace, 1761

The prominent occurrence of 1761 was neither military nor naval. It was diplomatic and political. From the end of March to the end of September attention was focused on the Anglo-French peace negotiation. All countries were tired of the war, and it seemed that the opportune moment had finally arrived. From The Hague on 10 March Joseph Yorke wrote to his father: 'All the World is full of Peace, and the people concerned in Stocks who buy the Secrets of Courts, and feel the pulses of their Purses, are quite sanguine about it.'[1] Three weeks later the British secretaries of state received from Versailles overtures which looked promising. Yet six months later peace was not achieved. Instead, France acquired Spain as an ally and the scope of the war enlarged. Given the expectations, this outcome was extremely disappointing and someone had to be blamed.

For almost two centuries public attention has focused on the causes of war. In the eighteenth century when wars were more common and peace was always negotiated, greater attention was focused on how wars ended. A failed negotiation brought great disappointment. Accusations flew in all directions; one side or the other was said to be too aggressive or too much under the influence of an ally. Yet statesmen had good reasons not to forgo military operations during a negotiation (assuming no cessation of arms had been arranged), and certainly did not wish to disappoint an ally or fail to preserve ongoing war-making capability unless the negotiation's success could be considered certain. In sum, the task of negotiating the end of a war was politically, militarily and diplomatically complicated. Mistaken assumptions, wilful deceptions and sometimes betrayals were part of the process.

[1] Yorke to Hardwicke, 10 March 1761, BL Add. 35,358 fo. 157.

The Seven Years War between Britain and France did not end in 1760 but, as is generally agreed, should have ended in 1761. The much-publicized negotiation that might have ended it in 1761 is the main theme of this chapter. According to most histories it was Britain's fault that the negotiation failed, and William Pitt was responsible. Unquestionably, Pitt was a demanding negotiator, and there can be no doubt that he sought a peace that reflected the impressive measure of British military success and naval dominance. The war had been expensive, and he wished to secure advantages that would diminish the future maritime and commercial capabilities of France, just as the empress-queen at Vienna wished to diminish the future power of Prussia. In one important respect the cases were different. By 1761 Britain had achieved militarily the maritime and colonial advantages that Pitt had sought, but Maria Theresa had not yet attained her goals. She assumed, however, that with Russian assistance her army could defeat the king of Prussia, whose ability to continue the war was seriously eroding. With respect to war aims, therefore, Austria had a strong reason to keep the war going, Britain much less so.

What about France? She still had a strong army, but no money to rebuild her navy, and Britain's unchallenged naval supremacy was bound to reduce her colonial possessions further if the war continued. Although the French monarchy's financial situation was dire, it was painful for Louis XV, Pompadour and Choiseul to allow financial concerns to determine whether France should make peace. The common view has been that Pitt's 'stiff and haughty diplomacy' drove Choiseul, 'who . . . sincerely desired that peace which France so badly needed', to move towards an alliance with Spain for continuing the war.[2] Choiseul was by nature an optimistic gambler; he knew that the French army was strong, and that the British seemed to be tiring of the expensive German war. He was susceptible to the idea that Spanish assistance could help France secure better terms. The question of how much these considerations influenced his conduct of the negotiation forms a prominent theme of this chapter.

Antecedents: Spain, Austria, Russia and Ferdinand's winter campaign

In February 1760 when the duc de Choiseul learned that the king of Spain had withdrawn his offer to serve as mediator he was, as we have seen,

---

[2] The words are Rohan Butler's when reviewing Rashed's book, *Peace of Paris*, in *English Hist. Rev.* 68 (1953), 445.

extremely upset. He demanded that Carlos III go ahead with the offer of mediation anyway and, if the British did not accept, declare war. D'Ossun, the ambassador, knew that Spain needed time to build up her forces and was in no position to go to war, but Choiseul persisted, writing letters to d'Ossun which denounced Carlos. The ambassador held back these angry comments, for he knew that in his heart the king of Spain wished to side with France. Ricardo Wall, the leading minister, answered Choiseul's impatient demands by bluntly telling d'Ossun in October that if Spain were to agree to an early declaration of war, her nascent navy would be wiped out. Choiseul tried every argument: the Spanish empire would certainly be attacked next; by allowing trade with Britain Spain was enriching the wrong country; it was the Spanish king's duty to step forward to save Europe from British maritime and colonial dominance now that France was unable to keep up the war at sea. In mid-November he was so anxious for the Spanish king to go to war that he urged him to attack and annex Portugal; France, he promised, would provide 15,000 troops to assist the invasion as well as ships of the line to help conquer Brazil. He also mentioned the possibility that France would invade the Netherlands. This amazing letter could hardly be taken seriously, but it contained a credible threat: 'If the king of Spain cannot declare himself efficaciously, the king [of France] will be forced to pursue, cost what it will, a negotiation of peace.'[3]

Months before, Ricardo Wall had reasoned that if Spain were to incur the expense of mobilizing her army and navy, it should be done for the sake of Spanish objectives, not French ones. Accordingly Spain chose to pursue long-standing complaints against Britain. Everyone at Madrid believed that the British would not take these Spanish grievances seriously unless they feared the prospect of France and Spain joined in wartime alliance. On 28 November d'Ossun reported that Carlos III understood that it was desirable for him to act alongside Louis XV because as soon as France made peace the English would fall on him, but 'unfortunately he was not yet ready': Havana was defenceless and Spanish 'arsenals were empty'.[4] Still, Carlos looked towards closer cooperation and acceded to France's request, made months before, for a new ambassador. Pablo Jerónimo Grimaldi y Pallavicini, marquis de Grimaldi was accordingly transferred from The Hague to Versailles.

---

[3] Choiseul to d'Ossun, 14 Nov. 1760, Waddington, *Guerre*, IV, 423–4.
[4] D'Ossun to Choiseul, ibid. IV, 425–6.

He was known to be hostile to Britain. His instructions, written by Wall on 14 January 1761, advised that if Spain hoped to obtain satisfaction for her grievances, steps needed to be taken well before France was on the point of making peace with Britain. Grimaldi was ordered to get things started by suggesting informally, as if on his own, that Spain might eventually fight alongside France; perhaps Minorca could eventually be transferred to Spain as a reward. In any case the ambassador should suggest that Spain would look forward to joining with France in an offensive and defensive treaty. This marked a decisive turn in Spanish policy.

How did Spain arrive at this hostile posture towards Britain? The ostensible reason as stated by the Spanish court was her sense of outrage at the British government's haughty dismissal of her grievances. These included the chronic problem of Spanish ships captured illegally by British privateers. Pitt had tried his best to curb such abuses and Wall could perceive the sincerity of his efforts; both men knew that there were always disputes over the legitimacy of captures. About the other grievances it is difficult to give a satisfactory answer. They were incorporated in a memorial which had been presented by a new ambassador to London, Joaquin Atanasio Pignatelli de Aragon y Moncayo, conde de Fuentes, on 9 September 1760. In it the Spanish government asked that all British settlements on the coasts round the bay of Honduras be immediately removed, and declared that only after this was done would Spain discuss the right of British subjects to cut logwood on those coasts. Logwood was an essential source of blue dye for woollen cloth, Britain's major industry. Another request was for Spain to have a share in the fishing off the Newfoundland banks. Pitt replied to these requests (which the Spanish termed grievances) in a letter dated 26 September to the British ambassador at Madrid, George William Hervey, Earl of Bristol. The fishery, he wrote, was 'a principal basis of the maritime power of Great Britain [and not] to be in any degree pared off and divided'. Spanish exclusion from it was embodied in the treaty of Utrecht, as the court of Madrid knew, and no British minister could think of making such a concession. As for logwood, although Britain was willing to remove the shore establishments, he strongly objected to the demand that they be removed before the British right to cut logwood could be discussed. In addition, there was an aspect of Spain's proceedings that had made Pitt very angry: Fuentes informed him that a copy of the memorial concerning the fishery was also being sent to Versailles. Pitt called this a 'strange step', remarking that it was diplomatically imprudent and perhaps indecent.

He warned that if Madrid was 'hoping to intimidate' London in this way, it would be counter-productive.[5]

Lord Bristol received this letter on 22 October, but it was not until 6 November that he and Wall were able to have a thorough conversation about it. Pitt had thought it wise to restrict discussion to ministerial and ambassadorial conversations and avoid written exchanges; he therefore told Lord Bristol not to let the Spanish minister have a copy of his letter, a proceeding that Lord Hardwicke (whom Pitt kept informed) approved. Wall and Bristol read it side by side. The Spanish minister was courteous but upset that he could not be permitted a copy. All along, Ricardo Wall was pleading for some sign of British flexibility. Unwillingness to provide him with a copy, he said, looked like 'trifling' with Spain's grievances, and in fact this mattered a great deal to him because his influence had been diminished by the death of Queen Amelia on 27 September. Lord Bristol had not believed that her passing harmed British interests, but he was wrong: she was conversant with policy issues and the king listened to her, and although she was an offspring of the French royal family, she was wary of French inclinations to use Spain for her own purposes. In fact, when the French government requested loans from Spain in February and April 1760 she had stepped in to prevent their being made. Wall had reason to worry, and told Bristol in December that the French interest at the court of Madrid was 'constantly endeavouring to get Him removed'.[6]

Because of unfortunate delays Pitt's letter allowing Bristol to give Wall a copy of the written response did not reach Madrid until 10 January 1761. By this time Wall was bending to the king's pro-French wishes. Bristol thought that he remained steady. He had not only misjudged the role of the queen but badly misread how much royal pressure there was on Wall. In mid-January his eyes were at last opened. Wall asked him some blunt question and took the occasion to ask, if logwood was essential to Britain's principal industry, were not fish essential to a Catholic country like Spain?

In retrospect it is evident that Pitt did not handle these relations with Madrid well. Although Hardwicke had approved the procedure of denying Madrid a written response, he had also warned that Wall might be losing influence. Pitt had neglected to take this into consideration. He was certainly ill-served by Bristol, and the ambassador's lack of perspicacity

---

[5] Pitt to Bristol, 26 Sept. 1760 in Thackeray, *History*, I, 487–92. Hardwicke to Pitt, 29 Sept. 1760, Yorke, *Hardwicke*, III, 250–1.
[6] Aiton, 'Diplomacy', p. 706. Bristol to Pitt, 16 Dec., 22 Dec. 1760, TNA, SP 94/162.

was especially harmful because London's communications with Madrid were slow: the couriers dared not travel through France and went by sea from Corunna to Falmouth. It took almost two months, sometimes longer, for a dispatch from London to receive an answer whereas the overland return trip between Madrid and Paris took only about fifteen days. On 19 January Bristol finally reported that Wall's attitude had changed for the worse. It was a clear indication of trouble. But the letter did not reach Pitt until 10 March.

Historians have usually supposed that a more generous and accommodating mode of diplomatic exchange on Pitt's part would have prevented Spain from becoming alienated. But no one in the British cabinet would have yielded to the fishery demand (Wall probably knew this), and although Pitt's handling of the logwood issues seems too stiff, he had cabinet support, not only from Hardwicke but also from the Duke of Devonshire, who told Fuentes that he 'could not advise Mr. Pitt to send orders for evacuating the coast [of the bay of Honduras] without some satisfaction given at the same time to us'.[7] There was an underlying question of whether, if London ordered an evacuation, the court of Spain would see it as a sign of weakness and push for more. But Wall needed some sort of favourable signal and did not get it.

Logwood-cutting encroachments on imperial territory were symbolic of a larger Spanish concern: fear of Britain's penetration of trade in their empire. Economic reform had been much in Carlos III's mind before his accession. He did not require French prodding to seek to oppose British commercial penetration. He had personally resented the British for a long time. Although British trade was generally profitable for Spain and her empire, the king in his heart was decidedly anti-British. Only the unreadiness of his armed forces restrained him from waging war alongside France. Military and naval weakness was Wall's only effective argument for restraint.

Unfortunately for Spain, Carlos III was inclined to believe that the British government would not stand up to a Franco-Spanish combination. He may have mistaken London's steady policy of trying not to antagonize Spain over maritime issues as signifying weakness. If so, it was a serious miscalculation. It was encouraged by naive reports from Fuentes, which Wall tried his best to counter.

What use the duc de Choiseul would make of Spain's willingness to engage in an offensive and defensive alliance will be seen shortly. The fact is that during the same months in which he was inciting Spain to war and

---

[7] *Devonshire Diary*, pp. 59–60 (15 Nov. 1760).

encouraging a military alliance he was urging Austria and Russia to plan for peace. When the ambassador, Starhemberg, said that Austria wished to fight on, Choiseul answered that France could not support another year's campaigning: 'What do you want me to do? We have no money, no resources, no navy, no soldiers, no generals, no heads, no ministers', he said (with exaggeration). 'You can count on it that I am going to employ all means possible to make peace as soon as I can.' He followed this up with a formal memoir which reported that France was out of money and barely holding on in Hesse, accumulating debts and unable to revive commerce. He saw no possibility of benefiting from continuing the contest either in America or Europe. Maria Theresa, he wrote, should declare at the end of the 1760 campaign that she will make peace with Prussia if England and France were to make peace.[8] Vienna did not send a formal reply until 22 October; it indicated no interest in peace.

By December, however, the attitude at Vienna changed dramatically. On 3 November Frederick II had achieved an unexpected victory at Torgau, thus retaining his hold on most of Saxony for the winter. Soon after news of the battle reached Vienna the empress-queen was shaken by a long interview with Marshal Daun. He informed her that the monarchy's finances were seriously depleted and recruiting was faltering. Maria Theresa, for the first time, conceded that the reconquest of Silesia was probably not possible. Kaunitz was of the same mind; on 31 December he declared that domestic considerations (chiefly financial problems) must take priority over foreign policy goals. He resurrected the proposal of a general congress, and proposed Augsburg as its site. Russia would probably agree with the proposal but would have to be consulted. The empress-queen was perplexed: she hoped to avoid the expense of mobilizing for a 1761 campaign, but because communications with St Petersburg were slow she might have to mobilize anyway. Ironically, just when everyone in London seemed to be convinced of the probability of Prussia's defeat the imperial government at Vienna was concluding with regret that Austria could not continue the contest. At the beginning of 1761 both France and Austria seemed to want peace, and Russia would probably have to go along.

There were, however, sharp disputes between Paris and Vienna over timing and method. Choiseul was determined to ward off a general congress, and in January he had the nerve to suggest that France would

[8] Starhemberg to Kaunitz, 28 Aug. 1760, Choiseul's memoir of 9 Sept., Waddington, *Guerre*, IV, 442, 446.

take charge of negotiating for her allies, ignoring the fact that by this point France's contribution to the war against Prussia was minimal. He proposed to accomplish this in a format of two congresses, one in London the other in Paris. He also proposed a suspension of arms. Kaunitz accepted the idea of a suspension (for six months) but rejected Choiseul's two congresses. Russia took the same position. At St Petersburg, however, the French found a way to gain their point: the Empress Elizabeth had fallen ill and was too sick to conduct business. Choiseul's special envoy, Louis-Auguste Le Tonnelier, baron Breteuil, managed, by dispensing suitable bribes, to gain Russia's assent to Choiseul's scheme of two congresses as preliminary to the general congress. He also obtained approval of something else Choiseul wanted: that the Russian ambassador in London should present a French memoir proposing peace negotiations to the British secretary of state. Meanwhile Kaunitz was growing very tired of hearing Choiseul's stream of criticisms and accusations. For three months, Kaunitz complained, Maria Theresa had been patiently receiving from him proposals that were both repugnant and ever-changing. Expressing his disgust, he said to the French ambassador: 'It is a principle of mine that truly great finesse is not to have any. The empress and I do not wish to deceive anybody.' He reminded the ambassador that she had not broken any of her promises. But she steadily rejected the idea of two congresses.[9] It was now February 1761. Vienna continued to insist on a general congress but was now backing away from an armistice because the procedural disputes had stretched out so long that Austria had no choice but to prepare for another campaign.

During late February and March the letters to Vienna from Versailles expressed urgency, even panic. Choiseul pushed for an immediate armistice, and when his wishes were not met his anger became so extreme that it aroused Kaunitz's suspicions: 'The duke', he wrote to Starhemberg, 'exceeds all limits of appropriateness and discretion; this leads me to believe that he must have conceived the hope of again putting on foot his great project of making himself master of the whole peace negotiation and of realizing his monstrous proposition of the double congress.' Kaunitz knew the man. Choiseul had just attempted to insert in his letter to Pitt a clause intimating that France was authorized to negotiate for all her allies, an attempt that Starhemberg alertly thwarted.[10] And so it appeared that

[9] Choiseul-Praslin to Choiseul, 15 Feb. 1761, ibid. IV, 480.
[10] Kaunitz to Starhemberg, 29 March, Starhemberg to Kaunitz, 26 March 1761, ibid. IV, 488–9.

Choiseul was foiled in his attempt to make himself master of the entire peace negotiation. As will be seen, however, he would eventually manage to obtain much of the control he desired.

What provoked Choiseul's urgency in late February and the first weeks of March? The likely cause was extreme anxiety over events in Hesse. Prince Ferdinand had launched an attack. Aware that the French in possession of Göttingen posed great danger to Hanover, he had tried in late autumn 1760 to dislodge them, but incessant rains made transport impossible and forced him to quit. Without doubt the French were planning to attack Hanover in the coming year with two great armies, one from the lower Rhine, one from Göttingen and Hesse. The correct strategy for the weaker army was to disrupt that offensive before it started; so, after communicating with Frederick II, Ferdinand decided upon a daring winter offensive. The attack went forward on 11 February. The French, as Ferdinand expected, were scattered in winter quarters. His two columns moved south, quickly bypassing Kassel on each side, overrunning enemy depots, and capturing supplies from some of them before the French could burn them. His eastern column of 12,000 men, initially assisted by 5,000 cavalry loaned by Prussia, reached Fulda; the western column of 17,000 men established itself on the Ohm River by the end of February, in both cases well south of Kassel. Ferdinand retained a force of 18,000 under his own command; he detached 10,000 men to conduct a siege of the city, and the rest were positioned south of it. Had the eastern column been strong enough to establish a cordon, Kassel could have been sealed off.

Although the French general, the duc de Broglie, was taken by surprise, he quickly grasped that Ferdinand was not making a mere temporary disturbance and issued urgent orders to rally troops from near and far. Nevertheless, for security of command he pulled his headquarters back from Kassel towards Frankfurt. All in all, the first week of March was a dark moment for the French. In retreating they had been forced to burn food and forage depots which had been very expensive to stock. Nevertheless, this was Broglie's finest hour. He acted promptly and wisely, making few mistakes – Ferdinand himself would praise his generalship – and managed to put his army in a position to take advantage of the attackers' key vulnerability, their becoming over-extended southwards. Ferdinand understood that unless he possessed Kassel he could not keep his army in Hesse, certainly not in wintertime. Broglie had placed a substantial winter garrison in the fortified city with ample provisions, and the garrison executed some devastating sorties. Moreover, the French commissariat, reformed by Marshal Belleisle, served Broglie well, while the supply system administered by the British Treasury was unable to cope. Transport was a key problem. A well-stocked allied depot on the Weser was only 20 miles from Kassel, but a supply of horses and wagons that were expected to come from Hanover failed to arrive.

Nevertheless, the siege of Kassel might have succeeded if the terrain had remained frozen, but in mid-March there was a thaw accompanied by incessant rain. Siege equipment could not be moved, and deep mud prevented carts from distributing provisions. As Broglie's forces gathered they began to prevail in minor battles and skirmishes. His men were in better condition than their opponents, who were cold, sickly and hungry – the penalties of a winter offensive. On 23 March Ferdinand gave the order to withdraw. His men pulled back in good order; the guns were floated down the Weser. Knowing that his opponent would leave very little fodder in the direction of a counter-attack, Broglie decided to re-turn his army to winter quarters. This gave Ferdinand time to restore his exhausted troops to health. His venture had not been entirely useless. Destruction of French supply depots served to delay the start of the French campaign of 1761.

The winter offensive thoroughly frightened people at Versailles. Knowing that word of it was spreading among the public, the court blamed Vienna, saying that the Austrians had failed to order the imperial army to block Prussian participation in the offensive. Expressing indigna-tion, Choiseul openly remarked that if French troops were forced back across the Rhine they 'would never recross it to enter Germany again'. Otherwise he affected to be unconcerned. Joseph Yorke, who had been receiving regular reports of Ferdinand's progress, wrote to his brother on 20 February: 'If Prince Ferdinand succeeds . . . the best thing they [the French] can do will be to make Peace . . . money is every day scarcer both at Versailles and at Vienna.' A week later: 'I see strong symptoms of Peace at Versailles.'[11] On 26 March Choiseul dispatched three documents to Russia's ambassador in London, count Galitzin: a broad declaration inviting participation in a general congress, and a letter accompanied by a memoir from Choiseul addressed to Pitt and Bute proposing a separate Anglo-French negotiation.

---

[11] Barbier, *Journal*, VII, 337. Yorke to Royston, 24 Feb., 27 Feb. 1761, BL Add. 35,365, ff. 280, 283.

Choiseul's two negotiations

When the marquis de Grimaldi arrived at Versailles as Spanish ambassador in early February 1761 his instructions were to find out how far France had proceeded towards opening a negotiation with Britain and also to seek an alliance. Choiseul could honestly assure him that discussions with Britain were not in progress. When Grimaldi suggested that Spain and France might wish to enter into an offensive and defensive treaty, Choiseul was wary. He asked whether Spain would support France if Britain were to reject a French peace overture. Grimaldi said he must refer the question to Madrid. They talked about drawing up a commercial treaty. Choiseul welcomed the idea, but both men understood that it would take many weeks to work out the details, and Grimaldi clearly wished for an early commitment. On 3 March Choiseul, though not prepared to make a commitment, handed him a paper that raised the possibility of an offensive and defensive alliance. This was sent to Madrid.

No reply to it had come by 26 March when Choiseul sent off to London the documents inviting a peace negotiation. His memoir contained a simple proposal well calculated to get the attention of the British ministers: it was a specific timetable providing dates after which new conquests could not be used as counters for exchange. This formula swept away London's anxiety that France might remain unwilling to recognize the measure of British military success. Specifically, nothing conquered in America and the West Indies after 1 July 1761, in India after 1 September and in Europe after 1 May could count at the peace table. The dates were curiously ordered because 1 May 1761 was only a month away, but the British cabinet had to assume that this was intended. Pitt did not like it because when the memoir came to his hand on 31 March the Belle-Île expedition had just sailed and he wanted to give it more time. Still, the memoir allowed the British to suggest other dates for demarcating the *uti possidetis* (a principle in international law specifying that a territory belongs to its current possessor, including by military conquest, unless provided for by treaty). Pitt's memorial in reply welcomed the proposal, but did not suggest alternative dates except to say that such dates might best be chosen at the moment when a preliminary agreement was reached; undoubtedly he was thinking that Britain might make further conquests. Choiseul answered that France had 'reason to recall the whole proposition, if the king of England does not acquiesce to the epochs annexed to it'. Pitt responded by quoting the portion of the original memoir that expressly provided for negotiating different dates.

He added that 'his Britannic Majesty . . . was ready on his part to enter, with speed and sincerity, upon the proposed negotiation.'[12] By this time it was the end of April.

There was another source of the delay, however. The original memoir contained a puzzling phrase. It stated that the *uti possidetis* pertained to conquests that Britain and France made upon each other. Did this wording exclude conquests made upon each other's allies? In early April Pitt spent hours with Hardwicke, who had also spotted the problem, discussing how he should respond. They both believed that the memoir could not really intend to exclude conquests France made upon Britain's German allies because the French would wish to use their conquests in Hanover and Hesse to offset colonial losses. But perhaps the French foreign minister hoped to exclude these German issues from the separate Anglo-French settlement. He had tried to do this a year before, but London had protested. Hardwicke agreed with Pitt that the question was vital and thought that the obscurity should be cleared up straightaway, saying: 'we were warranted to insert words to render clear and plain, what might be ambiguous in the paper'.[13] But because this was the first response to a welcome overture, there was reason to worry about the danger of inserting words which might be ill-received and off-putting. With Hardwicke's assent he avoided the question in his reply and substituted the idea that the two courts should send envoys to each other as soon as possible.

The other ministers agreed with this proceeding. They were happy to see Pitt's readiness to pursue the French peace proposal, and they all assumed that when the French envoy arrived the uncertainty would be quickly cleared up. Arrangements for sending the envoys took time, and in mid-May, Hardwicke, still waiting for the French envoy's arrival, noted much to his annoyance that after forty days this 'fundamental part of the French offer' was still not resolved. It was fundamental because, if the French were determined to leave the contest in Germany out, the British could not continue this separate negotiation. He regretted that he had not pushed Pitt more earnestly about it: 'I would have had our first answer stated in such a manner as to have obliged France to explain herself on that Question immediately; and it is to me surprising that it is not found out yet.'[14]

---

[12] Memorials from Pitt 8 and 28 Apr., memoir from Choiseul 19 April 1761, Thackeray, *History*, II, 512–18.

[13] Hardwicke to Newcastle, 6 April 1761, BL Add. 32,921, fo. 341.

[14] Hardwicke to Newcastle, 16 May 1761, BL Add. 32,923 fo. 126.

The French envoy, François de Bussy, arrived in London on 3 June. When questioned he said he had no instructions on the German issue and also said that because Britain had not accepted France's proposed dates for the *uti possidetis* it was not in force. The British ministers were astonished. Hardwicke wrote:

I hope he means to include in that separate Peace the Landgrave of Hesse, and the Duke of Brunswick, as well as the King in quality of Elector, for otherwise I do not see how the work can be done. This was yielded to by Mons. d'Affry at the Hague. As to the other Point, it is a Chicane to say that the uti possidetis *at first offered, is absolutely at an end by our Court not accepting the particular epochs then proposed, because those very Epochs were by Mon. Choiseul's first Memorial expressly offered to be treated upon. If the* uti possidetis *is entirely laid out of the Case, there is at present no Basis for the Treaty, and everything is quite at large, and subject to discussion upon the whole.*[15]

Bussy's statements were guided by the instructions Choiseul had given him, and in fact the foreign minister had shaped his envoy's role in a way that made him largely useless. The British ministers soon realized that nothing helpful could be expected from Bussy. Choiseul's plan was to conduct the negotiation through the envoy Britain sent to Versailles, a method that would keep the meaningful discussions under his control. It also served his need for secrecy, as Austrian, Russian and Spanish ambassadors at Versailles were by prior agreement receiving copies of everything he sent to London, including his letters to Bussy. But those ambassadors did not have access to the British envoy's correspondence with Pitt.

The envoy was Hans Stanley, a junior lord of the Admiralty. He had no experience as a diplomat but was well attuned to French manners and culture, had excellent command of the language, and discernment enough to raise tough questions. Pitt trusted his acumen and honesty. It should be noted that he chose a man who would earnestly work for peace. Since all decisions would be made by the government in London it was essential for Stanley to report his conversations with Choiseul fully and accurately. Stanley was impressed by Choiseul's intelligence and charm while noting his impulsive and talkative manner, but also made an interesting observation: he is 'frank enough in talk, meaning often what he says at the time, but fickle, very indiscreet'.[16] From his many letters one can

[15] Hardwicke to Newcastle, 3 June 1761, BL Add. 32,923, fo. 367.
[16] Stanley to Pitt, postscript 9 June 1761, Thackeray, *History*, I, 522.

see that Stanley, though he used the word 'often', wanted to believe the French minister and trust in his good faith.

He was instructed to get both aspects of the *uti possidetis* clarified as soon as possible. In their first business meeting of 7 June Choiseul sensibly suggested that Pitt should now offer specific dates. (The cabinet replied on 17 June, suggesting 1 July for Europe – news of Belle-Île's capitulation had arrived – 1 September for the West Indies and 1 November for the East Indies.) When Stanley informed Choiseul that Bussy was saying that the *uti possidetis* was not in force, Choiseul blamed his envoy for making this assumption but excused him by reference to Pitt's failure to name specific alternative dates.[17] On the 17th when Stanley told him that London was upset about the unresolved question concerning the *uti possidetis* and German conquests, Choiseul admitted that he had stated his original memoir in an awkward chronological style and introduced deliberate ambiguities so that France's 'allies might not entirely understand it'. He also said that because these allies were directly interested in questions of how France's conquests in Germany would be resolved he had withheld an answer. In fact, he still did not wish to provide a written answer. Instead, he asked Stanley to pledge that he would not tell what he was about to say to anyone at the French court, that it would pass to London 'in profound secrecy', and that knowledge of it would be confined to the narrow circle of cabinet ministers. Moreover, if any of them were to speak with Bussy, they must behave as if nothing of the kind had arrived because Bussy would inform allied and Spanish ambassadors in London. Stanley agreed, but on condition that he could write down specifics.[18] Accordingly, Choiseul dictated to him a brief note sketching France's terms. Stanley enclosed this in his letter to London dated 17 June.

Almost three months had been used up. Choiseul had been content to allow the possibility that the *uti possidetis* might not be in force to linger on (his blaming of Bussy was a ploy). And in order to avoid criticism from France's allies he had left unanswered the question of whether French conquests made in Germany were to be included in it.[19] Yet Pitt also contributed to the delay by his failure to offer specific alternative dates and by suggesting that clarification should await the arrival of the envoys. Pitt wished to keep British options open and the other cabinet members wished

---

[17] Stanley to Pitt, 16 June 1761, copy in BL Add. 32,924 ff. 118–19.

[18] Stanley to Pitt, 18 June 1761, Thackeray, I, 539–42.

[19] His intention to leave it unanswered is made clear in his instructions to Bussy, printed in *Recueil des Instructions: Angleterre*, pp. 382–3.

to avoid all possibility of giving offence. While they waited for answers Choiseul employed the time in developing a Spanish alliance.

Concerning Choiseul's suggestion of 3 March about a possible offensive and defensive alliance Wall told Grimaldi that it was too broad: only maritime issues and overseas possessions should be covered. He further suggested that if war were to erupt between Spain and England, Minorca should be reserved for return to Spain. Wall, nevertheless, gave the ambassador permission to pursue an agreement so long as he did not irrevocably engage the Spanish court. In late April when Grimaldi suggested that France should refrain from signing a peace with Britain unless Spanish grievances were satisfied, Choiseul became indignant, and not without reason: Spain had refused his entreaties to join France in the war and was now trying to benefit by being included in the peace. Grimaldi's suggestion would undoubtedly render peace with Britain harder to achieve. Shortly afterwards Choiseul informed the council of state that he favoured the principle of forming a Spanish alliance. He did not mention Grimaldi's suggestion that Spanish grievances should be included in the Anglo-French negotiation. Even so, three members of the council – Puysieulx, Berryer and d'Estrées – said that no alliance of any kind should be made while the negotiation with London lasted.

Choiseul went ahead anyway. In early May he informed the council of a plan for making two alliances with Spain. One would be defensive and would take effect only after peace was made with Britain. The king warmly approved of it and wished to call it a *pacte de famille* (between Bourbon monarchs). By the other alliance, as Choiseul subsequently described it in his instructions for Bussy, Spain would hold herself ready to enter the war, but no offensive arrangements would be adopted until the degree of British unwillingness to accept reasonable peace terms was found out. Choiseul provided an outline of this possible military convention to Grimaldi, and on 2 June he sent a copy to d'Ossun while Grimaldi sent one to Wall. The proposed military convention stated that if France did not achieve a peace settlement by 1 May 1762, Spain must go to war against Britain. In order to obtain Madrid's assent Choiseul pledged that he would allow Spanish grievances to be included in the current Anglo-French peace negotiation; he went so far as to state that France would make no agreement with Britain which did not satisfy Spain's requirements. This was an amazing commitment. Even Alfred Bourguet, ordinarily lavish in his praise for Choiseul's acumen, called it 'bizarre'. Choiseul seems to have been aware of its hazards. He made a note on the office copy of the offer saying that it was sent to Madrid 'on the order of the king', but there is no clear evidence that the council of state knew about it. The king of Spain was delighted and indicated his acceptance by express.[20]

Choiseul cannot be faulted for turning Carlos III's aspirations into a potential military benefit for France. It was his duty as a statesman to improve France's power position until peace was assured. But he secured this benefit by pledging to mix Spanish claims into the Anglo-French peace negotiation. The British government's aversion to this proceeding was well known, and he thereby hazarded the success of the negotiation. Did he suppose, as Grimaldi and Fuentes apparently did, that when threatened by a Franco-Spanish combination the British would yield? If Choiseul had confidence in this threat he should not from the viewpoint of power politics have kept the military convention secret, yet he was exceedingly careful to do so. Alternatively, did he suppose that if France and Spain were allied in an ongoing war, France would gain better terms than under Pitt's guidance Britain was likely to allow? It seems so. In an explanatory memoir which he wrote for Louis XV four years later he mentioned that he had intended the inclusion of Spain in order to 'second' France in the negotiation (the practical meaning of this is unclear), but added another reason: if the negotiation were to fail, Spain would be obliged to enter the war and thus help France recover her losses.

Belle-Île and Westphalia

As the planning for the Belle-Île expedition was already accomplished, Lord Ligonier was able to get the transports loaded promptly. On 25 March orders were given for the expedition to depart. A hundred transports, eleven ships of the line, and a dozen smaller warships got under way from Spithead on 29 March and made good time, reaching Belle-Île on 7 April. The commanders, Brigadier General Studholme Hodgson and Commodore Augustus Keppel, had both been present at the failed Rochefort expedition and understood the drawbacks of delay. They quickly decided on a landing site, Port-Andro at the eastern end of the island, and wasted no time. Fifty flat-bottomed boats were put in the water the next day, each carrying 60 soldiers. Warships opened fire on the small fort that commanded the bay and beaches, silencing its four guns in half and hour.

[20] Bourguet, *Choiseul et l'alliance espagnole*, p. 213; Ozanam, 'Les origines', pp. 329–30.

Seamen rowed the troops ashore without many losses, but the operation turned into a disaster. Rising ground formed an amphitheatre round the bay. The French had scarped the cliff at the bottom to create a nearly vertical wall, and at the top over 1,000 French troops were entrenched. Although 60 British grenadiers found a way up over rocks on the right, they were quickly overwhelmed and 40 were captured. The main body was pinned down under the cliffs. Seeing the impossibility of success, General Hodgson wisely signalled retreat. Two ships of the line had been able to anchor close enough for naval gunfire to be effective (contrary to Admiral Hawke's October report) and the French were thus prevented from falling upon the soldiers as they boarded the boats. Nevertheless, British casualties were quite heavy: of the army, 72 killed, 72 wounded and 246 taken prisoner; of the navy 15 killed, 29 wounded and 19 missing. French casualties were negligible.

This attempt on 8 April was definitely an 'opposed landing'. The defenders were French regulars, not the usual sort of untrained men who served on coastal watch, and their guns and muskets were in good order. Moreover, the governor and military commander, Gaetan Xavier Guilhem de Pascalis, chevalier de Sainte-Croix was an intelligent, capable, experienced officer. The French had been hard at work improving the existing masonry defences since October when Hawke's ships came to make a survey. Since Port-Andro had long been reckoned to be the most obvious landing site, Sainte-Croix placed most of his troops there; he was not distracted by the British feint at Sauzon in the island's north-western sector.

Although an overnight storm destroyed twenty flat-bottomed boats, the expedition's leaders did not give up. They had brought 7,000 troops plus 1,000 marines. Ships' companies, which totalled about 7,500 men, could contribute to the effort, especially by handling ordnance and conveying supplies. (Keppel's instructions specified that the navy should assist the army ashore as well as afloat.) The senior officers of both services scrutinized the entire shoreline of the island (about 28 miles long and 6–10 miles wide) looking for places to land. The result was very discouraging. As Hodgson remarked, 'the whole island is a fortification', made such by nature: rocky shores and high cliffs left few places of access, and the French had taken steps to defend those. Nevertheless, the arrival of reinforcements with two more ships of the line encouraged the British commanders to make another attempt.

They focused on three locations. One was Sauzon; the other two were not far from Port-Andro, one just to the north of it to which the largest force was assigned, the other further to the right, round the tip of the Kerdonis peninsula on the rocky north coast at La Perrière where there was a small cove. On the morning of 22 April the sea was calm, ideal for boats going ashore. Fog enabled the warships to take their stations undetected. When the fog cleared they opened fire on the enemy batteries. The flat-bottomed boats carrying the largest force gathered offshore north of Port-Andro, but Sainte-Croix had to be ready to defend all the beaches south of this position as well. Although the French defenders were bombarded by three ships of the line, one of which was the 90-gun *Sandwich*, Brigadier General John Crauford could see that an attempt to land would incur enormous casualties.

In early afternoon while the flat-bottomed boats lay off the eastern beaches, soldiers and marines in ships' boats on the other side of Pointe de Kerdonis (then called Pointe Locmaria) were being rowed towards La Perrière, located a few hundred yards west of the point. Two ships of the line under the direction of Sir Thomas Stanhope, captain of the *Swiftsure* (70 guns) supported them. One detachment of grenadiers was driven off with some loss, but another got ashore at a nearby spot called the Dog's Tooth (la Dent du Chien) without opposition. The soldiers climbed over the rocks and found a narrow path leading upwards to the peninsula's plateau, 40 feet above sea level. A detachment of marines followed close behind. Seeing this success and noticing Stanhope's signals, other boats steered for the site. Although the attackers were met by 200 French regulars at the top, they found a low wall for a shield and held their ground. Meanwhile more troops hurried up the path. All in all, 600 marines took part in this landing – an early instance of the kind of mission for which they would become famous – and together with the army regiments they beat off a French counter-attack. It is not clear when the British commander in this sector, Brigadier Hamilton Lambert, arrived at the top. Sainte-Croix, whose headquarters were not far away, was taken completely by surprise. When he realized what had happened he ordered troops from Port-Andro to come up the hill and attack, which they did, but they were routed by a timely counter-attack. Warship signals alerted Crauford, and direction was given to the oarsmen of his flat-bottomed boats to row round Pointe de Kerdonis to the landing place, a distance of about 2 miles. By evening British troops on the island outnumbered French two to one and were strongly encamped 3 miles inland.

This landing on 22 April was the decisive event of the campaign. It succeeded for the same reason Wolfe's at Quebec had succeeded: the weather was favourable; it occurred at a place where the enemy supposed the cliffs to be insurmountable; the troops promptly and bravely seized the opportunity; and the sailors rowed vigorously to the point of attack. Hearing of its success, Sainte-Croix pulled all his troops back to the fortress city of Le Palais, and except for its immediate environs the whole island was soon in British hands.

The siege of the great citadel would require six weeks of tedious labour. Enormous quantities of powder and shot would be expended, but because the expedition had plenty of resources and lots of time the outcome was never in doubt. As the days passed supplies arrived from England – also a few more troops and warships. The British naval force was powerful and numerous enough (usually fifteen ships of the line and eight frigates plus many smaller warships) to prevent French reinforcement from the mainland.

Did the French seriously try to reinforce Belle-Île? A reliable answer is unlikely to be discovered. The duc d'Aiguillon was responsible for defending Brittany. In December he had ordered a large stock of provisions and an additional battalion on to the island. Consequently, Sainte-Croix had enough provisions to last a year, a considerable store of powder and shot, lots of small arms in good repair and 3,400 regular troops. There were 1,000 militia, mainly useful as lookouts and messengers. It appears that Sainte-Croix and d'Aiguillon assumed that the island had enough troops because when the British forces arrived the duke did not have reinforcements at hand. In justifying himself to Choiseul, d'Aiguillon explained that he had proportioned the number of troops to the size of the citadel, a criterion not in accordance with a memorandum of 1753 which had declared prevention of a landing to be the essential concern.[21] Had the duc de Belleisle not died in January, the defence might have been better looked after because his grandfather had owned the island and built the citadel.[22] But the new war minister, Choiseul, was focused on Germany and left few good troops to defend the coasts. When he learned that a large British force was anchored off Belle-Île, his reaction was to dismiss the threat as being of no importance. D'Aiguillon naturally hurried to gather what troops and vessels he could. According to rumours in Paris he planned to send 1,000 men plus cattle and ammunition by night during the first week of May. The distance from the tip of the Quiberon peninsula to the

[21] Marion, *La Bretagne*, pp. 164–5.
[22] The spelling of Belleisle takes many forms. Throughout this book the island's name matches what appears on modern French maps and the marshal's is spelled as one word, but his title came from the island.

harbour at Le Palais is 8 nautical miles and from Port Louis 24; it was understood that such an attempt would be perilous.

The successful British landing shocked Versailles. Emergency council meetings resulted in orders to Brest and Rochefort to fit out squadrons of men-of-war, six of the line at Brest and five at Rochefort. After receiving intelligence of these orders Keppel reinforced the small squadron watching Brest and sent six of the line to watch Rochefort. Because Pitt and Anson were determined to keep Keppel's force strong the commodore still had enough warships to maintain a blockade of the island. If rumours were correct, d'Aiguillon by late May had a convoy at Port Louis ready to sail and was not inclined to wait for a naval escort, but the winds continued 'to be English'. In any case the venture would have been extremely hazardous.

From 23 to 28 April the British troops lay exposed to wind and rain, stormy weather preventing tents from being landed, but on 29 April the weather came fair. Since everything had to be hauled up the slopes the siege preparations were toilsome. (Seamen lent a hand and Keppel rewarded them with a double ration of wine.) General Hodgson complained of inadequate resources and was convinced that Ligonier and the Ordnance department had let him down. He was particularly vexed to find that the young engineers assigned to the expedition, though full of book knowledge, lacked practical experience. Nevertheless, the commander of the engineers, Brigadier Thomas Desaguliers, grandson of a Huguenot refugee, was very capable and there were a number of dedicated officers among the regulars. Brigadier Generals Guy Carleton and William Howe (both of whom would become well known in the American Revolutionary War) acquired first-hand experience in this operation that would be useful a year later at Havana.

The great citadel of Le Palais was made formidable by Nicolas Fouquet in the mid-seventeenth century and improved by the great Vauban. The British bombardment from land-based mortars began on 5 May. Bomb vessels near shore joined in two days later. It appears that Ligonier underestimated what was required to batter the citadel into submission, and it did not help that the 24-pounder brass cannon supplied by the Ordnance department were unserviceable after minimal usage. Yet Hodgson's complaints against Ligonier were really of no significance so long as he could draw on the navy, and Keppel was generous. In fact, borrowed naval guns – 32- and 24-pounders – played a principal role in blasting the breach through the fortress wall which produced surrender. Throughout the operation there was almost perfect harmony between Hodgson and Keppel, and the army and navy (and marines) at all levels. Despite this indisputable fact, myths about army–navy friction circulated in England as an explanation of why the siege took so long.

The French defence of Le Palais was stubborn and well conducted, the only lapse being a failure to prevent two outer redoubts from being captured on 13 May, which necessitated a general withdrawal into the citadel. Over the next ten days the town below the citadel came into British possession, and trenches and batteries moved closer. Eventually, heavy naval guns were placed only 400 yards from a vulnerable wall and were ready to fire on 23 May. At the end of the month Sainte-Croix resolved that he would surrender when a significant breach was made unless reinforcements arrived. His men were suffering severely under the bombardment and were no longer able to harass the British gunners, being immediately targeted by British marksmen whenever they showed their heads. On 6 June a breach was opened and on the morning of the 7th the citadel flew the white flag. That evening articles of capitulation, hurriedly drawn up by Hodgson and Keppel, were signed. Full honours of war were allowed; the 2,000 surviving French troops were not made prisoners of war but carried, along with 400 women and children, to Port Louis by British transports.

During the entire two months the British army suffered 283 killed and 456 wounded, to which may be added the navy's losses of about 15 killed and 30 wounded. Though statistics are lacking it has been deduced that French losses were three times these figures. The French spent money fitting out ships (a few of which would be useful later) and soon undertook costly measures to defend Rhé and other offshore islands in the Bay of Biscay against attack. In estimating the monetary cost of the expedition to the British it is to be remembered that much of the naval expenditure was fixed and would have been incurred if the fleet had remained at its bases. Moreover, and this is a point of importance, the army gained experience that became highly useful a year later at Havana.

Versailles was quick to allow the *Gazette de France* to publish an account of the repulse of the attempted landing on 8 April, but after that it was silent about Belle-Île, as Jacques Barbier noticed (he was hearing the adverse news from other sources). Acknowledgement of the loss was unavoidable, however, and when the regime did so it showed a clever sense of public relations: Sainte-Croix was celebrated as a hero. British officers' commendations of his conduct during the siege were published; he was awarded a promotion and pension by the court; and on 9 July he was given a glorious welcome by a large Paris crowd. Compared with the treatment given to most French generals who surrendered a fortress this was highly unusual. And also dubious, as he yielded as soon as a wall was breached when other officers were estimating that the citadel could hold out for three months. Although the public denigrated the duc d'Aiguillon, the court did not; he was protected by Pompadour.[23]

In England, press and public followed the progress of the expedition avidly. Some people grumbled that it was not worth the cost.[24] Newcastle's long-standing aversion to the expedition was well known. Upon hearing of the capitulation he wrote to Hardwicke: 'The news of the taking Belleisle brings me up to Town tomorrow, for Fear of being thought Disaffected.' A month earlier he had admitted that there was a benefit, especially upon receiving intelligence that the French were ordering men-of-war to be fitted out and shifting troops westwards from the Rhine and Flanders: 'Your Lordship [Hardwicke] sees, what a wonderful Diversion, if true, this famous Attack has already made.'[25] Yet he adhered to his opinion that the expedition was a mistake even though it succeeded, and he accepted the idea propagated by the French that the capture only served to make the court of Versailles angry and thus injured prospects of peace.

Massive French preparations to invade Westphalia had not made British observers angry but certainly made them apprehensive. At the beginning of the year Hardwicke believed it was essential to reinforce Ferdinand's army. Otherwise, he thought, the French were bound to occupy Hanover, and he doubted that they would enter 'so seriously into a separate Treaty with England, as to preclude themselves from so probable a Chance of getting possession of the Electorate'. Intelligence from Versailles in February confirmed that the aim was to become 'Masters of the Electorate' with all the troops that could be assembled, 'being convinced this is the last campaign'. In mid-January the duc de Broglie had written to Choiseul: '[M]ake peace, M. le Duc; that will be more valuable than a campaign, however honourable it could be for the generals.' But

[23] Barbier, *Journal*, VII, 359–60, 369, 375–6, 380–1; also Marion, *La Bretagne*, pp. 167–8.
[24] Among these was Horace Walpole; he was answered by his correspondent, Horace Mann: 'But after all could our fleet have been employed in any useful expedition? During a war I look upon inaction to be the worst situation' (Lewis, ed. *Walpole Correspondence*, V, 519).
[25] Newcastle to Hardwicke, 14 June 1761, BL Add. 32,924, fo. 87; 14 May, BL Add. 32,923, fo. 68.

Choiseul, who would become minister of war after Marshal Belleisle's death in late January, pressed Broglie to prepare his army for going forward despite its fatiguing exertion in repelling Ferdinand's winter offensive.[26] In late April, after the negotiation with Britain commenced, intelligence from Versailles described a divided court, one group wishing to end the war, the other arguing: 'it is Madness, now the Money for the Expence of the campaign is raised, not to profit of our Superiority, as that is the surest Way of obtaining a better Peace.'[27]

The French planned to invade Germany with two armies. On the lower Rhine under the prince de Soubise 100,000 men were gathered; on the upper Rhine there were 60,000 under Broglie, headquartered at Frankfurt. Soubise was scheduled to begin the offensive from Wesel before mid-May, but he was delayed by accidental burning of the barges that had brought the fodder supply. His army finally crossed into Westphalia on 12 June and marched eastwards between the Lippe and Ruhr rivers. At Unna he stopped to wait for Broglie, who also got a late start with his army that needed to recover from winter operations. On 15 June Broglie began to march northwards, first to Paderborn and then westwards towards Soubise.

The delays gave Ferdinand's army a chance to recuperate, but his army of 77,000 – 28,000 Hanoverians, 23,000 from Brunswick and Hesse, 18,000 British (under Granby) plus 8,500 light troops – was clearly outnumbered. His best option was to attack one of the French armies before they joined. He adopted a bold plan – to sweep north around Soubise's army to a point near Dortmund and thus come upon it from the rear. In short, he planned to outflank an entire army. Leaving their fires burning to deceive the enemy his troops decamped on the night of 1–2 July. Ferdinand's attempt to achieve surprise failed, however, partly because the circuitous march was slowed by drenching rain but mainly because broken terrain inhibited the transport of guns and prevented effective use of cavalry. Nevertheless, a position was gained west of Soubise's forces. In response Soubise correctly marched east towards Broglie; the French armies joined on 8 July.

Although at this point Ferdinand had only 65,000 men against 90,000 French, he chose to accept battle. At the village of Vellinghausen, halfway

[26] Hardwicke to Newcastle, 3 Jan. 1761, BL Add. 32,917, fo. 95 [ms nearly illegible]; Versailles intelligence, 6 Feb., BL Add. 32,918, fo. 307; Broglie to Choiseul, 14 Jan., Waddington, *Guerre*, IV, 287.
[27] Versailles intelligence, 24 April 1761, BL Add. 32,922, fo. 165.

between Hamm and Lippstadt, he anchored his left on the Lippe, which was full to overflowing, and extended his eastward-facing defensive line southwards across the smaller river Ahse. Soubise and Broglie carefully discussed and agreed on a battle plan. Broglie would attack between the rivers on the 15th while Soubise advanced along the south side of the Ahse to threaten the enemy's right flank. It was agreed that the main assault by both armies would occur on the 16th. But Broglie found his initial attack on the 15th to be unexpectedly successful, and late in the day he went on to push the defenders out of Vellinghausen. During the short July night the fighting became intense, but there was a five-hour pause (10 p.m. to 3 a.m.), and Ferdinand used it to advantage by bringing a considerable reinforcement from south of the Ahse to his lines near the village, enabling him to launch a morning counter-attack. As a result Broglie was forced to pull back at about 10 a.m. During all this time Soubise did almost nothing. At 9 a.m. he advanced, but when he received word that Broglie was pulling back he broke off and retreated. His plea afterwards was that Broglie had ruined their plan because the main attack was not scheduled to occur until the 16th. The French suffered 4,700 casualties, three-quarters of them in Broglie's army. Ferdinand's troops suffered 1,400.

Broglie was a general of proven abilities and known to be energetic, while Soubise was inclined to caution and inertia. Although Broglie's excessive and premature commitment during the night got him into trouble, it induced Ferdinand to weaken the southern part of his line, a sector that Soubise might have profitably attacked in the early morning hours. But Soubise was not a man to grasp a tactical opportunity. Although he was senior commander, he did not behave like one, for he was disposed to let Broglie's actions determine the outcome. Soubise was a decent and intelligent man, but here was another instance of the ill-effects of placing him in command, done to satisfy the wishes of madame de Pompadour. In fact, the whole command structure was seriously flawed: each army received separate orders from the war minister; fifteen days were needed for a courier's return journey to Versailles; staffs were saturated with lieutenant generals and marshals de camp, each staff despising the other. It was difficult enough to carry on a campaign in Germany without such complications.

The news of the outcome of the battle, so contrary to expectations, stunned Versailles; recriminations were intense. Still, French forces continued to enjoy superiority. Choiseul sent advice that called for keeping the armies in touch and cooperating, but his letters were not received by the two marshals before they decided to campaign separately. Broglie would lead a penetration eastwards with the goal of occupying Hanover and Brunswick. Soubise would operate in Westphalia. Since Broglie's task would entail long supply lines Soubise transferred 30,000 troops to his command. The campaigning east of the Weser was exhausting for both sides. Ferdinand's strategy was to threaten Broglie's supply lines in Hesse and thereby force him to divert troops from his principal objective. His second diversion towards Kassel did not succeed, however, in protecting the duchy of Brunswick. In October French troops occupied Wolfenbüttel and laid siege to the city of Brunswick. Ferdinand raced north and by a brilliantly executed night encirclement of the besieging army saved the city. The city of Hanover was not occupied by the French. In late October Ferdinand counter-attacked but failed to make significant progress, and in November both sides went into winter quarters. During all this time Soubise accomplished very little. His threat to Münster was not sufficient to draw troops from Ferdinand's main force. In late August he was short of food and forage and ranged northwards for resupply, briefly occupying Emden and annoying the people of East Friesland. He opted for winter quarters before Broglie did.

In May, hearing reports of the massing of French troops on the lower Rhine, Horace Walpole had offered a prediction about the likelihood of a successful negotiation:

I am not among the credulous, not conceiving why the Court of Versailles should desire a peace at the beginning of a campaign, when they will have so much more in bank to treat with at the end of it. They will have Hesse and Hanover – shall we have the rock of Belleisle?[28]

At the end of it the French still had Hesse, but not Hanover, and the British had Belle-Île. Walpole's implication was that the island was useless, which was the common opinion at the time. Yet it was not without strategic value. It was defensible by sea power and could be used – Pitt was intrigued by this – as a base from which to menace the entire coast from Lorient to Bayonne. Its principal value, however, lay in naval support. In the early years of the war the Western Squadron, while providing the crucial foundation of British superiority at sea, had been unable to prevent French warships from leaving ports and bases south of Brest. The solution, as we have seen, was to send ships inshore – to anchor in Basque Roads, for instance – but trying to cover this coast still presented an arduous naval challenge. Occupation of Quiberon Bay helped, but

[28] To Horace Mann, 14 May 1761, Lewis, ed. *Walpole Correspondence*, V, 504–5.

the critical ingredients for keeping ships on station – water and fresh provisions – came from England, and were often delayed by contrary winds and storms. Belle-Île could function as a repository. Moreover, it was large enough to enable cattle to graze and vegetables to be grown in quantity, and, perhaps most important, it could supply water. In this regard it proved to be unexpectedly bounteous: a reservoir with conduit pipes leading to the shoreline had been built for the French navy! Since warships, large and small, could take shelter in the lee of the island, the possession of Belle-Île made possible a comprehensive and continuous watch on the French Atlantic ports.

The Anglo-French negotiation

During his conversation with Stanley on 17 June Choiseul decided to wipe the slate clean. Stanley's instructions allowed him to receive any proposal that might lead towards peace, and Choiseul, realizing that he could no longer delay giving the British government a clear and substantive response to its questions about French conquest in Germany, took advantage of Stanley's offer to start afresh. As we have seen he demanded complete secrecy. When Stanley insisted on recording the specific terms in writing Choiseul reluctantly dictated them and then approved what the envoy wrote down. The result was a brief note that Pitt when he saw it called the 'little leaf'.[29] The British ministers understood Choiseul's anxiety for secrecy because they could guess the attitude of Austria.

In this 'little leaf' of 17 June Choiseul essentially asked for the return of Guadeloupe, Marie Galante and Gorée in exchange for Minorca; was willing to cede Canada but not Cape Breton (while accepting that Louisbourg would remain demolished); wished to retain the Newfoundland cod fishery as allowed by the treaty of Utrecht; but would give up the conquests France had made upon Britain's allies in Germany. After reading it over, Stanley remarked that too much was being asked in exchange for Minorca, that France should not count on getting Cape Breton back, and that the fishery request would pose difficulties. But the offer to give up the conquered German territories was heartening.

The British cabinet, convened as a council, discussed its response in two long meetings. On the following points everyone agreed: Canada

---

[29] See above, p. 524, and Stanley to Pitt, 18 June 1761, Thackeray, *History*, I, 539–43; the 'little leaf' is on p. 543.

in its entirety must be ceded to Britain, and the French must not suppose that the Ohio country could be included in Louisiana. Cape Breton and all the islands in the Gulf of St Lawrence, the straits and passages leading to it, and the right of fishing in the gulf and on those coasts must belong solely to Britain. Both Senegal and Gorée were to be kept. Belle-Île would be exchanged for Minorca. If the French wished to recover Guadeloupe and Mari Galante, they should pledge an immediate evacuation of the occupied territories of Britain's German allies and agree to Britain's retention of her conquests in India as determined by the *uti possidetis*.

The most difficult decision concerned the fishery off Newfoundland. For several weeks Pitt had been telling various colleagues that he wished to deny France all cod fishing areas. Two meetings of the council were held. Near the beginning of the first Pitt said that his private opinion had not changed and that he was prepared to break off negotiations on the matter of the fisheries, but he added that 'if the Council differed with him, he should acquiesce and execute what *they* should advise'. Granville, Hardwicke, Halifax, Bedford and Newcastle spoke in favour of letting the French have the Newfoundland fishery. Without it the French would be left with no fishing at all in the New World. This would be intolerable to them not only because, unlike the fur trade of Canada, the fishery was highly profitable, but also because it was vital for training up skilled seamen, the key ingredient of naval power. France's inevitable refusal would risk breaking the peace negotiation. An opportunity to end a successful and expensive war on good terms might be lost. It was decided, however, that the fishery should not be simply yielded. Since France requested its restoration in accordance with the treaty of Utrecht, Britain, they reasoned, had a right to ask for compliance with an article in that treaty which required demolition of Dunkirk's fortifications. Everyone agreed on this formula.[30]

Pitt called a second meeting to review his draft of a response. The fishery was again earnestly discussed. Bute suggested that a 'trial' should be made of denying it to the French to see if they might give in. He added that he had spoken with the king, who favoured such a trial; the demand could be dropped later if necessary. Pitt welcomed Bute's support but was firmly against asking for something the council was prepared to drop, and after much altercation he won his point. After the meeting Pitt phrased the response in a way that demanded the demolition at Dunkirk but did not clearly state that France might thereby gain the fishery. Thus, the terms

[30] Newcastle to Devonshire, 28 June 1761, BL Add. 32,924, ff. 311–21, esp ff. 313–14.

conveyed with Pitt's letter to Stanley of 26 June 'by the king's command' were demanding, and Pitt's language, declaring that on six major points 'his Majesty's intentions will be found fixed and unalterable', made them sound like an ultimatum.[31]

Stanley met with Choiseul on the 29th and wisely softened Pitt's hard-edged language as he read it to him. Although their long conversation did not cover all the key issues, some important points emerged. After a 'very obstinate struggle' Choiseul agreed to give up Cape Breton if French fishermen were allowed an *abri*, that is, a sheltered port where they could have a settlement and dry their codfish. He insisted, however, that the Newfoundland fishery was to be allowed to France. As for Dunkirk, he claimed that because of silting it was no longer a useful port; the British had no need to insist on a demand that was unnecessary and humiliating to France. In all other important respects, although he wished to recover Gorée, Choiseul seemed to accept Britain's terms. Stanley was informed that a formal response would soon follow, but in his long letter reporting the conversation he warned Pitt that the French would absolutely insist on some share of the fishery. He met again with Choiseul on 4 July to have him read through his letter for verification. Writing a postscript immediately afterwards, Stanley repeated his warning with respect to the fishery: the French 'would hardly relinquish it totally if an army was in the heart of their country'. In the same postscript he reported that Choiseul had mentioned to him that, if necessary, France could continue the war and might have 'new allies'. Stanley saw that he meant Spain, and observed that Grimaldi seemed 'more ungenerous and malicious' than the Austrian ambassador.

Newcastle was encouraged by Stanley's letters to be optimistic. Hardwicke disagreed. He thought the French had been delaying and would continue to do so. He had seen Pitt at court on the 6th and said it was likely that 'Choiseul waited for events in Westphalia'. Pitt 'owned that it looked so', and Hardwicke replied: 'the very thing we were afraid of'. Hardwicke also worried about Choiseul's inflexibility about Dunkirk, commenting that although its use might be impaired by shifting sands, a refusal would 'create great difficulty here' (England had long experience of Dunkirk as an enemy privateering base). Furthermore, he judged Stanley's warning about the Spanish ambassador's intrigues 'most

---

[31] Thackeray, *History*, I, 548. Unless otherwise cited, the quotations from letters and formal memoirs exchanged during the negotiation are taken from Thackeray, *History*, vol. I after p. 506, vol. II after p. 507.

material'.[32] Meanwhile, Newcastle hoped that Devonshire could change Bute's attitude about the fishery. Bedford joined the effort and wrote Bute a long letter, pacifistic and defeatist. In reply Bute said that he was opposed to giving the French sovereignty over even a small sector of Newfoundland. As for the possibility that France might break off the negotiation, he commented: 'Your Grace must allow that an ultimatum from a beaten enemy is most unusual in the beginning of a treaty.' He was sure that the usual course of negotiation would follow. In any case, Bute added, the British government had nothing but conversational remarks to go on (Stanley had reported a comment by Choiseul that 'his words do not bind him as a Minister'), so it was necessary to wait for France's formal response, soon expected.[33]

But it did not come, and the worried ministers wondered why. While Newcastle fretted that Pitt's strong language might be the cause, other ministers had their minds on reports from Germany indicating that Soubise and Broglie were closing in on Prince Ferdinand. On 15 July Newcastle, Hardwicke, Devonshire and Bute were at court and talked about the delay. Newcastle said that he had asked Bussy that morning why the promised French response had not come. When Bussy could not explain it Newcastle had told him 'we should not sit still any longer and see France take all the Electorate, without availing ourselves in the part where we were strongest' ('the part' meaning the maritime and colonial war). The four ministers informally discussed terms on which they would be willing to make peace and reached agreement on key points briefly stated by Bute: 'The Fishery with a place for them on the Banks of Newfoundland; Dunkirk as the Treaty of Aix[-la-Chapelle specified]; a port in lieu of Goree; Newport and Ostend not to remain in the hands of France after the general peace is concluded.' Devonshire proposed sending these terms to Paris straightaway together with a declaration that France should not expect anything better.[34] Pitt was not present, but they all knew that he desired speedy action. In fact, on the 17th Pitt drew up explicit orders for attacking Martinique; these were dispatched with a convoy of transports heading

---

[32] Hardwicke to Newcastle, 8 July 1761, BL Add. 32,924, fo. 444. Choiseul received a strong protest from the people of Dunkirk asking that the fortifications be preserved for the sake of commerce; intelligence from Paris, 13 July 1761 (BL Add. 32,925, fo. 38).

[33] Bedford to Bute, 9 July, Bute to Bedford, 12 July 1761, *Bedford Correspondence* (cited in Chapter 15), III, 22–34.

[34] *Devonshire Diary*, pp. 101–2.

for New York to pick up some of Amherst's troops and carry them to the Caribbean.[35] Thus, the leading ministers believed that the French were stringing them along – delaying in order to gain advantage from an anticipated military success in Germany. A council meeting was scheduled for 21 July to decide what to do about the French delay.

After three weeks of uncertainty events moved rapidly. On 20 July news reached London of two victories overseas. One was the capitulation of Pondicherry. In Paris shareholders of the French company contemplated total loss. The other was the capture of Dominica. Pitt's message of January had reached Amherst in time for him to gather 2,000 men under Andrew, Lord Rollo plus artillery and dispatch them to Guadeloupe where they met with Sir James Douglas, the admiral in command on the Leeward Islands station. From there, one 64-gun ship, three of 50 guns and three frigates sailed without delay to Dominica and anchored off Roseau on 6 June. When an invitation to surrender was refused the troops were landed, and although it was late in the day Rollo ordered an immediate attack on the four lines of trenches manned by the defenders. The British regulars overwhelmed them with very few casualties and the French commander was taken prisoner; the surrender was received the next day. A mountainous neutral island which the French had gradually occupied, Dominica was certainly not an acquisition of importance, but Pitt had not counted on the success so soon.

On the evening of 20 July France's response finally arrived. Clerks were undoubtedly up all night making copies for the council meeting that was already scheduled for the next day. The formal memoir, dated 13 July, insisted on the Newfoundland fishery as expected, and still expected the British to give back Cape Breton. No mention was made of Dunkirk. An article proposing that peace in India should be based on the Godeheu–Saunders truce of late 1754 appeared to ignore the military contest in south India entirely and looked ridiculous when read the day after news of Pondicherry's surrender arrived. Minorca would be exchanged for Guadeloupe and Marie Galante. Nothing in this document moved closer to agreement, in fact the opposite. A very troubling article was one stipulating that the French would continue to occupy Wesel and other territories belonging to the king of Prussia. This was a retraction from what Choiseul had dictated to Stanley in the 'little leaf', and the council members knew that they could not accept it without violating the Anglo-Prussian alliance. The next day news arrived of a third victory.

[35] Kimball, ed. *Correspondence of Pitt with America*, II, 452–4.

To everyone's astonishment Prince Ferdinand had defeated the French armies that were massing against him at Vellinghausen. Hardwicke wrote, with elation: This news 'changes the situation, and France will become more reasonable. How happy it is that Mons. de Choiseul has waited for his own Humiliation!'[36]

If France's most recent terms had to be viewed as a step backwards, what occurred on 23 July appeared utterly disruptive. Bussy presented two supplemental memoirs. One stated that Vienna's permission to make a separate peace with Britain was granted on two conditions: first, after the peace was made, France would continue to retain Wesel and other Prussian territories in reserve for Austria to dispose of, and secondly, Britain must not allow any of Prince Ferdinand's troops to serve the king of Prussia or give any other assistance to Prussia. France would similarly agree to give no assistance to Austria. The French termed this arrangement 'natural and equitable', but of course the British subsidy to Prussia far outweighed anything the French were then giving Austria. The second memoir from Versailles opened by stating that the peace could be made more durable if Spain were to guarantee it, but then came the bombshell: a listing of Spain's three grievances against Britain and the requirement that those grievances had to be settled within the current negotiation. This memoir shocked every member of the council.

Pitt refused to receive either memoir. He bluntly told Bussy that the British government would not 'suffer the disputes with Spain to be blended, in any manner whatever, in the negotiation of peace between the two crowns' and that the proposal should not be mentioned again.[37] The council's disappointment over the retraction regarding the Prussian territories escalated to outrage when it learned of these supplemental memoirs. France seemed to be chiefly concerned, not with peace, but with solidifying her Austrian alliance and backing the king of Spain. In a meeting of 24 July the council unanimously approved Pitt's actions and words.[38] All agreed that inclusion of a neutral power's (Spain's) complaints against a belligerent in an ongoing peace negotiation between two belligerents was highly improper. Stanley had mentioned in his letter of 14 July his success in persuading Choiseul to remove some lines that addressed Spain's concerns from the memoir of terms. France was now introducing the same subject by a different instrument. The ministers also

---

[36] Hardwicke to Newcastle, 22 July 1761, BL Add. 32,925, fo. 260.
[37] Pitt to Bussy, 24 July 1761, Thackeray, *History*, II, 554.
[38] As Newcastle informed Bussy, 29 July 1761, BL Add. 32,926, fos. 50–1.

believed that French delay in responding was deliberate. Pitt's letter to Stanley of 25 July began with a detailed account of why the entire council felt a sense of outrage. He bluntly accused France of delaying to 'gain time . . . to be able to push her one great operation in Germany' and noted that her engagements with Spain 'had been . . . disingenuously suppressed' until this important moment. As for the proposed guarantee of the peace by Spain, he thought it a 'strange idea'. When ministers read copies of Pitt's letter after it had gone off, some considered its tone too harsh, but they had all agreed with its criticisms of France's conduct. They hoped that Stanley could soften the effect of the language.

With this letter Pitt enclosed a 'paper of points' in answer to France's memoir of terms dated 13 July. It essentially reiterated Britain's terms of 26 June, but in the meeting of 24 July the ministers had wished to clear away all obscurity from the offer that would allow Frenchmen to 'fish and dry their fish on part of the banks of Newfoundland' according to the treaty of Utrecht if Dunkirk were reduced to the level specified in that treaty. In the 'paper of points' Pitt, however, did not express the offer as a clear quid pro quo, and when Hardwicke read the paper after it had been sent off he remembered that the ministers had unanimously agreed that all points should now become clear and specific propositions; he was incensed when he saw how Pitt had made the offer seem problematical.[39] In the meeting the ministers had also wished to allow the French to reduce Dunkirk's fortifications to the more moderate level required by the treaty of Aix-la-Chapelle, but Pitt had persuaded them to instruct Stanley to mention this only if it appeared to be the only thing standing in the way of an accommodation. In the event, since Choiseul would not budge on the issue concerning the Prussian territories, Stanley decided, with regret, that he must keep it to himself.

Lord Bute might have prevented Pitt's distortion of the consensus; he had seen the final drafts and allowed them to go forth unchanged because he agreed with Pitt in wanting to hold firm on the fisheries. He thought that because Canada's trade yielded very little while the fisheries produced a very large revenue for France, 'if we had not the Fishery we really got nothing'. When Newcastle complained about Pitt's wording Bute replied that the duke and other ministers should have stayed in London to read the documents instead of departing for their country houses

---

[39] Hardwicke to Newcastle, 2 Aug. 1761, BL Add. 32,926 fo. 140; Yorke, *Hardwicke*, III, 318–19.

after the meeting (on the 24th, a Friday afternoon in high summer).[40] Despite the wording of Pitt's 'paper of points', Newcastle believed that 'the Event in Germany, and the great one in the East Indies, would and must produce the best Consequences in our Pacifick Negotiations'. France's 'Great Superiority in Germany', he went on, had yielded her no benefit, so peace was inevitable.[41] Moreover, the French could observe that despite the recently reported victories the British government was not raising its demands, and it was possible to hope that Pitt's misconduct had been nullified because some cabinet ministers, speaking hastily with Bussy after the meeting of the 24th, informed him of the council's true consensus: if France would consent to put Dunkirk in a condition that would not give anxiety to the English nation and could agree on evacuations in Germany, London would allow her the Newfoundland fishery and nearby islands for refuge and drying, as well as arrangements for conducting an African slave trade.[42] Clearly, the ministers wished to keep the negotiation alive.

It is likely that Choiseul read Bussy's letter before he received Pitt's reply of the 25th, but if so, it made no difference. On 29 July when the packet arrived from London Stanley noticed Choiseul's emotional reaction straightaway. It was 'extremely plain and obvious' that the French minister seemed 'entirely determined to continue the war'. At court Choiseul fulminated against Pitt, and the next day, 30 July, he wrote letters to the French ambassadors at Madrid and Stockholm. A similar letter went to Vienna two days later. The letters stated that France had decided to end the negotiation, Choiseul added: 'It is important to hide this resolution from the court of London for a month. We shall keep up the negotiation several more weeks before breaking it off.'[43] This was done. Henceforth the negotiation, which London continued to take seriously, was a sham. Its purpose was to delay possible British military and naval initiatives and to gain further concessions if possible.

[40] *Devonshire Diary*, pp. 108–9; Newcastle to Hardwicke, 1 Aug., Newcastle to Devonshire, 5 Aug. 1761, BL Add. 32,926, ff. 125, 187–9.
[41] Newcastle to Joseph Yorke, 31 July, to Hardwicke, 1 Aug. 1761, BL Add. 32,926, ff. 95–6, 125.
[42] Bussy to Choiseul, 26 July 1761, Waddington, *Guerre*, IV, 564; Black, *Pitt the Elder*, p. 213.
[43] Choiseul to d'Ossun, 30 July 1761, Rashed, *Peace of Paris*, p. 92. Also Waddington, *Guerre*, IV, 569–70.

Choiseul and the lost chance of peace

It has been easy to suppose that Pitt destroyed the negotiation. He made no secret of his wish to deny the fishery to France. In April he had said that he wanted to 'keep all North America and the Fishery on the Banks of Newfoundland'.[44] During the negotiation he was clearly prepared to risk losing the chance of peace in hopes of withholding the fishery. Some of his language in the 26 June response had the character of an ultimatum. The 'paper of points' that he drafted a month later was written 'in a very haughty and dictatorial style'; it also failed to make clear, as the council wished, the terms by which the French could obtain the Newfoundland fishery and a shelter for drying the fish.[45] Pitt's drafting of the 'paper of points' was inexcusable, but the letter accompanying it expressed angry frustration on the part of all the ministers. Moreover, they thought they were being generous by not raising Britain's terms in the light of France's notable defeats in Germany and India. Both Newcastle and Hardwicke believed that those defeats must compel France to accept the terms Britain was offering; they could not believe that France would suddenly break off. Choiseul's letter of 30 July to Stockholm (which reported his decision to seek peace no longer but hide the fact and continue negotiating) had been intercepted by a British agent.[46] Yet when Newcastle read the deciphered letter he was so anxious for peace and so completely focused on overcoming what he believed to be the true obstacle, Pitt's resistance, that he did not let it influence him.

From Choiseul's emotional reaction on 29 July it appeared that Pitt's conduct provoked his decision to terminate the quest for peace, but he was strongly inclined in this direction at least two weeks earlier. It was a question of priorities. First, he had been very careful to avoid injury to the Austrian alliance. He knew how much it meant to Pompadour and that the separate Anglo-French negotiation made Vienna nervous. Kaunitz and Maria Theresa wanted the delays that a general congress would entail. To secure their assent Choiseul had permitted the ambassador, Starhemberg, to read everything he transmitted in writing to London. This was inhibiting. Choiseul got round it as best he could by confining the give-and-take to

---

[44] *Devonshire Diary*, 9 April 1761, p. 92; Middleton, *Bells*, p. 184; Peters, *Pitt and Popularity*, pp. 194–200.

[45] Hardwicke to Newcastle, 2 Aug. 1761, Yorke, *Hardwicke*, III, 318–19.

[46] Choiseul's intercepted letter to Ambassador Louis de Cardevac, marquis de Havrincourt at Stockholm may be seen in BL Add. 32,926, fo. 67.

his conversations with Stanley. Secondly, he also wanted a safeguard – something to fall back on in case Britain proved unwilling to grant a 'reasonable' peace. The safeguard of course was the alliance with Spain. Choiseul did not share the view of Fuentes and Grimaldi that the threat of a Franco-Spanish combination would both induce the British government to settle Spanish grievances and gain better terms for France, but he seemed to think that France and Spain in alliance could defeat Britain in an ongoing war. Thirdly, he hoped to gain better terms through a successful military campaign in Germany. Large and expensive as it was, Choiseul as war minister earnestly pressed for it. He knew that Louis XV and Pompadour wished to see the reputation of French arms restored, particularly Soubise's reputation.

Fulfilling all these goals within the time available was scarcely possible. Shortly after the initiating documents were dispatched to London on 26 March Starhemberg remarked to him, 'now we are about to conclude peace'. Choiseul replied:

Peace? Oh we will perhaps not make it soon; there is nothing pressing yet. The démarche that we made by our offer was necessary to ease our conscience; it was Easter time, one needed to put one's soul in repose; but as for peace, that's another thing, and we are still in control of making it only when we wish.[47]

The delay stemming from British uncertainties about the *uti possidetis* played into his hands. By mid-June, however, he had lost control of the timetable. On one hand the offensive in Germany had made a slow start. On the other his dealings with Spain moved quickly; in fact, Choiseul tried to slow Grimaldi down by telling him that the agreements they reached on 2 June must be embodied in formal conventions signed at Madrid. All too promptly the signed documents, slightly amended, were returned. In his accompanying letter Wall bluntly sketched the position to Grimaldi: he could say that 'from now on the negotiation [France's] with England was tied to ours, because the King has agreed to enter the war . . . the 1st of May 1762, if by chance . . . the current negotiation fails'. This reached Choiseul's ears precisely when he could no longer avoid discussing terms with the British. When the British memorial of 26 June arrived he delayed France's answer, but time was short. Grimaldi, who believed correctly that a serious negotiation with Britain was in progress, continually asked

[47] Szabo, p. 327; Starhemberg, 9 April 1761, in Arnold Schaefer, *Geschichte des siebenjährigen Krieges* 2 vols (Berlin, 1867–74), II, pt. 2, 200–1.

him when he was going to keep his promise and introduce Spain's
grievances. He felt cornered, telling Grimaldi that he did not know how
to extricate himself without breaking his word.[48] Stanley, in his postscript
of 5 July, had reported a parting remark from Choiseul: 'Give us the fishery,
and save us the point of honour respecting Dunkirk, for it is only in this
way that peace can be made.'[49] It sounded hopeful, but the next response
reaching London contained the disappointing retraction regarding Prussian
territories and was soon followed by presentation of the two memoirs that
the British would predictably consider offensive.

Choiseul had an additional reason to worry at this time: the parlement of Paris was assertively resisting an extension of some important
taxes. Would lack of money for continuing the war compel France to
accept onerous terms? Full of anxiety Choiseul told Grimaldi that he
must backtrack, that he now wished to modify the military convention
to eliminate the requirement that Spanish grievances be satisfied within
the Anglo-French negotiation. It is possible that if full control of policy
had been in his hands, he would have pressed Madrid to withdraw the
requirement, but he could not ignore Louis XV's warm enthusiasm for the
pacte de famille. According to some reports, the king was even urging that
the memoir proposing to settle Spanish grievances within the negotiation
should be sent off to London forthwith. Choiseul complied. In a private
letter he told Bussy to consult with Fuentes about whether and when
to present it, but this was lame: he knew very well what Fuentes would
say. Having thus placed the negotiation at risk to satisfy Spain, he saw
no point in failing to satisfy Austria and approved sending the memoir
stating Vienna's conditions. It is not possible to know (unless further
research uncovers new evidence) whether the above were really Choiseul's
thoughts, but it is undeniable that his arrangements put peace at risk,
especially because of Louis XV's enthusiasm for the Bourbon Family
Compact.

Choiseul's complicated plan required an offer of terms from London
that was both prompt and attractive – so attractive that he could tell
Grimaldi and Starhemberg, as well as Louis XV, that France could not
afford to miss this opportunity and therefore, regrettably, could not adhere
to the engagements that had been made. The response from London did
come in good time, but it was not generous enough. On 21 July the
parlement of Paris's resistance to extending the taxes was nullified by

[48] Grimaldi to Wall, 21 June 1761, Ozanam, 'Les origines', p. 332.
[49] Stanley to Pitt, 5 July 1761, Thackeray, *History*, II, 542.

a *lit de justice*. Choiseul could now consider taking the easiest path out of his predicament. When Pitt's letter of 25 July expressing the British ministers' indignation (which should not have surprised him) arrived along with the irritating 'paper of points', he had in hand an excuse for doing what he had been preparing to do. At this point he doubted that an accommodating response could come from London: he probably expected the British to raise their terms because of their latest military successes. His anger on 29 July was undoubtedly genuine, and the military defeat at Vellinghausen had not improved his mood, but anger was not the cause of his decision. As we have seen, he informed three ambassadors that the war would continue. To d'Ossun he added that he no longer wished to escape from the commitment that had secured the secret military convention and was ready to see it signed as it stood, along with the *pacte de famille*.

After casting aside the chance of peace Choiseul understood that he must try to hide his conduct from a disappointed French and European public. Back in June he had already conceived of a plan. This was reported to London by the informant at Versailles: 'But in case of a Refusal, they will then publish a sort of appeal to the Nation, that will serve to clear them of the odium of continuing the War; they . . . will attribute the Continuance . . . to the ambition of your Court.'[50] Such a plan was put into effect after the British government recalled Stanley. Over his own name Choiseul published a little book entitled *Mémoire historique sur la négociation* that purportedly traced its entire course.[51]

The book consisted of documents interspersed by explications and commentary. Stanley's letters (which contained the essence of the Anglo-French contentions) were not printed. Choiseul probably did not have copies of them, or a copy of the 'little leaf' which he had dictated in mid-June. In the *Mémoire historique* he summarized the 'little leaf' in a way that did not indicate a pledge that Prussia's Rhineland territories as well as those belonging to Hanover and Hesse would be evacuated. Thus, no one outside the British governing circle could know that France's formal memoir of 13 July (which he did print, dating it 15 July) withdrew such a

---

[50] Versailles intelligence, 19 June, received 30 June 1761, BL Add. 32,924 fo. 172.

[51] Choiseul, *Mémoire historique*. Because the documents Choiseul chose to print accorded with archival originals Rashed (*Peace of Paris*, p. 112) infers that it was a reliable account. Chaussinand-Nogaret has disagreed, remarking that Choiseul employed his innate sense of propaganda and placed the entire responsibility on Pitt (*Choiseul*, p. 140).

pledge. He did not print the supplemental memoir prompted by Vienna, or mention it, but printed the memoir regarding Spanish grievances. Recognizing that this memoir was widely considered to have spoiled the negotiation, he managed as best he could with weak arguments: he criticized 'the English Minister' for rejecting 'with hauteur' the French king's idea that Spanish participation could contribute to a solid and durable peace by preventing an Anglo-Spanish war from occurring, and went on to claim that Madrid had told Versailles that Spain's grievances should no longer be included if they might embarrass the negotiation.[52] He claimed in closing that neither the Austrian alliance nor the invitation to Spain could have prevented the achievement of peace. No mention was made, of course, of the secret military convention. In conclusion he posed the question which he said everyone was asking: What was the motive for the rupture of the negotiation? His answer: 'the absolute opposition of the Court of London to peace'.[53]

It is interesting that Choiseul excluded Britain's formal response of 26 June from his *Mémoire historique*. He certainly possessed a copy and must have known that it belonged in his little book, but it is missing; instead, some parts of it are summarized and presented as if spoken in conversation by Stanley.[54] Many historians have blamed the failure to make peace on this document. The argument is that its terms were so demanding, and presented in such severe language by Pitt, that they caused Choiseul to give up hope of peace and play the Spanish card. And yet Choiseul chose not to print it. Probably he wished to avoid any hint that he might have given up on peace so quickly. He knew that the 26 June memorial was Britain's first declaration of terms, made in response to an informal statement that he dictated to Stanley on the 17th. He had warned Stanley that this statement was merely preliminary, a point he confirmed in his *Mémoire historique* (pp. 76–7). In deciding not to print the 26 June memorial it seems that Choiseul realized that the

---

[52] Choiseul, *Mémoire historique*, pp. 188–9. Choiseul's public claim that relations with Spain had no impact was prearranged. Grimaldi wrote to Fuentes: '. . . it should not be said that peace has not been made on account of our differences with England'; he told Choiseul that it would be sufficient to order Bussy privately 'not to sign any thing without the accommodation of matters with Spain', on the understanding that the French commitment still stood; from a 13 Sept. 1761 letter that was intercepted and deciphered (*Chatham Correspondence*, II, 142).

[53] Choiseul, *Mémoire historique*, p. 195.

[54] Ibid. pp. 77–80.

British ministers' first declaration of terms could not reasonably be treated as their last. This opinion was held by Stanley and clearly expressed by Bute. It is entirely possible of course that Choiseul did in fact decide to abandon hope of peace upon receiving the memorial. If he did, however, it raises the question of whether he had given himself any chance of making a different decision. After all, Choiseul wanted not only the fisheries but an *abri* on Cape Breton island, and anyone in Britain could have told him that the latter was impossible. Even the Duke of Bedford was against giving back Cape Breton. Therefore, further negotiation would have been inevitably necessary, and Choiseul's goals could not have been attained quickly.

The French minister was convinced that Pitt was an implacable enemy who would never wish to give France what was needed.[55] Whether Choiseul realized that Pitt respected the system of cabinet government enough to yield to the wishes of his colleagues and the king if it seemed necessary cannot be known because his arrangements did not allow time for this to be found out. He gave peace a very narrow window of opportunity, one that made no allowance for the operation of British governmental institutions.

As a statesman Choiseul had to consider the interests of France as a great power. When he made the commitment to Spain in early June he must have believed that a Franco-Spanish alliance would be militarily successful and thereby make the English, as he put it, more reasonable.[56] If so, he misjudged the future, but as a policy choice it was in principle justified. It does not follow, however, that he was justified in placing the blame for the lost chance of peace on the British government, notwithstanding Pitt's failure to employ conciliating language. It is indisputable that Choiseul gave priority to alliances over peace, and his claim that the British were 'determined to perpetuate the war' was disproved by their willingness to continue the negotiation after he had thrown it over. As will now be seen, the British cabinet, believing or at least hoping that the ongoing negotiation was genuine, would grant many of the concessions that the French foreign minister had originally sought.

---

[55] For Choiseul's view of Pitt see Dziembowski, *Un nouveau patriotisme français*, pp. 280–1.

[56] Muret (*La prépondérance anglaise*, p. 558) has asked whether Choiseul, in early June, might have preferred war in alliance with Spain to the peace terms he thought he could get in 1761. Chaussinand-Nogaret (*Choiseul*, pp. 138–9) believes that he counted on continuing the war.

Pitt's resignation and the path to war with Spain

In a hurriedly written postscript, dated 1 August, Hans Stanley reported that the duc de Choiseul was complaining strenuously because the British were not offering an *abri*. His gloomy letter of 6 August reiterated how angry Choiseul was about this, and also reported his complaint about the inflexible language of the 'paper of points' with its frequent use of words like *must* and *never*. At this time an 'ultimatum', dated 5 August, was dispatched from Versailles. It led to five long and contentious council meetings in London from 13 to 24 August; ten to twelve members were present at each. The council quickly resolved to make it clear that the French could dry their codfish on some part of Newfoundland and that the standard of Aix-la-Chapelle was sufficient regarding Dunkirk. The French reiterated a former demand that access to fishing inside the Gulf of St Lawrence should be permitted. In July, even Newcastle had objected to allowing this, and Hardwicke had observed that their claimed 'immemorial' right to fish inside the Gulf was nonsense: the basis of such a claim must rest on possession of the surrounding shores, which they had lost and Britain was not going to give back. But on 18 August when Bute and Pitt met with the king, Bute had been persuaded by Devonshire to allow it. The king expressed his distress at seeing the acrimonious division of his council, and in three meetings between the 19th and the 24th fishing in the Gulf was granted, Pitt reluctantly agreeing for the sake of unity. On 30 August London sent an ultimatum allowing fishing inside the Gulf and for an *abri* on the island of St Pierre, just south of Newfoundland.

Choiseul's fraudulent continuation of the negotiation and his emphasis on the fishery question yielded positive results for France, because when genuine negotiations resumed in 1762 they commenced from the position at the end of August. During this month the French minister realized that the British might unexpectedly meet his terms, but he avoided embarrassment by adhering to demands which he knew to be unacceptable, such as prohibiting Prince Ferdinand's German troops from eventually serving the king of Prussia, or by introducing new ones, such as a claim that the Ohio territory was to be deemed part of Louisiana. (In refuting French claims about the American interior the British ministers made use of Amherst's map of Canada's limits as indicated by Vaudreuil.) Machiavelli correctly remarked that 'fraud . . . in the management of war . . . is laudable'. It has rarely been considered so in the making of peace, where it is commonly counter-productive, but Choiseul got away with it because most of the British ministers were earnestly hoping that a peace settlement could be negotiated.

The whole process brought out the worst in Pitt. His colleagues dreaded the effect of his imperious language on the French, and he was harming his relations with them. Hardwicke saw no excuse for the way he had obscured the offer of the Newfoundland fishery. By not expressing the true sense of the meeting in the 'paper of points' he had betrayed an elementary requirement of cabinet government, which he professed to uphold. Bute had allowed it to pass, but Hardwicke directed his anger at Pitt, the undoubted originator, and Pitt made the mistake of heatedly arguing with the old lawyer.[57] For Pitt to lose Hardwicke, who had so long and so often supported him against Newcastle's criticisms, was a serious, self-inflicted injury.

As for the others, Pitt could not bear to listen to the Duke of Bedford, who seemed intent on enabling France to escape the consequences of his success as director of the war. Bedford, for his part, did not disguise his dislike of Pitt. Newcastle, eager for the negotiation to succeed, declared that Stanley had 'constantly' given assurances 'of the sincerity of Mon. Choiseul, in which I have believed him, from the Beginning to this Day, notwithstanding the opinion of Great Men here, and of my good Friend Sir Joseph, at the Hague'.[58] (In fact, Stanley had sometimes doubted Choiseul's sincerity.) Convinced that the war's continuance was Pitt's fault, Newcastle moaned about the burden of having to find money to wage it and spoke of resigning the Treasury. Devonshire saw no reason to stop negotiating and endeavoured to prise Bute away from Pitt, who soon came to the conclusion that everyone on the council except his brother-in-law, Temple, was opposed to him. Pitt believed that the French were playing his colleagues for fools and scorned the concessions being made: 'These relaxations', he said, 'have not only spoiled this treaty, but will spoil all future treaties.' Hardwicke maintained his reserve. He remarked to Newcastle that the French would be foolish to continue the war, given their problems. He added, however: 'Much will now turn upon their boasted union with Spain which, I fear, has gone a great way.' In a meeting of 24 August, Lord Granville agreed: he said that further concession would 'have no effect' because of 'the union formed with Spain'. Pitt said:

[57] Middleton, *Bells*, p. 191.
[58] Newcastle to Yorke, 1 Sept. 1761, BL Add. 32,927 fo. 332.

'If the French should reject and the war be continued, I had rather it should be with France and Spain jointly, than with France alone.'[59]

On 2 September Stanley gained brief access to a paper, evidently part of a larger document, which confirmed that France was committed to supporting Spanish claims in the current negotiation with Britain. On the 6th he reported that an agreement between France and Spain was actually drawn up and needed 'only the last hand and signature'.[60] In fact, both the *pacte de famille* and the secret military convention had been signed on 15 August. Shortly after receiving this letter from Stanley, Pitt was reading an intercepted and deciphered letter from Grimaldi to Fuentes (dated 31 August) which confirmed the same French commitment to Spain. Pitt and Bute suggested that Stanley should be recalled. Newcastle opposed this, but Hardwicke thought that failure to recall Stanley would indicate such 'a want of firmness' that the French would become 'more obstinate'. Devonshire agreed, and at the end of a long discussion on 15 September the council ordered the recall.[61]

The question of what to do about Spain remained. Pitt came to the council meeting on 18 September with a letter just received from Lord Bristol stating that when he asked Wall, according to Pitt's instructions, whether Madrid had approved of the memoir presented by Bussy on 23 July, the answer was affirmative, and without apology. Wall had added that Spain had no hostile intentions towards Britain. Pitt asked his colleagues to pay no attention to this and reminded his colleagues of the intelligence that had come from Stanley – that a Franco-Spanish agreement was all but signed. He considered France and Spain to be clearly united, and proposed that Lord Bristol should be ordered to leave Madrid so that hostilities could begin. The other ministers disagreed. Hardwicke pointed out that going to war with Spain was 'very different from any other power' because Britain's Spanish trade was so valuable. Since many British merchants would be put at risk they should be forewarned. Everyone was apprehensive about the addition of a major enemy, but Pitt argued that 'an immediate action gives us the best chance to extricate ourselves'. Hardwicke considered the grounds for doing it insufficient.[62]

---

[59] Hardwicke to Newcastle, 22 Aug. 1761, Yorke, *Hardwicke*, III, 322; the other quotations are from Hardwicke's notes of the 24 Aug. meeting, ibid. III, 272–3.
[60] Thackeray, *History*, I, 578; II, 617.
[61] *Devonshire Diary*, pp. 119–25.
[62] Ibid. pp. 126–31.

The next day Bute, Devonshire, Mansfield (who had been brought onto the council after George III's succession) and Newcastle met privately; Hardwicke was not present because his wife was dying. None supported Pitt's proposal of immediate hostilities, but all except Newcastle thought that the conduct of the Spanish 'by their engagements with France and their avowal of the memorial presented by M. Bussy was so offensive' that they must be required to give a satisfactory answer regarding their intentions, and if none was received it was to be taken as a declaration of war. Newcastle realized he must acquiesce.[63] On the 21st the council proposed that Lord Bristol should be instructed to obtain a categorical answer to the question whether Spain was 'under any engagement to take part with France in the present war against England'.[64] Pitt and Temple considered this insufficient and it became clear that they were likely to resign; in fact, they drew up an 'advice in writing' addressed to the king which stated their position. The next day a letter from Stanley arrived which carried hints from Choiseul that he sincerely wished for peace and could find ways towards an accommodation. Newcastle and others, including the king, welcomed this last-minute glimmer of hope. Pitt could not believe that Choiseul's remarks were honest, and when Stanley reached London on the 30th, he still had nothing in writing and had to admit that there was no hope.

Another meeting was called. Before it convened Bute informed most of the council members that the king wanted Pitt out of office, and each agreed to go to the king and declare his opposition to Pitt's policy. This method avoided written responses to the 'advice in writing' (which the king had refused to receive). Pitt came to the meeting of 2 October prepared to resign his office unless the council agreed to recall Lord Bristol. Opinion quickly mounted against him. Hardwicke doubted that the Spanish desired war at this time and adhered to his opinion that the diplomatic grounds for declaring Spain a hostile power were insufficient. All were aware that Pitt was hoping that the silver fleet known to be coming from the West Indies could be intercepted. (No one in London knew that it had got safely into Cadiz on 12 September.) Anson, having earlier given an overestimate of the strength of the French and Spanish fleets, said that his ships were not yet in condition to undertake the contest. Ligonier warned (mistakenly) that Spanish land forces were quite formidable.[65] Pitt spoke

---

[63] Newcastle to Hardwicke, 20 Sept. 1761, Hunt, 'Pitt's Retirement', 122–4.
[64] *Devonshire Diary*, p. 134.
[65] Newcastle's notes of the meeting, Hunt, 'Pitt's Retirement', 130–2.

clearly and courteously, as he had done in the last two meetings. As for taking on an additional enemy, Spain was already an enemy, he said. It is 'the worst species of war' for Spain 'to abet France with her full weight. Cover her trade and lend her money and abet France in negotiation. You are now at war with the House of Bourbon. You are prepared, and she is not.'[66] In closing he made a speech in which he insisted that if he were to bear responsibility for affairs, he must have the direction of them. It was his familiar claim, but he also believed that he must persuade his cabinet colleagues rather than dictate to them. Moreover, in this case his claim to direct affairs was somewhat inappropriate because the council had been specifically empowered by the king to make all decisions in these negotiations. Lord Granville firmly reminded him of this. With good grace Pitt departed, and three days later he formally resigned.

In seeking to avoid immediate hostilities with Spain the council was prudent and Pitt unwise. Pre-emptive war almost always incurs significant diplomatic disadvantages and is best justified by acute danger. Pitt did not believe Britain was in danger; he saw opportunities. Furthermore, although he could point to strong indications that Spain was militarily committed to joining France, he did not possess evidence that could be publicly exhibited. The council realized that there was a preliminary step that could be taken: Lord Bristol could ask a categorical question concerning Spain's engagement to France to which an unsatisfactory answer could be deemed equivalent to a declaration of war. All except Newcastle appeared to favour this course (Bedford was not present). By insisting on immediate action Pitt pushed it aside.

Pitt had drawn the line over the wrong issue at the wrong time. After he left the meeting on 2 October the ministers decided to order the fleet at Gibraltar under Saunders to be reinforced. But now that Pitt was gone they became hesitant about sending the instruction requiring Lord Bristol to ask for a categorical answer. Hardwicke 'doubted much whether Spain would declare war against us, and [pointed out] that it had been constantly the view of France to encourage Spain to take such steps as . . . might animate us to begin [war] with them'.[67] In fact, Choiseul was urging Spain to speed up her war preparations; Pitt would have done the French minister's work for him. No instructions went to Lord Bristol for another month. Even then, the letter of 2 November did not threaten consequences if Madrid's reply was evasive. It was not until 19 November that the

---

[66] Hardwicke's notes of the meeting, Temperley, 'Pitt's Retirement', 329–30.
[67] Newcastle's notes of the 2 Oct. meeting, ibid. 130–1.

new secretary of state, Charles Wyndham, Earl of Egremont demanded a categorical answer. By this time the cabinet needed to have an answer in order to map out strategy for the coming year.

On 29 September Choiseul advised d'Ossun that Spain should go to war no later than December. When d'Ossun's reply indicated that Madrid intended to wait until the date required by the secret convention, Choiseul was alarmed. If the Spanish waited until May, he protested, they would not be able to wage war effectively until 1763, by which time the English would seize what was left of France's colonial empire. Carlos III was willing to go to war, but his ministers, led by Wall, put it off: the defences of the Spanish Caribbean were still inadequate and the armed forces were far from ready. Besides, Spain would need to develop offensive plans. Portugal was a logical if diplomatically questionable target. Other ideas proliferated, perhaps encouraged by Wall, who was privately against going to war. Spain, it was suggested, might attack Ireland, Gibraltar or Jamaica. In some cases orders were given, but few preparations were actually made. At length it was decided to increase the navy to 54 ships of the line, raise some recruits for the army, and send 8,000 troops to the Portuguese frontier.

Earlier, on 30 July, Choiseul had empowered d'Ossun to suggest quietly to the Spanish minister of finance that France would cede Louisiana to Spain if he would arrange a large loan. At the same time Choiseul pledged to reserve Minorca for eventual return to Spain if the Spanish would promptly declare war against Britain. When the silver fleet arrived Spain granted a loan, at 5 per cent interest, of half the cargo's value, to be transferred in six instalments during the first half of 1762. The actual value amounted to less than anticipated, and delays at Madrid caused Choiseul to fear that the Spanish might back out of their commitment. Like most people who did not know about the secret Franco-Spanish military convention, Joseph Yorke strongly doubted that Spain would go to war. It would be absurd for them to do it, and his opinion, he said, was shared by 'all the great Traders in Holland, who smell a war out as fast as anybody, and who would have been speculating without end'.[68]

One reason why it was hard to believe that Spain would be willing to go to war as France's ally was the low condition of the French navy. Choiseul, who had taken over as naval minister from Berryer in mid-October, decided to remedy this, or at least its perception. He had prepared the ground by his *Mémoire historique*, which attributed the failure

[68] Yorke to Royston, Nov. 1761, BL Add. 35,365, fo. 365.

of the negotiation to inflexible British demands. He thereby generated a renewed wave of Anglophobia and drew upon it to provide for the navy. To the archbishop of Narbonne, president of the Estates of Languedoc, he covertly suggested that the provincial representatives at the next meeting might choose to fund the cost of a new ship of the line. The proposal was voted by acclamation on 26 November. A report was printed in the *Gazette de France* of 5 December that encouraged emulation all over France. Other provincial estates, cities, financiers, the farmers general, corporations of skilled artisans, and even individuals joined in offering contributions to build ships of the line. These were to be named accordingly: *Languedoc, Bretagne, Bourgogne, Bordelais, Marseillais, Ville de Paris, Citoyen.* Smaller cities and organizations contributed frigates. Throughout the winter contributions poured in, about 16 million livres, which would amount to more than two-thirds of naval spending in 1762. A sign of the intense patriotism was seen at Bayonne where the public welcomed some ships bringing in timber as if they were a triumphant squadron.

The scheme, brilliantly conceived and executed, was a tremendous success. Given the time needed to build a ship of the line, however, it is not surprising that only two were launched before the war ended. The money enabled resupply of the dockyards and the mobilizing of small squadrons for sea, but it could not produce ships in time to help the Spanish navy in its coming struggle against Britain. Of political interest: the patriotic effusions boosting it spoke of the nation rather than the king, and the enthusiasm for supporting the navy can be taken as a popular commentary on the monarchy's emphasis on campaigning in Germany.

As it happened the British government pushed Madrid into commencing hostilities. When Lord Bristol carried out Egremont's instructions on 7 December and asked for a categorical answer, Wall would not provide one. Yet he realized that delay was no longer possible, and the next day Madrid sent orders to Spanish ports that all British ships should be seized and also to stations overseas that they should consider attacking as well as defending. Fuentes was told to leave London, but first he was to warn Spanish captains in the Thames to sail immediately. When Bristol made a second visit to Wall on 10 December he was handed a note which acknowledged the breaking of relations and blamed it on the insult implied by the British government's insistence on a categorical answer. The ambassador took his leave. When trying to depart he found that he and his courier were forbidden the usual mode of transportation to the Portuguese border. He did not reach Elvas until 26 December, where he dispatched warnings to British shipping and a message to Admiral Saunders.

On the 8th Wall had sent an interesting letter to Grimaldi in Paris. It was motivated partly by the fact that he had not told Lord Bristol the truth when asked whether the treaty with France contained anything offensive against Britain. Although he was able to say truthfully that the *pacte de famille*, signed on 15 August, was defensive and would not take effect until the war was over, he knew that the secret military convention, signed the same day, was decidedly hostile and of immediate relevance. He informed Grimaldi that there was a solution to the problem that could be adopted without risk. To establish that there was no other treaty signed on the 15th 'we have agreed to postdate the convention, so that it would appear to have been made after the rupture of the negotiation of the French and English'. Wall went on to point out that by this means Pitt's claim that Spain was determined to make war on England would appear false. He asked Louis XV and his foreign minister to approve of the post-dating. Grimaldi and Choiseul, at Versailles, worried over what the Austrians would think about this Franco-Spanish military convention. After many secret exchanges between Paris and Madrid in which documents were rewritten to remove clues that could betray the true date of execution, a substituted convention was eventually approved on 29 March 1762. It was given the more plausible date of 4 February and filed accordingly in the Spanish archives. But the drafts at the French foreign ministry were not purged, so the true date of signing, 15 August, has been revealed to posterity.[69]

London first learned that war with Spain was certain when Fuentes presented a memoir from Wall on Christmas Day. The 'insulting' categorical demand was blamed for the severing of relations. The memoir also stated that Spain's treaty relations with France were confined to the defensive *pacte de famille* which would not take effect until after the present war ended. No one in London knew about the secret convention, but Hardwicke was suspicious. When Newcastle wrote expressing his wish that the categorical demand had not been made, Hardwicke responded immediately: 'It is plain that Nothing would have satisfied Spain.' As for removing the logwood-cutting settlements he asked, 'What English Minister or Ministers would have ventured to have signed orders for that purpose?' He reminded Newcastle of Choiseul's letter of 30 July to Stockholm (which had been intercepted) 'wherein mention was made of training on the Negotiation between England and France till the latter end

---

[69] Waddington, *Guerre*, IV, 625–6. Aiton, 'A Neglected Intrigue', 388–92.

of September, when the Flota should be arrived'. It deserved, he added, 'more weight . . . than we were willing to allow it at that time'.[70]

In a morning meeting of 26 December, Newcastle, thinking of finances, declared 'the Impossibility of supporting this War', but no one paid attention. On the 29th Egremont called on Hardwicke for advice about answering Wall's memoir and drafting a declaration of war. The old man's response: Do not bother to answer the memoir and instead write a strongly worded declaration. Thanking Hardwicke, Egremont mentioned that the cabinet was about to order the Admiralty to commission privateers immediately, especially for the West Indies. The government intended to fight the war against Spain vigourously.

The British declaration of war against Spain was issued on 2 January 1762. Six weeks later Newcastle still believed that it could have been avoided, citing 'the universal opinion . . . that we have hastily and unnecessarily brought on the Spanish war'. The statements from Madrid joined to wishful thinking had persuaded him and many other Englishmen of this. Hardwicke firmly disagreed; he had talked with many who believed that the 'French faction in the Court of Madrid were determined to have the war, tho' possibly they wished to gain a little more time to be better prepared'.[71]

---

[70] Hardwicke to Newcastle, 25 and 26 Dec. 1761, BL Add. 32, 932, ff. 349, 367, Yorke, *Hardwicke*, III, 341.

[71] Newcastle to Devonshire, 26 Dec. 1761, Hardwicke to Newcastle, 29 Dec. 1761, BL Add. 32, 932, ff. 363, 400, Hardwicke to Newcastle, 16 Feb. 1762, BL Add. 32,934, fo. 381 and Yorke, *Hardwicke*, III, 342.

CHAPTER 15

Peacemaking, 1762: concessions before conquests

On 8 October 1761, three days after Pitt's resignation, Lord Bute told a political friend that the war must be carried on with determination.

You, my dear Lord, cannot dislike it more than I do; but as we have to do with a most treacherous enemy, whose infamous prevarications have been so lately experienced, we must act with redoubled vigour and spirit, before we can hope to bring them to such a peace as, from our repeated conquests, this country has a right to expect . . . This being so, the change of a Minister cannot at present make any remarkable change in measures. I sigh after peace, but will not sue for it; not out of pride . . . but from a thorough conviction that begging it from France is not the readiest way to come by it.[1]

When Bute wrote this he was afraid of Pitt in opposition, and initially supported vigorous war measures. But only six weeks after writing it he started a process that came very close to begging for peace. By a secret channel he reopened the negotiation that had lapsed in early September. The channel ran through Count Viry in London (whose capacity for intrigue has already been observed) and the Sardinian ambassador at Versailles, Roberto Ignazio, marquis Solaro, called the bailli de Solar, who happened to be a close confident of Choiseul's.

---

[1] Bute to Dodington, 8 Oct. 1761, Garswell and Dralle, eds, *Political Journal of . . . Dodington* (cited in Chapter 6), p. 425.

Back in 1759 when the king of Spain raised the question of peace Pitt's reply was that because Britain had major operations under way in North America any discussion of the subject must be delayed. In late 1761, without any request from Versailles or Madrid, Bute initiated a resumption of peace negotiations while a major British expedition was on the way to Martinique, an objective of great consequence. In fact, Viry sent a message in December informing Solar that British ministers hoped to reach a settlement before news came of Martinique's capture; the terms would be based on those established in early September. In other words, if France were to lose Martinique, it would not matter. Bute composed this message and had it sent; George III knew of it, but no other cabinet minister did. Months later, when a formidable expedition was heading for Havana, Bute similarly tried to get a settlement in place before news of Havana's conquest could reach London. The usual diplomatic pattern, of course, was and is for the side enjoying military advantage to await word of a probable military success before concluding a settlement. Under Bute's direction the British government proceeded in reverse order.

Bute and some of his colleagues almost managed to hand military success in Germany to the French. At the beginning of 1762 he announced to his fellow ministers that he wished to be rid of the German war as soon as possible. He thereby split the cabinet. Some members believed that Britain could not afford war with Spain while maintaining the war in Germany. Like Bute, they chose to ignore the serious military, moral and diplomatic consequences that a sudden, unilateral withdrawal of British troops from Prince Ferdinand's army would entail. Eventually, Newcastle, Devonshire and Hardwicke would be able to prevent it from happening, but not without significant political repercussions. They were unable, however, to prevent cancellation of the Prussian subsidy.

It is not an exaggeration to state that in the year 1762 British arms prevailed in all theatres of the war, without exception. (This was the case even in Portugal where, after a long struggle, the Anglo-Portuguese defence was successful.) Bute's eagerness to make peace explains why the terms of the treaty of Paris did not reflect Britain's record of triumph in this final year of the war. To be sure, Choiseul managed French diplomacy expertly, but it was not hard to look like a negotiating genius when dealing with an opponent so eager to please. One understands why Choiseul feared political restoration of Pitt more than he feared military defeat. Yet as the disappointments and defeats accumulated he realized that the war's continuation could not improve upon the generous terms that London was offering, and would probably make them worse. At this point, however, he was obstructed by the king of Spain. Although the Spanish could not cope with a British onslaught that was focused chiefly on them, Carlos III was reluctant to admit defeat. But London insisted that peace with France must be accompanied by peace with Spain. In the end the most challenging test of Choiseul's diplomatic resolve would not be his negotiation with London, but with Madrid.

Aftermath of Pitt's resignation

When Pitt formally resigned on 5 October 1761 the king expressed a hope that he would be willing to accept suitable honours or emoluments. Bute sent Gilbert Elliot to consult with him, and soon the king offered a pension of £3,000 per annum for Pitt, his wife and their eldest son as well as the elevation of his wife (but not himself) to the peerage. Hester would soon become Baroness Chatham. In this way Pitt could keep his seat in the House of Commons. With a growing family to support he needed money; he had not enriched himself in office beyond his salary as secretary of state. The resignation and the rewards were announced in the *Gazette* of 10 October, which also contained an extract of a letter from Madrid stating the Spanish government's peaceful intentions. Horace Walpole concluded that the combination of announcements was designed to harm Pitt, 'to blast his popularity'.[2]

No one in England – or abroad for that matter – foresaw Pitt's resignation. In view of the rewards it was widely assumed that he had been induced by Bute and the king to sell out. The torrent of condemnation, most of it spontaneous, was so great that he was persuaded to publish an explanation. He addressed a letter to Alderman William Beckford, his leading ally in the City of London, and it was conveyed to the *Public Ledger*, which, on 17 October, sold 3,000 copies in a few hours. Pitt began the letter by justifying his decision to write it: 'the most gracious and spontaneous marks of his Majesty's approbation of my services . . . have been infamously traduced, as a bargain for my forsaking the public'. He then explained that an important 'difference of opinion with regard to measures to be taken against Spain' caused him to resign; he and Lord Temple, after putting their views in writing for presentation to the king, were 'over-ruled by the united opinion of all the rest of the King's servants', and he resolved not to remain responsible for measures which he was 'no longer allowed to guide'. He was 'proud to have received' what

[2] Walpole, *Memoirs of King George III*, I, 57.

had been given him by 'the best of sovereigns'.[3] The letter carefully adhered to the pledge he had made to the king and others upon resigning that he would not seek to embarrass the ministry and would speak out only in defence of his reputation.

The only point that could reasonably have annoyed the king was his mention of the presentation of his views in writing; nevertheless, George III considered the letter offensive. The letter certainly achieved its object, as London opinion swung strongly in Pitt's favour. Bute reacted: he commissioned pamphlets. Some, like those written by William Guthrie, were substantive and closely argued; others were scurrilous and filled with false accusations. Pitt's adherents answered, but they laboured under disadvantages.

The most obvious disadvantage arose from his acceptance of the pension. Pitt thought of it as his due. He respected royalty and greatly preferred to receive recognition and reward from the monarch rather than from some wealthy magnate. He honestly claimed that he had not asked for the favours, yet it was only after he had expressed his intention not to act in opposition that they had been offered. Although he fully deserved the pension, it was indisputably designed to hold him to his stated intention, and acceptance of a royal pension was especially damaging to a man who had built his political career on ostentatious avoidance of material rewards. One of the most damaging pamphlets was titled *The Right Honourable Annuitant Vindicated*, the final word intended as mockery. A second disadvantage was the timing of his resignation. It dismayed and disarmed his supporters, most of whom looked to him to organize the very challenging war effort that now appeared necessary; he was accused of deserting the nation in time of great need.

The press battle raged for three months and was as vitriolic as any in the eighteenth century. In the midst of the furore Choiseul's *Mémoire historique sur la négociation* appeared in Britain, printed in English and French, conveying its point that Pitt's haughty stance was the cause of failure.[4] The idea that Pitt was responsible for prolonging the war was certainly something Bute wanted to promote, and he was not confident that Pitt would remain politically inactive, especially after seeing the enthusiasm that Pitt's letter to Beckford generated in the City. Despite

---

[3] Pitt to Beckford, 15 Oct. 1761, *Chatham Correspondence*, II, 158-9.
[4] Horace Walpole, who ordinarily did not trust the French, thought it was convincing; to Horace Mann, 14 Nov. 1761, Lewis, ed. *Walpole Correspondence*, V, 546.

the presence of strong bodyguards Bute's carriage was dangerously mobbed on the way to the Lord Mayor's reception in early November.

A key point of argument in the press war was whether Pitt had unnecessarily alienated the Spanish. Lord Hardwicke's eldest son, like Newcastle, was convinced that Pitt was to blame for Spain's hostile posture. Hardwicke did not rebuke his son, but did not agree. Although he had strongly differed with Pitt about the prudence of going to war immediately, he still thought that Spain had probably made a hostile pact with France. No one in England had proof that this was the case. Since the strongest current of public opinion blamed Pitt for the war with Spain, the House of Commons asked to see the relevant correspondence with Madrid. George Grenville was ready to comply but was overruled by the cabinet after Hardwicke argued convincingly against allowing it while diplomatic relations with Spain were still unsettled. In late December, upon leaving London, the ambassador, Fuentes, added fuel to the fire by issuing a statement claiming that the breaking of relations was Pitt's fault. Horace Walpole saw the diplomatic impropriety of this: 'it is properly the declaration of the King of Spain against Mr Pitt'.[5] After war was declared Grenville renewed Parliament's demand for the 'Spanish papers'. Pitt asked: 'If . . . they do come, shall it be with no farther retrospect than Bussy's memorial [in July]?' Judging correctly that this was the case, he added: 'how futile! how unsatisfactory!'[6] Pitt considered it improper to speak about the diplomatic exchanges that had put Spain and Britain at odds as early as January 1761, nor could he prove that France and Spain had signed a military convention – a treaty signed in August that at this moment, in late January 1762, Madrid and Paris were arranging to post-date so that British suspicions would seem unwarranted.

The bitter press war that came in the wake of Pitt's resignation was harmful, but there was another source of political trouble – disagreement on terms of a peace settlement. George III and Bute were determined to make the accomplishment of peace the political task of 1762. Serious disagreements over whether the cost of the war was sustainable, what to do about allies, and which treaty terms were essential would be inevitable, and opinions among the ministers differed widely. Bute was extremely impatient to end the war, especially Britain's role on the continent, but was fearful of popular criticism if he failed to adopt a strong military posture overseas and against Spain. The Duke of Bedford, who became

[5] Walpole to Mann, 28 Dec. 1761, ibid. p. 559.
[6] Walpole, *Memoirs of King George III*, I, 90.

Lord Privy Seal after Hardwicke refused the office, wanted to end the war everywhere and immediately. His defeatism was intense; he predicted failure in every theatre of war, particularly in Germany. Inclined to Francophilia, he inexplicably viewed French power as unbeatable yet somehow harmless. Newcastle, despite his pacifism and complaints about the war's expense, consistently upheld the war on the continent. Grenville, in complete disagreement, was prepared to abandon the German war, while considering overseas conquests to be the best method of ending the war on beneficial terms. Devonshire, though almost as pacifistic as Newcastle, was not inveterately opposed to overseas undertakings but joined Newcastle in supporting the German war. Egremont desired peace, but not at any price.

Making the needed compromises without serious disharmony would therefore require trust, good faith and political courage. These would be lacking – a second major cause of trouble. Bute, Newcastle and Grenville formed the foundation of the ministry: Bute the king's favourite, Newcastle the manager of patronage and parliament, and Grenville the spokesman in the House of Commons. The fundamental flaw was that neither Bute nor George III was minded to encourage a climate of trust. Their aim, whether they admitted it or not, was to divide, and this affected the way they thought about the cabinet. Newcastle, wishing to be in touch with everyone, might have served as a unifier, but Bute could not disguise his long-incubated hostility to the man. Devonshire tried to encourage harmony; he told Newcastle to stifle his petulant complaining and stop dropping hints about resigning (which no one believed) lest the government fall apart, and asked Bute to give Newcastle what he craved most – verbal tokens of royal approbation. But Bute could not bring himself to do it, one reason being that the king found it hard to be nice to someone he had been taught to despise from boyhood. Cabinet government would be corroded in 1762, not so much because of the vitriol of the press war or the attempt to blame Pitt for inviting the Spanish war, but rather because of the personal outlook of Bute and George III, combined with the painful project of making peace.

Pitt, now on the outside, was an unpredictable player. On 13 November 1761 when Parliament assembled he had been called upon to speak. He understood that he must mention something about his conduct with regard to Spain, but said that he would leave it to the members and the public to reach their own conclusions after reading the diplomatic correspondence. What is most remembered from this speech was a remark he made about the war in Germany: '*America had been conquered in*

Germany', Pitt declared, adding: 'Prince Ferdinand had been the saviour of Europe, and had shattered the whole military power of that military monarchy, France.'[7] No sentence from Pitt's Seven Years War speeches has been more commonly quoted than the first – usually to prove that his view of grand strategy was almost as 'Continentalist' as Newcastle's. Such an idea, as preceding chapters show, could not be correct. He made this declaration in a particular context: to counter the surging tide of opinion that was flowing against the war in Germany. His strong feelings led him into rhetorical extravagance. A clue to what underlay those feelings is found in the seldom quoted sentence that followed where he declared that Prince Ferdinand had 'shattered the whole military power' of France. To say that Ferdinand had done this was another exaggeration, yet Pitt's essential point was valid: Ferdinand had succeeded year after year, with inferior numbers, in frustrating the French army's effort to conquer in Germany. The French made that effort in order to gain compensation for losses in America. Pitt did not want his audience to forget this.

On 9 December 1761 in the debate on the army and navy estimates he returned to the subject. Calmly and without rhetorical flourishes on this occasion, he presented a fact-filled, comprehensive argument that reviewed the whole history of Britain's engagement in Germany. The engagement, he explained, was reluctant, necessary and ultimately beneficial. The original challenge facing the British government had been to 'make the German war useful to the interests of this country as a subordinate measure, while our marine and colonies should be the principal object'. Since England single-handed was not a match for France in Europe, 'You must always cast out work for France upon the continent whenever you go to war with that country; and when you do so, it does not much matter who are your allies, provided that they are such as will act strenuously against France and the allies of France.' This was the rationale for supporting the army in Westphalia and the Prussian alliance. In neither speech did he mention the balance of power. The object was to divert French resources, and also, although he did not wish to say it, to prevent French occupation of Hanover. In both speeches he lavished praise on Ferdinand, 'one of the greatest generals of the age'.[8] Pitt supported war in all theatres and did not mind the expense. By his resignation the strongest advocate for sustaining the German war was removed from the ministry, but his voice on

---

[7] In the Commons debate on the Address, at the opening of Parliament, *Proceedings and Debates*, I, 362–3. Emphasis in the original.

[8] Schweizer, 'An Unpublished Parliamentary Speech', 100, 102–4.

9 December 1761 ensured that the million pounds for supporting the 'foreign troops' of Ferdinand's army would be voted unanimously.

The German war and the Prussian subsidy

Those in Britain who opposed the German war and the Prussian subsidy generally saw the two issues as one. For instance, the Earl of Shelburne in a debate of 5 February 1762 simply said that 'whatever inconvenience may attend our stopping' was less dangerous than continuing.[9] He did not specify what was to be stopped. Like Shelburne, the public saw both issues as parts of a single continental commitment that had become extremely costly and appeared to have outlived its usefulness. Historical discussion has followed the same path, lumping both together. Yet the predictable strategic and diplomatic impact of ending the German war was quite different from that of withholding the Prussian subsidy.

In March 1761 Pitt had left a negotiation with Prussia regarding renewal of the alliance and subsidy unresolved. When Lord Bute took it up in November Frederick II's military situation had become more desperate than ever. He had lost the Silesian fortress of Schweidnitz and could not relieve Kolberg, a Baltic port only 150 miles from Berlin, which was under Russian siege. Frederick had done nothing during the year to assist Prince Ferdinand, yet under Article IV of the alliance treaty he had the right to be consulted regarding peace terms that Britain might arrange with France. This now seemed absurd.

On 29 December a proposal arrived from Berlin which asked Britain, in the event of an Anglo-French peace, to continue to support Prussia financially and diplomatically until its interests were satisfied. The Prussians were overreaching, and Bute, who was eager to end Britain's continental commitment, reacted sharply. There would be no renewal of the alliance treaty, he told the Prussia's London envoys, nor any promise of providing for Prussia after Britain and France made peace. The £670,000 annual subsidy for the coming year would be paid, but by means of a parliamentary grant without reference to a treaty. The envoys, knowing that Prussia desperately needed the money and observing Bute's anger, wrote to Berlin recommending acquiescence.

Bute's decision was not unreasonable, but he conveyed it without courtesy, and from this point forward his attitude towards the king of Prussia was transparently hostile. His letter to Andrew Mitchell of

[9] Schweizer, 'The Bedford Motion and House of Lords Debate', 116.

8 January 1762 announced the decision to pay the subsidy by a grant while omitting mention of any further assistance in case of an Anglo-French peace. Bute might have provided justification for the new policy merely by citing the new burden of war with Spain – in the manner practised by Choiseul when reducing France's treaty commitments to Austria in 1758 – but he did not confine himself to this. He told Mitchell to advise Frederick to adjust his terms of peace 'to the means, that may be in his power, of enforcing his demands by the sword'.[10] Nothing could have offended Frederick more. Finally (this was also conveyed to the Prussian ministers in London), the king of Prussia should be told to report his military resources and plans; in other words, the paymaster was asking to know in advance how the money that he had not yet committed would be spent. Bute seemed to think that a satisfactory reply could come soon, seemingly mindless of the fact that a return dispatch from Breslau where Frederick was in winter quarters would take at least a month.

Two days before writing this letter Bute had startled the cabinet by calling the German war into question. At the close of a meeting called to discuss military operations against Spain he threw out 'the Great Question, *for consideration only*, of withdrawing all our troops from Germany and giving up the German War'. Newcastle vehemently opposed the idea and so did Devonshire, who gave a passionate summary of the argument against withdrawal:

I spoke my opinion strongly against the measure; that it was making the King act a most dishonourable part in abandoning his allies and leaving them to the mercy of their enemies, when they had suffered so much on our accounts in a cause entirely foreign to them; that no power would ever again trust this country; that for the sake of bringing home 20,000 men, we should dissolve an army that had obliged France to employ in Germany a force that she called 150,000 men, and that in my opinion the consequence would be that France, absolute masters of the Continent, would dictate to the Dutch and every other power in the same manner as she and Spain are treating Portugal.

By the king's allies he meant Hanoverians, Hessians and Brunswickers. Grenville supported Bute, but the other cabinet members except for Newcastle sat silent.[11]

---

[10] Bute to Mitchell, 8 Jan. 1762, Schweizer, *Frederick the Great*, p. 190.

[11] Middleton, *Bells*, pp. 205–6; *Devonshire Diary*, 6 Jan. 1762, p. 154.

For the moment Bute did not pursue it, and Newcastle looked for ways to diminish the drain caused by costly supply arrangements in Germany, but a few days later the Duke of Bedford took up the question, announcing that he would introduce a motion in the House of Lords to recall the British troops. Bedford was stubbornly confident in his opinions – that they were often proved incorrect seemed not to discourage him – and no one could persuade him to drop the idea. When Bute complained to Devonshire about this, the latter's blunt reply was that the idea 'had taken its rise from him' and he could stop it. At bottom, the only reason for withdrawal was to save money. The coming campaign in Germany was estimated to cost £4 million, six times as much as the Prussian subsidy.

There were good reasons in addition to loyalty, good faith and national honour for continuing to support His Britannic Majesty's Army in Germany. One of these was brought forward from The Hague by Sir Joseph Yorke: The 'People of this Country [the Dutch Republic] look upon the King's Army as their Bulwark' against French demands; its removal would 'change the Nature of the War'.[12] Another reason was that the continental situation had been strikingly altered by the death of the Empress Elizabeth of Russia on 5 January. Her successor, Peter III, was a known admirer of Frederick II.

Bedford stubbornly refused to admit that these things changed the picture, and on 5 February he introduced his motion. His speech repeated Mauduit's arguments, to which he added a tale of woe about national finances. Bute spoke after him. Although Bute wished to avoid debating the substance of the issue, he made, nevertheless, a few comments about it. He noted that Parliament had hitherto steadily supported the German war and said he was aware of the 'universal contempt and indignation, which we must incur by at once deserting a cause which we have so strenuously supported'. Britain should avoid 'giving cause to our enemies to exult'. He also observed that recent developments (the change in Russia) suggested the value of a 'steady adherence to our German allies' for gaining a speedy and permanent peace.[13] These were strong arguments. Newcastle was nevertheless upset by Bute's avoidance of a vote on the merits (the motion was dismissed by a procedural ploy). Bute pretended afterwards that such a vote would have been lost.

Notwithstanding his February speech, in mid-April Bute spoke to his colleagues about withdrawing the troops. He cited Bedford's assertion

[12] Yorke to Newcastle, 2 Feb. 1762, BL Add. 32,934, fo. 146.
[13] Schweizer, 'The Bedford Motion and House of Lords Debate', 114–15.

that trying to pay for both Portugal's defence and the German war would bring national 'bankruptcy'. In reality, the money supporting the German troops was already committed, and an immediate withdrawal of the British troops would not save £4 million, only £2 million at most (according to Newcastle's calculations) because much of their cost in Germany was already incurred and if brought to England they would have to be paid anyway.[14]

It was necessary to ask the House of Commons for a Vote of Credit for defending Portugal. Grenville proposed a figure of £1 million. Newcastle believed that a vote of £2 million was needed. He was convinced that Grenville, with Bute's support, was asking for too little with the intention of closing out the German war. Hardwicke pointed out to Newcastle that the Treasury estimate on which he was relying yielded a total not far apart from Grenville's figure and cautioned him not to make an issue of it; instead the duke should look closely to see if it was 'possible to confine the Vote of Credit to one million'.[15] But Newcastle was not thinking tactically. He considered himself to be upholding the German war while also asserting his authority as First Lord of the Treasury against what he supposed to be unwarranted meddling by Grenville.

On 12 May, when the Vote of Credit was scheduled for debate, Pitt was in attendance. In support of it he posed the question, 'Should we sit with folded arms, while the two branches of Bourbon [*sic*] . . . would exclude us from neutral ports?' It was obviously necessary to 'set Portugal on its legs'; in any case, old treaty ties still bound Britain to Portugal. He brought up the German war, remarking that he was elated 'to find Lord Granby was going to it' at last. He ended by urging support of both spheres: 'Give the million to the war at large, and add three, four or five hundred thousand pounds more to Portugal – or avow to the house of Bourbon that you are not able to treat at the head of your allies.' Horace Walpole judged it a powerful speech: 'so artful, elevated, so much in character, and so distressful' to the ministers who were 'endeavouring to steal disgrace upon themselves and their country in the face of the world'.[16] It did not alter the Vote of Credit but may have played a role in preventing the troops from being recalled.

Newcastle decided that he must resign. Bute and Grenville were going behind his back to obtain figures from his departmental secretary, and he

[14] BL Add. 32,934, fo. 414.
[15] Hardwicke to Newcastle, 18 April 1762, BL Add. 32,937, fo. 204.
[16] Walpole, *Memoirs of King George III*, I, 105–7.

was afraid that they would succeed in terminating the German war. He was determined not to acquiesce. George III accepted the resignation courteously but without hesitation, and the duke felt deeply wounded. On 26 May 1762 his 45-year career at the highest levels of government came to an end.

In his speech of 12 May Pitt had noted that the king of Prussia had been 'ill treated' and asked, 'would we throw such a power out of our alliance, only to save 3 or £400,000?'[17] He did not know that the decision not to pay the Prussian subsidy had just been taken. It was Bute's final step in a policy that had some justification but was executed with a blinding antipathy – which George III fully shared – and it planted in the mind of Frederick the Great a deep and durable resentment. For a time Newcastle had also shared this attitude towards Frederick, and would accede to Bute's policy to a greater degree than he would later admit.

In mid-January Bute had ventured an overture to Vienna. Forwarded through The Hague, it was based on an assumption that the empress-queen was greatly troubled by the Bourbon *pacte de famille*, both as a power threat in general and as a challenge in Italy (where Spain and the Habsburg empire had long engaged in territorial disputes). When Newcastle learned of Bute's interest in making such an overture he seized upon the idea with gusto. Sir Joseph Yorke was to act as a key intermediary. To him Newcastle privately communicated his expansive enthusiasm for the project; the duke envisioned no less than a Mediterranean war wherein the British navy might assist the Austrians militarily in Italy, as had been done in the 1740s – this from a man who had objected strenuously to going to war with Spain. He included a suggestion that in order to win over the Austrians Britain might 'come to some regulation with regard to Silesia as should be satisfactory to them'.[18] He was obviously swayed by his affection for the 'old system'; he had always preferred Austria to Prussia. Bute was more circumspect: he limited his official instruction to Yorke to discovering whether Vienna might be interested. But Sir Joseph unwisely mentioned the products of Newcastle's imagination to the Dutch stadtholder, Prince Louis of Brunswick, who in turn spoke to the Austrian ambassador at The Hague, who wrote to Vienna. After many weeks the rebuff came. Kaunitz regarded the overture as a ploy to disrupt Austria's alliance with France. Although Bute claimed that the initiative was not diplomatically objectionable, he had not informed the king of Prussia.

[17] Ibid. I, 106.
[18] Quoted by Dorn, 'Frederick the Great and Lord Bute', 536.

Frederick learned about it in mid-March and exploded in anger, not least because of what was hinted about Silesia. His information had come from more than one source. The greatest blunder in all this was Newcastle's, but everyone involved should have realized that a secret overture of such great potential importance channelled through The Hague was bound to leak out. The British ministers had behaved carelessly, but Bute made no apology: he merely offered Frederick a technical justification.

As Newcastle would later observe, he was already inclined to treat the king of Prussia 'rather as an Enemy, than an Ally'.[19] There were personal reasons, but just as powerful was Bute's belief, which George III shared, that Frederick II was the arch-enemy of peace. When word came to London that Peter III had ordered the Russian army to withdraw from the war, George III's first thought was that it would cause Frederick to 'breathe still stronger revenge against ... Vienna'. He added: *therefore 'tis our business* to force him to peace'.[20] Like most of his ideas this came from Bute, who attempted to translate it into policy.

One approach was to hold back the subsidy. When Bute had asked Frederick to report his military resources and plans there could be no mistaking his purpose; he wanted to know whether Prussia intended to make war or peace. This was conveyed in Bute's letter of 8 January. When it reached Frederick he knew about the amazing upheaval at St Petersburg. The news naturally lifted his spirits and led him to take a misstep. He addressed a letter to George III which glowed with exultation over the chance each country now had to end the war by establishing supremacy in its sphere. (He saw the Spanish war as a great opportunity for Britain in the maritime sphere.) When this letter reached London on 21 February the king, bent on peace, viewed it with abhorrence. Its effect was all the more disastrous because everyone incorrectly assumed that this was Prussia's answer to the request for information about plans. At this time Bute was also reading some intercepted and deciphered letters written by the Prussian ministers in London that contained insulting remarks about himself and his colleagues. Much offended, Bute demanded that the subsidy should be withheld until the king of Prussia gave satisfactory answers about his plans. Frederick had realized that any response other than one which pointed towards peacemaking would be thought unsatisfactory. He considered the demand arrogant and improper.

[19] Newcastle to Hardwicke, 25 April 1762, BL Add. 32,937, fo. 349.
[20] George III to Bute, 5 Feb. 1762, Schweizer, *Frederick the Great*, p. 228.

Newcastle approved of Bute's proceedings, and in the closing days of February Hardwicke worked his pen feverishly to convince the duke that he was wrong. No one at court, Hardwicke noted, seemed to consider the king of Prussia's situation. How could he be expected to adopt a military or diplomatic plan until he could be more certain of Russian policy? Could he make plans without knowing whether he would actually receive the British subsidy? Did the British ministers think that he would make sacrifices for peace with Austria now that Russia had apparently ceased to be a threat? There were other considerations: Would not Britain's failure to grant the subsidy raise Austrian hopes and thus prolong the war? How would the new tsar react to this show of British indifference to its Prussian ally? He reminded Newcastle that Russian friendship had always been valuable to Britain. Above all, Hardwicke did not think the subsidy could 'be refused consistently with the King's honour', the reason being that the king of Prussia had accepted, without conditions, the proposed method of paying it. In short, he had agreed to a deal. Newcastle conveyed the old lawyer's arguments to Bute, who called on Hardwicke, and after a long conversation 'seemed to be convinced that the subsidy must finally be given', to which Hardwicke answered, 'the sooner the better'.[21]

As for Russia, Frederick had reason to suspect that Bute was trying to employ the tsar in an endeavour to force him into making peace. On 6 February, Bute had scheduled an interview with Galitzin, the Russian ambassador, who had been ordered home and was about to depart. Exactly what Bute told him became a matter of prolonged historical dispute, but it is now established that Galitzin introduced his own ideas alongside Bute's when he reported the interview to St Petersburg. Thereafter an abridged version was generated which combined both sets of ideas as if Bute had uttered them. In this version Bute was represented as suggesting that the Russian army should continue to occupy East Prussia. This was something that Galitzin wanted, for he hoped that the new tsar would retain Russia's conquests from Prussia, but there is a strong case that Bute did not actually say it. The document that Frederick saw in mid-March made it appear that he did.

Bute had taken a diplomatic risk in talking with Galitzin, whom everyone knew to be pro-French and anti-Prussian, and the outcome was similar to that produced by the overture to Vienna. Frederick sensed betrayal – that Britain was ready to abandon him. Naturally, under the new circumstances generated by the change at St Petersburg the idea of approaching

[21] Hardwicke to Newcastle, 23 and 25 Feb. 1762, Yorke, *Hardwicke*, III, 343–6.

Vienna was more disagreeable to him than ever, and if he was about to lose his only ally, the necessary move was to solidify relations with Russia. Peter III, whose native land was Holstein, had grievances against Denmark. Frederick did not really want to participate in a war against Denmark, but he could not afford to displease the tsar.

Bute was sure that Prussia was cooperating with Russia in plotting war against Denmark, and thereby found another reason for denying the subsidy. Aware of this and of Bute's hostile attitude towards Prussia, Hardwicke, who ordinarily preferred to avoid direct participation in high politics, scheduled a meeting with the minister on 13 April. During the conversation it became clear that Bute had given up hope of influencing Frederick and was emphasizing the importance of saving money (the issue on which Newcastle would choose to resign). In a second meeting Hardwicke advised Bute that money problems, possibly exaggerated, together with the 'behaviour of the King of Prussia and his ministers towards the King and his ministers' were weak grounds for so critical a step as breaking the promise to pay the subsidy; that the question should be 'determined upon higher and larger principles, and that the eyes of the whole nation and of all Europe were on the English ministry'.[22] Hardwicke's efforts failed. Bute was determined and had cabinet support. On 30 April five cabinet members voted against asking Parliament to grant the subsidy money. Only Newcastle, Hardwicke and Devonshire dissented.

By this time the only motive aside from personal pique for cancelling the subsidy was to save money. In short, financial distress of Europe's richest Treasury was given as an excuse for breaking the British government's word. To be sure, Frederick's record of diplomatic breaches of faith was notorious, but Britain was supposedly above such conduct. Frederick made sure the facts became known, and the notoriety of this transaction echoed down through the centuries. More immediately, the potentially valuable good will of both Prussia and Russia was sacrificed.

On the issue of whether to recall the British troops Bute continued to waver. In early June the Duke of Bedford believed it would be done, but no order was given. Earlier, Lord Hardwicke had feared that if it should happen that the king of Prussia was 'no longer to be supported by England . . . [the] Army in Germany would immediately be dissolved'.[23] He was wrong; Frederick understood that the army in Westphalia and Hanover

[22] Hardwicke to Newcastle, 14 and 18 April 1762, Yorke, *Hardwicke*, III, 348–51.
[23] Hardwicke to Newcastle, 27 Feb. 1762, BL Add. 32,935, fo. 98.

was useful to Prussia for defending her western flank and perhaps for securing her Rhineland territories at the end of hostilities.

The question of troop withdrawal was in some degree settled by the troops themselves. The French armies in Germany were late in getting organized because after the duc de Broglie's dismissal it took time to persuade the experienced marshal d'Estrées to accept a joint command with Soubise. Eventually the main army assembled ten miles north of Kassel. Ferdinand ranged his troops along the Diemel river east of Warburg and was careful to prevent French patrols from detecting his presence. After marching under a full moon and crossing the river at first light on 24 June, Ferdinand's army took the French by surprise. The French right under d'Estrées was able to organize a counter-attack and then pull back. The French left, comprising elite troops, was strongly positioned to resist a frontal attack, but was surprised from the rear by Granby's corps which, according to plan, had circled round. It partially extricated itself in fierce combat but lost 1,500 killed or wounded, and had more than 2,000 taken prisoner. In this action, called the battle of Wilhelmsthal, the allied forces lost a total of 700 men of which 530 were Granby's, and the French army lost 3,600, of which 2,700 were prisoners. The news reached London on 30 June. Hardwicke observed to his son, 'Such a victory happening so early in the campaign . . . must have a great effect in France.' It certainly ruined French offensive plans in Germany and led eventually to Kassel's coming under siege. To Newcastle Hardwicke remarked: 'What will your friend the Duke of Bedford say to this? I suppose, *all for the worse*.'[24]

Ferdinand had acted on his own. During the winter and spring London had provided no guidance. Ferdinand's letters apparently annoyed Bute, who criticized his attitude.[25] Granby's orders to join were issued so late that he arrived less than three weeks before the battle. It is astonishing to discover that after the victory at Wilhelmsthal Bute wrote a confidential letter to Choiseul deploring it and urging that the French army should make a strong stand against Ferdinand's forces lest his personal position in the ministry be destroyed by what he called 'the Prussian party' linked with Pitt.[26] Evidently, for Bute the victory was indeed '*all for the worse*'.

---

[24] Hardwicke to Royston, 1 July 1762, to Newcastle, 1 July, Yorke, *Hardwicke*, III, 398–9.

[25] Yorke to Hardwicke, 16 July 1762, ibid. III, 400. It will be remembered that Bute was a close friend of Sackville's.

[26] Ibid. III, 369; Schaefer, *Geschichte* (cited in Chapter 14), II, pt. 2, p. 552.

Martinique conquered

La Galissonière had warned in 1750 that if the British in North America were no longer threatened by Canadians and Indians, they could 'make formidable *armements*' on that continent, and from there it would 'take them so little time to carry large forces either to St. Domingue or to the Island of Cuba, or to our Windward islands' that defence would be very difficult and expensive.[27] In 1761, with Canada conquered, British troops from North America attacked the most important of the French Windward Islands, Martinique. Pitt approved Amherst's suggestion that Monckton, now 35, should be military commander of the expedition. Although Monckton had performed flawlessly in the field, the Duke of Cumberland considered the choice inappropriate. But the duke no longer made such choices.

Pitt wanted 2,000 men to depart early to attack Dominica, and directed Amherst to assemble at least 6,000 more for Martinique. In June he ordered empty transports at Belle-Île to cross to New York. By early October Amherst was personally at the camp on Staten Island where the men would embark, but the transports did not arrive until the 20th, having been severely mauled by an Atlantic storm. It took three weeks to make them fit for sea, so the convoy, escorted by three ships of the line and a frigate, did not sail until 19 November. The Admiralty had initially suggested Guadeloupe as the rendezvous. Learning of this, Sir James Douglas, the British commodore in the eastern Caribbean, became alarmed. On his own responsibility he wrote to Amherst and Monckton, warning them that if the convey went to Guadeloupe it would be leeward of Martinique. He suggested Barbados. The 64 transports carrying Monckton and 7,400 British regulars, plus artillery and engineers, arrived at Barbados on 24 December 1761.

This North American element, the largest, was the last to arrive. Douglas's squadron arrived first. Next came the ships from England under Rear-Admiral Rodney. Anson appointed him naval commander of the expedition. Rodney was under Newcastle's patronage and had just won a parliamentary seat in a costly borough election, but before this he had spent a total of twelve months cruising off Le Havre performing the kind of tedious and unrewarding service that Anson so greatly appreciated. After leaving Spithead on 14 October with four ships of the line, two bomb vessels and transports carrying 2,000 troops, he picked up two more of

---

[27] See above Chapter 1. In French terminology *armements* included mobilizing troops. The French Windward Islands are in the Lesser Antilles.

the line at Plymouth and headed for open sea. A hard gale soon scattered the ships. Rodney in the *Marlborough* (an old 90-gun ship rebuilt for 68 guns) reached Carlisle Bay on 22 November; the others all straggled in by 9 December. On the 14th came the *Téméraire* (taken from the French in August 1759) escorting a convoy with 2,000 troops from Belle-Île. Transports carrying 1,200 men from Guadeloupe, Antigua and Dominica spent a month working upwind to Barbados. With the arrival of the convoy from North America on the 24th there were in Carlisle Bay over 13,000 troops, thirteen ships of the line, a dozen frigates and sloops of war, and numerous smaller vessels. About 1,000 blacks, some of them slaves, some freedmen, were added to the force. Total naval manpower including marines amounted to about 11,000 men. Thus, from all over the Atlantic a huge force of 25,000 men was assembled in good time. In the age of sail it was an impressive achievement, made possible not only by naval dominance in the Atlantic, a secure North America, and developed administrative expertise, but also by timely and effective planning under Pitt's direction.

So vast an enterprise could not be kept secret, and in fact the French had long expected a second effort against Martinique. Versailles had sent out a new governor to replace Beauharnais. Captain LeVassor de la Touche was a navy man with practically no experience in land warfare. He had been born and brought up in the island, and Versailles supposed that he could motivate the inhabitants to mount a strong defence. Only about 750 regulars came from France to the island in 1760 and 1761, so a great deal would depend on the armed militia and local privateersmen. The citadel overlooking the town and harbour of Fort Royal, it may be remembered, was almost impossible to approach by water. On land, dense foliage enabled marksmen to stay hidden, and hilly, broken terrain made it very hard for an assault force to draw heavy guns to within range of the citadel – conditions which had defeated the British attempt in 1759.

La Touche arrived in a merchant ship from Bordeaux in January 1761. His defensive plan naturally relied on the terrain but also counted upon reinforcement from France, for, unlike Quebec, Martinique had been given assurance of strong support. A letter to La Touche from Versailles dated 28 September 1761 promised artillery, ordnance stores and three battalions (more than 2,000 regulars), all of which were to be conveyed by a squadron then fitting out at Brest. It would also bring an experienced general.[28] A second squadron, nine ships of the line and two frigates,

---

[28] Banbuck, *Histoire*, p. 132.

would bring three more battalions and was scheduled to leave Rochefort in December. (The second squadron never sailed because British warships in Basque Roads blocked it.) The comte de Blénac commanded the squadron at Brest – seven of the line and four frigates. It waited for essential supplies during the late autumn and after that for a favouring wind. A violent storm during the night of 11–12 January drove the watching British squadron to the English coast for refuge but also damaged one of Blénac's ships. He did not sail until 24 January.

On 6 January the British armada of 175 sail left Barbados and reached Martinique the next day. Rodney's first move was to spread small squadrons all round the island to alarm the inhabitants. British privateersmen went ashore under naval protection and raided some plantations near the coast. Consequently La Touche was pressured into keeping some of his defensive force distributed. The first landing of troops occurred on the 8th near the south end of the island. After the small batteries were silenced – a 64-gun ship fatally struck a reef in the process – 1,200 men got ashore at Sainte-Anne without difficulty, but finding no prospect of penetrating to Fort Royal Bay they soon re-embarked, and the fleet moved 12 miles up the western coast to Petit Anse d'Arlet. Here and at nearby Grand Anse 2,000 troops went ashore and climbed a high hill overlooking Pigeon Island (Île de Ramiers) where heavy batteries guarded the bay's entrance on the south side. An effective French counter-attack involving volunteers and slaves rewarded with money caused numerous casualties, and again the British troops re-embarked. The main reason for withdrawal, however, was not military opposition but the very steep terrain which prevented heavy artillery from being positioned to bear on Pigeon Island. Although the commanders' dispatches do not explain why they chose to begin in the southern sector, the likely reason was an awareness that the more direct approach from the Case Navire shore had led to frustration and failure three years before.

Besides, the shoreline there bristled with batteries, and Monckton's engineers doubted that naval gunfire could neutralize them. Rodney was confident, however, that his guns could accomplish the task. Monckton accepted his opinion, and early on 16 January ten ships of the line were arrayed about a quarter of a mile offshore. By early afternoon the batteries were silenced. In late afternoon and throughout the night boats ferried men and supplies ashore. By morning a force of 14,000 including two battalions of marines had been landed. There were practically no losses, and the early arrivals soon penetrated inland. A few French regulars with militiamen were on the scene and eager to harass the British troops as they

landed, but La Touche denied permission. He stuck to his plan of awaiting reinforcements from France.

The British not only landed unopposed but were given plenty of time
to prepare a well-planned assault on the initial objective, Morne
Tartenson, the heavily defended hill that caused the 1759 expedition to
turn back. To threaten the objective from the rear troops moved 3 miles
northwards to the base of the mountains. Monckton and his engineers
spent seven days preparing a four-pronged assault by the main body. One
brigade would push along the road by the sea on the right; another would
approach from elevated ground on the left. Between them two direct
thrusts would be made past a village, across a ravine and then straight up
the hill. Since these men would be mowed down by fire from the hillside
unless its trenches and breastworks were brought under heavy bombardment, four of the days were spent erecting two batteries. On 23 January
these were ready, and after daybreak on the 24th they kept up an
incessant fire while the four elements advanced. Luckily for the British,
the defenders in one sector had left their posts before their reliefs
arrived. When Captain Adam Williamson, leading an assault in that
sector, saw that enemy fire was concentrating on the other attacking
column he hurried his troops up the hill and found a deserted breastwork.
From there his men moved quickly from one entrenchment to another.
Thus the enemy's centre was overrun. On the flanks the attacks were
slowed by French musketry and artillery, but Monckton reinforced and
pressed the men forward. By nightfall Morne Tartenson was in British
hands.

But the hill was under heavy fire from batteries on Morne Garnier,
lying three-quarters of a mile to the east, and Monckton's field artillery
lacked sufficient range and power to neutralize them. Morne Garnier
would therefore have to be overcome. It lay across a deep ravine and was
being reinforced by troops drawn from the citadel's garrison. On the 27th,
however, La Touche made a serious tactical error – for which he had no
excuse because it ran contrary to his principle of awaiting reinforcement
from France. Under his encouragement over four hundred privateersmen
and regulars advanced towards one of the British batteries. They did not
realize how many British troops were hidden in a nearby woods, and
when they enthusiastically charged forward were caught in an ambush.
Half of them were killed or made prisoner and the rest fled to Morne
Garnier, but under hot pursuit they failed to regroup in order to hold the
hill. The next morning the British were amazed to see the 'works and
cannon which', as Captain Williamson commented, 'they precipitately and

most shamefully abandoned'.[29] Everyone agreed that this ill-considered French attack on the 27th saved the British from incurring heavy casualties in a direct infantry thrust at Morne Garnier.

Yet it is possible that Monckton would not have mounted such an assault. He had the option of reducing Morne Garnier's defences by bombardment, for he could count on seamen of the fleet to prepare heavy batteries. As Rodney later reported, the seamen 'made no difficulties in transporting numbers of the heaviest mortars and ship's cannon, up the steepest mountains at a very considerable distance from the sea, and across the enemy's line of fire'. An infantry officer who was an eyewitness wrote to a friend:

You may fancy you know the spirit of these fellows; but to see them in action exceeds any idea that can be formed of them. A hundred or two of them, with ropes and pullies, will do more than all your dray-horses in London. Let but their tackle hold, and they will draw you a cannon or mortar on its proper carriage up to any height, though the weight be never so great . . . We had a thousand of these brave fellows sent to our assistance by the admiral; and the service they did us, both on shore and on the water, is incredible.[30]

Naval guns – 24- and 32- pounders – plus heavy mortars positioned on Morne Tartenson would probably have made Morne Garnier untenable. Six hundred blacks from Barbados plus some from other British islands helped bring up ammunition, provisions and water. On the 30th the new batteries began firing upon the citadel. La Touche pulled all but 400 men from its garrison and retreated to the mountains. On 4 February, as the British were building closer batteries capable of breaching the citadel's wall, Fort Royal surrendered.

The militiamen went home to protect their property. Deputies from outlying districts came to make submission to Monckton. Troops landed at La Trinité on the east coast and subdued it. La Touche tried to persuade the merchants of St Pierre to hold out until the relief squadron arrived, but they doubted not only its arrival but whether it could deliver troops and supplies in the presence of the strong British naval force. Their warehouses were near the waterside, and Rodney sent a warning that his ships were prepared to bombard them. Urged to surrender by the inhabitants,

---

[29] Captain Williamson's letter to Newcastle, 5 Feb. 1762, BL Add. 32,934, fo. 186.
[30] Rodney to Admiralty, 10 Feb. 1762, Syrett, ed. *Rodney Papers*, I, 440. The infantry officer's letter of same date is quoted in Godfrey Basil Mundy, *The Life and Correspondence of the later Admiral Lord Rodney* 2 vols (London, 1830), I, 74.

La Touche signed a capitulation of the whole island on 15 February. As it happened, the relief squadron did not appear for three more weeks. Quickly learning that the island was in British hands, Blénac followed his orders to sail to Saint-Domingue. By the terms of capitulation French regulars were shipped home in British transports while members of the organized militia and privateersmen were made prisoners of war. For the inhabitants the terms were moderate, and Monckton proved to be as careful in administering pacification as he had been in conducting military operations. When he departed in June to take up the governorship of New York the merchants of St Pierre expressed their gratitude by presenting 'an elegant service of Plate'.[31]

All French and Neutral Islands in the eastern Caribbean readily submitted to British control once they knew that Martinique had capitulated. When Captain Augustus Hervey went to St Lucia the commandant initially refused to surrender, but did so immediately when Hervey's ship approached the fort with guns run out. Grenada surrendered on 5 March to a squadron commanded by Commodore Swanton, and St Vincent on the 12th. La Touche had certainly made mistakes, but given the size and capabilities of the British expedition, and the credible promises he had received from Versailles, he could hardly be blamed for building his defensive plan on support from France. Fundamentally, Martinique was lost because Blénac failed to get clear of Brest in time.

After the conquest Rodney sent a private letter to Newcastle in which he outlined Martinique's great value. The duke forwarded a copy to Hardwicke, whose strong reaction took him by surprise: 'This is really important in the superlative degree', Hardwicke wrote, 'for if Admiral Rodney is right, it gives the King the Key of the West Indies as much as Gibraltar does that of the Mediterranean; and it certainly might give England, in effect, the whole Sugar Trade of the World, except what remains in St. Domingo.' Hardwicke went on to suggest that the question of keeping Canada versus Guadeloupe should be reopened. (He was conversant with the earlier pamphlet controversy about this.) Some of Pitt's enemies, he remarked, said that he preferred keeping Canada only

out of partiality to his Friend Beckford, and out of Condescension to the particular Interests of our Sugar Colonies; but in that I suppose they did him wrong. . . . I allways suspected that one Reason why he contended so much for the Totality of the Fishery, impracticable to be obtained, was that he saw the Country of Canada was not greatly worth keeping.

[31] Gipson, VIII, 196.

. . . The Question now may come between [keeping] Canada, or a great part of Canada, and all the French Sugar Colonies, except St. Domingo.[32]

There were also strategic reasons for keeping all of France's eastern Caribbean islands as well as the Neutral Islands. One was protection of British trade from French privateers, which were a serious wartime menace and almost impossible to chase down before they entered harbour. Saint-Domingue was far to leeward, and neither its privateers nor any that might come from France could long remain in the eastern Caribbean without a base. Moreover, French fleets from Europe counted on Fort Royal as their initial port of call for crew refreshment and water replenishment. It was a very secure port and very difficult to blockade. In a later letter Rodney pointed out how much better the harbour at Fort Royal was to serve as a naval base than English Harbour on Antigua. It was commodious (English Harbour was too confined to clean the largest ships at the careening wharf), essentially impregnable, and better sheltered from hurricanes. He also pointed out that the presence of French power in the region would always discourage planters from developing any Neutral Islands that Britain retained.[33]

It was true that Jamaica planters feared that the produce of new acquisitions would undercut their sales in the British market, but the planters at Barbados, Antigua, Nevis and St Kitts were inclined to favour safety over marketing advantage.[34] If the British had resolved to keep all the French islands in the eastern Caribbean, the contest for dominance of trade in the West Indies would have been transformed. None of this, however, became a subject for discussion in London (nor has it ever gained historical attention), the reason being that the Bute administration was rushing headlong towards peace, and it was common knowledge that the French were ready to give up Canada but not their possessions in the West Indies.

The secret negotiation

Lord Bute hoped that with Pitt out of the way Britain and France could quickly reach a peace agreement. Choiseul's *Mémoire historique sur la négociation* had blamed the British, led by Pitt, for the failure. With Pitt

---

[32] Hardwicke to Newcastle, 2 April 1762, BL Add. 32,936, ff. 310–11. This important letter is printed in Pease, *Boundary Disputes*, pp. 411–14.

[33] Rodney to Lord Lyttelton, 29 June 1762, Phillimore, ed. *Memoirs and Correspondence of . . . Lord Lyttelton* (cited in Chapter 8), II, 632–5.

[34] Ibid. II, 633–4; Pares, *War and Trade*, pp. 191–4, 219–26.

out of office Bute was full of optimism about peace and decided to use the secret channel developed by the Sardinian ambassadors. He asked Viry in mid-November 1761 to write to Solar in Paris saying that it was unfortunate that the peace negotiation had been broken off before Pitt's resignation. His suggestion was that a secret negotiation should begin. Bute did not realize that France was committed by a secret military convention to continue the war with Spain as an ally.

In December the duc de Choiseul acknowledged the message, yet the overture puzzled him. He penned a brief note to Solar on 23 January in which he observed that there could be only three possible reasons for it: desire to alienate France from her allies, dissension in the British cabinet, or discovery that the burden of the war had become too heavy. Otherwise he could not understand it. He added that because of her allies France was not in a position to speak first, and ended by remarking that his policy would not change regardless of whether Martinique was captured.[35] This note was sent to London along with a letter from Solar reporting on a conversation he had had with both the duc and the comte de Choiseul. (The count, who would soon become duc de Praslin, was a cousin; Choiseul arranged to have Louis XV appoint him foreign minister in mid-October because, although he kept Spanish affairs in his own hands, he wished to concentrate on his duties as head of the naval and war ministries.) Solar's letter reaffirmed that France would not be the first to make an offer of terms.

These papers did not reach Viry until 2 March. Bute was shocked and wounded when he saw that Choiseul was treating his earnest initiative with cynical contempt. Declaring the papers 'insolent to the last degree', he told Devonshire that 'while France held such haughty language, it was in vain to think of treating with them'. Newcastle found Choiseul's note 'full of impertinence' but did not wish to see the secret channel closed. Hardwicke commented that although the note was addressed to Solar, Choiseul must have realized that it would be transmitted to London and wondered why the French minister had risked sending it. Was he not worried about the consequences of the tsarina's death? Upon investigation the old lawyer assembled conclusive evidence showing that Versailles had not yet received the news from St Petersburg when Choiseul wrote.

---

[35] The original French version of Choiseul's note of 23 Jan. 1762 is printed in George Thomas, Earl of Albemarle, *Memoirs of the Marquis of Rockingham, and his Contemporaries* 2 vols (London, 1852), I, 97–9.

Bute's desire for peace was strong and he overcame his resentment; he began discussing with Viry the terms that Britain might offer. Newcastle had thought that the British should not be the ones to propose terms, but was soon willing to go ahead regardless.[36] Two meetings – attended by Bute, Egremont, Devonshire, Newcastle, Hardwicke and Grenville – were held in mid-March, and a letter suggesting terms was prepared by Egremont to be conveyed via the secret channel. Before it was sent, however, news of Fort Royal's surrender arrived. Everyone was relieved that the letter had not been sent because, as Bute remarked to his colleagues, 'what would people say if we had made such offers after the success of Martinico'? He supposed the secret negotiation should be dropped, but Devonshire, supported by Newcastle, urged that a letter be sent without offering terms to express a desire for a reasonable peace. Hardwicke and Grenville preferred making no answer at all.[37] Bute also wished to keep the communications alive, and an opportunity was created by releasing the comte d'Estaing, whose second capture – the first occurred during the siege of Madras – had revealed a violation of parole.

Choiseul responded to this gesture warmly. France's international position had suddenly become very worrisome. The startling change in Russia indicated that peace in central Europe might come quickly without France playing a role, an occurrence that would undermine Louis XV's claim to be 'arbiter of Europe'. In addition, France's territorial conquests in Germany were likely to become of no account, and, strategically, Britain would be able to focus entirely on the maritime war and thus make it impossible for France to repair 'the dreadful loss of Martinique'.[38] Seeing that the Austrians were no longer confident of success, Choiseul told his ambassador at Vienna to do everything in his power to prevent them from making peace. Believing that if at all possible an Anglo-French peace should precede an Austro-Prussian one, Choiseul's attitude towards the secret negotiation changed dramatically. But how could he persuade the Spanish that peace was now essential? On 17 April he met with Grimaldi and told him that France was in negotiation with Britain (but did not say when the process had begun). The Spanish ambassador was dismayed. Up to this time Madrid had been urgently prodded by

[36] Hardwicke to Newcastle, 3 March 1762, Newcastle to Bute, 4 March, to Hardwicke, 8 March, BL Add. 32,935, ff. 160–1, 172, 249–50; *Devonshire Diary*, pp. 160–1.

[37] *Devonshire Diary*, pp. 161–2.

[38] Rashed, *Peace of Paris*, p. 136.

Versailles to make war to the full and invade Portugal without delay. The Spanish had almost finished positioning the forces for that invasion, and now they were expected to consider a possible peace.

The French minister ignored this and asked Solar to tell the British that France would accept the final agreements of September 1761 as a basis for further negotiation. This meant that terms were now to be seriously discussed and, as Hardwicke advised, it was time to involve the cabinet. Moreover, it was important that the language of diplomatic exchange should be exact and clear. Viry and Solar had been trying to disguise their letters as a business correspondence, the French ministers being referred to as merchants of Lyons.

A cluster of cabinet meetings took place between 23 and 30 April to discuss the terms that the secretary of state, Egremont, was to convey to Viry. There was not much debate about adding the island of Miquelon to that of St Pierre for French fishermen to use as a base, but a heated controversy arose over whether Britain should require 'some Considerable Equivalent for Martinico'. Choiseul's proposal had implied that France would get Martinique back for nothing. The cabinet decided that the equivalent should be either Guadeloupe or Louisiana. Grenville strongly pressed for retaining Guadeloupe. Newcastle feared that demanding either Guadeloupe or Louisiana would break the negotiation, and was upset to find that Hardwicke disagreed with him on this question. In fact, it seemed that Newcastle was more pacifistic than Bute; the duke complained that Bute talked like Pitt when describing 'the Demands of M. de Choiseul as proper to come from a Conqueror, and not from a Power that had suffered so much since the Breaking off the last Negotiation'. Over-estimating the military capabilities of France and Spain, Newcastle predicted that continuation of the war would carry Britain to destruction.[39] He was relieved when he found that Bute wished to adopt easier terms: Britain should neither keep Guadeloupe nor ask for Louisiana but instead keep all the Neutral Islands and also require that the Mississippi River should mark a western boundary of British territory in North America from the point where the Ohio joined it to the Gulf of Mexico. The cabinet adopted these terms on 30 April and Egremont gave them in writing to Viry the next day.

No reply came from Paris for a month, and when it came it made most of the ministers furious. To an offer that they had considered generous

---

[39] Newcastle to Devonshire, 23 April, to Hardwicke, 25 April 1762, BL Add. 32,397, ff. 324, 349–50.

Choiseul responded with a memoir reopening matters which everyone considered settled. For instance, he asked that the shores of Cape Breton should be made available to French fishermen; in India every French trading station of significance was to be restored (although both sides had agreed to leave this subject for later negotiation); and Prussian lands near the Rhine were to remain occupied by French or Austrian troops until a general peace was established, a demand that Britain had consistently rejected. In addition, the memoir insisted that both banks of the Mississippi River must belong to France. Choiseul added a gratuitous statement that concessions formally made by France in September were really of no account because they had been made merely to gain sympathy for France in Europe – an astonishing utterance. At first, Bute tried to pretend that the French memoir was reasonable, but the other ministers sharply disagreed, especially Grenville and Egremont, both of whom proposed that, in retaliation, Britain's offer of 1 May should be withdrawn.

Since the duc de Choiseul was anxious for peace at this time, why did he dispatch so exasperating a memoir? The probable answer is that the British government, guided by Bute and Newcastle, was clearly indicating that excessive demands entailed no hazard; he could be confident that after the outrage cooled negotiations would always be resumed. And Choiseul had particular proof of Bute's submissiveness. Fearing that Britain might join Russia and Prussia in a Northern alliance (designed to counter the Bourbon–Austrian connection), he had instructed Viry to preach the importance of British and French solidarity against such an alliance – clear proof that Viry was not just an agent of peace but also an agent of France – and Bute was receptive even to the point of considering a post-war British alliance with France. Choiseul therefore exploited Bute's naivety to the full.

By its proposal to keep all the Neutral Islands the British cabinet clearly intended to hold St Lucia. This was not just another plantation island. It lay precisely south, therefore slightly to windward, of Martinique, and its commodious north-western harbour, capable of sheltering a large naval squadron, opened on to the passage commonly used by French fleets bound for Fort Royal. Choiseul was aware of its strategic importance, once declaring, with typical exaggeration, that Martinique was useless without St Lucia. George Grenville, who had been a member of the Admiralty Board, was adamant that it should be kept. In late June, the cabinet, deeply annoyed by the most recent memoir from France, sided with Grenville and resolved that Britain should hold firm to its 1 May offer in every detail. Meanwhile, Viry was telling the British ministers that France would break off rather than allow Britain this island.

Bute wanted to give it up, but everyone else in the cabinet had objected. He thereupon took a step that no British minister would have dared to take without being able to count absolutely on royal support. Even then it was politically dangerous. He resolved to bypass the cabinet. His method, in which Viry's cooperation was essential, was to inform the French privately that Britain would give up St Lucia on condition that they would not obstruct a peace agreement on any other grounds. Bute had just taken over from Newcastle as head of the Treasury and had therefore become more powerful than ever, but a valid diplomatic offer could only be transmitted by a secretary of state. When the meeting ended Bute persuaded Egremont to join the scheme and go immediately to the king. George III reported the conversation: He 'desires that I will order him to give Viry a hint that St. Lucia will be yielded if all the articles are agreed to; the reason for this is to prevent Greenvilles [Grenville's] knowing it to be his own thought.'[40]

Naturally the deception thus begun had to be continued. The French were told that their formal responses must be written as if St Lucia had not been granted; otherwise the documents could not be shown to the cabinet. The duc de Choiseul accepted the need for silence about St Lucia, but he did not meet the requirement that France should let nothing else stand in the way of peace. In his memoir dated 25 May Choiseul had accepted the Mississippi River boundary without realizing that New Orleans was on the east bank. Now, in his reply of early July to the British offers just received, he insisted on keeping New Orleans. Egremont insisted that France had ceded it. He considered Britain's willingness to return Martinique very generous; keeping New Orleans was therefore justified. He did not know that Bute had been lured by Viry, under instruction from Versailles, into allowing the boundary to follow a line traced from the Mississippi above New Orleans along the Iberville River and through Lakes Maurepas and Pontchartrain to the Gulf of Mexico. The French pretended that the passage was navigable. Today the Iberville River disappears in a bayou, and the French had never used it as a ship channel. Although ignorant of the detailed geography, Egremont was determined to obtain reliable sea access to the Mississippi, and the issue grew into a serious obstacle to peace, for it soon became evident that Spain would vigorously oppose not just British access to the river but any British presence on the Gulf coast whatsoever.

[40] George III to Bute, 5 p.m. 21 June 1762, Sedgwick, ed. *Letters from George III*, pp. 118–9.

When Choiseul accepted the proposal of the Mississippi River boundary he was conceding something that concerned Spanish imperial interests, and he had kept Madrid completely in the dark about his peace negotiation with London. It was not until the end of April that d'Ossun received a letter mentioning it. Until then, all the letters from Versailles had encouraged Carlos III to think about the spoils of war: for instance, Spain's recovery of Minorca (pledged in the secret military convention) and the advantages to be gained by annexing Portugal. Now Versailles was suddenly talking peace. The Spanish army had hardly fired a shot and still had high hopes of prevailing in Portugal. Spain had gained nothing as yet, while France was on the verge of obtaining comfortable terms despite adverse developments in Russia and her dreadful losses in the Caribbean.[41]

The Bourbon alliance required that the Spanish king must consent to any negotiated peace between France and Britain, and the British were making it clear that their peace with France and Spain must occur simultaneously. Choiseul was thus in a bind. He could not avoid asking Grimaldi to state Spain's terms, and they were predictably aggressive. The old claims concerning fishing off Newfoundland and logwood-cutting were repeated. Among the newer points was an emphatic declaration that the British must be barred from holding territory on the shores of the Gulf of Mexico. This prohibition was not just Grimaldi's idea. Ricardo Wall had insisted on it. The court of Madrid considered the Gulf a Spanish preserve; any foreign vessel that ventured within it could be arrested on the ground – often true – that it was illicitly trading with the Spanish empire. Grimaldi readily perceived that the French were willing to allow the British access to the Gulf, and he was adamant that France should not offer Mobile. Choiseul presumed, correctly, that Britain would summarily reject Spain's demands.

He had no good solution to the problem. He forwarded Grimaldi's memoir to London without comment, or rather with the nonchalant advice that Britain should accept Spain's terms but depend upon the honour of the king of France to ensure that those terms would not actually appear in the peace preliminaries. He hoped the British would ignore Spain's demands for the time being and proceed immediately to naming an ambassador plenipotentiary to go to Paris, just as a French plenipotentiary would go to London, to negotiate the final details of the preliminaries. But he realized that London would probably not follow

[41] As the comte de Choiseul remarked in May; Rashed, *Peace of Paris*, p. 144.

this advice, and two days after dispatching the papers to London he wrote, on 20 July, a long, anxious letter to d'Ossun. It pointed out the dangers France would face if the war were to continue another year. All that was left to her in America was Saint-Domingue, and if the British were to capture Havana, it would be impossible to defend it. Nothing was left in Africa, and in Asia only the Mascarene Islands remained, which would certainly be taken within a year. If the troops in Germany could not hold Kassel, they must winter in France, and then 'the war will be fought on our frontiers and in our provinces'.[42]

The French dispatches, including Grimaldi's memoir, reached London on 24 July, and the council met on the 26th. When Bute opened the meeting by saying that peace was assured, the other ministers erupted in disagreement. They were most offended by the Spanish memoir. Rebuffing Bute's optimism, Granville, Lord President of the Council, pointed out 'that nothing was done with Spain and till those disputes were accommod-ated, there could be no peace with France; for if you gave them up their seamen (prisoners), they might immediately join the Spaniards; that his Lordship might be duped by France but by God he would not'.[43] Everyone opposed Bute on the issue of giving France St Lucia and New Orleans. Feelings ran high. In despair he wrote to Egremont asking for his support. Two more meetings were held, and in the intervals Bute, Viry and the king succeeded in pressuring everyone into submission. George Grenville was told that yielding St Lucia – he did not know about the secret agreement – was the vital step that would encourage Choiseul to force Spain to drop her impossible demands and make peace. The dissenting voices were muffled: in the council meeting of 31 July it was agreed that France could have St Lucia and New Orleans. The island of Miquelon was added to St Pierre for drying codfish. In Europe, Prussia's Rhineland territories were to be evacuated upon ratification. Other terms were based on the agreements of September 1761. Egremont, expressing strong suspicions about the Iberville River route, insisted on stipulating that British ships should be allowed the same access to the Mississippi River used by the French. As for the Spanish, the French were expected to persuade them to join in a simultaneous peace and were asked, if unsuccessful, to pledge that they would give no assistance to Spain in a continuing war with Britain. The Duke of Bedford had accepted Bute's invitation to go to Paris

---

[42] Choiseul to d'Ossun, 22 July 1762, Blart, *Rapports*, p. 31; also Rashed, *Peace of Paris*, pp. 160–1.

[43] *Devonshire Diary*, p. 175.

as British plenipotentiary. He was given the additional assignment of negotiating a Spanish peace with Grimaldi.

With the king's support Lord Bute had prevailed. He had succeeded in hurrying forward the progress towards peace (though at considerable political risk to himself). He had persuaded the secretary of state, Egremont, to participate in a secret offer of an important concession that the council had not granted, a proceeding which, as Viry warned Solar, would ruin both men if revealed.[44] His underlying concern was to avoid giving the French 'any bad impression'. Granville and Grenville, he said, should not worry about 'the supposed duplicity of Choiseul'. Because the French had transmitted the Spanish memoir without comment Bute realized that Versailles would probably not 'openly abandon her ally' despite earlier promises that Spanish and French peace agreements would go hand in hand.[45] But this did not deter him.

After the departure of Newcastle his unpopularity grew and he could see that his peace terms might encounter dangerous political opposition. He tried to bring Newcastle back into the cabinet and asked Hardwicke to call on him. In the conversation, on 28 July, Bute pretended that he and the king much regretted Newcastle's resignation, which, he said, had occurred for minor reasons. Hardwicke's response was unequivocal: Newcastle had resigned, first, because he found himself opposed on a Treasury matter, and secondly, because he profoundly disagreed about 'support of the German war and the preserving of the connection with the King of Prussia, united as he is with the Emperor of Russia, and England's availing itself of both those persons in war and in peace'.[46] Soon afterwards the king invited Newcastle to an interview and discreetly put an offer of office to him directly. The duke was tempted, but Hardwicke advised him to decline, pointing out that the purpose was to have him share blame for what had the appearance of a mishandled peace negotiation.

Lord Granville was right about the Spanish. Grimaldi firmly adhered to his demands and to the prohibition of British presence on the Gulf coast. The question in London was: were the French truly prepared to force peace on the Spanish? Hardwicke thought not; it was 'the wildest of all imaginations to fancy that France will just now break with Spain'.

[44] Pease, *Boundary Disputes*, p. cxlii.
[45] Bute to Egremont, 26 July 1762 at night, Sedgwick, ed. *Letters of George III*, pp. 127–8.
[46] Hardwicke's memorandum of the conversation, Yorke, *Hardwicke*, III, 402–3.

He remembered that in their conversation Bute had informed him that 'the Duc de Choiseul keeps everything tending to that [i.e. coercing Spain] in dark hints, thrown out in private notes to Solar', and puts none of it in the formal dispatches. Hardwicke had no faith in the French promise not to assist Spain afterwards and had reminded Bute, as Granville had done, that when Britain made peace with the French 'the great number of their seamen prisoners here' would be released.[47] Of course, the French government could easily claim that it was powerless to prevent them from enlisting in the Spanish navy.

The exchange of plenipotentiaries meant that the forwardness of the negotiation could no longer be hidden from the public. In any case Bute wanted people to think that peace was at hand. Common speculation in London held, however, that the Spanish would not give up their campaign to subdue Portugal. As for Havana, opinions differed over whether British arms would succeed. Bute, Bedford and the king hoped to get the peace preliminaries signed before news of a success at Havana arrived. The cabinet had insisted that Bedford must be instructed to inform the French upon his arrival in Paris that if Havana were captured, substantial compensation would be required for its return. Knowing that this might prevent an early settlement from being reached, George III hoped for failure; in mid-August he wrote to Bute: 'I was much hurt on receiving Ld. Halifax's account of the appearance of success at the Havannah.'[48] This attitude was not only disloyal to his own armed forces but also unwise, for the loss of Havana would enable Choiseul to compel the Spanish to accept peace.

The defence of Portugal

For two years Choiseul had been urging the king of Spain to attack Portugal. The Spanish army would obviously outnumber the Portuguese and the invasion could proceed on land. After the Spanish declaration of war against Britain Choiseul accelerated his demand for quick action. His impatient letters implied that the Spanish were hopelessly incompetent. But the 40,000 men that Spain was mobilizing – the largest Spanish army ever to take the field in the eighteenth century – was not easy to assemble on the Portuguese frontier. Almost two-thirds of the troops came from

[47] Hardwicke to Newcastle, 28 July 1762, Yorke, ibid. III, 402–4.
[48] To Bute, Sedgwick, ed. *Letters of George III*, p. 130. Halifax, after Anson's death, became First Lord of the Admiralty.

faraway posts in Catalonia and Valencia. The main source of artillery was Barcelona, so thousands of mules were needed to pull the guns and the wagons with ordnance stores almost 500 miles across northern Spain. The chief marshalling point, Salamanca, was in barren country, and depots well stocked with provisions were mandatory. All in all, the mobilization was a remarkable achievement for a country that had been militarily inactive for decades. In any case, the invasion of Portugal could not have started much before late April because Carlos III needed time to justify it. The queen of Portugal was his sister; Portugal had tried to be inoffensive and stay neutral.

Since 1756 the Portuguese prime minister had been Sebastião de Carvalho, conde de Oeiras. He was the most important man of eighteenth-century Portuguese history, who later would be known, famously, as the marquis de Pombal (the name that will be used here instead of Oeiras). He had served as an envoy in London, studied English writings on commerce, and was convinced that British merchant domination of the trade of Lisbon and the wine trade at Oporto was bad for the country's economy. He would have been happy to see limits put on British merchants, but the kingdom's survival was now at stake and British protection indispensable. Portugal had suffered severely from the earthquake of 1755, and in the ensuing economic crisis its army, never well organized and but poorly trained, had been reduced by half. The Spanish said that their troops assembling at Salamanca would enter the country as friends to help drive British merchants from the ports, but the Bourbons obviously intended to take control, and if that happened, the British would feel free to use their naval supremacy to take over the Brazil trade with its coveted gold and silver. Thus, the kingdom would be run as a conquered country, and the wealth of Brazil would end up in British hands. The only choice, as Pombal realized, was to appeal to the British to help defend the kingdom.

Pombal avoided giving a firm answer to the French and Spanish envoys for as long as he could, protesting (dubiously) that Portugal's alliance treaties with Britain, which dated back a half-century or more, were not offensive, as the Bourbons claimed, but defensive. He concealed the fact that since November 1761, when war between Spain and Britain seemed certain, Portugal had been asking the British government to come to the rescue. His delaying tactics were brought to an end by a third Bourbon ultimatum of 27 April 1762, this one overtly menacing. In rejecting it King Joseph I used strong words; he declared that he would defend his kingdom to the last tile of his palace.

The British response to Portugal's request for military assistance was favourable, but soon a problem arose because Bute, supported by Grenville, wished to treat aid to Portugal as an alternative to the German war. Although a grant of £200,000 was quickly approved, the British ministers, observing the pace of Spanish mobilization, saw no urgent need to send troops until late March. At this time Newcastle was intent on upholding the effort in Germany. Hardwicke warned him that he must not allow German concerns to obstruct assistance for Portugal. The Portuguese trade, he pointed out, yielded supplies of gold and silver that were absolutely vital to Britain. (Peru's silver came to Brazil to avoid British cruisers watching Panama.) Since Spain was now an enemy Portugal was Britain's only source of 'Treasure . . . a very serious Consideration'. How many troops Britain was formally obligated to send was not clear. The treaties spoke of 12,000, but half of those were perhaps meant to be Dutch. (The old lawyer complained that Paul Methuen, when drafting the famous treaty of 1703 that bore his name, had not made this point clear.[49]) As it happened, however, Pombal chose not to base his request on the treaties, probably because he did not want to validate English merchant privileges contained in them. Instead, he spoke of common interests and the 'common cause'.

The Portuguese army was nominally 31,000 strong, but in reality it could muster only 16,500.[50] It had not seen combat in decades, and, as the king and Pombal realized, there was no one competent to be made commander-in-chief. James O'Hara, Baron Tyrawley, a British army professional who had spent many years in Portugal, appeared to be the ideal choice, and he was initially nominated, but his health was poor and his attitude became uncooperative, so it was necessary to replace him. Count Wilhelm von Schaumburg-Lippe, a grandson of George I by a mistress, the Duchess of Kendall, might appear to be a dubious choice, but he proved to be an excellent one. He was an intelligent British army professional serving with Prince Ferdinand's army and was expert in matters of artillery and engineering. He also possessed considerable talent for leadership. British officers as well as Pombal and the Portuguese court learned to think highly of him. After he arrived he managed to thwart the ultra-conservative resistance of Portuguese senior officers (poorly paid and uncooperative) by dividing each regiment into two brigades and

---

[49] Hardwicke to Newcastle, 28 March, 1 April 1762, BL Add. 32,936, ff. 172, 260–2.
[50] Figures reported by the Portuguese ambassador in London; Black, 'British Expeditionary Force', 66.

putting his own nominee in charge of one of them. But Count Lippe did not arrive until 9 July and in the meantime the need to prepare the defences of Lisbon was urgent. Pombal supervised the city's preparation, and Charles O'Hara, a natural son of Lord Tyrawley by a Portuguese mother, was made a colonel in the Portuguese army. Also promoted was Major Charles Rainsford, who knew Spanish and learned Portuguese. They set to work on bolstering a defensive position 80 miles up the Tagus River at Abrantes.

The first British troops, two untrained regiments from Ireland plus Brigadier John Burgoyne's well-trained light cavalry with some grenadiers, arrived on 6 May. On 11 June Lord Loudoun, appointed commander of the British forces, received orders to take artillery, stores and four regiments from Belle-Île. His convoy was held up by contrary winds in the Channel and did not sail until 28 June; it finally reached Lisbon on 26 July. Sir Edward Hawke brushed off worries about an invasion by French troops gathered at Dunkirk – Choiseul never gave up schemes of this sort – and covered the convoy by positioning his ships near Cape Finisterre, ready to pounce on Spain's Ferrol squadron if it emerged. Admiral Saunders at Gibraltar sent cruisers to the Algarve coast to prevent a seaborne attack from Cadiz. One happy result of this for Saunders and the cruiser commanders was the capture of the *Hermione* which, loaded with silver, had come round Cape Horn from Peru. She was only a day's sail from home, but her captain had no idea that Britain and Spain were at war. The net value of the prize at condemnation was over £500,000.

Although Pombal had made a good beginning by preparing forts near Lisbon, when the Spanish crossed the border on 5 May the kingdom as a whole was practically defenceless. The first British troops arrived in Lisbon at almost the same moment, but nothing was ready for supporting them inland. The main Spanish thrust passed through Ciudad Rodrigo. The aim was to neutralize the fortress of Almeida, and then march southwards with Lisbon as the objective. Then Madrid changed the plan. The strongest force would now proceed 39 miles north to Zamora, cross into Portugal and besiege the frontier fortress of Miranda; the idea was to occupy the northern province of Trás-os-Montes and push down the Douro River to Oporto. This strategy had the advantages of putting Spain immediately in possession of some Portuguese territory, threatening British merchants at Oporto (their warehouses full of valuable wine), and avoiding, at least for a time, violence at Lisbon. Its disadvantage was that the Portuguese and British were given more time to prepare a defence of Lisbon.

The fortress of Miranda was arguably the strongest in Portugal and was expected to delay enemy progress significantly. It might have done so but for a tragic accident. The defenders, as the British minister at Lisbon reported, were 'using Ladles for want of Cartridges', and some powder 'which had carelessly dropt out of the Ladles took fire, and the whole Magazine blew up. Several Hundred Men were buried under the Ruins of the Citadel, and two Breeches were made in the Walls.'[51] The place surrendered the next day. This occurred in the last week of May and it seemed that nothing could stop the Spanish advance. British residents at Oporto began to move their families to Lisbon and put out panicked calls for transports to carry away their wines, worth perhaps £500,000. Although the Spanish army paid generously for provisions it obtained locally, the inhabitants nevertheless abandoned their villages, and Colonel O'Hara was able to recruit 2,000 men who, helped by women and children, watched river crossings and entrenched themselves on hilltops and cliff edges. Boats on the Douro were removed or destroyed. Under peasant harassment Spanish provisioning could not keep up with the advancing forces, and in June a body of 1,500 light troops which got as far as Villa Real nearly starved. The Spanish had launched the invasion with no maps of the region and no realization of how mountainous the route to Oporto was. When the commander-in-chief, Nicolás de Carvajal, marquis de Sarria, had asked about the roads in the region, no one could inform him.

Lord Loudoun spent the month of August remonstrating about the inadequacy of provisions and mules which the Portuguese had agreed to provide. He asked for many more mules than anyone at Lisbon expected, and he did not like the ones he saw, not realizing that in Portugal the typical scrawny mules were more efficient for most purposes. There was a language problem. Loudoun's French was second-rate and he switched to writing in English, which he knew Pombal could read, but clerks and other ministers could not and people got very upset. The king became involved. To Edward Hay, the British minister at the court, Pombal suggested that the business should be done in conferences, but when Hay spoke with Loudoun the general talked of 'his Instructions and responsibilities' and need for clear and explicit answers. Fortunately, however, he agreed to a conference with Pombal, and the points in dispute were settled in two hours.[52] It appears that the man who so annoyed American

---

[51]   Edward Hay to Egremont, TNA SP 89/56, 29 May 1762, fo. 113.
[52]   Hay to Egremont, 23 Aug. 1762, TNA SP 89/57, ff. 138-9.

MAP 16 *The invasion of Portugal*

officials had not changed much, but in Portugal he did no serious harm. He recognized that Lippe was an able commander and served him effectively.

In July the Spanish, frustrated in the Douro offensive, planned to occupy the region round Coimbra, where local food supplies would be available and from which the army might threaten either Oporto or Lisbon. Securing the main supply line for ammunition and other stores (through Ciudad Rodrigo) required the capture of the frontier fortress of Almeida. It was strongly situated on a high mound and the garrison numbered 4,000 with British officers present; cannon, ammunition and provisions were ample.

Yet, on 15 August, only ten days after the Spanish opened the trenches, the Portuguese governor surrendered. He had unwisely allowed women and children to come within the walls; the bombardment frightened them and he yielded to their entreaties. At this time the besieging army was amplified by the arrival of 8,000 French regulars commanded by Charles Juste, prince de Beauvau. The troops had left St Jean Pied-de-Port in early June and marched with three rest periods 380 miles in summer heat.[53] At about the same time General Sarria was replaced by Pedro Pablo Abarca de Boles, conde de Aranda, a distinguished soldier who had fought in Flanders in the 1740s.

At the beginning of September new orders came from Madrid. The move to Coimbra was cancelled. Instead, the main army was to head south to the Tagus River and then strike eastwards towards Abrantes. Lippe, evidently having intelligence of French plans, had positioned much of his force to protect Coimbra, but in late September he realized that enemy troops were heading southwards through the Beira province. Their line of advance towards Castelo Branco appeared to include Sabugal and Penamacor. Lippe, who had ordered Loudoun to go north with some British regiments, now suddenly called them back, and on 30 September they began a forced march towards Castelo Branco to guard the pass at Sobreina Formosa, 16 miles east of it. The fight to keep the French away from the upper Tagus had begun.

Lippe while focusing on the defence of Coimbra had not, however, completely forgotten Beira and Alentejo provinces. He had evidently feared a Spanish thrust through the defile where the Tagus knifed through the mountains and had received reports that the Spanish frontier town of Valencia de Alcántara was well stocked with grain and forage. He sent Burgoyne to raid it. In late August with 400 men, some of his grenadiers riding with the dragoons (two to a horse), Burgoyne advanced rapidly over the mountains and surprised the town. No magazines were found, but the garrison was decimated; Spanish confidence was undermined, and Portuguese spirits were lifted. In September Burgoyne employed his small force of British and Portuguese troops to guard the upper Tagus. He could not prevent the Spanish from occupying Vila Velha on the north bank, but thanks to Rainsford's reconnaissance it was realized that the road to Abrantes ran through a gorge that could be commanded by artillery on the south bank.

[53] Pajol, *Guerres*, VI, 132–3.

The campaigning in central Portugal during the months of September and October featured seemingly endless marching and counter-marching. The main cause was the Spanish high command's inability to discover a workable strategic plan. It could not solve the problems posed by harsh terrain, long supply lines, and scarcity of local food and forage. Its campaign in the Beira involved a great deal of road improvement and continual difficulties in bringing up provisions. As Spanish plans changed the British and Portuguese had to respond. They defended escarpments and passes, and concentrated near potential river crossings. In the end Spanish forces were unable to penetrate more than 10 miles west of Castelo Branco, and they never did break through to the more productive agricultural regions of the kingdom. The record does not indicate that the 8,000 French regulars provided significant help. On both sides the troops suffered great hardship: shoes were completely worn out – there was no resupply even for the British – and many men were felled by the hot climate and bad water. A list of British troops in early September showed 862 sick out of 5,212.[54]

Throughout this book it has been observed that rivers were often essential keys to offensive penetration. The east-to-west flowing Douro and Tagus would appear to have suited the Spanish ideally. Yet they were unable to make much use of them. One reason was the 90-mile supply line over very bad roads from the frontier pass near Ciudad Rodrigo to the Tagus at Vila Velha; another was the steepness of the rock-lined banks of Portugal's rivers in the interior and the scarcity of practical crossings. Surmounting these problems required thoughtful planning and special equipment, but these had been notably lacking. Near the end of the campaign, when Aranda saw that in the less broken country south of the Tagus his army might best employ its cavalry and infantry, he obtained Madrid's permission to cross the river, but he was unable to construct the intended road and pontoon bridge.

In early October British merchants in Lisbon were shaken by rumours, 'it being . . . reported that the Spanish army are in full march towards Abantes'. On the 9th the consul wrote to Loudoun, pleading with him to help people 'separate truth from falsehood' and report whether Lisbon was in immediate danger. On the 5th Burgoyne had overrun a Spanish camp near Vila Velha.[55] The danger to Lisbon was imaginary. In mid-October the seasonal rains began. Further Spanish advance was

---

[54] Francis, *Portugal*, p. 154. Burgoyne's men were not included.

[55] Black, 'British Expeditionary Force', 71–2.

unthinkable, and in early November Aranda withdrew the army into Spain where, on 24 November, they learned that the peace preliminaries had been signed.

The capture of Havana

On 6 January, two days after the declaration of war against Spain, Newcastle, Devonshire, Bute, Egremont, Grenville, Anson and Ligonier met and discussed Anson's bold scheme for capturing Havana. (At the same meeting Egremont mentioned a project presented to him by Colonel William Draper for capturing Manila and no objection was made to it. The results of the Manila operation were not known in London until after peace was made; it will be discussed in the concluding chapter.) Because both Anson and Ligonier supported the Havana venture the cabinet readily approved it, though Newcastle later regretted his acquiescence. Lieutenant General George Keppel, 3rd Earl of Albemarle, was appointed commander-in-chief, Admiral Sir George Pocock would command the naval force with Commodore Augustus Keppel to assist him, and Major-General William Keppel was selected to command the army. Since a conquest of Havana was bound to be lucrative the Keppel brothers were greatly favoured. Albemarle, 38 years old, had little experience of any kind as a field commander. He was the Duke of Cumberland's political secretary. A number of generals who had been successfully involved in amphibious operations were ignored, but, as we have seen, Augustus Keppel had a good record in conducting these, and because he was Albemarle's brother he would facilitate cooperation between the navy and the army. Pocock had commanded bravely and successfully in India, and deserved a reward.

The preparations were completed with admirable speed. By 22 February transports were ready to receive the 4,400 men who had been marched to Portsmouth. The victualling and store ships, some carrying special siege equipment, were efficiently readied in London, but their arrival at Spithead was delayed a week by adverse winds. Anson, though not in good health, journeyed to Portsmouth with two Admiralty Board members to make difficult decisions if necessary. All was ready when the wind came fair on 5 March, and after a fine passage the convoy reached Barbados on 20 April. Six days later the ships were at Martinique where they replenished water. Monckton had received orders to prepare all troops for embarkation who were not needed for garrisoning the conquered island. The orders clearly stated that the expedition held priority over completion of the conquest of Martinique, but this had been completed. The troops at Martinique, numbering over 8,000, formed the largest element of the expeditionary army; with the 4,400 from England and 4,000 which were to come from North America – half regulars, half provincials – the total land force would amount to 17,000.

The achievement by the administration was comparable to what had been done under Pitt's direction, except for one point: the ordering of the North American troops was mishandled. Egremont's orders to Amherst to gather the 4,000 men at New York and arrange transports were issued 13 January. Many regulars would have to be marched from Canada or brought from Nova Scotia, and recruiting the provincials could take time, yet all the men, plus warships from Halifax to escort the transports, were to be ready to go by 1 May. Amherst did not receive these orders until 1 April, however – six weeks late because Egremont's original dispatch was lost in transit. The orders should have been conveyed at once by two different fast vessels, and it is reasonable to think that Pitt would have done this. The orders permitted Amherst to employ two convoys. The first sailed on 9 June. Although the troops for the second sailing were at New York by 12 June, there were not enough transports – a problem that Pitt had taken special precautions to avoid – and the troops did not sail until the 30th.

When Pocock and Albemarle reached Martinique they found that Monckton had already embarked the troops, believing correctly that they would be healthier on board ship than in tents ashore. (Over 1,000 were already sick.) Pocock expected to find Rodney's squadron at Martinique, since most of its ships were assigned to his expeditionary force, but it was absent. Rodney had responded to an urgent plea from Jamaica's governor, who believed that Blénac's force at Saint-Domingue would combine with Spanish forces at Havana to assault the island. He had tried to persuade Monckton to send troops to Jamaica, but the general refused to make so significant a move without orders from home. Rodney was undeterred and departed for Jamaica. His hopes of becoming naval commander at Jamaica were soon dashed when on 26 March the frigate *Richmond* reached him off St Kitts. It was carrying an Admiralty order requiring him in no uncertain terms to be at Martinique to supervise the preparation of ten ships of the line and three or four frigates, plus bomb vessels and ships to be loaded with various stores, all of which were to proceed on a secret expedition. Notwithstanding these orders Rodney sent ten ships of the line to Jamaica. Knowing that his presence in person at Martinique was mandatory, he put them under the command of Sir James Douglas.[56]

The absence of those ships troubled Pocock. His orders were to escort the huge expeditionary force to the rendezvous off Cape St Nicolas, the north-western point of Hispaniola, where the transports from New York would join, from whence he would proceed through the dangerous Old Bahama Channel along Cuba's north coast to the objective. The trouble was that Blénac's squadron, thought to be eight ships of the line, lay upon his route at Cap Français, and Pocock had come out from England with only six counting his flagship, the 90-gun *Namur*. The mission was already being delayed at Martinique by Albemarle's decision to rearrange troops on board the transports. Pocock took a risk when he sailed on 6 May in order to avoid further delay, and he was certainly justified in adding Rodney's flagship *Marlborough* to his squadron and relegating the disgruntled rear-admiral who would remain behind to a 64-gun ship.

It was fortunate that Commodore Douglas became the man responsible for making strategic decisions at Jamaica. After obtaining intelligence that Blénac's forces were not prepared to make an attack and that Jamaica was therefore safe, he decided that he should 'keep the squadron to windward . . . the sooner to join Sir George Pocock when he comes'. A report that a convoy was expected 'from North America under a weak escort, to come down on the north side of Hispaniola' convinced Douglas that he must set aside Rodney's order to defend Jamaica; he put most of the squadron under Augustus Hervey off Cap Français to protect Pocock's convoy. He guessed that the rendezvous would be 'at or near the west end of . . . Hispaniola' and stationed a ship there. Finally, after learning from a ship that came from Governor Shirley of the Bahamas bringing local pilots who might be familiar with the Old Bahama Channel, and finding that the pilots confessed to having no knowledge of it, he made an important decision on his own initiative. He ordered the frigate *Richmond* to proceed westwards through that channel all the way to Cay Sal. Her captain, John Elphinston, was 'to take the utmost care in drawing sketches of the land and remarking the bearings and distance of one island from the other', and 'then to return off Cape St. Nicolas, or wherever you hear Sir George Pocock is' to report his findings. All these orders, based on intelligent inferences from fragmentary information, were issued between 8 and 19 April.[57] They perfectly suited Pocock's needs.

---

[56] Syrett, ed. *Rodney Papers*, I, 437, 447–8.

[57] Syrett, ed. *Siege and Capture*, pp. 83, 87, 91–2.

On 23 May Douglas met the great convoy off Cape St Nicolas. He soon returned to Jamaica with trading vessels which had joined it. Pocock, though expected by the Admiralty (with Lord Anson's encouragement) to use Old Bahama Channel, had the option of proceeding via the safe and familiar route: south of Cuba to Cape St Antonio, and then to Havana. One disadvantage of the safe route was that a fleet of 180 ships including large men-of-war, making its way slowly upwind from that cape, would inevitably be identified as enemy. Any chance of surprise would be lost. The other disadvantage was that it would take time. Noting 'the advancement of the season, and the increase of sickness among the soldiers', which could jeopardize success, Augustus Keppel observed that using the more direct Old Bahama Channel would result in fewer losses to sickness. Pocock agreed. The fleet sailed into the channel with small warships and longboats positioned out ahead. Both naval commanders fervently hoped that they would soon meet the *Richmond*. On the 29th they did, and after delivering his sketches and bearings Elphinston was soon ordered to lead the way. An enormous column, ships of the line inserted between groups of transports with frigates on the flanks, moved downwind north of Cuba. Boats marked the course and limits; they showed lights at night, and a bonfire was kept going on Cay Lobos where the passage narrowed. The precaution of anchoring at night was not adopted.

Ten days later on the morning of 6 June the great expeditionary force was off Havana. The lookouts on Morro Castle reported it and Governor Don Juan de Prado came from the city to observe. The ships were identified as British but the governor assumed them to be a trade convoy heading home from Jamaica. He returned to the city, attended mass at the cathedral, and was not disturbed until 12.30 p.m. when he was urgently summoned again. It has been commonly supposed that the authorities at Havana did not even know that war between Britain and Spain had been declared. This was not true: notification reached Havana overland from Santiago on 26 February. Spanish complacency stemmed fundamentally from a belief that no one would attack Havana because it was considered invincible. The appearance of so great an enemy force was therefore truly astonishing, and there had been no warning. It had met with a few Spanish ships east of Matanzas, but British warships had captured or diverted all of them.

With scarcely any opposition or losses the British landed almost 4,000 troops the next morning 2 miles east of the Cojimar River, 5 miles from Morro Castle. A small stone fort at the river mouth prevented their crossing towards the fortress. It was quickly made untenable by naval gunfire and marines sent in by Augustus Hervey secured it. Instead of quickly occupying the unfortified Cabaña ridge which bordered the entrance channel, Albemarle ordered most of the troops 6 miles south to Guanabacoa. After they repulsed an attack by militia cavalry, many of them were left there under General George Eliott to secure the besieging army against an attack from inland. Thus 2,500 men were assigned to defend in strength against an attack that the enemy had neither men nor means to mount. Meanwhile the Spanish authorities, having a hundred richly laden merchant ships in harbour and twelve ships of the line, installed a chain across the channel and sank three of the line to block it. Realizing that they had neglected the Cabaña ridge, they dispatched 1,000 troops and seamen with guns from the warships to defend it, but a British night reconnaissance frightened them off and left the strategically vital position undefended. A force under Colonel Guy Carleton occupied it on the 11th. (After the war the Spanish spent many years and much money constructing an extensive fort on La Cabaña.) As a diversion for Carleton's operation, Pocock's ships, anchored west of the city, began a bombardment and landed marines, who found that landing there was unexpectedly easy, and they seized the fort at Chorrera. Spanish ships opened fire on the British occupiers of La Cabaña, but British howitzers and heavy mortars soon compelled them to withdraw deeper into the harbour.

At this point Albemarle concentrated on preparing siege batteries. His object was to blast a breach in the landward face of El Morro. It was a hopeless undertaking, partly because the stone walls were immensely strong but also because there was a huge ditch at the base, at least 40 feet wide and 40 feet deep, and in places much wider and deeper.[58] From it much of the stone used to build El Morro's walls had been quarried. Its size meant that troops could not exploit a breach made in the walls above, but since no one had been assigned to penetrate the thick, bushy woods far enough to survey the ditch Albemarle did not know how large it was. On 11 June seamen began to land heavy guns and ammunition at a location west of Cojimar. When the surf was moderate landing the 24-pounders was, Keppel reported, 'the least of our difficulty'; it was 'the roads and distance to draw them' on land that made him apprehensive. The roads had to be hacked through thick woods and paved with logs. Although the distance from the shore to the batteries was less than 3 miles and the neat was intense, the sun at noon shown directly overhead.

---

[58] Dimensions are given in Syrett, ed. *Siege and Capture*, p. xxx.

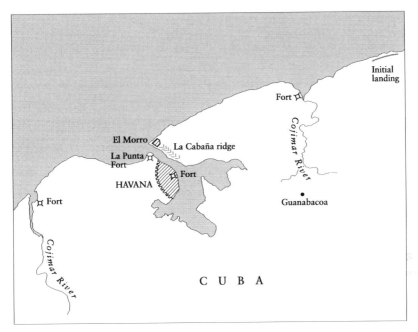

MAP 17 *Havana*

By the 18th Keppel had 1,000 seamen employed in hauling cannon. Until this moment rainwater was available, but now the rains practically ceased. Conditions were good for getting work done, but within two days the men were desperately thirsty and began to suffer from dehydration. Some died from drinking the polluted water of the Cojimar River, of which there was now very little. Albemarle asked Pocock for water from the ships. Shipboard supplies could not last long, but the Chorrera River, which was secured by Pocock's forces on the 15th, afforded fresh water, and for the rest of the campaign seamen were busy filling casks and shuttling them by boat to Cojimar. Without this the siege could not have continued.

Day after day the troops and the ships' working parties laboured to construct batteries and bring up guns and ammunition. Near the end of June two substantial batteries were almost ready, and the generals asked whether warships might close in to attack the fortress to divert attention to seaward at the time when their batteries were scheduled to unmask and commence firing. Augustus Hervey was eager to try, and Keppel and Pocock, though sceptical, let him. Three ships anchored close to El Morro's walls on 1 July. Their guns could not sufficiently elevate and their shot had no effect on the masonry, a fact obscured by smoke. Hervey's *Dragon* lost its anchors and grounded; the *Cambridge* suffered severely, her captain killed and rigging destroyed; the *Marlborough* also suffered. At the end of the day the three ships had 48 killed and 148 wounded. Albemarle thanked Pocock, saying that the effort had lightened fire upon the land batteries, but the benefit did not justify the cost.

General Keppel's twelve 24-pounders were not effective against the fortress walls, and Albemarle asked Pocock for 32-pounders. Two weeks without rain had allowed the protective fascines (bundles of sticks) of the British batteries to dry out, and on 2 July they caught fire. The fire was initially suppressed but that night the smouldering embers ignited the wood platform, and it was entirely consumed. It was a terrible setback. El Morro's garrison had a chance to remount many guns, and the reconstruction of batteries (their positions now known to the enemy) was exposed to cannonading both from El Morro and across the channel. Sickness began to take a heavy toll, and the navy had to provide still more manpower. A battery of four 32-pounders was entirely manned by seamen, who achieved a rapid rate of fire that the artillerymen had not hitherto witnessed. On 15 July Albemarle was discouraged; the soldiers, he informed Pocock, 'fall sick very fast'; he had 'called on the Guanabacoa people' but they were 'not sufficient', and the men from Keppel's ships were 'distressed from constant work'. He asked for a loan of seamen from the ships on the west side.[59] The body of soldiers at Guanabacoa was insufficient because they had been dying fast, probably from yellow fever. In contrast, although the men building the batteries became ill from heat, thirst, overwork and dysentery, they did not usually die, probably because the rocky ground where they worked was dry and inhospitable to mosquitoes. On the 17th Albemarle wrote to Egremont: '[I]f the North Americans do not arrive, and very soon, I shall be at a great loss how to proceed.' He and Pocock dispatched emergency requests to Jamaica for men and ammunition.

Although progress towards making a breach was disappointing, in mid-July twenty guns and numerous mortars prevented the fortress garrison from remounting and manning its guns. It was time to push closer. The solid rock would not allow trenches, and very little soil to fill biscuit bags serving as gabions could be found, so it was fortunate that the homeward-bound Jamaica trade, which then appeared offshore, happened to be carrying bales of cotton. Commodore Douglas also

[59] Albemarle to Pocock, 15 July 1762, Syrett, ed. *Siege and Capture*, p. 242.

brought 600 blacks from Jamaica, hired by Albemarle's order. The cotton bales became the chief means of protecting the troops as they made their way forward.

The only tactical option was to proceed 950 feet to the right and attack the sea bastion. Finally, the besiegers were in luck: on the seaward side there was a wall across the ditch to block out sea water, and it was just wide enough on top for men to cross it in single file and reach the base of the bastion. The location was not easily fired upon from the fortress, and the British brought up a couple of guns and small mortars to provide countering fire. Keppel issued a call for 40 miners. 'Your own ship [the *Namur*]', he informed Pocock, 'is the most likely to be able to furnish [them] as she did belong to a Cornish chief, Admiral Boscawen.' Before long the recruited miners dashed 60 feet across the top of the wall, losing only 4 men to musket fire from above. Although the miners struggled 'with very large stones which cost them much labour to remove', they accomplished their task of undermining the bastion in about a week. When the Spanish realized the danger they sent, in the early morning darkness of 22 July, about 1,500 men silently across the channel who attacked in three different locations. Those who tried to dislodge the miners were driven off by musket fire from the grenadiers covering them.[60] A second attack was to follow, but the losses of the first on all three fronts were heavy and it did not come. Floating batteries which emerged from the channel at first light on the 30th were quickly repulsed. That afternoon at about 2 p.m. the mines were sprung.

The explosion brought down enough of the sea bastion to provide a suitable breach. It was followed by a brief cannonade. British regulars then

filed off quickly man by man across the ledge of rock, scrambled up a difficult slope of rubbish, and gained the platform of the bastion, where 15 or 16 men were arrived before they were opposed by the enemy now coming out of their casemates, in which they had taken shelter dreading another explosion. A very desperate and critical conflict here took place, but our men . . . reinforced as fast as their comrades could follow . . . drove the enemy into the hollow part of the fort.[61]

---

[60] Keppel to Pocock, 20 July, and Mackellar's Journal, 21 and 22 July 1762, ibid. pp. 255–8; also p. 320.
[61] David Dundas's memorandum, ibid. pp. 319–21.

After an hour's close combat the British lost 14 killed and 28 wounded. The victors recorded Spanish casualties as 130 killed, 37 wounded, 326 captured and 213 shot or drowned while attempting to cross to the city.[62] During this combat, the garrison commander, Don Luis de Velasco, was mortally wounded. He was a navy captain. In fact, almost from the outset the entire defence had been placed in the hands of naval officers. Velasco had performed brilliantly. Ever since, as first decreed by Carlos III, many ships of the Spanish navy have carried his name.

Velasco had possessed certain advantages. Bombardment was said to have cost the garrison 1,000 casualties, but every four to six days fresh men came from the city and the warships. Supplies also came. Thus, the garrison could not be worn out by sleepless fatigue, its complement of about 700 could be maintained, and ammunition and provisions replenished. The relief came across the channel at night. Why the British were unable to hinder it is an unanswered question, for there is no evidence that they tried. Velasco's other great advantage was the inherent strength of El Morro, plentifully supplied with water from its cisterns and nearly impregnable. It has therefore been reasonable to criticize Albemarle for his exclusive concentration on besieging it and paying no attention to the alternative of attacking the city.

Patrick Mackellar was chief engineer and Albemarle appears to have followed his recommendations. The initial landing at Cojimar enabled the army to exploit the Spanish failure to fortify the heights of La Cabaña. But once this vital ridge was secured and fortified, it would have been wise to consider, indeed to reconnoitre properly and learn, how formidable El Morro with its great ditch was, and also to survey the anchorage and landing areas at Chorrera in the western sector. Mackellar had been informed that the western landing area was seriously inferior to that at Cojimar. It was not true. When Pocock was able to land there without difficulty a direct attack on the city became an option. Water was a major factor, and Mackellar knew that the western sector was well supplied while the situation in the eastern sector was doubtful. He did not realize how thin and decayed the city's walls were.[63] Successful occupation of the city would remove the supply base from which El Morro drew sustenance.

To be sure, this strategy would have given the campaign a very different form. The distance from the landing place to the city was considerably greater than comparable distances in the eastern sector, and, as Mackellar

[62] Keppel, *Three Brothers*, p. 72.
[63] Mackellar's memorandum is printed in Syrett, ed. *Siege and Capture*, pp. 151–8.

pointed out, an army attacking the city's north wall would be subjected to enfilading fire from El Morro, and at the west wall from the anchored warships. Havana's defending force was thought to be numerous, many sorties from the city were to be expected, and Spanish cavalry might cause trouble. But in fact, most of the defenders were militia and there were fewer than 3,000 serviceable muskets. The British would come forward mainly at night of course, and it would not take much for guns to smash a breach or two in the city wall. If the British occupied the city, the Spanish would then confront the agonizing question of whether to bombard it from El Morro. As for a strategy of attacking the eastern and western sectors simultaneously, it was thought to require more men than Albemarle and Pocock possessed. If the North Americans had been present from the outset, the dual strategy might have been considered.

The first convoy from New York did not arrive until just before El Morro surrendered. Pocock had failed to send Elphinston in the *Richmond* soon enough to meet it before it attempted to navigate the Old Bahama Channel and some of its transports ran aground. No lives were lost, and eventually the *Richmond* helped rescue the stranded men and bring them to Havana. The second convoy unluckily encountered a strongly escorted trade convoy from Cap Français when coming through the Caicos Passage. Six transports carrying 488 troops, most of them regulars, were taken; the rest escaped. All in all, 3,267 healthy provincials and regulars came to assist the depleted army, the first convoy arriving on 28 July, the second on 2 August. They played almost no role in the conquest, not even in the final phase in which the city was compelled to surrender.

After the fortress capitulated the British spent ten days repositioning guns, mortars and howitzers, and built batteries in the western sector. Historians have often said that the British army was on the verge of collapse from sickness, but the Spanish had suffered almost 3,000 casualties as well as ravages from yellow fever (probably introduced by reinforcements and labourers brought from Mexico) and in early August had only 770 regulars fit for duty. Ammunition for only a few days remained. On the British side, the ships' companies had totalled about 11,000 men, now lessened by 1,000 who were sick or dead, most of them marines. Of course the arrival of the North Americans underlined the hopelessness of the Spanish situation.

After Albemarle's invitation to surrender was honourably rejected by the governor the British batteries opened fire from three sides on the morning of 11 August. The fort at La Punta and the city walls were the main targets; after three hours the fort was untenable, and in three more hours it was obvious that the city walls were inadequate. Prado requested a cessation. Albemarle and Pocock offered terms that allowed the residents to keep their money and property, and granted honours of war to the fighting men, but insisted on acquiring all warships and merchant ships with their cargoes – a point the Spanish conceded only after more bombardment was threatened.

Nine ships of the line were captured; three had been sunk to block the channel; two large ships under construction were destroyed. The Spanish navy thereby lost one-fifth of its ship strength. The cargoes of the merchant ships were highly valuable, and there was a large quantity of treasure in the city. The prize money from all this was staggering, and when the accounts were finally settled years later more than £737,000 had been distributed to the captors. According to prior agreement Albemarle and Pocock shared equally; each receiving £123,000. Commodore Keppel and General Eliott got £24,540 each. Albemarle, unlike Monckton, was a much disliked conqueror; he high-handedly offended the bishop of Havana and infuriated British and American suppliers by imposing special levies which were later judged illegal. Commodore Douglas, whose intelligent initiatives had greatly contributed to the success, tried to claim a share but was turned down. Private soldiers each received just over £4 and seamen £3 16s. – if they lived.

An October report listed 560 of the army killed in action and 4,708 dead from disease; the navy had 86 killed, and 800 seamen and 500 marines victims of disease. This was certainly not the end of the death toll. Yellow fever killed thousands afterwards. Although attacking the city instead of El Morro would have required less hard labour and probably less time, lots of men would nevertheless have died of yellow fever because the germ was already present in Havana when the expedition arrived. The North American troops inevitably served as an occupying force. Many died at Havana, others during the voyage back to New York where they continued to die in barracks which Amherst converted to hospitals. Of 207 Rhode Islanders who went to Havana 86 died of disease. The regulars appeared to suffer even worse: the New York Independent Companies were so devastated that they had to be disbanded. Of the 11,576 regulars of the primary invasion force only 2,067 were fit for duty in October.[64] Plainly, the men who bravely rose to the challenge paid a terrible price. Prize shares for the rank and file were always low in those

[64] See Syrett, 'American Provincials', 388–9.

days, but in view of the wealth acquired by the commanders were disgracefully low.

Peace with bitterness

On gaining the council's permission to exchange plenipotentiaries Bute declared that the peace was 'made'. Throughout 1762 it was the policy of Bute and George III to treat France generously, and now, despite cabinet objections, St Lucia was to be given to France and she was to keep New Orleans. The public did not know this, and by putting the notoriously pacifist Duke of Bedford in charge of final negotiations Bute gave the impression that peace was certain.

It was not, although Choiseul unquestionably wanted it. France had nothing left but Saint-Domingue, no active navy, no money to activate one, and no good prospects in Germany. The Austrians had lost their Russian partner and were down to 'their last florin'. The Spanish army in Portugal was not doing well. Choiseul's immediate problem was that Spain was tenaciously adhering to its demands: removal of logwood-cutting settlements; affirmation of the right to fish off Newfoundland; denial of British presence on the shores of the Gulf of Mexico; and, with new emphasis, early cancellation of existing Anglo-Spanish commercial treaties. How could he persuade Spain to agree to a simultaneous peace? In his letter of 31 July Egremont reminded him that Britain required this, but he mentioned a possible alternative: France might make a separate peace with Britain if she pledged not to assist Spain afterwards.

Earlier Choiseul had planned to sign a separate peace with the British and leave it to them to deal with Spain. Bute had been willing to allow this but was overridden in council. Egremont's proposed alternative posed the risk that France would make the pledge not to assist Spain with no intention of honouring it. Choiseul might have done this, but he knew that the British would insist on a formal and public statement. Instead, he urgently summoned a council of state and asked Louis XV to write a letter to Carlos III to impress on him the desirability of making peace. Choiseul considered this letter to be so important that he volunteered to carry it to Madrid personally, but the council would not permit the leading minister to leave Paris, so the former ambassador to Portugal, Jacob O'Dunne, carried it. His departure for Madrid became known in England. Viry tried to pretend that O'Dunne's journey was of no consequence – that peace with Spain's approval was assured – but Hardwicke soon penetrated what was going on: the French ministers 'saw that, if they should stipulate not to assist Spain in her war against England . . . they should ipso facto be guilty of an Infraction of their last Treaty with Spain; and forfeit all the advantages of the Family-Compact, which Mon. de Choiseul was determined not to do'. O'Dunne's mission therefore indicated that the Spanish had not yet agreed and that Versailles was pressing them hard.[65] As it happened, to avoid appearing uncooperative Carlos III had already agreed to allow the exchange of plenipotentiaries and had granted Grimaldi plenipotentiary powers to negotiate with Bedford. But he made no promises about terms.

The two dukes, Bedford and Nivernais, crossed the Channel in early September. Bedford, after being warmly welcomed at Calais, reached Paris on the 12th. He was a startling choice. When Hardwicke learned that Bedford was to be given this responsibility he wondered why an administration would trust so delicate a business to someone so arrogant and unpredictable. 'I am sure', he told Newcastle, 'I should not wish to be the Secretary of State to have the Correspondence with Him.'[66] That task fell to Egremont who, it may be confidently presumed, would have chosen a different man. Egremont drafted very exacting instructions for Bedford. These conveyed 'the King's express commands that you do insist upon signing the preliminaries with France and Spain at the same time'. They also emphasized the importance of careful wording regarding 'the navigation of the Mississippi . . . in case that that [sic] which is proposed thro' the River Ibberville and the Lakes Maurepas and Pontchartrain should prove insufficient for the purposes of commerce'.[67] Moreover, in a supplemental letter, Bedford was told that the final draft of the preliminaries must have London's approval before being signed – a condition that Egremont and Grenville managed to get Bute to accept, which Bedford resented.

During September Egremont awaited Bedford's letters with anxiety. They finally arrived on the 24th. Egremont was annoyed to see that the duke had yielded some minor points, but what was truly upsetting was a new French draft of preliminaries which Bedford conveyed without comment. Egremont was already upset because Nivernais, on instructions from Versailles, had presented a paper that added new items, such as 'the Indians between the Lakes of Canada and the Mississippi should remain neutrals'. He told George III that he did not dare meet with Nivernais

---

[65] Hardwicke to Newcastle, 21 Aug. 1762, BL Add. 32,941, ff. 325–8.
[66] Rashed, *Peace of Paris*, p. 167.
[67] Wickham Legg, ed. *British Diplomatic Instructions*, pp. 64–5.

because he 'was so heated that he should have gone out of one door if the Frenchman had entered in the other'. In the new draft the French were reopening matters that Egremont considered settled. Bute was angry too, and let Bedford know it: 'I should think myself highly criminal, both to my King, and country, were I ever to advise his Majesty to depart from a single Article already conceded by the French.' George III took a different view: in his opinion Bedford was 'too highly fetter'd', and when Egremont suggested a procedure whereby the preliminaries would be drawn up in London ready for signing, the king ridiculed this by saying, in that 'case a boy of ten years old would be' fit to serve as plenipotentiary.[68]

Perhaps Bedford's pacifist reputation led the French to test the British government's resolve, but their military record and prospects put them in a very weak position. In Germany their army had hurriedly retreated from Göttingen and was moving back through Hesse towards the Rhine, leaving Kassel cut off. Choiseul was informed by d'Ossun and officers of the French auxiliary force in Portugal that Spanish supply difficulties were mounting.

There was a gleam of hope in Newfoundland, however. On 8 May two ships of the line, a frigate, and two warships *en flûte* carrying 570 troops had escaped from Brest. Their orders were a well-kept secret and when they reached Newfoundland on 23 June they surprised the 200-man British garrison at St John's. Lord Colville's squadron at Halifax had provided convoy escorts for the Havana expedition and was much reduced in strength. When the alarming report from Newfoundland reached him he alerted the governor of Massachusetts, whose message to Amherst arrived at New York on 15 July. Amherst acted immediately. He appointed his capable brother Colonel William Amherst to command a hurriedly gathered force of 1,500 troops, 500 of them Massachusetts provincials from the Halifax garrison. He borrowed the Massachusetts warship *King George* to escort the transports. Meanwhile, the French assault force had quickly compelled St John's to surrender and ravaged the British fishing fleet and shore facilities. The French began preparations for wintering on the island. Learning of the success, Choiseul ordered out reinforcements, but these (the frigate *Zéphir* and a privateer carrying provisions, clothing, ammunition and 93 more troops) were captured off Brest.

When Colville's small squadron appeared off St John's in early September the French naval commander, Captain Charles-Henri-Louis

---

[68] George III to Bute, 25, 26 Sept., Bute to Bedford, 28 Sept. 1762, Sedgwick, ed. *Letters from George III*, pp. 137–9.

d'Arsac, chevalier de Ternay, planned to give battle, but just before he got under way lookouts reported that the enemy had acquired an additional warship accompanied by nine transports. These, of course, carried Colonel Amherst's troops. Ternay gave up the idea of battle and made no serious attempt to prevent the troops from landing. When it became obvious that the arriving army would prevail he resolved to save his ships from capture, and under foggy conditions he evaded Colville's blockade. (In this kind of operation he was expert, having been instrumental in getting the trapped ships in the Vilaine River to sea.) Two days later the French garrison was compelled to surrender. It was bound to happen anyway because Ternay's ships had been spotted heading westwards after leaving Brest, and the Admiralty ordered a small squadron to cross the Atlantic. It arrived just after the French garrison surrendered.

Soon after his arrival in Paris Bedford learned to his astonishment that Grimaldi had been told nothing about the negotiation concerning the Mississippi boundary and British access to the Gulf of Mexico. Choiseul asked Bedford not to bring the subject up. In talking with Grimaldi, Bedford was struck by his tenacity and rudeness, and taken aback when Grimaldi demanded that existing Anglo-Spanish commercial treaties must terminate. He informed Choiseul that his instructions allowed no room for compromise on either this or the more familiar Spanish issues.

Choiseul wrote to d'Ossun to tell him that Madrid must not think of altering particular terms; the British were presenting them as sine qua non. He put the position bluntly: 'Does the king of Spain want war or peace? If he wants the latter . . . he must adopt the articles. If he wants war, he must reject them; there is no middle ground.' As for permitting 'the English to establish themselves at the mouths of the Mississippi' he added, 'I warn you that we will not allow peace to be lost' for this reason, because 'Louisiana belongs to us in all sovereignty'; the king would not let it be used in a manner contrary to France's interests. A further warning: if the Spanish king wished to continue the war, he should no longer count on assistance from France.[69] Upon reading this on 28 September Carlos III assured d'Ossun that he would not let Spanish claims prevent France from making peace. He left it to France to look after Spain's interests.

Choiseul was extremely anxious not to lose the favourable terms Britain was granting to France. Military and naval prospects were worsening, and letters from Nivernais were disturbing. He reported that Bute and Egremont were afraid to make further concessions and were anxious to

---

[69] Choiseul to d'Ossun, 20 Sept. 1762, Blart, *Rapports*, pp. 32–3.

make peace before the opening of Parliament. Nivernais supposed that if this did not happen, Pitt would return to office – Choiseul's greatest fear.[70] His determination to increase the pressure on Spain was made before news of Havana's capture arrived.

The event was decisive nevertheless. London learned of it on 29 September. Bute was inclined to give Havana back to Spain without compensation. So was Bedford, who feared that the negotiation with France would be broken off. Grenville, who had steadily protested against the sacrifice of British overseas conquests, would not hear of it, and Egremont and the other ministers agreed with him. Even George III chose not to side with Bute on this question. It was agreed that Spain must cede either Florida or Puerto Rico. Hoping to speed up the Bourbon response, Bute quietly conveyed this information through Nivernais to Versailles.

The news of Havana's capture reached Paris on 3 October. Choiseul was shocked; he had been confident that the place would hold out. When Carlos III heard the news on the 9th he reacted passionately. He said that Spain would keep fighting until her terms were accepted. He commented to d'Ossun that lack of success was part of war, and added: 'I never slept more tranquilly than last night.'[71] Calculations of the new military and naval requirements that would be required left him unmoved. Meanwhile, Choiseul was advising Louis XV to offer Louisiana (the western part that remained) to Spain, ostensibly in gratitude to Carlos for his loyal support and in recognition of his losses, but also of course to persuade him to accept peace. On the 15th he informed Madrid that the British would accept either Florida or Puerto Rico in compensation for Havana and advised the Spanish to cede Florida. Carlos put himself in Louis XV's hands and ordered Grimaldi to sign whatever the French required.

While these orders were on their way to Paris the British cabinet met. Grenville had suggested to Bute that the preliminaries should first be examined and approved by Parliament. His proposal was rejected, but Egremont's instructions of 26 October showed the influence of Havana's capture: concessions that Bedford had made to France were wiped out, and Britain's terms were framed as an ultimatum. To make sure the pacifist duke understood, George III added a personal letter saying that if the terms were not accepted the war would continue. Clearly, the British council was now standing firm. And yet, one last time, Bute passed cards under the table to please the French, and once again Choiseul employed

[70] Dull, *French Navy*, pp. 238–9.
[71] Blart, *Rapports*, p. 39.

diplomatic deceit. Without informing his colleagues or Bedford, Bute secretly let the French know which points Bedford was allowed to yield. Choiseul in his final meeting with Bedford told him that his yielding on these points would give more force to France's effort to gain Spanish consent. He kept secret the fact that a dispatch confirming Spain's consent had just arrived from Madrid.[72] As a result, French fishermen were allowed more scope and less supervision in the Gulf of St Lawrence. Bedford justified his conduct as follows:

I can with truth assure your Lordship, that had I not ventured to take the liberty to relax in some very few points of no great importance to us, but of great moment in the eyes of the French king and his ministers, I should never have been able to have got that court to have spoke so roundly to the Spanish minister as they have done.[73]

He had been tricked. Bute had invited it; his policy of gratifying France continued to the last moment.

The preliminaries were signed at Fontainebleau on 3 November. Bute had the king ratify them before Parliament met (after managing to delay its opening). As a result Parliament was prevented from altering particular articles. Nevertheless, broad approval was required and a favourable vote was by no means assured because by this time the Bute administration was deeply unpopular.

The original cause of unpopularity was Bute's decision to worry Newcastle into resigning and to supplant him at the Treasury. Thereby the royal favourite became in effect prime minister, and during the summer the pro-Pitt *Monitor* and a new weekly, the *The North Briton*, attacked him more intensively as a favourite and a Scotsman. The cleverest and most unscrupulous essays were written by John Wilkes, who would soon become notorious but was currently unknown. He was covertly subsidized by Earl Temple. Details of the peace negotiation were not public knowledge, Bedford's pacifism was, and his appointment in early September ignited an explosion of outrage.

We have seen that although Newcastle favoured continuation of the German war and good relations with Prussia, he was otherwise almost as eager for peace as Bedford. Bute because of his desire to make concessions to France found himself without supporters on the council. When he told Devonshire about this the latter's response was: 'What, my Lord, your

---

[72] Rashed, *Peace of Paris*, pp. 184–5.

[73] Bedford to Egremont, 3 Nov. 1762, *Bedford Correspondence*, III, 145.

own Council?'[74] (All the members except Lord Granville were Bute's own choices.) So Bute had tried to bring Newcastle back. Hardwicke, as we have seen, advised the duke against it, and not only did Newcastle refuse, he began to criticize the peace terms that were being offered.[75] But Havana's capture generated enormous public excitement, and secretary of state George Grenville, who was also responsible for dealing with the House of Commons, wanted to bring the whole Whig triumvirate onto the council to broaden support.

Instead, Bute narrowed it. He promptly got rid of Grenville, forcing him to change places with the First Lord of the Admiralty, the Earl of Halifax. For the crucial task of gaining parliamentary approval of the peace preliminaries he called on Henry Fox. The political world was dismayed and puzzled by these moves because George III was known to despise Fox, and, as Horace Walpole remarked, 'Unpopularity heaped on unpopularity does not silence clamour.'[76] A second shock soon followed. Near the end of October when Devonshire, still officially a member of the council, declined to attend a meeting to discuss the final version of the preliminaries, the king rudely dismissed him from his court employment. This was an unheard of insult to one of the greatest Whig families in England.

Newcastle, reacting with outrage to this treatment of a close friend and colleague, was strongly disposed to act in opposition. Hardwicke cautioned him; he should wait until the articles of the preliminaries were known: would they be 'admissible'? As matters stood, they might differ very little from terms Newcastle had supported while in office. That would be used against him. Another consideration was public and parliamentary opinion. Hardwicke's impression was that the public very much wanted peace. Unless the terms when revealed were clearly inadmissible Newcastle would not be able to count on broad support for continuing the war. Hardwicke also reminded him that the situation was not what it had been in 1757: Newcastle had then enjoyed a close relationship with the king, whereas the new king seemed to dislike him. Moreover, George III would contend mightily to keep his favourite at the Treasury. Hardwicke ended on a personal note: he had no heart for opposition; he was old and felt tired. Undoubtedly he was also thinking of his sons' careers.

[74] Yorke, *Hardwicke*, III, 406.
[75] On 4 Sept. in a conversation with the king, and in letters to Hardwicke, 18 and 30 Sept. 1762, BL Add. 32,942, ff. 149–56, 290–1, 427–30.
[76] Quoted in Lawson, *Grenville*, p. 142.

Hardwicke agreed with his son Charles that no plan of opposition could succeed without Pitt. He tried to tell Newcastle this, but the duke did not want to hear it. He was afraid of Pitt, considered him a war-monger, and could not accept the idea of a partnership that would allow Pitt the power he had formerly exercised. Pitt, for his part, did not forget how Newcastle at the beginning of the new reign had allowed Bute to gain high office. Seeing Bute now installed in the most powerful office of all, Pitt vowed that he would neither do anything to assist the favourite's 'transcendency' nor join with the man who had paved the way for it. Instead, he would stand independent. As for opposition, Pitt was well aware that the king disliked him and dreaded the idea of 'holding office against the good will of the Crown'.[77] As Newcastle drifted towards open opposition, he made no serious attempt to gain Pitt's cooperation.

Yet the duke pressed his closest friend to speak out against the peace preliminaries in the House of Lords. Very reluctantly Hardwicke agreed to do it. His notes for the speech have survived. He began by mentioning the desirability of peace, but commented: 'I wished from [the bottom of] my soul, that advantage had been taken of the successes of the last year . . . to have varied, to have abated' concessions. 'Look round the globe – all the French sugar islands taken from them except St. Domingo'; the 'dominions of King and his allies in Germany recovered . . . before those Articles were settled' so that France had nothing to offer in compensation for all that Britain had given up. Havana was conquered, 'an immense and insurmountable loss to Spain' and also distressing to France because of her share in Spanish commerce. 'I do not see', he said, 'that the least advantage has been made of this situation, in respect of France.' He went further:

If no concessions could be obtained of France by force of this conquest, surely it was the strongest reason why no new concessions should be made in her favour. But I fear that is the case. Several very material points given up to France, which I never heard of till just before the preliminaries were signed, nor were ever fully explained, till they came over actually signed.

Hardwicke also mentioned: St Lucia being given up, an important island; no proper inspection of the fishing station of St Pierre though France had agreed to it; restoring to France her *comptoirs* in India (What did the

---

[77] Account of Thomas Walpole's conversation with Pitt, 13 Nov. 1762, Yorke, *Hardwicke*, III, 430–1.

word include? he asked). He also noted that good relations with Prussia and Russia had been 'totally neglected'.[78] His speech was merely an act of loyalty and a marker for posterity. The House of Lords accepted the preliminaries without a vote.

On the same day, 9 December 1762, Pitt spoke in the House of Commons. He was dreadfully afflicted by gout, arrived late, had to be steadied on his feet by friends, and was allowed at times to sit down. His voice was weak, but he spoke for three and a half hours. As expected, he emphasized the fisheries, saying that the French were being given much more than he had very reluctantly agreed to allow them when in office, especially in the Gulf of St Lawrence. By giving up the Caribbean conquests as well as restoring access to the fisheries, the treaty would leave France with her maritime and commercial strength intact. His other criticisms were similar to Hardwicke's. Both men dwelt on how little advantage had been made of the year's military successes; both worried that the complete success in India might be compromised; both agreed that diplomatic opportunities on the continent had been thrown away. Pitt reiterated his belief that the German war had made overseas conquests possible. His voice could not produce the old thunder, but the unmistakable style remained. Why, he asked, were the terms no better than those of 1761, after a year in which the French 'had put you to the expense of fourteen additional millions, and after your arms had been crowned with such advantages?' He ridiculed the attitude that produced the concessions: 'We must, say the French, have St. Lucia, for *cela bouche Martinique* [it shuts up Martinique]; is that a reason to be given to a British Parliament?' He noted that the article concerning India spoke of 'mutual restitution of conquests' and asked, 'what were the conquests which France had to restore?' Regarding Europe he observed, 'The branches of Bourbon were united; we and our allies disunited!' – the king of Prussia 'disavowed! given up! sacrificed!'[79] As he declared that he stood independent, everyone realized that the government would prevail. The vote of thanks which signalled acceptance was overwhelming: 319 to 65.

This lopsided vote had three causes: first, Newcastle and Pitt failed to unite; second, Britain had won and most people wanted peace; third, members of Parliament realized that the political penalty for voting against the government was likely to be severe. In respect of the third, the

---

[78] *Parl. Hist.* XV, 1251–8.

[79] *Proceedings and Debates*, I, 416–23 contains Horace Walpole's record (in *Memoirs of King George III*). Some quotations are from *Parl. Hist.*, XV, 12 63–7.

favourite minister not only held the whip hand but was clearly in earnest on this major issue. Since the king was young, an opposition vote could lead to decades in the political wilderness. There was also danger of immediate retribution. Hardwicke and Devonshire thought that the appointment of Fox would backfire because he was so thoroughly disliked, but they were wrong. The rude dismissal of Devonshire and Fox's hints that he was prepared to be ruthless spread fear. In the event fear was justified. Many members who voted with the opposition, if they held offices under royal control, were dismissed. Even minor civil servants lost their positions, especially if they were dependants of Newcastle. The king removed Devonshire and Newcastle from their Lord Lieutenancies. All in all, the vote on the peace preliminaries in December 1762 produced the greatest political purge since the Hanoverian Succession in 1714.

Despite pride in the achievements of British arms and a return of peace, the concessions to France and the coercive politics used by the government to gain approval of the preliminaries sowed a great deal of bitterness in England. At Madrid there was bitterness over humiliating losses, as well as frustration because the war was unexpectedly terminated in less than a year. The king of Prussia was bitter not only about Bute's treatment of him as an ally but also because the preliminaries put his Rhineland territories at risk. According to the terms the French were required to evacuate them, but it was widely predicted that the French would delay their evacuations until Austrian troops from the Netherlands were ready to take over. Prussian units were scraped together from Prince Ferdinand's army in hopes of preventing this, but they were insufficient and could not march soon enough to succeed. In the end the Austrians restored the territories in the treaty of Hubertusburg (15 February 1763), partly because Frederick agreed to put a stop to the brutal ravaging of Saxony by Prussian forces. In France people were very happy to see the war end even though it had gone badly. Choiseul wrote to d'Ossun on the day the preliminaries were signed: 'Spain is treated a little hard; as for us, the conditions are better than those of the year past and those that we could hope for next year.'[80] His claim of better terms than 'those of the year past' was dubious.

It remained to execute the definitive treaty. Bedford's instructions asked him to remove the words that defined the Iberville River as a Louisiana boundary. It was not done, but he did manage to insist on altering the article relating to India. When anxious for France to agree to the

---

[80] Choiseul to d'Ossun, 3 Nov. 1762, Rashed, *Peace of Paris*, p. 186.

preliminaries Bute and Egremont had put pressure on the East India Company to give France generous terms, but the company spokesmen would not agree. In the relevant preliminary article Egremont inserted vague language that, some said, might prove advantageous to the French. (Robert Clive voted against the preliminaries.) But when terms of the definitive treaty came under consideration in London the question was reopened. As a result, Bedford was sent instructions which enclosed the letters the company had written to Egremont making its case. Bedford seemed to understand what was wanted. How he proceeded is not known, but, although the French vehemently protested, he gained some key points (to be examined in the next chapter). The final treaty, signed on 10 February 1763, certainly deserved to be called the Peace of Paris, for it was there that Choiseul had assiduously kept the negotiations.

CHAPTER 16

Conclusion and aftermath

When the Seven Years War began France was the strongest power in Europe. Her economy was advanced and diverse, her population three times that of Great Britain and Ireland. With a large peacetime army, readily expandable, her military power was vastly greater than Britain's, whose peacetime army was small and means of military recruiting constricted. Without doubt Britain had the superior navy, but the war began badly for the British even in the maritime and colonial sphere. In 1757 it seemed obvious that France would win the war.

Yet, within three years British forces comprehensively defeated French forces everywhere in the world, on land and sea. By the end of 1759 Fort Duquesne and Fort Niagara were in British hands, thus cutting off French communications with the western interior of North America, and Quebec had just been occupied by a British army which could safely move upriver to Montreal the following spring. Thousands of British regulars and provincials could be mobilized in northern New York and provisioned from colonial resources to complete the conquest of Canada. The defenders lacked numbers and food, and had very little chance of receiving help from France. In Germany, a French effort to occupy Hanover had been turned back by Prince Ferdinand's army at Minden. French preparations to invade the British Isles in 1759 were rendered useless by British sea power. The *coup de grâce* was Sir Edward Hawke's great victory at Quiberon Bay on 20 November 1759. Guadeloupe in the Caribbean, and Senegal and Gorée in West Africa were in British possession. In India, Madras had withstood a dangerous siege and Bengal had come under British control; the latter's resources, valuable in themselves, would help prevent the French from conquering the Carnatic. Finally, a 'violent crisis in French finances' – Berryer's description – occurred at the end of 1759. The situation had long been building up thanks to the vast quantity of uncashed and overdue short-term paper, but the crisis was triggered on 15 October by news of Montcalm's defeat at Quebec. With finances in disarray and its naval ports now closely watched, Versailles decided to cut the naval budget to practically nothing. French colonies overseas were left to fend for themselves. France's European allies would not help her because they were concentrating on defeating Prussia.

Why did this happen? Political leadership was a key factor. As Sir Herbert Richmond observed (see Chapter 1), errors of policy and strategy have the most far-reaching effects. The errors made at Versailles in the Seven Years War were due partly to overconfidence and partly to flawed high-level leadership. Policymaking at Versailles was not only opaque but often ill-considered and incoherent. Louis XV allowed Madame de Pompadour to exercise a strong influence over key appointments and in some instances policy. She tended to assume that French power was inexhaustible and invincible. Although she wished for France to flourish as a great power, she steadily sought to advance the careers of her favourites and looked to her own political needs, for she could never feel that her position was secure. The system – or non-system – resulted in narrowly considered actions that often invited poor military performance. When Choiseul became leading minister he consistently gave priority to France's interests as a great power – perhaps his greatest merit as a statesman – and appeared, especially late in the war, to possess unfettered control of policy (although the king and Pompadour probably prevented him more than once from pursuing the policy he preferred). Yet his leadership was not without flaws, since his skill in diplomacy generally failed to overcome his strategic misjudgements.

In contrast, Britain's high-level leadership after 1757 was remarkably competent. The key figure was Pitt, but his strategic acumen was significantly complemented by the sagacity of Hardwicke, and the cost of his expansive war plans was made possible by Newcastle's management of Parliament and skill in dealing with George II. Although at the beginning of the war Newcastle was inclined to bend to George II's concern for Hanover in ways that Hardwicke criticized, it is nevertheless obvious that these three men always considered their main goal to be the improvement of Britain's power position. They never ceased to share with members of Parliament and the public a dread of French power.

Fundamental causes of British military success

Political leadership would have been of little use without a powerful and efficient war machine under the direction of able officials and commanders.

To begin with the Royal Navy: it possessed an experienced officer corps, well-equipped dockyards, victualling facilities, overseas bases, and a remarkable capacity to build warships in private yards. Its greatest problem was finding crews upon mobilization, and full mobilization in this case required three years. In the spring of 1756 the scarcity of manned ships forced Lord Anson to choose, and he made a mistake: he overrated the active strength of the Brest squadron and kept the Western Squadron strong instead of sending three or four more ships to Byng's squadron in the Mediterranean. A shortage of ships also contributed to the Admiralty's failure to prevent the French navy from gathering a strong force at Louisbourg in early 1757.

Full British mobilization combined with French naval weakness transformed the strategic picture. By spring 1758 the Royal Navy counted 70,000 seamen (eventually the figure would reach 84,000). Many of these were landsmen trained at sea. The French navy could no longer man the ships that it had. The French seafaring population was not large – only about 60,000 – and the navy did not have many opportunities to train landsmen. To make matters worse, 10,000 French seamen were in British prisons in the spring of 1758, and thousands of men who had sailed to Louisbourg in 1757 had died of disease. Consequently, French naval capability was not just overtaken; it collapsed. The Royal Navy could now guard the Straits of Gibraltar properly and was able to disrupt French preparations in Basque Roads, thus restricting the French naval presence at Louisbourg to six ships of the line and 3,500 men (in 1757 there had been sixteen ships and 13,000 men). In 1759 the Royal Navy accomplished the following: assisted at the capture of Guadeloupe; dominated the Coromandel Coast; carried Wolfe's army up to Quebec; destroyed or captured five of the Toulon squadron's ships of the line off Lagos; and maintained a blockade of Brest while also watching the troop transports in the bay of Morbihan.

The blockade of Brest in 1759 was uniquely tenacious, but even so, Conflans could have evaded it if his mission had pointed him to the ocean instead of requiring him to turn east. In truth, although the Western Squadron could delay sailings, it could not prevent French warships and fast merchant ships from escaping to the open ocean. Quiberon Bay was a decisive battle – for two reasons: it thwarted a planned invasion and, for a time, eliminated the Brest squadron. In this battle of 20 November 1759 seven French ships of the line were sunk, wrecked or captured; six took refuge in the Vilaine River and eight fled to Rochefort; in both locations they were bottled up by British warships. Before it, trying to prevent

French expeditions from going overseas was very difficult and demanding. After it, the task was much easier, because the Brest squadron was sharply reduced, money for restoring it was withheld, and ports in the bay of Biscay could be easily monitored. In the final years of the war British cruisers and privateers maintained a close watch on the entire French Atlantic coastline, exercising a level of command of the sea that was unequalled at any other time in the eighteenth century.

As a naval strategist Anson was too conservative. To get ships assigned for service in distant seas someone like Pitt was needed to override the First Lord's inclination to keep them near home. But when it came to blockading Brest the First Lord was in his element. His greatest single contribution to strategic success lay in his readiness to support Hawke's requests for special victualling and refitting arrangements; these sustained the huge squadron that cruised off Brest in 1759. In fact, British naval success in general stemmed not from Anson's strategic decisions, but rather from his ability as a first-rate administrator and trusted leader. His selection of admirals and commodores for important commands was admirable: Boscawen, Saunders, Howe, Keppel and especially Hawke, on whom he relied heavily. (His only significant mistake was Byng.) The best testimony to his professionalism in these matters was his appointment of Augustus Hervey to important commands despite Hervey's known personal hostility.

Suppression of French shipping did not require full naval mobilization in the Seven Years War. The danger of confronting strong British squadrons and perhaps the Western Squadron, its location not known with certainty, caused French naval ministers to shy away from sending out squadrons to harass British cruisers and privateers. For the same reason, the French navy no longer provided strong escorts for convoys. Outward-bound French merchant ships sailing in small groups commonly escaped interception, but because so many British armed ships cruised off the French coast they were often captured on the return voyage. By the end of 1757 French merchants discontinued Atlantic commerce almost entirely. In contrast, British commerce thrived throughout the war.

It was not accidental that the earliest and most significant British victories in North America – Nova Scotia, Louisbourg and Quebec – were operations in which the troops and supplies came by sea. A good deal of attention has been paid to British ignorance of suitable combat tactics in wilderness warfare, but the fundamental problem in the interior was logistical – how to supply an advancing army safely. Since the British were committed to offensive operations they had to solve it. The solution required a body of scouts with special skills for protecting supply lines and gathering intelligence. Indians knew the terrain and could find their way. Lacking them the British had to create the ranger companies. American provincials were best suited to the task, but continuous service was required, and Lord Loudoun, to his credit, promptly instituted rangers as a branch of the regular army. The same sort of permanence was desirable when it came to teams and wagons as well as bateaumen. The most important contribution of John Bradstreet, who is best known for his successful raid on Fort Frontenac, was his energetic and competent management of the unruly assemblage of bateaumen.

The tasks of building roads, garrisoning depots, escorting supply convoys, guarding horses and building stockades, bateaux and armed lake vessels required thousands of men. Pitt was right when he gave colonial authorities incentives to provide provincial soldiers. Provincials often proved to be brave and effective when tested in combat, but their main contribution was to perform these services. The Duke of Cumberland had not understood the reasons why provincials were needed. His overly ambitious war plan based mainly on regular troops was seriously defective.

Braddock was not the only second-rate commander in America in the beginning years. In one way or another they all were, and except for Shirley they were Cumberland's choices. It was fortunate for British military prospects in North America that in the wake of the Rochefort debacle Pitt, Hardwicke and Newcastle were able to persuade the king to give Ligonier the power to recommend. He chose Amherst who, as commander-in-chief, has been commonly criticized for being too cautious, but caution was needed in North America. It was time to stop giving the Canadians easy opportunities to thwart expeditions and replenish their dwindling resources by capturing British supplies. This was a crucial consideration. Although Versailles might have wished to convey more troops across the Atlantic – in fast ships it probably could have been done – Canadian agriculture could not support them, and it was not safe or practicable to ship large quantities of food from the home country. Vaudreuil understood that Canadian strategy required raiding – not just for the purpose of disrupting enemy supply lines, discouraging enemy efforts and gaining Indian allegiance, but for bringing back captured guns, ammunition and, above all, provisions. Amherst did not like Indians. Like Montcalm, he did not trust them, but he made strategic choices that took them into account. Forbes, also selected by Ligonier, was similarly cautious about his supply lines and never doubted that well-organized Indian hostility could overturn a campaign.

Given the huge preponderance of British America's resources and British sea power's inhibiting effect on supplies from France it is easy to suppose that nothing could have saved Canada from conquest. It seems certain that the British would have captured Louisbourg and Quebec since these operations were supplied by sea. Even so, if Versailles had replaced Montcalm with Lévis, Wolfe might not have achieved his brilliant surprise at Anse au Foulon, and, in any case, during those final hours Lévis would probably have made better use of the available French and Canadian troops than Montcalm did.

The French ministers had hoped that Britain's military potential in North America would be irrelevant. They planned to end the war quickly in Europe by occupying Hanover. The attractiveness of this strategy was enhanced by an expectation that Austria, Russia, Sweden and France would speedily crush Prussia. The Dutch Republic would then be compelled to submit to France, and if the British chose to continue fighting, French financial resources could be applied to the maritime and colonial sphere.

There was a diplomatic complication. France had no right to attack Hanover. As Maria Theresa pointed out, it would violate a long-standing guarantee of the peace and integrity of the Empire. Besides, Hanover had assiduously avoided provocation, shunning cooperation with Prussia. On a practical level Vienna worried that a campaign against Hanover would delay French assistance against Prussia. But Austria needed the subsidy money and the empress-queen yielded under French pressure. However, when word reached Paris that Prague was under siege Louis XV, aware that the French war plan deviated from his treaty pledge, felt honour-bound to send the army then gathering under Soubise to assist the Austrians. French strategists did not want Soubise to commit his forces, but the signals from Versailles were muddled, and an order to Richelieu to detach 12,000 of his troops to Soubise (probably issued at Pompadour's urging) proved fatal. It made possible the battle of Rossbach (5 November 1757) – not remarkable in terms of numbers but enormous in terms of consequences because in its wake the plan for wintering Richelieu's army in the heart of Germany became untenable.

Rossbach led to the retreat of Richelieu's army, and this became the truly decisive campaign of the German war. According to Clausewitz, destruction of the enemy's army is the principal goal of military action, and the winter retreat of early 1758 was a prime instance although it did not feature a great battle. It somewhat resembles Napoleon's retreat in Russia but has no recognized name, and the general who brilliantly took advantage of the French army's wintering difficulties, Ferdinand of Brunswick, is scarcely known to history. The destructive rout pushed the French army all the way across the Rhine, and the dream of a short war evaporated. It was too soon, however, for Bernis's recommendation of peace to be accepted at Versailles, and France turned to a desperate strategy of invading the British Isles, according to a plan concocted by Choiseul and Belleisle which had almost no chance of success.

To Belleisle's credit the French army in Germany was in due course restored. At about 150,000 it steadily outnumbered His Britannic Majesty's Army under Ferdinand which grew to about 100,000, but it never managed to overcome its weaker opponent. The German war continued for four more years, each side unable to establish a decisive advantage. In Hesse the French could hold on, but in Westphalia and Hanover local resources of provisions and forage were insufficient, while Ferdinand's army had access to supplies coming up rivers from the North Sea. Westphalia was not, therefore, a good choice for a decisive theatre. Conceivably, the French army might have succeeded if its commanding generals had been disposed to cooperate, but because each general's staff was associated with a faction at Versailles non-cooperation was endemic. Pompadour's unwavering determination to have Soubise assigned to important commands aggravated the problem.

Apart from naval superiority, there were two keys to British success in the West Indies: careful operational planning and proficiency in amphibious warfare. Pitt rather quickly learned the planning requirements. He alerted the Admiralty, Ordnance and War Office as soon as he could about equipment and transport needs, and gave timely warning to military commanders abroad about preparing troops. He developed a good understanding of the rhythms of preparation required in the age of sail. His finest effort was his last: the Martinique expedition of 1761–2. Amphibious operations have always required a measure of luck, but in this war the British not only planned a timely assemblage of forces but also developed skills and special equipment for accomplishing an efficient landing. After 1758 British performance in all these respects progressed to a level unmatched in the world. The consistent high level of cooperation between the land and sea services in the Seven Years War (after the Rochefort debacle) is particularly noteworthy. Such cooperation not only supported successful landings but afforded timely naval services after the troops were ashore, such as landing naval guns, sending sailors to haul them and sometimes serve as gun crews, and providing ample ammunition for long sieges (crucial at Martinique and Belle-Île). By 1762 marines were often functioning in the role for which they later became famous, though not in great numbers.

The foundation of military success in India was money, because most of what was needed to wage war could be purchased locally. Even if Lally had been temperamentally suited to gaining the cooperation of company officials at Pondicherry, he would have been at a disadvantage because French company funds could not come close to matching what was available to his opponent. Although London sent funds, the English company continued to trade profitably during the war, especially in Bengal, and was able to send money from Bengal to Madras to assist the conquest of the Carnatic. The total expense for military operations and subsidies during the war is not easy to discover, but it appears to have been very considerable. After Lally's siege of Madras failed, superior British naval and financial resources made the ultimate surrender of Pondicherry inevitable – so long as the British general conducted his forces alertly and cautiously, as Eyre Coote did. The Royal Navy always had nine to eleven ships of the line in the Indian Ocean from 1758 to 1763. British naval expense for the East Indies during the year 1760 was calculated at £557,491, a figure only slightly less than the figure for the West Indies and somewhat greater than that for North America.[1] We have seen that when funds came from France in the middle of the contest the French admiral spent most of it on his squadron. Neither in blood nor money was the war in India cheap.

Why peace was delayed

Interwoven in the history of the last three years of the war is a basic question: Why was peace not made? Explanations usually focus on Pitt. The usual narrative has emphasized his goal of reducing French maritime power as a reason to keep the war going. It has not been difficult to support this approach by citing criticisms of Pitt's conduct culled from Newcastle's letters and memoranda as well as Bedford's letters and Devonshire's diary. These were not unbiased witnesses. Bedford was a dedicated pacifist, Newcastle generally so inclined, and Devonshire almost as eager for peace as Newcastle. Yet even these sources testify that in most instances Pitt's actions were solidly supported by his cabinet colleagues. The history of the failure to make peace is complex, and a summary of each government's conduct in 1760 and 1761 is in order.

[1] BL Add. 33,047, fo. 371.

At the end of the campaigning season in 1759 Pitt was willing to contemplate negotiations. Otherwise the Anglo-Prussian Declaration would not have been made. In some histories the declaration has been dismissed as a dodge for evading Spanish mediation, but in fact it was much desired by Frederick II, and Pitt, his fellow ministers and comte d'Affry at The Hague believed that it provided a viable path to peace. The militarily inactive winter months were the appropriate time for a peace congress to be organized; an accompanying cessation of arms was possible. The declaration was evaded by the duc de Choiseul and the Austrian ambassador Starhemberg, who saw danger in it and immediately conspired to formulate a counter-declaration.

When Pitt received the king of Spain's offer to serve as mediator, the whole cabinet agreed with his decision to turn it down; they all judged that the Spanish king could not possibly be impartial. The same ministerial unity was evident when the French government refused to allow Prussian interests to be considered: the cabinet agreed that Yorke should tell d'Affry that Britain could not simply set aside its Prussian ally. (The ministers assumed, correctly, that France would not risk offending Austria.) Even Newcastle had to admit that there was no acceptable basis for a peace negotiation in 1760 other than the Anglo-Prussian Declaration.

Although Pitt felt the pull of popular enthusiasm for more overseas conquests in the wake of the victories at Quebec and Quiberon Bay, he also realized that there were no British troops available to send to the obvious popular theatre, the West Indies. The large army in North America was committed to completing the conquest of Canada, and the few regiments remaining in England would be needed to counter the strong offensive that France was preparing to launch in Germany. He dreaded the necessity of sending these troops to Germany. Committing British money and blood to the defence of Hanover was always unpopular, and he could no longer credibly claim that it was being done to assist Prussia because everyone knew that Prussia, under severe pressure from Russia and Austria, had become an ally of dubious value. All in all, Pitt did not look forward to the campaigning year of 1760, and the public's positive response to Mauduit's arguments, published after the campaigning season ended, would confirm that his worries were justified.

Since France showed no signs of quitting, Pitt had to assume that Versailles's idea of a reasonable and honourable peace would not allow Britain to retain many fruits of her military success. Not until Choiseul made his *uti possidetis* proposal of late March 1761 did France clearly indicate that the conquests mattered. Pitt welcomed the overture but was hesitant as to how to proceed and so was Hardwicke because the applicability of the *uti possidetis* was unclear. The two statesmen (unlike Newcastle) did not trust Choiseul, who later admitted that the obscurity was deliberate – designed to allay criticism by Vienna. The British ministers did not feel similarly constrained by the king of Prussia, who had told them that he trusted the future of his Rhineland territories to their care.

Heartened by a brief sketch of terms which Choiseul (reluctantly) dictated to Stanley in mid-June, the British government responded ten days later. Some of the language drafted by Pitt in this response dated 26 June 1761 was severe, and he failed to make a crucial point clear: that the French could have the Newfoundland fishery if they agreed to demolish the fortifications of Dunkirk. In this Pitt was at fault, though Bute approved the language. This document is often said to have caused the ruin of the negotiation. Yet Stanley, the British representative in Paris, explained to Choiseul that fishing off Newfoundland would be allowed and that a suitable *abri* would be provided (though Cape Breton was out of the question) if France were willing to satisfy Britain on the matter of Dunkirk. No one in the British cabinet, except Bedford afterwards, believed that this response might cause France to break off the negotiation. Everyone viewed it as an initial statement of terms, and all were mindful that the peace overture had originated at Versailles. A useful counter-response was expected.

What happened thereafter dismayed the entire cabinet: first, there was a delay during which the ministers feared that the French were waiting for news of a victory in Germany; then, when the response of 13 July arrived, it not only continued to insist on the return of Cape Breton but also retracted other points that the British considered settled. Soon afterwards the Spanish and Austrian memoirs were delivered. The ministers were angry, and Pitt's letter of 25 July expressed everyone's anger. But the letter also pointed out that Britain was not raising her terms despite three recently reported military successes. In his letter Pitt was once again guilty of obfuscating the cabinet's offer to allow the Newfoundland fishery in exchange for reducing Dunkirk. Although his colleagues had specified that the offer was to be made clear, he did not faithfully comply. His colleagues did not disguise their annoyance, and his acceptance of more extended fishery concessions near the end of August seems to have been aimed at repairing damaged relations.[2] At Versailles Choiseul angrily gave

---

[2] Devonshire's effort, employing the king's influence, to restore ministerial cohesion in a way that led to Pitt's willingness to yield is made clear in Schweizer, 'Cabinet Crisis' (cited in Chapter 14).

the impression that his decision to turn away from the quest for peace was provoked by Pitt's dispatches of 25 July. His peacemaking efforts in 1760 and 1761 deserve close examination, however.

Was Choiseul serious about making peace in early 1760? His plan called for an armed Spanish mediation to force Britain into granting favourable terms. His response to the Anglo-Prussian Declaration was to conspire with the Austrian ambassador Starhemberg in order to evade it. When the Anglo-French talks at The Hague were thwarted by disagreement over allowing Prussian concerns to be discussed, he summarily ended them and reassured Vienna that nothing would be done. Thereafter he urged Spain to invade Portugal. In short, his proceedings in 1760 were not designed to bring peace.

No one knows why Choiseul made his overture to London in late March 1761. Perhaps he was alarmed by Ferdinand's winter offensive in Hesse. When he learned that it was halted he became less eager to negotiate. All along he was afraid that Pitt would not allow France suitable terms. The Austrian alliance was a problem: he promised Starhemberg that he would let him see all communications sent to London. He used the three-month delay in the spring to engage Spain more closely. Of crucial importance, on 2 June he pledged to Grimaldi that he would introduce Spanish concerns into the Anglo-French negotiation if Spain were to agree to a military alliance. It seems that the council of state was not informed of this amazing commitment. Even so, three council members voted against forming any sort of alliance with Spain at this time lest it undermine the chances of peace. On 22 June word arrived from Madrid that approved the Grimaldi–Choiseul agreement.

Choiseul probably believed he was keeping his options open, but he had manoeuvred himself into a corner. Any offer from London granting terms advantageous enough to justify breaking his agreement with the Spanish would have to come quickly, but the British would certainly not give back Cape Breton, and how quickly could a substitute location for an *abri* be agreed upon? All the while Grimaldi was reminding him of his pledge to resolve Spanish concerns in the negotiation, a proceeding that, as Choiseul knew, the British would consider intolerable. To back away from the pledge would put at hazard the Bourbon family pact, which Louis XV warmly desired, and would deprive France of a possible military ally. Moreover, Choiseul was fully aware that the Austrians were not inclined towards peace. With the window closing, he chose alliances over peace. France's mid-July response was careful to protect Austrian claims to conquered Prussian Rhineland territories (terms differing from those he had dictated on 17 June), and the memoir stating that Spanish grievances must be included in the Anglo-French negotiation was sent off to Bussy. Choiseul cannot have reasonably expected a British reaction very different from the one he received, but he fulminated about Pitt's reply and resolved to continue the war, announcing this decision to key French ambassadors secretly on 30 July.

Shrewdly he kept on negotiating with Britain, both to delay any British military initiatives until the campaigning season was over and to see what better terms might be obtained. Actually, by the end of August the British cabinet granted most of what France appeared to want, but Choiseul had not allowed enough time for the British cabinet to gain Pitt's acquiescence. Practically everyone in France had wanted the war brought to an end except himself, Louis XV, Pompadour, and the Austrian and Spanish ambassadors. Having kept the negotiation entirely under his control, he was able to throw the blame for the rupture on the British by publishing his *Mémoire historique sur la négociation*. It was a tremendously successful piece of propaganda, in Britain as well as in France. At the same time he cleverly raised special contributions for the navy and urged Spain to begin hostilities as soon as possible.

The significance of 1762

At the start of 1762 Britain's outlook seemed bleak. The British ministers faced war with Spain and the danger that Portugal, a country whose independence was of vital commercial and strategic importance, would be overrun. According to well-established patterns of trade and traffic Lisbon 'could be considered an English Atlantic port'.[3] The cabinet quickly decided that 6,000 British troops must be sent to help the Portuguese army withstand a Spanish invasion. Although Prussia's situation was dire, her fate did not directly concern Britain, and in north-west Germany the position remained stalemated, but the immense cost of Prince Ferdinand's army had become a great burden, and the expense of trying to defend Portugal now had to be added to it.

France's situation, however, was worse. The French knew that a mighty expedition was on the way to Martinique. Choiseul pretended to make light of the possibility that it could be conquered, but he knew that its loss would be devastating. All French trading centres in India had been

---

[3] Ian K. Steele, *The English Atlantic, 1775–1740: An Exploration of Communication and Community* (New York and Oxford, 1986), p. 72.

seized, and without a naval force further overseas losses were inevitable. Although he intended to use the French army in Germany aggressively, Choiseul had to wonder whether George III and his new set of ministers might be indifferent to Hanover. How much would they give up for its evacuation? As he had done in early 1759, he sketched out a desperate plan to invade the British Isles. Considering the weakness of France's naval forces, it depended upon not only a high level of deception but also a degree of operational coordination which could not possibly be achieved in the sailing-ship era. Choiseul was a skilled propagandist and clever foreign minister, but an execrable war minister whose instinct to gamble overwhelmed his strategic judgement. In any case, before the slightest move could be made for executing a literally fantastic invasion plan, France's war prospects sank to the bottom. On 5 January 1762 the Empress Elizabeth died and was replaced by Peter III, who completely reversed Russian policy. On 15 February Martinique surrendered, and soon afterwards all French controlled islands of the eastern Caribbean were in British hands. Austria, financially exhausted, revealed that she was ready to quit the war, and within a few weeks there were strong indications that Spain's invasion of Portugal was likely to falter. It had quickly become obvious that Choiseul's decision to extend the war was militarily disastrous.

Yet, thanks to the Bute administration's strategic and diplomatic policies France did not suffer the full consequences. The British government's offensive strategy was aimed not at French possessions, but at Spanish. The Martinique expedition was an exception – aimed at a key French colony – but it had been launched by Pitt. Moreover, amazingly, the Bute administration was prepared to abort it: the commanders of the Havana expedition were given orders to take away the troops if the conquest was not yet complete when they arrived. These orders never became controversial because Martinique surrendered before Albemarle and Pocock arrived.

All things considered and despite a high risk of failure, the decision to attack Havana was nevertheless justifiable, because the ministers had to anticipate Spanish success in Portugal. By taking Havana the British would have an asset important enough to compel Madrid to withdraw. Manila was another matter. As the Spanish entrepôt in the Far East it was an eye-catching target and the Spanish would be shocked by its loss, but eighteen months were likely to pass before news of its conquest could reach London to influence a peace negotiation. Manila's commercial value to the British, as officials of the East India Company pointed out, was very doubtful, and in any case there was little prospect of its being retained after the return of peace. Two arguments in favour of the project were that the required naval force was already in the Indian Ocean and that much of the military expense could be shouldered by the East India Company. The same advantages, however, would apply to an attack on the Mascarene Islands. Admiral Samuel Cornish, in response to a request from Pitt, had already worked out a plan for attacking Mauritius when Colonel William Draper arrived at Madras with orders changing the objective to Manila. Mauritius was recognized as strategically valuable for securing East India commerce – when the British captured the island in 1810 they held on to it – and word of its capture would almost certainly reach London and Paris in time for any peace negotiation. But Île de France (Mauritius) was of course French. The Bute administration, focusing on Spanish objectives, chose Manila. The enterprise was backed by Lord Anson who called upon East India Company officials more than once to persuade them to support it. In his younger days he had captured a silver galleon from Mexico in the Philippine Islands and acquired an immense fortune thereby. Undoubtedly he believed that this was a useful sort of wartime mission. So did Draper, who proposed the scheme to the cabinet with himself as its military commander.

The operation moved forward quickly. Draper, promoted to brigadier general, left England in late January and arrived at Madras on 10 July. Governor Pigot and Admiral Cornish accomplished the preparations in just twenty days, and, despite navigational hazards, nearly all the ships – eight of the line, three frigates, two Indiamen – reached Manila Bay on 23 September. It was learned that the Spanish did not even know that war had been declared; no cannon were mounted on the city's walls, which in any case were not formidable. Draper therefore decided upon a direct attack. On the 25th troops landed unopposed at a beach about a mile away. Despite a couple of days of heavy surf a battery of eight 24-pounder naval guns was established at a range of 300 yards and ready to open fire on the 29th. The assault force consisted of 1,960 men including 679 seamen, 338 marines and 780 Asians (mostly sepoys) plus the soldiers – too few to perform both guard duty and siege preparation. The men became fatigued, and the local natives were absolutely hostile. Nevertheless, a suitable breach was made, and on the morning of 6 October the men poured through it.

The city was at the attackers' mercy and they did not show any. Pillaging continued for thirty-six hours until Draper obtained a ransom of $4 million dollars (almost £1 million) from the governing archbishop in return for halting the depredations. Half of the sum was to be paid immediately, the other half in bills on Madrid. Draper's own profit was huge. Cornish made a small fortune from the ransom and his share of the capture of the *Santissima Trinidad* (filled with goods from China) as well as stores captured in the Cavite navy yard. Prize money shares for the ordinary soldiers and sailors were somewhat larger than those awarded at Havana. The ships, most of which were in bad condition when the expedition set forth, benefited greatly from overhaul at Cavite, but the East India Company, even though it received by prior agreement a third of the ransom money, was never adequately compensated for its expenses. Draper sailed in a sloop of war on 11 November and made a remarkably fast voyage home but did not arrive until 16 April 1763. Mainly because Manila's hinterland was controlled by extremely hostile and well-organized Filipino guerrillas, there was no hope of profitable trading, and in any case the conquest occurred too late to be legitimately retained. Madrid, notwithstanding repeated demands from London, never paid the balance of the ransom.

The choice of Manila was in accord with the Bute administration's policy of avoiding offensive operations against the French. Although Prince Ferdinand would continue to combat the French army effectively, Bute's secret apology to Choiseul after Ferdinand's victory at Wilhelmsthal suggests that he would have preferred to see no offensive action taken against the French army in Germany. This one-sided approach to strategy was matched by the pattern of British diplomacy.

It was soft against France, stiff against Spain. From the outset Bute aimed to provide France with terms so attractive that she would eagerly make peace. Consequently, while Britain's forces were steadily winning in 1762 her government was negotiating with France as if losing. At the same time, Spain's negotiating demands were ignored: British policy depended upon France to compel Spain to make peace, offering terms to France so advantageous that Choiseul would not wish to lose them.

From the outset Bute's policy of appeasing France had been supported by Newcastle and Bedford. Newcastle's principal motive was fear that the Treasury could not meet the additional expense of a war with Spain. Bedford expressed his defeatism in predictions that French arms would prevail, and demonstrated his pacifism by suggesting that French power was either not dangerous – he was inclined to Francophilia – or that nothing could be done about it. Objecting to the proposal to deny the fishery to France, he wrote in July 1761:

[T]he endeavouring to drive France entirely out of any naval power is fighting against nature, and . . . must excite all the naval powers in Europe to enter into a confederacy against us, as adopting a system viz.

*that of a monopoly of all naval power . . . [which would be] as
dangerous to the liberties of Europe as that of Louis XIV was,
which drew almost all Europe upon his back.*[4]

This statement, a criticism of Pitt, has been frequently quoted and sounds reasonable and admirable as a reminder that a victorious power should wisely consider peace rather than try to crush an opponent. But Bedford was also echoing a common theme of French propaganda. Not even Pitt envisioned a complete monopoly. The policy of British governments before, during and after the Seven Years War was to keep the Royal Navy preponderant while treating neutral powers as gently as circumstances allowed. It was understood that in wartime the ships of those powers would have to choose between the profits of neutral shipping or, in alliance with France, a pounding by the guns of the Royal Navy. Pitt and Bedford despised each other not just because of personal antipathy but because Pitt believed that France was a very dangerous enemy whose naval capabilities ought to be reduced and Bedford did not. Lord Bute did not share Bedford's fears of military defeat by France – if anything, he feared British victories – but he agreed with Newcastle that the war had become too expensive.

Here lay the pragmatic rationale for ending the war promptly. Britain's annual war expenses had become much greater than France's. There were two major causes: the British were maintaining a fully mobilized navy while the reduced French navy cost very little, and Britain's expenses in Germany were much greater than France's. In 1761 Newcastle remarked that in Germany Britain was paying six times France's expenditure – probably an exaggeration, but four times might have been a reasonable estimate. A summary of expenditure on British armed forces in 1761 showed that the navy cost £3,817,701, the army in North America £1,371,862 and Prince Ferdinand's army £4,802,035.[5] Although figures are lacking for estimating French war expense at this time, it probably amounted to less than half the British figure.

British advocates of peace talked of national bankruptcy, but there was no financial crisis. As will be seen in a moment, British finances could support an ongoing war. It has been suggested that Parliament and the public would not accept the expense. Yet even Newcastle, while casting an anxious eye on the national debt like everyone else, admitted that there

---

[4] Bedford to Bute, 9 July 1761, in John B. Hattendorf *et al.*, eds, *British Naval Documents, 1204–1960* NRS (Aldershot, 1993), pp. 332–3.

[5] In Newcastle's papers, BL Add. 33,048, ff. 158, 172–4.

was money enough to support new loans, and in May 1762 he was so eager to sustain the German war that he proposed a supplementary vote of credit of £2 million instead of £1 million. Clearly, the dispute between the duke and Grenville at that time was about strategy, not money.

Grenville's preferred strategy was similar to Mauduit's in *Considerations*: to wind down the effort in Germany and concentrate on hostilities upon and across the seas where Britain with naval supremacy could do as she pleased. The cost would be limited. Grenville might even have concluded that new expeditions would not be necessary, as the government could have issued a simple declaration saying that Britain would continue to hold all West Indian conquests indefinitely.

The problem was how to end the costly German war. Bute, Bedford and George III hoped to end it in 1762 but were forced to see the impracticality of doing so. Clearly, they were determined not to allow it to continue into 1763, and most Englishmen agreed. Bute's solution was to make peace with France, but there was a possible alternative approach. At the end of April, Joseph Yorke reported the French to be saying that Peter III's reversal of policy meant that there would 'certainly be an end put to the War in Germany, either by the Czar or by Negotiations with England'. He commented:

for my own part I should like the first way best, that is to say that the Czar should help us to drive the French out of Germany, and then we begin to negotiate; that would make short work of the Negotiation, and we might without difficulty I believe prescribe the Terms.[6]

Presumably he did not mention the possibility of asking not just Russia but also Prussia to assist Ferdinand's army because he knew that good relations with Prussia were no longer possible. For Bute had made nothing out of the stunning event at St Petersburg: instead of suggesting to Frederick II that he might think of lending assistance to Ferdinand against the French (the kind of move Choiseul would have made), he persisted in urging him to go on his knees to Vienna. Bute's hatred of Frederick and strong prejudice against European involvement also infected his treatment of Russia. Joseph Yorke, when he wrote his letter, did not realize that Peter III had also been offended. In July, Newcastle remarked to Hardwicke: 'What a Confusion have these new Ministers brought things to, by their Ignorance? When, if they had taken our Advice, and availed themselves of Russia and Prussia . . . we might have had a general Peace

[6] Yorke to his eldest brother, 27 April 1762, BL Add. 35,366, fo. 70.

by the End of the Campaign.'[7] Perhaps Newcastle and Yorke were too optimistic, but the existence of a possible alternative should not be ignored.

As the months passed, getting Spain to accept peace became the main problem, for both London and Versailles. With Russia out of the war, Austria exhausted, and the prospect of Spanish success in Portugal disappearing, Choiseul was eager to accept Bute's terms, but he was reluctant to force the Spanish king to quit a war that he had encouraged him to fight. Hardwicke believed that peace was as far away as ever. Then the news from Havana arrived. Choiseul thereupon presented Madrid with an ultimatum along with a gift of the remainder of Louisiana. A British military victory had thus brought an end to diplomatic delay.

The post-war significance of 1762 arises almost entirely from actions taken by the Bute administration. First, there was an eclipse of British influence in Europe. Pitt had not wanted to risk a confrontation with Russia by sending a fleet to the Baltic. Newcastle also, as Hardwicke reminded Bute, had wanted Britain to be able to count on good relations with Prussia and Russia 'in war and in peace'.[8] Bute and George III spurned Prussia and sowed suspicion in Russia. Secondly, Britain no longer tried to avoid offending Spain. Pitt was much annoyed by Carlos III's belligerence, but the Bute administration went further, adopting a policy of pointed hostility towards Spain which had lasting consequences. Thirdly, Bute's peace negotiation left France's commercial and maritime resources substantially intact. As Pitt, commenting on the peace, observed:

France is chiefly, if not solely, to be dreaded by us in the light of a maritime and commercial power . . . [and] by restoring to her all the valuable West-India islands, and by our concessions in the Newfoundland fishery, we had given to her the means of recovering her prodigious losses and of becoming once more formidable to us at sea.[9]

British arms had captured all the French islands of the eastern Caribbean. The decision to return them could be ranked, as Pitt appeared to rank it, alongside the fishery concessions. Fourthly, in the year 1762 the British government acquired a vast expanse of North American territory, stretching all the way to the Mississippi River and including Florida and the Gulf

---

[7] Newcastle to Hardwicke, 29 July 1762, BL Add. 32,941, fo. 108.

[8] On 28 July 1762, Yorke, *Hardwicke*, III, 405.

[9] Quoted in Baugh, 'Great Britain's "Blue-Water" Policy' (cited in Chapter 1), p. 45, and Scott, 'Importance', p. 17.

coast. This territory became British because the French and Spanish, forced to yield something, chose to give it up and the Bute administration accepted it. The implications, immediate and distant, were profound.

A fifth significance of 1762 was its impact on British domestic politics. Bute's single-minded pursuit of peace pushed the limits of constitutionality and carved deep political wounds. He sought concessions for France that more than once put him at odds with his entire cabinet, and he twice arranged concessions without cabinet knowledge. By appointing the Duke of Bedford to complete the negotiation of the preliminaries he stirred a public outcry. His fixed intention was to prevent parliamentary review of the preliminaries, and he took the startling step of appointing Henry Fox to manage the vote. As Newcastle observed and Hardwicke agreed, the ministry had chosen to gain parliamentary acceptance of its peace terms by *power*, by which they meant the king's patronage power to bestow or deny, as managed by Bute and Fox.[10] Hardwicke did not think this method would succeed, but it did. Bute guessed correctly that the opponents of the preliminaries would be divided and that the stark choice of peace or no peace joined with fear of royal anger, as exhibited in the dismissal of Devonshire, would prevail. Many commentators have seen Bute's end as justifying his means, and it is true that in a parliamentary government the politics of fashioning a negotiated peace were complex. Yet moderate men viewed Bute's conduct with abhorrence, and it is interesting that neither he nor George III gave any sign of thinking or caring about the political consequences of what they were doing. In fact, they made those consequences worse by abetting Fox's extreme purge, high and low, of those who opposed their will, the litmus test being how a member of Parliament voted on the preliminaries. This was simply persecution – unnecessary because Newcastle and his friends and followers had been crushingly defeated. Members could only conclude that any opposition to the government's measures in future would be severely punished. The political system that had reached compromises to win the war's great successes was replaced by one dominated by the king and his favourite under which dissent could be very costly.

Outcomes: peace terms, finances, navies, Spain and France

By the treaty of Paris, 10 February 1763, France ceded to Great Britain all Canada including the Great Lakes, the Ohio territory and Acadia (the

[10] Yorke, *Hardwicke*, III, 424.

maritime provinces). French vessels were allowed to fish on the New-foundland banks and in the Gulf of St Lawrence, in the latter no closer than 9 miles from land. Unfortified French possession of the islands of St Pierre and Miquelon was allowed for shelter, drying fish and habitations. (The islands are a department of France to this day.) Britain acquired Louisiana east of the Mississippi River, including Mobile on the Gulf coast. France kept New Orleans and the delta area south of the Iberville River, but with a proviso that British vessels must have equal access to the Mississippi from the sea. In a separate agreement France ceded her remaining portion of Louisiana to Spain. From Spain in exchange for Cuba Britain received Florida, which included the peninsula and the Gulf coast to the Mississippi delta. All French and Spanish inhabitants of British North America were given liberty to practise the Roman Catholic religion. Spain was required to leave Portugal as if untouched. Belle-Île was returned to France, and Minorca returned to England. The seaward fortifications of Dunkirk were to be demolished according to the treaty of Aix-la-Chapelle. In Germany the lands of the Elector of Hanover and his allies were restored to George III while Prussian territories near the Rhine were to be evacuated. Mere evacuation would have allowed occupation by Austria, but Halifax, as secretary of state, worked out a separate agreement with Versailles that helped to solve Prussia's problem. In India there was a return to the status quo at the beginning of 1749 (before Dupleix's acquisitions); the French also acknowledged Muhammed Ali Khan and Salabat Jang as lawful rulers of the Carnactic and the Deccan respectively. In Bengal the French were allowed to trade but forbidden to erect fortifications or maintain troops. In Africa, Britain returned Gorée but kept Senegal. The British were allowed to cut logwood and build store-houses in Honduras, but could not build forts. It was in the West Indies that France received the most generous terms. Martinique, Guadeloupe and Marie Galante were returned, and the Neutral Island of St Lucia was assigned to France. Britain gained undisputed possession of Dominica, St Vincent and Tobago as well as Grenada.[11]

Some controversial concessions to France did not prove to be of great importance. Fishing inside the Gulf, already declining before the war compared to the Newfoundland fishery, continued at reduced levels. New

---

[11] The official treaty was recorded in French. Corbett prints a full text of the definitive treaty in English (II, 377–90). He also describes Halifax's arrangement, for which Frederick II was grateful (p. 364).

Orleans ended up under Spanish rule and was not a British concern except that the Iberville River boundary was a nuisance. Frenchmen at New Orleans had ways of making Britain's access to the Mississippi River impracticable, and British post-war attempts to make the Iberville River into a canal were (not surprisingly) thwarted by natural obstacles. Since the Spanish usually welcomed French settlers in Louisiana, Acadians migrated there in considerable numbers, first directly from their original home, then from France where they disliked the meagre plots of land made available to them; also they were socially reluctant to assimilate. The last wave of these people, who came to be called Cajuns, arrived in the mid-1780s. With respect to commerce the most important treaty result was one that the British retrieved in the definitive version: the clause forbidding a French military presence in Bengal. In general no one denied that France had lost the war. Although Choiseul took credit for the peace terms he secured, they were no better than those he missed obtaining in August 1761 – arguably worse.

An early war of revenge was not possible, chiefly for financial reasons. The monarchy had managed to support its army during the war's final three years by curtailing the naval budget and postponing payments on countless bills and other short-term obligations. The crisis of late 1759 had constricted currency, which inhibited tax collection. Bertin, the new controller-general, reported that many people were unable to pay the one-third in silver that some levies required; he claimed that increased taxes on tobacco and other consumables were self-defeating because they diminished consumption. A key fact, he informed the council of state, was that only about half the proceeds from existing taxes and loans actually reached the treasury. In short, the usual financial methods no longer functioned. He therefore recommended limiting the war effort to the least costly operations and seriously thinking of peace. Choiseul – the two men were rivals – cut the navy's budget but was unwilling to make peace. The king sided with Choiseul and therefore could no longer avoid asking the parlement of Paris to approve substantial new taxes.

Bertin negotiated long and hard with the parlement's leaders. Just when he thought he had gained their assent the *parlementaires*, on 18 February 1760, demanded an account of the king's expenses. Everyone knew that Louis XV had bluntly refused to provide such an accounting in 1756. Berryer angrily remarked that the parlement of Paris wanted to be like an English one, and Pompadour taunted Bertin by a furious note: '[Y]ou see how wrong you are to be honest with them; I cannot repeat too much that it is necessary to deal with them with an iron bar.'[12] But Bertin could not ignore reality. He patiently resumed negotiations in late February and obtained registration without need for a *lit de justice*. Plenty of trouble remained, however. The provincial parlements opposed the new taxes with greater resolution than Paris had shown. During the summer of 1760 the parlements at Rouen (Normandy), Rennes (Brittany) and Dijon (Burgundy) were particularly vociferous and intransigent. The king was firm. When a deputation from Normandy came to Versailles on 3 August Louis XV responded: 'I am your master, I should punish you for the audacity of your principles: return to Rouen, register my edicts without delay. I want to be obeyed.'[13] They did not obey, and the edicts were registered by royal command. The new taxes were a third *vingtième* and double *capitation* which, to gain acceptance, Bertin confined to the years 1760 and 1761. By these taxes France kept the war going.

In mid-June 1761, when the peace negotiation was in earnest, the royal council issued a declaration that the same taxes must be extended for two more years. To avoid an avalanche of publicized remonstrances which could undermine France's negotiating position as well as damage French credit in Holland, Bertin asked the king to resort immediately to a *lit de justice*. It was executed on 21 July; on this occasion protest in the parlement of Paris was muted, partly because Choiseul had indicated to the *parlementaires* that he would not oppose measures against the Jesuits but also because peace seemed to be at hand. (The Jansenists and other opponents of strict Roman Catholicism in the parlement wanted to see the power of the Jesuits eclipsed.) When the estates of Normandy objected, the king thought fit to write a letter, read at Rouen on 5 August, in which he condescended to mention his policy and asked for help in ending the war more favourably by extending the taxes, thus 'letting our enemies see that we are in condition to resist them'.[14] The parlement at Rouen did not know that Choiseul had already decided against peace.

The extension of the *vingtièmes* and *capitations* supported continuation of the war, but these were Extraordinary taxes, supposedly levied for emergencies and not to persist in time of peace. In early 1763, after the peace treaty was signed, Bertin recognized that the third *vingtième* and second *capitation* must expire, but he proposed to make the first *vingtième* perpetual and to extend the second to 1768; he also called for

[12] Alimento, *Réformes fiscales*, pp. 104–5.
[13] Kwass, *Privilege*, p. 176.
[14] Swann, *Politics*, pp. 190–1; Kwass, *Privilege*, pp. 179–80.

an updating of the land assessments on which these taxes were based. This programme was presented to the parlement of Paris in April. Bertin again asked the king for a speedy *lit de justice*, which was executed on 1 June. Protest in Paris nevertheless continued, and provincial parlements' protests were heard throughout the realm. Many provincial members considered royal bankruptcy preferable. Why, they asked, should landowners and small country proprietors be taxed to pay off Parisian bond-holders, monied men and privileged officeholders? The parlement of Rouen requested a royal budget, which was of course refused, and soon issued an *arrêt de défense* forbidding collection of the disputed taxes in Normandy. Some other provincial estates also took this unprecedented step. It was a blatant challenge to royal authority, and was accompanied by claims about 'liberty'. This crisis of 1763 was widespread and publicized; many of the remonstrances were printed. In the end Bertin obtained the taxes, but not the land survey. Choiseul pocketed the fiscal success and used Bertin's unpopularity to force his resignation.

Still, these taxes could not cope with the mass of accumulated short-term debt. It included 72 million livres in frozen requisitions; 42 million in naval and colonial bills left unpaid for years; many millions more in artillery and ordnance bills; and a mass of bills, estimated at 90 million, issued in Canada. The last category was reduced by a commission appointed to investigate and punish Canadian officials, of whom fifty were arrested. The commission assumed that their bills were either fraudulent or padded with excess charges. Its calculations ignored wartime shipping costs, inflation and losses caused by delayed payment. Officials were accused of profiting privately, and undoubtedly they had done so, but this was a practice that was generally overlooked. Not in this case: Bigot, the Canadian intendant, was given a death sentence on 23 August 1763, though it was not carried out. The commission achieved the purposes for which it was constituted: the Canadian debt was reduced to 37.6 million livres and blame for the loss of Canada was diverted from the government at Versailles to allegedly corrupt Canadian administrators.

As the years passed it became clear that the monarchy could not meet its financial obligations. Some of the bills were converted to long-term loans which paid a below-market interest rate. New short-term paper was substituted for old; much of the new paper eventually became almost worthless. An expert has described the proceedings as 'a long bankruptcy on the instalment plan'.[15] Because the French treasury was continually

---

[15] Le Goff, 'How to Finance', pp. 378–9, 396–7, 409.

scraping an empty barrel it was impossible to avoid dependence on financiers possessing their own resources like Laborde (see Chapter 12). The French state's credit became more intertwined with financiers' private business than ever. In the late 1780s this played a central role in undermining the monarchy and bringing on the French Revolution; the word 'liberty', uttered in provincial parlements in the 1760s, would acquire extraordinary power.

An extremely large short-term debt at the war's end also confronted the British government. The navy's unfunded debt peaked above £7 million in 1763, mainly because it was suddenly swollen by the charge for seamen's wages as ships were being paid off. Some of these ships had been stationed abroad and their crews' wages had not been fully paid for years. There were also unpaid bills for provisions and stores. Unlike the situation in France, these bills did not represent an accumulation of many years. Throughout the war such bills had been paid 'in course', that is, in an unalterable sequence from the date of issue. After a specified number of months the bills began to earn interest. Since payment was assured they were assignable with confidence and merchants could obtain cash by selling them at a discount (which varied according to an estimated time of payment).

Military and naval spending rose from £7.3 million in 1757 to £16 million in 1761, while revenue increased only from £8 million to £9.6 million, so the revenue from taxes was obviously insufficient.[16] Long-term borrowing was necessary, and without doubt long-term loans were the foundation of British war finance. The system, which dated from the 1690s, was founded on interest-paying annuities backed by Parliament. Some investors looked for bonds that the government could not choose to redeem, but Treasury officials were reluctant to issue them: they wanted to retain the option of calling them in after the war when interest rates fell. Every long-term loan issue had to have a tax assigned to pay the interest, and the most painful decisions, subject to debate in the House of Commons, involved selecting a suitable source. Usually an excise tax was imposed on an item of consumption. Long-term annuities and other securities could be sold on the London stock exchange, which began in Jonathan's Coffee House. Prices fluctuated according to fortunes of war and expectations of peace. (The terms 'bull' and 'bear' were already in use when the war began.) In the Seven Years War there was almost always plenty of money in London to purchase new issues. It arose chiefly from profits of British

[16] Mitchell and Deane, *Abstract*, pp. 387–8, 398.

commerce, but over a quarter came from abroad, much of it funnelled through Amsterdam. Parliament voted £3 million in 1763 to convert navy bills on which 5 per cent interest was being paid to 4 per cent annuities.[17] A further funding of navy debt was approved by Parliament in 1765 at 3 per cent. Investors purchased these securities despite the fact that the national debt had swollen to £134 million from £72 million before the war.[18]

As First Lord of the Treasury, Newcastle had no great expertise in finance, but he could rely on a knowledgeable Treasury secretary, James West. Monied men in the City trusted Newcastle, and West was in regular contact with them. Among them was Samson Gideon, born in Barbados of Spanish Jewish lineage, and noted for his market wisdom. Newcastle and West valued his advice, but the finances of the British state did not depend on him; the City's wealth was well distributed, and the Bank of England, founded in 1694, was a stabilizing element.

There was one task that Newcastle did not handle well – administering military expenses in Germany. Except for supplying ordnance, the British army, unlike the navy, did not possess established systems for procurement. Providing flour, meat, fuel, fodder and forage was the Treasury's responsibility and had to be carried out by contractors. In parts of the world where there were garrisons, contractors had learned the requirements. In North America, after initial incompetence, the contracts worked reasonably well. But Germany was a new kind of challenge. Supplying a very large army consisting of German and British troops deployed in unexpected locations in an unfamiliar theatre, and often on the move, posed unprecedented problems. There was a 'shortage of honest men with the necessary triple qualification: skill at business, competence in German, and tolerance for discomfort'.[19] Germans without proper qualifications often had to be employed. Money was provided plentifully, and everyone knew that the main concern was to make sure the troops were supplied. Prince Ferdinand's complaints, which alternated between reporting shortages and criticizing ridiculous waste, were echoed by Pitt, and Newcastle was naturally frightened and wounded. The criticisms were often valid. Unfortunately, Newcastle had no head for envisaging an effective administrative structure and received more bad advice than good, so the commissariat in Germany drifted from one failed arrangement to another.

[17] Wilkinson, *British Navy and the State*, pp. 106–14.
[18] Mitchell and Deane, *Abstract*, pp. 398, 402. Most accounts at the time put the post-war national debt at £146 million.
[19] Browning, 'Newcastle and . . . Germany', 27.

On the whole, the army was well supplied, but fraud was uncontrollable and notorious. Joseph Yorke could not help thinking: 'the Maladministration . . . has disgusted every body and made this second war of Diversion a real Burthen'.[20] Thomas Pownall, formerly governor of Massachusetts, was sent to Germany in 1761 to establish a properly administered commissariat; it became operational just as the war ended. Pownall stayed on as a member of a commission charged with sorting out which claims were valid. The job took three years and saved the government millions.

The British navy remained strong in the post-war years. Despite the national debt (interest charges consumed 45 per cent of total spending) the navy received suitable funding. The First Lord of the Admiralty, John Perceval, 2nd Earl of Egmont, used the money wisely. Because a ship of the line required a major repair every twelve to fifteen years, it was estimated that the dockyards could maintain a fleet, active and reserve, of about 90 of the line. New construction was planned accordingly. Until the eve of the American Revolutionary War superiority in numbers over the navies of France and Spain combined was maintained. The Admiralty did not lose sight of the Royal Navy's enormous refitting demands in wartime: it asked for considerable sums to improve dockyard facilities at Portsmouth and Plymouth.

During the war's last three years the French navy had been neglected. In 1763 the list showed 60 ships of the line, a figure that included 15 donated ships under construction. Choiseul, the naval minister, believed the number could be increased to 80 in five years. Three years later, however, there were only 62 considered fit for service. Shortage of funds was the principal reason why progress was disappointing. In April 1766 Choiseul resigned as naval minister to focus on foreign affairs. His discouragement had been deepened by the Spanish navy's slow recovery. After the fall of Havana when he was pressuring the king of Spain to make peace he had mentioned that a war of revenge could be mounted within five years. Spain and France should therefore rebuild their navies and be ready for an opportunity. Privately, however, he had his doubts: 'I assure you', he told d'Ossun, 'that if I had known what I know now, I would have been very careful not to propose to the king that a power should join the war which, by its weakness, could only bring loss and ruin to France.'[21] Because there was insufficient Spanish and French post-war naval progress Choiseul repeatedly postponed the war of revenge.

[20] Yorke to his brother Lord Royston, 27 April 1762, BL Add. 35,366, fo. 70.
[21] Choiseul to d'Ossun, 9, 20 Oct. 1762, Blart, *Rapports* p. 42.

Spain's lack of progress in the early 1760s arose almost entirely from the naval situation. The royal treasury had been able to pay the entire cost of the land campaign against Portugal from a vast reserve fund of gold and silver that had been established to cope with military emergencies, but there was no reserve to restore the navy, which had lost 12 ships of the line at Havana. By summer 1765 the Spanish navy possessed only 37 of the line. In the last half of the 1760s, however, Spain did build up her fleet, and when the British remonstrated against Spanish expulsion of their tiny garrison in the Falkland Islands Madrid considered taking strong action. Versailles could not agree. In the summer of 1770 it was found that 10 ships of the line on the French list had to be condemned and 9 needed rebuilding, and it was known that the Admiralty under Sir Edward Hawke had 16 guardships ready to be manned. In September the cabinet called for mobilizing 22 more. Although Portsmouth dockyard suffered a disastrous fire that July, which consumed most of the stores in reserve, Britain's mobilization went forward unabated; private shipyards assisted. Realizing that the French fleet and dockyards could not possibly match the British, Choiseul urged the Spanish to stand down.

Spain's naval weakness was not the only reason why France was disappointed by the Bourbon alliance. The French had been hoping that it would serve to increase their exports to Spanish markets. They were soon dismayed to find that Carlos III, eager to build up domestic industry, was allowing his officials to obstruct their trade. Over the years French merchants had gained a privileged position in Spain, but an article in the *pacte de famille* stated that they should have equal standing with their Spanish counterparts, and this article was being used to take away the special privileges. After two years during which French exports made scant progress Choiseul's patience evaporated. France, he wrote to d'Ossun, had a right to expect Spain to open her markets, domestic and imperial, to French goods and close them to the British. Although the alliance required France to go to war for Spain's sake, he commented, Spain would 'only be a dead body in wartime, with forces it would be absurd to count on, and which will only play a role by their losses in coming wars'.[22] He told d'Ossun that since Spain would be useless in a war of revenge, the main concern now was to make sure of French advantages in Spanish markets.

---

[22] Choiseul to d'Ossun, December 1764, Scott, 'Destins parallèles', p. 216; also Brown, *Studies in the History of Spain*, p. 49.

French producers could supply many of Spain's needs, but the Spanish had become used to receiving imports from Britain. During the peace negotiations Carlos III had tried his best to get existing commercial treaties with Britain nullified, but the Bute administration declared resolutely that the treaties must stand. It may seem strange that the British, after hammering the Spanish militarily and negotiating with them obstinately, could suppose that treaties thus insisted upon would be of any practical value. But the history of Anglo-Spanish relations was filled with instances in which commercial treaties imposed by military and diplomatic pressure had produced beneficial results for British merchants. The underlying reasons were Spanish preference for many kinds of British goods and British credit facilities. Carlos III probably would have preferred to see French goods replace British, but it was very difficult to make this happen. The period of British occupation of Havana was an eye-opener. With British credit, supplies from North America, and slaves from Jamaica, the Cuban economy suddenly blossomed. For the Spanish authorities it was an amazing yet disturbing scene. The king of Spain had more to think about than the admission of French goods to his dominions.

In the realm of strategy Choiseul's immediate post-war concern was defence of the Windward Islands, which had been so quickly lost and fortunately returned. He knew the French navy would remain inferior and had no reason to think that fortified garrisons could hold out, so he decided to prepare means for a counter-strike by troops located nearby. A large colony of white settlers in French Guiana (suitably upwind of the vulnerable islands) could provide such a force. Noting how many recent immigrants to the British American colonies had come from Germany, he ordered handbills to be printed in German and other languages as well as French for recruiting colonists. These announcements advertised Guiana in glowing terms and promised that the French government would support emigrants, including wives and children, for two and a half years. It would cover the cost of their travel to Rochefort as well as their transatlantic voyage. The planned social composition of the settlement accorded with Enlightenment ideals; there were to be no slaves. Although the proposed site near the mouth of the Kourou river was just 5 degrees north of the equator, many educated men approved the project, some of whom had experienced life in the tropics. The planning was hurried and faulty. Preliminary preparations at the site were made late, and settlers began arriving before responsible authorities did. Most important, the number of recruited colonists was far too large. It is estimated that 17,000 persons walked across France to Rochefort and nearby ports where officials, anxious to get rid of them, promptly put them aboard vessels. The first convoy sailed on 17 May 1763, and by July 1764 almost 14,000 people were at Kourou. The layout of the settlement was too confined and sanitation was a serious problem. Water and food soon became contaminated, and within a few months 9,000 were dead. The lethal disease was not malaria or yellow fever but typhoid fever which the immigrants brought with them; tropical dysentery then prevented recovery. Official blame for the catastrophe fell on everyone except the planners at Versailles. Choiseul claimed that he had been given bad advice, undoubtedly true, but he had been in a hurry and the size of the venture was his idea. Managing this large-scale venture, even if it had been destined for a temperate climate, was far beyond the regime's administrative capabilities. Étienne-François Turgot, older brother of the famous economist and statesman, had been appointed governor of the colony. He was rightly criticized for not arriving in Guiana until December 1764, but his comment was correct: 'the project of sending a large number of men all at once could not have succeeded'.[23]

Choiseul's fear that the British might attack in the Caribbean was unfounded, but both sides were on edge. Successive British governments ordered naval squadrons to trouble spots, real and imagined: Turks islands, Honduras, the Gambia River, Newfoundland. George Grenville, as leading minister in 1763 and 1764, acted without hesitation. He also sought payment of money owed by the French government. The treaty of Paris had required each side to reimburse the cost of maintaining prisoners of war until they were repatriated, but in respect of French troops who became prisoners in Canada the French government would not honour the bills drawn for the purpose. Grenville demanded a payment schedule from Versailles and received one that looked satisfactory, but soon found that the French intended to reduce the value of the bills to near nothing, just like the other bills from Canada. His protests yielded nothing but promises, excuses and delays. In early 1766, after Grenville's administration had been replaced by Lord Rockingham's, the secretary of state, Henry Seymour Conway, notified the French that it was 'a National Concern . . . of a very serious nature' which, unless they agreed immediately to pay the bills at a reasonable discount, would be brought before Parliament. It was hinted that Pitt would take the matter up. Choiseul's fear of Pitt was enough to produce prompt satisfaction.[24]

[23] Rothschild, 'Horrible Tragedy', 89.
[24] Félix, 'Finances, opinion publique et diplomatie', pp. 140–51.

In 1768 Choiseul sent troops to occupy Corsica and got away with it. Information on whether the republic of Genoa had actually handed Corsica over to France was initially uncertain. Subsequently, cabinet opinion was divided on whether to dispatch a fleet because it might mean war. Cabinet members who were the Duke of Bedford's adherents kept him informed about the discussions, and he spoke with the French ambassador; as a result Choiseul knew that it was safe to proceed with an otherwise risky move. In all other cases, however, the government adhered to a policy of prompt and vigorous response. When it looked as if the French were gathering forces in the Mascarene Islands for an attack on India in the later 1760s, British countermeasures were timely, as they were in the Falkland Islands crisis.

Britain and North America

Lord Bute resigned on 8 April 1763. He was tired and frustrated by the day-to-day burdens of office and felt that he had completed his great work, the achievement of peace. He had also been recently denounced for allowing unnecessarily large fees to the underwriters of a loan. Perhaps his Treasury honestly miscalculated the impact of peace on the market, but the transaction appeared scandalous. Worse, the loan's interest was to be covered by an excise tax on cider. The bill allowed excise commissioners (whom the public reviled) to enforce it by entering private dwellings and imposing penalties. The West Country where cider was produced erupted in violent protests, and when the House of Commons debated the tax Pitt was in his best form and made the most of the sanctity of an Englishman's dwelling.

The circumstances of the loan were sharply dissected in *The North Briton* Nos 42 and 43, the weekly publication which had been attacking Bute for months. But it was *The North Briton* No. 45, published on 25 April after Bute's resignation, that changed British political history. With biting sarcasm and invective its author, John Wilkes, attacked the King's Speech of 19 April. The speech (upon the closing of Parliament) had bragged about the peace treaty. It spoke of 'the happy effects which the several allies of my crown have derived from this salutary measure', and mentioned that it helped the king of Prussia obtain satisfying terms. Aware that Bute had in reality tried to obstruct Prussian success, Wilkes asked: 'What strain of insolence, therefore, is it in a minister to lay claim to what he is conscious all his efforts tended to prevent?' As for the speech's claim that the peace was 'beneficial' to the English people,

No. 45 pointed out: 'All our most valuable conquests were agreed to be restored, and the East India company would have been infallibly ruined' if the definitive treaty had not set matters right. Although Wilkes stated at the outset that the King's Speech was understood to be written by the ministry, this did not shield him. Bute's resignation had made George III distraught, and No. 45 made him angry – partly because of the implied insults to the royal personage, but also because it denigrated the peace treaty of which his 'dearest Friend' was immensely proud. Grenville, who replaced Bute at the Treasury, moved quickly to have Wilkes arrested for seditious libel and sent to the Tower – too quickly because Wilkes was apprehended under a General Warrant and the arrest was mismanaged. Wilkes had the wit and daring to make the most of it. There is no question that the language in the paper was outrageous, and according to law as it then stood it merited prosecution for libel. But prosecution was complicated because Wilkes was a member of Parliament.

That the famous No. 45 was a response to the court's inflated claims about the peace treaty, and that seven earlier numbers of *The North Briton* had attacked the peace preliminaries, are facts not generally known. It is the arrest of Wilkes that is remembered, for very good reasons. His legal contestations combined with his success in politically energizing an enlarging urban middle class under the banner of 'liberty' had lasting importance. The London mob was far from new in English politics, but Wilkite crowds were different: they were literate and they became organized. They added an unsettling dimension to the complexities of governing and of political affiliation at a time when calm vision and deliberation were much needed.

Grenville's secretaries of state were Egremont (his brother-in-law) and Halifax. Everyone considered this administration too narrow; it was quickly called a triumvirate. Some considered it incapable of maintaining reliable majorities in Parliament, but in the near term this was not as great a problem as it appeared because potential opponents were frightened; they remembered the fate of members who had voted against the peace preliminaries. But in the long run the administration seemed vulnerable. Soon after the vote on the cider excise, which the government won, Pitt went to dinner at Devonshire House, the first time he had sat down with Newcastle and the Whig lords since his resignation. To the administration this was an ominous sign, and with the king's permission Egremont visited Hardwicke three times in hopes of recruiting him. In the first conversation on 13 May 1763, after due civilities they 'fell upon the never-failing and inexhaustible topic of Mr Wilkes', Egremont mentioning 'that his Master was extremely hurt and provoked with it'. Hardwicke, whose son Charles was Attorney-General and intimately involved, offered no opinion. In response to the main reason for the visit the old man said that he could not join the government unless his colleagues came with him. He explained why. Egremont, he said, 'knew as well as anybody that in this country there were such things as honourable connexions, which some might represent under the odious name of faction, but might really be only necessary engagements in order to carry on and effectuate right and necessary measures'. Individuals who came 'naked', he added, would 'be rendered unable to serve either the King or themselves'. In a second conversation, on 1 August, Egremont proposed that Hardwicke should become Lord President of the Council, but admitted 'that the King could not bring himself to submit to take in a party in gross'.[25] It was obvious that Hardwicke's conception of collective ministerial responsibility in which personal and political affiliation would help sustain the government was not acceptable to George III: it would threaten his 'independency'. What the king really wanted was the return of Lord Bute to high office.

On 21 August 1763 Egremont died of a stroke. Aware that the king detested Grenville, whose lengthy, lawyer-like briefings were insufferably tedious, Bute got in touch with Pitt. Their long conversation on 25 August was promising and led to a royal interview on the 27th in which it was agreed that Newcastle, Hardwicke and Devonshire would join the council but not hold key offices. Pitt would be a secretary of state. Two of Bute's adherents would keep their places. Pitt stated that he did not want anyone in his ministry who had played an important role in the peace negotiation. The king seemed content and the interview went well. Newcastle, Hardwicke and Devonshire were urgently summoned from their country houses to London. On arrival, however, they found that it was all off. Pitt's second interview with the king, on the 29th, was chilly: George III had changed his mind, and to this day no one really knows why. It is sometimes supposed that in the second interview Pitt raised his requirements, but he had no motive for doing this and all available evidence is against it. What is certain is that the king met with Bute on the 28th. Quite possibly they were troubled by the exclusion of anyone who was involved in the peacemaking. It would leave no one to inhibit a parliamentary inquiry into the negotiation, and Bute might be in danger, something George III could not bear to contemplate.

[25] Hardwicke to Newcastle, 13 May, to his son Royston, 5 Aug. 1763, Yorke, *Hardwicke*, III, 495–6, 512–16.

This may not be the correct explanation, and the episode may seem trivial – until it is considered that on this occasion a broad-based administration representing considerable wisdom might have been substituted for a narrow one under Grenville to which the king reverted, and that Grenville's administration went on to enact the most momentous legislation in the history of Anglo-American relations. Admittedly, the broad-based administration, if installed, might not have lasted – six weeks later Hardwicke was confined to his bed by a fatal cancer, dying on 6 March 1764, and Devonshire, only 44, died in early October 1764 – but George III might not have felt that his only choice afterwards was to stick with Grenville.

Important groundwork for Grenville's American measures was laid down at the end of 1762 when it was decided that 10,000 regular troops should be stationed across the Atlantic. The decision was made by the king and Bute. There would be twenty battalions in America; they would carry a full complement of officers but a reduced number of troops. Ample evidence reveals that George III immediately and eagerly engaged in awarding posts to particular officers and deciding which regiments that had been added during the war would remain active. Many army officers sat in Parliament, and if there were 85 regiments instead of 67 (as in 1749), fewer officers would be disappointed by demobilization. This would mean a considerable expansion of royal patronage and also of the military budget. On grounds of expense Newcastle thought the 'Court Plan for the Army' should be opposed, as did most Tories, but when the estimates were debated on 4 March 1763 worries about expense were diminished by a hint from the administration that the cost of these battalions would be borne by American colonists. Besides, Pitt spoke out in favour of the plan, arguing that the peace treaty had left France and Spain strong enough to take the offensive. This smothered opposition.

The plan called for 7,500 troops in North America (the rest in the West Indies), and to most people this seemed obviously necessary. Very briefly the arguments were as follows. First, an estimated 75,000 Canadians were now under a conqueror's governance; they should know that British soldiers were at hand. Secondly, the vast territory acquired in the peace treaty would, if left unguarded, be vulnerable to attack by France and Spain. Thirdly, Indians of the interior needed to be treated with firmness and fairness under military administration; otherwise they might find French support and would conduct the kind of raiding that occurred in the early years of the war.

The first requirement was not, in reality, as demanding as it seemed. Canadians had seen enough of war's hardships. Moreover, they had reason to feel that France had let them down. The monarchy's spurning of Canadian bills of exchange that they considered legitimate was a further source of grievance, and they urgently needed money for post-war recovery. Under Article IV of the treaty of Paris they were explicitly allowed their Catholic religion and its institutions. Those who wished to leave Canada could sell their real property and take with them their personal property without hindrance. They had been led to expect cruel treatment, but soon began to realize that Amherst's promises were being genuinely upheld by General Murray, who was, among other things, wise enough to leave local government in the hands of the parish organizations. The Canadian people were of course traumatized by the conquest, but the French language was allowed to prevail, and although British rule barred them from higher office and would in due course put them at a commercial disadvantage (most shifted their focus to agriculture), their way of life was basically unaltered. The situation did not, in fact, require a large army of occupation.

Regarding the second argument, we have seen that France and Spain were in no condition to go to war; furthermore, interior North America was the last place they would wish to begin. Those who imagined Bourbon intervention in the interior were 'fighting the last war', supposing that what happened in 1753–4 could easily happen again. The frontier between British and Spanish Louisiana was subject to minor disturbances, but nothing substantial could be done by the Bourbon powers without use of the two great rivers, and Britain's navy could control access to them (a fort at Natchez might be needed). As a knowing observer pointed out, superiority at sea prevented the continent from 'being invaded by a formidable enemy; and 'tis needless to erect forts to keep ye trees in subjection'. Britain's territorial gains had left the Thirteen Colonies with 'no internal enemy but Indians, who may be easily made friends'.[26] The king and his ministers may have believed that interior North America was under threat from Bourbon forces, but they made no more effort to examine the question than Pitt did, and there is ample evidence to suggest that they were guided by other motives.

The third argument cannot be easily dismissed. Making friends with the Indians was certainly the sensible policy, but what were the best means

[26] Baugh, 'Maritime Strength', p. 205, from a memorandum in Charles Jenkinson's papers dated 10 March 1763, author unknown.

of doing it? As it happened, Amherst made a terrible blunder. He should have paid attention to the warning Forbes sent him from Pennsylvania just before dying: 'I beg . . . that you will not think triflingly of the Indians or their friendship, when I venture to assure you that twenty Indians are capable of laying half this province waste.'[27] Amherst, however, after completing the conquest of Canada and sending off a portion of his army to the West Indies, could be sure that London authorities would ask him to reduce expenses in North America. He decided to curtail the gifts that had been regularly given to the Indians. He also planned to make it difficult for them to trade for firearms and gunpowder, which they absolutely needed for survival. Sir William Johnson warned him not to do these things, but Amherst's thoughts were focused on the fact that the Cherokee nation had just been subdued by force on the South Carolina border; a thousand regulars had burnt their villages and crops. That this method had required two expensive campaigns did not give the commander-in-chief pause, nor did the difficulty of applying it in the vast trans-Appalachian interior. Prejudice ruled Amherst's mind on this issue: he had a low opinion of Indians as fighting men, partly because they used treachery to avoid casualties. By the end of 1762 the cessation of presents and difficulty of access to ammunition were creating great anxiety among the western tribes.

On 14 May 1763 an Ottawa leader named Pontiac at the head of 600 warriors put the fort at Detroit under siege. The uprising immediately spread, and before long eight small forts to the north and west and also in western Pennsylvania were overwhelmed, entry in some cases being gained by deception or deceit. Amherst's critics accused him of failing to react promptly, but as soon as he received confirmation of rumours he issued appropriate orders despite the distressing inadequacy of his forces. Enlistments were expiring, and some units were under orders to go home, but loss of men to disease at Havana was the truly dreadful factor. Of those who had returned many died and the rest were convalescents – physically weak and subject to a recurrent illness, which suggests malaria. Yet Amherst had no choice but to send them inland. Relief for Detroit could come via Lake Erie, but Fort Pitt, under siege in July, could only be saved by a cross-country march from Philadelphia. This was led by Colonel Bouquet whose men, many of them sickly, were ambushed at Bushy Run (25 miles east of the fort) by a large body of Indians. Bouquet formed a defensive circle with packhorses and cattle, and an

---

[27] See above, end of Chapter 10.

inner breastwork of sacks of flour, and then waited patiently while taking casualties from hidden musketry. The plan he executed the next day lured the Indians into the open where they were devastated by surprise flanking fire which was followed by a bayonet charge. In this action of 5 and 6 August Bouquet lost 50 killed and 60 wounded of his 400 men, but the survivors reached Fort Pitt, which held out. Detroit also held out: its garrison was bolstered by troops coming from Niagara in bateaux, and its provisions were replenished by armed lake vessels. Shortly after a vessel carrying desperately needed supplies arrived in October, ablaze with flaming arrows, Pontiac abandoned the siege.

Amherst had ordered that the Indians should be punished. Johnson and Bouquet were wiser. Johnson used his Iroquois connections together with gifts to calm the rebellious Senecas, and the next year he brought the weight of the Six Nations into the balance against the insurgents. Also in 1764 Bouquet tempered force with negotiation, gifts, and promises of access to trade goods to recover captives and bring peace to the Ohio territory. It helped significantly that French officials in Illinois and Louisiana, aware that the Peace of Paris had been signed, refused to supply gunpowder to Pontiac and his followers. The rebellion lost energy, and Pontiac himself became an agent of peacemaking.

While 'Pontiac's rebellion' was raging Lord Halifax at the Board of Trade was working up a plan for governing the new American territories. The result was the Royal Proclamation of 7 October 1763. East Florida, West Florida, the ceded islands in the Caribbean, and Nova Scotia with the maritime regions were constituted as provinces. In these provinces civil government was to be established and immigration encouraged. The huge expanse of wilderness from the Appalachians to the Mississippi River was left to the Indians. Settlement by colonists and European immigrants was prohibited. The motive was to honour Indian treaties made before and during the war, and eliminate occasions for violence. Another motive, though not explicitly stated, was to prevent settlement from occurring far inland; it was supposed that distant settlements would not be markets for British manufactured goods because the settlers would develop their own – an anxiety which revealed London's abysmal ignorance of frontier economics. Following a recommendation from Johnson trading would be restricted to licensed traders at posts linked to forts. Thus, the vast interior was closed to settlement and unregulated trading.

All in all, it was an honourable plan, but it was seriously flawed and impracticable. The main flaw was that there was no provision for civil government and thus for enforcement. The army was the supervising agency, but under English law the army had no peacetime authority to punish would-be settlers and misbehaving traders who were civilian subjects of the king. It was impracticable because land speculators, some of whom had political influence in Britain, could not be easily curbed, and although there was still a great deal of land east of the mountains for a growing population – immigration to the Thirteen Colonies was strong during the war – the pressure to move west would be irresistible. There was also the question of cost, which was bound to arise when people realized that defence of the interior against French or Spanish attack was unnecessary. The cost of employing the army to regulate the Indian trade greatly exceeded the trade's commercial value. The principal forts at Oswego, Niagara, Pittsburgh and Detroit, as well as a presence in Canada, needed to be maintained, but otherwise, why incur a huge military expense in the interior of North America? The purpose of expelling the French from the continent had been to diminish the cost of colonial defence, not to increase it. Would it not be better simply to assemble forces to defend the frontiers if a need arose? These questions were beginning to be considered in the autumn of 1765 when riotous protests broke out in the eastern ports. The concern for security shifted from the wilderness to the populated seaboard.

The immediate cause of rioting was the Stamp Act, the project of George Grenville, who enjoyed drawing up regulations and had happily accepted the challenge of imposing stricter supervision on the American colonies. As First Lord of the Admiralty he had instituted measures to curtail American smuggling, which he believed had been carried on extensively during the war. (Undoubtedly there had been a good deal of trading with the enemy at Saint-Domingue, but Grenville must have been aware that trade with Guadeloupe and Marie Galante became legal in 1759, as did trade with the rest of the French Windward Islands in early 1762.) In any case, with Bute's assistance he obtained a statute that permitted ships of the Royal Navy to enforce customs collection. Captains were authorized to search vessels entering harbour and would be awarded half the value of any cargo judged to be illicit. In effect, this provided prize money in peacetime.

Customs duties collected in America scarcely covered the cost of collection, and when Grenville moved from the Admiralty to the Treasury in April 1763 he was determined to rectify this. The most notorious uncollected duty was the 6d. per gallon on molasses from the foreign West Indies. Established in 1733, this very high rate was intended to be prohibitive; the West Indian planter interest had prevailed on Parliament to enact it. The government understood, however, that New England exports and shipping depended heavily on molasses imports (used to make rum), and that rum sales enabled colonists to buy British manufactured goods. British planters were not reliable suppliers of molasses; they sold most of theirs to England, but French planters could not send theirs to France because the cognac interest prohibited importation. Smuggling French molasses to the American mainland was therefore quietly permitted after 1733; the British Atlantic economy in general benefited thereby and British planters in the Caribbean were not significantly injured.

Grenville was determined to collect the duty. When naval enforcement began in the summer of 1763 Governor Francis Bernard of Massachusetts could not understand what London was thinking. No one, he said, could profitably afford to pay a duty of 6d. a gallon; if the goal was revenue, the rate should be one penny. He sounded an alert to a Treasury official: 'The publication of orders for the strict execution of the Molasses Act has caused a greater alarm in this Country than the taking of Fort William Henry in 1757.'[28] Grenville was aware that the rate needed to be lowered. With the aid of Treasury officials he was busily drawing up what would become the American Revenue Act, more commonly known as the Sugar Act. It passed through Parliament easily and became law in April 1764. Its details were designed to defeat all the smuggling tricks that Grenville had heard about. But he was not as capable an administrator as he thought he was. He did not know or seem to care about the ways colonial shipping actually operated. The statute required certificates, bonds and 'cockets' (documents detailing cargo), many of which could not in practice be executed according to the rules, and in small ports the documents were unobtainable. Coastal shipping would be strangled. As for French molasses, the act lowered the duty to 3d. Nearly everyone – Grenville consulted quite a few experts – recommended 2d. or lower. His decision to set it at 3d. was deliberate, not an ignorant mistake. He later claimed that he had thought it necessary to compromise with the West Indian interest, but he of all people must have recognized that the planters had no moral or economic claim on an administration which had decided in the peace negotiation not to keep some highly productive French sugar islands, and had also granted their primary wish, a prohibitive import duty on foreign sugar.

Why, then, did he choose the 3d. rate? He claimed that it would yield more revenue. Yet he also wanted the revenue to be coerced. He felt that setting a lower rate was equivalent to giving in to the smugglers, and he

---

[28] Letter of January 1764, Stout, *Royal Navy in America*, pp. 39–40.

was obsessed with defeating smugglers. Naval enforcement would prevent smuggling. Colonial rum distillers would find ways, he was sure, to make a profit at the 3*d*. rate. If the effect would be to reduce commerce, it did not seem to bother him; it was a necessary cost of bringing colonial trade under proper control. He believed that century-old laws of trade which for many decades had been relaxed to promote shipping growth and general prosperity should now be enforced. Whatever his motives, it was obvious to colonial merchants and shippers that the government's measures would result in constricting the very commerce that it had been the war's ultimate objective to increase. In the colonies puzzlement gave way to alarm, then mistrust, and eventually to anxieties that the London government was both ignorant and incompetent.

Then came the Stamp Act. When putting forward the Sugar Act in March 1764 Grenville introduced the idea of a colonial stamp tax, saying that the colonists were certainly prosperous enough to pay it and in all fairness should do so: 'We have expended much in America. Let us now avail ourselves of the fruits of that expence.'[29] Stamped paper would be required for licences, shipping clearances, deeds and other legal documents, but also for newspapers, the cost varying according to the nature of the item. Currency drain would be avoided because the revenue would stay in the colonies to support the army. Colonial agents agreed with Grenville that a tax of this kind was fair and reasonable, but they suggested that because it was an internal tax it ought to be levied by colonial legislatures, not by the British Parliament. Agents of Massachusetts and some other colonies tried to persuade him to let their legislatures vote the tax, but he blocked this proposal. Unquestionably he knew that the issue of whether Parliament had a right to impose this tax was controversial in the colonies. To fend off possible controversy in London he began his speech of 6 February 1765, which introduced the bill, with a long and rather boring catalogue of legal precedents purporting to show that Parliament's right to impose it was beyond doubt. He dismissed the possibility that the measure would cause serious discontent in the colonies. In any case, he asked, 'But as to this objection, when will the time come when enforcing a tax will not give discontent, if this tax does produce it after what we have done and suffered for America?'[30] The constitutional issue was thus placed in the forefront straightaway, along with a hint from

[29] Gould, *Persistence*, p. 110. On the act's passage see Bullion, *Great and Necessary Measure*, pp. 114–63.

[30] *Proceedings and Debates*, II, 9–11.

Grenville that it should be settled now or never. Although the administration had recently received warnings from colonial representatives in
London that the act would provoke a strong protest, Grenville did not
mention this in the speech or debate.

The bill passed easily and became law on 22 March 1765. When word
of its passage crossed the ocean colonial leaders were at first hesitant.
Some had signed up to be distributors of the stamps. Despite a legendary
(and evidently misreported) speech by young Patrick Henry, the four
resolves announced by Virginia's burgesses stopped short of declaring that
such a tax could be levied only by the colony's legislature, but a version
containing a fifth resolve, which stated this, was soon printed in newspapers and made a strong impression in New England. Since the stamps
would not be required until 1 November there was time to organize a
broad colonial protest. A circular letter from the Massachusetts assembly
in July resulted in a Stamp Act Congress in New York in October. Nine
colonies sent delegates; the other four sent letters of support. Claiming the
rights of Englishmen, the congress declared that only colonial legislatures
could impose such a tax. At this point mobs became the instrument of
protest. Some of the men who had signed up to distribute the stamps saw
their houses burned. All distributors were compelled to resign. Governors
could not expect obedience from militia units, and despite the army
commander-in-chief's readying of regular troops they dared not call upon
them. Colonial leaders feared mobs as much as their counterparts in
England did, but these mobs responded to their guidance. Colonial business
came to a halt. Without proper stamps ships could not be cleared to leave
port. The crucial next step was to persuade local judges to grant official
status to documents lacking stamps, and this was done, but before it could
take effect a great deal of commerce was suspended. As a result, orders for
manufactured goods dried up, and soon production in Britain declined
sharply. Suddenly there was distress in British manufacturing districts.

Fundamentally, the Anglo-French Seven Years War had begun because
of the importance of the North American market for British exports, and
the Stamp Act suddenly ruined that market. Trade recession and unem-
ployment in Britain were the reasons why the act was promptly repealed.
The Rockingham administration brought in merchants and manufacturers
– Edmund Burke assisted in organizing this – who testified to Parliament
about not only the dire effects of the Stamp Act but also some of the trade-
restricting features of the Sugar Act. The molasses duty was lowered to
1*d*., a level at which it became the largest contributor to colonial customs
revenue. Grenville in opposition tried to defeat these measures. He did not

appear to like merchants. (He had been unwilling to involve Parliament to intimidate Versailles in order to help merchants holding Canadian bills relating to prisoners of war.) Although, in 1766, Parliament saw the need to repeal the Stamp Act, it passed the Declaratory Act to maintain its theoretical right to tax the colonies. So the issue remained, and it was ineradicable. The colonists saw it as a standing menace to their right of self-government.

By tradition and political instinct the Thirteen Colonies had remained disunited. Grenville united them. He also alienated colonial elites, who were the only people who might be able to keep the diversified and growing population of British America in a functioning imperial relationship. Because colonial elites did not wish to separate from the British empire the relationship could continue so long as both sides avoided provocation, but because it was a question of rights there were bound to be groups on both sides ready to test the limits. Moreover, fundamental conditions generated by the war and post-war British policies were making imperial cohesion harder to maintain.

First, Americans (the term was coming into use) began to perceive that the British people and their government did not care about their welfare. They were alarmed by the level of London's ignorance about America. It was evident that Englishmen gave them no credit for helping to win the war. London newspapers had focused on the British army, especially at Louisbourg and Quebec; the contributions of provincial troops in the interior seemed to be unknown or else characterized – especially by British army officers in Parliament – as inadequate and inept. This was insulting. That British subsidies covered less than half the cost of the colonial war effort and that a tenth of Massachusetts's male population answered a call to arms were facts to be ignored. The British people, including educated men, assumed that all Americans had illegally traded with the French in the Caribbean. All this was probably more irritating and worrying to Americans than lack of parliamentary representation. Secondly, traditional channels of communication across the Atlantic were losing vitality; the means of quietly avoiding provocation in advance, particularly through the Board of Trade, were closing down. Thirdly, if Americans were upset by the 'posture of hostility' toward the colonists (that startled Benjamin Franklin when he was in London in 1766), Englishmen were upset by the manner in which Americans seemed not to know their place. American did not display the measure of social deference that prevailed in England and often behaved, so it seemed, like Wilkite crowds, which made the impression worse. Fourthly, there was in England an underlying assumption, given credence by British army officers, that an American rebellion could be easily put down.

Perhaps a statesman of the stature of Pitt, still admired on both sides of the Atlantic, could have found a way to halt the slide towards rebellion and revolution, but Pitt soon became a burnt-out shell. After becoming head of government (as Earl of Chatham) after Rockingham in July 1766, he was utterly incompetent. Chronic illness had taken its toll: his personal flaws as a colleague became exaggerated, his knowledge outdated, his judgement on matters of policy erratic. Above all, his health broke down after only three months, and his mind then drifted into a depression so deep that he could not bear the thought of public business and was absent from London for weeks on end. Nevertheless, George III, considering him the shield of his 'independency', did not want him to resign. Only after Chatham finally resigned did his mental recovery progress, whereupon, in a July 1769 interview with the king, he denounced the government's hostile attitude toward Wilkes and the American colonists. After hearing this George III wanted nothing more to do with him.

The Seven Years War profoundly altered great-power circumstances in Europe. Russia had acquired capabilities that placed her among the great powers, and Prussia after a harrowing experience nevertheless emerged as strong as ever, while Austria needed time to recover. Most important, France desired peace on the continent. Britain's primary continental interest was always to contain French aggression, especially in the Netherlands, and to enlist allies which could divert French resources, but Russia, Prussia and Austria were no longer afraid of France. They were, in fact, afraid of allying with Britain because Anglo-French rivalry seemed likely to embroil them in war, and they did not want war. A major effect of the war, not visible on a map, was the financial exhaustion of all the continental powers. British diplomats and statesmen including Chatham were inclined to think that a continental alliance was worth pursuing, but when it came to assessing potential benefits and liabilities the government found the price too high. Subsidy money was the main motive behind a European power's willingness to ally with Britain, for Britain was the one country that still had money. Russia under Catherine II (later called 'the Great'), who had allowed her husband to be murdered, was the only European power that would consider a British alliance – hoping for money and naval assistance against the Turks – but statesmen in London remained wary of peacetime subsidies and did not want to injure Britain's trading interests in the eastern Mediterranean.

A long-standing argument for Britain's maintaining alliances in Europe was the need to make sure that its trade would not be shut out. Before the Seven Years War the central concern had been the export trade to the Netherlands. After the war, however, this market ceased to be so important. Trade with Russia remained vital since the navy and shipping industry depended upon Russian materials; in 1766 the old Anglo-Russian commercial treaty was renewed. Between 1750–1 and 1772–3 Britain's exports to Europe declined by 9 per cent (of the 1772–3 figure re-export of products brought from across the oceans accounted for almost half) while in the same span of years Britain's exports to North America, the West Indies and India more than doubled. French trade followed a different pattern. While Britain's exports to her colonial world were 62 per cent greater in value in 1764–9 than in 1750–5, France's exports to her colonies were 21 per cent less. Regarding Europe, Britain's exports declined 2 per cent while France's increased by 8 per cent.[31] Thus, British trade was shifting from Europe to the wider world and France's was not, though in the 1770s and 1780s the colonial trade of both countries increased significantly.

The enduring fundamental concern of British policy was to preserve and enhance maritime commerce, which was seen as essential to prosperity and national survival. Almost no one in Britain disputed it, but in this regard the government of France was ambivalent. Although by mid-century the French people commonly recognized Britain as their main rival, which suggested a need to develop maritime capabilities, many of the elite at Versailles did not consider such capabilities to be essential to national survival, and Louis XV's notions of greatness centred on his army and France's standing in Europe. At the end of the war Choiseul tried to turn the Spanish alliance to commercial account, but met with frustration. France preserved her West Indian production and commerce (which in due course would grow prodigiously) as well as access to the North Atlantic fisheries, but in all other respects she saw her position in the world beyond the seas seriously impaired, and the monarchy's post-war financial weakness inhibited remedies. In the eyes of the French people the war discredited the Bourbon monarchy; try as it might, its shortcomings in managing war could not be masked.

Although Britain fought the Seven Years War ostensibly over trade, the conflict, ironically, began with a dispute over the Ohio territory and ended

[31] Mitchell and Deane, *Abstract*, p. 312 plus private communication from Javier Cuenca.

with a peace treaty which implied that the purpose had been to acquire half of North America. Commerce was far from forgotten, however. No longer disposed to treat Spain delicately, the British explored the Pacific – the 'Spanish lake' – in search of new opportunities. An aggressive policy in India was pursued with London's approval. Who exactly in the British government pressed for the change in the definitive treaty that forbade a French military presence in Bengal remains obscure, but Egremont appears to have thrown his influence behind it, and Grenville soon turned the government's support away from those directors of the East India Company who had acquiesced in Bute's supine policy and towards those who favoured Robert Clive and his party. Clive sought an unrivalled supremacy in Bengal, and obtained it. As in North America the French were closed out, and kept out by British naval superiority. By making use of indigenous merchants and bankers, company officials developed the richest trade in India. Moreover, Bengal under British control yielded a territorial revenue capable of supporting a large army, which was deemed necessary for defeating external military challenges and keeping internal order.

The British took over all of Canada and vast stretches of territory in the North American interior mainly because this was what the French were willing to give up. The territorial acquisitions in North America helped to turn British thoughts on policy and power more emphatically towards the wider world and away from involvement in Europe's great-power contentions.

It also encouraged already existing ideas about a need for control. In North America the rationale for control was far less clear than it was in India. The need for a British army to defend against external attack was doubtful (though few statesmen in London realized this), and internal order was maintained by American colonial authorities. Grenville believed that colonial trade should be more narrowly confined. (The commercial and maritime benefits of doing this were non-existent.) Taxation was an important issue. Almost all Englishmen felt that the Americans must pay duties and taxes to support their defence, and the coercive tone of Grenville's policies was popular. Some people worried that the North American colonies, rapidly growing in population and wealth, would become the centre of the British empire, that London would eventually become a mere satellite. If Grenville's policies were influenced by this last consideration, the effect of them was to convert a long-term danger into an immediate one. Within a decade the British government made a decision, commonly fatal to empires, of attempting to put down a distant rebellion by sending a substantial army. This decision presented France with an opportunity that was too attractive to let pass, and led to Britain's nightmare scenario of a war begun when the combined navies of France and Spain enjoyed a tonnage advantage one-third greater than Britain's. This war cost Britain its American colonies, but in its aftermath Britain's productive manufacturing industry and unmatched commercial and financial capabilities, shielded by the Royal Navy, recaptured the dynamic American market. These capabilities would shape the future of world politics for two centuries.

Abbreviations and short titles

Amer. Hist. Rev.	*American Historical Review*
Anderson, *Crucible of War*	Fred Anderson, *Crucible of War: The Seven Years's War and the Fate of Empire in British North America, 1754–1766* (New York, 2000)
Antoine, *Louis XV*	Michel Antoine, *Louis XV* (Paris, 1989)
Barbier, *Journal*	Edmond Jean François Barbier, *Chronique de la régence et du règne de Louis XV (1718–1763); ou, Journal de Barbier* 8 vols (Paris, 1857–1866)
Beatson, *Naval and Military Memoirs*	Robert Beatson, *Naval and Military Memoirs of Great Britain from 1727 to 1783* 6 vols (London, 1804)
BIHR	*Bulletin of the Institute of Historical Research*
Black, *Pitt the Elder*	Jeremy Black, *Pitt the Elder* (Cambridge, 1992)
BL Add.	British Library Additional Manuscripts
Blart, *Rapports*	Louis Blart, *Les Rapports de la France and de l'Espagne après le pacte de famille, jusqu'à la fin du ministère du duc de Choiseul* (Paris, 1915)
Carter, *Dutch Republic*	Alice Clare Carter, *The Dutch Republic in Europe in the Seven Years War* (London, 1971)
Casgrain, *Montcalm et Lévis*	H.-R. Casgrain, *Guerre du Canada 1756–1760: Montcalm et Lévis* 2 vols (Quebec, 1891)

Chatham Correspondence	William Stanhope Taylor and John Henry Pringle, eds. *Correspondence of William Pitt, Earl of Chatham* 4 vols (London, 1838–40)
Chaussinand-Nogaret, *Choiseul*	Guy Chaussinand-Nogaret, *Choiseul (1719–1785): Naissance de la gauche* (Paris, 1998)
Clowes	W. Laird Clowes, *The Royal Navy: A History from the Earliest Times to the Present Day* 7 vols (Boston and London, 1897–1903, repr. London, 1996), vol. 3
Corbett	Julian S. Corbett, *England in the Seven Years' War: A Study in Combined Strategy* 2 vols (London, 1907)
Dann, *Hanover and Great Britain*	Uriel Dann, *Hanover and Great Britain, 1740–1760, Diplomacy and Survival* (Leicester, 1991)
DCB	*Dictionary of Canadian Biography*
Devonshire Diary	Peter D. Brown and Karl W. Schweizer, eds. *The Devonshire Diary: William Cavendish, Fourth Duke of Devonshire, Memoranda on State of Affairs, 1759–1762* Royal Hist. Soc. (London, 1982)
Doran, *Andrew Mitchell and Anglo-Prussian Diplomatic Relations*	Patrick Francis Doran, *Andrew Mitchell and Anglo-Prussian Diplomatic Relations during the Seven Years War* (New York and London, 1986)
Dorn, *Competition*	Walter L. Dorn, *Competition for Empire, 1740–1763* (New York, 1940)
Dull, *French Navy*	Jonathan R. Dull, *The French Navy and the Seven Years' War* (Lincoln and London, 2005)
Dziembowski, *Un nouveau patriotisme français*	Edmond Dziembowski, *Un nouveau patriotisme français, 1750–1770: La France face à puissance anglaise à l'epoque de la guerre de Sept Ans* Voltaire Foundation (Oxford, 1998)
English Hist. Rev.	*English Historical Review*

Gipson	Lawrence Henry Gipson, *The British Empire before the American Revolution* 15 vols (New York, 1958–70)
Hamilton, ed. *Adventure in the Wilderness*	*Adventure in the Wilderness: The American Journals of Louis Antoine de Bougainville, 1756–1760* trans. and ed. by Edward P. Hamilton (Norman, OK, 1964)
Hispanic American Hist. Rev.	*Hispanic American Historical Review*
HJ	*The Historical Journal*
Ilchester, *Henry Fox*	Giles Stephen Holland Fox-Strangways, Earl of Ilchester, *Henry Fox, First Lord Holland, his Family and Relations* 2 vols (London, 1920)
Intl. Hist. Rev.	*The International History Review*
Jennings, *Empire of Fortune*	Francis Jennings, *Empire of Fortune: Crown, Colonies, and Tribes in the Seven Years War in America* (New York, 1988)
JICH	*Journal of Imperial and Commonwealth History*
JMH	*Journal of Modern History*
JSAHR	*Journal of the Society for Army Historical Research*
Kennett, *French Armies*	Lee Kennett, *The French Armies in the Seven Years' War: A Study in Military Organization and Administration* (Durham, NC, 1967)
Kimball, ed. *Correspondence of Pitt with America*	Gertrude Selwyn Kimball, ed. *Correspondence of William Pitt When Secretary of State with Colonial and Military and Naval Commissioners in America* 2 vols (New York, 1906)
Lacour-Gayet, *Marine Militaire*	Georges Lacour-Gayet, *La Marine Militaire de la France sous le règne de Louis XV* (Paris, 1902)
Lewis, ed. *Walpole Correspondence*	W.S. Lewis, *Horace Walpole's Correspondence with Sir Horace Mann* 11 vols (New Haven, 1954–1971)

Mackay, *Admiral Hawke*	Ruddock F. Mackay, *Admiral Hawke* (Oxford, 1965)
Mackay, ed. *Hawke Papers*	Ruddock F. Mackay, ed. *The Hawke Papers, A Selection: 1743–1771* NRS (Aldershot, 1990)
Masson, ed. *Mémoires et Lettres de . . . Bernis*	Frédéric Masson, ed. *Mémoires et Lettres de François-Joachim de Pierre, Cardinal de Bernis* 2 vols (Paris, 1878)
Middleton, *Bells*	Richard Middleton, *The Bells of Victory: The Pitt–Newcastle Ministry and the Conduct of the Seven Years' War, 1757–1762* (Cambridge, 1985)
MM	*Mariner's Mirror*
Namier, *England in the Age*	Lewis Namier, *England in the Age of the American Revolution* 2nd ed. (London, 1961)
NRS	Navy Records Society
NYCD	E.B. O'Callaghan *et al.*, eds. *Documents Relative to the Colonial History of the State of New York* 15 vols (Albany, NY, 1853–87)
ODNB	*Oxford Dictionary of National Biography*
Pares, *War and Trade*	Richard Pares, *War and Trade in the West Indies* (Oxford, 1936, repr. London, 1963)
Pargellis, *Lord Loudoun*	Stanley McCrory Pargellis, *Lord Loudoun in North America* (New Haven, 1933, repr. Hamden, CT, 1968)
Pargellis, ed. *Military Affairs*	Stanley M. Pargellis, ed. *Military Affairs in North America, 1748–1765: Selected Documents from the Cumberland Papers in Windsor Castle* (New York and London, 1936)
Parkman, *Montcalm and Wolfe*	Francis Parkman, *Montcalm and Wolfe: The French and Indian War* [Boston, 1884] 2nd repr. ed. (Cambridge, MA, 2001)

Parl. Hist.	William Cobbett, ed. *The Parliamentary History of England from the Earliest Period to the Year 1803* 36 vols (London, 1806–20)
Pease, *Boundary Disputes*	Theodore Calvin Pease, ed. *Anglo-French Boundary Disputes in the West, 1749–1763* Illinois State Historical Library, vol. 27 (Springfield, IL, 1936)
Peters, *Pitt and Popularity*	Marie Peters, *Pitt and Popularity: The Patriot Minister and London Opinion during the Seven Years' War* (Oxford, 1980)
Pritchard, *Louis XV's Navy*	James F. Pritchard, *Louis XV's Navy, 1748–1762: A Study of Organization and Administration* (Kingston and Montreal, 1987)
PRO	Public Record Office, London (now The National Archives)
Proceedings and Debates	R.C. Simmons and P.D.G. Thomas, eds. *Proceedings and Debates of the British Parliaments Respecting North America 1754–1783*, vols I and II (Millwood, NY and London, 1982)
Rashed, *Peace of Paris*	Zeneb Esmat Rashed, *The Peace of Paris, 1763* (Liverpool, 1951)
Savory, *His Britannic Majesty's Army*	Lt-Gen. Sir Reginald Savory, *His Britannic Majesty's Army in Germany during the Seven Years War* (Oxford, 1966)
Scott, *Birth*	H.M. Scott, *The Birth of a Great Power System 1740–1815* (Harlow, 2006)
Sherrard, *Lord Chatham*	O.A. Sherrard, *Lord Chatham: Pitt and the Seven Years' War* (London, 1955)
Showalter, *Wars of Frederick the Great*	Dennis E. Showalter, *The Wars of Frederick the Great* (Harlow, 1996)
Shy, *Toward Lexington*	John Shy, *Toward Lexington: The Role of the British Army in the Coming of the American Revolution* (Princeton, 1965)

Stanley, *New France* — George Stanley, *New France: The Last Phase, 1744–1760* (Toronto, 1968)

Steele, *Betrayals* — Ian K. Steele, *Betrayals: Fort William Henry and the 'Massacre'* (New York, 1990)

Szabo — Franz A.J. Szabo, *The Seven Years War in Europe 1756–1763* (Harlow, London and New York, 2008)

Thackeray, *History* — Francis Thackeray, *A History of the Right Honorable William Pitt, Earl of Chatham* 2 vols (London, 1827)

TNA — The National Archives, Kew (formerly Public Record Office, London)

Vigié, *Dupleix* — Marc Vigié, *Dupleix* (Paris, 1993)

Waddington, *Louis XV et le renversement* — Richard Waddington, *Louis XV et le renversement des alliances: Préliminaires de la Guerre de Sept Ans 1754–1756* (Paris, 1896, repr. Elibron Classics, n.d.)

Waddington, *Guerre* — Richard Waddington, *La Guerre de Sept Ans: Histoire diplomatique et militaire* 5 vols (Paris, 1899–1914, repr. Elibron Classics, 2005–6)

Walpole, *Memoirs of King George II* — Horace Walpole, *Memoirs of King George II* ed. by John Brooke 3 vols (New Haven and London, 1985)

Walpole, *Memoirs of King George III* — Horace Walpole, *Memoirs of the Reign of King George III* ed. by Derek Jarrett, 3 vols (New Haven and London, 2000)

Whitworth, *Ligonier* — Rex Whitworth, *Field Marshal Lord Ligonier: A Story of the British Army, 1702–1770* (Oxford, 1958)

Williams, *Life* — Basil Williams, *The Life of William Pitt, Earl of Chatham* 2 vols (London, 1913)

WMQ — *William and Mary Quarterly*

Yorke, *Hardwicke* — Philip C. Yorke, *The Life and Correspondence of Philip Yorke, Earl of Hardwicke, Lord High Chancellor of Great Britain* 3 vols (Cambridge and Chicago, 1913)

Notes on sources

Chapter 1 Introduction

Richard Waddington's *Louis XV et le renversement des alliances* and *La Guerre de Sept Ans*, six volumes in all, are still after 100 years indispensable for examining the French side. An up-to-date study focusing on the French side is Jonathan Dull's *The French Navy and the Seven Years' War*, a work of thoroughgoing research with a superb bibliography. Most histories of the Anglo-French Seven Years War concentrate heavily on the British side. Of the biographies of Pitt, I have frequently consulted Basil Williams's two volumes and O.A. Sherrard's second volume, *Lord Chatham: Pitt and the Seven Years' War*. Lawrence Henry Gipson's great work on *The British Empire before the American Revolution* is remarkable both for its scope (it pays attention to the French side) and detail, though it was written when research in European archives was difficult for Americans. I have consulted volumes 4 to 8. Fred Anderson's *Crucible of War* is now the best study of the war in its British and American colonial contexts. (For full bibliographical citations of these works see the Abbreviations and short titles list.)

North America's emerging importance

The ideas were developed in Daniel A. Baugh, 'Maritime Strength and Atlantic Commerce: The Uses of a "Grand Marine Empire"' in *An Imperial State at War: Britain from 1689 to 1815* ed. by Lawrence Stone (London, 1994), esp. p. 203. See also Bruce P. Lenman, 'Colonial War and Imperial Stability, 1688–1793' in P.J. Marshall, ed. *The Oxford History of the British Empire, Volume II: The Eighteenth Century* (Oxford, 1998), pp. 154–9.

Canada's utility for France

La Galissonière's memorandum of December 1750 is fully printed in English translation in *NYCD* X, 220–32, but the translation is poor, sometimes seriously flawed. Dual-language extracts may be found in Pease, *Boundary Disputes*, pp. 5–22, but Pease did not always indicate where he chose to omit. I have used the French version in Roland Lamontagne, ed. *Aperçu structural du Canada au XVIIIe siècle* (Montreal, 1964). Pierre Henri Boulle includes a useful account of the memorandum in his Ph.D. dissertation, 'The French Colonies and the Reform of their Administration during and following the Seven Years' War' (University of California, Berkeley, 1968), pp. 437–40. For the broader French background: Jean Bérenger and Jean Meyer, *La France dans le monde au XVIIIe siècle* (Paris, 1993).

A global contest

A comparison of the British and French navies is offered in Daniel A. Baugh, 'Naval Power: What Gave the British Navy Superiority?' in *Exceptionalism and Industrialisation: Britain and its European Rivals, 1688–1815*, ed. by Leandro Prados de la Escosura (Cambridge, 2004), pp. 235–57. This essay cites sources dealing with the French navy. Also important: Dull, *French Navy* (2005), and Christian Buchet, *La Lutte pour l'espace Caraïbe et la façade atlantique de l'amerique centrale et du sud (1672–1763)* 2 vols (Paris, 1991). Buchet has also contributed significantly to British naval history, notably by 'The Royal Navy in the Caribbean, 1689–1763' *MM* 80 (1994), 30–44, and *Marine, économie et société: Un exemple d'interaction: l'aitaillement de la Royal Navy durant la guerre de sept ans* (Paris, 1999), pp. 329–43, an important study of British naval victualling.

Logistics in America: Edward P. Hamilton, *The French and Indian Wars: The Story of Battles and Forts in the Wilderness* (New York, 1962), Chapter 1: 'They Went by Water' sketches the problem and includes a description of bateaux.

French logistics in Europe: Kennett, *French Armies* is indispensable; see esp. pp. 99–129. Also relevant: Christopher Duffy, *The Army of Frederick the Great* 2nd ed. (Chicago, 1996) pp. 198–204; the supply and transport challenges characteristic of the Seven Years War are clearly described, but one should bear in mind that the Prussian army's system was much more efficient than the French.

Geography and policy

Here I have drawn mainly on my own writings. For geography: Daniel A. Baugh, 'The Atlantic of the Rival Navies, 1714–1783' in Nancy L.

Rhoden, ed. *English Atlantics Revisted: Essays Honouring Ian K. Steele* (Montreal and Kingston, 2007), pp. 206–31. For geopolitics: Daniel A. Baugh, 'Great Britain's "Blue-Water" Policy, 1688–1815' *Intl. Hist. Rev.* 10 (1988), 33–58, and 'Withdrawing from Europe: Anglo-French Maritime Geopolitics, 1750–1800' *Intl. Hist. Rev.* 20 (1998), 1–32. Also Baugh, 'Maritime Strength' and 'Naval Power', both cited above. John Brewer, *The Sinews of Power: War, Money and the English State, 1688–1783* (New York, 1989) explains how Britain's system of taxation and finance gained political acceptance and administrative efficiency in the half-century before the Seven Years War began.

Chapter 2 Statesmen and regimes

The Duke of Newcastle

This is based fundamentally on the Newcastle Papers in the British Library manuscripts division, especially his correspondence with Hardwicke. Reed Browning's *The Duke of Newcastle* (New Haven and London, 1975) is a first-rate biography. See also his article on Newcastle in the *ODNB*, and Ray A. Kelch, *Newcastle, A Duke Without Money: Thomas Pelham-Holles, 1693–1768* (Berkeley, 1974).

The Earl of Hardwicke

The basis is Hardwicke's correspondence with Newcastle in the Newcastle Papers and the letters from Joseph Yorke to his father, brothers and sister in the Hardwicke Papers (all in the British Library). P.C. Yorke's three-volume *Life and Correspondence of . . . Hardwicke* published in 1913 (full reference in Abbreviations and short titles) draws mainly on these letters and is an invaluable source. For Hardwicke's personal life and career see particularly vol. II, 501–2, 529, 563–97. The assessment of Hardwicke as a strategist is in Richard Pares, 'American versus Continental Warfare 1739–63', *English Hist. Rev.* 51 (1936), reprinted in *The Historian's Business and Other Essays* (Oxford, 1961), p. 168. Sir William Holdsworth, *A History of English Law* vol. 12 (London, 1938), pp. 237–97 discusses 'Lord Hardwicke and his Contribution to the Formation of the Modern System of Equity'. Peter D.G. Thomas's article on Hardwicke in the *ODNB* is useful, but its conclusion concerning Hardwicke's character quotes the Earl of Waldegrave without mentioning that the two men were political adversaries.

William Pitt

Basil Williams's two volumes were written at a time when the British Empire was not deplored, but the biography is not as uncritically worshipful of Pitt as is sometimes supposed and it remains a valuable guide to Pitt's conduct of the war. Kate Hotblack, *Chatham's Colonial Policy: A Study of the Fiscal and Economic Implications of the Colonial Policy of the Elder Pitt* (London, 1917, repr. Philadelphia, 1980) remains informative, but she perceives a degree of coherence in Pitt's thought that may be questioned. Middleton's *Bells* is a careful, detailed and highly useful study of Pitt as a wartime administrator which corrects the old idea that Pitt somehow supervised everything that led to success. Marie Peters's concluding chapter of *The Elder Pitt* (London and New York, 1998) takes a more cynical view of Pitt's political manoeuvring than is to be found in the conclusion of her *Pitt and Popularity*. The manic-depressive disorder is briefly addressed by Brian Tunstall in *William Pitt, Earl of Chatham* (London, 1938), p. 12, and also in Stanley Ayling, *The Elder Pitt, Earl of Chatham* (London and New York, 1976), pp. 144–51. Vere Birdwood, ed. *So Dearly Loved, So Much Admired: Letters to Hester Pitt, Lady Chatham from her relations and friends 1744–1801* (London, 1994) has fine illustrations and prints a good deal of her correspondence, but disappointingly reduces her correspondence with her husband to snippets.

The duc de Choiseul

Biographical and background information is drawn chiefly from Rohan Butler, *Choiseul: Volume I, Father and Son 1719–1754* (Oxford, 1980), esp. pp. 133–43. Unfortunately, only the first volume of this great work has appeared. For Choiseul's character and behaviour see Michel Antoine's *Louis XV*, pp. 750–3, and Guy Chaussinand-Nogaret's *Choiseul*, pp. 16, 78–90. On Louis XV as correspondent and his desire to repossess his letters see Antoine, pp. 450–1. The council of state (or *conseil d'en haut*) is discussed in Rashed's *Peace of Paris*, pp. 230–2. Dull, *French Navy*, pp. 20–24, examines its composition in 1755.

Chapter 3 Origins: the contested regions, 1748–54

Acadia and Nova Scotia

Gipson's narrative (V, 167–206), based on detailed and wide-ranging research, continues to be a valuable guide; for the Indians informing the

Acadians that they would be regarded as enemies if they went back to Nova Scotia see pp. 203–4. Recent and valuable is John Mack Faragher, *A Great and Noble Scheme: The Tragic Story of the Expulsion of the Acadians from Their American Homeland* (New York, 2005), pp. 245–77. Also: Stanley, *New France*, pp. 58–75, and Guy Frégault, *Canada: the War of the Conquest* (Toronto, 1969), pp. 164–200. Winthrop Pickard Bell, *The 'Foreign Protestants' and the Settlement of Nova Scotia: The History of a Piece of Arrested Colonial Policy in the Eighteenth Century* (Toronto, 1961) is highly informative on many subjects but especially the recruiting and transporting of German Protestant farmers to settle at Halifax and elsewhere on the east coast. For New England's role: George A. Rawlek, *Nova Scotia's Massachusetts: Study of Massachusetts–Nova Scotia Relations, 1630 to 1784* (Montreal and London, 1973), pp. 193–216. On Le Loutre: *DCB, IV*: Introduction, 'Acadia' and also 'Le Loutre'; J.C. Webster, *The Career of Abbé Le Loutre in Nova Scotia with a translation of his autobiography* (Shediac, 1933). Original letters involving Le Loutre are found in Edouard Richard, *Acadie: reconstitution d'un chapitre perdu de l'histoire d'Amérique*, 3 vols (Quebec, 1916), II, 445–65.

The New York frontier

Gipson, V, 88–112. Stanley, *New France*, pp. 78–90. Steele, *Betrayals*, pp. 3–10. Waddington, *Louis XV et le renversement*, pp. 17–18. For the policy of the Iroquois nations see Jon Parmenter, 'After the Mourning Wars: The Iroquois as Allies in Colonial North American Campaigns, 1676–1760' *WMQ* ser. 3, 64 (2007), esp. pp. 63–6.

Ohio: the French predicament

In explaining why the Ohio region became the centre of attention and subject to military occupation after 1748 countless historical writings, both general and particular, have blamed the governors (Duquesne and Dinwiddie) for acting without authorization from home, and have also stated that the French were actuated by a need to oppose English territorial settlement. Jennings (*Empire of Fortune*), for instance, uses the word 'penetration' in ways that imply encroachment by English settlers. Patrice Louis-René Higonnet, 'The Origins of the Seven Years' War' *JMH* 40 (March 1968), despite its helpful research, is misleading (pp. 60–8). For the French concern to eradicate English trading as a sine qua non of bringing the resident Indians under a Canadian-dominated tranquillity see Richard White, *The Middle Ground: Indians, Empires, and Republics in the Great Lakes Regions, 1650–1815* (Cambridge, 1991), pp. 127–238. White carefully weighs the French policy alternatives: fear and force versus generosity and negotiation. Also useful is Michael N. McConnell, *A Country Between: The Upper Ohio Valley and Its Peoples, 1724–1774* (Lincoln and London, 1992), pp. 54–88. Background on governing New France: Guy Frégault, *Le Grand Marquis: Pierre de Rigaud de Vaudreuil et la Louisiane* (Montreal, 1952).

Original sources: Theodore Calvin Pease and Ernestine Jenison, eds, *Illinois on the Eve of the Seven Years' War, 1747–1755* in *Collections of the Illinois State Historical Library* vol. 29 (Springfield, IL, 1940); the volume contains extracts of correspondence of Canadian officials with each other and with the minister of marine and colonies, printed in French and English. The significant parts of Céloron's journal, translated into English with supplementary material, are printed in *Ohio Archaeological and Historical Quarterly* vol. 29, 4 (October, 1920).

Ohio: the French solution

My account is principally based on Donald H. Kent, *The French Invasion of Western Pennsylvania, 1753* (Harrisburg, PA, 1954) and on letters printed in Pease and Jenison, eds. *Illinois on the Eve*. Preparations ordered by Duquesne during the autumn, winter and spring may be traced in letters printed in Fernand Grenier, ed. *Papiers Contrecoeur et autres documents concernant le conflit anglo-français sur l'Ohio de 1745 à 1756* (Quebec, 1953). Also useful: Sylvester K. Stevens and Donald H. Kent, eds, *Wilderness Chronicles of Northwestern Pennsylvania* (Harrisburg, PA, 1941), pp. 37–86.

Virginia responds

Gipson, VI, 20–43. For George Washington: Douglas Southall Freeman, *George Washington: a biography* (New York, 1948–57) vols 1 and 2; Charles H. Ambler, *George Washington and the West* (Chapel Hill, NC, 1936), esp. pp. 30–91. On Jumonville and Fort Necessity: Marcel Trudel, 'L'Affaire Jumonville', *Revue d'histoire de l'Amerique française* VI (1952–3), 331–51. Also Anderson, *Crucible*, pp. 5–7 and Frank W. Brecher, *Losing a Continent: France's North American Policy, 1753–1763* (Westport, CT and London, 1998), pp. 51–8. Trudel's article, which Brecher dismisses too lightly, asks and answers some key questions. Brecher's analysis of the use the French made of the Jumonville affair (p. 55) deserves serious attention.

Duquesne's letters to Contrecoeur are in *Papiers Contrecoeur*, cited above. Guy Frégault, *François Bigot: Administrateur français* 2 vols. (Montreal, 1948), I, 51–79, reveals Rouillé's anxiety to diminish expenses. Simultaneously, however, Rouillé's instructions mapped out expensive missions and he continued to support these missions financially, as is pointed out by Matt J. Schumann in 'Mercantilism, Communications and the Early Prehistory of the Seven Years' War, 1749–1754', *Nuova Rivista Storica* 89 (2005), 92, 98. Schumann cites articles by Catherine M. Desbarats: 'The Cost of Canada's Native Alliances: Reality and Scarcity's Rhetoric' *WMQ* ser. 3, 52 (1995), 609–28 and 'France and North America: The Net Burden of Empire during the First Half of the Eighteenth Century' *French History* 11 (1997), 1–28.

A contest in India: Dupleix's project

My account of Dupleix's project, its British opposition, and his recall is based principally on Marc Vigié's carefully researched biography, *Dupleix* (Paris, 1993), pp. 295–521. Prosper Cultru, *Dupleix: Ses plans politiques; sa disgrace* (Paris, 1901), pp. 244–373 has also been consulted, particularly for details of Dupleix's negotiations with Chanda Sahib and the development of his project (pp. 244–88), the quality of French sepoys (pp. 312–13), what the directors in Paris knew and when (pp. 337–43), and the 1753 negotiation in London (pp. 359–61). Cultru's account of Dupleix's recall differs somewhat from Vigié's. I have benefited immensely from the penetrating assessment of the French company's fundamental problems in Catherine Manning, *Fortunes à faire: The French in Asian Trade, 1719–48* (Aldershot, 1996), Chapter 10 'From Trade to War', pp. 195–218. Also useful are Alfred Martineau's Chapter 6, 'Dupleix and Bussy', in H.H. Dodwell, ed. *The Cambridge History of India, Volume V: British India, 1497–1858* (Cambridge, 1929), pp. 125–40, and Henry Dodwell, *Clive and Dupleix: The Beginning of Empire* (New Delhi, 1989), a reprint of Dodwell's *Dupleix and Clive* (London, 1920), pp. 31–137. For detailed accounts of the military campaigns see Sir George Forrest, *The Life of Lord Clive* 2 vols (London, 1918), I, 110–216. On discussions in Paris concerning Dupleix's recall, Philippe Haudrère, *La Compagnie française des Indes au XVIIIe siècle* 2 vols, 2nd ed. (Paris, 2005), II, 738–45 is particularly useful.

Chapter 4 Risking war, 1754–55

Unreadiness of the British colonies

Canadian readiness: W.J. Eccles, 'The French Forces in North America during the Seven Years War', *DCB*, IV, xvii–xviii. Eccles, *France in America*, rev. ed. (East Lansing, MI, 1990), pp. 71–5, 116–20. Duquesne: *DCB*, IV, 'Duquesne', by Pierre-L. Côté, esp. pp. 256–7. Guy Frégault, *François Bigot* (cited in Chapter 3), II, 58–69.

British colonial obstacles: the account is based mainly on Gipson, V, Chapters 4 and 5. Also Kent, *French Invasion of Western Pennsylvania*, pp. 45–51, cited in Chapter 3 above. The deliberations of Lord Halifax and Newcastle are examined in Alison Gilbert Olson, 'The British Government and Colonial Union, 1754' *WMQ* ser. 3, 17 (1960), 22–34. See also the Memorandum of points for consideration at Albany in July 1754 by John Pownall; *Pennsylvania Archives*, VI, 199. On Dinwiddie's excessive optimism, *The Official Records of Robert Dinwiddie: Lieutenant-Governor of the Colony of Virginia* 2 vols (Richmond, VA, 1883–4), I, 58, 215. Virginia's military unreadiness: James Titus, *The Old Dominion at War: Society, Politics, and Warfare in Late Colonial Virginia* (Columbia, SC, 1991), pp. 1–4, 14–16, 22–32, 37–42, 47–51, 64.

Britain raises the stakes

The account essentially follows T.R. Clayton, 'The Duke of Newcastle, the Earl of Halifax, and the American Origins of the Seven Years' War' *HJ* 24 (1981), 571–97. This article establishes the roles of Newcastle, the Duke of Cumberland and Henry Fox in the proceedings and effectively refutes Patrice Higonnet's argument (cited in Chapter 3) that the war's escalation was foisted on the administration by British colonial governors and Lord Halifax.

The futile negotiation

The essential sources are: Pease, *Boundary Disputes*; and Waddington, *Louis XV et le renversement*. Gipson closely examines the conduct of the boundary commissioners (V, 298–338). Max Savelle's *The Diplomatic History of the Canadian Boundary 1749–1763* (New Haven and Toronto, 1940), Chapter V has been superseded by his later work, *The Origins of American Diplomacy: The International History of Angloamerica, 1492–1763* (New York and London, 1967), pp. 309–19; these pages provide a clear account of the complicated territorial proposals and are especially valuable for showing what Robinson was prepared to offer, to no avail, after mid-March. Clayton's 'Duke of Newcastle ... and the American Origins' is important on this subject, esp. pp. 597–601. For the recent map, Edmund Berkeley and Dorothy Smith Berkeley, *Dr. John Mitchell: The Man Who Made the Map of North America* (Chapel Hill, NC, 1974), pp. 190–213.

Britain and Europe

The peace negotiations at Aix-la-Chapelle are clearly set forth in M.S. Anderson, *The War of the Austrian Succession, 1740–1748* (London and New York, 1995), pp. 193–209. For British anxieties see William Coxe, *Memoirs of the Administration of the Right Honourable Henry Pelham* 2 vols (London, 1829), I, 456–65; II, 14–37, 314–27. The letters involved in the dispute between Hardwicke and Newcastle of 1749 are partly printed in Yorke, *Hardwicke*, II, 16–23, but for Newcastle's responses in full see BL Add. 35,410, ff. 140–54; a copy is also in BL Add. 32,719. Reed Browning, 'The British Orientation of Austrian Foreign Policy, 1749–1754' *Central European History* 1 (1968), 299–323 shows that Newcastle's imperial election scheme did not play a role in alienating Austria from Britain. On the Dutch Republic's weakness and reluctance, see Alice Clare Carter, *Neutrality or Commitment: The Evolution of Dutch Foreign Policy, 1667–1795* (London, 1975), pp. 72–81. The substantial influence of Hanover on Newcastle's policy is shown by Dann, *Hanover and Great Britain*, pp. 81–9. There is useful material in Jeremy Black, 'Anglo-French Relations in the Mid-Eighteenth Century 1740–1756', *Francia* 17/2 (1991), 45–79. For a broad view see: Paul Langford, *The Eighteenth Century 1688–1815* (Basingstoke and New York, 1976), pp. 128–32, 138–9, and Scott, *Birth*, pp. 64–74, 84–6. On Spanish policy: Jean McLachlan, 'The Seven Years' Peace, and the West Indian Policy of Carvajal and Wall', *English Hist. Rev.* 59 (1938), 457–77 is important. A detailed, comprehensive and penetrating account of Anglo-Spanish relations during the period from 1748 to 1755 is provided in Pares in *War and Trade*, pp. 517–57. He points out Newcastle's omissions in 1748 that were largely remedied by Keene. For the 1752 treaty of Arunjuez and the dismissal of Ensenada in 1754 see Richard Lodge, ed. *The Private Correspondence of Sir Benjamin Keene* (Cambridge, 1933), pp. xvii–xx. This book contains many letters from Keene to his friend, the British consul at Lisbon.

London under pressures, Versailles under illusions

On the British press and public opinion: Bob Harris, *Politics and the Nation: Britain in the Mid-Eighteenth Century* (Oxford, 2002), pp. 106, 117–21, 236–55, 332. Kathleen Wilson, *The Sense of the People: Politics, Culture and Imperialism in England, 1715–1785* (Cambridge, 1995) uses the concept of 'empire' broadly and shows how it captivated the British public mind.

As my footnotes indicate, Pease, *Boundary Disputes* (cited above) and Waddington, *Louis XV et le renversement* are essential sources for examining Rouillé's conduct of the early 1755 negotiation. See also Black, 'Anglo-French Relations' (cited above). Fascinating insights and opinions relating to transactions and rumours at Versailles may be found in René-Louis de Voyer, marquis d'Argenson, *Journal et mémoires du marquis d'Argenson, publiés . . . par E.J.B. Rathery* 9 vols (Paris, 1859–67), vols 8 and 9. Pre-war opinions in Paris about the problem of Britain's growing commercial and naval power, and in favour of resisting expansion of the British American colonies, are noticed in Baugh, 'Withdrawing from Europe' (cited in Chapter 1), pp. 13–16. As this book was about to be sent to the publisher, a very recent and important article was brought to my attention: John Shovlin, 'Selling American Empire on the Eve of the Seven Years War: The French Propaganda Campaign of 1755–1756' *Past and Present* 206 (February 2010), 121–49. The title speaks for itself; the role of the *Observateur hollandois* is accented. For the influence of these ideas on policy see pp. 126, 129–32, 147–48.

Chapter 5 War without declaration: North America, 1755

The French navy gambles and wins

For the British side: Corbett, I, 53–9; and Peter K. Kemp, 'Boscawen's Letters to his Wife, 1755–1756' in *The Naval Miscellany Volume IV*, ed. by Christopher Lloyd, NRS (London, 1952), pp. 172–96. The French side: Étienne Taillemite's article on 'Emmanuel-Auguste de Cahideuc, Comte Dubois de La Motte' in *DCB*, III, 92–3. A minor portion of Jacques Aman, *Une Campagne navale méconnue à la veille de la guerre de Sept Ans: L'escadre de Brest en 1755* (Vincennes, 1986) deals with Du Bois de La Motte's transit across the Atlantic.

Nova Scotia

For the history of British–Acadian relations and the carrying out of the massive expulsion my account relies very much upon John Mack Faragher's carefully researched *Great and Noble Scheme* (cited in Chapter 3). British official policy towards the Acadians is also exhibited in Bell, *'Foreign Protestants'* (cited in Chapter 3), pp. 64–83, a book which, as its title implies, thereafter gives a thorough account of the establishment of Halifax and other Atlantic coast settlements. Naomi E.S. Griffiths, *The Acadian Deportation: Deliberate Perfidy or Cruel Necessity* (Toronto, 1969) remains a valuable introduction and guide. Regarding the Anglo-French confrontations in Nova Scotia after 1748 including the capture of Fort Beauséjour I have consulted Gipson, VI, 243–85; Stanley, *New France*, pp. 70–5, 108–23; and Ian K. Steele's article on 'Robert Monckton' in *DCB*, IV, 540–2.

Braddock and disaster

For readability, sense and vividness, Parkman's Chapter 7 in *Montcalm and Wolfe* remains unsurpassed. Further research may be guided by Paul E. Kopperman, *Braddock at the Monongahela* (Pittsburgh, 1977), which evaluates the various accounts and prints long extracts from them while also providing a good bibliography. Long extracts from British officers' journals are printed by Charles Hamilton, *Braddock's Defeat* (Norman, OK, 1959). Freeman's *George Washington* (cited in Chapter 3), II adds interesting details, especially regarding the preparations and march. For Washington's letters W.W. Abbot, ed. *The Papers of George Washington* 10 vols (Charlottesville, VA, 1983–1995), I. Dinwiddie's report is in *Official Records* (cited in Chapter 4), II, 258. Stanley Pargellis, 'Braddock's Defeat' *American Historical Review* 41 (1936), 253–69 makes a convincing case that an experienced British officer like Braddock should have known what precautions to take, but the article does not address the challenge posed by fighting in that particular woodland situation. See also Pargellis, ed. *Military Affairs*, pp. 112–29; and Robert L. Yaple, 'Braddock's Defeat: The Theories and a Reconsideration' *JSAHR* 46 (1968), 194–201. Peter E. Russell, 'Redcoats in the Wilderness: British Officers and Irregular Warfare in Europe and America, 1740 to 1760' *WMQ* ser. 3, 35 (1978), 642–3 is informative; it tends to support Pargellis's analysis. Matthew C. Ward, *Breaking the Backcountry: The Seven Years' War in Virginia and Pennsylvania 1754–1765* (Pittsburgh, 2003), pp. 45–73, 132–48 provides a penetrating history of French-abetted Indian raiding on the frontiers of these colonies in the aftermath of Dunbar's retreat.

Campaigns in northern New York

For these campaigns printed documentary sources are quite abundant, most notably NYCD, vols 6 and 10; The Papers of Sir William Johnson 14 vols (Albany, NY, 1921–65), II; and Charles Henry Lincoln, ed. Correspondence of William Shirley, Governor of Massachusetts and Military Commander in America 2 vols (New York, 1912), II, esp. pp. 289–92. Gipson's account of Shirley and Oswego (VI, 127–77) is valuable though inclined to excuse Shirley's mistakes and to blame Johnson and DeLancey for his difficulties. For a countering view, and a richer and more reliable account of the Lake George encounters, see Milton W. Hamilton, Sir William Johnson: Colonial American, 1715–1763 (Port Washington, NY, 1976), which also treats the Canadian side more fully. Steele, Betrayals, pp. 28–56 provides a valuable narrative. An excellent brief guide to both sides may be found in his Warpaths: Invasions of North America (New York and Oxford, 1994), pp. 190–4. Parkman's chapter 'Dieskau' in Montcalm and Wolfe is one of the best in the book, but Parkman demoted the importance of Iroquois intentions as well as the contribution of Captain Eyre. Parkman's perceptions are enhanced by his personal survey of the topography of the region from Fort Edward to Crown Point at a time when it remained in semi-wilderness. The present writer, who resides in 'Iroquois country', has viewed parts of the area from the Mohawk's headwaters to Oswego. The Oswego River is now improved for boat and barge navigation, and joined to the Erie Canal; five locks are required to take it to the level of Lake Ontario.

Chapter 6 Indecision in Europe: May to December 1755

The seizure of French shipping, 1755

Operations at sea: Mackay, Admiral Hawke, pp. 114–34 is the principal source for the British side; also Mackay, ed. Hawke Papers, pp. 113–28. On the French side the account relies on Aman, Une Campagne navale méconnue (cited in Chapter 5), passim but especially the chart on p. 189. For an excellent brief account in English see Dull, French Navy, pp. 35–6; p. 38 gives details of France's loss of seamen, and see p. 303, n. 103.

Corbett's narrative (I, 68–72) lacks crucial dates and is marred by factual errors as well as unwarranted speculations.

Meetings of the Regency Council: Evan Charteris, *William Augustus Duke of Cumberland and the Seven Years' War* (London, 1925), pp. 162–5 provides a useful narrative, more accurate than Corbett's, but it is pre-judiced in favour of Cumberland and makes no mention of 6 August. John Carswell and Lewis Arnold Dralle, eds. *The Political Journal of George Bubb Dodington* (Oxford, 1965), pp. 314–21, contains Fox's recollection of Anson's remark that the war will begin 'next week'. See also J.C.D. Clark, ed. *The Memoirs and Speeches of James, 2nd Earl of Waldegrave, 1742–1763* (Cambridge, 1988), pp. 69–70. Newcastle discussed whether prizes were to be made and whether the orders should extend, not just to the ships under Hawke's command, but to all commands and individual captains, in his letters to Hardwicke of 22 and 23 August 1755, BL Add. 32858 ff. 243, 259–60. Hardwicke's letter to Newcastle of 4 August discussed the inevitability of giving 'further orders' to Hawke notwith-standing the delay caused (BL Add. 32857, ff. 540–1).

Admiral John Byng's reports from his station off Ushant in autumn 1755 are in PRO Adm 1/88. For the 1755 propaganda campaign stimulated by the French government see Dziembowski, *Un nouveau patriotisme français*, pp. 62–72.

The Netherlands and Hanover

The main sources are Carter, *Dutch Republic*, esp. Chapter 3; Waddington, *Louis XV et le renversement*, pp. 126–55; and Dann, *Hanover and Great Britain*, especially Chapter 4. D.B. Horn, *Sir Charles Hanbury Williams and European Diplomacy (1747–58)* (London, 1930), pp. 178–205 pro-vides a detailed narrative. Lodge, ed. *Private Correspondence* (cited in Chapter 4). For brief and penetrating broader interpretations see Dorn, *Competition*, pp. 292–5, and Scott, *Birth*, pp. 82–90.

Pitt and the Russian subsidy

The letters in Yorke, *Hardwicke*, II, 228–49 provide the foundations for what appears in this section. A rich narrative is found in Williams's *Life*, I, 259–85. He is inclined to give Pitt the benefit of any doubt, and on this issue the judgement of Marie Peters, *The Elder Pitt* (cited in Chapter 2), pp. 63–5 is more balanced. The political negotiations involving Newcastle, Hardwicke, Pitt and Fox are dissected in detail by J.C.D. Clark, *The*

Dynamics of Change: The Crisis of the 1750s and English Party Systems (Cambridge, 1982), but his account is conceived within a narrowly political focus and also tends to ignore Hardwicke. On the negotiation of the Russian treaty see Horn, *Sir Charles Hanbury Williams and European Diplomacy*, pages cited above.

Paralysis at Versailles

The indispensable source for the French government's pacifistic indecision is Waddington, *Louis XV et le renversement*, pp. 156–96, who made considerable use of Frederick's letters to Knyphausen. See also Gipson, VI, 381–8. For the constitutional crisis see John Rogister, *Louis XV and the Parlement of Paris, 1737–1755* (Cambridge, 1995), and for 1754–6 Barbier's *Journal* vol. 6. D'Argenson's *Journal et mémoires* (cited in Chapter 4) records rumours of peace and war during 1755, vol. 8, pp. 467 to end; vol. 9, x–161. Pierre de Nolhac, *Madame de Pompadour et la politique* (Paris, 1928), pp. 130–40 discloses the covert Austrian diplomatic initiative and its reception. British intelligence received from the French court: BL Add. 32857, fo. 524, 1 Aug. 1755. Suggestions submitted to the king regarding choices of strategy are summarized in Dull, *French Navy*, p. 37.

Frederick II's dislike of France's elaborate diplomatic schemes of the early 1750s, and French contempt for his refusal to accept them, are traced in Robert Nelson Middleton, 'French Policy and Prussia after the Peace of Aix-la-Chapelle: A Study of the Pre-History of the Diplomatic Revoltuion of 1756' (Columbia University Ph.D. dissertation, 1968). Middleton considers Frederick to have made a mistake, but amply exhibits the presumptuous attitude of the French court that annoyed him.

The story of the duc de Duras's stumble at Madrid is told in Waddington, *Louis XV et le renversement*, pp. 115–25.

Chapter 7   French triumphs, British blunders, 1756
France's initial war plan

Naval preparations for sending troops and officers to America are described in *Mémoires du duc de Luynes sur la cour de Louis XV (1735–1758)* 17 vols (Paris, 1860–5), vol. 15, pp. 29–31, 41. The threat of an invasion of the British Isles is sketched in intelligence reports in the Newcastle papers BL Add. 32,862–4, *passim*; these include the intercepted dispatches from Bunge, the Swedish envoy at Versailles, to his chief, Baron Höpken, at Stockholm. Additional intelligence reports are printed in H.W. Richmond, ed. *Papers Relating to the Loss of Minorca*, NRS (London, 1913), pp. 149–202. Sir Julian Corbett took the invasion seriously and built an elaborate strategic analysis upon it (I, 83–95). Mobilization and embarkation for Minorca may be traced in Lacour-Gayet, *Marine Militaire*, pp. 252–65, and in more detail in Raoul de Cisternes, *La Campagne de Minorque* (Paris, 1899), pp. 83–123. Shortage of seamen is analysed in Timothy J.A. Le Goff, 'De la paix à la guerre: les origines des équipages de la marine de commerce en Méditerranée pendant les guerres du XVIIIe siècle' in *Guerre et commerce en Méditerranée: IXe–XXe siècles* (Paris, 1991), pp. 279–308, esp. p. 301.

France and the Diplomatic Revolution

Scott (*Birth*, pp. 81–92) offers a valuable brief general guide. My account of negotiations with the Dutch is based on Carter, *Dutch Republic*, supplemented by the letters of Joseph Yorke to Newcastle (BL Add. 32, 862–3). For France's role in the Diplomatic Revolution the essential authority remains Waddington, *Louis XV et le renversement*, pp. 247–371. Also informative are the letters exchanged by Baron Knyphausen and Frederick II, printed in *Politische Correspondenz Friedrichs des Grossen*, ed. by Johann Gustav Droysen *et al.*, vol. 12 (Berlin, 1884). Nolhac, *Madame de Pompadour* (cited in Chapter 6) describes the meeting of 19 April. Gaëtan de Raxis de Flassan printed excerpts of Starhemberg's letter to Pompadour of 20 April in vol. VI of *Histoire générale et raisonnée de la diplomatie française, ou de la politique de la France, depuis la fondation de la monarchie, jusqu'à la fin du règne de Louis XVI* 7 vols, 2nd ed. (Paris, 1811). Although Waddington could not discover the original, he judged the letter to be probably genuine. The importance of the Austrian alliance to Pompadour for retaining her power at court is brought out in John D. Woodbridge, *Revolt in Prerevolutionary France: The Prince of Conti's Conspiracy against Louis XV, 1755–1757* (Baltimore and London, 1995), pp. 29–30, 45–6. Walter Dorn's brief appraisal of the diplomatic revolution, in *Competition*, pp. 292–308, is penetrating and judicious.

Admiral Byng and the French conquest of Minorca

Chiefly I have drawn on my 'John Byng' article in the *ODNB*. The best informed and most judicious account of the British response to the

French threat is Brian Tunstall's *Admiral Byng and the Loss of Minorca* (London, 1928). Dudley Pope, *At Twelve Mr Byng was Shot* (London and Philadelphia, 1962) is closely researched and provides countless details not found elsewhere but is strongly biased in Byng's favour (one instance: his account of General Blakeney's court-martial testimony omits key elements that may be found in Tunstall's). Gipson's narrative (VI, 403–17) attempts to justify Byng's conduct. Regarding the Admiralty's failure to provide a sufficient squadron soon enough, the introduction by Captain (later Admiral) Herbert Richmond to *Papers Relating to the Loss of Minorca* (cited above) continues to be the most exacting analysis. Also informative is the well-researched account in Ilchester, *Henry Fox*, I, 322–33. Corbett (I, 126–7) provides a sketch of what Byng might have done to harass French supply lines.

There is no published modern history of the siege. Raoul de Cisternes, *La Campagne de Minorque* (Paris, 1899) may be supplemented by T.H. McGuffie, 'The Defence of Minorca, 1756' *BIHR* 23 (1950), 182–90. McGuffie's article contains valuable statistics and details but adheres closely to an interpretation shaped by Major William Cunningham's resentment of General Blakeney. Chapter 9 of Desmond Gregory, *Minorca, the Illusory Prize: A History of the British Occupations of Minorca between 1708 and 1802* (Rutherford, NJ and London, 1990) provides background and contains a penetrating discussion of public criticisms made of Blakeney after the event (pp. 170–2). For a brief account of the massive improvements the British made to the castle's fortifications see Bruce Laurie, *The Life of Richard Kane, Britain's First Lieutenant-Governor of Minorca* (Rutherford, NJ, 1994), pp. 227–33.

Anyone who has read Dziembowski's *Un nouveau patriotisme français* will recognize how much my closing observations owe to it.

Oswego destroyed

Supplies and the supply line to Oswego: Gilbert Hagerty, *Massacre at Fort Bull: the de Lery expedition against Oneida Carry, 1756* (Providence, RI, 1971). Chapter 5 of Pargellis, *Lord Loudoun* is titled 'Shirley and Oswego'. An essential primary source is Lincoln, ed. *Correspondence of William Shirley* (cited in Chapter 5). On French-Canadian military capabilities I have relied on W.J. Eccles, *The Canadian Frontier, 1534–1760* rev. ed. (Albuquerque, NM, 1983), Chapter 8, esp. pp. 166–71. See also Eccles, 'The Social, Economic, and Political Significance of the Military Establishment in New France', *Essays on New France* (Toronto, 1987), pp. 110–24 and his summary in *DCB*, III, xv–xxiii (cited in Chapter 4). French planning and preparations for the attack are carefully traced in D. Peter MacLeod, 'The Canadians against the French: The Struggle for Control of the Expedition to Oswego in 1756' *Ontario History* 80 (June 1988), 143–57. Anderson, in *Crucible of War*, pp. 150–7, provides an excellent brief account of Oswego's hopeless resistance. See also Stanley, *New France*, pp. 138–47. Original documents on the British side, including the journal of Patrick Mackellar, are printed in Pargellis, ed. *Military Affairs*, pp. 187–221. On the French side there is Hamilton, ed. *Adventure in the Wilderness*, pp. 22–8. The slaughter of up to 100 men by the allied Indians (not mentioned in Bougainville's journal) is pointed out by Anderson. Jennings (*Empire of Fortune*, pp. 294–6) detects the attempted cover-up by Montcalm and Vaudreuil. William G. Godfrey, *Pursuit of Profit and Preferment in Colonial America: John Bradstreet's Quest* (Waterloo, 1982), pp. 76–85, probes the causes of the failure to relieve Oswego and the circumstances that allowed the blame to fall on Shirley. See also Gipson, VI, 205–9.

British and American armies

The British army: Alan Guy, 'The Army of the Georges 1714–1783' in David Chandler and Ian Beckett, eds. *The Oxford Illustrated History of the British Army* (Oxford, 1994), pp. 92–110; Tony Hayter, *The Army and the Crowd in Mid-Georgian England* (London, 1978), pp. 20–5; Stephen Brumwell, *Redcoats: The British Soldiers and War in the Americas, 1755–1763* (Cambridge, 2002), esp. pp. 11–26. Loudoun, provincials, recruiting and the colonies: Anderson, *Crucible of War*, pp. 135–49; Alan Rogers, *Empire and Liberty: American Resistance to British Authority, 1755–1763* (Berkeley and Los Angeles, 1974), Chapters 4–7; Pargellis, *Lord Loudoun*, pp. 82–210. Indentured servants: Rogers, pp. 42–4; Karl Frederick Geiser, *Redemptioners and Indentured Servants in the Colony and Commonwealth of Pennsylvania* (New Haven, 1901), pp. 39, 71, 94–101. On migration and settlement of recruits from Germany see Alexander V. Campbell, 'Atlantic Microcosm: The Royal American Regiment, 1755–1772' in Rhoden, ed. *English Atlantics Revisited* (cited in Chapter 1), pp. 284–309. The difference in quality between New England's provincials and those raised in Pennsylvania and Virginia, especially before 1757, is set forth in Ward, *Breaking the Backcountry* (cited in Chapter 5), pp. 104–22. Building Fort William Henry: Steele, *Betrayals*, Chapter 3. Activities of the

French at Ticonderoga: Hamilton, ed. *Adventure in the Wilderness*, pp. 33–98.

Chapter 8 France's new war plan, 1756–57
Pitt attains his goal

The account in Clark, *Dynamics of Change* (cited in Chapter 6), pp. 225–326 is thoroughly researched and reliable; the briefer treatment in Sherrard, *Lord Chatham*, II, 124–62 is also helpful. Hardwicke's correspondence with Newcastle is of the first importance; see Yorke, *Hardwicke*, II, 275–80, 318–39, 375–83. See also Ilchester, *Henry Fox*, I, 329–60, II, 1–21, and William James Smith, ed. *The Grenville Papers: Being the Correspondence of Richard Grenville Earl Temple, K.G., and the Right Hon. George Grenville, Their Friends and Contemporaries* 4 vols (London, 1852–3), vol. I.

War begins on the continent

Diplomatic antecedents: Doran, *Andrew Mitchell and Anglo-Prussian Diplomatic Relations*, pp. 59–69; Scott, *Birth*, pp. 94–5. A penetrating analysis of Prussia's situation may be read in Dorn, *Competition*, pp. 311–17; also in Herbert Butterfield, 'The Reconstruction of a Historical Episode: The History of the Enquiry into the Origins of the Seven Years War' in Butterfield, *Man on his Past: The Study of the History of Historical Scholarship* (Cambridge, 1969), pp. 142–70, which traces historians' attempts to discover whether Prussia was truly under threat. On the Prussian army's 1756 campaign: Showalter, *Wars of Frederick the Great*, pp. 135–45, and Szabo, pp. 36–47.

France's support of Austria: John Charles Batzel, 'Austria and the First Three Treaties of Versailles, 1755–1758' (Ph.D. thesis, Brown University, 1974), pp. 147–206; Waddington, *Louis XV et le renversement*, pp. 462–77; Dull, *French Navy*, pp. 68–70.

France's new war plan

France's determination to attack Hanover and her resulting strained relations with Austria are exhibited in Batzel, 'Austria and the First Three Treaties', pp. 206–39, 249–93 and Waddington, *Guerre*, I, 58–106.

On Pompadour's immense influence, particularly after the dismissal of Machault and d'Argenson, and also on the recalcitrance of the parlements in 1756, see Julian Swann, *Politics and the Parlement of Paris under Louis XV, 1754–1774* (Cambridge, 1995), pp. 53–6, 141–82. That Louis XV's court perceived a Protestant-based conspiracy in both the parlement's resistance and the assassination attempt is pointed out by Woodbridge in *Revolt in Prerevolutionary France* (cited in Chapter 7), pp. 69–80.

The trial of Admiral Byng

Chiefly based on: Tunstall, *Admiral Byng and the Loss of Minorca* (cited in Chapter 7) and my 'John Byng' article in *ODNB*. Original sources: Beatson, *Naval and Military Memoirs*, III, 329–36; Walpole, *Memoirs of King George II*, II, 163–75, 198–244. Lord Lyttelton's comment is in Robert Phillimore, ed. *Memoirs and Correspondence of George, Lord Lyttelton* 2 vols (London 1845).

Pitt, George II and Germany

Clark, *Dynamics of Change*, pp. 321–444; Sherrard, *Lord Chatham*, II, 163–213; Williams, *Life*, I, 303–25; Yorke, *Hardwicke*, II, 360–412. On the House of Commons enquiry see the authoritative summary in Richmond, *Papers Relating to the Loss of Minorca* (cited in Chapter 7), pp. xxi–xxvii; also Walpole, *Memoirs of King George II*, II, 252–4. Fact-filled parliamentary papers generated by the inquiry are printed copiously in *The History, Debates, and Proceedings of both Houses of Parliament of Great Britain from the year 1743 to the year 1774* 7 vols (London, 1792), III, 292–389.

The French invasion of Germany

Waddington, *Guerre* (I, 380–475, 527–57) remains the unmatched source. For Cumberland and his army: Savory, *His Britannic Majesty's Army*, pp. 11–46; Evan Charteris, *William Augustus, Duke of Cumberland* (London, 1925), pp. 250–90. On logistics and winter quarters: Kennett, *French Armies*, pp. 99–111. Richelieu's fear that Cumberland might receive reinforcements by sea is mentioned by Corbett (I, 224–6). An essential source: *Correspondence particulière et historique du maréchal duc de Richelieu en 1756, 1757 et 1758, avec M. Paris du Verney* 2 vols (London, 1789), I, 98–251.

Prague and Kolin: Showalter, *Wars of Frederick the Great*, pp. 148–67; Szabo, 56–64.

A Hanoverian policy

Politics and diplomacy: Dann, *Hanover and Great Britain*, Chapter 5; Yorke, *Hardwicke*, III, 157–89; BL Add. 32,872–5 *passim*; Doran, *Andrew Mitchell and Anglo-Prussian Diplomatic Relations*, pp. 120–32.

Louisbourg and Lake George

Louisbourg expedition: Gipson, VII, 101–16; J.S. McLennan, *Louisbourg from its Foundation to its Fall* (London, 1918, repr. Halifax 1979), pp. 202–5; Pargellis, *Lord Loudoun*, pp. 229–43, but Pargellis attributes the failure to bad weather rather than France's naval achievement.

Fort William Henry: Steele, *Betrayals* is essential (pp. 57–128). Also useful and well considered is Chapter 19 of Anderson's *Crucible of War*. Francis Parkman's Chapter 15 in *Montcalm and Wolfe* is not only beautifully written but quite informative regarding the French and Indian side of the campaign. Original sources concerning Loudoun's and Webb's failures are found in Kimball, *Correspondence of Pitt with America*, I, 36–73 *passim*; Pargellis, *Lord Loudoun*, pp. 243–51; Pargellis, ed. *Military Affairs*, pp. 313–25, 370–9, 396–7.

The Rochefort expedition

The Baltic squadron issue: Karl W. Schweizer, *Frederick the Great, William Pitt, and Lord Bute: The Anglo-Prussian Alliance, 1756–1763* (New York, 1991), pp. 55–7; Doran, *Andrew Mitchell and Anglo-Prussian Diplomatic Relations*, pp. 144–9. Sherrard (*Lord Chatham*, II, 216–24) also discusses the expedition's political background and preparation.

On the operation's conduct I have used: Mackay, *Admiral Hawke*, pp. 160–80; Mackay, ed. *Hawke Papers*, pp. 149–82; and W. Kent Hackman, 'The British Raid on Rochefort' *MM* 64 (1978), 263–75. Also, *The Report of the General Officers, appointed by His Majesty's Warrant of the First of November, 1757, to inquire into the Causes of the Failure of the late Expedition to the Coasts of France* (1758), of which there were many printings, is a rich primary source though not all of its facts were accurate. Corbett's Chapter 9 (vol. I) is informative, but Corbett managed to believe that the expedition was a successful diversion. The French side is not well studied, but see Lacour-Gayet, *Marine Militaire*, pp. 304–10, and G. Tulau, 'La Flotte anglaise sur les côtes d'Aunis et de Saintonge en 1757' *Revue maritime et coloniale* 114 (1892), 114–20.

On the public furore see Peters, *Pitt and Popularity*, pp. 94–102, and Smith, ed. *Grenville Papers* (cited above), I, 212–27. Woodbridge, *Revolt in Prerevolutionary France* (cited in Chapter 7) gives a useful and detailed account of the furore and of Pitt's suspicion of treachery on the part of the army and the Duke of Cumberland (pp. 120–34), but his effort to show that the expedition counted on organized Huguenot assistance ashore is unconvincing. That cabinet members were deeply worried by the public furore and upset by the generals' conduct is plainly revealed in their letters (BL Add. 32,874–5 *passim* and Yorke, *Hardwicke*, III, 186–90). Although P.C. Yorke undoubtedly read these letters, he nevertheless wrote a highly distorted account of the expedition (III, 116–18). Concerning the inquiry, the *Report of the General Officers* is a basic and important source. Middleton, *Bells*, pp. 42–3, provides a summary of Mordaunt's court-martial.

Chapter 9 The tide turns, 1758

The French army in Germany: defeat and disaster

The foundation is Waddington, *Guerre*, I, 380–446, 458–79, 491–559, 587–685, 728–45; II, 2–67; for the conduct of relations with Austria: I, 543–6, 558–72. Camille Rousset, *Le Comte de Gisors, 1752–1758* (Paris, 1868) contains letters Gisors wrote to his father, Belleisle, while serving in Richelieu's army. On aspects of supply in 1757 and 1758 Kennett, *French Armies* is essential (pp. 43, 92–111). The basic difficulty of French campaigning in Germany is summed up in pp. 291–4 of H.M. Scott, 'Hanover in Mid-eighteenth Century Franco-British Geopolitics' in Brendan Simms and Torsten Riotte, eds. *The Hanoverian Dimension in British History, 1714–1837* (Cambridge, 2007), pp. 275–300.

Reconstituting the Army of Observation: Dann, *Hanover and Great Britain*, pp. 116–18. Appointment of Ferdinand of Brunswick: Szabo, p. 94. On the achievements of Ferdinand's army from late November 1757 to April 1758 nothing matches the account in Savory, *His Britannic Majesty's Army*, pp. 47–68. The capture of Emden: Corbett, I, 248–52. Frederick II's victories at Rossbach and Leuthen: Showalter, *Wars of Frederick the Great*, pp. 185–206; Szabo, pp. 96–112.

War in India: Bengal

The duration of voyages was calculated from examples of the 1740s and 1750s in Anthony Farrington, *Catalogue of East India Company Ships' Journals and Logs 1600–1834* (London, 1999). Rex Whitworth, ed. *Gunner at Large: The Diary of James Wood R.A., 1746–1765* (London, 1988) prints a daily journal of an outbound voyage (pp. 73–93). My discussion of routes and seasons is based chiefly on Vigié's in *Dupleix* (pp. 32–6).

Campaigns: Forrest, *Life of Lord Clive* (cited in Chapter 3) provides clear, detailed narratives (I, 256–460). An admirable brief account is offered by Michael Edwardes in *The Battle of Plassey and the Conquest of Bengal* (London, 1963). My figures concerning British casualties are drawn from H.C. Wylly, *A Life of Lieutenant-General Sir Eyre Coote, K.B.* (Oxford, 1922), pp. 31, 34, 42. Concerning negotiations with the nawab of Bengal and the conspiracy mounted against him I have relied chiefly on J.H. Little, *The House of Jagatseth* (Calcutta, 1967), pp. 168–200 and Mark Bence-Jones, *Clive of India* (London, 1974), pp. 100–32, a book that has also been a key source for glimpses of Clive's personal life as well as the battle of Plassey (pp. 133–43). For certain particulars I have consulted S.C. Hill, ed. *Bengal in 1756–1757: A Selection of Public and Private Papers Dealing with the Affairs of the British in Bengal during the Reign of Siraj-upduala* 3 vols (London, 1905, repr. New York, 1968), especially vol. 2.

For the larger picture: P.J. Marshall, *The Making and Unmaking of Empires: Britain, India, and America c. 1750–1783* (Oxford, 2005), Chapter 4, 'War and its Transformations, India 1754–1765'.

Achieving naval superiority

Manning: Daniel A. Baugh, *British Naval Administration in the Age of Walpole* (Princeton, 1965), Chapter 4. Stephen F. Gradish, *The Manning of the British Navy in the Seven Years' War* (London, 1980) is an important monograph on the Royal Navy's mobilization. A table based on the work of David J. Starkey showing the growth of the seafaring population may be found in Daniel A. Baugh, 'The Eighteenth-Century Navy as a National Institution, 1690–1815', Chapter 5 of J.R. Hill, ed. *The Oxford Illustrated History of the Royal Navy* (Oxford, 1995), pp. 133–9. Manning the French navy: Timothy J.A. Le Goff, 'Problèmes de recrutement de la marine française pendant la Guerre de Sept Ans' *Revue historique* 283 (1990), 205–33; also Le Goff, 'Les gens de mer devant le système des classes (1755–1763): résistance ou passivité?' *Revue du Nord*, no. 1 spécial hors série (1986), 463–79; this article explores the great difference between the Atlantic and Mediterranean situations. Chapter 4 of Pritchard, *Louis XV's Navy* is packed with valuable information; he emphasizes the French navy's failure to pay its seamen.

Ships, their numbers compared, and aspects of durability: Clive Wilkinson, *The British Navy and the State in the Eighteenth Century* (Woodbridge, 2004), pp. 67–80, 84–94. Jean Meyer and Martine Accera, *Histoire de la Marine Française des origines à nos jours* (Rennes, 1994), pp. 100–10. I have made considerable use of Dull's lists of active British and French warships (*French Navy*, pp. 255–86).

For a general comparison of the missions, facilities and attributes of the two navies, see Baugh, 'Naval Power' (cited in Chapter 1), pp. 235–57; this essay cites numerous sources of information on the French navy. For the Royal Navy see the bibliography associated with Baugh, 'The Eighteenth-Century Navy as a National Institution'. See also N.A.M. Rodger, *The Command of the Ocean: A Naval History of Britain, 1649–1815* (London, 2004), pp. 291–311, and his article, 'The Victualling of the British Navy in the Seven Years' War' *Bulletin du Centre d'Histoire des Espaces Atlantiques* No. 2 (Bordeaux, 1985), pp. 37–53. Rodger's *The Wooden World: An Anatomy of the Georgian Navy* (London, 1986) is an incomparable study of shipboard life, manning and naval careers, and happens to be focused on the era of the Seven Years War. Regarding the French ordnance problem, manning, naval finance, officer corps and naval authority see Pritchard, *Louis XV's Navy*, pp. 37–88, 143–59, 184–205; also, Dull, *French Navy*, pp. 45–49.

Raids on the French Channel coast

The complexities involved in developing the subsidy treaty with Prussia are laid out in Carl William Eldon, *England's Subsidy Policy towards the Continent during the Seven Years' War* (Philadelphia, 1938), pp. 108–18. Pitt's comments about Mitchell in his letter to Newcastle of 28 January 1758 are printed in Doran, *Andrew Mitchell and Anglo-Prussian Diplomatic Relations*, p. 167. On the timing of the first raid to coincide with Ferdinand of Brunswick's offensive see Corbett, I, 266–9, 275–81.

My account of the raids mainly follows W. Kent Hackmann, 'English Military Expeditions to the Coast of France, 1757–1761' (University of Michigan Ph.D. thesis, 1969), Chapter 3. It is supplemented by Middleton,

Bells, pp. 64–78, 81–5; Barthélemy Pocquet, *Histoire de Bretagne* vol. 6 (Rennes, 1914), pp. 256–74; and A.W.H. Pearsall, 'Naval Aspects of the Landings on the French Coast, 1758' in *The Naval Miscellany, Volume V*, ed. N.A.M. Rodger, NRS (London, 1984), pp. 207–43. Pearsall discusses the design and hurried construction of flat-bottomed boats, and also provides precise details, drawn from officers' logs, of the operational role of Howe's ships.

France in distress

On military operations near the Rhine, including the battle of Krefeld and its aftermath see Savory, *His Britannic Majesty's Army* pp. 67–115, and Waddington, *Guerre*, II, 60–7, 112–87. Bernis's despair and his reasons for the necessity of peace may be read in his correspondence from May through October 1758 with Stainville (Choiseul). An English translation is K.P. Wormeley, *Memoirs and Letters of Cardinal de Bernis* 2 vols (Boston, 1901), II, 181–251. I have translated quotations, however, from Masson, ed. *Mémoires et Lettres de . . . Bernis*.

Austria's military recovery: Szabo, pp. 126–8. Regarding negotiations between Vienna and Versailles: Batzel, 'Austria and the First Three Treaties' (cited in Chapter 8), pp. 375–96, 409–13, 418–29, 452–84, 498–9, 512–25. (Starhemberg's personal dislike of Choiseul is revealed on pp. 513–14, 518–19.) Waddington, *Guerre*, II, 415–85 is an equally essential source. For Choiseul's deft manoeuvring amidst contradictory advice from Versailles see Chaussinand-Nogaret, *Choiseul*, pp. 68–75.

State finances: Austria's efforts toward improvement are summarized in Szabo, pp. 123–6. On Louis XV and the parlement of Paris see Waddington, *Guerre*, I, 124–33. Bernis's negotiations with the parlement are discussed by Swann, *Politics and the Parlement of Paris* (cited in Chapter 8), pp. 148–55.

Chapter 10 The Atlantic and North America, 1758

Sea power and shipping

Comprehensive studies: Patrick Villiers, *Marine Royale, corsaires et trafic dans l'Atlantique de Louis XIV à Louis XVI* 2 vols (Villeneuve d'Ascq, [2002]), II, 445–60. Patrick Crowhurst, 'The Admiralty and the Convoy System in the Seven Years War' *MM* 57 (1971), 163–73. The British fleet's blockading ineffectiveness prior to 1759 is carefully traced in

Richard Middleton, 'British Naval Strategy, 1755–1762: The Western Squadron' *MM* 75 (1989), 351–60.

British privateering: David J. Starkey, *British Privateering Enterprise in the Eighteenth Century* (Exeter, 1990), pp. 161–92, gives a penetrating account of its incidence, modalities and permutations in this war. I am grateful to Jeremy Michell for sharing with me his forthcoming article 'British Prize-taking during the Seven Years' War, 1755 to 1762', which includes valuable statistical compilations. See Gomer Williams, *History of the Liverpool Privateers and Letters of Marque* (Liverpool and London, 1897, repr. Montreal and Kingston, 2004), pp. 79–178 on privateers engaging in combat. Also valuable is A.G. Jamieson, *A People of the Sea: The Maritime History of the Channel Islands* (London and New York, 1986), pp. 154–7.

French West Indian trade: François Crouzet's chapters in F-G. Pariset, *Bordeaux au XVIIIe Siècle* (Bordeaux, 1968), esp. pp. 194–205, 221–34, 287–300. Pierre H. Boulle, 'Patterns of French Colonial Trade and the Seven Years' War' *Histoire Sociale* 13 (1974), 48–86, esp. 50–62, 73–5, 79–80. Pares, *War and Trade* (pp. 322–43, 359–62) is indispensable, though his view of the strategic utility of disrupting the French West India trade (pp. 390–3) is quite narrow.

Neutral shipping and the French West Indies: Richard Pares, *Colonial Blockade and Neutral Rights 1739–1763* (Oxford, 1938, repr. Philadelphia, 1975) is the pioneering study (see esp. pp. 180–309); it covers the policy problems and places the legal arguments within a broad military and diplomatic context. On this subject see also: Pares, *War and Trade*, pp. 362–75; Carter, *Dutch Republic*, pp. 121–8; Joseph Yorke's letters to Hardwicke, BL Add. 35,357, ff. 287–341 *passim*; Williams, *Life*, I, 401–2.

Neutrals and naval stores: Carter, *Dutch Republic*, pp. 72–3, 88–121; H.S.K. Kent, *War and Trade in Northern Seas* (Cambridge, 1973), pp. 130–9. Pares's discussion in *Colonial Blockade*, pp. 245–55 is essential, but some of its interpretative comments seem to be undermined by his own evidence. Supplies of naval stores at the French dockyards: information on masts is scarce, but see James Pritchard, 'Fir Tree, Financiers, and the French Navy during the 1750's' *Canadian Journal of History* 23 (1988), 351–2. On anchors: Paul Walden Bamford, *Privilege and Profit: A Business Family in Eighteenth-Century France* (Philadelphia, 1988), pp. 125–8. On timber: Bamford, *Forests and French Sea Power, 1660–1789* (Toronto, 1956), pp. 57–69 is excellent.

The French effort to support Canada: John F. Bosher, 'La ravitaillement de Québec en 1758' *Histoire Sociale* 5 (1972), 79–85; *The Canada Merchants, 1713–1763* (Oxford, 1987), pp. 14–22, 174–201; and *Business*

and Religion in the Age of New France (Toronto, 1994), especially
Chapters 14 'Success and Failure in Trade with New France, 1660–1760'
and 21 'Shipping to Canada in Wartime 1743–1760'. See also Jean de
Maupassant, *Un grand armateur de Bordeaux: Abraham Gradis* (Bordeaux,
1931); Stanley, *New France*, pp. 191–200, 211–13. The Admiralty's
assignment of cruisers to cover the French Atlantic coast at this time has
never been studied systematically; Captain Geary's reports in 1757 (Adm
1/1833) are detailed but of limited scope.

West Africa

James L.A. Webb, Jr., 'The Mid-Eighteenth Century Gum Arabic Trade
and the British Conquest of Saint-Louis du Sénégal, 1758' *JICH* 25
(1997), 37–56, and A.J. Marsh, 'The Taking of Goree, 1758' *MM* 51
(1965), 117–30. Beatson's narrative (*Naval and Military Memoirs*) remains
useful (II, 140–9); see also III, 184–9 where an account of the *Litchfield*
shipwreck by a survivor is printed.

Changing conditions of warfare in North America

Canadian food shortage: Jean Elizabeth Lynn, 'Agriculture and War in
Canada, 1740–1760' *Canadian Historical Review* 16 (1935), 123–36;
Gilles Archambault, 'La Question des vivres au Canada au cours de
l'hiver 1757–1758' *Revue d'histoire de l'Amerique française* 21 (1967–8),
16–50. Indian support: Parmenter, 'After the Mourning Wars' (cited in
Chapter 3), pp. 70–2.

Pitt's encouragement of provincials and recall of Loudoun: Anderson,
Crucible of War, pp. 166–8, 200–1, 209–14, 219–31; Pargellis, *Lord
Loudoun*, pp. 336–48. Pargellis's well researched account, though partial
to Loudoun, is nevertheless first rate.

Ligonier's elevation: in addition to the letters between Hardwicke and
Newcastle cited in the footnotes there is an account in Whitworth,
Ligonier, pp. 219–25.

The conquest of Louisbourg

On the French navy's frustrated efforts see François Caron, *La guerre
incomprise ou les raisons d'un échec (Capitulation de Louisbourg, 1758)*
(Vincennes, 1983), pp. 277–97, 310–16, and also the summary of the
voyages in Dull, *French Navy*, pp. 106–7.

Basque Roads, 4–7 April 1758: Mackay, *Admiral Hawke*, pp. 189–92. The Mediterranean: Corbett, I, 255–60; Ch. Chabaud-Arnault, 'Études historiques sur la marine militaire de France: La marine française avant et pendant la guerre de Sept ans, IV' *Revue Maritime et Coloniale* 114 (1892), 490–1.

The assault upon and defence of Louisbourg: McLennan, *Louisbourg from its Foundation to its Fall* (cited in Chapter 8), pp. 238–93 is the principal authority. On the hazardous landing see also J. Mackay Hitsman with C.C.J. Bond, 'The Assault Landing at Louisbourg, 1758' *Canadian Historical Review* 35 (1954), 314–30.

Ticonderoga and Frontenac

Ticonderoga: Ian M. McCulloch, '"Like roaring lions breaking from their chains": The Battle of Ticonderoga, 8 July 1758' in Donald E. Graves, ed. *Fighting for Canada, Seven Battles, 1758–1945* (Toronto, 2000), pp. 23–80; and Nicholas Westbrook, '"Like roaring lions breaking from their chains", The Highland Regiment at Ticonderoga' *Bulletin of the Fort Ticonderoga Museum* 16 (1998), 17–91. British campaign preparations: Gipson, VII, 212–18. French defence: Stanley, *New France*, pp. 176–8; Bougainville's journal in Hamilton, ed. *Adventure in the Wilderness*, pp. 205–32; Parkman, *Montcalm and Wolfe*, pp. 352–70.

Fort Frontenac: my account mainly follows that in Godfrey, *Pursuit of Profit* (cited in Chapter 7), pp. 123–34, but is supplemented and amended by documents printed in Richard A. Preston and Leopold Lamontagne, *Royal Fort Frontenac*, Champlain Society (Toronto, 1958), pp. 78–80, 256–8, 262–71.

Mountains and Indians: the road to Fort Duquesne

The sketch of the frontier situation is based on printed sources in Sylvester K. Stevens and Donald H. Kent, eds. *Wilderness Chronicles of Northwestern Pennsylvania* (Harrisburg, PA, 1941), pp. 93–115. Choice of route and progress of the road: S.K. Stevens, Donald H. Kent and Autumn L. Leonard, eds. *The Papers of Henry Bouquet, Volume II: The Forbes Expedition* (Harrisburg, PA, 1951), cited as *Bouquet Papers*, II, is the indispensable source. Forbes's letters to Governor Denny, General Abercromby and William Pitt are printed in Alfred Proctor James, ed. *Writings of General John Forbes* (Menasha, WI, 1938). For the correspondence of George Washington with persons other than Bouquet:

Abbot, ed. *Papers of George Washington* (cited in Chapter 5), vols. 5 and 6. Volume 6 contains a useful map of the roads. The best secondary accounts are Gipson, VII, 247–86, and Niles Anderson, 'The General Chooses a Road: The Forbes Campaign of 1758 to Capture Fort Duquesne' *Western Pennsylvania Historical Magazine* 42 (1959), 109–38, 241–58, 383–401. Archer Butler Hulburt, *Historic Highways of America, Volume 5: The Old Glade (Forbes's) Road* (Cleveland, OH, 1903) is a remarkable product of archival research for its time and despite its nationalistic rapture remains useful, especially for relating primitive to modern place names. For Major Grant's battle and the two subsequent skirmishes: Gipson, VII, 268–70, 273–4, 282–3; for the November skirmish: Freeman, *George Washington* (cited in Chapter 3), II, 357–9. Negotiations with the Delawares and Shawnees, and Christian Frederick Post's journeys: Gipson, VII, 275–81; Anderson, *Crucible of War*, pp. 268–82; Jennings, *Empire of Fortune*, pp. 374, 384–7. My account was written before I was aware of Matthew Ward's *Breaking the Backcountry* (cited in Chapter 5); his chapter concerning this campaign, which discloses Forbes's conception of the mission and Bouquet's expertise, should be first on anyone's list of further reading.

Chapter 11 The West Indies and North America, 1759
Martinique and Guadeloupe

West Indies naval background: Corbett, I, 351–70. Adoption of the project and Pitt's motivations: Corbett, I, 371–6; Peters, *Pitt and Popularity*, pp. 128–32.

Operations: the best-researched account by far is Marshall Smelser, *The Campaign for the Sugar Islands, 1759: A Study of Amphibious Warfare* (Chapel Hill, NC, 1955); see pp. 57–9 for French reports about Martinique's weak means and will to resist. See also: Corbett, I, 377–95; Beatson, *Naval and Military Memoirs*, II, 228–49, III, 210–20, 361; and the dispatches in Kimball, ed. *Correspondence of Pitt with America*, II, 20–31, 83–4, 94–106, 141–2, 174–7.

Niagara and Lake Champlain

Niagara: I have basically relied on Brian Leigh Dunnigan, *Siege – 1759: The Campaign Against Niagara*, rev. ed. (Youngstown, NY, 1996). Milton W. Hamilton, *Sir William Johnson* (cited in Chapter 5), pp. 241–63 adds useful details. An essential primary source is Pouchot's *Memoirs on the Late War in North America between France and England*, translated by Dunnigan (Youngstown, NY, 1994) with valuable footnotes, pp. 188–235. For La Corne's raid on Oswego: Gipson, VII, 356–7.

Lake Champlain: my account is drawn mainly from Amherst's journal, *The Journal of Jeffery Amherst*, ed. by J. Clarence Webster (Toronto and Chicago, 1931), pp. 130–98; and Daniel John Beattie, 'General Jeffery Amherst and the Conquest of Canada, 1758–1760' (Ph.D. dissertation, Duke University, 1975), pp. 137–98. Lawrence Shaw Mayo, *Jeffery Amherst: A Biography* (New York and London, 1916), pp. 122–65 offers a reliable guide. For the French side, see C.P. Stacey's 'Bourlamaque' in *DCB*, III, 84–7; and David Lee, 'The Contest for Isle aux Noix, 1759–1760: A Case Study in the Fall of New France' *Vermont History* 37 (1969), pp. 96–101.

Montcalm, Vaudreuil and the defence of Canada

Interrelations of French and Canadian soldiers: Jean Berenger and Philippe Roy, 'Les relations des troupes reglées (troupes de terre et de la marine) avec les Canadiens' in Jean Delmas, ed. *Conflits de sociétés au Canada français pendant la guerre de sept ans et leur influence sur les operations* (Vincennes, 1978), pp. 19–40.

Montcalm versus Vaudreuil: W.J. Eccles, 'Montcalm', *DCB*, III, 458–69. For Montcalm's early life and career see Marie-Magdeleine Del Perugia, *Louis-Joseph de Saint-Véran: Marquis de Montcalm* (Paris, 2004), pp. 17–21. Eccles, 'Rigaud de Vaudreuil', *DCB*, IV (relevant pages 669–72). Roger Michalon, 'Vaudreuil et Montcalm: les hommes, leurs relations, influence de ces relations sur la conduite de la guerre 1756–1759' in Delmas, ed. *Conflits*, pp. 41–140. Frégault, *Canada: the War of the Conquest* (cited in Chapter 3), pp. 63, 123–4, 151–3, 228–30, 242–3. *NYCD*, X, 687–926 passim.

Bougainville at Versailles: Casgrain, *Montcalm et Lévis*, II, 36–42; Étienne Taillemite, 'Bougainville', *DCB*, V, 102–6; Hamilton, ed. *Adventure in the Wilderness*, pp. 296–311, 322–4; Waddington, *Guerre*, III, 252–61; Pierre-Georges Roy, 'La Mission de M. De Bougainville en France en 1758–1759' *Rapport de l'archiviste de la province de Québec* 4 (1923–4), 1–70; *NYCD*, X, 906–7.

Defence of Canada: in addition to Eccles's *DCB* articles on Montcalm and Vaudreuil, and Michalon's 'Vaudreuil et Montcalm' see Eccles's important essay, 'The French forces in North America during the Seven Years' War' in *DCB*, III, xv–xxiii.

The capture of Quebec

The indispensable study is C.P. Stacey, *Quebec, 1759: The Siege and the Battle* (Toronto, 2002); this edition of a book first published in 1959, edited by Donald E. Graves, contains valuable appendices, among which are Stacey's subsequent contributions and a chapter by Graves on naval aspects. My account is principally based on materials in this book, but an original source of importance is *An Historical Journal of the Campaigns in North American for the Years 1757, 1758, 1759, and 1760 by Captain John Knox* (cited as *Knox's Journal*), 3 vols edited by Arthur G. Doughty for the Champlain Society (Toronto, 1914). These volumes contain valuable supplementary material; vol. I, 328–456 and vol. II, 3–252 are directly relevant. I have also consulted Ian K. Steele, 'Monckton' and G.P. Browne, 'Murray', *DCB*, IV, 540–2, 569–7, and C.P. Stacey, 'Townshend', *DCB*, V, 822–3. The night approach downriver to the Anse au Foulon is analysed in Donald W. Olson, William D. Liddle, Russell I. Doescher, Leah M. Behrends, Tammy D. Silakowski and François-Jacques Saucier, 'Perfect Tide, Ideal Moon: An Unappreciated Aspect of Wolfe's Generalship at Québec, 1759' *WMQ* 59 (2002), 957–74.

For the battle on the Plains of Abraham: Tom Pocock, *Battle for Empire* (London, 1998), pp. 172–9; Stanley, *New France*, pp. 221–34; and the remarkable essay by Eccles, 'The Battle of Quebec: A Reappraisal' in his collected *Essays on New France* (Toronto, 1987), pp. 125–33. My assessment of Wolfe's plan differs from Eccles's but is essentially in agreement with his view of Montcalm's decision to attack Wolfe's line.

For the French side, in addition to Stacey I have consulted Casgrain, *Montcalm et Lévis*, II, 55–294, and the 'Journal de Foligné' in Arthur B. Doughty and G.W. Parmelee, *The Siege of Quebec and the Battle of the Plains of Abraham* 6 vols (Quebec, 1901) IV, 163–217.

William Wood, ed. *The Logs of the Conquest of Canada*, Champlain Society (Toronto, 1909) is a useful guide to St Lawrence River navigation in the age of sail and prints excerpts from the logs of many British warships involved in the operation. Corbett, I, 396–476 provides interesting details concerning the role of the navy in the campaign, but his speculations about Wolfe's ideas and intentions should not be credited.

Chapter 12 The British victory at sea, 1759

Invasion threat and blockade of Brest

French plans: P. Coquelle, 'Les Projects de Descent en Angleterre' *Revue d'histoire diplomatique* (1901); Lacour-Gayet, *Marine Militaire*, pp. 318–25;

Marcel Marion, *La Bretagne et le duc d'Aiguillon, 1753–1770* (Paris, 1898), pp. 94–106; Guy Le Moing, *La Bataille navale des 'Cardinaux' (20 novembre 1759)* (Paris, 2003). Claude Nordmann, 'Choiseul and the Last Jacobite Attempt of 1759' in *Ideology and Conspiracy: Aspects of Jacobitism, 1689–1759* (Edinburgh, 1982), pp. 201–17; this article also touches on negotiations with Sweden and Swedish politics. A copy of Choiseul's letter of 11 October to Havrincourt (intercepted) may be found in BL Add. 32,897, ff. 1–4.

British squadron off Le Havre: David Spinney, *Rodney* (London, 1969), pp. 148–71. David Syrett, ed. *The Rodney Papers*, NRS (Aldershot and Burlington, VT, 2005), I, 287–391 covers both the raid and the prolonged watch afterwards.

British coastal defence: Middleton, *Bells*, pp. 107–12; Williams, *Life*, II, 399–408; J.R. Western, *The English Militia in the Eighteenth Century* (London and Toronto, 1965), pp. 146–61.

Blockade of Brest: Mackay, *Admiral Hawke*, pp. 200–38; Mackay, ed. *Hawke Papers*, pp. 207–338; Marcus, *Quiberon Bay* (cited below), pp. 23–114; Richard Middleton, 'British Naval Strategy, 1755–1762: The Western Squadron' *MM* 75 (1989), 360–7.

Lagos Bay and Quiberon Bay

Gibraltar and Lagos Bay: Ch. Chabaud-Arnault, 'La marine française avant et pendant la guerre de sept ans' *Revue Maritime* 115 (1892), 411–15; Clowes, III, 210–15. I am grateful to Dr Clive Wilkinson for providing me with data from a *Namur* logbook on wind direction and strength for 17–19 August 1759.

La Clue's orders: Lieut. Costet, 'Un erreur historique: la destination de l'Escadre de Toulon en 1759' *Revue Maritime* n.s. 119 (November 1929), 637–44.

Quiberon Bay: principal sources: Mackay, *Admiral Hawke*, pp. 239–54, Mackay, ed. *Hawke Papers*, and Le Moing, *La Bataille navale* (cited above); supplemented by Lacour-Gayet, *Marine Militaire*, pp. 329–34, Geoffrey Marcus, *Quiberon Bay: The Campaign in Home Waters, 1759* (London, 1960), pp. 134–68, and Marion, *La Bretagne* (cited above), pp. 106–13. My reconstruction of the battle (about which so much remains uncertain) has greatly depended upon intercommunication with Dr Ruddock Mackay, whose book, co-authored with Michael Duffy, *Hawke, Nelson and British Naval Leadership, 1747–1805* (Woodbridge, 2009), provides a more detailed and comprehensive narrative.

France defeated: the war lost

Minden and its aftermath: see generally Piers Mackesy, *The Coward of Minden: The Affair of Lord George Sackville* (London and New York, 1979); Savory, *His Britannic Majesty's Army*, pp. 166–89; Waddington, *Guerre*, III, 24–109. Aftermath of Quiberon Bay: Mackay, ed. *Hawke Papers*, pp. 350–63; Le Moing, *La Bataille navale*, pp. 92–9. Thurot: Lacour-Gayet, *Marine Militaire*, pp. 348–51; Corbett, I, 88–91.

French finances. On revenue inadequacy: Joël Félix, *Finances et politique au siècle des Lumières: Le ministère L'Averdy, 1763–1768* (Paris, 1999) offers detailed information on Seven Years War revenues (pp. 37–58); also useful: Richard Bonney, 'Towards the Comparative Fiscal history of Britain and France during the "Long" Eighteenth Century', in Prados de la Escosura, ed. *Exceptionalism and Industrialisation* (cited in Chapter 1), pp. 197–99. For Silhouette's analysis: James C. Riley, *The Seven Years War and the Old Regime in France: The Economic and Financial Toll* (Princeton, 1986), pp. 148–58. Coping with military expenses in Germany: Kennett, *French Armies*, pp. 42–5, 92–5. International connections: Jacob M. Price, *France and the Chesapeake: A History of the French Tobacco Monopoly, 1674–1791, and of Its Relationship to the British American Tobacco Trades* 2 vols (Ann Arbor, 1973), I, 579–85. On Pâris de Monmartel (or Montmartel): Robert Dubois-Corneau, *Paris de Monmartel (Jean), Banquier de la Cour* (Paris, 1917), pp. 250–75. Bernis's 1758 letters to Stainville convey a sense of impending crisis: Masson, ed. *Mémoires et Lettres de . . . Bernis*, II *passim*. On the need for specie: Yves-René Durand, 'Mémoires de Jean-Joseph de Laborde' in *Annuaire-Bulletin de la Sociéte de l'Histoire de France, années 1968–1969* (Paris, 1971), pp. 154–60; also Barbier's *Journal* vol. 7, pp. 194–208. For insight into borrowing expedients see David D. Bien, 'Offices, Corps, and a System of State Credit: The Uses of Privilege under the Ancien Régime', in Keith Michael Baker, ed. *The French Revolution and the Creation of Modern Political Culture* vol. 1 (Oxford, 1987), pp. 89–114. The problem of wartime outflow of specie is analysed with respect to Britain for an earlier period in D.W. Jones's pioneering study: *War and Economy in the Age of William III and Marlborough* (Oxford, 1988).

Naval finance and the bankruptcy crisis: Pritchard, *Louis XV's Navy*, provides an excellent and detailed overview (pp. 192–201). Especially for the linkage of commerce and naval finance see J.F. Bosher, *The Canada Merchants*, pp. 191–201, and 'Financing the French Navy in the Seven Years' War': *Beaujon, Goossens et Compagnie* in 1759' in *Business and Religion*, pp. 349–371 (both Bosher titles cited in Chapter 10). See also, Henri Legohérel, *Les Trésoriers généraux de la Marine (1517–1788)* (Paris, 1965), pp. 175–6, 180–7, 198, 205–6, 244–52, 262. Berryer's frustration: Pares, 'American versus Continental Warfare 1739–63' (cited in Chapter 2), 155–8; Pierre Henri Boulle, 'The French Colonies and the Reform of their Administration during and following the Seven Years' War', Ph.D. dissertation, University of California, Berkeley, 1968, pp. 150–4. On causes of the bankruptcy crisis see Félix, *Finances et politique* (cited above), pp. 54–8. I am grateful to Prof. Félix for a private communication concerning the perceived shortage of metallic money.

Chapter 13 Britain conquers afar, disunity looms at home

Choiseul's approach to peace, 1759–60

Spanish mediation and talks at The Hague: my account of the British side rests substantially on manuscript sources in the Newcastle papers (BL Add. 32,897–32,904) and *Devonshire Diary*, pp. 33–4. Other sources: Rashed, *Peace of Paris*, pp. 23–58; Waddington, *Guerre*, III, 427–41, 508–45; Roger H. Soltau, *The Duke de Choiseul* (Oxford, 1909), pp. 42–56. Alfred Bourguet, *Études sur la politique étrangère du Duc de Choiseul* (Paris, 1907), pp. 136–77 deals with the conversations at The Hague. Rohan Butler disclosed the deep roots of Carlos III's friendship with France in 'The Secret Compact of 1753 between the Kings of France and Naples' in *Royal and Republican Sovereignty in Early Modern Europe*, ed. by Robert Oresko, G.C. Gibbs and H.M. Scott (Cambridge, 1997), pp. 551–79. French dealings with Spain: André Soulange-Bodin, *La Diplomatie de Louis XV et le Pacte de Famille* (Paris, 1894), pp. 98–137, and Alfred Bourguet, *Le Duc de Choiseul et l'alliance espagnole* (Paris, 1906), pp. 90–118. (Unfortunately Bourguet did not always date his extracts from Choiseul's correspondence with d'Ossun.) François Rousseau, *Règne de Charles III d'Espagne (1759–1788)* 2 vols (Paris, 1907), I, 46–51 provides a detailed account of d'Ossun's effort to obtain permission to mention Spanish mediation in the counter-declaration but is otherwise not reliable.

Choiseul's dealings with Austria and Russia: Waddington, *Guerre* is the essential source (III, 440–54, 472–508; IV, 438–93). Choiseul–Bernstorff, *Correspondence*: Johann Hartvig Ernst von Bernstorff, *En brevvexling mellem Johan Hartvig Ernst Bernstorff og Hertugen af Choiseul, 1758–1766* (Copenhagen, 1871). (The letters are in French.)

War in India: the Coromandel Coast

My approach has been significantly influenced by background provided in articles by G.J. Bryant, particularly: 'British Logistics and the Conduct of the Carnatic Wars (1746–1783)' *War in History* 11 (2004), 278–306; 'Asymmetric Warfare: The British Experience in Eighteenth-Century India' *Journal of Military History* 68 (April 2004), 431–69; and 'The Cavalry Problem in the Early British Indian Army, 1750–1785' *War in History* 2 (l995), 1–21.

Although the histories and biographies mention money shortages, they do not consistently integrate this element into the military narrative.

The most important study, for both sides, is Dodwell's *Clive and Dupleix*, originally *Dupleix and Clive* (cited in Chapter 3), pp. 54–83. Robert Orme, *A History of the Military Transactions of the British Nation in Indostan from the Year MDCCXLV* 2 vols (London, 1778, repr. New Delhi, 1973) remains the most detailed record; it is difficult to use but indispensable.

For the French side I have relied chiefly on Tibulle Hamont, *La fin d'un empire français aux Indes sous Louis XV: Lally-Tollendal d'après des documents inédits* (Paris, 1887), and Waddington, *Guerre*, III, 380–421, V, 2–38. G.B. Malleson, *History of the French in India from the Founding of Pondicherry in 1674 to the Capture of that Place in 1761* 2nd ed. (London, 1909, repr. Delhi, 1984) seems not very reliable when checked against Dodwell, Hamont and Waddington. A lucid article by Sidney James Owen, 'Count Lally' *English Historical Review* 6 (1891), 495–534 relies heavily on Hamont's book. Owen explores, as Hamont did, the troubled relationship of Lally and Bussy, in which the recall of Bussy from the Deccan played a pivotal role. Dodwell (pp. 178–80) was strongly of the opinion that Lally made a wise decision when he recalled Bussy, but almost no one has agreed with him on this point. Although Owen is inclined to denigrate Bussy and excuse Lally, his scholarship is balanced and provides evidence which undermines some of his arguments. All historians agree that the process leading to Lally's execution was scandalous and shameful; see especially the accounts in Hamont and Owen.

For the British side: Wylly, *Life of Lieutenant-General Sir Eyre Coote* (cited in Chapter 9), is not strictly confined to Coote and his operations, and is essential reading (pp. 59–109, 382–95). The best account of Forde's expedition to the Northern Circars is Forrest's in *Life of Lord Clive* (cited in Chapter 3), II, 76–85, 104–16. For details of all the campaigns see vol. 2 of Orme's *Military Transactions* (cited above), which also provides troop numbers and casualties on both sides, including naval casualties.

The above works all take cognizance of naval operations. For movements of the squadrons Corbett (II, 120–35) is most informative. For the naval battles see Waddington, Hamont, Dodwell, Clowes (III, 174–82, 197–200) and Pocock, *Battle for Empire* (cited in Chapter 11), pp. 125–48. The impact of Lally's style of governance and the last grim months of Pondicherry under siege were recorded in fascinating detail in *The Private Diary of Ananda Ranga Pillai*, ed. by J. Frederick Price and K. Rangachari (ed. by H. Dodwell from vol. 4 onward), 12 vols (New Delhi, 1985), vols 11 and 12.

The conquest of Canada, 1760

Gipson, VII, 428–67, despite a few mistakes, is an excellent guide to events on both the British and French sides. Chapters 29 and 30 of Parkman's *Montcalm and Wolfe* are not only evocative but still generally accurate. Doughty, ed. *Historical Journal . . . by Captain John Knox* (cited in Chapter 11), vol. 2, is a remarkable source for the folowing: winter in Quebec, 241–376; battle of Ste-Foy and French siege of the city, 377–430; arrival of British ships and Swanton's resolve to sail upriver immediately, 414–30; the siege raised and movement of Murray's force upriver to Montreal, 430–522; and the articles of capitulation, 566–89. See also C.H. Little, 'Dispatches of Rear-Admiral Lord Colville, 1759–1761', Maritime Museum of Canada Occasional Papers (Halifax, 1958), pp. 15–28. The preparation and progress of Amherst's army in 1760 may be traced in Webster, *The Journal of Jeffery Amherst* (cited in Chapter 11), pp. 199–251.

For the French side: Waddington, *Guerre*, IV, 332–92 is valuable; also Casgrain, *Montcalm et Lévis*, II, 331–410; and Stanley, *New France*, pp. 242–58. On the feeble French rescue attempt and its delayed departure: Waddington, *Guerre*, IV, 333–4; *NYCD*, X, 1065–9; and Jean de Maupassant, 'Les deux expéditions de Pierre Desclaux au Canada (1759 et 1760)' *Revue historique de Bordeaux*, 8th year (1915), 313–30. See also Gustave Lanctot, *Réalisations françaises de Cartier à Montcalm* (Montreal, 1951), pp. 160–5, which also covers the subsequent destruction of the French ships in the Ristigouche River (pp. 166–81).

Pitt and the German war

Public opinion: Peters, *Pitt and Popularity*, pp. 154–82. Pitt's reluctance to send troops: Sherrard, *Lord Chatham*, pp. 354–6; Middleton, *Bells,* pp. 148–51, 155–6, 165–6. The 1760 French offensive and Ferdinand's defensive operations: Szabo, pp. 301–9; Savory, *His Britannic Majesty's Army*, pp. 202–79. On the dispute over sending an expedition to Belle-Île the best account is in Mackay, *Admiral Hawke*, pp. 267–73, supplemented by Whitworth, *Ligonier*, pp. 334–7 and Middleton, *Bells*, pp. 166–9. On the pamphlet by Israel Mauduit, *Considerations on the Present German War* (London, 1760) and its impact: Peters, *Pitt and Popularity*, pp. 182–6.

The Pitt–Newcastle administration undermined

Pitt's relations with Bute and Newcastle in 1760: Sherrard, *Lord Chatham*, pp. 349–50, 353–4, 360–7; on Pitt's (earlier) good relations with Bute: Romney Sedgwick, 'Letters from William Pitt to Lord Bute, 1755–1758' in Richard Pares and A.J.P. Taylor, eds. *Essays presented to Sir Lewis Namier* (London, 1956), pp. 108–66. Sackville's trial: Mackesy, *Coward of Minden* (cited in Chapter 12), pp. 158–242; Whitworth, *Ligonier*, pp. 320–4; Walpole, *Memoirs of King George II*, III, 101–5. Bute, Pitt and Newcastle in the new reign: my account is based on Namier, *England in the Age*, pp. 120–67, and *Devonshire Diary*, pp. 45–91. Sherrard (pp. 387–95) portrays the Duke of Devonshire as chiefly responsible for succumbing to Bute's intrigues, but Reed Browning (*The Duke of Newcastle* (cited in Chapter 2), pp. 274–5) attributes it to Newcastle's reacting to an imagined threat to his power, as he usually did.

Chapter 14 The chance of peace, 1761

Antecedents: Spain, Austria, Russia and Ferdinand's winter campaign

Dealings with Spain: Waddington, *Guerre*, IV, 415–29; Bourguet, *Choiseul et l'alliance espagnole* (cited in Chapter 13), pp. 119–89; Allen Christelow, 'Economic Background of the Anglo-Spanish War of 1762' *JMH* 18 (1946), 22–7. Queen Amelia's blocking of the loans: Arthur S. Aiton, 'The Diplomacy of the Louisiana Cession' *Amer. Hist. Rev.* 36 (1931), 706.

British policy: Waddington, as above; Yorke, *Hardwicke*, III, 250–2; Thackeray, *History*, I, 484–92; TNA SP 94/162 (State Papers); *Devonshire Diary*, p. 59. Disagreements between Vienna and Versailles: Waddington, *Guerre*, IV, 438–93. Ferdinand's winter campaign: Savory, *His Britannic Majesty's Army*, pp. 280–308; Waddington, *Guerre*, IV, 287–321.

Choiseul's two negotiations

Negotiation with Spain: the indispensable work is Didier Ozanam, 'Les origines du troisième Pacte de famille (1761)' *Revue d'histoire diplomatique* 75 (1961), 322–31. See also Bourguet, *Choiseul et l'alliance espagnole* (cited in Chapter 13), pp. 190–220, and Rashed, *Peace of Paris*, pp. 61–3, 75–9. Waddington's account (*Guerre*, IV, 428–35) lacks Spanish sources.

Negotiation with Britain: Rashed, *Peace of Paris*, pp. 70–5 provides a basic guide. Thackeray, *History* prints most of the documents (I, 506–43, II, 507–24). Choiseul's instructions to Bussy are printed in *Recueil des Instructions . . . XXV, 2: Angleterre*, ed. Paul Vaucher (Paris, 1965), pp. 372–85. Hardwicke's correspondence with Newcastle in BL Add. 32,921–3 is important.

Belle-Île and Westphalia

The best general accounts of the expedition are Hackmann 'English Military Expeditions to the Coast of France' (cited in Chapter 9), pp. 164–85, and F.J. Hebbert, 'The Belle-Ile Expedition of 1761' *JSAHR* 44 (1986), 81–93. An officer's journal of the operation is printed in 'The Siege and Capture of Belle-Isle' *Royal United Service Institution Journal* 43 (1899), 161–83, 520–33. On the navy's role Corbett, II, 158–70 may be consulted, but I have relied mainly on Keppel's letters to the Admiralty (TNA Adm 1/91, ff. 229–318), and to a lesser extent on Thomas Keppel, *The Life of Augustus Viscount Keppel* 2 vols (London, 1842), I, 302–29; also Whitworth, *Ligonier*, 348–52.

Information on the French side is scarce. Captain H. Binet's article, 'Les anglais at Belle-Isle-en-Mer (1761–1763)' *Revue de Bretagne* n.s. 49 (1913), 123–47 gives precise place names on p. 133 and these match an old map reproduced in *Vauban à Belle-Ile: Trois cents ans de fortification côtière en Morbihan*, Congrès de l'Association Vauban, May 1989 (Le Palais, 1990), p. 88. Maps, plans and photographs of fortifications may be found in *Vauban à Belle-Ile*.

On lack of reinforcement from the mainland: Marion, *La Bretagne* (cited in Chapter 12), pp. 164–8; see also the intelligence letters from Versailles (BL Add. 32,922, ff. 326–7 and 32,923, ff. 117–18), especially those dated 4 May and 16 May. The intelligence reports from French ports are less reliable but those of 4 May and 30 May 1761 (BL Add. 32,922, fo. 332 and 32,923, fo. 296) are of particular interest; the winds continuing 'to be English' is mentioned at fo. 296.

The campaign in Westphalia and the battle of Vellinghausen: Szabo offers an excellent brief account (pp. 350–3, 358–61); see also Savory, *His Britannic Majesty's Army*, pp. 310–62. Waddington, *Guerre*, V, 58–214 is the best source for the French side. For Bute's apology: Arnold Schaefer, *Geschichte des siebenjährigen Krieges* 2 vols (Berlin, 1867–74).

The Anglo-French negotiation

This section is based on primary sources. Nearly all the letters that passed between Pitt and Stanley (the latter reporting what Choiseul said in conversation) as well as the relevant memoirs are printed in Thackeray, *History*, I, 539–57; II, 524–65. Newcastle's papers (BL Add 32,324–6), are essential for revealing the British ministers' perceptions; they also contain some letters from Stanley not printed by Thackeray. *Devonshire Diary* is an essential source (pp. 92–116), and it supplies highly informative footnotes by Peter D. Brown and Karl W. Schweizer. For the letters of Grimaldi, Fuentes and Wall that were intercepted see *Chatham Correspondence*, II, 89–107, 137–44. The best history of the negotiation remains Rashed's *Peace of Paris*, pp. 75–114. Despite a tendency to take Choiseul's statements at face value, it is a work of thorough scholarship and thoughtful interpretation; French and Spanish archival sources as well as British are consulted, and she does not neglect the work of other historians (but is sometimes misled by them). The account in Middleton, *Bells*, pp. 182–92, lacks knowledge of the French side. Alfred Bourguet, 'Le Duc de Choiseul et l'angleterre: la Mission de M. de Bussy à Londres 1761' *Revue historique* 71 (1899), 1–32 gives an exaggerated impression of Bussy's role but contains useful information. Also W.L. Grant, 'La Mission de M. de Bussy à Londres en 1761' *Revue d'histoire diplomatique* 20 (1906), 351–66. Dull (*French Navy*, pp. 196–205) succinctly traces the terms offered.

Choiseul and the lost chance of peace

Karl Schweizer's 'Lord Bute, William Pitt, and the Peace Negotiations with France, April–September 1761' in Schweizer, ed. *Lord Bute: Essays in Re-interpretation* (Leicester, 1988), pp. 41–55, is brief and penetrating. He seems to agree with the many historians (p. 54, n. 37) who have claimed that Pitt's 26 June statement of terms caused Choiseul to turn towards Spain, but he also points out that Choiseul had other priorities and did not allow enough time (pp. 45–6). Max Savelle provides a detailed account of the negotiation in *Origins of American Diplomacy* (cited in Chapter 4), pp. 467–85; he consistently blames Pitt and justifies Choiseul, and seems not to realize that Choiseul was no longer negotiating for peace after 30 July. Williams, *Life* (pp. 80–102) and Peters, *Pitt and Popularity*, (pp. 200–1) have not found Pitt solely to blame, nor have Ozanam ('Les origines' (cited above), pp. 327–35), Chaussinand-Nogaret (*Choiseul*, pp. 135–40), and Pierre Muret, *La Prépondérance anglaise (1715–1763)* 3rd ed. (Paris, 1949), pp. 557–60. In contrast, P.C. Yorke's pertinacious blaming of Pitt (*Hardwicke*, III, 281–91) is carried to the extent of omitting important letters in which Hardwicke agreed with Pitt. Duc de Choiseul, *Mémoire historique sur la negoçiation de la France et de l'Angleterre, depuis le 26 mars 1761 jusqu'au 20 september de la même année, avec les pièces justificatives* (Imprimerie royale, Paris, 1761) may be read on Google Books, and a facsimile edition has very recently been printed in Breinigsville, PA.

Pitt's resignation and the path to war with Spain

Negotiations from 1 August onwards: Thackeray, *History*, II, 565–626; Newcastle's correspondence in BL Add. 32,326–8 (esp. Hardwicke's of 8 August, BL Add. 32,926, ff. 308–310, and Devonshire's of 9 August, fo. 322). *Devonshire Diary*, pp. 118–40 includes notes taken in meetings. Newcastle's notes of meetings are in Yorke, *Hardwicke*, III, 275–80 and also in William Hunt, 'Pitt's Retirement from Office, 5 Oct. 1761' *English Hist. Rev.* 21 (1906), 119–32, which may be read alongside Hardwicke's notes published by H.W.V. Temperley in 'Pitt's Retirement from Office, 5 Oct. 1761' in the same volume, 327–30. See also Hardwicke's notes of August meetings in Yorke, *Hardwicke*, III, 271–4. On Devonshire's role in persuading Bute and Pitt to grant favourable terms to France concerning the fisheries see K.W. Schweizer, 'The Cabinet Crisis of August 1761: Unpublished Letters from the Bute and Bedford Manuscripts' *BIHR* 59 (1986), 225–9.

Pitt's resignation: Some of Pitt's correspondence with Lord Bristol may be found in Thackeray, *History*, I, 560–67, 579–88. Corbett (II, 190–208) presents a useful account despite his occasionally questionable judgements. Richard Pares's treatment in *War and Trade* (pp. 580–90), based on French and Spanish as well as English original sources, is perceptive, but some of his broader statements seem inconsistent with his evidence. For London's dealings with Madrid after Pitt's resignation see Waddington, *Guerre*, IV, pp. 619–27.

Choiseul's efforts to coax Spain into hostilities: Blart, *Rapports*, pp. 17–24 is essential. See also Aiton, 'Diplomacy' (cited above), pp. 705–9.

The donated warships: Lacour-Gayet, *Marine Militaire*, pp. 390–2; Pritchard, *Louis XV's Navy*, pp. 204–5; Dziembowski, *Un nouveau patriotism français*, pp. 458–70.

Postdating the secret convention: Arthur S. Aiton, 'A Neglected Intrigue of the Family Compact' *Hispanic American Hist. Rev.* 11, 3 (1931), 387–93; Waddington, *Guerre*, IV, 625–6.

Chapter 15 Peacemaking 1762: concessions before conquests

Aftermath of Pitt's resignation

Pitt's situation and the press war: Peters, *Pitt and Popularity*, pp. 202–41 is the essential source; see also Williams, *Life*, pp. 114–23. Disunity of the ministry: Namier, *England in the Age*, pp. 302–10; *Devonshire Diary*, pp. 156–7. The 'Spanish Papers' called for by Parliament are printed in *Parl. Hist.* XV, 1128–210. For Pitt's speeches and the political background see Walpole, *Memoirs of King George III*, I, 56–107. Also Karl Schweizer, 'An Unpublished Parliamentary Speech by the Elder Pitt, 9 December 1761' *Historical Research* 64 (1991), 92–105. This long and impressive speech was recorded with great care by young Charles Jenkinson, Bute's secretary, who many years later (as Earl of Liverpool) became prime minister.

The German war and the Prussian subsidy

As the footnotes suggest, my principal sources for British decision-making, particularly relating to the German war, are the Newcastle Papers (BL Add. 32,934–40) and Yorke, *Hardwicke*, III, 295–303, 341–59, 368–9, 391–406; also *Devonshire Diary*, pp. 154–61, 166–8, 170–1. Karl Schweizer's 'The Bedford Motion and the House of Lords Debate 5 February 1762' *Parliamentary History* 5 (1986), 107–23 is an important article. For the demise of the Prussian subsidy see Schweizer, *Frederick the Great, William Pitt, and Lord Bute* (cited in Chapter 8), pp. 142–321, and Doran, *Andrew Mitchell and Anglo-Prussian Diplomatic Relations*, pp. 295–341. Walter S. Dorn, 'Frederick the Great and Lord Bute' *JMH* I (1929), 529–60 carefully examines the British overture to Austria; he emphasizes Newcastle's blundering role and tends to excuse Bute.

The view in Schweizer (pp. 172–81) is more balanced, and Herbert Butterfield's critical and penetrating analysis in 'British Foreign Policy, 1762–5' *HJ* 6 (1963), 131–6 should not be missed. On Treasury estimates and Newcastle's resignation see Namier, *England in the Age*, pp. 309–26. The battle of Wilhelmsthal and its antecedents: Savory, *His Britannic Majesty's Army*, pp. 362–76.

Martinique conquered

There is no definitive study of this expedition. Brief accounts may be found in Corbett, II, 209–11, 218–26 and Gipson, VIII, 187–96. In Pargellis, ed. *Military Affairs* there is a detailed description of Monckton's attack plan against Morne Tartenson (pp. 450–5). Captain Adam Williamson's letter to Newcastle offers an eyewitness account of the fighting (BL Add. 32,934, ff. 185–7). Colonel Hunt Walsh's memoir, ed. by W.Y. Baldry in 'The Expedition Against Martinique, 1762' *JSAHR* 1 (1921), 244–5 is less informative. The above three sources differ on material points. Regarding the French defence: M. Sidney Daney, *Histoire de la Martinique depuis la colonisation jusqu'en 1815* (Fort Royal, 1846, reprinted 1963), 5th part, Chapter 17 remains indispensable. C.A. Banbuck's contribution in *Histoire politique, économique et sociale de la Martinique sous l'Ancien Régime (1635–1789)* (Paris, 1935), pp. 131–40 depends greatly on Daney but adds some interesting items, especially regarding reinforcements from France. For naval aspects and the occupation of nearby islands see David Spinney, *Rodney* (London, 1969), pp. 172–90 and David Syrett, ed. *The Rodney Papers: Volume I, 1742–1763*, NRS (Aldershot, 2005), pp. 264–6, 422–47. For the expedition's preparations an important source is Kimball, ed. *Correspondence of Pitt with America*, II, 384–7, 403–19, 442–5, 452–86; also N.A.M. Rodger, ed. 'The Douglas Papers, 1760–1762', *The Naval Miscellany*, V, NRS (London, 1984), pp. 244–83. See Pares, *War and Trade* for discussions of West Indian peace terms (pp. 216–26), island defence (pp. 249–52), and Blénac's delayed sailing (pp. 590–1).

The secret negotiation

Four narratives have been consulted: Rashed, *Peace of Paris*, pp. 115–61; Pease, *Boundary Disputes*, pp. cxxi–cxlvii; Corbett, II, 327–50; and Savelle, *Origins of American Diplomacy* (cited in Chapter 4), pp. 489–503. Rashed is the best source for relations between France and Spain, but her narrative is not easy to follow. A clearer if much briefer account is in Blart, *Rapports*, pp. 24–31. Although Savelle's narrative is orderly and closely researched, it lacks insight from the French and Spanish sides. Pease's introduction is perceptive in a number of ways, especially with regard to the Mississippi boundary, but not comprehensive. Corbett, despite sententious pronouncements and occasional exaggerations, addresses the secret negotiation with clarity and insight. The above narratives disagree quite a bit on facts and interpretations, probably because the archive of Viry–Solar correspondence, which all four authors consulted (but I did not), is so copious and complex. My primary research in this case is focused on the rather amazing history of the British side; footnotes indicate my sources. Romney Sedgwick, ed. *Letters from George III to Lord Bute, 1756–1766* (London, 1939), pp. 113–29 carefully traces the sequence of events in June and July. Also useful are the transcriptions of some of Viry's and Choiseul's letters (translated), in Pease, *Boundary Disputes*, pp. 409–504.

The defence of Portugal

Spain's challenging problem of mobilizing an invasion army near the Portuguese border is examined in Augustin González Enciso, 'Spain's Mobilisation of Resources for the War with Portugal in 1762, in *Mobilising Resources for War: Britain and Spain at Work During the Early Modern Period*, ed. by H.V. Bowen and A. González Enciso (Pamplona, 2006), pp. 159–89.

Kenneth Maxwell, *Pombal: Paradox of the Enlightenment* (Cambridge, 1995), pp. 111–15 provides valuable insight into Portugal's situation. On the British contribution see A.D. Francis, 'The Campaign in Portugal, 1762' *JSAHR* 54 (1981), 25–42. David Francis's book, *Portugal 1715–1808* (London, 1985), contains a chapter entitled 'The 1762 War with Spain'; it is similar but not identical to his article. Jeremy Black, 'The British Expeditionary Force to Portugal in 1762: International Conflict and Military Problems' *British Hist. Soc. of Portugal Annual Report and Review* (1989), pp. 66–75 is a useful supplement. Naval protection is discussed in Corbett, II, 314–22.

It is not easy to keep track of the central Portugal campaigns of September–October in Francis's writings, which often fail to specify time and place. Rousseau's brief narrative in *Règne de Charles III* (cited in Chapter 13), I, 73–82, which is based on Spanish histories, provides a measure of clarity. On the British and Portuguese side, the reports of

Edward Hay to Egremont in TNA SP 89/55–7 are very helpful. Charles
Pierre Victor, comte de Pajol's chapter 'Campagne de Portugal (1762)' in
Les Guerres sous Louis XV 7 vols (Paris, 1881–91), VI, 123–53 is based
on French war department correspondence. Although its treatment is fragmented, it reports on the French auxiliary force and Spanish strategic
plans, and sketches the Spanish army's situation during the final weeks of
the campaign.

The capture of Havana

The essential source is David Syrett, ed. *The Siege and Capture of Havana
1762*, NRS (London, 1970). The documents are mainly naval, but Syrett's
introduction is comprehensive, and many of the documents provide
detailed information on land operations. Sonia Keppel's brief and reliable
Three Brothers at Havana 1762 (Salisbury, 1981) traces the progress of
the campaign ashore and discusses political aspects. Regarding preparations, decisions at Martinique, passage through the Old Bahama Channel
and execution of the landings Syrett's documents provide the essential
details. Spanish prior awareness and initial reactions at Havana have been
carefully investigated by David F. Marley in 'Havana Surprised: Prelude
to the British Invasion, 1762' *MM* 78 (1992), 293–305. David Syrett,
'American Provincials and the Havana Campaign of 1762' *New York
History* 49 (October 1968), 375–90 covers the assembling of all North
American troops, their passage to Havana, and return. Rousseau, *Règne
de Charles III* (cited above), pp. 82–8 offers statistics relevant to the
Spanish defence. Francis Russell Hart, *The Siege of Havana, 1762* (Boston
and New York, 1931) is of little value except for exhibiting the defenders'
impotence on the eve of capitulation.

Peace with bitterness

Of the four narratives listed above in 'The secret negotiation' Corbett's
(II, 346–65) is the most forcefully presented. Rashed's (*Peace of Paris*,
pp. 159–200) pays close attention to France and Spain, but the interplay
of the negotiation between Britain and France is better laid out in Savelle,
Origins of American Diplomacy, pp. 492–510. Pease's discussion
(*Boundary Disputes*, pp. cxxxvii–clxxi) is similarly well presented; it also
mentions facts drawn from the Viry–Solar archive that are not reported
elsewhere. Although I disagree with some of its conclusions, Jonathan Dull's
brief but closely researched account of this phase of the negotiations

(*French Navy*, pp. 236–43) is a valuable guide. See also Blart, *Rapports*, pp. 31–41. Bedford's instructions are printed in L.G. Wickham Legg, *British Diplomatic Instructions 1689–1789, Volume VII: France, Part IV, 1745–1789* Camden Soc. 3rd ser. vol. 49 (London, 1934), pp. 55–78. These should be read in conjunction with *Correspondence of John, fourth Duke of Bedford* (cited as *Bedford Correspondence*), ed. by Lord John Russell, 3 vols (London, 1842–46), III, 88–148.

Newfoundland: Evan W.H. Fyers, 'The Loss and Recapture of St. John's Newfoundland in 1762' *JSAHR* 11 (1932), 179–215, and Georges Cerbelaud Salagnac, 'La reprise de Terre-Neuve par les Français en 1762' *Revue française d'histoire d'outre-mer* 63 (1976), 211–22.

British politics and the peace: O.A. Sherrard, *Lord Chatham and America* (London, 1958), pp. 36–94 offers a readable narrative. In Sedgwick, ed. *Letters from George III* (cited above), pp. 130–75, one may observe how closely the king followed the proceedings. His readiness to be politically vindictive is revealed in Jeremy Black, *George III: America's Last King* (New Haven and London, 2006), pp. 62–5. A succinct but important source is Philip Lawson, *George Grenville: A Political Life* (Oxford, 1984), pp. 132–47. The expectations of Newcastle and Hardwicke are displayed in Yorke, *Hardwicke*, III, 406–54. Namier (*England in the Age*, pp. 333–61, 367–406) focuses on Newcastle's drift into opposition but largely omits his thoughts about peace terms which may be found plentifully in the same collection (BL Add. 32,941–5). In his *Memoirs of King George III* (I, 110–31) Horace Walpole exposed the degradation of the government under Lord Bute at this time with merciless derision and quite often with accuracy. My account of the East India Company's dissatisfaction with the peace preliminaries is based on Lucy S. Sutherland, *The East India Company in Eighteenth-Century Politics* (Oxford, 1952), pp. 92–9. The definitive treaty of Paris is printed in Corbett (II, 377–90).

Chapter 16 Conclusion and aftermath

'Fundamental causes of British military success' is derived from chapters throughout the book, and 'Why peace was delayed' from Chapters 13–14.

The significance of 1762

Choiseul's invasion plan is described by Corbett (II, 301–8), who seemed to take it seriously. The Manila expedition: Nicholas Tracy, *Manila Ransomed: The British Assault on Manila in the Seven Years War* (Exeter, 1995); Nicholas P. Cushner, ed. *Documents Illustrating the British*

Conquest of Manila 1762–1763, Camden Soc. 4th ser. vol. 8 (London, 1971). On French hopes that minor naval powers would join with France against Britain see Baugh, 'Withdrawing from Europe' (cited in Chapter 1), pp. 13–15.

Outcomes: peace terms, finances, navies, Spain and France

The French fisheries after 1763: Jean-François Brière, *La pêche française en Amerique du Nord au XVIIIe siècle* (Quebec, 1990), esp. pp. 183, 214–15. Louisiana: Douglas Steward Brown, 'The Iberville Canal Project: Its Relation to Anglo-French Commercial Rivalry in the Mississippi Valley, 1763–1775' *Mississippi Valley Historical Review* 32 (1946), 491–516. Acadian settlement: Faragher, *Great and Noble Scheme* (cited in Chapter 3), pp. 428–36, 451–2.

French finances. Bertin's diagnosis and efforts: Félix, *Finances et politique* (cited in Chapter 12), pp. 39–58, 136–7. Antonella Alimento, *Réformes fiscales et crises politiques dans la France de Louis XV: De la taille tarifée au cadastre général* (Bruxelles, 2008), pp. 98–108. Joël Félix, ed. 'Les Rapports financiers des contrôleurs généraux des finances: Deux rapports financiers de Bertin à Louis XV', *Études et Documents VII*, CHEFF (Paris, 1995), pp. 517–36. Joël Félix, 'Verifier, liquider, amortir: La dette et l'économie politique de la dette au XVIIIe siècle' in *Les modalités de paiement de l'État moderne* (Paris, 2007), pp. 145–77, esp. pp. 172–4. See also Swann, *Politics and the parlement of Paris* (cited in Chapter 8), pp. 185–244. For the provincial parlements: Michael Kwass, *Privilege and the Politics of Taxation in Eighteenth-Century France: Liberté, Égalité, Fiscalité* (Cambridge, 2000), pp. 95–103, 155–89. Post-war debt: T.J.A. Le Goff, 'How to Finance an Eighteenth-Century War' in *Crises, Revolutions and Self-Sustained Growth: Essays in European Fiscal History, 1130–1830* ed. by W.M. Ormrod, Margaret Bonney and Richard Bonney (Stamford, 1999), pp. 377–413. On Canadian bills see J.F. Bosher, 'The French Government's Motives in the *Affaire du Canada*, 1761–1763' *English Hist. Rev.* 96 (1981), 59–78.

British finances: P.G.M. Dickson, *The Financial Revolution in England: A Study in the Development of Public Credit 1688–1756* (London and New York, 1967) is the truly important general work, particularly relevant here for its attention to investment from abroad and the stock exchange. Reed Browning, 'The Duke of Newcastle and the Financing of the Seven Years' War' *Jour. of Economic History* 31 (1971), 344–77; for a less positive view see Middleton, *Bells*, pp. 113–18. Statistics:

B.R. Mitchell and Phyllis Deane, *Abstract of British Historical Statistics* (Cambridge, 1962). Army supply in Germany: Reed Browning, 'The Duke of Newcastle and the Financial Management of the Seven Years War in Germany' *JSAHR* 49 (1971), 20–35; Gordon E. Bannerman, *Merchants and the Military in Eighteenth-Century Britain: British Army Contracts and Domestic Supply 1739–1763* (London, 2008), esp. pp. 18–19, 31–9, 148–50; H.M. Little, 'Thomas Pownall and Army Supply, 1761–1766' *JSAHR* 65 (1987), 92–104. Dealing with post-war naval debt: Wilkinson, *British Navy and the State* (cited in Chapter 9), pp. 106–14.

Post-war navies. British: Baugh, 'Naval Power' (cited in Chapter 1); Wilkinson, *British Navy and the State*, pp. 105–164; Mackay, *Admiral Hawke*, pp. 303–8, 326–7. French and Spanish navies: H.M. Scott, 'The Importance of Bourbon Naval Reconstruction to the Strategy of Choiseul after the Seven Years' War' *Intl. Hist. Rev.* I (1979), 17–35.

Spanish trade: Blart, *Rapports*, pp. 43–53; H.M. Scott, 'Destins parallèles ou solidarité politique? Choiseul et le Troisiéme Pacte de Famille' in *La Présence des Bourbons en Europe: XVIe–XXIe siècles*, ed. by Lucien Bély (Paris, 2003), esp. pp. 214–20; Vera Lee Brown (Holmes), *Studies in the History of Spain in the Second Half of the Eighteenth Century*, Smith College Studies in History, XV (Northampton, MA, 1929), pp. 7–62.

French post-war overseas ventures. The French Guiana project: R. John Singh, *French Diplomacy in the Caribbean and the American Revolution* (Hicksville, NY, 1977), pp. 61–129. Emma Rothschild, 'A Horrible Tragedy in the French Atlantic' *Past and Present* 192 (2006), 67–108. British responses: Nicholas Tracy, *Navies, Deterrence, and American Independence: Britain and Seapower in the 1760s and 1770s* (Vancouver, 1988), pp. 42–105; Tracy, 'Parry of a Threat to India, 1768–1774' *MM* 59 (1973), 35–48. Failure to prevent the French from acquiring Corsica: H.M. Scott, *British Foreign Policy in the Age of the American Revolution* (Oxford, 1990), pp. 115–22. Canadian bills owed to British merchants: Joël Félix, 'Finances, opinion publique et diplomatie: Le *Committee of Canada Merchants* et la question du remboursement par la France des "billets du Canada" de propriété britannique 1763–1775' in *Le négoce de la paix: Les nations et les traités franco-britanniques (1713–1802)* (Rouen, 2008), pp. 127–64, esp. 137–52.

Britain and North America

British politics: John Brewer, 'The Misfortunes of Lord Bute: A Case-Study in Eighteenth-Century Political Argument and Public Opinion' *HJ* 16

(1973), 3–43. *The North Briton* and Wilkes: George Nobbe, *The North Briton: A Study in Political Propaganda* (New York, 1939), pp. 101–20, 184–224; Yorke, *Hardwicke*, III, 468–74, 495–532. A careful argument for supposing that George III and Bute were afraid of a parliamentary inquiry is found in D.A. Winstanley, *Personal and Party Government: A Chapter in the Political History of the Early Years of the Reign of George III, 1760–1766* (Cambridge, 1910), pp. 156–86.

An army for North America: John L. Bullion, '"The Ten Thousand in America": More Light on the Decision on the American Army, 1762–1763' *WMQ* 43 (1986), 646–57. The essential work is Shy, *Toward Lexington*, pp. 45–320. For Pontiac's rebellion: Anderson, *Crucible of War*, pp. 535–53, 617–37. My account disagrees with the geopolitical assessment of the North American situation offered in John L. Bullion, 'Security and Economy: The Bute Administration's Plans for the American Army and Revenue, 1762–1763' *WMQ* 45 (1988), 499–509; see Baugh, 'Maritime Strength' (cited in Chapter 1), pp. 203–14.

Grenville's American measures: Neil Stout, *The Royal Navy in America, 1760–1775: A Study of Enforcement of British Colonial Policy in the Era of the American Revolution* (Annapolis, MD, 1973), pp. 1–90. On colonial trade with the enemy: Rogers, *Empire and Liberty* (cited in Chapter 7), pp. 90–104. John L. Bullion, *A Great and Necessary Measure: George Grenville and the Genesis of the Stamp Act, 1763–1765* (Columbia, MO, 1982) includes a careful examination of the Sugar Act as well as the Stamp Act. For the impact in America: Edmund S. and Helen M. Morgan, *The Stamp Act Crisis: Prologue to Revolution* (New York, 1963). Attitudes in England are explored in Eliga H. Gould, *The Persistence of Empire: British Political Culture in the Age of the American Revolution* (Chapel Hill, NC and London, 2000), pp. 106–47. P.D.G. Thomas's *British Politics and the Stamp Act Crisis: The First Phase of the American Revolution, 1763–1767* (Oxford, 1975), which strives to excuse Grenville, is the indispensable study of the Act's repeal.

Broader interpretations: Bernhard Knollenberg, *Origin of the American Revolution 1759–1766* (New York, 1960). John M. Murrin, 'The French and Indian War, the American Revolution, and the Counterfactual Hypothesis: Reflections on Lawrence Henry Gipson and John Shy' *Reviews in American History* 1 (1973), 307–18. Jack P. Greene, '"A Posture of Hostility": A Reconsideration of Some Aspects of the Origins of the American Revolution' *Proceedings of the American Antiquarian Society* 87 (1977), 27–68; and Greene, 'The Seven Years' War and the American Revolution: The Causal Relationship Reconsidered' in *The*

British Atlantic Empire before the American Revolution, ed. by Peter Marshall and Glyn Williams (London, 1980), pp. 87–108. Also John Shy, 'The American Colonies in War and Revolution, 1748–1783' in Marshall, ed. *Oxford History of the British Empire: Volume II* (cited in Chapter 1), pp. 300–24, esp. 305–12. Alison Gilbert Olson, *Making the Empire Work: London and American Interest Groups, 1690–1790* (Cambridge, 1992) examines the deteriorating means of communication and negotiation (esp. pp. 134–73). On Pitt's (Chatham's) debility and depression see Ayling, *Elder Pitt* (cited in Chapter 2), pp. 338–76.

Scott, *British Foreign Policy in the Age* (cited above) examines the post-war circumstances of the European powers. I am grateful to Professor Javier Cuenca for providing me with figures for comparing patterns of British and French trade before and after the war. See also his chapter, 'Comparative Patterns of Colonial Trade: Britain and its Rivals' in Prados de la Escosura, ed. *Exceptionalism and Industrialisation* (cited in Chapter 1), esp. pp. 51–9. On British policy in Bengal see Marshall, *Making and Unmaking* (cited in Chapter 9), pp. 147–57.

Index

Printed in Great Britain
by Amazon

12835822R00427